THE AMATEUR GARDENER

THE
AMATEUR GARDENER

by

A. G. L. HELLYER, M.B.E., V.M.H., F.L.S.

COLLINGRIDGE BOOKS

Published for
Collingridge Books by
The Hamlyn Publishing Group Ltd
Hamlyn House, 42 The Centre
Feltham, Middlesex
Printed in Great Britain by
Robert MacLehose and Co. Ltd
The University Press Glasgow
First published 1948
Second Edition, Tenth Impression 1968
© *Revised, A. G. L. Hellyer* 1964

Preface

I STILL RECOLLECT vividly my introduction to gardening. It was in 1915 or 1916 when I was no more than a small boy. My family, in common with tens of thousands of others, started to dig up the lawn and grow vegetables as our own small answer to the U-boat menace. We were endowed with much enthusiasm and a complete lack of knowledge and I do not think our efforts were crowned with much success. But I do remember in the intervals of struggling with the unkindly London clay spending happy hours poring over the pages of Cousins' *Chemistry of the Garden* and H. H. Thomas' *Complete Gardener* and finding a new world of delight which has remained with me ever since.

Looking back now those seem very distant days. This is not merely due to the normal passage of time but rather to the immense changes which have taken place in almost every aspect of gardening during the intervening years. Two wars and the necessity to fight for our national existence in a world of growing scarcities and bitter competition have given an immense impetus to agricultural and horticultural research with the result that our knowledge of plant behaviour and our control over much that occurs in the garden is far greater than it was in the early part of the century.

Side by side with this technical development has come a great increase in the number and variety of the plants which may be cultivated—an increase partly due to the diligent searching of plant collectors in remote parts of the world but even more to the untiring and highly skilled work of plant breeders. As a result there never was a time when the gardener had such a choice of good material, nor so great a need of help in making a wise selection from it.

It is my hope that into the present volume I have compressed sufficient (and sufficiently up-to-date) information to be of value to a wide circle of readers whose interest in gardening is essentially practical rather than theoretical and who seek a guide book for everyday use. While much scientific information has been included I have tried to avoid scientific terms and to write in the language of everyday so that the book may be sufficiently simple to be understood by all.

In those sections devoted to flowering plants it has, of course, been necessary to make use of botanical names, for in many cases these are the only ones which permit accurate identification of the plants in question. But even here I have always employed what might be termed

5

the 'popular botanical' names, that is to say those in general use in gardens and nurseries, rather than those more strictly scientific names which have the latest blessing of the botanical pundits.

The plan of the book, in separate sections each devoted to one aspect of gardening, and in chapters devoted to one class of plant or one particular problem, such as pruning or the use of fertilisers, will, I hope, make for easy reference, more particularly as within the chapters an alphabetical sequence has been followed wherever it seemed helpful. However, a comprehensive index has been provided in addition in case any particular item should elude the reader.

The labour has been long but pleasant. It will be well rewarded and my purpose fully served if some readers find this volume one half as useful and enthralling as I did those two books that introduced me to the joys of gardening thirty odd years ago.

A. G. L. HELLYER

Rowfant,
Sussex.

Contents

PART I. A GENERAL SURVEY

PART II. THE ORNAMENTAL GARDEN

PART III. GARDENING UNDER GLASS

PART IV. VEGETABLES

The Amateur Gardener

PART V. FRUITS

PART VI. DEALING WITH FOES

Photographic Illustrations

Photographic Illustrations

11

Photographic Illustrations

12

PART I

A GENERAL SURVEY

CHAPTER I

Why Cultivation is Necessary

IT IS quite possible to grow plants successfully without any soil at all. This is done on a large scale in some places and for special purposes in others and this kind of gardening is sometimes known as hydroponics. There are several different systems but all are alike in providing the plants with some non-nutritive roothold, such as a bed of sand or ashes or a wire framework, and then surrounding their roots with a solution containing all the essential plant foods. A good many advantages can be claimed for this kind of cultivation, but invariably it suffers from one grave drawback, namely that the plant is entirely dependent upon the gardener for everything it requires. One slip or oversight on his part may bring about catastrophe.

Now, in the garden this is not the case. Ordinary fertile soil contains all the ingredients a plant requires for life and health and it is only in comparatively small matters that the gardener's interference is necessary. It is even possible for him to leave the garden alone for considerable periods and still get good results. All the time he is taking advantage of the natural resources of his land instead of relying exclusively on his own skill and knowledge as is essential with so artificial a system as soilless culture.

These comments are not made with any intention of running down soilless culture or belittling its value under certain circumstances. What I am anxious to do is to emphasise, by means of contrast, the unique value of fertile soil, and the importance of understanding its nature and the means by which it may be maintained.

WHAT, THEN, IS FERTILE SOIL? That is not an easy question to answer but broadly speaking it will consist of a mixture of sand, clay and humus. The last is the term used by the gardener to describe any well decayed organic matter, for example leaf mould, dung, peat and the dead bodies of small animals. Fertile soil, in addition to containing a great number of chemicals, some of them in such minute quantities that it is very difficult to measure them, also teems with microscopic organisms known as bacteria. Like other living things these multiply under favourable conditions and what they require is warmth, moisture and air.

When the soil was first studied scientifically the importance of these living organisms was not recognised and it was only the chemical

15

constituents that were taken into account. As a result many of the age old practices of the gardener were hard to explain and some of them came to be regarded as mere prejudices. It is only of comparatively recent years that the conception of 'living soil' has become widespread. With it has come the understanding of much that was previously obscure.

This idea that the soil is alive may puzzle the beginner but it is a fact which he must recognise for it explains a great deal of the work which he will have to do. For example, much of the cultivation that he carries out has for one of its objects the aeration of the soil in order that useful bacteria may be encouraged to breed more rapidly. The dung and other humus forming materials which he digs into his garden are not only intended to feed plants and improve the texture of the soil but also to stimulate those bacteria which are most beneficial to it.

I can imagine someone saying at this point: 'Are soil bacteria really essential to plant life and if so where do they find a place in the science of hydroponics?' The answer is that they are not essential to plants though they are essential to soil fertility. In hydroponics they are ignored but without them the gardener has to provide his plants with a much greater variety of artificial foods and take elaborate precautions to prevent the accumulation of poisonous substances. Briefly what these bacteria do is to manufacture plant foods from substances which contain the essential elements but in unsuitable forms or combinations, and to neutralise or render positively beneficial substances which might do harm. Without bacteria even the richest natural soil would become infertile in a very short time.

By no means all bacteria are beneficial from the gardener's point of view. Some reverse the work of the useful kinds, wasting plant foods, producing acids and in other ways damaging the soil. Fortunately these harmful bacteria only get the upper hand in soil that is badly supplied with air or heavily saturated with water. In other words they will only be found in dangerous numbers on those types of land which gardeners refer to as waterlogged, sour, or badly aerated. A great deal of cultural work is directed towards correcting these natural faults.

FROST, WIND AND RAIN. Weather plays a big part in improving the fertility of soil. Frost penetrates unyielding clods of clay and chalk, expands the moisture within them and bursts them asunder just as it bursts our water pipes. Any observant person will have noticed the way in which freshly dug ground tends to crumble on the surface after a spell of frosty weather.

Wind has a similar effect and the drying east winds which are such a common feature of the English spring, and usually annoy the

Successive layers of soil in an excavation made in uncultivated woodland. First there is a layer of dead, undecayed leaves. Next come several inches of dark top soil rich in the humus formed by decaying leaves. Then there is a layer of much closer soil which is lighter in colour and lacking in humus. Finally the spade has uncovered solid clay.

Ridging a plot in early winter so that as great an area as possible may be exposed to the beneficial influence of wind, frost and rain

A first step in digging any plot of ground. A trench 1 ft. wide and 10 in. deep is opened across one end of the plot

The work of digging proceeds by turning the soil, spadeful by spadeful, forward and over into the trench which is always kept open for this purpose

Half trenching in progress. In this illustration the bottom of the first trench
is being broken up with a fork

A further stage in trenching. After weed or grass has been skimmed off
the surface, top spit soil is turned forward into the first trench

Spreading a mulch of well-rotted dung around and between raspberry canes

A well-built compost heap. It has been built with vegetable refuse alternate layers of which have been dusted with sulphate of ammonia and lime

Making a junction between land drain pipes   Laying land drain pipes in rubble or clinkers

Heavy clay soil treated with lime to break it up and make it more workable

Applying sulphur dust to strawberries with a handy type of hand duster

A pneumatic type of knapsack sprayer in use on roses

Planting a rose bush: preparing the planting hole

Straggling or broken roots are removed before the rose bush is planted

The bush is gently jerked as soil is returned around the roots.

The soil is made thoroughly firm by pressure with the foot.

23

A lily-of-the-valley root as lifted from an old bed

The same root split up into single crowns and replanted in shallow trenches ready to be re-filled with soil

non-gardener quite a lot, are really most helpful in crumbling the surface soil and so preparing it for seed sowing and planting.

Rain is the most vital of all because plant roots can only absorb food in solution and so practically everything they need from the soil must first be dissolved by the rain which falls on the soil. I say 'practically everything' advisedly because the root hairs themselves do excrete weak acids which are capable of dissolving some chemicals without the agency of external water. That explains why one will sometimes find the fine network pattern of a root system covering the surface of a soft stone or lump of chalk turned up in the garden. The acids of the root hairs have etched themselves into the stone.

The purpose of cultivation is to aid and abet all these natural forces. For example land is dug early rather than late in the winter in order that as much of the surface as possible may be exposed for a long period to the beneficial effects of wind and frost. Drains are made in order to remove surplus water, so warming the soil, allowing air to enter, and encouraging the beneficial types of bacteria. In summer soil is hoed or lightly forked in order to break the surface crust and let in air, so again stimulating bacterial activity and quickening the release of plant foods.

TYPES OF SOIL. Briefly one may classify four basic types of soil from which the rest are built up. They are sand, clay, chalk and peat or humus. Loam, of which we hear so much, is a mixture of sand, clay and humus, while marl, famous for its use as a top dressing for cricket pitches, is a mixture of clay and chalk.

Of course no fertile soil is pure sand, pure clay, or, for that matter, pure anything else. These basic ingredients will not by themselves support plant life. But when the gardener refers to a certain soil as being of this or that type he means that this or that ingredient predominates. In practice the terms are extremely loosely used.

Loams are of innumerable different types varying from sandy loams in which sand may form 80 per cent. of the complete bulk, to heavy loams, in which clay is predominant. Lime may be almost entirely absent or it may be present in considerable quantity. Fertile chalk soils are always mixed with a certain amount of sand or clay, sometimes both. Good peaty soils also often contain a high percentage of sand. It is, in fact, not possible to draw a hard and fast line between one type of soil and another and this must always be borne in mind when the terms are used.

The characteristics of the different types are important. Sandy soils are in general rather lacking in plant food and they tend to lose quickly whatever is put into them. In consequence they are constantly in need of

B   25

feeding with dung, fertiliser, etc. This is what the gardener means when he describes such soils as 'hungry'. Sandy soils are dry by comparison with other types and, because of this, they are easily worked and become warm early in the year, which means that they are very suitable for the cultivation of early crops.

By contrast clays are generally well supplied with plant foods and they hold easily whatever is put into them but they are wet, cold, late and difficult to work.

Chalk soils have many of the bad points of both sand and clay. Like the former they are often poor and particularly wasteful of one important plant food, nitrogen, for reasons which will be considered later. They have not the compensating earliness of sand though they are not as a rule as cold and late as clay but they are often sticky and difficult to work in winter.

Peat soils, when first cultivated, are usually poor but they improve rapidly and repay the gardener well for intelligent treatment. They are easy to work and, though often wet, can frequently be drained easily. The principal trouble with peat is that it is as a rule very acid and this is a condition inimical to healthy bacterial activity and to most plant life.

The ideal soil is the good loam of which the gardener so often talks but is so seldom able to produce. Theoretically it should be a mixture of about equal parts sand and clay with plenty of humus and sufficient lime to correct any tendency to acidity. In actual fact even the best garden soils are generally a little deficient in one or other of these qualities and one of the gardener's first tasks is to discover just what this deficiency is and then make it good.

WHAT IS SUB-SOIL? When one has walked over a piece of ground and classified the soil as regards type one has not said all that there is to be said about it. To begin with the surface soil is only one part of the problem. What lies beneath is of equal importance. Technically this is known as the subsoil and it may differ strikingly from what appears on top. For example, it is quite possible to have a dark, spongy, humus laden top soil overlying a bed of solid, cheese-like clay. Not only are the two soils quite different in appearance and texture but they vary in every other respect, chemical as well as physical.

Nor is there any particular level at which the subsoil begins. In some cases it may be within two or three inches of the surface, in others there may be two or three feet of top soil before the subsoil commences. Sometimes the change between top soil and subsoil may be sudden and sharply defined like layers in a cake; at others the one may gradually merge into the other, without any clear line of demarcation. The only way to settle these points is to dig a number of deep holes in various parts of the garden, continuing to delve downwards until the subsoil is reached.

ACIDITY AND ALKALINITY. Another matter of great importance is the degree of acidity or alkalinity of the soil. For the sake of the non-technical reader let me explain first that acidity is the opposite of alkalinity and that a substance which is neither the one nor the other is described as neutral. Most garden crops, including ornamental plants and fruit trees, thrive best in soils which have a very slight degree of acidity or are neutral. This characteristic can be measured in various ways, is expressed numerically and is described as the pH of the substance. $pH7$ represents neutrality. Figures below 7 denote increasing degrees of acidity, above it increasing degrees of alkalinity. The ideal garden soil will have a pH reading of between 6·5 and 7. Real trouble begins to arise when the reading gets below 5·5 or above 8. Without going into a great deal of unnecessary detail I may say that below the 5·5 limit soils become definitely acid, many crops fail to grow and various undesirable organisms multiply. Plant disorders of one kind or another are also apparent above the 8 limit, some plant foods become locked up or are wasted at an altogether unreasonable rate.

There is, as a matter of fact, a great deal of difference between the tolerance of one plant and another for acid or alkaline soils. To give an example, rhododendrons and heathers have adapted themselves to grow in regions which are too acid for many other plants and they have to be given these conditions when they are brought into gardens or they fall into ill health. At the other end of the scale there are plants such as chicory and red valerian which are naturally found on chalk downs or in limestone cliffs which prefer conditions of comparatively high alkalinity.

An accurate test of the pH of a soil is really a matter for a trained chemist but a rough guide can be obtained by one or other of several means. The simplest, but least satisfactory, is to place a sample of soil in a tumbler and pour some dilute hydrochloric acid over it. If the acid bubbles and froths freely there is free carbonate of lime in the soil and it is alkaline. If there is no effervescence the soil is either neutral or acid but that is as far as the test will take one. It cannot tell one anything about the degree of acidity or whether it is serious or not.

A better method is to pour distilled water over the sample in the tumbler, shake this up vigorously for a minute or so and then leave it to settle. When the water is clear, dip a piece of blue and a piece of pink litmus paper into it. If the blue litmus paper turns pink the soil is acid, if the pink litmus paper turns blue it is alkaline.

The third, and by far the most accurate means of testing for the amateur is by means of a barium sulphate soil testing outfit. In this a special soil indicator is used with distilled water to give a certain colour which varies from pink in cases of extreme acidity through green where the soil is only slightly acid, to blue for alkalinity. Without any special skill a result can be obtained to within half a point. It must be observed, however, that to give an accurate result this test must be carried out with distilled water which is itself neutral in reaction. If the water has been standing long in a badly stoppered glass bottle it may be markedly acid or alkaline and will in consequence falsify the result if it is used, without correction, for a soil test.

THE VALUE OF LIME. When soils are seriously acid they can be corrected by dressing them with lime and that is, in fact, one of the main purposes for which lime is used in the garden. It will be readily understood from what has already been said that an excessive use of lime can be quite as harmful as lack of lime and it is therefore wise before applying it to get some idea of the condition of the soil. This matter is further dealt with in the chapter on manures and fertilisers (see p. 60).

In addition to its effect in counteracting soil acidity lime also has a very remarkable physical influence on heavy soils. Clay is sticky when wet because the particles of which it is composed are so fine that they are held together by the surface tension of the water covering them. When lime is added to clay these minute particles group together into small crumbs or 'flocks' less influenced by surface tension and consequently neither so slippery nor so close in texture. The scientist terms this process flocculation and the gardener uses it to very great advantage to improve the working of difficult soils.

EVEN COLOUR COUNTS. It might not appear that the colour of soil could be of any importance, but practice shows that it has a considerable effect upon the growth of plants. The reason is that dark soil tends to absorb sun heat whereas a light coloured soil reflects the sun's rays. In consequence, other things being equal, dark soils are warmer and earlier than light soils. That is one reason why the addition of humus-forming substances such as compost, dung, leaf mould and peat, are valuable, because humus is dark in colour. Soot also helps in this respect besides having important manurial properties.

CHEMICAL ANALYSIS. So far I have said nothing about chemical analysis as a means of arriving at a conclusion regarding the quality and character of soil. This is not because of any poor opinion of analysis but rather because I feel it to be out of reach of most of my readers. A detailed analysis of even one sample of soil will cost several guineas. As soil may vary considerably from one part of the garden to another, a single sample is not of much value.

There are other difficulties about soil analysis which are not always recognised. An ordinary, straightforward analysis will give the total quantity of the more important elements which exist in the soil but it will not tell the gardener in what form they exist. It may well be that a great deal of what the analysis shows to be present is in forms which make it unavailable as plant food at any rate for the time being. This drawback can be overcome to some extent by special methods of analysis designed to show available rather than total plant food and the ideal is to have both kinds of analysis carried out.

Finally there is the difficulty of interpreting the analysis and using it to devise a plan of action. I am afraid that in many cases this is impossible for anyone but a trained soil chemist, and the best solution would be for the chemist who carries out the analysis to state plainly what it implies in terms of garden practice; for example that there is a marked deficiency in nitrogen and therefore immediate dressings of some nitrogenous fertiliser are required. Unfortunately my own experience is that chemists seldom give such practical advice. However, if the reader happens to belong to the Royal Horticultural Society he can get his soil analysed by that body for quite reasonable fees and the experts who carry out this work will interpret the results.

LEARNING FROM WEEDS. Nevertheless I believe that for most gardeners more is to be learned from a general study of the soil and of the weeds and plants that grow in it than from chemical analysis. I will give a few examples of how this works out in practice. Clover shows a considerable intolerance of acid conditions. In consequence if clover grows naturally and freely on the ground it is a fairly certain indication that it is not highly acid. In contrast to this most heathers and rhododendrons cannot thrive on an alkaline soil, and do not even like one that approaches neutrality. These plants favour land with a marked degree of acidity. Weeds which may be associated with them are the common sheep sorrel, foxglove, bracken and spurrey. Wild gorse and broom will also be found under similar conditions.

Soils which contain large amounts of lime and are in consequence markedly alkaline will produce the wild clematis freely (this is the plant often known as old man's beard or travellers' joy) while other vegetation that is characteristic is bird's foot trefoil, kidney vetch, centaury, bladder campion and chicory.

Loamy soils that are in reasonably good condition will produce luxuriant examples of the sow thistle. Groundsel will spring up freely and become very strong. Chickweed and fat hen or goosefoot are also likely to be abundant.

On badly drained land rushes and sedges will appear while on peaty soils sphagnum moss may be abundant. Common moss is usually a sign of poverty and/or poor aeration and green scum appears on the surface under similar conditions.

I have dealt with the symptoms of chemical deficiency which crops may show in the chapter on Manures and Fertilisers.

WEEDKILLERS. One purpose of cultivation is to clear land of weeds but, on occasion, this can be done by other means than digging, forking or hoeing. Weedkillers are available but they must be used with understanding of their individual characteristics. They can be divided into selective and non-selective types.

Selective weedkillers kill particular classes of plants. Some such as 2,4-D and MCPA kill most broad leaved plants but do not harm grass. They are therefore very useful for clearing meadow grass of weeds and converting it to good lawn turf and they can also be used to keep established lawns weed free. Some, such as 2,4-5-T, are particularly effective in killing nettles, brambles and brushwood and are useful in the preliminary clearing of rough ground. In contrast dalapon kills grass but is much less poisonous to broad leaved plants so it can be used to get rid of unwanted grass around fruit trees or in shrubberies.

Non-selective weedkillers kill everything, plants and weeds alike. The most familiar is sodium chlorate which is usually dissolved in water at from 4 to 8 oz. per gallon and sprayed or lightly watered on the weeds to be killed. It needs to be used with great care because if applied in excess it can be washed through the soil and damage plants it was not intended to touch.

Simazine by contrast has little tendency to move through the soil and is extremely persistent. It is particularly effective in preventing the growth of weeds on ground already dug or hoed.

One non-selective weedkiller, paraquat, kills all plants it touches but is rendered innocuous by the soil. It can, in consequence, be used around growing plants so long as it is not permitted to fall on them.

All weedkillers should be used strictly in accordance with manufacturers' instructions. Sodium chlorate is inflammable but can be purchased in formulations which include an anti-fire chemical.

CHAPTER II

How Soil is Worked

SOIL TILLAGE resolves itself into two main parts, autumn and winter working on the one hand and spring and summer cultivation on the other. At the former period the soil can be far more thoroughly broken up than at other times of the year. I do not say that it is never possible to carry out deep cultivation in spring or summer but it is the exception rather than the rule and in a broad way the distinction I have made can stand as a useful classification for methods of work.

Autumn and winter cultivations can again be sub-divided into five distinct operations, forking, digging, half trenching, trenching and ridging. I will deal with these individually.

FORKING AND DIGGING. These operations are very similar. In both cases the object is to break the ground up to a depth of 10 in. or so, that is to say to the full length of the tines of a fork or the blade of a spade. In both cases, also, an attempt is made to turn each spade or forkful of soil right over so that the part which was on top at first is buried when the operation is completed. In this way weeds are turned in and killed and the lower soil is brought to the surface there to be exposed to the beneficial influence of weather (see Chap. I).

In practice it will be found more difficult to carry out this ideal of turning the soil right over with a fork than with a spade and for this reason I advise digging rather than forking whenever possible. Nevertheless the fork has two advantages. Firstly the work is less laborious and can, in consequence, be done more rapidly; and secondly it is possible to work with a fork ground that is too sticky or hard to be turned over with a spade.

In both cases the same general method should be followed. Start by digging out across one end of the plot a trench approximately 10 in. deep and 1 ft. in width. This initial trench is most important for upon it depends a good deal of the success of the rest of the work. The soil removed from the first trench is wheeled to the far end of the plot. In the case of a very large piece of ground it is more economical to divide it into several fairly narrow strips and deal with each separately. In this case the soil from the first trench is wheeled to the opposite side of the plot, as shown in diagram overleaf, instead of to the far end.

31

Now start at one end of the trench, face it and thrust in the fork or spade to its full depth and about 6 in. back from the edge of the trench. Lever the soil up by pulling backwards on the handle. Slip one hand well down the shaft, lift the spadeful of soil and turn it right over, at the same time throwing it well in front of you into the trench. Continue in this way right across the plot until the whole of a 6 in. wide strip has been dug forward into the previously made trench. If this work is properly done there will still be a trench 1 ft. wide and 10 in. deep into which the next 6 in. of soil can be turned in the same manner. Operations proceed in the same manner, strip by strip, until the whole plot has been dug, when the last trench is filled with the soil removed from the first trench.

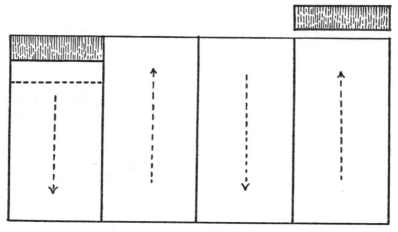

DIVIDING A LARGE PLOT FOR DIGGING

The two shaded rectangles indicate the first trench opened and the position of the soil wheeled from it. The work of digging proceeds as indicated by the arrows.

One mistake which the beginner makes is that of failing to throw the soil sufficiently far forward so that the trench becomes blocked up and there is no room to work. Another fault is that he does not turn each spadeful right over, with the result that some grass and weed is left on the top. Yet another point to watch is that the spade or fork is thrust vertically into the soil to its full depth. If it is pushed in at an angle, the ground will be covered more rapidly but cultivation will not be anything like so deep or thorough. The last error to avoid is that of taking too much soil at a time; six inches is quite enough; more makes heavy going and bad work.

HALF OR BASTARD TRENCHING. This is a method of breaking up the ground more deeply than by forking or digging, and yet avoiding the danger of bringing relatively infertile subsoil to the top. It is really quite a simple operation but a little difficult to describe in words and far easier to understand from a diagram, so I have provided one herewith.

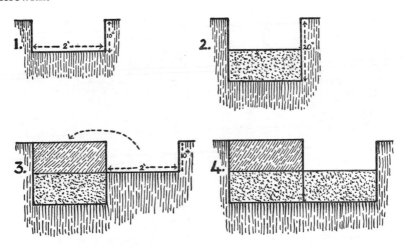

THE METHOD OF HALF TRENCHING

1. The first trench is 2 ft. wide and about 10 in. deep. 2. The subsoil is broken. 3. Another 2 ft. strip of top soil is turned over. 4. More subsoil can be broken up. The work proceeds in the same way throughout the plot.

Briefly the method is as follows: Start as for digging but make the trench 10 in. deep and 2 ft. wide. As before the soil displaced should be wheeled to the far end of the plot, or the far side if the plot is big and to be worked in strips. Now get into the bottom of the trench so formed and fork or dig it from one end to the other. To do this it will be necessary to face at right-angles to the position adopted for the preliminary digging. In this way the soil is broken up a further 10 in. deep but is still left lying in the bottom of the first trench. Mark out another 2 ft. strip behind the first trench. Turn the top soil from this, spadeful by spadeful, into the first trench on top of the broken up subsoil. When this second trench is finished, get into the bottom of it with spade or fork and break it up as before. The work continues in this way, one 2 ft. strip after another, until the whole plot has been trenched. Again the soil displaced from the first trench will be used to fill the last one.

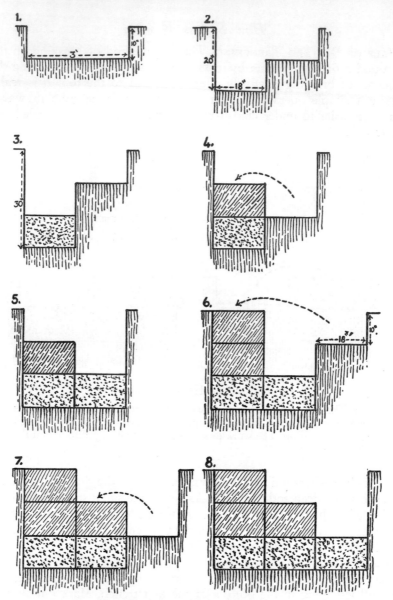

THE METHOD OF FULL TRENCHING

1. The first trench is 3 ft. wide and 10 in. deep.

2. A second trench 18 in. wide is opened.

3. Subsoil is broken up.

4. Second spit soil is turned on top of broken subsoil.

5. More subsoil is broken.

6. A further 18 in. wide trench is opened and the first spit thrown forward.

7. The second spit soil is dealt with.

8. More subsoil is broken up.

The work proceeds in the same way throughout the plot.

34

FULL TRENCHING. This adopts the same principles as half trenching but carries them one stage further so that the soil is broken up to a depth of approximately 30 in. or three spade depths. Again a diagram will probably be more helpful than words and one is provided on p. 34.

To start full trenching excavate the first strip 10 in. deep and 3 ft. wide, that is to say 1 ft. wider than for half trenching. Remove this soil to the end or side as formerly, and make it into a very distinct heap. The bottom of this 3 ft. wide trench must be divided in half longitudinally by stretching a line from one end to the other. Get down into the trench and dig out the forward half of it a further 10 in. deep, barrowing the soil away to the end or side, but tipping it in a heap entirely distinct from the bigger heap of top soil.

The result of this operation will be to form a step within the first trench, the lower part of which will be 20 in. below ground level and 18 in. in width. Get into this deeper and narrower trench and break up the bottom of it with fork or spade as in half trenching. Now stand on the upper part of the step and turn this over with a spade on to the lower portion which has just been forked. In this way a fresh piece of subsoil will be exposed and this in turn will be broken with a fork or spade.

Next step up to ground level again and mark out a new strip but this time only 18 in. wide. With a spade throw the top soil from this strip right over on to the raised step of second spit soil in the first trench. Turn the second 10 in. of soil on top of the broken subsoil in the first trench and finally break up the newly exposed subsoil with spade or fork. The work proceeds in 18 in. strips by the same method until the plot is completed when the smaller heap of second spit soil is used to fill in the bottom of the last trench and the larger heap of top soil is used to finish it off.

RIDGING. Another important item of autumn or winter cultivation is known as ridging. The object in this case is not so much directly to break up the soil as to expose as large a surface as possible to the pulverising action of weather.

There are several methods of ridging, but I think it will suffice to describe one which can be adapted to requirements as may seem necessary. The ground is first divided into 3 ft. wide strips, each of which is dealt with separately. Start at the end of one of these strips and take out a trench 1 ft. wide and about 10 in. deep across it, i.e. the whole trench will be 3 ft. long. Now work back down the length of this strip as for ordinary digging, turning the soil forward and over but bringing the spadefuls from each extremity of the short trench towards the centre.

In this way a ridge will be built up as the strip is dug. Each strip is dealt with in the same way until the whole plot is turned up into a series of ridges which should be as steep as possible. The illustration below will help to make this process clear.

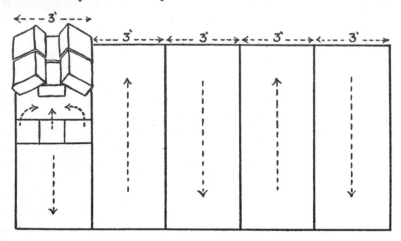

A Diagrammatic Illustration of Ridging

Each strip is 3 ft. wide and is dug lengthwise, the centre spadeful of soil being turned forward and the left and right turned inwards. The work proceeds up and down strips as indicated by arrows.

Spring and Summer Cultivations. These mainly consist in forking, raking and hoeing with the object, first of breaking down clods left by the winter digging and, secondly, of destroying weeds and maintaining a loose, finely broken layer of soil on the surface. This last is known as a dust mulch and its object is to keep the lower soil cooler than it would otherwise be and so check the rate of evaporation from the surface. The finely broken soil is full of air spaces and, as with a woollen or cellular garment, these air spaces interpose a barrier to the passage of heat.

I will deal first with the breaking down of clods left by winter cultivation. Two tools may be used for this purpose, the fork and the Canterbury hoe. The latter is rather like a short, three-pronged fork with its tines set at right-angles to the handle. It is a very good tool indeed for this particular purpose and it can be used with quick, swinging blows to break down even the stiffest lumps of clay. When using a Canterbury hoe work forwards across the ground and deal with one small strip at a time.

The fork is used with a swinging motion from side to side when breaking down lumps and it is the backs rather than the points of the tines which do the work. Again I think the illustrations on p. 546 will prove more helpful than a great deal of description.

Do not, at this first breaking down, attempt to get the soil too fine. For a great many plants and even for the sowing of large seeds, very finely broken soil is a drawback rather than a help, as it tends to set badly after heavy rain. It is only when sowing small seeds such as those of the onion, lettuce, cabbage, flax, poppy and godetia, that an extremely fine seed bed is essential and then only because otherwise it would be impossible to sow the seeds sufficiently near the surface.

Another important point is that this spring preparation must be done when the soil is in just the right condition, which will be when it is drying out rapidly on the surface after a short period of drying sun or wind. Very often in March and April there are long periods when an east wind blows and though it is cold it is also extremely drying and generally provides ideal conditions for final planting preparations.

RAKING. This is an art which is very little understood by most amateurs. The tendency is to use the rake to remove lumps from the surface rather than to break them up, which is the purpose for which it should really be employed. The rake should be used with long strokes both towards and away from the operator. Just as much power should be employed in the movement away from the body as towards it and in fact it is in this second part of the action that most of the breaking up takes place. If raking is properly done very few lumps of soil will be removed from the surface and it will mainly be stones that will remain to be gathered up at the finish. Once again I have tried in a series of illustrations to show how this work should be done.

HOEING. There are three distinct reasons for hoeing; *one*, to kill weeds by disturbing seedlings and severing larger weeds; *two*, to thin out plants and particularly to 'single' i.e. reduce to one every few inches, seedlings sown in rows; and *three*, to break down lumps. A fourth use for the hoe is to draw seed drills.

There are also two main types of hoe, the Dutch hoe with blade set roughly on the same plane as the handle, and the draw hoe with blade set at right angles to the handle. The former is used by pushing it away from the body and then drawing it back again, all the time moving slowly backwards across the ground. It is most serviceable for weed eradication between plants growing in straight rows. The draw hoe is used by pulling it towards the body with chopping and 'drawing' motions and is most serviceable for singling, breaking down lumps and killing weeds between plants not in regular rows.

CHAPTER III
Drainage Problems

WATERLOGGING IS very bad for soil even if it occurs at times of the year when there are no crops actually in the ground. If this seems to require a little explanation I would refer the reader back to what I have already said in Chapter I about soil bacteria and their activities in the soil. I would repeat that bacteria, though they are probably most familiar to us as agents of disease, are by no means all harmful. Many are absolutely essential to the health of the soil and without them the best land will soon become infertile. On the other hand there are other kinds of bacteria which are harmful to the soil, wasting plant foods, producing poisons and quickly preventing all satisfactory plant growth. It so happens that the useful bacteria require air, whereas most of those that are harmful only thrive where there is little or no air. What, you may say, has this to do with waterlogging? Simply that if soil is completely saturated with water all the air will be driven out of it. The useful bacteria will perish and the harmful ones will obtain the upper hand.

That is just one of the evils of waterlogging. Another is that it chills the soil, while a third and equally vital point is that roots, as well as bacteria, require air and that when deprived of it they also will die. It is no uncommon thing to see whole groups of trees in low-lying orchards burst into bud in the spring and then suddenly wither and die without apparent cause. So frequent is this in some places, and so destructive of trees that it has been dubbed 'The Death' and various causes have been suggested. The true explanation in almost every case is that this particular area has been waterlogged for some period during the winter, that all fine roots have died in consequence, and that the brief burst of activity in the spring was simply made on the stored up sap in the branches, which, once exhausted, left the trees without means of sustenance.

CULTIVATION TO IMPROVE DRAINAGE. By no means all soils require drainage, nor even is this always necessary on soils which show a certain degree of winter waterlogging. Where the trouble is not very serious it can often be overcome by thorough cultivation, particularly if this can be accompanied by generous dressings of dung, well rotted compost, straw, peat or leaf mould, any of which will improve texture and allow water to flow more freely. Heavy liming will often effect a wonderful improvement on clay soils for the reasons I have already explained in the section on lime, p. 28. In fact I would go as far as to say that unless there are obvious reasons for believing that such treatment will not effect a remedy, cultivation and the addition of extra lime and humus should always be tried first as a remedy for waterlogging. I say this because drainage is invariably an expensive undertaking and frequently a difficult one, especially in small gardens.

One problem which is often hard to overcome is to find any suitable outlet for the water once it has been collected in drains. In fields and large estates there are other ditches or main drains into which subsidiary drains may be directed but the owner of a small garden seldom has any such facilities. It is against the law to open a sewer for the purpose of running a land drain into it and the only alternative as a rule is to dig a soakaway which must be of considerable size and depth if it is to be of any practical value.

LAND DRAINS. The method of draining land is to dig narrow trenches at intervals of about 12 ft. and to a depth which will be dictated by the depth of the subsoil. A point to bear in mind here is that soil becomes waterlogged because the subsoil is so compact that water cannot soak through it and in consequence it forms a pan on which the water lies. A drain, to be effective, must be laid at just about the level of this pan, neither higher nor lower. If the drain is too deep, it will itself be protected by the pan and very little water will get into it. If, on the other hand, it is too high, water will still stand below it and the evil will not be fully overcome. As a rule the top of the really impervious subsoil is anything from 1 to 2 ft. below the surface and that is approximately the depth to which land drains should be dug. Each drain must have a continuous slope in one direction, though it need not be greater than 1 ft. in 40 ft. Frequently it is most convenient to have a number of subsidiary drains communicating with a central drain, in which case what is termed the herring-bone pattern shown in diagram overleaf is generally followed.

When the drainage trenches have been dug, something must be put into them to keep them open at the bottom and provide a free passage for the water. There are several alternatives. The best, but also the most expensive, is the earthenware land pipe which is simply a cylindrical length of earthenware pipe without joints or flanges. To be fully effective it should be laid on a clinker or stone bottom with more hard rubble surrounding and covering it. The pipes are butted end to end but there is no attempt to make the joints between the pipes tight for it

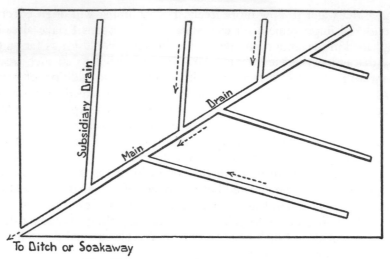

To Ditch or Soakaway

THE HERRING-BONE SYSTEM OF DRAINING

is through them that the water seeps into the pipes. The purpose of the surrounding rubble is to prevent earth being washed down into the drain and silting it up. The very best drains have the rubble graded, the coarsest pieces surrounding the pipes and the finer material being used on top to act as a filter. Finally the trenches are refilled with soil and the work is completed.

Where one pipe drain leads into another the joints are made by cracking the pipes with a hammer and covering them with a few potsherds or crocks as shown in the illustration on p. 21.

An alternative to pipe drainage is a plain stone drain. In this case the bottom of the trench is filled for 8 or 9 inches with fairly large clinkers, brick ends or other coarse rubble. Then the material is gradually graded off to finer samples with breeze or gravel on top to make the filter. The efficiency of stone drains depends a great deal on the type of material used. The harder and more angular it is the better and there is nothing to beat well burned boiler clinkers. If the rubble is too small or smooth the drain tends to silt up after a few years and then has to be re-made.

Very often the cheapest method of all is to fill the bottoms of the trenches with faggots laid end to end. These can be made from almost any brushy wood, but hazel, when available, is preferable to most other kinds. It is a great advantage if turfs can be laid grass side downwards on top of the faggots before the soil is returned to the trenches. Well made faggot drains will remain effective for years but if insufficient wood is used or it is too soft and unbranched the drain soon collapses and is useless.

THE SOAKAWAY. I referred earlier in this chapter to a soakaway. This is a device for collecting surplus water and allowing it to drain away slowly into the more porous layers which often underlie the first subsoil. The effectiveness of a soakaway will depend partly on its size but even more upon whether it can be driven right down through the subsoil to a more open layer beneath. In some cases it is possible to penetrate the impervious subsoil by digging a hole 4 or 5 feet deep but in other places—my own garden is an example—one has to go down at least 12 ft. before getting to anything through which water can flow freely. In diameter the soakaway may be of any convenient dimensions but it is seldom wise to have it less than 3 ft. across; 6 ft. is a more usual measurement. It is, in effect, a well, but it differs from a well in that once it has been dug it is immediately filled up to within a foot or so of the surface with large stones, clinkers or other hard rubble and is then topped over with soil. The soakaway is, of course, made at the lowest part of the ground to be drained so that all drains may eventually discharge their water into it.

CHAPTER IV
Paths and Path Making

I AM CONVINCED that paths do not, as a rule, receive the careful consideration which they merit. They are so permanent a feature of the garden and have such a tendency to dominate the rest of the layout that it certainly pays to think twice—and then think again—before deciding where they shall go and of what material they shall be made.

And yet, having delivered this warning, I find it next to impossible to give any further advice on the matter except to suggest that common sense is often the best guide in these matters and that the services of an expert garden designer can often be obtained quite cheaply. There are, I know, various stock rules about the siting of paths; that they should be centred on a main window or door: that they should lead somewhere and not just meander about aimlessly; that there should not be too many of them and, in particular, that they should not be permitted to cut the garden up into awkward shapes or leave narrow, useless borders against fences. But there are so many exceptions to all these generalisations that I feel they may be more hindrance than help to the garden planner, and I am thrown back on the simple statement that each problem must be solved in its own way according to the obvious needs of the situation.

When it comes to the matter of path construction it is possible to be far more precise. Even the width of a path is a matter upon which some fairly definite statements can be made. Main paths should seldom be less than four feet wide; five or six feet is often better. Side paths can sometimes be as little as two feet in width but this is about the minimum except for the little tracks that are often used to give access to out-of-the-way parts of the rock garden.

Again one can dogmatise to some extent regarding materials. Main paths do need to be made of something that will stand up to heavy wear. That rules out thin paving slabs set in sand and also grass paths, attractive though these can be in the right place. Asphalt has the necessary wearing qualities but does not blend well with the garden and in my opinion is only suitable for car drives. Gravel can be costly in upkeep though modern weed killers have eased this problem a little. Nevertheless I do not favour gravel around the house because of its tendency to pick up on boots and get carried into the house.

42

By this process of elimination one is left with three obvious possibilities—thick paving slabs preferably set in cement; paths made entirely of concrete, and old brick paths. The last can be charming in the right setting but suffer from one fatal drawback, a tendency to become dangerously slippery in wet weather. Concrete by itself is the solution which thousands of small garden owners have accepted in the past and no doubt will continue to accept in the future. It has the merits of cheapness, durability and safety and the added advantage that any handyman can lay it himself. Its one great drawback is that it does not look very sightly. This can be overcome to some extent by careful tinting—but beware of overdoing this or the cure can be very much worse than the trouble. Nevertheless when all is said and done it must be admitted that concrete does not weather in the pleasant manner natural to stone and so this leaves us with paving slabs, either rectangular or crazy, of suitable thickness (at least 2 in. in my estimation) and either wholly or partially set in concrete as providing the best possible path surface in positions near the house and likely to be much in use. Further off, in vegetable and fruit garden, gravel may provide a perfectly satisfactory material, provided it is of the type that will bind when rolled and not remain permanently loose as is the case with sea shingle. I know of nothing more tiring to walk on than this.

As regards the details of construction it can be stated emphatically that every path needs a good foundation—or, to be more precise, a good 4 in. of hard rubble below the surfacing material. Without this there is bound to be trouble in winter when water will collect beneath the surface and heave it up whenever there is a sharp frost. Incidentally a well-made path with a good depth of clinker or brick ends beneath it can act as a very serviceable garden drain and considerably improve the surface condition of a wet plot, especially if the lowermost part of the path can be made to communicate with a soakaway or ditch.

When gravel is used for surfacing there should be a good 2 in. of it on top of the foundation layer, and it should be well watered and rolled as it is spread. One inch of asphalt will make an excellent path so long as it is bedded on a good solid layer of hard rubble; in fact $\frac{1}{2}$ in. of asphalt will do for paths that will not receive a great deal of wear. It must be well tamped down as it is laid and all asphalt paths should be given a distinct camber i.e., slope downwards from centre to sides, so that they throw off water readily. Water collecting and freezing beneath asphalt can cause disaster in no time.

Bricks can be laid in a variety of ways; flat, on edge, in straight rows, herringbone fashion, in squares and so on. Moreover they can simply be bedded in sand, with more sand brushed down into the crevices between them, or they can be set in cement which, of course, makes a far stronger but also considerably more expensive job. Another possible drawback of cement setting is that it limits the possiblity of establishing small creeping plants, such as thymes and sandworts (*arenaria*) between the bricks. However this can be overcome to some extent by leaving uncemented crevices here and there and confining the plants to these chosen spots.

Paving slabs can be bedded in sand or ashes, a method which provides almost endless possibilities in planting. Moreover the plants, as they become established, will help to bind the paving slabs in position. Nevertheless there is always some danger of slabs working loose, and even one rocking or sticking up a little above its neighbours can be a source of considerable danger. It is for this reason that I prefer to bed the slabs on all main paths in cement, though an occasional pocket can be left in which to introduce a few plants.

The preparation of good concrete, either for path making by itself or as a setting medium for bricks or paving slabs, is not quite so simple a matter as might appear. The first essential is to purchase really fresh cement. If it is 'hot' from the kiln, so much the better. Old cement, though it may still be powdery and apparently in good condition, never gives the hard 'set' possible with a fresh sample. The other two ingredients, ballast and sand, should be mixed in the proportions of two parts by bulk of the former to one of the latter. To this the cement is added at the rate of one part to six of the aggregate.

Be sure that all the ingredients are thoroughly mixed while still dry. Then add water, a little at a time, turning the heap meanwhile and continue in this way until the whole mass is wet without being sloppy. This is rather important. If too little water is used, the cement will not set properly; if too much is applied, it will tend to float up on top of the concrete when it is laid and later it will scale off, leaving a very bad surface. The navvy describes the correct condition of wetness as 'greasy'. It is a little like that; but perhaps it will help the novice more to say that it should have the consistency of very stiff porridge.

When bricks or slabs are laid in concrete it is wise to scrape out the joints as one goes along and fill them up later (this is known as pointing) with a specially fine mixture made with three parts sand to one of cement. This, or the concrete itself for that matter, can be tinted by mixing in a very small quantity of any of the recognised painter's pigments, such as Venetian Red or Yellow Ochre. Add this while mixing the dry materials. The right proportions will have to be ascertained by experiment.

44

Paths and Path Making

Two last points about the laying of crazy paving paths. Start with the bigger slabs and fill in the spaces afterwards after the style of a jig-saw puzzle. Sometimes there is a lot of clay adhering to the slabs. This should be removed first as if left it makes it very difficult to bed them level and firm.

CHAPTER V
Manures and Fertilisers

I DO NOT think that any very hard and fast dividing line can be drawn between a 'manure' and a 'fertiliser'. Broadly speaking 'manure' is used by gardeners to denote the bulkier soil foods of organic origin such as dung, leaf mould, compost, spent hops, etc., while 'fertiliser' is taken to denote more concentrated forms of inorganic food such as superphosphate of lime, sulphate of ammonia and muriate of potash. But there are plenty of examples which do not fit neatly into either of these groups and in the following notes I shall not attempt to make any distinction between them. Instead I shall confine myself to explaining the particular value and the method of use of each substance named in alphabetical order.

At the outset it may be well to consider why it is necessary to apply manures and fertilisers at all. Under natural conditions there is no such addition or, at any rate, it is not very obvious to the casual observer, yet weeds and grasses appear to thrive quite satisfactorily.

The explanation is two-fold. First of all even in uncultivated soil manuring of a kind does go on, partly by the agency of earthworms which pull decaying leaves and other vegetation into the soil, but also by the surface decay of vegetation and myriads of insects etc. Secondly the gardener requires a much more intensive rate of cropping than is carried out under natural conditions and this exhausts the soil of certain vital plant foods more rapidly than would otherwise be the case.

A point I want to drive home at this juncture is that every fertile soil, besides containing enough plant food in suitable form for immediate use, also holds immense reserves of all the essential chemicals and that in time these will be rendered available by the action of weather and soil organisms, such as the bacteria discussed in Chapter I. All the gardener has to do is to supplement these natural supplies and particularly to balance them where one tends to be in excess of another.

It is, I think, useful to draw a distinction between feeding the soil and feeding plants. Both are necessary in certain circumstances but the former is considerably the more important of the two. By feeding the soil I mean adding to it substances which will enrich it chemically for a considerable time and also, in many instances, stimulate the living organisms which form so vital a part of it. Dung and compost come into this category and so do nitrogenous fertilisers applied with a green manure (see p. 57) to assist in its decay.

When the rapid feeding of plants is essential the gardener must make use of chemicals which are either immediately available for absorption by the roots or can be changed into suitable forms by one or two simple stages and in a short time. Nitrate of soda is an example of such a food. In solution it can be absorbed by the roots at once and an effect may be observed in increased growth and deepened colour of foliage within three or four days. Contrast this with the effect of bone meal which is not soluble in water and only liberates the useful phosphoric acid it contains after a long period of disintegration in the soil. Even when bone meal is very finely ground so that the greatest possible surface is exposed to the action of soil acids and bacteria it may be months before any appreciable benefit is observed in the growth of plants.

INORGANIC VERSUS ORGANIC MANURES. In case any of the foregoing remarks, either in this chapter or Chapter I, should be misinterpreted, I must make it absolutely plain that I am not one of those who believe that only organic manures are beneficial and all inorganic ones are harmful. A great deal of controversy has raged on this point and there are some 'experts' who hotly contend that no inorganic fertilisers should be countenanced in the garden; they even go so far as to claim that plants grown with such fertilisers have lower food value than those produced with organic manures, and may encourage disease in those who consume them. There is not the slightest evidence for any of these statements and both classes of manure have their value in the garden.

ESSENTIAL FOODS. It is not known exactly how many chemicals are essential in the soil for the growth of plants. Up to the time of writing it has been shown that something like fifteen or sixteen substances appear to be vital but additions are still being made to this list and much has yet to be learned. From the gardener's point of view, however, the four most important foods are nitrogen, phosphorus, potassium (potash) and calcium, with magnesium running these a close fifth and sulphur, iron, boron, manganese, copper, zinc and molybdenum tagging along somewhere in the rear. It is common to refer to the first six of these as major and the remainder as trace elements. This is a fair enough description provided it is understood that all are equally essential to healthy plant growth and that what makes the first group take precedence over the second is simply that these elements are needed in greater quantity. The first four, nitrogen, phosphorus, potash and calcium, are most likely to be deficient in soil, and are, in consequence, those which the gardener will most frequently need to supply.

At this point I must explain another matter. Nitrogen, phosphorus, calcium, etc. are elements which, as a rule, cannot usefully be supplied to the soil in their pure state. Nitrogen, for example, is a gas which forms a major portion of the air that we breathe and it would be quite impossible to put it into the soil as nitrogen. But all these elements combine with others to form salts or organic compounds and it is in these forms that the gardener puts them into the soil. Nevertheless even when one has got a salt of one of these elements and has discovered that this particular salt is soluble in water, it does not follow that the plant will be able to make use of it. Plants are finicky in this respect. They like their foods in certain well defined forms and if the wrong form is supplied it must remain in the soil until it is changed into the right form. Sometimes this takes a long time and that is one reason why some fertilisers are quicker acting than others.

BALANCED FEEDING. Before I attempt to explain what effect each particular food has upon the plant I must make it clear that lack of any one food may affect the usefulness of all or any of the others, while contrariwise an excess in one direction may produce an apparent shortage in another. Sometimes it is the balance or proportion between foods which is vital. Let us consider an example. We will imagine first a soil which contains a normal quantity of nitrogen and potash, both in suitable forms for use as plant food. In consequence plants grow normally and show no signs of starvation. Then for some reason or other the quantity of nitrogen is greatly increased. As one result there may be immediate signs of potash deficiency which will only disappear when the potash content of the soil is also raised above the normal. An understanding of this truth will explain many otherwise inexplicable soil problems and will also answer the question why it is just as necessary to keep feeding a garden that is in a high state of cultivation as one in which the soil is comparatively poor. It also follows that, though one may speak of this or that effect being the *principal* one produced by any particular food it is quite wrong to think of it as the *only* effect produced.

WHAT EACH FOOD DOES. Bearing that last warning in mind here are some indications of the way in which some of these foods influence growth.

Nitrogen has its most marked effect upon rate and vigour of growth and the colour of foliage. When nitrogen is in short supply plants tend to be stunted, leaves are small and pale or bluish in colour. Add nitrogen in a suitable form and the rate of growth immediately increases, the leaves becoming large, lush and dark green.

Phosphorus also has a considerable effect upon growth though not quite so markedly as in the case of nitrogen. Nevertheless when phosphorus is very deficient there will be many of the symptoms of nitrogen starvation. Perhaps the most spectacular effect of phosphorus is on roots which grow freely when it is abundant but are poor and stunted when it is lacking. That is one reason why fairly large doses of phosphatic fertilisers are always advised for root crops. Phosphorus also has a considerable effect on the satisfactory ripening of seeds and fruits though curiously enough it does not appear to be very important in the case of orchard cultivation.

Potash is, however, the principal fruit forming fertiliser. As I have already suggested there is a close linkage between the effect of potash and nitrogen on plants. When the proportion of nitrogen is increased the potash must be added also or it will appear to be deficient though it was present previously in adequate quantity. When there is insufficient potash in the soil in relation to the nitrogen present, fruits tend to be poorly coloured and lacking in flavour, faults which disappear directly potash is added. Potatoes in potash-starved land cook badly, turning black and soapy though others nearby with plenty of this element are white, floury and of first class quality. Potash also has a striking effect on foliage for when it is deficient leaves, particularly of fruit trees, become scorched at the edges much as they would be scorched by drought or excessive heat.

Calcium is the element which the gardener adds to the soil when he limes it, for quicklime is calcium oxide while chalk and limestone are calcium carbonate. It enters into the constitution of all plants and is essential to them, but there is generally sufficient in the soil for their needs. Lime must be regarded as one of the major soil foods because of its importance in the soil itself where, as I have already explained, it flocculates clay and corrects acidity thereby stimulating bacterial activity and aiding the liberation of other plant foods.

Magnesium plays a vital part in the formation of chlorophyll, the substance which makes leaves green. When magnesium is in short supply chlorophyll is only partially formed and leaves develop patches of yellow. This condition, incidentally, can equally easily be caused by lack of iron or by excess of lime which results in a reduction of available iron.

Boron is one of the so-called 'trace' elements, that is to say it is only required in very minute quantities above which it acts as a plant poison. It is only of recent years that its importance has been recognised but some conditions which were formerly regarded as diseases, notably Brown Heart in turnips and swedes, have been shown to be due to lack of this element. Nevertheless the amateur must go carefully in using it because the maximum dose required does not usually exceed 2 oz. to 30 sq. yd. and even this may prove too much. Other considerations apart it is a difficult matter to distribute 2 oz. of any material evenly over 30 sq. yd. of ground and the only satisfactory way of doing it is to mix it intimately and evenly with a suitable carrier such as fine sand.

Zinc, copper and manganese also come into this class of trace elements but are best left alone by the gardener unless he has reliable information that they are required.

'COMPLETE' OR COMPOUND FERTILISERS. These terms are used to describe any mixtures of chemicals which provide nitrogen, phosphorus and potash in reasonable quantity. It will be observed that such mixtures are not complete in the sense of supplying all plant foods which may possibly be deficient in the soil. In fact the terms arose many years ago before the science of plant feeding had been adequately studied and at a time when it was supposed that these three elements were the only ones about which the gardener need trouble. It still remains true that they are the three most likely to be in short supply and in consequence that the so-called complete fertiliser is the best general standby for the gardener.

FERTILISER ANALYSIS. Under the Fertilisers and Feeding Stuffs Act it is necessary for every manufacturer to declare the amount of available nitrogen, phosphorus and potash in the fertiliser which he sells. Sometimes a fertiliser will be described solely in the terms of this analysis. For example a writer will refer to the use of 4 : 8 : 4 mixture as being wise at this or that stage of growth. Invariably in such cases the quotation is for nitrogen, phosphoric acid and potash in that order. Such reference tells one nothing about the actual ingredients used which may be of any kind that when mixed will give this final analysis, 4 per cent. nitrogen, 8 per cent. phosphoric acid, 4 per cent. potash. Nor does it tell one whether the fertiliser contains any other useful elements. Nevertheless the three-fold ratio is a useful method of abbreviation and one which should be understood by the gardener.

MIXING FERTILISERS. Not all chemicals which are themselves suitable as fertilisers can be mixed satisfactorily. In some cases there is an immediate and very noticeable chemical reaction, as, for example, when sulphate of ammonia is mixed with lime, the result of which is to liberate quantities of ammonia gas which is most unpleasant, causing choking and watering at the eyes. Ammonia lost is nitrogen lost. In other cases the reaction is less obvious though not necessarily less serious. For example, if lime is added to superphosphate of lime much of the soluble phosphoric acid will be converted into insoluble calcium phosphate which will not become available as plant food for a very long time: for these reasons it is wise to stick to well tried or properly recommended formulae.

Another important point about mixing one fertiliser with another is that each ingredient must be ground as finely as possible and that the whole lot must be mixed intimately. If this is not done one part of the soil will get an excess of one chemical, another of some other chemical. That is one advantage of purchasing proprietary compound or complete fertilisers. These are ground and mixed by machinery with better results than can be obtained by hand. Nevertheless it is quite possible to make satisfactory mixtures at home especially if a hard, concrete floor is available on which the lumps can be broken up with a hammer or the back of a shovel and on which the heap of chemicals can be turned over and over until they are intimately blended.

Some mixtures which are otherwise satisfactory tend to set hard a few days after they have been made. This will occur, for example, with a simple 'complete' fertiliser prepared with superphosphate of lime, sulphate of ammonia and sulphate of potash. If the lump is then broken up it will not set again and there will not have been any loss in fertilising value. Incidentally this kind of setting can be prevented by adding a small quantity of fine bone flour when mixing.

AN ALPHABETICAL LIST OF
MANURES AND FERTILISERS

BASIC SLAG. This is a waste product of industry obtained from the lining of blast furnaces. It contains varying quantities of phosphoric acid which is only liberated slowly in the soil. In practice the usefulness of this fertiliser is in direct proportion to the fineness of grinding and all samples should be guaranteed to pass a 100 mesh sieve. Finely ground basic slag looks rather like soot, is extremely heavy and not very pleasant to handle. It has the merit of adding lime as well as phosphoric acid to the soil and is, therefore, particularly useful on the more acid types of soil in which, incidentally, its solubility is increased. Solubility also varies from one sample to another and should be quoted by the manufacturer. Over 80 per cent. soluble is good, whereas below 40 per cent. is very poor. Analysis for phosphoric acid may vary from as little as 8 to as much as $18\frac{1}{2}$ per cent. This fertiliser has little immediate action and is most suitable for autumn or winter application on heavy or peaty soils. Rates may vary from 4 to 8 oz. per square yard.

BLOOD. Fresh blood contains quite a lot of plant food in the form of nitrogen but is extremely unpleasant to handle and is seldom used in the garden. Where it is employed a trench can be kept open for it and the blood poured in as received and covered with soil. A pleasanter method is to add 1 lb. freshly slaked lime to each gallon of blood, stir well, pour into a shallow box or tray and cover with a further thin layer of lime.

Leave the mixture until dry, then crumble and use at 4 oz. per sq. yd. Huge quantities of blood are dried commercially and marketed as a fine, granular, dark red powder which is clean to handle and has no unpleasant smell. This powder is not as a rule fully soluble in water but can be used to make liquid manure if it is well stirred and applied at once. A good sample will have an analysis of about 12 per cent. nitrogen. This is fairly readily available and in consequence dried blood can be used as a spring and summer fertiliser either before sowing or planting or to plants in growth. Rates will vary from 1 to 3 oz. per sq. yd. or ½ to 1 oz. per gallon of water.

BONES, DISSOLVED. Although a great many advantages have been claimed for dissolved bones at one time or another these do not appear to be established by any scientific test and from the garden standpoint they may be regarded as identical with superphosphate of lime. If they can be purchased at the same or a cheaper price, well and good, but if they cost more, they should be left alone.

BONE FLOUR, STEAMED. From the point of view of the plant food it contains and the action which it has on plant growth, steamed bone flour is identical with a fine grade of bone meal and likely to contain from 15 to 32 per cent. of phosphoric acid in rather slowly available form. The steaming results in the extraction of all gelatine from the bones and the flour is in consequence very dry and excellent for mixing with other fertilisers to prevent them from binding.

BONE MEAL. This is a favourite phosphatic fertiliser with gardeners and has the merit of being extremely steady in action. The phosphorus which it contains is liberated slowly over a long period. The rate of its release is increased by fine grinding and an acid soil. The analysis varies greatly from one sample to another, extremes being about 15 to 32 per cent. phosphoric acid. Bone meal prepared from raw bones also contains small quantities of nitrogen (from 1 to 5 per cent.) but in steamed bones the nitrogen has been removed. Like basic slag, bone meal is most useful for autumn and winter application as it has little immediate effect on growth. It can be used at rates of from 4 to 6 oz. per sq. yd. or 3 to 4 oz. per bushel of potting soil.

CALCIUM CYANAMIDE. This is a by-product from hydro-electric works and in some districts is much used as a nitrogenous fertiliser. It has the merit of combining lime with nitrogen and therefore being particularly serviceable for use on acid soils. Drawbacks are that it is an extremely fine and dusty powder, difficult to spread evenly, rather unpleasant to use and with a caustic effect on foliage. In consequence it is most suitable for application to vacant ground in late winter and early spring. It may also be used as a weed killer and fertiliser combined and at rates of 2 to 3 oz. per sq. yd. is effective in killing the smaller annual weeds. Analysis shows 20·6 per cent. nitrogen and about 22 per cent. free lime. Rates of application as a fertiliser only will vary from $\frac{1}{2}$ to 2 oz. per sq. yd. Calcium cyanamide is also a useful rotting agent for compost heaps (see below) for which purpose it should be sprinkled freely over each 6-inch layer of material.

CHELATES. See Sequestrenes.

COAL ASHES. These have no value as a fertiliser though gritty ashes from a furnace with a quick draught are useful for lightening heavy soil. Ordinary domestic coal ashes are too soft and fine in texture to have any useful effect of this kind.

COMPOST. This is a general name given to any decayed organic matter, for example leaves, grass mowings, hedge clippings, refuse from the vegetable garden or even animal refuse such as that from the slaughter house, fish shop, etc. All these materials may be dug into the soil in their natural state but it is usually better to convert them into compost first by one of the controlled processes of decay. In practice there does not appear to be much difference between the results obtained from many of these methods. Provided the final result is a dark brown or blackish mass in which there is little trace of the original ingredients, e.g. un-decayed leaves, stems, etc., the compost may be applied in the same way and at the same rate as animal manure with similar results.

As air is necessary for healthy decay it is inadvisable to make compost heaps too wide or too high, though they may be of any convenient length. Usually 3 ft. should be regarded as the maximum width and height of a heap when first built.

The rate of decay can be increased and incidentally the quality of the compost improved by treating it with nitrogen and lime in one form or another. The purpose of the first is to feed and thereby stimulate bacteria and of the second to counteract acidity. A number of excellent proprietary accelerators are marketed or use can be made of one or other of the fertilisers which provide these substances, e.g. calcium cyanamide, nitro-chalk or nitrate of lime. A third alternative is to dust alternate layers of the heap as it is built with a nitrogenous fertiliser such as sulphate of ammonia and some form of lime such as quicklime or hydrated lime.

Other essentials to satisfactory and rapid decay are warmth and moisture. In consequence the compost heap should be built in a sheltered position, though not a sunny one, and any parts of it which appear dry should be thoroughly soaked with water. More even decay is obtained if the heap is completely turned after about one month, the interior portion being brought to the outside and the latter turned inwards. At the same time any parts which appear dry should be thoroughly moistened with water or liquid manure (urine or stable drainings).

COMPOST MADE BY THE INDORE PROCESS. This is a system of compost making which has had a great deal of publicity. It was devised by Sir Albert Howard after extensive experiments carried out in India in the state of Indore from which it takes its name.

Briefly this system differs from that outlined above in not making use of any chemical fertilisers to speed decomposition and in insisting upon the importance of mixing vegetable and animal wastes in every compost heap. According to Sir Albert Howard the ideal proportion is about three parts by bulk of mixed vegetable waste (the more mixed the better) to one part of animal waste, for preference strawy manure from the stable or byre. If no animal waste is available Sir Albert Howard recommends sprinkling each 6 in. layer of vegetable refuse with a thin film of dried blood, hoof and horn meal or fish manure or moistening the heap with bedroom slops.

The compost is kept at as even a temperature and degree of moisture as possible, either by preparing it in concrete pits in the case of large quantities or in wooden bins about 4 ft. square and 3 ft. high on a garden scale. It is changed from one pit or bin to another about six weeks after it is first put down to decay. This removal takes the place of the ordinary turning given to outside heaps. In the first pit or bin air shafts are driven right down into the compost at frequent intervals with a wooden stake or crowbar but in the later stages of decomposition when the compost reaches the second pit or bin no shafts are made.

Sir Albert Howard states that under his system there should be no unpleasant smell and no flies will be attracted to the heap for breeding purposes. If either of these things occurs the pit or bin should be emptied at once and refilled. As in other systems the dry refuse must be moistened but a special point is that very green, succulent leaves should first be withered and then wetted again before being used as compost.

COW MANURE. The value of cow manure as plant food will depend partly upon the way in which the cattle from which it was obtained have been fed and also upon the manner in which it has been stored.

Fresh cow manure from cake fed beasts will have the highest analysis and may contain something like o·8 per cent. of nitrogen, o·4 per cent. of phosphoric acid and o·6 per cent. of potash. It is, therefore, a well-balanced plant food.

There tends to be a rapid wastage of plant food elements, and particularly of nitrogen, if the manure is exposed to air and rain. The best method of storing farmyard manure so that it does not deteriorate is to build it into a compact stack under a roof of some kind and then to cover it all over with at least 6 in. of soil beaten down hard.

As animal manure decays it loses bulk and it is possible, because of this, that an old sample may show a higher chemical analysis than a fresh sample, but this should not be allowed to obscure the fact that some of the valuable plant food originally contained in the manure has been lost. Undoubtedly the most economical method of using this or any other form of animal manure is to dig it in fresh. Unfortunately there are two drawbacks; first that the plant foods contained are not immediately available but must first be liberated by bacterial action, and second that in the process of decomposition excess acids may be formed in the soil and prove harmful to plant life. In time they will be washed out and they will also be neutralised if there is sufficient active lime in the soil but the use of fresh manure is not desirable on soils that are already known to be acid.

Where it is essential that the manure used shall have an immediate effect on plant growth it is necessary to make use of samples that have already decayed to a condition where they are of an even texture throughout without any straw or other bedding remaining readily identifiable as such. Such manure can be used as a top dressing to plants in growth either alone or mixed with an equal bulk of soil or can be dug into the ground at rates up to 1 cwt. to 6 sq. yd.

Fresh cow manure is best applied to vacant ground in autumn or early winter.

FEATHERS. All types of these are rich in nitrogen and in consequence valuable as a soil dressing. 1 cwt. of feathers is sufficient for from 8 to 10 rods of ground, or a plot about the size of an ordinary allotment. The average analysis is about 8 per cent. of nitrogen, which is liberated steadily over a period of many months. The smaller the feathers the quicker the action, as decay is more rapid.

FISH WASTE. This, like other organic matter, contains a lot of potentially valuable plant food. The flesh and offal is particularly rich in nitrogen while the bones contain a high percentage of phosphorus. Fresh fish refuse of all kinds may be dug into the soil as a substitute for animal manure and is estimated to have approximately the same chemical value, though its mechanical effect upon the texture of the soil is not so good as that of stable or farmyard manure prepared with plenty of straw. It is very unpleasant stuff to have lying about for any length of time and the best method of using it is to keep a trench open on a vacant plot of ground and throw the refuse into this as it becomes available, turning soil on top of it at once. The rate of application will be the same as for animal manure, that is to say 1 cwt. may be spread over from 6 to 24 sq. yd. of ground according to the poverty of the soil and the type of crop to be grown. As a rule such refuse will contain more nitrogen than either phosphorus or potash and so for crops which require a balanced food supplementary dressings of phosphoric and potassic fertilisers should be given at the appropriate season.

Fish guano is a name given to fish waste prepared in special factories. It is dried and granulated and can be kept for long periods without decaying or becoming unpleasant. It is much richer in plant food than fresh fish waste and though analysis will vary from sample to sample an average will be somewhere in the neighbourhood of: nitrogen 8 to 10 per cent., phosphoric acid $4\frac{1}{2}$ to 9 per cent., potash 2 to 3 per cent. It should be used like a fertiliser as a dressing at the rate of 3 or 4 oz. per sq. yd. in late winter or early spring on ground that is about to be planted or sown.

Fish manure is a name given to a mixed, or complete fertiliser prepared with a fairly high percentage of dried fish guano but with added phosphorus and potash to make it a better balanced plant food. As the formula will vary according to the ideas of the manufacturer his instructions regarding use must always be followed.

FLUE DUST. This must not be confused with soot. The latter is the deposit taken from the chimneys of ordinary open fire-places whereas flue dust is a name given to deposit from the chimneys of boilers with a forced draught. In all cases this results in a much greater loss of nitrogen and on this account most flue dust has no value at all as a fertiliser. But in certain specialised industrial plants the flue dust does contain, in addition to other ingredients, quite considerable quantities of potash in forms suitable for application to the soil. These dusts are of value as garden fertilisers solely on their potash content and should be purchased according to their analysis. A really good sample may contain as much as 8 per cent. of potash and will be worth about one sixth the price, weight for weight, of sulphate or muriate of potash. A poor sample may have as little as 2 per cent. of potash and will be hardly worth purchasing. Similarly the rate of application will vary according to the analysis from as much as 1 lb. per sq. yd. in the case of low grade dusts to 5 or 6 oz. for best quality. All flue dusts are most suitable for autumn or winter application as it may be some time before all the potash they contain is available as plant food.

GREEN MANURE. Farmers make a great deal of use of quick-growing crops which can be ploughed in while still green and succulent and which will then rot rapidly in the soil and provide humus. It should be observed that with the exception of green crops belonging to the pea family, e.g. vetches, clover and annual lupins, green manures cannot add any chemical to the soil which was not there already. The reason for the exception in the case of the pea family is that most members of this have developed an association with certain bacteria which live in nodules on their roots and have the remarkable power of being able to fix free nitrogen from the atmosphere. It is a fact, therefore, that ground into which a crop of clover, lupins, etc. has been dug, is actually richer in nitrogen than before and the amount under favourable conditions may be quite considerable, say the equivalent of a dressing of sulphate of ammonia at the rate of 1 oz. per sq. yd.

It may be argued that if other forms of green manure add no new chemicals to the soil they are of no value. This is incorrect. They have, in fact, three separate uses, first to improve the texture of the soil by enriching it with humus, secondly and by the same means, to increase the rate of bacterial activity and thirdly to convert into temporarily insoluble forms chemicals which might otherwise be washed out of the soil by rain.

This last point is important and often overlooked. Perhaps it can best be illustrated by a concrete example. Let us imagine that a considerable quantity of nitrate of soda or sulphate of ammonia has been used for the summer feeding of crops and that the gardener believes a surplus remains in the soil at the end of the summer. If he does nothing about it, most of this food will have disappeared by the following spring, but if he immediately plants a quick-growing crop such as mustard or rape, which will absorb the surplus nitrogen and if, in addition, he digs this in when it is a few inches high, the nitrogen will still be there the following year.

Almost any quick-growing green crop may be used as green manure but the four most favoured varieties are mustard, rape, vetches and annual lupins. The advantage of mustard is that it is the quickest growing crop of all and may be sown as late as the end of August for autumn digging. Rape makes abundant foliage but does not grow quite so fast and should not be sown later than the end of July, which is also the

D   57

final sowing date for annual lupins. Vetches need an even longer growing season and are best sown in the spring. In most cases it is a considerable advantage, though not a necessity, to dust the ground at the rate of 2 oz. per sq. yd. with calcium cyanamide, Nitro-chalk or sulphate of ammonia as the green manure is dug in. Any of these will feed the bacteria needed to bring about the decay of the green manure in just the same way as they will in a compost heap (see p. 53), thereby producing more rapid and more complete decomposition. It does not matter how early a green crop is turned into the soil but it should not be left after the stage at which it starts to form flower buds. Later than this the tissue becomes very tough and woody and decays too slowly to be of real value.

GUANO. Originally this name was applied solely to the dried deposit left by sea birds on certain points along the coast of Peru. This is an almost rainless district and as a result the bird droppings remain for many years and retain their manurial value. This natural guano is a rich, complete manure containing on the average about 10 to 14 per cent. nitrogen; 9 to 11 per cent. phosphoric acid and 2 to 4 per cent. potash. It can be used in the preparation of ground at the rate of 2 to 3 oz. per sq. yd., but is particularly valuable as a summer feed or top dressing to plants in growth at rates of about 1 oz. per sq. yd. or 1 oz. per gallon of water.

The natural deposit has, however, become very scarce and expensive and in many cases what is sold now as guano is not really bird droppings at all but a mixture of various chemical fertilisers giving approximately the same analysis as natural guano. Such fertilisers should be bought and used solely on published analysis.

HAIR. This is most likely to be available mixed with some skin in the form of scrapings from hides. Hair contains a considerable quantity of nitrogen which is of value to many crops, but it is rendered available rather slowly. In consequence hair and hide scrapings are most suitable for autumn and winter application. They may be dug in at rates up to 1 cwt. to 30 sq. yd. Incidentally they have a very important effect upon the texture of heavy soils for which they are particularly suitable.

HOOF AND HORN MEAL. Finely ground hooves and horns make a valuable fertiliser containing an average of 12 to 14 per cent. of nitrogen which becomes available steadily over a period of several months. It is a rather expensive fertiliser but is specially valuable for potting composts with which it may be used at rates varying from 1½ to 4 oz. per bushel. Outdoors the usual rate of application is 2 oz. per sq. yd. It may be used at any time of the year. The finer the grinding the more rapidly will the nitrogen be liberated.

HOPS. Spent hops as obtained from the brewery have not much value reckoned purely as plant food but they have a most useful effect upon the texture of almost all soils. They tend to lighten heavy clay and yet render light, sandy soils more retentive of moisture. Hops should always be allowed to weather for three or four months before use, after which they can be dug in at any time of the year at rates up to 1 cwt. to 15 sq. yd.

Hop manure is quite a different proposition. In this case the hops have been treated chemically to improve their value as plant food. There are numerous proprietary brands, and as treatment varies considerably, analyses will also differ widely. All should be applied strictly in accordance with manufacturer's instructions, which may vary from as little as 4 to as much as 12 oz. per sq. yd. As the chemicals used are generally of a very soluble character, hop manures are not particularly suitable for autumn or winter application but are excellent in early spring and may also be used as top dressings to plants in growth.

HORMONES. Plant hormones are not fertilisers in the ordinary sense of the word but are substances which have a very marked controlling effect upon growth, comparable in some ways to that of the hormones secreted by certain glands in human beings and animals. Those of most interest to the gardener are the root forming hormones such as beta-indole-acetic acid and alpha-naphthalene-acetic acid. When these are applied to plant tissues in extremely dilute solutions they have the effect of inducing or hastening the formation of roots. In greater concentration they act as plant poisons.

The best of these root forming hormones have been prepared in various proprietary brands and are offered under trade names with full instructions regarding use. Some are sold as liquids for dilution with water, others as powders to be applied direct to the plant. In the case of the liquids the usual method of application, after appropriate dilution, is to stand cuttings erect for 24 hours in about 1 in. of the solution, after which the cuttings are inserted in the soil in the ordinary way. In many cases cuttings treated in this way will root in half the time that will be taken by untreated cuttings. There is no harmful effect arising from correct use of these substances. See also page 72.

HORSE MANURE. Weight for weight horse manure is usually richer than cow manure but once again samples are likely to vary a great deal according to method of feeding and the way in which the manure has been stored. All the remarks made in this connection about cow manure apply equally to dung from the stable. Horse manure is dryer and more open in texture and therefore better in its mechanical effect upon heavy soils. It is also the only kind of natural manure which is reliable for the cultivation of mushrooms. In this connection, however, it should be noted that it is now possible to grow mushrooms on straw or chaff compost prepared by rotting with special chemicals (see p. 595). Horse manure that is to be used for mushroom culture must be fresh, prepared with straw bedding, and from animals that are in good health. For other purposes horse manure is used in the same way as cow manure.

KAINIT. This is a natural deposit which is quarried in France and Germany. It contains about 14 per cent. of potash in the form of sulphate of potash and in addition as much as 60 per cent. common salt (sodium chloride) and 20 per cent. sulphate of magnesium. It is used principally as a potassic fertiliser though the sodium chloride and magnesium sulphate also have value as plant foods. Kainit is apt to have harmful effects on plant roots if used in too great strength and is most suitable for autumn and winter application, particularly to vacant ground or to robust subjects such as orchard trees. Rate of application is from 2 to 4 oz. per sq. yd. This substance is closely allied to that sold as 'potash salts'.

LEATHER. This, like most other animal products, contains nitrogen which can be made use of by plants as food. Unfortunately in the case of leather this nitrogen is liberated so slowly that it is not of much value as a fertiliser. Fragments of leather may remain undecomposed in the soil for many years. Fine leather dust yields up its nitrogen more rapidly but even so it is not likely to show any immediate return. However, leather dust is sometimes useful to give bulk to more highly concentrated fertilisers and thus render even distribution a simpler matter. Analysis of leather dust varies from about 3 to 6 per cent. of nitrogen according to methods of manufacture. Rates of application may be up to 1 lb. per sq. yd. at any time of the year.

LIME. As I have already pointed out in Chapter I, lime is very much more than a plant food, though it is a plant food, and this point must not be ignored. Its other uses are as a corrector of soil acidity and an improver of soil texture. The former it does by neutralising acids formed in the soil and the latter by flocculating (that is to say turning into small flocks or granules) the very fine particles which characterise clay soils.

Strictly speaking lime is the popular name for calcium oxide (quick-lime) and calcium hydroxide (slaked lime). The latter is obtained by slaking quicklime, also known as burnt lime or lump lime. In the garden 'lime' is used more broadly to cover practically any substance which has the same general effect upon the soil. Thus when the gardener applies chalk or ground limestone he still says that he is 'liming' the soil.

There is a good deal of misconception as to the relative value of the different forms of lime, using the term in this broad sense. It is often stated that quicklime is swifter in action than any other form of lime and that chalk and limestone are comparatively slow. In actual practice this is not found to be the case to any very marked degree provided the chalk or limestone is sufficiently finely ground. The main advantage of quicklime is that, directly it comes in contact with moisture, even the moisture of the atmosphere, it very rapidly crumbles to an extremely fine powder which can be mixed most intimately with the soil. It takes good machinery to grind chalk or limestone to anything like the same degree of fineness and coarser samples cannot be mixed so evenly and intimately with the soil and therefore do not affect it so rapidly. It is not correct to say that quicklime, nor yet slaked lime (calcium hydroxide), the form in which lime is usually applied in gardens, are any more beneficial in their action on the soil than chalk or limestone.

In this connection it is interesting to note that, when applied to soil, all types of lime tend to turn rapidly into one or other of two distinct forms. If the soil to which the lime is applied is acid, a certain percentage, sufficient to correct this acidity, is absorbed into the soil and becomes combined with the humus and finest particles of soil (colloids). All this absorbed lime is termed 'active' lime (sometimes it is referred to as exchangeable lime) and this is the only part which is of immediate value to the soil and the plants growing in it. It is this 'active' lime which reacts with other chemicals in the soil, liberating plant food, stimulating bacterial activity and itself becoming available as plant food. The remaining, or surplus lime, after acidity has been corrected, is rapidly converted into chalk or, more technically, calcium carbonate. This surplus lime has no immediate effect on plants or soil but forms a store from which more 'active' lime can be absorbed as required.

The lime test which I described in Chapter I as being carried out by pouring dilute hydrochloric acid on to the soil can only reveal the presence of free calcium carbonate, i.e. any reserve of lime on the lines I have just described. Now it is quite possible for a soil to have ample active lime and yet have no 'reserve' or 'free' lime capable of being revealed by the acid test. That is, in fact, the principal drawback of this test.

Another point which must be borne in mind is that, though a little free lime does no harm to many crops, an excessive amount of it may cause a lot of trouble. It will tend to destroy humus, waste nitrogen, lock up iron and bring about various conditions of plant starvation, some of which may be revealed by the foliage turning yellow or white (chlorosis). It is just as easy to do harm by giving too much lime as by not giving lime at all.

I am often asked whether applications of lime can be directly related to the known *p*H reaction of the soil. The answer is that they can, but not quite so easily as might at first appear. One cannot say straight away, for example, that because the *p*H is 5·5, 12 oz. per sq. yd. of burnt lime must be given to make the soil neutral. To understand why this is so I must refer the reader again to what I have said regarding the nature of the active lime in the soil. It is in combination with the humus and very fine particles of soil. Now he will remember from what was said about soils in Chapter I that there are far more fine particles in a clay soil than in a sandy one and that the largest amount of humus is likely to be found in peaty soil. It follows from this that soils which contain a lot of clay or peat can absorb more lime than soils of a more sandy and consequently coarser nature. Because they can take in so much active lime, such soils, once they have become neutral, will continue a long time, even under heavy cropping, before they become acid, but once they do become acid it will take a lot of lime to make them neutral again. In contrast to this a sandy soil which has few fine particles and little humus and, therefore, little chance of absorbing lime, will soon be exhausted and need replenishing. It is precisely the difference between filling and emptying a large reservoir and a small one. That is why the gardener's rule must be little and often when liming sandy soils though he can afford to give heavier applications at less frequent intervals on clay or peat. I have attempted to show the working out of this in the following table.

TABLE FOR LIME DRESSINGS

Dressings of ground quicklime necessary to correct varying degrees of acidity on soils of different types. All figures are for oz. per sq. yd.

*p*H	Sand	Light loam	Medium loam	Heavy loam	Peat	Clay
6·5	4	5	6	7	8	9
6·0	5	6	7	8	9	10
5·5	6	7	8	10	12	12
5·0	7	8	10	12	14	14
4·5	8	10	12	14	16	16
4·0	10	12	14	16	18	18

The principal types of lime in use in the garden are burnt or lump lime, also known as quicklime (calcium oxide); slaked or hydrated lime (calcium hydroxide); limestone and chalk, both of which are regarded by the chemist as having the same chemical constitution, namely calcium carbonate; and magnesium limestone, which may be obtained in natural, burnt and hydrated forms.

In considering the relative value of these different kinds of lime two points should be taken into account; first the amount of calcium oxide, either actual or equivalent, which each contains, and secondly the fineness of its particles. In this latter connection it must be recollected that burnt lime, though at first in large lumps, rapidly disintegrates into a very fine powder on exposure to the air. Other things being equal the sample with the highest percentage of calcium oxide and the tiniest particles is the best to use. There are only two qualifications to this statement. The first is that burnt lime scorches foliage and for this reason cannot be used with safety on land on which plants are growing. The second is that magnesium limestone, besides enriching the soil in lime, also provides it with magnesium, which is valuable if the soil is lacking in that ingredient but may be dangerous if the soil already has enough magnesium. It is quite possible to work out the unit valuation for any kind of lime on the basis of its price and percentage of calcium oxide and I have tried to show how this is done in the accompanying table.

TABLE OF LIME EQUIVALENTS

All figures represent oz. per sq. yd. Figures in vertical columns show relative dressings of different forms of lime required to produce the same effect.

Quicklime	1	2	3	4	5	6	7	8
Hydrated Lime	1⅓	2⅔	4	5⅓	6⅔	8	9⅓	10⅔
Finely Ground Chalk	2	4	6	8	10	12	14	16
Finely Ground Limestone	2	4	6	8	10	12	14	16
Coarsely Ground Chalk	3	6	9	12	15	18	21	24
Coarsely Ground Limestone	3	6	9	12	15	18	21	24
Lump Chalk	4	8	12	16	20	24	28	32
Quicklime	9	10	11	12	13	14	15	16
Hydrated Lime	12	13⅓	14⅔	16	17⅓	18⅔	20	21⅓
Finely Ground Chalk	18	20	22	24	26	28	30	32
Finely Ground Limestone	18	20	22	24	26	28	30	32
Coarsely Ground Chalk	27	30	33	36	39	42	45	48
Coarsely Ground Limestone	27	30	33	36	39	42	45	48
Lump Chalk	36	40	44	48	52	56	60	64

The last point to consider in relation to lime is the best time of year at which to use it and the method by which it should be applied. Contrary to frequent advice it is not wise to give lime as a top dressing only. It should be worked, as thoroughly and evenly as possible, into the upper soil, to a depth of 3 or 4 inches. This fact is of more importance in fixing the time of application than almost any other. It will in general be easier to apply lime properly in the autumn or early spring than in the winter or summer for it is at the two former seasons that the ground can, as a rule, be most thoroughly worked. The only other matter of importance in this connection is that lime should not be applied at the same time as dung, particularly if the dung is fresh, nor at the same time as certain fertilisers, notably sulphate of ammonia. Lime liberates nitrogen from dung and sulphate of ammonia in the form of ammonia gas, which passes into the atmosphere and is lost. It is possible without much loss to give a moderate dressing of lime two or three months before or after applying manure or sulphate of ammonia but it is better policy to make the applications in separate years. Where rotation is carried out, see Chapter XXIII, it is good policy to give lime once in every third or fourth year, omitting dung altogether that season.

LIQUID MANURE. This may be prepared in a great variety of ways. Originally the term was confined to the liquid drainings from stables, cow sheds, etc. which were allowed to run into underground cess pits from which they were pumped on to the land from time to time. This kind of manure is still very valuable and though no hard and fast figures can be given for analysis it can in general be stated to be richer in plant foods, particularly potash, than an equivalent bulk of solid manure from the same source. It can also be used as a spring or summer feed for plants in growth for which purpose it should be diluted with several times its own volume of water.

A very good substitute for this kind of natural liquid manure can be made by steeping a small sack of well-rotted dung in a tub of water and using the latter in place of ordinary water for plants in full growth. Like the liquid referred to above it must be well diluted, approximately to the colour of straw, otherwise it is liable to be too strong and cause injury to delicate roots.

Liquid manures can also be prepared with almost any soluble chemical fertilisers but great care must then be exercised not to increase the strength too much. In the case of proprietary fertilisers the manufacturers generally give instructions for the preparation of liquid manures and these must be followed to the letter. Failing any such instructions it is generally safe to use a complete fertiliser containing up to 10 per cent. nitrogen, phosphoric acid and potash at the rate of 1 oz. to the gallon of water, though more dilute solutions employed in greater quantity give better results. Single chemicals such as nitrate of soda, sulphate of ammonia, etc. should seldom be employed at a strength above ½ oz. per gallon.

A point of importance is that most of the plant foods in dung are only liberated after fairly prolonged decomposition. As a consequence it is useless to prepare liquid manure from undecayed animal droppings.

MEAT MEAL. Pure meat meal, like hoof and horn meal, is mainly a nitrogenous fertiliser but its analysis will vary greatly according to the proportion of other ingredients it may contain. For example most manufacturers include a proportion of bones in their meat meal and these will give a phosphatic as well as a nitrogenous content. All such fertilisers should be purchased against their published analysis. In general they are somewhat slow in action but safe and valuable foods if not too expensive. They are most suitable for potting composts and for winter or early spring use outdoors, approximate rates being 2 to 3 oz. per bushel of potting soil or per sq. yd. of ground.

MINERAL PHOSPHATE. Vast natural deposits of phosphatic rock are found in certain parts of the world, notably North Africa. Naturally the analysis of this rock varies from one sample to another, extremes being from as low as 25 to as high as 39 per cent. phosphoric acid. In all cases the phosphate is only very slowly available, this rate being increased in proportion to the fineness of grinding. In this respect the material may be compared with basic slag. Mineral phosphate is most suitable for use on the more acid types of soil and should be applied in autumn or winter. Rates of application are from 3 to 4 oz. per sq. yd. This is a material from which superphosphate of lime is manufactured by treatment with sulphuric acid and in general superphosphate is a more suitable fertiliser for the garden.

MURIATE OF POTASH. Chemically muriate of potash is potassium chloride and because it contains chlorine it is liable to act as a root irritant if used in too great quantity. For this reason muriate of potash is not quite as safe or satisfactory a fertiliser as sulphate of potash which it resembles in other respects. The potash analysis is 50 per cent. Muriate of potash is well held in the soil and can, in consequence, be applied at any time of the year. Rate of application is from ½ to 2 oz. per sq. yd. It is said that, unlike sulphate of potash which tends to make potatoes more floury, muriate of potash tends to increase the firmness of the flesh and render it more waxy when cooked, but I have not been able to confirm this in practice.

NITRATE OF POTASH. This chemical is far better known as saltpetre, the substance used for making touchpaper and an ingredient of old-fashioned gunpowder. It is rather too expensive for widespread use as a fertiliser but as it contains both nitrogen and potash in readily available forms, it is a useful food for special purposes. In particular it makes a first rate liquid manure. For this purpose it should be used at the rate of $\frac{1}{2}$ oz. per gallon. Dry it can be applied at rates up to 2 oz. per sq. yd. The analysis is nitrogen $12\frac{1}{2}$ per cent., potash 40 per cent. This chemical must not be confused with Chilean potash nitrate, which is quite a different substance with, on the average, a much lower potassic content.

NITRATE OF SODA. This is one of the two most used nitrogenous fertilisers in the garden. It is readily soluble and probably the quickest acting of all fertilisers. Under favourable conditions some effect may be observed three or four days after use. Because of its ready availability care must be taken not to use too much at a time, nor should it be applied in autumn or winter when it would be washed out of the soil before the plants had time to benefit from it. If applied direct to foliage it is inclined to scorch, while another fault is that it makes clay soils even stickier than before. Nevertheless it is the best of all fertilisers for giving a quick fillip to backward crops in spring and summer. Rates of application are up to 1 oz. per sq. yd. or $\frac{1}{2}$ oz. per gallon of water. The analysis is $15\frac{1}{2}$ to 16 per cent. of nitrogen. It is extremely deliquescent, that is to say it attracts moisture, even from the atmosphere, and the crystals will soon dissolve unless stored in a very dry place.

NITRATE OF LIME. This is a granular fertiliser which contains both nitrogen and lime and is consequently particularly suitable for application to the more acid types of soil. It should be compared with nitrochalk which it resembles in many respects. Analysis shows a variation of from 13 to $15\frac{1}{2}$ per cent. nitrogen. It is used as a top-dressing to crops in growth at rates up to 1 oz. per sq. yd. and, like every fertiliser containing both nitrogen and lime, is a useful accelerator of decay in the compost heap through which it may be sprinkled thinly. Like nitrate of soda it attracts moisture freely and must be stored in a very dry place.

NITRO-CHALK. This is a proprietary fertiliser which has the merits of being extremely clean and pleasant to handle, easy to spread evenly and containing both nitrogen and carbonate of lime in readily available form. It is most suitable for use on the more acid types of soil in spring or early summer. It attracts moisture readily and must be kept in a very dry place or it is soon reduced to an unpleasant wet paste. It should be used at rates up to 2 oz. per sq. yd. The analysis is $15\frac{1}{2}$ per cent. nitrogen, 48 per cent. carbonate of lime.

PIG MANURE. Chemically pig manure has very much the same value as that obtained from cattle and all the remarks made under the heading 'Cow Manure' regarding influence of feeding, storing, etc. on the value of the manure apply equally to this substance. The important difference between pig manure and that from the byre or stable is that it is much wetter and closer in texture and therefore less suitable for the heavier types of soil. For the same reason it is a particularly good dressing for light, sandy soils which dry out rapidly in summer. Pig manure may be used either fresh, to vacant ground only, or rotted, either on vacant or cropped land. Rates are the same as for cow manure.

POULTRY MANURE. Fresh poultry dressings contain a lot of valuable plant food though, as with other animal manures, the exact analysis will vary according to the method of feeding, etc. The highest grades are likely to be from birds that have been fattened under intensive conditions and these may reach $2\frac{1}{2}$ per cent. nitrogen, 1 per cent. phosphoric acid, and $\frac{1}{2}$ per cent. potash. This analysis is for the moist droppings. When droppings are dried slowly they lose bulk but not quality and therefore the analysis goes up. Taking the above sample as an example, when air dried the analysis would rise to $6\frac{1}{2}$ per cent. nitrogen, $2\frac{3}{4}$ per cent. phosphoric acid and $1\frac{1}{2}$ per cent. potash. Careful kiln drying would result in an even further extraction of moisture and a slight upward trend in the analysis. It will be seen, therefore, that an air-dried sample of poultry manure is worth, weight for weight, nearly three times as much as the same manure before drying.

There is a popular prejudice against poultry manure which is mainly unjustified. The only drawbacks to the use of poultry droppings are that they have not the useful mechanical effect of bulkier manures, they tend to make soil acid rather more rapidly and are, by comparison, somewhat poorly supplied with potash. The first drawback can be overcome by using straw, leaf mould, peat or compost in addition, the second by giving more frequent applications of lime and the third by supplying extra potash in the form of wood ashes, sulphate of potash, etc.

Fresh droppings can be dug in at any time of the year at rates up to 1 cwt. to 40 sq. yd., whilst dry droppings are most suitable for application in spring or summer at rates of 6 to 8 oz. per sq. yd., or may be used as top dressings to plants in growth at from 2 to 4 oz. per sq. yd.

PHOSPHATE OF POTASH. This is a highly concentrated and very soluble fertiliser which is, unfortunately, too expensive for general use though it is useful for application to special plants or crops particularly as a liquid manure during the season of growth. It contains both phosphoric acid and potash in readily available form, the analysis being phosphoric acid 51 per cent., potash 35 per cent. Use at the rate of up to $\frac{1}{2}$ oz. per gallon of water or 1 oz. per sq. yd of ground.

POTASH NITRATE. This fertiliser is often marketed as Chilean potash nitrate and is not the same thing as nitrate of potash. It is, in fact, a mixture of salts which occurs naturally in certain parts of Chile and elsewhere. Analysis differs greatly from one sample to another. Nitrogen averages 15 per cent. but potash may vary from 15 per cent. in poor samples to as much as 44 per cent. in best grades. Both potash and nitrogen are readily available and as the potash nitrate is very soluble in water it is best applied in spring or early summer. The rate of application is up to 2 oz. per sq. yd., or $\frac{1}{2}$ oz. per gallon of water.

POTASH SALTS. This rather vague name covers a variety of different mixtures of salts found in natural deposits in certain parts of Germany, France and elsewhere. Kainit (see p. 60) is one of these potash salts, though it is always marketed under its own special name. Why other grades have not also been given popular names is not at all clear. Potash salts should be purchased on their potash analysis which may vary from 20 to 30 per cent., the highest grade being worth just 50 per cent. more than the lowest. Other chemicals likely to be present include common salt and magnesium sulphate. Potash salts are all most suitable for autumn or winter use at rates up to 3 oz. per sq. yd.

RAPE DUST. This is a by-product obtained from oil mills and a good sample will contain from 5 to 6 per cent. of nitrogen which, however, is only available as plant food after a considerable period in the soil. The principal value of rape dust is to give bulk to more concentrated fertilisers and it is sometimes used for this purpose in commercial products. When applied by itself the rate is 4 oz. per sq. yd.

SALTPETRE. See Nitrate of Potash.

SALT (*Sodium Chloride*). Common salt, usually sold as agricultural salt, is principally employed in the garden as a weedkiller, although it also has some fertilising properties, for sodium is a plant food. Moreover the action of salt, especially on heavy land, is to liberate potash already there. It must be applied with a certain amount of caution, as too heavy a dose will cause damage. It is particularly serviceable for crops such as beet, seakale and asparagus, which are native to the sea coast, and during periods of potash scarcity, as, for example, in war time. Use in spring at rates up to 2 oz. per sq. yd.

SEQUESTRENES. Some chemicals required by plants become locked up in certain soils so that they are unavailable as food. A notorious example is iron on chalk or limestone soils. As a result of the lack of available iron leaves become yellow, growth is weakened and some plants, notably the so-called lime-haters such as many rhododendrons, heathers, camellias and lupins, may even die. It is no use giving soil dressings of ordinary iron salts as these are almost immediately locked up likewise. Feeding through the leaves by spraying with dilute solutions of iron salts may help but must be constantly repeated. A far more lasting remedy is to apply the iron in particular chemical combinations known as chelates or sequestrenes in which the iron is held against the normal reaction with the calcium carbonate in the soil. Various chelating agents are used, some more effective than others. Chelated iron or iron sequestrenes are applied like any other fertiliser to the soil and are entirely safe provided the rate of application advised by the manufacturers is not exceeded. They can be applied at any time of year and can be used for pot plants as well as for plants grown in the open.

SEWAGE SLUDGE. Of recent years this has been marketed in enormous quantities but it varies greatly in its value as a plant food. Much sewage sludge has been so washed by water that all soluble chemicals have been removed and little remains which can be regarded as plant food. Good samples may contain 2 or more per cent. of nitrogen and up to 1.5 per cent. of phosphoric acid and such have about twice the value of the average sample of farmyard manure. Sewage sludge should be dug in during autumn or winter at rates up to 1 cwt. to 20 sq. yd. It is a bulky, slow-acting manure, which has the merit of enriching the soil in humus. It should always be purchased against its published analysis.

SEAWEED. In seaside areas seaweed is often abundant and can either be collected by the gardener or purchased very cheaply. Analysis varies greatly according to the kind of seaweed which predominates and whether it is wet or dry. The seaweed richest in plant foods is that known as Laminaria, with long, broad fronds, usually with crinkled edges. Next in merit come the bladder seaweeds which are found in great quantities all round the British Isles. The least useful are the very fine, fern-like seaweeds. Dried seaweed will contain three or four times as much plant food per ton as a wet sample. An average analysis for fresh bladder seaweed is 0.3 per cent. nitrogen, 0.1 per cent. phosphoric acid and 1.0 per cent. potash. Note the comparatively high potash content which makes it an especially valuable manure for fruit trees and tomatoes. Fresh seaweed can be used at rates up to 1 cwt. to 6 sq. yd. and dry seaweed up to 2 cwt. per rod.

SHODDY. This is the name given to the waste from woollen mills. If it is used as a manure and dug into the soil it decays slowly and provides nitrogen over a long period. Moreover it has a most beneficial effect on the texture of almost all types of soil as it adds humus to them. Shoddy is, in fact, a very valuable manure and a useful substitute for dung, but unfortunately it is seldom available for private gardeners as all supplies are generally contracted for by market growers. Where it can be obtained it should be dug in during autumn or winter at rates up to $\frac{1}{2}$ cwt. per rod. Analysis varies considerably from one sample to another from as little as 5 to as much as 15 per cent. nitrogen.

SOOT. As a fertiliser soot is solely of value on the basis of the amount of sulphate of ammonia it contains. This may be as much as 30 per cent. in a good sample, giving a nitrogen analysis of 6 per cent., whereas a poor sample of soot, for example one which has been exposed to rain for some months, may have as little as 1 per cent. of nitrogen. Secondary uses are that it darkens the soil and so enables it to absorb more heat from the sun and that, when fresh, it destroys pests, especially slugs and snails. It can be used at any time of the year at rates up to 6 oz. per sq. yd.

SULPHATE OF AMMONIA. This chemical and nitrate of soda are the two most popular quick-acting nitrogenous fertilisers. Sulphate of ammonia has not quite so rapid an action as nitrate of soda but under favourable conditions will show an effect on the colour and vigour of growth in about a week. Unlike nitrate of soda it does not damage the texture of clay soils but it does tend to make acid soils even more acid. It must not be mixed with lime or ammonia gas will be given off which means the loss of nitrogen from the fertiliser. On the other hand, it is most effective on soils which contain an adequate quantity of available lime (see Lime). It is the best nitrogenous fertiliser for mixing with superphosphate of lime, sulphate of potash and muriate of potash and in consequence is employed in a great many complete fertilisers including proprietary preparations. It is most suitable for spring or early summer application and can be used by itself at rates up to 2 oz. per sq. yd., $\frac{1}{2}$ to 1 oz. being the usual dose. It is readily soluble in water and can be used in this way as a liquid manure at rates up to $\frac{1}{2}$ oz. per gallon. Sulphate of ammonia is not quite so deliquescent as nitrate of soda but nevertheless it must be stored in a dry place.

SULPHATE OF IRON. Iron is an important plant food and if it is deficient in the soil the plant reacts by failing to develop chlorophyll and in consequence has yellow or white leaves instead of green. When this condition occurs it has been suggested that dressings of sulphate of iron at rates up to 1 oz. per sq. yd. will serve as a corrective but it seems unlikely that this is, in fact, the case. Iron deficiency is generally due to excessive alkalinity of the soil rather than actual lack of iron and correction of this fault, as, for example, by discontinuing applications of lime, and giving heavy dressings of animal manure, leaf mould, peat, etc. and, possibly, in addition doses of sulphur will lower the *p*H (see Lime) and render iron in the soil available once more. If it does become necessary to give iron to plants it is most effectively done by spraying them occasionally with a solution of sulphate of iron, 1 to 2 oz. per 5 gallons of water, or by applications of sequestrenes in which iron is held against chemical interaction with calcium in the soil. See Sequestrenes.

SULPHATE OF MAGNESIUM. This chemical is better known as Epsom Salts. Besides its medicinal value it is a useful fertiliser in cases where magnesium is lacking. It is soluble and fairly quick-acting and consequently most suitable for spring and summer application. The commercial salt contains 10 per cent. of magnesium and should be used at the rate of 1 oz. per sq. yd. or in liquid manures at ½ oz. per gallon of water.

SULPHATE OF POTASH. This is the most generally useful form of potash as it is not only relatively pure but also contains nothing which can do any harm to plants. Moreover sulphate of potash can be mixed with such chemical fertilisers as superphosphate of lime and sulphate of ammonia. The analysis of pure sulphate of potash shows 48 per cent. potash. It can be used at rates up to 2 oz. per sq. yd. or in water at ½ oz. per gallon. As it is well held in the soil in spite of the fact that it is soluble it can be applied at any time of the year.

SUPERPHOSPHATE OF LIME. This is the most popular and generally useful fertiliser where phosphates are deficient. In spite of its name it contains no free lime and consequently it cannot be used to make good deficiencies of lime in the soil. Its value is solely for the phosphate which it contains and this varies according to sample from 12 to 18 per cent. in the form of phosphoric acid. Some manufacturers quote the phosphate content of this fertiliser on the basis of the amount of phosphate of lime it contains which gives to the uninitiated an exaggerated idea of the quality of the sample. The phosphate of lime content of any sample will always be just over twice that of the phosphoric acid analysis. For example, a sample of superphosphate of lime described as containing 40 per cent. phosphate of lime is the equivalent of another sample quoted as containing 18 per cent. phosphoric acid. Bear this point in mind when comparing prices.

Superphosphate of lime is a quick-acting fertiliser and is reasonably soluble in water. It can be mixed with safety with sulphate of ammonia, sulphate of potash, muriate of potash and bone flour. There is a tendency for mixed fertilisers containing superphosphate of lime to set after three or four days but the lump can easily be broken up by a blow with the back of a spade and the fertiliser will not set a second time unless it gets very damp.

Superphosphate, either by itself or in combination with other fertilisers, is most suitable for spring or early summer application. Alone it can be used at rates up to 4 oz. per sq. yd. or in water at 1 oz. per gallon.

TOWN REFUSE. Of recent years considerable quantities of town refuse have been converted into manure by local authorities. The value of this material depends entirely upon its origin and the way in which it has been prepared and an analysis should always be obtained before it is purchased. An average sample will contain about 5 per cent. nitrogen, $2\frac{1}{2}$ per cent. phosphoric acid and the same quantity of potash. This would have approximately five times the value of a good sample of farmyard manure and should be used at the rate of about $\frac{1}{2}$ cwt. per rod. Like dung it is most suitable for autumn or winter use and it adds humus to the soil besides enriching it chemically.

WOOD ASHES. A very useful source of potash which is present in the form of carbonate of potash. Unfortunately samples vary so much in the amount of potash they contain that it is impossible to give any general instructions regarding rate of application. A lot will depend upon the age of the wood burned, the rate of burning and the method of storage. In general old wood contains more potash than young growth, slow burning preserves more of the potash than rapid combustion and storage must be in a dry place or much of the potash will be lost. Best samples may contain as much as 7 per cent. of potash and can be used effectively at the rate of 6 to 8 oz. per sq. yd. at any time of the year. Poor samples may have as little as 1 per cent. potash and therefore seven times as much would be required to produce a comparable effect.

A small formal water garden planted with water lilies, rushes and other aquatics

Rose Shot Silk, a typical hybrid tea variety with showy pink flowers shot with gold. It is a first class bedding rose.

One of the best hedge shrubs is English yew but it is rather expensive to purchase and apt to exhaust the surrounding soil

Golden privet has the merit of being bright in colour and sturdy in constitution. Few shrubs stand up to town conditions better

A rock garden under construction. It is being built of medium size blocks of unweathered sandstone arranged to simulate a natural outcrop of rock

Easily grown rock plants used to clothe a low stone wall

A more elaborate rock garden built of weathered Westmorland limestone

A border of hardy annuals sown in irregular drifts

A herbaceous border in a small garden. It has been planted for a successional display

A herbaceous border planted in large drifts to give a bold colour display
at one season of the year

A border of Darwin tulips. These flower in May and can, if desired, be removed in time to make way for summer flowers.

Hyacinths used for spring bedding. The effect is usually most satisfactory when one colour only is used in a bed.

PART II

THE ORNAMENTAL GARDEN

CHAPTER VI

Flowers from Seed

I HOPE THAT the heading of this chapter will not prove misleading. It is, of course, true that most flowering plants can be raised from seed if one has the facilities and the patience to deal with them correctly. But it is not, on that account, my purpose here to enter into a general discussion of seed germination in all its more difficult or doubtful aspects. On the contrary this chapter is to contain only those plants that are so readily reared from seed and so quickly and satisfactorily attain flowering size that it has become the usual practice to renew them by this means annually.

The chapter includes all those plants known as annuals because they complete the cycle of their growth in one year and then die leaving their seed-produced offspring to perpetuate the race. But it goes beyond the rather narrow limits set by this definition and embraces in addition many plants not strictly speaking annuals though usually treated as such. Antirrhinums and lobelias are plants of this type which will immediately occur to the more knowledgeable gardener. It also includes biennials, i.e. those plants which complete their life in two years and then die like annuals having distributed their seed to germinate in due time. This group is also swelled by plants not strictly belonging to it though usually treated as biennial in gardens. The wallflower and the forget-me-not are two familiar examples. A point about biennials which the beginner should not overlook is that, despite the fact that they live for two years, it is necessary to sow seed every year if an annual display of flowers is to be produced.

All these plants which are so readily raised from seed have one point in common; they are comparatively cheap to produce. Hardy annuals and biennials in particular can be raised in hundreds from packets of seed costing no more than a few pence each and with little tax upon the gardener's skill beyond the preparation of a fine, crumbly seed bed. The half-hardy kinds need a little more care and must in most cases be raised under glass though often an unheated frame will provide quite sufficient protection. Millions of these plants are raised annually by nurserymen and offered for sale in the spring and early summer at very low prices. They often provide the best means of making a bright display during the summer and can be used with equal effect in formal bedding schemes or in the more 'natural' forms of gardening.

For the purpose of cultivation these plants may be most readily considered under three headings:

1. Hardy annuals and plants treated as such.
2. Half-hardy annuals and plants treated as such.
3. Biennials and plants treated as such.

HARDY ANNUALS

These are all plants which are hardy enough to be sown outdoors in spring without any protection in most parts of the country. Some, though not all, are hardy enough to pass the winter outdoors without protection. All complete their growth in a year or less. If they are sown in the spring they flower the following summer and ripen their seed before the winter. If they are sown about August or September they make small plants before the winter, almost stop growing from November to March, when they grow rapidly again and flower in late spring or early summer. Only the hardiest kinds should be chosen for this latter method of cultivation if it is intended to leave the plants outdoors all the winter, but any hardy annuals can be August or September sown for overwintering in a frame or cool greenhouse. Many of them make delightful pot plants grown in this way and potted on in October and March.

SOIL. Most hardy annuals will succeed in any ordinary soil. Germination is likely to be most rapid and successful in the lighter types of sandy loam particularly those soils which readily break down to a fine seed bed in spring yet do not easily set on the surface after a few heavy showers. Heavy, wet soils and those very liable to cake or 'pan' are the most unsatisfactory for this type of plant though they can be improved a lot by the free use of peat, leaf mould and sand.

A rich soil is not as a rule desirable as it tends to encourage leaves at the expense of flowers. For this reason dung should be used sparingly or not at all and should always be of the strawy rather than the concentrated sort. The quicker acting chemical fertilisers should, as a rule, be avoided for the same reason but slower kinds such as bone meal and hoof and horn meal may prove useful, especially on poor, sandy soils.

Beds for hardy annuals should be well dug or forked and then given a week or so to settle. If this is impossible, tread them well, first in one direction and then in another, to get a firm seed bed which will not sink unevenly at a later date. Rake the surface level and leave it loose and crumbly on top.

SOWING. It is of vital importance to choose a good period for sowing. As a rule from mid-March to late April is the best time but condition of soil matters far more than date. I would delay sowing until early May rather than put seed in when the ground was wet and lumpy.

Seed can either be sown in shallow drills, 6 to 18 in. apart according to the variety of annual to be grown, or can be scattered thinly all over the surface. The former method is usually best for formal beds and borders and the latter for irregular groups and patches either in borders of annuals by themselves or where annuals are grown with permanent plants such as herbaceous perennials and shrubs. If the seed is sown broadcast it can either be raked in or, a better method, can be covered by sprinkling some fine soil over it. Old potting soil is excellent for the purpose but ordinary garden soil can be used if put through a $\frac{1}{2}$ in. mesh sieve.

Germination is usually rapid. The seedlings must be thinned out directly they can be handled conveniently which is usually when they are an inch or so high. It is most important to give them sufficient room. One of the commonest mistakes is overcrowding which results in drawn, half starved plants which have a brief and comparatively poor flowering season. In many cases thinnings can be replanted to fill gaps or make further beds, but annuals with tap roots seldom transplant well. This is true of poppies, eschscholzias and godetias.

SUMMER CARE. Very little further care is required beyond occasional hand weeding or hoeing and the removal of faded flowers. This last is important because it greatly prolongs the flowering season. As I have already explained an annual's life is over once it has ripened its seed. If by the constant removal of faded flowers it is prevented from setting any seed it will often persist in the attempt to do so and go on producing more and more flowers.

Most hardy annuals will stand a good deal of sunshine and drought but in very dry weather it sometimes pays to water the beds thoroughly. The only drawback to this is that, once one starts to water, it is usually necessary to continue as the plants are encouraged to make more roots near the surface than they would otherwise do and so are less able to find their own supplies deep down in the soil.

SEED SOWING. If desired, seed can be saved from some of the plants to be sown the following year. All that is necessary is to cut off the seed pods, heads or whatever they may be when they turn brown or yellow, place them in paper lined trays in a sunny window for a week or so, and then shake or rub out the seed and store it in a cool dry place until sowing time. The drawback of home saved seed is that the different colours and forms of any one kind of annual usually intercross very readily and so, as a result, the next year's seedlings are 'hybrids' of very mixed appearance. As carefully selected seed from specially isolated plants can be purchased so cheaply it is seldom worth the trouble of saving seed at home.

HALF-HARDY ANNUALS

The chief difference in cultivation between these and hardy annuals is that most of the seedlings are raised under glass. Greenhouse sowing begins in January but the main sowings are seldom made before the last week in February or first in March. In either case a temperature of around 60° is desirable to ensure quick germination. A few weeks later seed can usually be germinated satisfactorily in a frame. Outdoor conditions are seldom sufficiently settled to justify sowing without protection before the first week in May and that means the plants will be late in flower. Nevertheless some kinds do well treated in this way and it is a useful means of extending the flowering season.

SOWING AND EARLY CARE. As regards the details of seed sowing and germination these are exactly the same as for greenhouse plants. The seed compost, John Innes (p. 423), or something closely resembling it should be used and placed in really well-drained seed trays or earthenware pans. Sow very thinly, cover lightly with fine soil and protect with panes of glass and brown paper to cut down evaporation. When germination occurs remove this covering and keep the seedlings in as light a place as possible.

Prick them off into deeper trays and a slightly richer compost when they can be handled conveniently and, after a further week or so in the greenhouse to get them growing strongly, remove them to a frame and gradually harden them off by increasing ventilation a little at a time as the weather improves. The object should be to get the plants thoroughly accustomed to the open air not later than the end of May. Many kinds can be put outdoors several weeks earlier, especially in the South and West.

SOIL AND PLANTING. The soil for final planting should be prepared in the same way as for hardy annuals but need not be quite so finely crumbled as the plants are by this time sturdy and able to fend for themselves. Plant with a trowel giving the roots plenty of space. Make very firm and water in freely. Thereafter treat exactly like hardy annuals.

HARDENING-OFF. The main difficulty with these half-hardy kinds is to get them thoroughly hardened off before they are put outdoors. If they are rushed along too quickly and are not gradually inured to the outside air they may receive a severe check after planting out. Then they are apt to hang fire for weeks and eventually come into flower so late that they give only a fraction of the display of which they are capable.

BIENNIALS

These are almost invariably raised in a reserve bed or in a frame from which they are first transplanted to another reserve bed and only to their flowering quarters when they have made quite big plants.

SOWING AND CARE OF SEEDLINGS. June is the busiest sowing month for biennials though some gardeners like to get their seeds in about a month earlier. This, I think, is wise on those soils which tend to delay germination. Seed can be sown in drills or broadcast as for hardy annuals but drills are better as it is easier to recognise seedlings from weeds and to keep the bed clean.

The seedlings must be transplanted as soon as possible to the nursery bed in which they will grow on. This should be sheltered and the soil should be reasonably rich and nicely crumbly. Lift the little plants with a small fork after first giving them a good soaking if the ground is dry. Replant them firmly with a trowel spacing them several inches apart each way so that they will have plenty of room to make strong plants. As a rule this transplanting can be carried out during July and August.

PLANTING. By October most of the plants should be ready for their final quarters. In these they should be planted just like hardy perennials either in straight rows if the object is a formal display or a supply of cut flowers, or distributed in irregular drifts if a natural effect is aimed at.

A SELECTION OF THE BEST KINDS

ACROCLINIUM. This is a pretty 'everlasting' flower. The blooms can be dried and will then retain their shape and colour for many months. Acrocliniums are hardy annuals. They grow about 1 ft. high and flower in June from an April sowing or July from an early May sowing. The flowers are daisy like, with stiff petals and the colours mainly shades of pink together with cream and white. Seed should be sown where the plants are to flower and covered very lightly. Give the plants a warm sunny place and lightish soil. Thin out the seedlings to 8 in. Cut the flowers for drying just before they are fully developed. Tie them in small bunches and hang them upside down in a cool airy shed. The dried stems are too thin to bear the weight of the flowers and must be replaced by florist's wires.

ADONIS (*Pheasant's Eye*). Plants belonging to the buttercup family and with distinctly buttercup-like flowers. These are deep crimson in colour in both the annual species to be found occasionally in catalogues. *A. aestivalis* flowers in early summer and *A. autumnalis* flowers principally in late summer. There is also a yellow flowered species, *A. vernalis*, but this is a perennial for the rock garden or part of the border in well drained soil. It flowers in spring. The annuals average 18 in. in height, have finely cut foliage which sets off the brilliant flowers charmingly, and succeed best in fairly warm places and well-drained soils. Sow where wanted to flower and thin to 8 or 9 in.

AGERATUM. One of those plants treated as half-hardy annuals though they are in fact perennials (in this case half-hardy perennials). Ageratums are for the most part compact, low growing plants with soft feathery heads of tiny bluish flowers. They are grand plants for edgings and groundworks to larger things for which purposes they rival the blue lobelia. The best forms do not exceed 6 in. in height but there are taller, more straggling varieties up to 18 in. Colours vary from pinkish mauve to a true if not very deep blue. All can be raised very readily from seed sown in a warm greenhouse in February or March or an unheated frame in early April. Prick the seedlings off 1½ in. apart each way into shallow boxes and harden them off to be planted out along with the other summer bedders in late May. Ageratums will succeed in any ordinary soil and sunny or partly shaded place and should be planted 6 in. apart. If desired specially good forms can be increased by cuttings of young growth.

ALONSOA. These very cheerful plants are regarded almost exclusively as subjects for the greenhouse, yet they will succeed well outdoors in sunny, sheltered places. For this purpose they should be treated as half-hardy annuals and raised under glass from a late February or early March sowing. Prick off in the usual way and plant out late in May, 6 or 8 in. apart. Heights vary from 12 to 30 in. for the species such as *A. acutifolia* and *A. Warscewiczii*, but there are improved garden forms of more compact habit, some of which do not exceed 9 in. Colours range from pink to bright scarlet and flowers are produced from June to August. When grown as greenhouse pot plants alonsoas are usually sown in August or September and then flower in spring. No heat is needed; only protection from frost.

ALTHAEA.—*See* HOLLYHOCK p. 106.

ALYSSUM. The yellow flowered alyssum is a perennial described under rock plants (see p. 189) but the sweet scented alyssum (*A. maritimum*) is a true hardy annual. It is probably the best carpeting annual with white flowers especially as there are now specially compact forms which do not exceed 4 in. in height. Incidentally there is also a lilac flowered variety but it is not nearly so effective as the white. All may be grown from seed sown in April or early May where the plants are to flower or, if preferred, seed may be sown in boxes in a frame or greenhouse in March the seedlings being transplanted a couple of inches apart into other boxes when they can be handled and hardened off for planting in flowering quarters in May. This is one of the hardy annuals which transplants really well. Plant or thin to 6 in. This alyssum will grow anywhere—sun or shade, heavy soil or light.

AMARANTHUS (*Love-lies-bleeding*). There are several species, all half-hardy annuals, but the one most commonly seen and, incidentally, most worth growing, is *A. caudatus*. This makes a bushy, leafy plant 2 to 3 ft. in height producing flowers in numerous very long, thick, catkin-like trails. In colour they are a deep plush purple, very striking if somewhat sombre. This is a plant that can be used effectively as an isolated specimen dotted about here and there in bedding schemes. Raise the plants from seed sown in greenhouse or frame in March and give the usual half hardy treatment of pricking off (or better still potting singly) and hardening for late May planting. A warm, sunny position and open but rather rich soil suits the plant best.

ANAGALLIS (*Pimpernel*). Everyone knows of the Scarlet Pimpernel and the pretty little native plant which provided his name, but many remain unacquainted with the far more showy garden pimpernels of which *A. linifolia*, also known as *A. Monellii*, is the best. There are blue, pink and scarlet flowered forms of this plant. The colours are very good and clear, the flowers are produced in profusion for a long time and the plants are easy to grow in any sunny place. They are perennials best treated as hardy annuals and raised each year from seed sown thinly in April where the plants are required to grow. Pimpernels are sprawling in habit and well fitted for the rock garden for use as edgings or for making a groundwork beneath taller plants. They seem to do particularly well in seaside gardens.

ANCHUSA (*Alkanet*). Mostly hardy perennials but one is treated as a hardy annual. This is *A. capensis* a perfect miniature of the big, perennial kinds with masses of bright blue, forget-me-not-like flowers on bushy, foot high plants. It will bloom in summer from an April sowing outdoors and should be sown where it is to grow for preference. It is not faddy about soil but likes a sunny place, as might be expected from a South African. Plant or thin to at least 9 in.

ANTIRRHINUM. Strictly speaking a nearly hardy perennial, that is to say it will live and flower for a number of years and will pass the winter outdoors without protection in some places. But it is not reliably hardy and more often than not disappears in winter especially if the weather is wet as well as cold and the ground is inclined to be heavy. In any case old plants tend to get straggly and are not so attractive as first year plants. For all these reasons and also because antirrhinums are very readily raised from seed sown in slight warmth and flower profusely in a few months they are almost invariably treated as half-hardy annuals.

Seed is sown very thinly during January, February or early March. Early sowing is advisable provided the necessary temperature of about 55° can be maintained as the early seedlings make the best plants and have the longest flowering season. Sow very thinly in well-drained boxes or pans and germinate on the greenhouse staging, covering with glass and paper. Prick off the seedlings when they have their first true leaves, spacing them 2 in. apart each way in ordinary seed trays or similar boxes using a slightly richer compost (see p. 422). Early sown plants may need to be potted singly into 2½ or 3 in. pots when they are about 3 in. high but as a rule March sown antirrhinums can be grown on in the boxes until planting out time. Water moderately throughout, give plenty of light and air, and get the plants into an unheated frame as early in March as the weather permits. Harden them off steadily so that they can be planted out as soon as the weather is favourable in May. In their flowering beds the plants should be spaced a foot apart each way, or 8 in. for the dwarf varieties.

Some gardeners pinch out the tip of each plant when about 6 in. high. This gives a very branching plant but the central spike is sacrificed and as this is always the biggest the practice does not appeal to me. It certainly should not be used by those intending to exhibit some flowers.

The only summer care needed is the constant removal of faded flower spikes. Rust, a disease which attacks the foliage first producing many rusty spots on the undersides of the leaves and then causing them to wither, is troublesome in some seasons particularly those that are hot and dry, and is difficult to keep at bay. Frequent spraying from April to August with Burgundy Mixture is the best remedy. Rust-resistant varieties are now available.

Varieties are very numerous and may conveniently be classified under three main headings, tall, intermediate and dwarf. The first are 3 ft. high, the second 15 to 18 in. and the last 9 in. There are also extra large flowered strains of the intermediate type which pass under various names such as Majestic and Triumph. In all these classes there is a great range of colour from white through pink, yellow and apricot to intense crimson. There are no better plants for summer bedding.

ARCTOTIS. A pretty half-hardy annual well worth growing. The flowers are like delicately formed moon daisies on slender stems and they vary in colour from silvery with blue reverse in the species *A. grandis* to white, yellow, orange and red in the numerous hybrids. *A. grandis* is 18 in. tall. The hybrids are mostly about half this height. All flower from July to September. They should be raised from seed sown in a warm greenhouse in February or March the seed being covered very lightly and watered rather sparingly at first. Prick the seedlings off 2 in. apart and harden them off for planting out at the end of May. Space them 1 ft. apart and give them a warm sunny spot in particularly well-drained soil. These are good plants for hot, dry banks as they are used to the heat of a South African summer.

ARGEMONE (*Prickly Poppy*). A race of sun loving American poppies. The best is *A. mexicana*, 2 ft. in height with big, lemon yellow flowers of the usual poppy type. Seed should be sown in March in a warm spot outdoors and light or ordinary soil. Do not transplant the seedlings but thin to 1 ft. apart. The plants commence to flower in July.

ARNEBIA (*Prophet Flower*). Those interested in novelty may like to have these plants with their yellow, black spotted flowers. *A. cornuta* is the species usually offered. It is about 2 ft. high and is a half hardy annual. Sow in a warm greenhouse in February or March and plant outdoors in a warm, sunny place late in May. Space 1 ft. apart. There is also a hardy perennial species named *A. echioides*.

ASPERULA (*Woodruff*). A big family containing a few remarkably pretty garden plants of which one, *A. azurea setosa* (or *A. orientalis*) is a hardy annual with myriads of little sky-blue, sweet scented flowers. It is about a foot high, has no particular fads and can be raised from seed sown outdoors from March to May where the plants are to bloom. Thin to 6 in.

ASTER. Favourite summer bedding plants correctly known as calli-stephus. The asters considered here are all true half-hardy annuals and not to be confused with the hardy perennial asters (Michaelmas daisies) described on p. 143. The botanist separates these annual asters in a different genus with the name callistephus but though this is some-times used in catalogues it has never become really familiar to gardeners.

Asters are of many different types but all can be raised from seed sown in a slightly heated greenhouse in late February or March, in an unheated frame in late March or early April or in a sheltered place outdoors in early May. Cover the seed very lightly and be sparing with water at first. Damp and heat are the enemies of seedling asters and will soon bring on an attack of damping off if permitted. For the same reason sowing should be specially thin and the seedlings pricked off as soon as possible. Personally I never sow asters until mid-March even in a warm greenhouse because with the longer days there is less trouble from damping off.

Space seedlings a good two inches apart when pricking off and use a rather open but fairly rich compost. Avoid checks to growth especially from chills or drought. Harden off steadily and plant out in late May. Asters like a sunny place but will often do quite well in light shade. The singles in particular will put up with a good deal of rough treat-ment.

If seed is sown outdoors in early May it is best to scatter it where the plants are to grow and so cut out the checks to growth caused by transplanting. Cover the seed with a thin sprinkling of fine soil. Thin out the seedlings to about a foot apart which is also the correct distance for planting out. Summer care consists solely in removal of faded flowers. If any plants wilt off in the beds, going black at or a little above soil level and quickly collapse they should be removed and burned at once and the soil soaked with a solution of Cheshunt Compound.

There are a great many different types, some with double and others with single flowers. All are serviceable for cutting as well as for garden display though some, such as Californian Giant, are grown principally for the former purpose. Ostrich Plume asters have big, fully double rather shaggy flowers. Comet asters are also double but the flowers have a firmer, more regular appearance. Both are about 18 in. in height. The Californian Giants and Mammoth asters resemble Ostrich Plume varieties in flower but the plants are nearly twice as tall. There are dwarf asters, usually about a foot in height, with double flowers of medium size. Another race of below medium height has small, button-like flowers and is known as Pompone. Then there are several strains of single flowered asters including the familiar *A. sinensis* with flat daisy-like flowers in a variety of colours and the bigger, shaggier Southcote Beauty. All flower from about August to October.

BALSAM.—See p. 440.

BARTONIA. The only species grown is *B. aurea*, a showy hardy annual with yellow, poppy-like flowers produced throughout most of the summer. It revels in light soils and sunny places and should be sown thinly in April where it is to flower. Thin the seedlings to at least 9 in. as the plants make a good deal of growth and will eventually be 18 in. in height. This is an easily grown annual which deserves to be a good deal better known than it is. Its one fault is that it is inclined to get straggly towards the end of the season but as much can be said against a great many more popular annuals.

BEGONIA. Most of the begonias are dealt with as greenhouse plants but one important species, *B. semperflorens* has become a very popular summer bedding plant and, though a half-hardy perennial, is almost invariably raised anew each year from seed. It is then treated as a half-hardy annual, the seed being germinated in February–March in boxes or pans in a temperature of about 60° and pricked off 2 in. apart each way into deeper trays to be hardened off in a frame ready for planting out in early June. If desired the best plants can be potted singly as I have advised for forward antirrhinums, so that bigger plants are available for putting out in the summer beds. The secret of success with these begonias is to use a rather open, leafy or peaty compost throughout and to give them plenty of sunlight and moisture. Plant 9 in. to 1 ft. apart each way in their final quarters. *B. semperflorens* itself has masses of small pink flowers all the summer. There are also good red and white forms.

BELLIS (*Daisy*). The common daisy is a perennial and a tough one at that, but the garden varieties to which it has given rise are often treated as biennials. There are some very good plants amongst these with fully double flowers, often of such size and brilliance that it is difficult to associate them with the humble lawn daisy. They make grand edgings or carpetings especially for spring bedding schemes with daffodils, tulips and hyacinths. The method of culture commonly used is to sow seed outdoors in May or early June, prick off seedlings a few inches apart each way in July in a nursery bed, also in the open, and remove the well-grown plants to flowering quarters in the autumn after the beds have been cleared of their summer occupants. The giant kinds

93

may be planted as much as 9 in. apart but the smaller varieties should be set 6 in. apart. All will grow in practically any soil and place. There are white, pink and red flowered varieties.

BRACHYCOME (*Swan River Daisy*). A blue or white 'daisy' which makes a bushy plant a foot in height. It is a sun lover and a half-hardy annual. Treat it just like an annual aster, raising the seed in a greenhouse or frame from a March or early April sowing, or sowing it in sheltered places outdoors in early May. The plants should be spaced 12 in. apart.

BROWALLIA. Though a greenhouse plant this may be treated success-fully as a half-hardy annual particularly in a good summer or a sheltered garden. Raise under glass in March and plant out as soon as all danger of frost is past. The best kind is *B. speciosa* which has showy white, lilac or deep blue flowers during August and September. It grows 18 in. or a little more in height.

CALANDRINIA (*Rock Purslane*). These are plants for the warmest places in the garden. They do well on sunny ledges in the rockery or may be sown on dry walls. Few of the species are true annuals but they may be treated as such and either be sown in greenhouse or frame for planting out in May or directly in the open in April, where they are to flower. The two best kinds are *C. grandiflora*, with showy reddish-purple flowers on foot high stems and *C. umbellata* with smaller but very numerous flowers of a penetrating shade of magenta. The last is a sprawling plant not exceeding 6 in. in height. Both flower in July and August.

CALENDULA (*Pot Marigold, Scotch Marigold*). The most easily grown of annuals but not to be despised on that account. The modern calen-dula is a really magnificent hardy annual, about 2 ft. high, with fully double flowers of great size and in a variety of fine shades of yellow and orange. Some have quilled and others flat petals. All can be raised with the greatest of ease from seed sown in March, April, May or early September where the plants are to flower. Cover the seeds with half an inch of soil and thin out the seedlings to at least 9 in. Most people leave calendulas far too thick with the result that they get starved and finish blooming sooner than they should do. While in flower they should be examined every day or so in order that all faded blooms may be removed. There is really no place in which calendulas will not grow but they are happiest in well-drained soils and full sun.

CALIFORNIAN POPPY.—*See* ESCHSCHOLZIA p. 102.

CALLIRHOË (*Poppy Mallow*). Plants for sunny places. They have brightly coloured, poppy-like flowers and make a good show in the garden. For June–July flowering sow in a frame or greenhouse in March and plant out in May. For July–August flowering sow outdoors in April and thin out the seedlings to about a foot. The plants are a little over two feet in height. Amongst the best kinds are *C. involucrata*, crimson and *C. Papaver*, magenta.

CALLISTEPHUS.—*See* ASTER p. 92.

CANARY CREEPER.—*See* TROPAFOLUM p. 128.

CANDYTUFT.—*See* IBERIS p. 107.

CANTERBURY BELL. To be 'correct' I should call the Canterbury Bell by its botanical name *Campanula Medium*, but this might be very confusing to readers in view of the popular association of 'campanula' with the perennial members of the race. The Canterbury Bell is a true hardy biennial though now a so-called annual strain has been raised which will flower in late summer from a spring sowing.

Seed of the ordinary biennial Canterbury Bell is sown in May or early June in a frame or sheltered border outdoors. In either case the soil should be rather light and as fine as possible. Sow in drills $\frac{1}{4}$ in. deep and about 6 in. apart. Prick off the seedlings into a bed of fairly rich, light soil when they have made three or four leaves each. Give them a watering first and another afterwards and space them 6 in. apart each way. They will soon grow into good, strong plants and can be put into their flowering beds either in October or March–April. Here they should be spaced a good foot apart each way for they will grow 3 ft. tall and make big, branching plants. They like well-dug, fairly rich soil and will succeed in sun or partial shade. Flowers are produced in June and July.

The annual Canterbury Bells are raised in a frame or greenhouse in March or early April. They should be pricked off and hardened off for planting out in May or early June when they will start to flower in August.

The annual Canterbury Bells are only available in the single flowered forms, though in a full range of colours including white, pink, rose, light blue and dark blue. The biennial Canterbury Bells not only have this colour range in single flowered forms but repeat them in varieties with fully double flowers, and again in the very attractive 'cup and saucer' varieties which are really semi-doubles with a second ring of petals behind the main bell forming a 'saucer' to its 'cup'.

CARNATION. In addition to the Border and Perpetual Flowering carnations described elsewhere there is an interesting and useful group of so-called annual carnations or Marguerite carnations. These will flower about August from seed sown in a warm greenhouse in January or February, pricked off into deep seed trays as soon as they can be handled and hardened off for planting outdoors early in May. They should be given an open, sunny position in reasonably good soil. Some of the best plants can be potted and used for cool greenhouse decoration in the autumn and winter. All flower very freely, have double flowers with fringed petals and they include a good range of colour such as white, pink, scarlet and yellow.

CASTOR OIL PLANT.—*See* RICINUS p. 120.

CELOSIA. One of the more difficult half-hardy annuals requiring a good deal of heat and moisture. It is more often seen as a greenhouse plant than outdoors but it can be used most effectively for summer beds if good strong seedlings are obtained by sowing in January or February in the greenhouse in a temperature of 65–70°. Keep the atmosphere of the house rather moist by frequent syringeings and dampings of walls and floors. Pot the seedlings singly in small pots as soon as they can be handled conveniently. Use rather rich soil for this. If necessary pot again into 4 in. pots should the smaller receptacles become filled with roots. Harden off very slowly and carefully and plant outdoors from the pots when all danger of frost is over and the weather is mild. It is usually wise to wait till at least the second week in June for this.

Give as sunny and sheltered a position as possible and keep the plants really well watered in dry weather.

The flowers of celosias are extraordinarily graceful and brilliant— feathery plumed in bright yellow, scarlet or glowing crimson. They are 12 to 18 in. in height and borne throughout the later summer and early autumn. There is another form, popularly known as Cockscomb, with stiff, curiously congested clusters of crimson flowers in place of feathery plumes.

CELSIA. The celsias are closely related to the mulleins and look like them. They have long, tapering spikes of flowers standing well up above the basal clusters of leaves. Though not true annuals they can be treated as such and this is the best method of culture when they are to be grown outdoors. Sow in a greenhouse or frame early in March and get the seedlings potted up singly and hardened off in time for planting out in late May. They will then flower in July. The two best kinds are *C. Arcturus* with 3 ft. spikes of yellow flowers, and *C. cretica* which is not much more than half this height but with larger flowers, yellow spotted with brown.

CENTAUREA.—*See* CORNFLOWER (p. 99) AND SWEET SULTAN (p. 126).

CHEIRANTHUS (*Wallflower*). In addition to the wallflower a few other species of cheiranthus can be raised from seed. Far and away the best is *C. Allionii* a brilliant, orange flowered plant usually known as the Siberian wallflower. It has the bushy habit of an ordinary wallflower, small, single, vivid orange flowers and an exceptionally long flowering season starting in April and often continuing till after mid-summer. In fact practically the only difficulty likely to be encountered with this grand plant is to make it fit into the rotation of bedding. If it is put out along with the other spring flowering plants it will be practically impossible to get it cleared away in time for the normal summer occupants of the beds, unless, indeed, one can bring oneself to sacrifice it while it is still in full bloom. *Cheiranthus Allionii* is not fragrant.

All wallflowers, including the familiar fragrant kinds derived from *C. Cheiri*, are really perennials but they tend to get straggly when old and are only reliable, year after year, on poor, exceptionally well-drained soils. In good garden soil such as is necessary to make them give their best display the first season, they are apt to grow lush and disappear the winter following flowering. In consequence they are almost always treated as hardy biennials. Seed is sown in May or June in an open position and well-broken soil, in drills ½ in. deep and 6 in. apart. The seedlings are transplanted when 2 or 3 in. high to another similar bed and spaced at least 4 in. apart in rows 9 in. apart. The tip of each plant is pinched out a few weeks later to make it grow bushy. In October the plants are finally removed to the beds in which they are to flower where they are spaced 9 in. to 1 ft. apart each way.

The common wallflower can be obtained in double flowered as well as single forms but the latter are the more popular. In addition to the more familiar yellow and crimson varieties there are many other more unusual shades such as rosy lilac, purple, ruby, orange and fiery red.

CHRYSANTHEMUM. The familiar perennial chrysanthemums have their counterpart in the world of annuals. These species are quite hardy and can be sown outdoors in March or April where they are to bloom. Broadcast the seed very thinly or sow in drills a foot apart, and cover with ¼ in. of fine soil. Choose a really sunny position for these plants. They are not particular as regards soil though they do best in those that are fairly light and open. With really good drainage

it is possible to sow in September as well as in spring and let the seedlings stand outdoors all winter. They will then flower early the following summer before the spring sown seedlings commence. All plants,
autumn or spring sown, should be thinned to about 1 ft. apart as they
bush out considerably and reach a height of anything from 18 in. to
3 ft. according to variety. There are single and double flowered forms.
White and shades of yellow are frequent in both but the singles are
often banded with a contrasting colour such as crimson or rose with,
in some instances, a central disc of yet another shade giving a tricolor
effect. The plant known in gardens as 'golden feather' and often clipped
as an edging or for carpet bedding is *C. Parthenium aureum*. It can be
raised from seed as above.

CLARKIA. Very easily grown hardy annuals which will thrive in
practically any soil and sunny, or even partially shady position. All
the garden varieties have double flowers carried in what, in the
non-technical sense, one would call a slender spike. From successional sowings made between mid-March and mid-May plants may be
flowered from July to October, while an early September sowing made
in a fairly sheltered place will provide flowers in May and June the
following year. All sowings should be made where the plants are
to flower as clarkias do not transplant well. Sow thinly $\frac{1}{2}$ in. deep and
thin the seedlings to about 9 in. Some seeds can also be sown in small
pots and potted on for flowering in the cool greenhouse.

There are a great many varieties in shades of pink and red and there
is also a good pure white. Heights range from about 18 to 30 in.

COBAEA SCANDENS. One of the few good annual climbing plants.
Strictly speaking it is not an annual at all but a half-hardy
perennial, but it is much more convenient in the garden to raise it
anew each year from seed rather than try to protect it during the
winter. Seed is sown in February or March in a greenhouse or frame
and the seedlings are potted singly in 3 or 4 in. pots and hardened
off for late May planting. Given good soil and a sunny place they
will grow very rapidly and one plant may easily cover a space 8 ft.
square in one summer. The flowers are not unlike those of the Canterbury bell and are either a rather pale violet-purple or white in colour.
A drawback is that, unless plants are got well forward and kept growing
steadily, flowering may start rather late in the summer.

COLLINSIA BICOLOR. A pretty little hardy annual with 9 in. spikes
of lilac and white flowers all summer. It should be sown thinly where
it is to flower and be thinned out to 6 in. Successional sowings can be

made from mid-March to mid-May with a further sowing in well-drained soil in early September to stand the winter outdoors and flower the following June.

CONVOLVULUS. Two showy hardy annuals pass in gardens under the names *C. major* and *C. minor*. They are convenient names for they do neatly convey the fact that one is big and the other small. But neither happens to be correct botanically. The first should be *Ipomaea purpurea* and the other *C. tricolor*. Both are easily grown in any ordinary soil and sunny place. *C. minor* is hardy and can be sown outdoors in March, April or even September where it is to bloom. *C. major* is not so hardy and should not be sown outdoors before early May. However, it grows so fast that late sowing is no great drawback. Alternatively it can be raised in small pots in greenhouse or frame from a March sowing. *C. minor* should be thinned to at least 9 in. and left to cover the ground with its spreading, bushy growth. *C. major* needs 2 ft. or more and its proper place is at the foot of a fence, screen or arch up which it can climb. This it will do very quickly to a height of 5 ft. or more. There are blue, pink and white varieties of *C. minor*; blue, pink and crimson of *C. major*. Both will flower all August and September.

COREOPSIS. In addition to the perennial varieties of coreopsis described in Chapter VII there are some excellent hardy annual kinds. These sometimes pass under the name 'Calliopsis', but coreopsis is correct. All have very showy flowers like big, broad-petalled daisies on slender but surprisingly strong stems 1 to 3 ft. in height according to variety. In some the flowers are wholly yellow; others are crimson, while yet others combine yellow and crimson. All flower from July to September. Sow successively from mid-March to early May, outdoors where the plants are to flower. Cover lightly and thin the seedlings to at least 9 in. apart. These annual varieties of coreopsis do best in a sunny place and are not in the least finicky regarding soil. They are excellent for cutting as well as being first rate bedding plants.

CORNFLOWER. This favourite hardy annual needs no description, though all readers may not be aware that in addition to the common tall, deep blue variety there are good pinks, lilacs and pale blues of similar height, a tall white and a blue flowered dwarf that does not exceed 12 in. in height. This last is excellent for bedding. The tall varieties can also be used for garden display but need careful staking. Their prime value is as cut flowers for which purpose they are unexcelled by any hardy annual. Sow seed thinly in March, April or early

September in drills ½ in. deep and 18 in. apart (9 in. for the dwarf variety). Thin the seedlings to at least 9 in. (6 in. for the dwarf) and place bushy hazel branches in the ground around the tall kinds to give them support. They will grow up through the twigs and soon hide them from view. An alternative is to strain a length of twine or wire between stakes down each side of the row, but this is not so neat. If the flowers are required for cutting, gather them regularly and do not let any form seed as this will shorten the flowering season. Seedlings from the September sowing will stand the winter outdoors without protection provided the soil is fairly light and well drained. These seedlings will start to flower the following June about a month ahead of the March sown plants. In spring sowing can be carried out in almost any kind of soil though light, not too rich soils give the best results. The position chosen should be open and sunny.

COSMEA (*Cosmos*). Half-hardy annuals with ferny foliage and flowers in a variety of shades of pink, rose, wine red, white and yellow. Double flowered varieties are also available. Seed should be sown in a temperature of 55 to 60° in February and the seedlings pricked off and hardened for planting out during the second half of May or early in June. Space them at least 9 in. apart in a sunny place and reasonably good soil. Some strains start to flower very late in the summer and should be avoided. This fault is often erroneously put down to faulty culture. A good strain will start to flower in June or at latest July and continue till September if faded flowers are removed regularly. Cosmeas are first rate for cutting because of their long, slender stems and are also good bedding plants for the centres of beds or the back of borders as they average 3 ft. in height and may exceed this considerably in rich soil or partial shade.

CYNOGLOSSUM (*Hound's Tongue*). *C. amabile* has brilliant blue forget-me-not flowers and it can be treated as an annual. Sow in the open ground in late April for August–September flowering or raise in boxes in a frame in March for planting out in May to give July–August bloom. The plants are bushy and about 2 ft. in height and will be all the better for a little support as, for example, from the tops of some hazel branches pushed into the ground around them while they are still fairly small.

DAHLIA. The many double flowered forms of dahlia I have dealt with elsewhere (see p. 343). Here I only want to mention the dwarf, single flowered bedding types which are being increasingly raised from seed and are often treated as half-hardy annuals. They are very easy to manage and make an unsurpassed display from about mid-July right on into October or even, in a very favourable autumn, until November. The best results are obtained by sowing seed in a greenhouse with a temperature of 60 to 65° in late February or early March but seed can be sown as late as mid-April in an unheated frame and produce plants which will flower freely the same year. Early raised seedlings must be pricked off 3 in. apart each way or potted singly in small pots but, if April sowings are made very thinly, the plants can often be allowed to stand undisturbed in the seed rows until planting-out time. This must not be before the first week in June as dahlias are very readily injured by frost. Give the plants a sunny place in good, rich soil and space them at least 1 ft. apart each way. They will attain a height of from 18 in. to 2 ft. If desired the tubers can be lifted in autumn as soon as the top growth has been blackened by frost and be stored like other dahlias, to be replanted or increased by cuttings the following spring. As a rule this is only worth while with exceptionally good colours or with plants that are outstanding in some other way. Colours are very varied including scarlet, pink, yellow and white. Seed can be purchased to colour but seldom breeds entirely true.

DAISY.—*See* BELLIS p. 93.

DELPHINIUM.—*See* LARKSPUR p. 108.

DIANTHUS. Most dianthuses are perennials and they will be found in other sections, but the genus includes one important group of half-hardy annuals. These are forms of *D. chinensis* and its variety *Heddewigii*. These grow about 9 in. high and look very much like pinks but are extraordinarily bright and varied in colour. There are vivid scarlets, rich crimsons, good clean pinks, salmons and various effective combinations of these. Flowers are also very varied in form, some being double, some single; some smooth petalled and others deeply slashed or fringed.

All can be sown in a warm greenhouse (temp. 60°) in January or February to be pricked off 2 in. apart in deep seed trays as soon as possible and subsequently removed to a frame in April for hardening off and planting outdoors late in May. They will then flower in July and August. Those who have no heat can sow in a frame or unheated greenhouse in July, overwinter the plants without heat and plant out the following May. For a massed display plant about 9 in. apart.

Dianthus Delight is a free-flowering and bushy hardy annual.

DIMORPHOTHECA (*Star of the Veldt*). South African daisies treated as annuals. They love warm places and light well-drained soils. Rightly treated they grow very fast and will commence to flower in June from a mid-April sowing outdoors. Sow very thinly where the plants are to bloom, cover with a thin scattering of fine sandy soil and thin out the seedlings to 8 or 9 in. Alternatively seed can be sown in March in greenhouse or frame, pricked off, hardened and planted out in May. The plants bush out a good deal and grow about 1 ft. high. Colours are always bright and pleasing and include fine shades of yellow, orange, apricot and buff.

ECCREMOCARPUS SCABER. A vigorous, half-hardy, perennial climber which, like *Cobaea scandens*, can be so readily raised and flowered from seed in one season that this is the practically universal method of growing it. It is a slender, twining plant with tendrils, the flowers are small, tubular and scarlet and they are at their best in August. The plant thrives in a warm, sunny place such as the side of a porch or arch facing south. Sow seed in a greenhouse early in March, pot the seedlings singly in 3 or 4 in. pots and harden them off for late May or early June planting. If the soil is reasonably good the plants will easily reach the top of a 10 ft. trellis in one season.

ECHIUM. These rather weedy plants have the merit of thriving in very hot dry places and poor soils, which improve rather than spoil them by keeping them compact and encouraging the freest production of their bright blue or red flowers. Heights vary from 1 to 2 ft. All are hardy. The best to treat as annuals are *E. creticum*, red and *E. plantagineum*, blue. These can be raised from seed sown in April where the plants are to bloom. Thin to about 9 in.

ERYSIMUM. Wallflower-like hardy perennials which are almost always treated as hardy biennials. Culture is exactly the same as for cheiranthus (see p. 97). *E. linifolium* is about 18 in. and has mauve flowers. There are also good forms of *E. suffrutescens* which are a little taller and have clear yellow or bright orange flowers. All bloom in late spring and early summer.

ESCHSCHOLZIA (*Californian Poppy*). For a warm, rather dry place there is no more easily grown or brilliantly coloured hardy annual than this. The widely opened, poppy-like flowers are in vivid shades of yellow, orange and red. They have the high gloss that one associates with buttercups and are admirably set off by the finely divided, grey green foliage. Eschscholzias grow 9 in. to 1 ft. tall, spread rather widely and should always be sown where they are to bloom as they resent root disturbance. Sow any time from mid-March to mid-May in the sunniest and warmest spot available. Thin the seedlings to 8 or 9 in. and then leave them to look after themselves. If faded flowers can be removed from time to time it will help but it becomes an almost impossible task after a while because of the freedom with which they are produced. Poor soil is an advantage rather than otherwise as it increases the rate of flowering and prevents undue growth of leaves. There are double flowered as well as single flowered forms.

EVENING PRIMROSE.—*See* OENOTHERA p. 115.

FELICIA. Daisy-like flowers which have obvious affinities with the Michaelmas daisies—so much so, in fact, that one species, *F. tenella*, has sometimes been known as *Aster tenella*. As with the true asters blue is the prevailing colour and some of the shades represented are exceptionally beautiful. One of the best in this respect is *F. amelloides* a popular greenhouse pot plant which is often known as *Agathaea coelestis*. It will flower the first year from seed if sown in warmth in February or March and it can then be hardened off for May planting outdoors. Several other species, such as *F. Bergeriana* and *F. rotundifolia*, can be treated in the same way. The average height of these dainty, free flowering plants is 1 ft. and spacing in the border should be about 9 in.

FORGET-ME-NOT.—*See* MYOSOTIS p. 113.

FOXGLOVE (*Digitalis*). A plant so well known under its popular name that one forgets it has a botanical one. In gardens the common magenta red foxglove of our woodlands and waste places has been transformed almost out of recognition. The flowers are not only bigger but their colours are much more varied embracing fine shades of pink and cream, besides white and many handsome spotted forms. One new race has flowers which are held out almost horizontally all round the stem instead of hanging downwards all round one side only. All can be raised without the least difficulty from seed sown outdoors in May or June in a cool place. Prick off the seedlings in July or early August in good rich soil and a half shady place, spacing them at least 6 in. apart and they will grow into sturdy plants for removal to flowering quarters in October or March. They will grow anywhere but are seen at their best in fairly rich, leafy or peaty soil and partial shade. Space them at least 15 in. apart as they will make big plants averaging 4 ft. in height. They are at their best in June.

GAILLARDIA. Do not confuse the gaillardias which I am about to describe now with the perennial kinds included in Chapter VII. These are half-hardy annuals and they must be raised anew from seed each spring like any annual aster or ten week stock. They are all showy plants with the large, daisy-flowers typical of the family. Some are wholly crimson and some wholly yellow but most are bicolored with red flowers tipped with yellow or white. Most of the best are varieties of *G. pulchella* and the form of this known as *picta* with coppery red and yellow flowers is especially good. All flower in July and August from a March sowing under glass and should be planted in a sunny place and ordinary soil. Height averages 18 in. The plants should be spaced 1 ft. apart.

GILIA. The finest species, *G. coronopifolia*, is treated as a half-hardy annual, seed being sown in a warm greenhouse in February and subsequently treated in the same manner as asters or stocks. The plants have finely divided leaves and the scarlet, pink, salmon or yellow flowers are borne in long slender spikes 3 to 4 ft. high. There are other hardy species, such as *G. tricolor* with white lavender-edged flowers on foot high stems and *G. capitata* which is blue and about 2 ft. high, but these are not so showy. They may be sown outdoors in April where they are to flower. All like sunny places and are not particular regarding soil.

GLAUCIUM (*Horned Poppy*). *G. flavum* (or *luteum*) is a handsome British plant which is worth a place in the garden especially in hot, dry places. It has yellow poppy flowers and grey green foliage and it is known as the 'horned' poppy because of the extraordinarily long, curved seed pods which suggest attenuated horns. Sow seed in June or July directly in the open ground where the plants are to flower the following year and thin the seedlings to 1 ft. or thereabouts. *Glaucium flavum* grows about 2 ft. in height and flowers in June and July.

GODETIA. This is one of the most useful of hardy annuals. It will succeed practically anywhere, in sun or shade, light soil or heavy and there are heights for all purposes. Varieties of the tall type may be anything from 2 to 3 ft. high and they carry their flowers in long spike-like sprays. In contrast there is a dwarfer type in which the plants seldom exceed 15 in. and are very bushy, the flowers being carried in short clusters all over the plant. Finally there are ultra dwarf varieties of the same general habit but not exceeding 6 or 8 in. in height. In each type there are both single and double flowered forms, and the colour range, though mainly in shades of pink and magenta, also includes crimsons and white. Seed of all may be sown any time from mid-March to mid-May or in September in any ordinary soil. Cover lightly with fine soil and thin the seedlings as soon as possible to 9 or 10 in. apart (6 or 7 in. for the very dwarf kinds). The seedlings do not transplant well as they have tap roots. Flowers are produced all summer if several sowings are made.

GOLDEN FEATHER.—*See* CHRYSANTHEMUM p. 97.

GYPSOPHILA. In addition to the perennial varieties described on page 157 there is a fine hardy annual species named *G. elegans*. This has single flowers each about half an inch across borne in loose, lavish and very slenderly built sprays. It is an ideal plant for cutting and is grown in immense quantities for market, especially for sale with sweet peas with which it associates well. It is also a pretty plant for massing in the garden though it does not last very long. Average height is 18 in. There are white and pink flowered varieties. In order to ensure a succession of bloom from mid-summer until the autumn frosts four or five sowings should be made at intervals of about a fortnight starting in mid-March with a final sowing in September to stand the winter and flower early the following summer. Choose a sunny spot and any ordinary, not too heavy soil. Sow thinly either broadcast or in drills 9 in. apart and cover with ½ in. of soil. Thin the seedlings to at least 6 in. apart.

HELIANTHUS.—*See* SUNFLOWER p. 124.

HELICHRYSUM. The best of the 'everlastings' with chaffy-petalled flowers, which will last most of the winter if cut in the right condition and dried slowly by being hung in small bunches head downwards in an airy shed. The flowers are like big double daisies in a great variety of bright colours including yellow, pink and scarlet. They are borne in profusion on bushy plants 2 to 3 ft. in height. Helichrysums are hardy annuals and may be sown in April or early May outdoors where they are to bloom though still better results are obtained by March sowing under glass for May planting. Give the plants a sunny, open position in well-drained soil, cover the seed lightly and thin the seedlings (or plant out those raised under glass) 9 to 12 in. apart. Cut the flowers for drying just before they are fully developed. For winter decorations their stems should be replaced by florist's wires. Average height is 2 ft.

HELIOPHILA. These sun loving South African annuals are more familiar in the greenhouse than outdoors but they can be grown as half-hardy annuals and used for summer bedding. The plants have very slender, branching stems terminating in loose sprays of small, bright blue flowers. *H. linearifolia*, self blue, and *H. leptophylla*, blue with a white eye are the two species most commonly seen. Both should be sown in March in greenhouse or frame and after potting two or three seedlings in each 3 in. pot, should be hardened off for May planting in small groups just as they come out of the pots. Space these groups 8 or 9 in. apart and give them a sunny position in light, open soil. Average height is 1 ft.

HELIOTROPE (*Cherry Pie*). Though this plant is a half-hardy perennial and I have included it amongst greenhouse flowers, it is so frequently treated as a half-hardy annual that I must mention it here also. When grown in this way seed should be sown during January, February or early March in a warm greenhouse (temp. 60–65°) and the seedlings be pricked off into boxes and later potted singly just like antirrhinums. Be very careful when hardening them off as they are sensitive to cold. For the same reason do not plant out until early June and then give as sunny a position as possible in reasonably rich and well-drained soil. If desired some of the plants can be lifted and potted in late September and transferred to the greenhouse to be propagated by cuttings the following spring. The greenhouse must, at the very least, be frost proof.

HELIPTERUM.—*See* ACROCLINIUM (p. 87) AND RHODANTHE (p. 120).

HIBISCUS. The hibiscus of romantic novelists is a tropical shrub or small tree and could not under any circumstances be treated as an annual but the family, which is a big one, contains several true annuals of which the best from the garden standpoint is *H. Trionum*. This is a rather straggly plant, about 18 in. high, which produces masses of fleeting, silken-textured flowers yellow with a showy central blotch of maroon. It should be treated as half-hardy, i.e. seed should be germinated in greenhouse or frame in March and the seedlings passed through the usual stages of pricking off and hardening in time to be planted outdoors in a sunny place and rather poor, sandy soil in May. Space them about 1 ft. apart.

HOLLYHOCK (*Althaea*). This hardy perennial is often treated as a biennial, seed being sown outdoors in May or June to provide seedlings which are transferred to a nursery bed in July and to flower beds the following October or March. Sow very thinly in drills ½ in. deep and 6 or 8 in. apart. Plant in the nursery bed at least 6 in. apart in rows 1 ft. apart and in final quarters at least 2 ft. apart. Both double and single flowered varieties can be raised from seed and great variety of colour can be obtained in both types all of which will breed very true to type if the seed has been carefully saved. If desired the best plants can be retained for flowering again in later years and may be propagated a hundred per cent true to type by means of root cuttings (see p. 138). It is also possible to flower hollyhocks the same year from seed if this is sown in January in a warm greenhouse, seedlings are pricked off into deep seed trays or potted singly and then carefully hardened off for planting out at the end of May.

All hollyhocks are most likely to prove really permanent in sunny, sheltered places and rather poor, well-drained soils. The flowers may be bigger and finer in richer soils but the plants grow too lush and are apt to rot off in winter. For this reason and particularly in cold districts, some gardeners prefer to overwinter their summer raised seedlings in frames and plant them out in March or early April.

HONESTY.—*See* LUNARIA p. 110.

HUMULUS (*Hop*). The common hop is not grown for ornament but the Japanese hop, *H. japonicus*, is used as a covering for arches, etc. It is a very quick-growing annual climber with big, pale green leaves which are variegated with white in one variety. Seed is usually sown in greenhouse or frame in March so that the seedlings can be potted singly in 3 in. pots and hardened off in time to be planted out towards the end of May. It is also possible to sow in early May directly in the open ground where the plants are to grow but they will not get so big from such a late sowing. Given good soil and an early start the plants may easily climb to a height of 15 ft. before the end of the summer.

IBERIS (*Candytuft*). This family includes several outstanding rock plants (see p. 210). There are, in addition, two exceptionally fine annuals, the common candytuft (*I. umbellata*) with flattish heads of white, lilac or purple flowers, and the rocket candytuft (*I. coronaria*) with big columnar spikes of pure white flowers. Both average 18 in. in height but there is a dwarf (9 in.) form of the first while the rocket candytuft will grow considerably taller in rich soil. All are quite hardy and can be sown outdoors in September if desired to stand the winter without protection and give a midsummer display the following year. For July and August flowering it is quite sufficient to sow in March and April where the plants are to bloom. Thinnings can be transplanted elsewhere. Space at least 8 in. apart (more for really big blooms) and give a sunny position in ordinary or rich soil. The common candytuft can also be used for filling blank places in the rock garden.

IMPATIENS.—*See* p. 475.

IPOMAEA.—*See* CONVOLVULUS p. 99.

JACOBAEA. Hardy annuals which should be more widely grown. They are easy to manage and make a great display with their highly coloured flowers borne in clusters on 18 in. stems throughout the summer. The best strains produce nothing but fully double flowers—

small but showy pompons in bright shades of rose, purple and crimson. There is also a pure white variety for contrast. Seed of all may be sown very thinly in April or early May where the plants are to flower, while, for an earlier display, seed can be sown in the greenhouse in March and given the usual 'half-hardy' treatment. Outdoors cover ½ in. deep and thin seedlings to at least 8 in. each way. Jacobaeas succeed best in warm, sunny places and rather well-drained soils. They are first class for cutting.

KOCHIA (*Summer Cypress*). One of the few annuals grown exclusively for its foliage. It makes a pyramidal bushling like a miniature conifer, up to 3 ft. high bright green at first but slowly changing to purplish crimson as the summer draws to a close. The colour is most highly developed in rather poor, dry soils. Sow seed in shallow boxes in a frame or airy greenhouse early in April, prick off the seedlings 2 in. apart each way directly they can be handled and transfer them to summer beds in early June. They are most useful dotted here and there amongst low growing plants. They also make pretty pot plants for the unheated greenhouse.

LARKSPUR. Really a hardy annual species of delphinium but I have kept to the popular name in this case to avoid confusion. Larkspurs carry their flowers in long spikes not unlike those of a perennial delphinium though considerably smaller, but they have very finely divided, ferny leaves. There are both single and double flowered forms but the latter are the more popular and certainly the more effective. All are about 3 ft. in height. They flower in July and August from a spring sowing or in June and July from an early autumn sowing. March, April and early September are the best times for sowing. Seed is usually sown directly in the beds in which the plants are to flower, the seedlings being thinned to 10–12 in. apart, but an alternative method is to sow in boxes, prick off like stocks or asters and plant out in May or early June. Nurserymen often raise small plants in this way for sale along with other popular summer bedding plants. Larkspurs do best in full sun and will succeed in most ordinary garden soils though they prefer those of an open textured but fairly rich nature.

LAVATERA ROSEA SPLENDENS. A vigorous hardy annual which is closely related to the mallows and looks very much like a mallow. The flowers are shaped like wide funnels and in the common type are a rather crude rose pink, but there are improved forms including one, appropriately known as Loveliness, in which the colour is both brighter and purer. There is also a white variety. All are plants for the back of the border or the centre of large beds. They grow about 3 ft. high and if given space, a single plant will cover a square yard of ground. Sow very thinly in April (or, in a sheltered place, in September) where the plants are to grow and thin to at least 18 in. Give as sunny a position as possible. *Lavatera rosea splendens* will grow in practically any soil but flowers most freely in those that are well drained and not too rich.

LAYIA. Only one species, *L. elegans*, is much grown; a hardy annual with daisy-like flowers mainly yellow but each with an outer rim of white. The plant is bushy and about 1 ft. in height. Layia lacks the brilliance to make it a really popular plant but it is a useful addition to the garden in summer and is easily grown in a warm sunny place and rather light soil. Sow seed in April or early May where the plants are to bloom and thin the seedlings to 8 or 9 in.

LEPTOSIPHON. An unhackneyed annual and a plant for warm, sunny spots. Leptosiphons are dwarf plants for edgings, carpetings or rock gardens. Their fragile stems are smothered by the small but showy flowers in a great variety of colours. Seed should be sown in April or early May where the plants are to bloom and the seedlings thinned to 4 or 5 in. No further attention is required.

LEPTOSYNE. The hardy annual species grown, *L. Stillmanii*, has bright yellow daisy flowers on 18 in. stems and will start to produce them five or six weeks after sowing in any ordinary soil and sunny, fairly warm position. April and early May are the months for sowing and the plant deserves to be more widely grown for it is showy and useful both for cutting and for garden display.

LIMNANTHES. One species is grown, *L. Douglasii*; a delightful hardy annual which will flower in early summer from a spring sowing or in spring from an early September sowing. It is a great favourite with bees, and beekeepers often grow it from an early autumn sowing so as to have something in bloom to stimulate activity at the commencement of the season. *L. Douglasii* is a low growing plant with masses of pale yellow and white flowers. It makes a charming edging to a bed or border and is a welcome change from more hackneyed subjects. Sow thinly $\frac{1}{2}$ in. deep where the plants are to grow and thin the seedlings to 6 in. It likes a sunny place but is not particular as regards soil.

LINARIA (*Toadflax*). In addition to the perennial linarias (see p. 163), there are some excellent annual varieties derived from *L. maroccana*. These have slender spikes of small, snapdragon-like flowers in a great variety of very striking colours including rich purples, wine reds and bright pinks. All are excellent for cutting besides making a grand display in the garden. Sow from mid-March to mid-May in a sunny place where the plants are to flower. Thin to 6 or 8 in. The plants average 1 ft. in height. No special soil or preparation is necessary.

LINUM (*Flax*). Another genus which, beside perennials, includes one fine hardy annual. This is *L. grandiflorum* the 'scarlet flax'. It is a fragile looking plant with thin, wiry stems about a foot in height clothed with narrow leaves and terminating in loose sprays of vivid scarlet flowers which individually do not last long but are produced in never ending succession throughout July and August. Seed should be sown very sparingly in March, April or early May in a warm sunny place and ordinary soil. Thin the seedlings to 6 in. and then leave them alone. They will do the rest unaided.

LOBELIA. The blue bedding lobelia needs no introduction. For years it has been the most popular of all edging plants for summer bedding schemes. Strictly it is a half-hardy perennial but it is almost invariably grown as a half-hardy annual. Seed is sown in boxes or pans in February or early March in a greenhouse with a temperature of about 60°. The seedlings are pricked off 2 in. apart each way into other seed trays while quite small and are removed to a frame towards the end of April. If steadily hardened off the plants will be ready for putting outdoors any time after mid-May. Plant 6 in. apart in any ordinary soil and sunny or even partially shaded position. Lobelias are excellent town plants withstanding the grimy atmosphere of great cities better than most. They can also be grown in pots and hanging baskets though for the latter purpose the trailing varieties derived from *L. tenuior* are to be preferred to the compact type derived from *L. Erinus* and favoured for bedding.

LOVE-IN-A-MIST.—*See* NIGELLA p. 115.

LUNARIA (*Honesty*). This old-fashioned plant is grown for the seed vessels which are like inch wide parchment discs. They will last most of the winter and make an attractive indoor decoration especially when associated with scarlet berries. But even in the garden in summer honesty is not without attractiveness. The flowers are not very big and are rather a crude magenta-rose but they are freely produced and look pretty enough in the right place. One of the merits of honesty is that it will grow in quite shady places and rough soils, even under trees, where few other plants would thrive. It is a hardy biennial easily raised from seed sown in May or June in a partially shaded place outdoors. Sow thinly and plant out the seedlings about 10 in. to 1 ft. apart when they have two or three rough leaves each. No further attention beyond occasional weeding will be necessary. Height is about 3 ft. For winter decoration cut in autumn when the seed vessels look like parchment.

LUPINUS. The perennial lupins are described on page 164. The hardy annual varieties with which we are concerned here are by no means so beautiful, their flower spikes tending to be small and ineffective by comparison with those magnificent giants, but improvements have been and still are being made and good strains are worth a trial especially in poor, sandy soils for which selection is necessarily restricted. Sow the seeds 1 in. deep in March, April or early May where they are to flower. The seeds are big and easily handled so it is usually most convenient to drop them in singly about six inches apart and subsequently remove surplus plants to leave the rest standing an average of 18 in. apart. Transplanting is seldom very satisfactory as the plants take too long to get over the check. These lupins are 2 to 2½ ft. tall and they flower in July and August. There are white, blue and pink varieties.

LYCHNIS COELI-ROSA.—*See* VISCARIA pp. 129-130.

MAIZE.—*See* ZEA p. 130.

MALCOMIA.—*See* VIRGINIAN STOCK p. 129.

MALOPE. A hardy annual much resembling *Lavatera rosea* and, like it, a member of the mallow family. It is a hardy annual and makes a bushy plant 2 to 3 ft. high and as much through. The flowers are rather crude in colour, a bright but harsh shade of rosy red with darker stripes. There are improved forms and a white. Seed should be sown very sparingly in March or April where the plants are to bloom and the seedlings thinned out to at least 15 in. apart. Malope likes plenty of sun and warmth but is not in the least particular regarding soil.

MARIGOLD.—*See* TAGETES p. 127 AND CALENDULA p. 94.

MATHIOLA.—*See* STOCKS p. 122.

MATRICARIA. The best-known kind is *Matricaria parthenioides*, a plant, often described as *M. eximia* or *Chrysanthemum Parthenium*, with strongly scented foliage and masses of small, daisy-like flowers which in many varieties have been developed into perfectly double, though miniature pompons. There are white and yellow flowered forms varying in height from 8 in. to close on 2 ft. The plants are bushy in habit and perennial in character, though usually treated as annuals and raised from seed sown in frame or greenhouse in March. The seedlings are given the usual pricking-off and hardening in readiness for May or early June planting in a sunny place and ordinary soil.

MENTZELIA.—*See* BARTONIA p. 93.

MESEMBRYANTHEMUM. This family is mainly composed of half-hardy perennials, many showy, others merely strange, but it includes one outstanding plant which is commonly grown as a half-hardy annual. I refer to *M. criniflorum*, a trailing plant only a few inches in height and with many large, brilliantly coloured flowers which might suggest showy daisies to the unbotanical observer. Penetrating shades of rose are common, also crimsons, apricots, softer shades of pink and even buff. This is a grand plant for edging sunny beds and borders or for planting on south slopes and ledges in the rock garden. In shade the flowers refuse to open and they will even remain closed on a dull day.

Sow the seed in boxes or pans in greenhouse or frame in March, prick off into deeper boxes as soon as the seedlings can be handled and complete the hardening off process in time to plant outdoors, about 8 in. apart, in early June. This is one of those rare plants which actually seems to do better in poor soil than in good, but it does need good drainage.

MIGNONETTE. This most fragrant of hardy annuals no longer appears to be as popular as it was. Perhaps colour is more esteemed to-day than perfume but, if so, it may be pointed out that some of the best modern varieties are not to be despised as flowering plants quite apart from their exquisite scent.

It is customary to state that mignonette will only grow where there is plenty of lime in the soil. My own experience does not bear this out. I have grown excellent spikes in distinctly acid soils without any special preparation. Nevertheless there is no denying the fact that mignonette usually does well in chalky or heavily limed soils and it is certainly one of the first annuals which should be considered by those faced with the problem of dealing with such soils.

Sow seed successively from late March to mid-May where the plants are to flower and thin the seedlings to at least 8 in. Most people leave the plants much too thick and so spoil the effect.

Mignonette also makes an excellent pot plant for the cool greenhouse. For this purpose the seeds are sown in boxes or pans and transferred singly to 2½ in. pots while still quite small. Later they can be moved on into 4 in. pots for flowering. Seed sown in August will give flowering plants in early spring.

MIMULUS (*Musk*). The true musk, famous for the scent which it lost owing, it is said, to hybridisation with another species, is *Mimulus moschatus*. This is purely a greenhouse pot plant but there are many other species of mimulus which are excellent plants for the open garden, some of them hardy perennials, some true annuals but all readily raised from seed sown in greenhouse or frame in March. All like moist, fairly rich soils and will thrive in sun or some shade. Many are first class at the waterside. The best of all for annual treatment are the large flowered hybrids with brightly coloured and usually spotted or blotched flowers which are commonly sold as *M. tigrinus*. They are 9 to 12 in. high and flower in July and August. Seedlings should be raised under glass and planted out, 9 in. to 1 ft. apart, in late May where they are to bloom.

MYOSOTIS (*Forget-me-not*). The spring bedding kinds are usually described as biennials. Actually they are hardy perennials though they often flower themselves to death or succumb to wet and cold in their second winter. In consequence, and also because young plants give the best display, they are almost always treated as hardy biennials. Seed is sown outdoors in an open or half shady place and ordinary soil towards the end of June or early in July. The seed should be covered with ½ in. of fine soil. The seedlings are pricked off 4 in. apart in rows 8 in. apart as soon as they have made two or three leaves and are removed to their flowering beds in October. Plant 8 in. apart for a massed display or use as an under planting or edging for tulips, wall-flowers, etc.

Forget-me-nots can often be naturalised in the wild garden, thin woodland or shrubbery and will seed themselves about and soon cover all the ground. This is particularly likely to happen if the soil is rather light and sandy but the position cool and a little moist.

NASTURTIUM. The plant we all know as nasturtium is not really a nasturtium at all but a tropaeolum and the true garden owner of the name nasturtium is quite a different thing, in fact none other than the refreshing watercress. But here I am defying the botanist and sticking to the popular usage of 'nasturtium'. And what a good plant it is. Listed as a hardy annual it is really only half-hardy—another confusion you see—but it can be sown outdoors from mid-April to mid-May without protection and will then flower from midsummer until the frosts of autumn put a finish to its gorgeous display.

Yellow and scarlet are the typical nasturtium colours, separately and together in a great variety of brilliant combinations but other and more unusual shades are available including salmon pink, orange pink and cherry. There are both tall and dwarf varieties with single flowers as well as semi-tall and dwarf varieties with double flowers. These last are often known as 'Gleam' nasturtiums after Golden Gleam the first of the class to become well known.

All will grow in any soil—in fact the poorer it is the more they seem to flower—and in practically any position, though they do better in sun than in shade. The tall kinds make good coverings for fences, trellises, screens etc., while the semi-tall and dwarf kinds are excellent bedding plants. Tall and semi-tall kinds should be thinned to at least 1 ft. or planted that distance apart. Dwarfs may be as close as 6 in.

An alternative method of cultivation to sowing where they are to bloom is to sow the seeds singly in small pots, or space them 2 in. apart in seed trays, germinate them in a frame or sheltered place outdoors and plant them out in their flowering quarters in late May or early June. They transplant well.

NEMESIA. One of the loveliest half-hardy annuals. Nemesias vary in height from 6 to 12 in., can be had in bloom outdoors at any time from June to October and, under glass, in winter or spring, and they make excellent pot plants as well as being grand for outdoor bedding.

For ordinary summer bedding seed should be sown thinly in boxes in late March or early April in greenhouse or frame without artificial heat. Prick off the seedlings 2 in. apart each way as soon as possible and harden them off steadily for planting out late in May or early in June. The secret of success is to keep the plants growing steadily all the time without any checks which may easily occur in the boxes through lack of water, poor soil or rapid fluctuations of temperature. Use a good compost (see p. 423) with enough peat to prevent rapid drying out, and do not leave the seedlings so long in the boxes that they commence to flower before they are put out. In the garden give them rather richer soil than is advised for most bedding plants and a sunny or half shady position with plenty of water in hot weather.

The short, trumpet shaped, broadly lipped flowers are carried in showy clusters and include a great range of good colours such as blue, scarlet, crimson, yellow, orange and white.

For winter flowering seed is sown in early August in a frame and the seedlings potted and later taken into a cool greenhouse. Spring flowers can be obtained in the same way by delaying sowing until about mid-September.

NEMOPHILA. Lovely hardy annuals for edgings and carpetings. *N. insignis* is the best species. It grows 6 in. high, has small, sky blue flowers in great profusion and may be sown successively from mid-March to mid-May where it is to bloom in any ordinary soil and sunny position. Broadcast the seed thinly and thin seedlings to at least 4 in. apart. The plants will commence to flower from ten or twelve weeks after sowing and continue for several weeks.

NICOTIANA. The commercial tobacco is a species of nicotiana but the kinds usually grown in our gardens for ornament are varieties of *N. affinis* (*alata*), the sweet scented tobacco and also of *N. Sanderae* a hybrid from *N. affinis*. These average 3 ft. in height, have long, narrowly tubular flowers widely expanded at the mouth, and include white, pink, carmine and crimson forms.

They will grow in any ordinary soils and sunny or partially shaded positions and are all treated as half-hardy annuals. Seed may be sown in boxes or pans in a temperature of 60° any time from mid-January to June but for outdoor planting a late March sowing is most satis-factory. Prick off 3 in. apart in deep seed boxes when the seedlings have their first true leaves and harden off for planting outdoors from the middle of May to the middle of June. Nicotianas also make excellent pot plants for flowering in the greenhouse during spring, summer or early autumn.

NIGELLA (*Love-in-a-mist*). A hardy annual with ferny foliage and blue flowers produced during most of the summer. The ordinary form is about 18 in. in height but there is also a dwarf of about half this height. Seed of all these should be sown sparingly where the plants are to grow, the seedlings being thinned to at least 9 in. Sow from mid-March to early April with a final sowing in August to stand the winter and flower the following June. Spring sowings give flowers in July and August. The flowers are excellent for cutting as well as for garden decoration.

OENOTHERA (*Evening Primrose*). A big family including excellent perennials for the herbaceous border and rock garden. But the true evening primrose, *O. biennis,* is a hardy biennial which will grow in the poorest and lightest of soils and either sunny or shady places. It is easily raised from seed sown in May or June, either directly where the plants are to bloom, or in a nursery bed for the seedlings to be pricked off when large enough and finally transplanted to flowering quarters in October or March. It is a tall plant, roughly 3 ft. when full grown, with masses of large, lemon yellow flowers with red calyces which help to set them off. The flowers open towards evening and are individually evanescent though they follow one another for many weeks, the flowering season being from June to August. *O. Lamarckiana* is an improved form of *O. biennis* with bigger flowers and more robust growth.

PANSY. To the botanist this is simply yet another species of viola and even to the novice gardener the similarity between the pansy and bedding viola must be obvious. But to avoid confusion and because pansies are so commonly raised from seed I am using the popular name here and have dealt with violas elsewhere (see p. 182).

Pansies can be treated as perennials and propagated by cuttings just like the best violas, and this in fact is just what is done with some of the outstanding show varieties. But pansies for summer bedding are generally treated as hardy biennials and are discarded after flowering.

The method is to sow the seed in June or early July in a frame or in seed boxes stood in a sheltered place outdoors. The seedlings are pricked off a month or six weeks later into a bed of finely broken but rather rich soil and a cool, shady position. If a little very old dung or mushroom compost can be worked into the bed some time prior to pricking off, so much the better as this will hold the moisture these plants so much like besides giving them plenty of nourishment. In exposed places the seedlings are usually pricked out in frames so that frame lights may be used to protect them from the most severe winter weather and, still more, from sudden alternations of rain and frost.

In April the plants are put out in their flowering quarters, still in fairly rich soil but either sun or shade. They are planted 6 to 9 in. apart and subsequently it is necessary to be very persistent in the removal of all faded flowers before seed sets. In this way the flowering season will be extended well on into the summer instead of being confined to May and June. For a really late summer display a further sowing can be made in a cool greenhouse or frame in March, the seedlings being treated like half-hardy annuals and planted out in late May or early June.

PAPAVER (*Poppy*). The big oriental poppies are perennials, and I have dealt with them elsewhere (see p. 168). Here I am concerned with the Iceland poppies, which although also strictly perennial are almost always treated as annuals or biennials in gardens, and the true annual poppies which come mainly from two sources, our own native scarlet field poppy and the big opium poppy of the East.

The Iceland poppy, *P. nudicaule*, is an outstanding cut flower and a useful garden plant. It can be raised from seed sown very thinly in boxes of fine soil in February or March, barely covered, and germinated in a cool greenhouse or frame. The seedlings are then pricked off 1½ in. apart each way like half-hardy annuals (see p. 86) and are hardened off for planting outdoors as early in May as possible. They like a sunny position and well drained, though not too dry soil. An open, sandy loam with some leaf mould or peat suits them admirably. Plant at least 1 ft. apart each way. Water well for the first few weeks should the weather be dry. Once established the plants grow very fast and will commence to flower in July or August. If the position is not too cold or badly drained many of the plants will survive till the following year when they will have made big clumps and will commence to flower in June. Colours are both brilliant and delicate ranging from vivid orange to soft shades of pink, cream, apricot, and maize.

The true annual poppies are amongst the easiest of plants to grow. They will thrive in almost any soil and sunny position, in fact they seem to have a preference for the poorer and drier places. Seed, which is extremely small, should be broadcast as thinly as possible during March, April and May, where the plants are to bloom, and covered with the merest sprinkling of fine soil. Thin the seedlings to 9 in. apart for the Shirleys or 1 ft. for the opium varieties. The seedlings do not transplant well. If flowers are required for cutting it is a good plan to char the ends of the stems directly they are gathered otherwise the blooms may fade very quickly.

There are double as well as single forms of the Shirley poppies while as a rule it is only the fully double varieties of the opium poppy that are grown. The latter is about 3 ft. high and the leaves are greyish green. The Shirleys are 18 in. to 2 ft. high with ordinary green foliage. Colours are extremely varied in both groups.

Annual poppies can also be sown in the same way in September to flower the following May and June.

PERILLA. One of the few annuals grown for its foliage and not at all for its flowers. *P. nankinensis* is a bushy plant, about 2 ft. high, with oval purplish-bronze leaves which look very effective in summer bedding schemes. It is grown from seed sown in a warm greenhouse (temp. 60–65°) in February, the seedlings being pricked off and hardened like any other half-hardy annual for final planting out in late May or early June when danger of serious frost is past. Plant 1 ft. apart for massed effect or use as dot plants between dwarfer subjects.

PETUNIA. These gorgeously coloured half-hardy perennials are almost always grown as half-hardy annuals in the garden. There are single and double flowered forms but the former are the more popular and generally useful. The singles may be further subdivided into large flowered and bedding types, the latter being particularly floriferous though the name must not be taken to imply that the large flowered varieties cannot also be used for summer bedding. There is also a race of dwarf petunias not exceeding 9 in. in height. The ordinary types average 1 ft. and reach 18 in. in some cases. Colours are mainly in shades of purple, violet, wine red and rose together with white and various combinations of these colours with white. Some of the effects are rather garish but many are extremely effective.

Sow seed in a warm greenhouse in January or February or a frame in March. Prick off the seedlings into deep seed boxes when they can be handled and harden off for planting out in May or early June. Some of the most forward plants can be potted singly if desired to keep them growing freely until planting-out time. Petunias like sun, warmth and good drainage. They need a moderately rich soil and should be planted 9 in. apart for a mass display.

All varieties may be used as pot plants for the greenhouse but the large flowered and double types are particularly suitable for this purpose.

PHACELIA. Only one species is commonly grown purely for ornament. This is *P. campanularia*, one of the outstanding 'blues' amongst hardy annuals. It is, in fact, a real gentian blue without trace of amethyst or mauve. The plant grows 6 to 9 in. high and, from a mid-April sowing, will be in full glory by July. Sow thinly where the plants are to flower, cover with ¼ in. of soil, thin out to 6 or 8 in. apart. This phacelia likes a sunny place and an ordinary but reasonably well-drained soil. *P. tanacetifolia* is a taller and far less showy hardy annual largely cultivated by beekeepers because of the quantity of nectar it contains.

PHLOX. Most of the phloxes are perennials for border or rock garden (see pp. 168 and 221) but one important species, *P. Drummondii*, is a very showy half-hardy annual. This is raised in exactly the same way as stocks or asters, that is to say seed is sown very thinly in February, March or early April in shallow seed trays and lightly covered with fine soil. Germination is effected in greenhouse or frame with a temperature of about 60°. The seedlings are pricked off 2 in. apart each way into deeper trays as soon as they can be handled conveniently and are steadily hardened off for planting in the open garden towards the end of May. They should be spaced about 9 in. apart and it is a good plan to peg the trailing growths of the taller kinds to the soil in such a way as to get a really good all over cover of the ground. A few plants can be trained up short canes to give the effect of dot plants rising above a carpet of bloom. There are also dwarf types not exceeding 6 in. in height which need no pegging or staking.

Flowers are very similar in shape to those of the herbaceous phloxes but are borne in smaller clusters on much thinner stems. Colours are varied and often extremely brilliant including shades of scarlet, crimson, carmine, rose, pink, violet, mauve, pale yellow and white. The plants bloom in the open from July to September or may be had a couple of months earlier in pots under glass from a September sowing.

POLYANTHUS. The right of this plant to be included in the present section may be open to doubt. However it is so often raised from seed and not retained after flowering that I have thought best to place it here. None the less it is a true perennial and one which may be grown as such with complete satisfaction.

Botanically it is a primula as is also our native primrose. It is quite possible to keep polyanthuses for many years and to propagate them by division and this, indeed, is the only practical method when some particular form must be kept exactly true to type. But for ordinary spring bedding it is simpler to raise stock from seed and seedlings are far less likely to fall into ill health.

Polyanthuses grow rather slowly so seed should be sown in a cool greenhouse or frame certainly in February or no later than March. Prick the seedlings off into good, rich, finely broken soil and cool, shady position outdoors, spacing them 3 in. apart in rows 6 to 8 in. apart. Water them freely in dry weather. By October they should have made strong plants which can be lifted, with as much soil as possible, and transferred to the beds in which they are to flower. These may be in sun or shade and the soil should be good and well supplied with leaf mould or peat. For a mass display plant 8 to 9 in. apart each way. In some gardens it may be necessary to thread black cotton between short sticks over the beds in spring to prevent birds from picking off the flowers.

A good mixed strain will give a great range of colours in shades of crimson red, orange, bronze and yellow. Separate colours can also be purchased and good strains of blue polyanthuses exist though seed is scarce and the plants sometimes prove less robust than those of other colours.

POPPY.—*See* PAPAVER p. 116.

PORTULACA. A showy half-hardy annual which needs a warm spot and rather light, well-drained soil to do itself justice. The small flowers are vivid orange scarlet and the bushy plants about 6 in. in height. Sow seed in a warm greenhouse in February or March and, after pricking off 1½ in. apart in light soil, harden off for planting out in late May or early June. This is a good annual for a sunny rock garden.

PRIMROSE. When used for spring bedding this may be treated in exactly the same manner as the polyanthus. The colour range is only slightly less extensive and some very fine strains of blue primroses exist together with others which are washy or impure in shade.

PRIMULA.—*See* p. 222.

RESEDA.—*See* MIGNONETTE p. 112.

RHODANTHE. An 'everlasting' grown for drying and subsequent use in winter decorations. The flowers are pink and smaller than those of the better known helichrysums. Rhodanthe is a half-hardy annual and should be grown in exactly the same manner as helichrysum.

RICINUS COMMUNIS. The castor oil plant of commerce, occasionally grown in this country for ornament on account of its big leaves, which are finely cut in some varieties and handsomely coloured bronze, crimson or bluish green in others. The plants grow very rapidly and may reach a height of 8 ft. and a diameter of 4 or 5 ft. in one summer. Seeds may be sown in a greenhouse or frame in March with little or no heat and the seedlings potted singly in 3 or 4 in. pots and hardened off for late May or early June planting. This plant is chiefly valuable for the sub-tropical effect which it can give to big summer bedding schemes.

RUDBECKIA. Most of these are perennials and have been described elsewhere (see p. 175), but there are also hardy annual species, and though some of these are rather coarse and unattractive there are a few excellent garden hybrids. These have showy yellow, bronze or crimson daisy-like flowers, often blotched or ringed with maroon. They are carried on branching stems from 18 in. to 4 ft. in height. Seed should be sown in late April where the plants are to bloom and the seedlings thinned to 15 to 18 in. apart. Alternatively seed can be germinated in a frame in March and seedlings treated like half-hardy annuals for May planting outdoors. These annual rudbeckias are not particular as regards soil but like sun and good drainage.

SALPIGLOSSIS. Half-hardy annuals about 3 ft. high, with widely trumpet-shaped blooms delightfully veined in contrasting colours.

Growth is slender and branching and the whole plant is slightly sticky. The salpiglossis belongs to the same family as the nicotiana and bears a general resemblance to it, though the flower colours and markings are totally different. It is more popular as a cool greenhouse pot plant than for the open garden but is, none the less, a good bedding plant in sheltered places. Too much wind will damage the rather slender growth. Amongst the many combinations of colour dark blue and gold, crimson and gold, and rose, crimson and gold may be noted as particularly effective.

All should be grown in exactly the same manner as nicotiana except that the plants have not the same tolerance of shady places, preferring sun and warmth.

SALVIA. This big genus includes the herb sage, many sub-shrubby and usually rather tender plants, some good herbaceous perennials and the brilliant *S. splendens*, a scarlet flowered, half-hardy bedding plant with which we are mainly concerned here. It is a true perennial and for long was propagated by cuttings like a geranium or marguerite. Gradually this practice has given place to seed rearing and the plant is now usually treated as a half-hardy annual. It needs a little more heat for germination than the general run of such plants.

Sow in January or early February in a temperature of 65°, pot the seedlings singly in small pots when they are a couple of inches high and work them on into 4 in. pots by late April or early May. All this time they need greenhouse protection and an average temperature of at least 60°. By early May they may go to a frame for hardening off but it is seldom wise to plant outdoors before the first week in June. They should then be spaced at least 1 ft. apart in any ordinary, not too rich soil and sunny, warm position. They will then commence to produce their spikes of tubular, vivid scarlet flowers in August and continue until the autumn frosts. At their best no plants, not even scarlet geraniums, are capable of making a more striking display.

Very different is *S. Horminum*, a hardy annual with flower spikes which would not be very noticeable were it not that each carries a pair of large, bright purple or deep blue bracts. The plant grows 18 in. high, looks much like a sage apart from its striking bracts, and is easily grown in any ordinary soil and sunny position. Sow seed in March or April, thin the seedlings to about 1 ft. apart, and then leave them alone to flower in July and August.

SAPONARIA. The one good hardy annual, *S. Vaccaria*, is a slender-stemmed plant 18 in. high or rather more with masses of dainty pink or white flowers which are almost as useful for cutting as those of the annual gypsophila and have much the same decorative effect. Sow seed sparingly in March, April and May for succession and thin the seedlings to 8 or 9 in. A sunny place and ordinary, not too heavy soil suits this annual soapwort best.

SCABIOUS. The Caucasian scabious is described on page 176, but the equally popular sweet scabious is usually treated as an annual and renewed each year from seed. It is an attractive plant and not at all difficult to grow. Sow it in boxes in greenhouse or frame early in March and make a further sowing in mid-April directly in the bed or border in which it is to flower. In this way a succession of bloom will be obtained. The box-raised seedlings will be pricked off 2 in. apart each way and hardened off for planting out in May 1 ft. apart each way. The open ground seedlings will be thinned to 1 ft. and the thinnings can, if desired, be replanted elsewhere. In this way there will be flowers for the garden and house from July to October.

The plants average 3 ft. in height, like sun but are not fussy about soil. The flowers are in a great variety of colours including some particularly rich shades of purple and crimson, good pinks, mauves, lavenders and a useful white.

SILENE PENDULA (*Catchfly*). A rather fragile hardy annual which, nevertheless, will grow in most places without any fuss. The flowers are pink, the plants vary in height from 6 to 12 in. and seed should be sown directly in the open ground where the plants are to flower. Sow successionally from mid-March to mid-May for an all summer display and thin to about 6 in.

STATICE (*Sea Lavender*). The annual statices are grown principally for cutting. The flowers have the papery texture which distinguishes the 'everlasting' and, if carefully dried, they will retain their colour for many months. The two kinds commonly grown are *S. sinuata* in shades of white, blue and pink and *S. Bonduellii*, yellow. All these are half-hardy annuals readily raised in the same manner as stocks or asters from February or early March sowings. After hardening off, plant them out in late May or early June in beds in the reserve or kitchen garden from which their flowers may be cut without loss. Plant 9 in. apart in rows 18 in. apart in as sunny a place as possible and well dug, open, but not over rich soil. For drying cut just before the flowers are fully open and hang head downwards in a cool, airy shed for several weeks.

STOCKS. The showy garden stocks of to-day may conveniently be split into three main races or types. First there are the Ten-week Stocks and Beauty of Nice Stocks all of which are half-hardy annuals derived in the main from a form of *Mathiola incana* named *annua*. Then there are the Brompton Stocks which have another form of *M. incana* named '*graeca*' for their principal parent and are hardy biennials. The Intermediate or East Lothian Stocks, derived from *M. sinuata,* show some features of each of these two first types and may be grown either as annuals or biennials. Very different from these is the inconspicuous but extraordinarily fragrant night-scented stock which is a species known as *M. bicornis* and a hardy annual.

The Ten-week Stocks are the familiar double flowered, fragrant and very handsome stocks of the summer garden. They are raised from seed sown during the latter half of March in boxes or pans in a greenhouse or frame with an average temperature of 55°. Do not sow too early and avoid high temperatures and stuffy atmospheres. Ten-week Stocks need to be grown steadily, without checks, but also without undue forcing. They damp off readily in a hot or stuffy place.

Prick them off 2 in. apart into deep seed trays directly they show their first true leaves. Give them as light a place as possible, not too far from the glass, and harden them off steadily for planting out towards the end of May. In the garden give them an open, sunny place in moderately rich but fairly open soil. Space them 1 ft. apart. Do not pinch out the tips of the plants or allow them to be damaged carelessly as this will prevent them from forming their central and best flower spikes. There are varieties ranging from 1 to 2½ ft. in height while colours include pink to crimson, pale lavender to purple, white, yellow and many art shades.

The Beauty of Nice Stocks can be grown in exactly the same manner as the Ten-week Stocks but they are also much favoured for winter flowering under glass for which purpose they are better than the ordinary annual varieties. For winter bloom seed is sown from mid-June to early August in an unheated greenhouse or frame, the seedlings are pricked off as already described and later are potted singly, first into 3 in. pots and, when these are nicely filled with roots, into 5 in. pots in which they will flower. Throughout they should be kept in an unheated frame or greenhouse with as much ventilation as is compatible with the maintenance of a minimum temperature of about 40° and an average of around 55°. Heights average 2 ft. Colours are as for Ten-week Stocks.

The Intermediate Stock can be grown in two ways. One is to treat as a half-hardy annual but to sow about a month earlier than the Ten-week Stocks. Otherwise the treatment is the same and the plants, put out towards the end of May, will flower in August and September after the Ten-week Stocks have finished. Alternatively seed can be sown in August, the seedlings transferred to an unheated frame in October, and removed to the open again the following April to bloom at about the same time as Ten-week Stocks. The plants are 12 to 18 in. high. White, mauve, purple, pink and red are the principal colours.

The Brompton Stocks have spikes of flowers, in good strains nearly as double and as showy as those of the annual stocks but with a woodier main stem and a more shrub-like habit. They are grown from seed sown outdoors towards the end of June or early in July, the seedlings being treated in exactly the same way as wallflowers (see p. 97) except that when planted in their flowering quarters, they should be spaced at least 15 in. apart. Though fairly hardy they will not stand very cold winters in damp places so in northern districts or on heavy soils it is safer to overwinter the plants in a frame and not finally plant them out until April. Heights average 2 ft. Colours are white, rose, scarlet and purple.

There is nothing showy about the small, dull lilac flowers of the Night-scented Stock and by day one might easily pass this plant by unnoticed. It is towards evening that it begins to exhale its powerful perfume. Sow it freely in March, April or May in any soil or situation, but particularly near the house and below living room windows where its fragrance can be appreciated to the full. Thin the seedlings to about 6 in.

SUNFLOWER. The immense sunflowers in which cottagers delight, and from the heads of which vast quantities of seed can be removed to feed poultry and parrots, is a true hardy annual. It is really astonishing that so large a plant can complete its life cycle in one short season of five or six months yet such is the case. Seed can be sown outdoors in April where the plants are to bloom and by August the stems will be anything up to 10 ft. in height each terminated by one immense, yellow flower which may easily measure a foot across. By early September the petals will have faded and the seeds will be commencing to ripen, and it is quite likely that by the end of that month the gardener will be able to cut off the seed heads and bring them indoors to dry. They should certainly be cut directly any of the seeds show signs of loosening.

There are a number of varieties of this sunflower differing in height (some are as dwarf as 4 ft.), colour (they are all yellow but some are pale and others dark) or form of flower (most are single but some double, semi-double or with twisted or slashed petals) but all needing exactly the same treatment. They like rather rich soil and plenty of sun and, though they can be transplanted when still tiny, they do better when allowed to grow on where sown. For this reason it is best to sow the seeds in twos or threes about 2 ft. apart and then single out the seedlings to the strongest at each station.

SWAN RIVER DAISY.—*See* BRACHYCOME p. 94.

SWEET PEA. No one will deny the sweet pea the title of prince of hardy annuals. No annual is more widely grown by both professionals and amateurs and certainly none has given rise to such keen rivalry in the production of super-excellent blooms. Every summer show has a class for sweet peas and very fine many of the exhibits are even in small village and suburban displays.

There is a very great difference in the methods necessary to produce exhibition blooms and those of ordinary quality. Where the object is simply to have a good show in the garden and some attractive cut flowers for the house it will be quite sufficient to treat the sweet pea much like any other hardy annual but to give it rather richer soil. Reduced to its bare outline this means that seed is sown outdoors in March or early April where the plants are to bloom, in a sunny place and soil that has been well dug and moderately enriched with dung or a compound fertiliser. No further attention is given, beyond sticking with brushy hazel branches in May and occasional weeding and hoeing. It is best to sow the seeds in double drills nearly 1 in. deep, the pair of drills being about 10 in. apart, with at least 4 ft. separating each pair from the next similar pair. The seeds are spaced 2 to 3 in. apart and no thinning is done.

Much more elaborate methods are used by the exhibitor. As a rule he sows his seeds, in early October, two or three together in small pots filled with an ordinary seed mixture (see p. 423). Germination is effected in a frame but the lights are used more to keep off excessive rain than to raise the temperature.

At the end of the year the tip is pinched out of each plant. As a result it will make several side growths but only one of these is retained, the rest being removed at an early stage.

Meanwhile the ground in which the peas are to be planted is very thoroughly prepared. It is dug deeply—often three spits deep—and plenty of well-rotted dung is worked in together with bone meal and wood ashes. As likely as not the grower will finish off with a top-dressing of superphosphate of lime and sulphate of potash, the first at 2 and the second at 1 oz. per. sq. yd. Often only a narrow strip of ground is prepared, sufficient for a double line of plants 10 to 12 in. wide. This method has one drawback, however, namely that a strip prepared in this way is apt to be surrounded by comparatively hard ground to which it acts as a drainage trench with disastrous results to the plants grown in it.

The seedlings are thoroughly hardened off for planting out during the latter half of March or as early in April as possible. The seedlings are planted singly, not in twos or threes as they come out of the pots. They are spaced at least 9 in. apart—often a good deal more—and each plant is provided with a bamboo cane or similar support at least 7 ft. high.

Each sweet pea is kept to a single stem and trained up its own cane. All side growths are removed, also tendrils. Even the flower buds are picked off until the plants have climbed about 3 ft. up the supports, or until a few weeks before the date of the principal show. In this way the whole strength of the plant is concentrated upon the production of comparatively few flowers each of which in consequence may be expected to develop to the fullest possible extent. Flower stems a foot or more in length carrying four to six flowers each are obtained.

Feeding of these exhibition plants is usually generous. It starts about May and continues all the time the plants are in bloom. As a rule the food is given in liquid form. Dried blood may be alternated with a compound fertiliser, with natural liquid manure made by steeping a bag of rotted manure in water for further variety. A close watch is kept upon growth and, if this appears to be getting too coarse, additional potash is supplied, as, for example, sulphate of potash 1 oz. to 4 gal. of water spread over 3 or 4 yd. of row.

An alternative to autumn sowing is to raise the seedlings in a slightly heated greenhouse in early January and harden them off for planting out in early April. The seedlings are stopped, in the same way as already described, when they are about 3 in. high. In other respects treatment is exactly the same as for the seedlings raised in the autumn.

If plants reach the top of their canes and still appear vigorous and capable of producing good flowers, they are carefully untied, the bottom three or four feet of stem is laid along the ground and the top part is secured to another stake further along the row. In this way more head room is obtained and the season further extended.

SWEET SULTAN. This is a species of centaurea and related to the cornflower. It is a hardy annual, excellent for cutting and for beds and borders. Sow it outdoors any time from mid-March to mid-April where it is to bloom and thin the seedlings to 8 or 9 in. apart. Give it as sunny a position as possible and be careful to sow when the surface is reasonably dry and crumbly, otherwise germination may be poor. Apart from this there is nothing special to be said about the culture of this lovely, old-fashioned plant with its deeply fringed flowers in shades of mauve, purple, wine red, blue, yellow and white. Average height is 18 in. and the plants are in bloom from July to September from spring sowings. For June flowering sow in early September in a sheltered place and particularly well-drained soil and thin out the following March.

SWEET WILLIAM. An old-fashioned plant but still popular. It is a hardy biennial and it is grown from seed sown outdoors in May or June. Sow in drills in the same manner as wallflowers and subsequently prick off the seedlings into a nursery bed also, like wallflowers, so that they grow on into sturdy plants for putting into their flowering quarters in October or March. Final planting distance should be at least 1 ft. apart each way, and the plants should be given as sunny a position as possible in ordinary well worked soil. Pink, scarlet, crimson and white are the basic Sweet William colours and very beautiful they are, but many delight still more in the varieties with flowers of mixed colours, such as the auricula-eyed types, each bloom of which has a clearly defined eye of a contrasting shade to that of the rest of the bloom. All are equally free flowering and easy to grow; all bloom in June and July, and their average height is 18 in. They are as useful for cutting as they are for bedding or for filling gaps in the herbaceous border.

TAGETES (*Marigold*). Here belong those showy half-hardy annuals the French and the African marigolds and that bright edging plant, *T. signata pumila*, but not the pot marigold which is a Calendula (see p. 94). All are lovers of sun and warmth. They will grow in practically any soil, except, perhaps, one that is damp to the point of being boggy, but they are happiest in the lighter and better drained types particularly if they are fairly rich into the bargain. At one time there was great competition in the production of show blooms and for these it is absolutely essential to have a well-nourished soil in tip top condition.

Usually these plants are treated as half-hardy annuals, seed being sown in a greenhouse in March in a temperature of about 55°, but it is possible to get quite good results in many districts by sowing outdoors at the end of April or during the first week in May where the plants are to flower. In the first instance the seedlings are pricked off two inches apart in deep seed boxes (or potted singly for show purposes) as soon as they can be handled, and are then carefully hardened off for planting out in May. From outdoor sowings the seedlings are simply thinned out and allowed to stand. Final spacing in either case should be 1 ft. for African and French marigolds, 6 to 8 in. for *Tagetes signata pumila.*

There is a miniature form of the French marigold which may be spaced at 8 in.

The African marigolds all have very big, double or semi-double flowers in shades of yellow and orange. There are both single and double flowered forms of the French marigold in cultivation and most combine yellow and chestnut-red, the markings often being very beautiful. The regularity of these markings is of paramount importance in the case of blooms required for show and, as this is a hereditary character, great care must be taken to obtain seed only from perfectly marked plants.

TROPAEOLUM. Most species I have described under the garden name 'nasturtium' but one popular annual climber must come here. This is *T. canariense*, the yellow-flowered 'canary creeper'. This can be raised from seed sown in a warm frame or greenhouse in early April the seedlings to be planted out at the end of May where they are to flower.

URSINIA. A family of South Africans with bright, daisy-like flowers. They are half-hardy annuals to be raised in the same way as Cosmeas and others of this class or, alternatively, they may be sown outdoors early in May in specially warm, sunny places and, after thinning, left to grow and flower where they stand. If given 9 to 12 in. space from plant to plant they will bush out and make a better display than if over-crowded. One of the best is *U. anethoides* with especially vivid orange flowers each a couple of inches across with a central band of crimson. It is 1 ft. in height.

VENIDIUM. Another family of brilliant South African daisies. All species have big, showy flowers in which a ground colour is contrasted with a central zone which in some varieties is black, in others maroon and in others a pale shade of yellow or orange. Heights range from 18 in. for *V. calendulaceum*, to 3 ft. for *V. fastuosum* and its varieties. All may be raised from seed sown in a warm greenhouse in April but *V. calendulaceum*, which is hardier than the rest, can be sown directly in the open ground in April like a hardy annual. *V. fastuosum*, with orange, maroon and black flowers 4 in. across, is the best of the bunch.

VERBASCUM (*Mullein*). While many are hardy perennials (see p. 181) a few are hardy biennials which must be renewed each year from seed. This is true of *V. Thapsus*, a giant of seven feet with densely grey woolly leaves and narrow spikes of yellow flowers; also of the hybrids Miss Willmott (white) and Harkness Hybrid (yellow) both 6 ft. or more in height. All can be raised very easily from seed sown in ordinary soil and open position outdoors in May. Seedlings should be transferred to a nursery bed in July and from thence to flowering quarters in October or March. These verbascums flower in July and are fine plants for the back of the border.

VERBENA. This family includes hardy perennials (see p. 181) but here I am only concerned with the half-hardy hybrids which are used for summer bedding as well as for greenhouse culture in pots. These are all perennials and as such can be kept from year to year and increased by cuttings, but in practice this is seldom done except with a few very choice varieties, the usual plan being to treat the plants as half-hardy annuals and raise a fresh stock annually from seed sown in a warm greenhouse any time from mid-January to mid-March. Germination may be slow and irregular unless a temperature of 60° or more can be maintained. Otherwise cultivation is much the same as for antirrhinums. The seedlings, either pricked off or potted singly, are hardened off for planting out in late May or early June.

Verbenas are somewhat sprawling in habit and look their best when planted fairly close (say 9 in. apart) so that they make a complete carpet over the soil. Every so often one plant can be tied up to a short cane to break the level. The flowers are borne in compact clusters all the summer and colours are both varied and brilliant, including many shades of pink, blue, purple and scarlet. For colour they rival the annual phloxes and both plants might be more widely used with advantage.

VIRGINIAN STOCK. This pretty little annual with confetti-like flowers is one of the most easily grown of plants. It is only necessary to sprinkle the seed thinly any time from March to June where the plants are to flower and either rake it in or cover with a thin scattering of soil. No thinning or after care is required. Plants average 6 in. in height and colours range from white through pink and mauve to crimson. There are few better annuals for sowing in crevices, between paving slabs or in odd corners where few other plants would find living room.

VISCARIA. The showy viscaria is a hardy annual which is both dainty and effective for garden or cutting. Seed can be sown in March, April or early September where it is to flower. The September sowings will stand the winter outdoors without protection and flower in June and July the following year, while the spring sowings will keep up the display until late summer. Stems are thin and wiry, not unlike those of the annual gypsophila which the plant also resembles in flower though colours are more varied including pink, carmine, scarlet and blue as well as white. Heights vary from 6 in. to 1 ft. All should be

H

thinned to 6 in. and will do best in a sunny place and open, well-drained soil. Incidentally botanists say that this plant is really a lychnis and should be known as *L. Coeli-rosa* but 'viscaria' seems to be too well established in the minds of gardeners to be weeded out.

WALLFLOWER.—*See* CHEIRANTHUS p. 97.

XERANTHEMUM. An everlasting flower with chaffy, daisy-like flowers which can easily be dried and kept for winter decorations. Colours are varied. The plant is a hardy annual and seed can be sown in April in any sunny, sheltered place and porous soil. Thin to 6 or 8 in. and support with short, bushy hazel twigs.

ZEA (Maize). This may be primarily regarded as a food crop, one variety of maize being the sweet corn which is occasionally grown in the vegetable garden. Here we are concerned with an ornamental variety with leaves broadly striped with creamy white. It is a handsome foliage plant attaining a height of several feet in a matter of weeks and consequently valuable for some summer bedding effects. It can be raised from seeds sown in early May where the plants are to grow, or in small pots in April in frame or greenhouse, the seedlings to be planted out in late May or early June. The variety grown is *Zea Mays variegata.*

ZINNIA. This most gorgeously coloured annual is a plant which well repays careful cultivation. The best modern strains of zinnia will produce very big, fully double blooms which are equally effective in the border and as cut flowers. Colours include white, yellow, pink, orange and scarlet and there are also a great number of intermediate or 'art' shades, some of them exceptionally beautiful.

Zinnias to be seen at their best need rich but porous soil and must be grown steadily and without check from start to finish. It is a mistake to sow seed very early. The first week in April is soon enough and a frame will often give better results than a heated greenhouse; indeed I have seen some of the best blooms on plants raised from seed sown outdoors early in May, the seedlings being left to grow on undisturbed like hardy instead of half-hardy annuals. In any case avoid rapid changes of temperature, do not let the plants get checked by lack of water and, if they are to be planted out, do this before they get starved in the boxes or pots in which they were pricked out. Give them good soil and a sunny place and water them freely in dry weather. The plants will grow nearly 3 ft. high and may want staking, especially if the position is a windy one. If two sowings are made, one in April the other in May, blooms may be had from July to September.

CHAPTER VII
Hardy Herbaceous Perennials

A HERBACEOUS PLANT is one that is soft in growth in contradistinction to a plant that is woody and is in consequence classified as a tree or shrub. A perennial is any plant which continues to live for a number of years irrespective of whether it flowers or not. In this it contrasts with the annual, which completes its life cycle in one year and then dies after flowering and producing seed, the biennial which has a similar life cycle but takes two years about it and the monocarpic plant which likewise dies as soon as it has flowered and ripened seed but may take an indefinite number of years before it does this.

From this it will be seen that a herbaceous perennial is a plant which is soft in growth and continues to live and flower for a considerable time. There are a great many plants which come into this category and they are subdivided again into hardy, half-hardy and tender kinds. These are relative terms with no very hard and fast dividing line between one and another. Broadly speaking a plant is regarded as hardy when it will normally live outdoors in most parts of the country without protection. It is said to be half-hardy when it can be grown outdoors in summer but must be put into a greenhouse or frame for the winter, and tender when it needs protection throughout the greater part of the year. Before leaving this point, however, I would like to make it quite plain that hardiness varies considerably even in one plant according to the condition of its growth. Young shoots are almost invariably much less hardy than those which are older and riper. It is no uncommon thing to see the young growth of even such native trees as oak and ash cut by frost in the spring and in exceptional circumstances young trees may even be killed in this way, yet no one on that account would dub oaks and ashes as half-hardy. It is a question of what is customary rather than what is exceptional.

In this chapter I am solely concerned with the hardy herbaceous perennial, a most important type of plant from the gardener's point of view because most of its members can be grown with very little difficulty and once established require less attention than any other single class of plants.

THE HERBACEOUS BORDER. It is only during the present century that the hardy herbaceous perennial has played a really big part in English gardening. It was very largely due to the prolific writings of William Robinson that the worth of the herbaceous perennial became widely recognised and the herbaceous border, that is to say the border devoted to the cultivation of this type of plant, began to be a feature of every garden. I am not sure that the process has not now gone rather too far, at any rate as far as the full-blown herbaceous border is concerned, for it has become so popular a feature that even in the smallest gardens there is often an effort to include it.

Now it is very questionable whether the herbaceous border can be a really satisfactory feature unless plenty of room is available. Personally I would not attempt to plant a herbaceous border in less space than 30 ft. length and 6 ft. width, and I would add that the width is even more important than the length. The reason for this is that a great many herbaceous plants have not a very long season of flower. They are magnificent while they last but the show is over in a few weeks.

There are two ways of overcoming this drawback. One is to plant a border entirely with varieties which flower at approximately the same time and arrange matters so that this border is a feature at its own season and can be ignored for the rest of the year. That works well enough in big places, but it is obviously impracticable for the small garden. Alternatively the plants may be assorted so that between them they cover a reasonably extended season and in addition to arrange them as far as possible so that the later flowering kinds grow up around the earlier sorts and thus screen their bareness from view. This latter is the scheme most commonly employed and it works very well provided there is room to plant on a generous scale, not as single plants of each kind but in groups of five, six or more. That is why I say that width is even more important than length for it is impossible to have several sizeable groups of plants one behind the other in a border that is no more than 3 or 4 ft. in width.

THE MIXED BORDER. There is an alternative to the pure herbaceous border and for want of a better name I call it the 'mixed border'. In this any type of plant is welcome, the only qualifications being that it will add to the general display and not interfere with its neighbours. In the mixed border one can add annuals, biennials and monocarpic plants together with shrubs and even, on occasion, small trees. Bulbs may figure quite largely and are particularly useful because their foliage takes up little room and they can, in consequence, sometimes be established under a carpet of other plants. The danger with a mixed border is that, with such a mass of material, the amateur becomes bewildered, has no idea what to put in or what to leave out and probably ends up with too many plants in too small a space to the detriment of all. However, this need not occur if a little extra forethought is brought to the task and particularly if expert advice is called in.

The best method of setting about the planting of any border is first to draw its outline to as large a scale as possible on a sheet of paper and then to write down the names of the favoured plants together with their height, colour and season of flowering on small slips of paper which can be moved about on the plan like the pieces in a jigsaw puzzle. In this way one can carry out a kind of experimental planning on one's study table, shifting the pieces around until one gets what appears to be a pleasing and satisfactory arrangement.

SPECIALISED BORDERS. There are other ways in which hardy herbaceous perennials may be used in the garden. Some of the most free flowering kinds, and particularly the comparatively limited number which have an extended flowering season, are excellent for massing by themselves. In fact they can be used instead of the more usual 'bedding' plants such as geraniums, marguerites, heliotropes and antirrhinums. The advantage of this scheme is that they do not have to be renewed every year or lifted in the autumn and replanted in the spring as is the case with the plants just mentioned. Care must be taken, however, to see that the plants chosen really have a reasonably extended flowering season.

HERBACEOUS PERENNIALS AS CUT FLOWERS. Quite a number of herbaceous plants are also excellent for cutting. Some of them, indeed, are so good for this that they have become popular with market growers and will be found in every florist's shop at their correct season. Examples of this type are pyrethrums, shasta and moon daisies, Caucasian scabious and the double flowered gypsophila. The amateur need not confine himself to these. There are many other charming hardy perennials which for one reason or another would not be a success commercially but can nevertheless be grown in private gardens for cutting. I think it is a great advantage, though, of course, by no means essential, if plants required specifically for this purpose can be grown by themselves in straight rows in a reserved part of the garden where their flowers will not be missed when they have been taken for the house.

ARRANGEMENT OF PERENNIALS. This raises another point, namely the actual arrangement of individual plants in the herbaceous border. I have on very rare occasions seen them planted in straight lines with reasonably satisfactory effect but usually it is much more effective to plant in

133

irregular groups and to avoid all semblance of regularity. In a general way the taller plants should be kept at the back and the dwarfer varieties in front but allowance must be made for the screening of earlier blooming kinds as I have already explained and also it is a good plan to bring some groups of taller plants forward to break the border up into a series of irregular bays. The illustrations of well-planted herbaceous borders which appear on pp. 78 and 79 will no doubt help to make this plain.

PREPARATION OF SOIL. The general cultivation of the majority of hardy herbaceous perennials is simple and follows the same basic plan. The ground need not be very rich but it should in most cases be well drained and contain sufficient humus to preserve it from severe drying out during hot weather. It must be borne in mind that once planted the border is not likely to be seriously disturbed for a number of years and that during that period it will only be possible to carry out superficial cultivation and feeding. The initial preparation should therefore be as thorough as possible and in particular great care must be taken to eliminate all persistent weeds such as couch grass, coltsfoot, ground elder and bindweed.

In the case of new gardens I favour delaying the planting of the herbaceous border for at least one year and utilising the ground the first season for vegetables or annuals. In this way at least two diggings can be given before the border is permanently planted and this will get the ground into a better state of cultivation than would otherwise be possible.

PLANTING. There are two principal seasons for planting herbaceous perennials, one the period when they are just starting into growth, roughly from the middle of March to the middle of April and the other at the time when they are just coming to the end of their growth towards the end of September and during the first half of October. I do not favour planting late in the year when the ground is cold and wet and roots no longer retain any activity. A few kinds can be planted satisfactorily in the height of summer as soon as they have finished flowering but this always necessitates a considerable amount of attention for the first week or so after planting. During this period the plants must be watered freely and frequently if the soil is at all dry.

The actual details of planting are much the same as for other types of plant. It is important to choose the right kind of weather or at any rate to avoid really bad conditions when the soil is wet and sticky. If plants arrive from a nursery when the soil is unfit for planting, line them out in a shallow trench and cover their roots with soil. Heeled in

like this they will keep in good condition for several weeks but should
be planted permanently directly the soil is fit.

It is very important to make holes sufficiently wide and deep to
accommodate all roots spread out in a natural manner. A trowel will be
the usual tool, but for big plants a spade may be even better. A dibber
should never be used. It makes far too narrow and deep a hole.

Depth can best be gauged by the old soil mark showing on the plants.
This should be covered with about ½ in. of soil. If the soil mark cannot be seen, make certain that the uppermost roots are covered with at
least 1 in. of soil or that the crown of the plant, that is the point from
which most of the basal shoots grow, is at or very slightly below soil
level.

Few beginners make the soil sufficiently firm round the roots after
planting. Except in the case of very small plants the foot rather than the
hands should always be used for this job. Soil that is left at all loose
dries out rapidly and growth is seldom satisfactory in it.

Spacing will, of course, vary according to the habit of the plant but
it will probably be somewhere between 6 and 9 in. for edging plants,
1 ft. to 18 in. for mid-border plants and 2 to 3 ft. for the occupants of
the back of the border.

Though one should never plant when the soil is wet it may sometimes be necessary to plant when the soil is rather too dry. In that case
and, indeed, whenever there is doubt as to there being sufficient moisture to keep the plants going, a thorough watering should be given
immediately after planting. Use a can without a rose for this job but
break the rush of water with a piece of sacking tied loosely round the
spout. One does not want to wash the soil off newly planted roots but
at the same time they must be given sufficient and the trouble with roses
is that they invariably give the surface a deceptively wet appearance,
leaving the lower soil comparatively dry.

THINNING. Many herbaceous perennials are all the better for a little
thinning in the early stages of their growth. This applies particularly
to free growing things such as Michaelmas daisies, delphiniums and
golden rod (*solidago*). Left to their own devices these make so many
shoots in the spring that they become overcrowded before their
flowers open and quality and display suffer. A little experience is necessary to learn how many shoots should be taken away but frequently a
reduction of as much as 75 per cent. can be made without harm, especially in the second year after planting.

STAKING. Tall plants will almost all need some staking, particularly
those which have been highly developed by breeding and have, in

consequence, very big, heavy flowering heads. This applies to all the modern delphiniums and also to quite a number of the taller, double flowered Michaelmas daisies.

As far as possible try to arrange stakes so that they are concealed by the growth as the stems lengthen. In general three or four stakes should be used per plant if it has more than one stem and these stakes should each be driven into the ground so that it leans out at the top, so tending to open the growth like the feathers of a shuttlecock rather than to bunch it together as is inevitably the case if only one stake is used.

PROPAGATION. The majority of hardy perennials can be increased readily by division of the roots at the ordinary planting season. Division simply means that the original large root is split into several pieces, each of which must be provided with at least one growing shoot or crown and some good roots. Small plants can usually be divided by hand but big, old clumps often get so tough that they must be split by some other means. One excellent scheme is to thrust two small border forks back to back through the centre of the clump and then lever their handles apart. Hand forks can be used in an identical manner for smaller plants. Very occasionally a knife may be required but should be used only to sever the hard, central crown of such a plant as a delphinium or peony. The trouble with knives is that they nearly always do more harm than good, severing roots from shoots in a most unexpected and disconcerting manner.

When dividing very old clumps, particularly of free spreading things such as Michaelmas daisies, moon daisies and heleniums, it is usually wise to discard the central portion of each clump altogether and retain only the outer pieces which are younger, more vigorous and less likely to be diseased or pest ridden.

Most herbaceous perennials can also be raised from seed. This is sometimes a slow method of increase for seedlings may take a couple of years to reach full flowering size; in fact in a few instances they may take at least one year to germinate. Seedlings can also be disappointing, especially in the case of highly developed plants such as many of those already mentioned. These are very hybrid and because of this mixed origin seedlings are apt to differ astonishingly from their parents. Occasionally a relatively pure-breeding strain can be produced even of a hybrid subject. For example quite good seed is often available of Geum Mrs. Bradshaw. Most of the seedlings will show so little variation from the parent plant as not to matter very much from the ordinary gardener's point of view. But nothing like this is possible at present with peonies, Michaelmas daisies, lupins or phloxes and the most that one can say is that the resultant seedlings will still be peonies, Michael-mas daisies, lupins or phloxes as the case may be. In all other respects they may be as different from their parents as the proverbial chalk and cheese.

Nevertheless seed is a very good method of perpetuating certain types of herbaceous perennials, particularly those that are naturally short-lived, such as hollyhocks, verbascums and aquilegias and those with which a certain degree of variation in colour, stature, etc., does not matter very much. Seedlings have the merit of being almost always vigorous and healthy and as a rule they can be raised very cheaply.

In general seed of herbaceous plants can be sown either under glass, as for example in a cool greenhouse or frame, during March or April, or outdoors in May or June. In a few cases March raised seedlings will flower a little in their first year but this is the exception rather than the rule. In most cases it will not be until the second year that there is any-thing like a full display.

In every instance the seedlings should be transplanted from the seed boxes or bed as soon as they can be handled conveniently and immedi-ately replanted in a bed of reasonably rich, finely broken soil situated in an open position. Give them plenty of space in this to grow on into sturdy plants by the following autumn or spring by which time most will be ready for transplanting to permanent positions.

A third method of propagation is by cuttings. As a matter of fact far more herbaceous plants can be raised in this way than many amateurs believe. Most people know that lupins and delphiniums can be increased by stem cuttings secured in early spring but not so many are aware that scabious, coreopsis and phloxes besides a great many other plants can be equally easily increased in the same manner. The method in these cases is to make cuttings from young shoots when 3 or 4 in. long. The shoots are cut off low down, even below soil level if possible, the essential point being that each must be firm and solid at the base. Each cutting is trimmed cleanly just below a joint and inserted in a bed of rather sandy soil. It should be put in just deep enough to keep it upright, which generally implies a hole 1 in. to $1\frac{1}{2}$ in. deep. Press the soil firmly around the base of the cutting and, when the whole bed is full, water thoroughly. Shade from direct sunlight until the cuttings no longer flag. Thereafter simply water regularly until sufficiently well rooted to be transplanted. Most of these cuttings do best in a frame but they can be rooted in the open if the weather is kind.

Root cuttings offer another very valuable means of increasing many herbaceous perennials and not, surprisingly enough, only those with thick, fleshy roots. Phloxes, which have comparatively thin roots, grow freely from root cuttings and so do gaillardias. More obvious kinds for this method of propagation are anchusas, hollyhocks, verbascums, oriental poppies and perennial statices of all kinds. It is odd that gypsophilas and lupins, which have likely looking roots for the purpose, fail completely.

Propagation by root cuttings is exceptionally easy. All that is necessary is to lift a good plant or so any time between December and March inclusive, cut up the roots into pieces 1 to 2 in. in length and place them in the soil. The thicker roots are, I think, most satisfactory when pushed into the soil vertically the right way up. As all the cuttings look exactly alike when prepared it is necessary to make some mark on them to know which is the top end if this method is to be employed. My method is to make a sloping cut at the bottom of each cutting and a square cut at the top. This gives the base of the cutting a pointed end which can easily be pushed into the soil. These vertical cuttings should be just covered with soil. The alternative, most suitable for thin cuttings, is to lay them horizontally on a flat bed of soil and cover with a further ½ in. of soil. Water moderately until shoots appear above ground. Then give more water and finally transplant to a nursery bed about May or June.

One advantage of raising perennials from cuttings, either stem or root, rather than from division, is that less of the old plant is carried over to the new individual and in consequence there is less likelihood of its being troubled with the pests or diseases which have afflicted its parent. This is very marked in the case of phloxes which have been crippled by eelworms. Completely clean stock can be raised even from heavily infested plants if root cuttings only are employed.

In the following alphabetical list of herbaceous perennials I have not attempted to include everything that might be grown but only plants of real merit which can be cultivated without undue difficulty and are available from most nurserymen specialising in such things. Rarities, novelties, etc. must be sought for in books dealing with such matters and also in the catalogues of trade specialists.

One other point about which I must warn the beginner at this stage is that in this list and in all subsequent selections of plants in this volume botanical names will be used—not exclusively but very largely. This is always a stumbling block at first as some of the names appear extremely difficult to anyone new to the subject. Unfortunately there is in many cases no satisfactory alternative. Numbers of the best flowers have no true popular names at all and even where common names are well established they are sometimes applied loosely to several different species and even, in some instances, to different families. In consequence it is quite impossible to be precise either in describing or ordering such plants unless they are specified by their correct botanical names.

Also, without going into great detail regarding the principles which govern the application of botanical names it may be helpful to explain that every plant has at least two names, the first a generic name and the second a specific name. The generic name identifies the bearer as belonging to a certain 'genus' or group of allied, but by no means identical plants. The specific name pinpoints it more accurately as a particular 'species' or member of that group. Thus *Lupinus polyphyllus* is the common herbaceous lupin, whereas the different though obviously allied tree lupin is identified as *Lupinus arboreus*.

Frequently a third name makes its appearance. Sometimes this follows the botanic style and sometimes it is of purely popular origin. In either case it serves to distinguish some special form or variety of a species. As an example there are a great many varieties of *Lupinus polyphyllus* distinguished by such names as Grenadier, Highlander, etc.

A SELECTION OF THE BEST KINDS

ACANTHUS (*Bear's Breech*). A small family of plants grown mainly for their foliage. The leaves rather suggest a milk thistle on an enlarged scale and it is said that one of the species served as a model for the scroll-like capital of the famous Corinthian column. The flowers of acanthus are curious rather than beautiful—stiff spikes of tubular blooms in a dull shade of purplish lilac, about 3 ft. in height. There are two species in common cultivation, *A. spinosus* and *A. mollis*, and both are equally worth growing. *A. mollis* also has a fine variety named *latifolius* with extra large leaves. All will thrive in any ordinary soil in sun or partial shade. Plant in autumn or spring. Propagate by seed or division in the spring, or by root cuttings in winter.

ACHILLEA (*Yarrow, Milfoil*). One species of achillea is a well known weed which can be a perfect pest on lawns. This is the common milfoil with soft, finely divided leaves and creeping stems which hug the soil and root as they go. In addition there are numbers of ornamental species mostly for the rock garden, though a few are suitable for the herbaceous border. All have iron constitutions, will grow anywhere and prefer sunny positions. Curiously enough some of the best have arisen as varieties from *Achillea Millefolium*, the weed just referred to. Like many other wild plants it is susceptible of improvement and such forms as Cerise Queen and Rose Queen, with flattish heads of carmine flowers on 18 in. stems make a fine display from June to August.

Other good kinds are *A. Eupatorium*, Parker's variety 4 ft. in height with mustard yellow flowers in heads as big as saucers, and *A. Ptarmica*, best planted in one of its double flowered forms such as The Pearl or Perry's White. These individual blooms are perfect pom pons, ½ in. across, white in colour and in loose heads on 2-ft. stems. All flower throughout the summer and may be planted at any time in autumn or spring. They are best propagated by division at either season.

ACONITUM (*Monkshood*). The popular name refers to the curiously hooded flowers which do suggest the cowl of a monk. They are carried in spikes not unlike those of the delphinium though on a smaller scale. All thrive best in rather moist soil though they will grow tolerably well under drier conditions. They will succeed in sun or partial shade and some species, including *A. Napellus*, may even be naturalised in thin woodland. This, incidentally, is the source of the drug aconite, a poison which permeates the whole plant. It is a handsome plant producing deep purple flowers on 3 ft. spikes in June and July. There are also allied kinds such as *A. bicolor*, white flowers edged with blue and Spark's variety, in which the normal purple colour deepens to indigo. The plants known in gardens as *A. Fischeri* and *A. Wilsonii* both flower in September and October, the first with rather stout, 3-ft. spikes of pale blue flowers and the latter twice as high and varying from pale blue to violet. There are a couple of yellow aconitums, *Anthora*, 2 feet, and *orientale*, 5 feet. All make underground tubers, dislike root disturbance, are best transplanted in spring and may be increased by seed or division at the same season.

AGROSTEMMA (*Campion*). More correctly this plant should be known as lychnis but the other name is so well established in gardens that I use it here to avoid confusion. The only species worth bothering about is *A. Coronaria*, a very well-known plant which makes a freely branched bush a couple of feet in height with grey foliage and, throughout July and August, vivid magenta flowers. It is an extremely striking plant, easily grown in ordinary or poorish soil and sunny position. It is best planted in spring and may be raised from seed sown at that time.

ALLIUM.—*See* p. 335.

ALSTROEMERIA (*Peruvian Lily*). All alstroemerias are extremely showy plants which would undoubtedly be much more widely grown were they easier to establish. It is the first couple of years that are difficult, for all dislike root disturbance, are slow to re-establish themselves and often do little or nothing at first. Being South American plants they delight in all the sun and warmth they can get and require deep, well-drained soil. The rather fleshy roots should be spread thinly at the bottom of a 5 or 6 in. deep trench and covered with soil. April is the best month for this work and thereafter the plants should be left severely alone for as many years as possible, with occasional hand-weeding the only attention necessary.

The best known species is *A. aurantiaca* with vivid orange flowers like small lilies in close spikes. It is in bloom in July and August and is about 3 ft. high. Other fine kinds of similar height are *A. chilensis*, in various shades of pink and salmon; *A. haemantha* in which the blooms are blood red with an orange throat, and *A. Ligtu*, a pink flowered species which has also produced a number of grand hybrids in shades varying from pink to flame. These are all rather more tender and difficult to grow than *A. aurantiaca*.

ALTHAAE. *See* HOLLYHOCK p. 159.

ANCHUSA (*Alkanet*). These handsome plants precede the delphiniums by a week or so, being at their best in early June, at which season they provide the best blue to be found in the border. Anchusas might be likened to enormous forget-me-nots with flowers nearly 1 in. across and stems 4 to 5 ft. in height. They make stout tap roots which thrive best in a rather light soil and dislike disturbance. Propagation by division is impossible. Seed germinates readily but seedlings vary quite a lot in the colour of their flowers. The best method of increase of named kinds is by root cuttings. The species of greatest importance is *A. italica*. It has produced quite a number of named varieties varying chiefly in the size and purity of colour of their flowers. The best are Dropmore, Opal, and Morning Glory. One other species, *A. myoso-tidiflora* is a very different sprawling plant with masses of small blue flowers in April and May. It is suitable for the front of the border in sun or shade.

ANEMONE (*Wind Flower*). Many of the anemones are woodland or alpine plants but one hybrid, commonly known as *A. japonica* but correctly *A. hybrida*, is a fine border plant. At its best during September it is a first class partner for the Michaelmas daisies. Height varies from 18 in. to 4 ft. according to variety and colour from pure white and palest pink to a rather deep wine red. None of these Japanese anemones likes root disturbance. All are best transplanted in spring and can be propagated by division at that season. They will thrive in any ordinary soil in a sunny or half-shady position. Outstanding varieties are Whirl-wind semi-double, pure white; Queen Charlotte, bright pink; and Alice, a deeper pink with semi-double flowers. *A. hupehensis* is closely allied, dwarf and rosy red.

ANTHEMIS (*Chamomile*). Here again there are many species for the rock garden but also a little useful material for the herbaceous border. Unlike most hardy perennials nearly all the chamomiles have a long flowering season. The flowers are daisy-like, of various shades of yellow and carried on long, stiff stems which make them very suitable for cutting. All do best in rather light, well-drained soils and full sun. They can be propagated by cuttings of firm, young growth rooted in spring or early summer much in the same manner as marguerites which they resemble in many respects without sharing their tenderness.

The best species is *A. tinctoria* which makes a compact, bushy plant a couple of feet or more in height and as much through. There are several varieties of this, notably Loddon Gold with golden yellow flowers and E. C. Buxton in which the colour is nearer lemon yellow. *A. Sancti-Johannis* is a showy plant similar in habit but with bigger and deeper yellow flowers.

ANTHERICUM (*St. Bruno's Lily and St. Bernard's Lily*). These are graceful plants with white, lily-like flowers. All will grow readily in any ordinary soil and reasonably open position. They have grassy foliage which dies down in winter and are best planted in spring, at which season they can also be increased by division. The two most usually seen are *Anthericum Liliago*, the St. Bernard's Lily, which is about 1 ft. in height, and *A. Liliastrum* (syn. *Paradisea Liliastrum*), the St. Bruno's Lily. This is rather bigger and taller. A third kind, *A. ramosum* spreads more rapidly than either of the others by means of underground stems which throw up fresh tufts of foliage all round the parent plant.

AQUILEGIA (*Columbine*). The common columbine will need no introduction to most readers. It is one of the most delightfully dainty of all border plants and its one drawback is that it is somewhat short lived. However it is readily raised from seed sown outdoors in May or June and an excellent range of colours can be obtained if seed is saved from a good strain. The old-fashioned columbine, *A. vulgaris*, has short spurs to the flowers and has been largely replaced in gardens by the more modern, long spurred hybrids of which Scott Elliott's is one of the most famous strains. In these the spurs are delicately formed and often as much as $1\frac{1}{2}$ in. long. Colours are mostly in pastel shades of salmon pink and yellow but there are also red and crimson forms. A comparative newcomer, *A. longissima* has the longest spurs of all and pale

142

yellow flowers. All bloom in May and early June. Selected varieties may be increased by careful division in spring. Mixed strains raised from seed can be planted in autumn or spring. All do well in sun or partial shade and like a light, but not excessively dry soil.

ARMERIA (*Thrift*). Most of the thrifts are rock plants but one species, *A. cephalotes*, is a handsome border perennial. It makes compact tufts of grassy foliage from which, in June, appear bare stems a foot or more long terminated by globular heads of bright rose flowers. This is the plant which has produced the even better and more widely grown Bees' Ruby with flowers of increased size and richer, almost crimson colour. All can be increased by division in spring, the best planting season, and thrive in full sun and rather light soils.

ARTEMISIA. For the herbaceous border easily the best artemisia is *lactiflora*, a really handsome plant of shuttlecock habit, 5 ft. high, each stem terminating in a loose plume of creamy flowers. It will grow anywhere, does not mind some shade and flowers in August. *A. gnaphalodes* is a useful, grey-leaved plant for a position towards the front of the border and is equally easy to grow. Either can be increased by division in spring.

ASCLEPIAS.—*See* p. 338.

ASPHODELINE (*False Asphodel*). *Asphodeline lutea* is a plant with bold tufts of narrow leaves, a little like those of a red hot poker. From these spear up in early summer a few stiffly erect 3-ft. spikes, a little sparsely set with starry yellow flowers which usually have rather a weedy appearance in the eyes of the ignorant though they are hailed with delight by the well informed. It would be wise to see the false asphodel in bloom before deciding to plant it. Culture presents no difficulty in any ordinary soil and sunny aspect and increase can be either by seed or division in spring.

ASTER (*Michaelmas daisy*). We are not here concerned with the annual or China asters which are dealt with in another chapter but with the perennial species of which the famous Michaelmas daisy is the best known kind. There is great variety in this family both in habit and character of flower. Best known are the true Michaelmas daisies raised from *A. novi-belgii* or *A. novae-angliae*, and the early flowering forms which trace their parentage to *A. Amellus*.

This Amellus group flowers in August and September. The plants are seldom above 2 ft. in height and usually rather more through, freely branched with big single flowers. Good examples are King

George, bluish violet; Ultramarine, deeper in colour, and Sonia, lilac pink. Spring is the correct season for moving or dividing the plants. All other Asters can be planted or divided in autumn or spring.

The *novae-angliae* and *novi-belgii* groups are in general taller, from 3 to 6 ft. in height with smaller, often semi-double flowers in massive branched heads. The main difference from the gardener's point of view is that the *novae-angliae* have slightly hairy, rough foliage and flowers which tend to close at night whereas the leaves of *novi-belgii* varieties are smooth and glossy and the flowers are open day and night. It is this latter group which has been most highly developed. Literally hundreds of varieties exist including in colour all shades from pink to a rather crude crimson, from palest lavender to violet and also pure white. As new varieties are introduced annually and old ones are superseded almost as fast as they become familiar, it would be a waste of time to give a selection, which can be made from the current catalogue of any specialist.

Then there are small flowered Michaelmas daisies, such as *A. ericoides* which branches stiffly and in October smothers itself in tiny white daisies. *A. cordifolius* and its varieties has similarly small and numerous flowers but in loose, arching sprays often 5 ft. long. Others of interest are *A. acris*, with narrow leaves and starry, blue flowers, *A. luteus*, 3 ft. high, bushy and smothered in tiny yellow daisies, and *A. Linosyris*, often known as Goldilocks on account of its masses of small, golden yellow flowers. *A. yunnanensis*, Napsbury has large, blue daisies on 18 in. stems in June.

All these perennial asters grow readily in any ordinary soil and sunny or partially shady position. They can be increased by division and, in the case of the vigorous growing kinds, it is advisable to divide fairly frequently before the old clumps get overcrowded.

Astilbe (*False Goat's Beard*). This plant is frequently called spiraea in gardens though botanically this is incorrect, the spiraeas forming a distinct genus. Astilbes are all true herbaceous plants. They have very elegant, fluffy plumes of small flowers and are in bloom during July and August. Though not faddy regarding soil they succeed best in fairly rich, moist loams and are excellent for planting at the waterside. They will grow in either sun or partial shade. Most of the numerous varieties grown are hybrids, often collectively known as *A. Arendsii*, raised by crossing three species—*A. Davidii*, with narrowly erect, magenta-crimson panicles 4 ft. in height; *A. astilboides* with wider and shorter plumes of creamy white, and *A. japonica* which is similar in habit but soft pink in colour. The hybrids have, in consequence, a wide range in colour and type, from the spreading white panicles of King Albert to the more columnar, crimson spires of Gertrude Brix. There are all manner of intermediates in colour and shape, some of the loveliest being those with graceful pink or salmon flowers obviously closely associated with *A. japonica.* Incidentally all make useful pot plants for the cool or unheated greenhouse and can be had in bloom a couple of months ahead of their season by gentle forcing. Plant in spring or autumn and increase by careful division in spring.

ASTRANTIA (*Masterwort*). These are curious rather than striking plants which have the merit of thriving in places too shady for most herbaceous perennials. They grow 1 ft. to 18 in. in height and have tiny, greenish flowers surrounded by a stiff ruff of pale pink or greenish bracts. The two species most usually grown are *A. maxima* and *A. major*; either can be planted in spring or autumn and increased by division at these times.

BAPTISIA (*False Indigo*). The true indigo, from which the famous dye was once obtained is *Indigofera tinctoria.* The false indigos are related and one, *B. australis*, is occasionally planted for ornament. It will grow in rough places, does not object to some shade and makes a very leafy plant 2 to 3 ft. high carrying a lot of small spikes of blue, pea-flowers in early summer. Plant it in spring or autumn and increase when necessary by division in spring.

BOCCONIA (*Plume Poppy*). The only species commonly cultivated in gardens is *B. cordata,* a very handsome plant worth growing for its heart-shaped, grey-green leaves alone. The flowers are small and amber coloured, not very remarkable individually but handsome in the mass. They are carried in enormous, loose plumes on stems of at least 6 ft. from mid-summer onwards for several weeks. This plant will thrive in either sun or half shade. Plant in spring and increase by division at the same time. The correct name is really *Macleaya cordata.*

BOLTONIA ASTEROIDES. A well-named plant for it does look very much like a perennial aster or Michaelmas daisy. It is 5 or 6 ft. high and has loosely branched sprays of small daisy-flowers which are at their best in early autumn. They are white, more or less tinged with pink or mauve. The competition of the beautiful garden forms of Michaelmas daisy has been too much for it but those who prefer undeveloped species will like to grow this boltonia and can do so in any reasonable soil and open, or even partly shaded, position. It can be planted and, if desired, divided in spring or autumn.

I   145

BUPHTHALMUM. Only two species are much grown, *Buphthalmum salicifolium*, a quick spreading plant with yellow flowers in shape not unlike those of the familiar moon daisy. and *B. speciosum* with large leaves and orange-yellow flowers. The plants are in bloom from about mid-summer until early autumn. They are very hardy and will grow anywhere, being particularly suitable for chalky soils. They can be planted and divided in spring or autumn.

CAMPANULA (*Bellflower*). A great many of the campanulas are rock plants but there are also numerous showy kinds for the herbaceous border. All are easily grown and several, notably *C. lactiflora* and *C. latifolia*, will thrive in considerable shade. All can be planted in spring or autumn and are increased by division at either season.

C. *carpatica* is 9 in. to 1 ft. in height, with blue, cup-shaped flowers of considerable size throughout the summer. There are also white and lavender forms. *C. latiloba*, also known as *C. grandis*, is very sturdy with numerous saucer-shaped, purplish flowers close-set on 3-ft. spikes in June. *C. lactiflora* is pale blue and the flowers are carried in loose sprays on 5-ft. stems. *C. latifolia* has the habit of *C. grandis* but with bell-shaped, drooping flowers. *C. persicifolia*, perhaps the most useful of the lot, varies from 2 to 4 ft. in height with erect spikes of widely open, bell-shaped flowers in colour varying from clear blue to deep blue and white. There are also double flowered forms. *C. caespitosa*, also known as *C. pumila* and *C. Bellardii*, is primarily a rock plant, but useful in the border as an edging. It suggests a neat harebell with the thinnest of wiry stems terminated by nodding blue or white flowers. *C. glomerata dahurica* has closely clustered heads of violet flowers on 18 in. stems in early summer.

CARNATION, BORDER. The Tree or Perpetual Carnation needs the protection of a greenhouse in winter so it must be sought in the chapter on greenhouse flowers (p. 449). Here I am concerned only with the hardy, or 'border', carnation which can be left outdoors all the year, though when grown for exhibition it is sometimes given greenhouse protection to keep the flowers as clean and perfect as possible.

The border carnation has been very highly developed with the result that there are a vast number of 'named' varieties to which newcomers are constantly added. The would-be winner of prizes must keep right up-to-date in this matter of variety for success depends not a little upon growing the right kinds, carnations having a nasty habit of deteriorating after a few years. That is one reason why no selection of varieties will be found in this book. It would be out of date too soon.

If you cannot get good advice any other way place an order for plants with one of the well-known specialists and leave it to him to send you the best.

Culture is fairly simple; indeed it is quite possible to grow good carnations simply by planting in ordinary, loamy soil in a sunny herbaceous border. The exhibitor usually gives them a bed to themselves, in a sunny place for preference, and prepares the soil by deep digging, moderate manuring and the generous use of bone meal and wood ashes. The plants are renewed annually from 'layers'; that is to say young, non-flowering shoots which are pegged down into the soil around the parent plant in July and are not severed from it until they are well rooted, a process which usually takes no more than six or eight weeks if the soil is kept nicely moist. Before they are pegged down the layers are slit with a sharp penknife for about half an inch right through a joint where they are to be buried in the soil. This hastens rooting by checking but not stopping the flow of sap.

When they are rooted the layers are severed from the parent plant and a week or so later are lifted with plenty of soil and either planted straight away in the beds in which they are to flower or else potted singly in 4-in. pots in ordinary potting soil (see p. 421) and wintered in a frame with plenty of ventilation whenever the weather is neither very wet nor very cold. This method is recommended in cold districts or where the soil is not too well drained. The potted layers are planted out the following March.

In either case space them at least 1 ft. apart and make them really firm. As the flower stems lengthen stake them singly but do not tie right up to the topmost bud. Let the last tie be a good 6 in. below this so that the stem arches over at the top and the expanding flower hangs a little on its side, so shooting off rain and escaping the full glare of the sun.

Remove all side buds so that the whole strength of the plant is concentrated in the terminal bud which will give the finest flower. It may be necessary to shade or otherwise protect the bloom for the last few days if it is being prepared for a show for no blemish can be tolerated.

For garden display disbudding is unnecessary and plants may be allowed to remain undisturbed for several years. Exhibitors usually discard all their plants as soon as layers have been secured, relying exclusively on year-old stock for their show flowers.

CATANANCHE. The effect of *C. caerulea* in bloom is very much that of a cornflower and it is, in fact, a member of the same family. It is a true perennial, 2 to 3 ft. in height and it flowers in August and September. Considerable improvement has been made on the original kinds and the best forms, such as Wisley Variety and *major*, have flowers of notably increased size and substance. All are first class for cutting. Plant in spring or autumn and increase by division in spring. The catananches succeed best in full sun and well-drained soil.

CENTAUREA (*Knapweed*). Another family of plants for a sunny position and light soil. All the garden knapweeds are very easy to grow and several are extremely handsome. The best known, *C. montana*, is a couple of feet in height and much like a cornflower. It starts to flower in May and continues most of the summer. There is a white form in addition to the typical blue and both are good for cutting. *C. dealbata* is a taller plant producing bigger, rosy-pink flowers around mid-summer. Even more striking is *C. macrocephala*, with yellow flowers almost as big as tennis balls on 4 to 5 ft. stems. All may be planted in spring or autumn and increased by division at either season.

CENTRANTHUS (*Red Valerian*). The common red valerian is a native plant which grows in great profusion in some parts of the country, particularly on limestone cliffs. It is extremely handsome and delights in warm, dry places. For the garden there are deeper coloured forms such as *C. coccineus*. All flower in June and July. They should be planted in spring or autumn and increased by division at either season.

CEPHALARIA (*Giant Scabious*). This is the plant that is often known as the yellow scabious. The flowers are very like those of the familiar blue scabious, but bigger and coarser and the whole plant is on a large scale, often 6 ft. in height and branching freely. Unlike the blue scabious it has only a short flowering season in July. It grows easily in any ordinary soil and sunny position, and can be planted in spring or autumn but should only be divided in spring.

CERASTIUM (*Snow-in-Summer*). See p. 196.

CERATOSTIGMA. *See* PLUMBAGO p. 171.

CHEIRANTHUS. This name is most usually connected with the common wallflower and the brilliant orange *C. Allionii*, both bedding plants, not to be included in our present list. There are, however, one or two useful herbaceous kinds properly to be considered here. Notable among these are the cheerful yellow Harpur Crewe, with double flowers; and *C. semperflorens*, with single flowers that are bronze at first, purple later. Both like sunny places and lightish, well-drained soils. They should be planted in spring and increased by cuttings in spring or early summer.

CHELONE (*Turtle Head*). For a long time chelones were known as penstemons, to which they are closely allied and bear much resemblance. Easily the best species is *C. barbata*, a graceful plant which deserves to be better known. It has slender but erect stems 3 ft. in height, bearing in summer almost throughout their length narrowly tubular scarlet flowers. It should be given a warm, sunny position in well-drained soil. Plant in spring and increase by summer cuttings made from non-flowering side growths or by careful division in the spring.

CHRYSANTHEMUM. The familiar greenhouse and 'border' chrysanthemums are outside the scope of this chapter though border varieties can be used in the herbaceous border to increase the autumn display. For the moment I am concerned solely with the entirely hardy and herbaceous kinds of which the native moon daisy (*C. Leucanthemum*) and the imported Shasta Daisy (*C. maximum*) are the best-known examples. Curiously enough the Shasta Daisy proves the easier to cultivate in gardens for it can be transplanted in spring or autumn and divided at either season, whereas all forms of *C. Leucanthemum* detest autumn root disturbance. All like good drainage and plenty of sun. *C. maximum* is coarse and strong with glossy leaves and very bold flowers. In some forms the petals are slashed. Examples are Beauté Nivelloise, with flowers 6 to 8 in. in diameter, Marion Collyer, and Phyllis Smith.

Kinds with plain petals are King Edward VII, Mayfield Giant and Superb. Esther Read and Pauline Read are fully double like pyrethrums, the former pure white and the latter creamy yellow. All bloom in July and August and will grow in practically any soil and reasonably open position. Another useful species is *C. uliginosum*. This has single white flowers on 5 ft. stems and they do not commence to open until the end of September.

C. rubellum is closely allied to the familiar 'border chrysanthemums' and flowers from August to October. It has multitudes of soft pink single flowers on branching, 2 to 3 ft. stems. Numerous forms have been raised, some with double flowers, which are almost indistinguishable from the dwarfer forms of Korean chrysanthemum. They are reasonably hardy and in many parts of the country may be grown in the herbaceous border without special protection. They can be increased by cuttings or division in spring.

CIMICIFUGA (*Bugbane*). In spite of their unattractive name Bugbane are very graceful and decorative plants, particularly valuable for the late summer border. They produce slender spikes of feathery flowers and thrive in sunny or partially shady positions. Though they are not particular as regards soil they do best in moist places. The best kinds are *C. japonica*, 3 ft. in height with erect spikes of white flowers; *C. simplex*, similar in stature and colour but with drooping flower spikes and *dahurica*, 3½ ft., creamy white flowers. Cimicifuga may be planted in spring or autumn and divided at either season.

CLEMATIS. In addition to the familiar climbing clematis there are two or three not so well-known herbaceous species. Of these the best are *C. heracleifolia Davidiana*, with 3-ft. spikes of tubular, blue flowers; *C. integrifolia*, a rather shorter plant requiring a few twiggy branches to hold it up, and *C. Durandii* a showy hybrid still more in need of support. All bloom in July and August. Plant in spring in ordinary soil and sunny position and increase by division at that season. Also prune back dead or thin growth at the same time.

CONVALLARIA.—*See* LILY OF THE VALLEY p. 163.

COREOPSIS. These are among the most free-flowering plants for the herbaceous border; in fact they tend to flower themselves to death and may need to be renewed from cuttings or by seed fairly frequently to maintain vigour. All have showy flowers on slender stems which are admirable for arranging in vases. They require a fully sunny position and rather light, well-drained soil if they are to be permanent. In heavier soils they are more than ever inclined to die out after the first summer. The most reliable and truly perennial is *C. lanceolata*, 3 ft. in height, yellow, and in bloom from June to September. There is a larger flowered form of this known as *C. lanceolata grandiflora*, not to be confused with *C. grandiflora* itself which is a different species and the showiest of the family. This last has several forms, some with double flowers, such as Perry's variety and *flore pleno*. A grand kind, known as *C. auriculata superba* (really *C. pubescens*) has a crimson blotch at the base of each yellow petal. All should be planted in spring. The single flowered kinds may be propagated by cuttings taken in April or seed sown in May; the double forms by cuttings only.

CORTADERIA.—*See* PAMPAS GRASS p. 168.

CRAMBE. *C. cordifolia* is a very handsome plant for the back row of the herbaceous border. It grows 6 ft. or more in height, has big, rounded leaves which are themselves an ornament to the garden and, in early summer, bursts into immense cloudy masses of small, white flowers giving rather the impression of a giant gypsophila. There is not the slightest difficulty in growing it for it is not fussy regarding soil or situation. Plant it in spring and, if you want more plants, lift an old clump at that season and divide it.

DELPHINIUM. This is one of the most important families of border plants and one which has been completely transformed by plant breeders. There are two main races for the herbaceous border, the giant delphiniums with massive spikes of bloom often 5 or 6 ft. in height, and the branching delphiniums known as the Belladonna group. These latter have much smaller and looser spikes and are fine for cutting or for the middle and front of the border. No useful purpose would be served by giving lists of varieties as these are further improved annually and catalogues quickly become dated.

All delphiniums thrive in light, loamy soils and sunny, open positions. They dislike bad drainage, particularly in winter, and are best planted in spring or, in the case of rooted cuttings, early summer. Propagation of named varieties must be done either by division or cuttings in spring and cuttings are preferable as the plants are healthier and more vigorous. The important point is to secure young shoots as cuttings before they have got hollow at the base, that is when they are about 4 in. long. They will root very readily in sandy soil in a shaded frame. Seed sown either as soon as ripe in July–August or in March, preferably in a frame but otherwise in a sheltered border outdoors, germinates well and will produce small flowering plants the following season, but seedlings show wide variation from their parents. When grown for exhibition the large flowered delphiniums are usually restricted to one spike for year-old plants and two or three spikes for two-year-old plants. Staking needs to be carefully done, one stake being used for each spike in the case of the large flowered kinds. The belladonna delphiniums can often be most effectively supported by means of short pea sticks pushed in around them at an early stage of growth.

DIANTHUS. Under this name the botanist includes plants more familiar to gardeners as pinks, border carnations and Sweet Williams. As I am certain that these will be the names to which readers will instinctively turn when requiring information on these plants I have used them and here shall only refer to the species which are commonly called 'dianthus' in gardens. A great many dianthuses are rock plants so the reader should also make reference to Chapter VIII.

The herbaceous border dianthuses are not numerous. *D. plumarius*, parent of the garden pinks, is the most important. It is a variable plant, always with the narrow grey leaves of the familiar pink but sometimes compact, at others straggling, with white, pink or carmine flowers, often deeply fringed though there are plain petalled forms as well. I like best the strain, known as Cyclops, in which each flower has a central zone or 'eye' of deeper colour. All shades of pink, rose and carmine are to be found in this and it is exceptionally free flowering even for a dianthus. Rather similar in flower character but much dwarfer and more compact in habit is *D. Winteri.*

Then there is *D. superbus*, a plant which might be grown in the rock garden but is also quite big enough to take its place in the front row of the herbaceous border. It looks like a rather slender pink, with big single flowers the petals of which are deeply, repeatedly slashed. The colour is unusual for the family—mauve, but distinctly more blue than pink. The flowers are deliciously fragrant.

All these herbaceous dianthuses will grow in any decent soil that is neither stagnant with moisture in winter nor parched by the first burst of summer heat. Most like lime but it is not essential to any. All can be raised very readily from seed, which may be sown in greenhouse or frame in spring. Cuttings of specially fine forms can be rooted in sandy soil under a handlight in early summer. For *D. Allwoodii* see Pinks p. 170.

DICENTRA (DIELYTRA) (*Bleeding Heart*). Three species of dicentra are commonly grown, namely *D. eximia*, *D. formosa* and *D. spectabilis*. All are graceful plants with delicate, fern-like foliage and arching spikes of pendent rose pink flowers, those of *eximia* and *formosa* being about 1 ft. in height while *spectabilis* is twice this stature. All three succeed best in rather cool, shady places and ordinary soil. They are in bloom from mid-July, may be planted in spring or autumn and divided at either season.

DICTAMNUS (*Burning Bush*). Distinctive plants which might be more widely grown for they have handsome, ash-like leaves and yard high spikes of quite showy flowers. These vary from white to plum purple in *Dictamnus albus*, and several forms have been selected under names such as *ruber*, red and *purpureus*, purple. All will grow in any sunny position and are not at all particular regarding soil. Seed sown in March in a frame usually germinates freely, or old plants can be lifted and carefully divided at the same period.

DIGITALIS (*Foxglove*). Though other species are occasionally found in gardens it is selected garden forms of the wild British foxglove that are most valuable. One of the best known strains is The Shirley but a more recent and very beautiful development is a strain known as Excelsior, in which the flowers are carried almost horizontally all round the stem instead of drooping on one side only.

All can be raised from seed sown outdoors in April or May. Colours vary from white and pale pink to crimson, many being most attractively spotted. The flowers are in general bigger than those of the wild plant. Like it, these garden foxgloves grow best in partial shade and will succeed in any ordinary soil. Seedlings should be ready for planting in their flowering quarters the autumn or spring after sowing.

DORONICUM (*Leopard's Bane*). *D. plantagineum* is one of the best early flowering border perennials. It has big, yellow, daisy-like flowers on 3-ft. stems and they commence to open towards the end of April in a normal season, continuing throughout May.

They are excellent for cutting besides being very decorative in the border. There is an important form known as *excelsum* or sometimes as Harpur Crewe which has bigger flowers than the type. All doronicums grow freely in any ordinary soil and sunny or half-shady position and can be increased by division in March. Plant in spring or autumn.

DRACOCEPHALUM.—*See* PHYSOSTEGIA p. 170.

ECHINACEA (*Purple Cone Flower*). In many gardens echinaceas are called rudbeckias and the relationship between the two genera is certainly close and obvious. *E. purpurea* is the species grown but there are several forms of it, all showy, late flowering plants. They average 4 ft. in height, have stiff, stoutish flower stems each terminated by a big daisy-type flower that has purple petals and a black central disk and are easily grown in any ordinary soil and open place. In some of the 'named' varieties to be found in gardens and nurseries the colour of the blooms is a good deal deeper and richer. All can be planted and, if necessary, divided in either spring or autumn.

ECHINOPS (*Globe Thistle*). Possibly it is the rather coarse foliage which prevents the globe thistle from becoming really popular for it is handsome, easily grown and well worth a place in the border. The flower heads are completely spherical, rather larger than a golf ball in good varieties and bright blue in colour. There are several species of which the best are *E. bannaticus* and *E. Ritro*, both about 4 ft. in height flowering in July. They make long tap roots and in consequence will grow in soils too dry for many other perennials. They like sunny, open positions and can be planted in spring or autumn and increased by careful division in the spring.

EPIMEDIUM (*Barrenwort*). The barrenworts are not showy perennials but they have a quiet beauty of foliage and flower which will appeal to those with eyes to see. An added merit is that they will thrive in quite dense shade, even under shrubs and trees, particularly if the soil contains plenty of peat or leaf mould. They are dwarf, bushy plants with yellow, pink, red or white flowers in spring and glossy, dark green leaves which turn to fine shades of bronze in autumn. Plant in spring and increase by careful division at the same time. The best kinds are *E. alpinum*, red, *E. pinnatum*, yellow and Rose Queen, rose.

ERIGERON (*Flea-bane*). The flea-banes have the appearance of dwarf Michaelmas daisies. Few exceed 18 in. in height. One species, *E. aurantiacus*, has orange coloured blooms and from this some useful hybrids in shades of pink and salmon have been raised. Another species, *E. philadelphicus*, has masses of small pink flowers. However, the most popular are the prevailingly blue kinds such as Quakeress, Merstham Glory, Antwerpia and mesa-grande. All are at their best during June and July and succeed in sunny, open positions and ordinary soils. They are suitable for the middle or front of the border and can be planted and divided in either spring or autumn.

ERYNGIUM (*Sea Holly*). These are most familiar as 'everlasting' flowers for autumn and winter decoration for which some species are grown on a commercial scale but they are also excellent border plants with handsome, spined foliage and teasel-like heads of flowers surrounded by spikey bracts often of an extraordinarily steely shade of blue. All succeed best in rather deep, light, well-drained soils and sunny positions. They do not like being disturbed and are best transplanted in spring at which season they can also be increased by careful division. They bloom from July to September. When required for winter decoration the flowers should be cut just before they are fully developed and suspended head downwards in a cool, dry, airy place to dry. Amongst the best of the numerous species are *E. amethystinum*, amethyst; *E. Oliverianum*, violet-blue; *E. Violetta*, one of the darkest in colour, and *E. planum*, which has comparatively small but very numerous steely-blue flower heads. An exceptional species with immense heads of creamy white flowers is *giganteum*. This is usually treated as a biennial.

EUPHORBIA (*Spurge*). This is an immense family of plants most of which are weeds from the gardener's point of view but a few are effective on account of the handsome bracts which surround the inconspicuous flowers. The two most frequently seen are remarkable in their difference one from the other. *E. Cyparissias* is an exceptionally graceful plant, 1 ft. high, with narrow, almost heather-like foliage, slender stems and bright yellow bracts in crowded heads. In contrast *E. Wulfenii* is a very bold plant, 3–4 ft. high and often double that through with stout, glaucous green foliage and immense heads of greenish yellow bracts. Both thrive in sun and ordinary soil and may be planted in spring or autumn and divided at either season. *E. pilosa* major and *E. epithymoides*, both about 18 in. high with soft yellow bracts are two others occasionally planted. They need similar treatment to the foregoing.

FILIPENDULA.—*See* SPIRAEA p. 178.

FUNKIA (*Plantain Lily*). To avoid confusion it may be well to mention that botanists have now accepted the name of Hosta for this family under which name it may appear in some up-to-date catalogues. The plantain lilies are chiefly valuable because they will thrive in damp, shady places unsuitable for most herbaceous perennials. They have broad, plantain-like leaves often of a grey or glaucous colour and spikes of tubular and as a rule not very showy flowers, though there are a few exceptions, notably *F. plantaginea* (*subcordata*), in which the flowers are white, fragrant and quite striking. Other good kinds are *F. lancifolia*, with pale mauve flowers on 18 in. stems; *F. glauca* (*Sieboldiana*), about the same size and lilac in colour, and *F. undulata* in which the glossy green leaves are striped with creamy white. All can be planted in spring or autumn and divided at either season. They flower in July and August.

GAILLARDIA. These are amongst the most gorgeously coloured flowers in the perennial border. The blooms are big and daisy-like, some plain yellow, some scarlet ringed with yellow and some a vivid tangerine. Unlike most perennials they flower continuously throughout the summer. There is, however, one drawback to this, namely that they tend to exhaust themselves in one season and die out the following winter. They are most permanent on light, well-drained soils and in very sunny positions, but even so it is advisable to maintain a succession of young plants either raised from seed or, in the case of named varieties, by careful division in spring or by root cuttings in winter. Heights average 2 ft. and as the stems tend to be too weak to support the heavy flowers it is advisable to supply some support which may take the form of the brushy tops of pea sticks pushed into the soil around the plants during April or May. Typical varieties are E. T. Anderton, pure yellow; Ipswich Beauty and The King, both scarlet and gold, and Tangerine, described by its name.

GALEGA (*Goat's Rue*). These are rather coarse perennials, by some considered too weedy to be admitted to the garden, but useful for rough places and particularly for soils too dry for choicer things. *G. officinalis* makes a bushy plant 3–4 ft. high, 2–3 ft. through, smothered throughout the summer with small pea-like flowers of rather too pale a shade of lavender. Better kinds are Her Majesty, which is a really good, soft blue and Lady Wilson, pale lilac. All can be planted in any soil and sunny position in spring or autumn and can be divided at either season.

GERANIUM (*Cranesbill*). Do not confuse these hardy geraniums with the so-called geraniums used for summer bedding. These latter are, in fact, not geraniums at all but pelargoniums, though it appears quite hopeless to eliminate the wrong and confusing name from gardens. The true geraniums with which we are concerned now are quite hardy plants which can be left in the border summer and winter. For the most part they are rather spreading and leafy with showy, saucer shaped flowers produced freely throughout the summer. Some, such as *G. armenum* and *G. phaeum*, are a rather crude magenta or port wine red, but others, notably *G. Endressii*, which is bright rose, and *G. pratense*, a deep lavender blue, are entirely charming. All grow readily in any ordinary soil and sunny or partially shady position. Plant in spring or autumn and increase by division at the same season.

GEUM. Like the gaillardias, geums suffer from the very freedom with which they flower and in rich soils tend to bloom themselves to death in one summer. They are happiest in rather light, well-drained soil and sunny positions. Unlike gaillardias they do not make good cut flowers as the blooms soon wither in water. Geums average a couple of feet in height, bloom from May to October and are amongst the best plants for the front of the border. There are a great number of garden raised varieties which must be increased by careful division in spring, the best planting season. Seed germinates readily in spring or early summer, either outdoors or in a frame, but seedlings tend to vary from their parents unless great care is taken in selection. Amongst the best kinds are Mrs. Bradshaw, vivid scarlet; Lady Stratheden, golden yellow; Prince of Orange, a clear orange, and Fire Opal, an effective coppery red. A notable species is *G. Borisii* which has small, single but very vivid orange red flowers.

GUNNERA. The gunneras are grown for their leaves. These are immense and very handsome. The general effect is rather like that of an unusually beautiful rhubarb magnified five or six times. Obviously these are plants that must be given plenty of space. They are seen to best advantage as isolated specimens and, as they like plenty of moisture, they are frequently planted at the waterside. A few well-placed gunneras and Royal Ferns will give an almost tropical luxuriance to the margin of any fairly large pool or stream. The species usually grown is *G. manicata*.

Gunneras are just a little tender and in all except the mildest parts of the country it is a wise precaution to build a shelter of twigs or wire netting covered with straw or bracken over them after their leaves have been removed in November. Do not let this covering press heavily on the crowns and be sure to remove it in April by which time the roots will be starting into growth again. Apart from this precaution gunneras are not difficult to grow, thriving in any good, loamy soil that does not dry out too much in summer. Spring is the best planting time and also the season for division when further plants are required.

GYPSOPHILA. From the ordinary gardener's point of view there are two gypsophilas which really matter, one the annual with which we are not concerned in this chapter and the other, *G. paniculata*, a perennial which makes a solitary tap root going 3 or 4 ft. down into the soil, and a bushy, freely branching plant with narrow, grey-green leaves and an immense number of tiny white flowers. It is the ideal foil for sweet peas and similar delicate summer blooms. The most popular forms of gypsophila are those with double flowers like tiny white pompons. Of these there is the ordinary 'flore pleno' and the newer 'Bristol Fairy' in which the flowers are at least twice as large as those of the older form. All need a deep, well-drained soil and sunny position. They like lime but can grow without it. They should be planted in the spring.

It is impossible to divide the solitary tap root and propagation must be by seed, which is unreliable in the case of the double kinds; by grafting small shoots of the double forms on to pieces of root of the single in early summer (not really a task for the amateur); or by cuttings taken in the following rather special way. A good plant is lifted and potted in spring and placed in a greenhouse or frame. All shoots are pinched when 4 or 5 in. long. Secondary shoots are pinched again when the same length. The next lot of shoots to appear are taken as cuttings when about 1½ in. long and are inserted in pure silver sand in a frame or under a hand light. They must be watered freely.

A break in the prevailing white of this family is made by the variety Rosy Veil, a lower growing and less robust plant with double flowers of a rather washy shade of lilac pink.

HELENIUM. These are among the most useful of summer flowering perennials, for they make a magnificent display from about midsummer until the early days of September. The first to flower is *H. pumilum aurantiacum*, which bears a mass of golden yellow flowers in June and early July. It is 2 ft. in height. Very similar but a month later is *H. pumilum magnificum*. Taller plants, up to 5 ft. high in good soil, are Riverton Beauty, Riverton Gem and *H. autumnale rubrum*, the last named wholly mahogany red, the two former combining crimson and gold. Other fine kinds are Moerheim Beauty, a brighter crimson than *rubrum*, and Crimson Beauty, bronze red, both about 2½ ft. high. All grow readily in any ordinary soil and sunny position and can be planted and divided in spring or autumn.

HELIANTHUS (*Sunflower*). There are both annual and perennial sunflowers. The former are dealt with separately in the chapter on annuals. Almost all those for the herbaceous border are big plants with massive golden yellow flowers, single in most cases but double in such varieties as Loddon Gold and Bouquet d'Or. Of the singles the most handsome is Monarch (syn. *sparsifolius*) with golden flowers as big as tea plates, each with a small black centre. It is more difficult than most sunflowers to grow, needing good drainage and, possibly, some winter protection. *H. rigidus*, Miss Mellish, tall and very showy, suffers from the drawback of spreading by underground stems and becoming rather a nuisance. *H. decapetalus* (*multiflorus*) is a dwarfer, bushier and less invasive plant. All flower from August to late October, like sun and, with the one exception mentioned, are not particular regarding soil. They can be planted and divided in spring, or in autumn after flowering.

HELIOPSIS. To the gardener these plants are extremely like the sunflowers just described. They average 4 ft. in height, have stiffly erect stems and large, deep yellow flowers. There are double and semidouble forms in addition to the singles of which *H. scabra* is the best known, though *H. laevis* and *H. patula* are also grown. All are useful for the middle and back of the border and should be treated in exactly the same manner as perennial sunflowers.

HELLEBORUS (*Christmas Rose, Lenten Rose*). There are a number of species of helleborus but two only are of general interest to the amateur gardener, the rest being plants for the collector and the specialist. These two species are *H. niger*, the Christmas Rose, and *H. orientalis*, the Lenten Rose. The first has pure white, saucer shaped flowers on stout 15-in. stems. It really does bloom at Christmas time in the open air and continues well on into January. There is a form of it named *altifolius* (or *maximus*) which is bigger, has flowers slightly spotted with rose and starts to bloom nearly a month earlier.

H. orientalis has many varieties and these are more familiar in gardens than is the true species. It is a little taller than the Christmas Rose, similar in general appearance but with flowers which are more often some rather dull shade of purple or maroon than white. All the same there are pure white Lenten Roses and yellowish ones into the bargain, while some of the purple shades are pleasing enough in their quiet way and certainly welcome in March and April.

All these hellebores like good, rich loamy soils and cool places. They have no objection to shade but they do object to root disturbance so should be left alone as long as possible. When they finally get overcrowded they can be lifted and divided very carefully after flowering, which is also the best planting time.

HEMEROCALLIS (*Day Lily*). These plants are known as Day Lilies because the individual flowers last for only one day. This matters little as fresh buds are produced in seemingly endless succession and the plants make a good display throughout June and July. The flowers are trumpet shaped and in various shades of yellow and orange. All have the merit of thriving equally well in sun or partial shade. They are not particular regarding soil but do best in a good loam. There are a great number of named varieties differing mainly in the size and shade of colour of the flowers. The average height is 2 ft. Planting can be done in spring or autumn and division may be carried out at either season.

HEUCHERA. Very graceful plants with somewhat the decorative effect of a large London Pride. They have sprays of small but numerous flowers on slender stems up to $2\frac{1}{2}$ ft. in height. The colour range is from palest pink to crimson. The most freely grown are forms of *H. sanguinea*, such as Edge Hall, a good pale pink; Shirley, scarlet and Pluie de Feu, crimson. *H. brizoides gracillima* is a particularly dainty kind, pale pink in colour, while *H. tiarelloides* is smaller, paler and of hybrid origin. All bloom in June and July, like sunny positions, are not faddy about soil and can be planted and divided in spring or autumn.

HOLLYHOCK (*Althaea*). These are frequently treated as biennials, the seed being sown one year for flowering the next, after which the plants are dug up and thrown away. Nevertheless all hollyhocks are true perennials and will continue to flower for many years if given good drainage and a sunny position. In addition to single flowering types there are others with fully double blooms. Specially selected forms are best increased by root cuttings taken in December or January. All flower in July and August, and are best planted in spring or early autumn. Seed should be sown outdoors in May or early June, seedlings being pricked off 6–8 in. apart each way in July or August and transferred to flowering quarters the following autumn or spring.

HOSTA.—*See* FUNKIA p. 155.

INCARVILLEA. When these do well they never fail to attract a great deal of attention for their big gloxinia-like flowers have an almost tropical splendour, unusual in a hardy plant. Yet perfectly hardy they are, if given a situation with good winter drainage and plenty of sunshine. All have tuberous roots which need sun warmth to ripen them properly. The best kinds are *I. grandiflora*, rosy-red, 12 in.; a dwarfer variety of it named *brevipes*, also with rosy red flowers both flowering in May and June; and *I. Delavayi*, rosy magenta in colour and 2 ft. in height. There is also a magnificent hybrid of medium height named Bees' Pink. It has soft pink flowers. All should be planted in spring and increased by careful division at the same time or in the case of the species, by seed sown in a frame or greenhouse in spring.

INULA. Rather coarse perennials with big, showy, daisy-like flowers. Some kinds may be naturalised in the wild garden or thin woodland while others may be used in the middle of the herbaceous border. The best is *I. Royleana* with large, orange yellow flowers on 2 ft. stems in July and August. No inula is particular as to soil or situation and all can be planted and divided in spring or autumn.

IRIS. This is an immense family including plants with bulbous roots which are dealt with separately in the chapter on bulbs. Here we are concerned only with those having ordinary fibrous roots or with fleshy rhizomes as in the common German or flag iris. It is from this last-named species that a great number of the best garden varieties have been and still are being produced. There are commercial specialists who grow nothing but this one flower and whose lists run to hundreds of varieties. Colours have been greatly extended beyond the prevailing purple of the common flag and now include excellent yellows, pinks, pale blues, coppery shades, wine colours and combinations of these. All these flag irises suffer the drawback of a rather short flowering season in late May and early June. Heights vary from 2 to 5 ft. All grow readily in any ordinary or rather light soils and sunny positions. They like lime but it is not essential to them. Contrary to popular belief they do not like shady places. They are best planted immediately the flowers fade towards the end of June but can also be planted in spring or early autumn. They are increased by division of the rhizomes and special care should be taken to break off all the old and half dead pieces of rhizome when dividing, keeping only a couple of inches from the base of the leaves. Plant firmly but only just cover the rhizomes with soil. They will work out on top in a short time and this is their natural position.

The dwarf 'Crimean' irises obtained from *I. Chamaeiris* (often erroneously called *I. pumila*) look and behave very much like dwarf flag irises and require identical treatment in the garden except that, as they are no more than 9 in. in height they must be planted at the very front of the border or, if preferred, can be grown in the rock garden.

Then there are two races of very beautiful but difficult irises known as Regelio-cyclus and Oncocyclus. *I. susiana,* the Mourning iris, so called because of its sombre colour scheme of heavy, almost black netting on a white ground, is the best known example of the first class while *I. Gatesii* is a typical Oncocyclus iris. These and their kith and kin are not beginner's plants. They need a gritty, well-drained soil and plenty of sun and warmth. In particular their rhizomes must be thoroughly ripened in late summer and for this reason it is an advantage to plant them on a sun-baked ledge or on top of a terrace wall or bank where the soil is likely to dry out thoroughly as the summer advances. Sometimes it may prove necessary to cover them with handlights or cloches after flowering to help this ripening process. All have very large flowers and are of medium height.

Apart from these types with thick rhizomes which store food and so help the plants over dry spells there are a great many irises with ordinary fibrous roots and these also vary greatly in their requirements. Some of them like plenty of moisture in the soil and may be planted near the pool or stream but with their crowns a few inches above the water. This is true of the so-called Japanese iris, *I. Kaempferi* with its very large, flamboyant, widely opened flowers in various shades of purple, violet, blue and pink. It grows 2½ to 3 ft. high and flowers about mid-summer.

I. laevigata, also sometimes known as the Japanese iris and rather similar in appearance but slighter in build, is even more of a moisture lover and may be planted actually in a pool or slow stream with its crown 2 or 3 in. below water level. It revels in a good, rich, loamy soil. Such conditions will also suit our own native yellow flag iris which grows 4 or 5 ft. high and flowers in May and June.

Either moist soil or quite ordinary border conditions will please the very graceful *I. sibirica* with its big clumps of grassy foliage and numerous small blue or violet 'flags', that make such delightful cut flowers. The giant *I. ochroleuca* (*orientalis*) with its narrow, corkscrewed leaves and 5 to 6 ft. stems terminated by pale yellow or whitish flowers is another of these accommodating irises for moist or ordinary soil.

Finally there are many species which will thrive best in porous soils and sunny positions. Good drainage is a first essential for most of these and the smaller kinds are as happy on the rock garden as in the border. A representative selection would include *I. gracilipes*, with grassy leaves and, in May, small lavender flowers on slender 9-in. stems; *I. Douglasiana*, 1 ft. high with violet flowers in June; *I. unguicularis* (*stylosa*), the winter flowering iris, with fine lavender or white flowers sometimes partly hidden amongst the abundant grassy foliage, a fault which can be overcome by planting it in poor, sandy or gravelly soil; and *I. tenax*, 15 in. high, carrying in June its beautiful lavender and rose flowers.

Unlike the rhizomatous irises all these fibrous rooted kinds should be planted in spring and can be divided at the same season.

KNIPHOFIA (*Red-hot Poker*). These plants were once called tritoma and may still be found under this name in some old-fashioned catalogues. They are all handsome if rather stiff plants with stout, sword-like leaves and sturdy stems topped by poker shaped heads of scarlet or yellow flowers. There are some much smaller kinds, mostly species, such as *K. rufa* and *K. Galpinii*, both a couple of feet in height with narrow, grassy leaves and comparatively slender flower stems, but unfortunately these are in the main more tender and difficult to grow than the bigger kinds. Of the latter the best are *K. Uvaria* (*alooides*), 5 ft. high, with scarlet and yellow flowers in August; *K. erecta*, similar in height but with the flowers gradually erecting themselves from the bottom of the spike upwards, a peculiarity which gives it a curiously rocket-like appearance; *K. nobilis*, 7-8 ft. high and late flowering, and *K. maxima globosa*, even later, often carrying its almost globular red and yellow heads into November. There are also many hybrids with 'fancy' names such as Royal Standard, Mount Etna, Sulphur Spire, etc. All should be grown in full sun and reasonably rich but well-drained soil. They need plenty of moisture while the flower spikes are forming but dislike a waterlogged soil in winter. They may be planted in spring or autumn, but are best divided in spring.

LATHYRUS (*Everlasting Pea*). A familiar sight in cottage gardens in summer is the so-called perennial pea, *Lathyrus grandiflorus*, a herbaceous climber, in habit not unlike a sweet pea though rather more robust and with very numerous pea-flowers which are either a rather harsh shade of rose or pure white. It is a pretty and useful plant which will grow in almost any soil and place. The perennial pea will climb to a height of about 8 ft. and can be used to clothe walls, arches, screens, sheds, etc. It can be raised readily from seed sown in a frame in March or outdoors in May.

LAVATERA. Most of these plants are annuals and therefore are dealt with separately, but one important species, *L. Olbia*, is an almost shrub-like perennial 6–7 ft. high and as much through, branching freely and producing from June to September big, rose-coloured flowers rather like small, single hollyhocks. It is most satisfactory in well-drained and rather poor soil. In rich ground it is apt to become too leafy and to die in winter. Plant in spring and propagate by cuttings of the young shoots taken in spring or early summer.

LIATRIS. These striking plants never fail to attract comment. If they were easier to grow they would doubtless be in every garden. Actually they require a combination of sun, moisture and good winter drainage which is often rather difficult to come by. The soil should be sandy but with plenty of humus, and water should be supplied freely from June to August if the weather is dry. The plants make a number of stiffly erect stems 2–3 ft. high, clothed for half their length in fluffy, rose-pink flowers which have a curious habit of opening from the top downwards. The two best kinds are *L. pycnostachya*, which is 3–4 ft. high and *L. spicata* which is considerably shorter. Both should be planted in spring and increased by careful division at that season.

LIBERTIA. Not a plant in the first rank but useful because of its graceful, narrow foliage, wand-like spikes of white flowers and the fact that it can be grown practically anywhere. It likes best a sunny position and light soil but is not a fussy plant. Spring is the best season both for planting and for dividing old clumps when further stock is required.

LIGULARIA.—*See* SENECIO p. 177.

LILY OF THE VALLEY. The lily of the valley, *Convallaria majalis*, is seldom grown in the herbaceous border though it is a true herbaceous plant. This, no doubt, is very largely because it is so valuable for cutting that it is more convenient to give it a bed to itself, often in an out of the way place from which blooms can be picked freely without spoiling the general garden display. Certainly the lily of the valley responds well to such treatment which permits it to be mulched liberally with well-broken, old stable manure and leaf mould each March and, if desired, to be covered with frame lights in spring to obtain earlier and cleaner blooms. Plant the crowns singly in October or early November about 6 in. apart in rows 9 in. apart and cover them with 1 in. of soil. Thereafter leave them to spread and multiply for years until the bed becomes so overcrowded that there is a definite falling off in the quality and quantity of bloom. Then lift in autumn, divide to single crowns and replant as in the first instance. The soil should be rich and deeply cultivated, the position sheltered but a little shaded or at any rate not very hot and dry. There is a rare form of this plant with pale pink flowers but it is not, in my opinion, as lovely as the common white variety.

LINARIA (*Toadflax*). The only two species of this very large family of interest for the herbaceous border are *L. dalmatica*, with narrow, grey-green leaves and slender spikes of bright yellow flowers rather like tiny antirrhinums, and *L. purpurea*, which is similar but with purple flowers. Both bloom continuously from July to September. The plants thrive in any ordinary soil and sunny position and may be planted and divided in spring or autumn.

LOBELIA (*Cardinal Flower*). Most amateurs think of lobelias solely as cheerful edging plants for summer bedding, but there are also some excellent hardy or nearly hardy kinds for the herbaceous border. In well-drained soil these often stand the winter without protection in mild districts. Elsewhere they should be lifted and placed in a frame from about October until April. The three important kinds are *L. cardinalis*, with slender 3-ft. spikes of vivid scarlet flowers; *L. fulgens*, similar but with beetroot red foliage, and *L. siphilitica*, which is a little shorter, less graceful and with rather washy blue flowers. There are numerous garden forms of all three plants, some of which are marked improvements on their parents. All may be planted and divided in spring. They flower from August to October and like plenty of moisture during the growing season; so much so, in fact, that in summer they can be given semi-bog conditions, though good drainage is essential in winter.

LUPINUS (*Lupin*). There are two very distinct species of perennial lupin in addition to the annuals dealt with elsewhere. One is the tree lupin which is almost a shrub, with a semi-permanent, woody framework. It has comparatively small spikes of yellow or white flowers in May and June and makes a big bush 5 ft. high and as much through. The other perennial species *L. polyphyllus*, is a true herbaceous plant, producing its flower spikes in May or early June on 3–4 ft. stems but dying down each autumn and sprouting up again the following spring. It has been much improved by breeders and a great many named varieties have been and still are being raised. A notable improvement was that made by Mr. Russell of York when he raised seedlings in which the upright or standard petals spread out fanwise so giving the whole spike a much more solid appearance than formerly. The present colour range includes white, yellow, mauve, lavender, purple, pink and crimson, in addition to a multitude of intermediate shades and combinations.

All lupins detest lime, like good drainage and do best in rather sandy or porous soils. They usually tend to flower themselves to death in a few years, and so should be renewed constantly either from seed sown outdoors in spring or early summer or by cuttings rooted in a frame in March or April. The cuttings are made from firm young shoots severed close to the crown of the plant. Selected or named varieties will not breed true from seed but must be increased by cuttings. All lupins like a sunny position and are best planted in spring.

LYCHNIS (*Campion*). These plants are closely related to agrostemma, in fact the latter genus is often included with lychnis. Two kinds are showy herbaceous perennials, namely *L. chalcedonica*, 3–4 ft. in height with flattish heads of geranium red flowers, and *L. Viscaria splendens plena*, 1 ft. in height with double, carmine flowers. Both flower in July and need soil well drained even to the point of poorness. They should be planted in spring and may be divided carefully at that season, or *L. chalcedonica* can be raised from seed sown under glass in March or outdoors in May. *See also* AGROSTEMMA p. 140.

LYSIMACHIA. The well-known Creeping Jenny is a species of lysimachia, but it is with the taller kinds that we are concerned at present. Three of the best of these are the common *L. vulgaris*, a rather rare British plant found by stream-sides and with 3-ft. spikes of bright yellow flowers in June and July; *L. punctata* (syn. *verticillata*) which is rather similar in effect but more slightly formed and with flowers and leaves in whorls; and *L. clethroides* with white blooms in slender spikes. All like damp, rich soils and cool, half shady positions, though they will also grow in quite dry places. They can be planted and divided in spring or autumn.

LYTHRUM (*Purple loose-strife*). Spike flowered perennials for sunny or half shady places and ordinary soils. The flowers of *L. virgatum* are small, rose magenta and carried in close, slender spikes 3 ft. in height. *L. Salicaria* is a rather looser, less compact plant with similarly showy but crudely coloured flowers. There are improved garden forms such as Rose Queen and Lady Sackville. All may be planted in spring or autumn and divided at either season.

MECONOPSIS (*Himalayan Poppy*).—*See* p. 215.

MEGASEA.—*See* SAXIFRAGA p. 176 and 227.

MERTENSIA. This is a family frequently recommended but seldom seen. Not all of its numerous species are worthy of the praise lavished upon them but there are good border plants amongst their number, notably *M. virginica* (*pulmonarioides*) with ample tufts of blue-green leaves and loose sprays of sky blue flowers in early summer. The plant is about 3 ft. high and grows readily in ordinary, well-drained soil and a sheltered, sunny position. It can be increased by careful division in spring but does not like root disturbance so should be left alone as long as possible. *M. sibirica*, often offered, is inferior in every way, making too much leaf in proportion to flower.

MIMULUS (*Musk*). When one has ruled out the musks which are annuals or treated as such (see p. 113) and those which are grown mainly in the rock garden (see p. 216) one is left with a few kinds for the herbaceous border or the edge of stream and pool. Of these far and away the most important is our own native *Mimulus luteus* which delights in very moist soil and in such places soon makes big, leafy clumps producing freely almost all the summer, bright yellow, pouched flowers on 18-in. stems. There are several colour forms in which the yellow ground is more or less heavily splashed with crimson or maroon. All can be increased by division in spring, the best planting time.

MONARDA (*Bergamot*). The leaves of these plants are very fragrant and the tubular flowers are produced in showy whorls, one above the other on a spike 3–4 ft. in height. The best-known and probably the best all-round kind is *M. didyma*. Its variety, Cambridge Scarlet, is as nearly pure scarlet as one can imagine and flowers from July to September. There are also many hybrids, some with flowers of rather doubtful amethyst blue shade and a white form which is not very effective. All should be grown in ordinary soil and sun or partial shade. Plant in spring or autumn and divide at the same season.

MORINA. One rather striking species, *M. longifolia*, is grown in borders. It has spiky, thistle-like leaves and stiff spikes of pink and white tubular flowers, the whole effect being not unlike a stiffer acanthus. Treatment is the same as for that genus. Propagate by seed in spring.

MYOSOTIDIUM. Imagine one of the giant leaved (megasea) saxifrages with pale, bluish flowers on a rather diminished scale in place of the normal ample blooms of pink and rose and you have a fair idea of *Myosotidium Hortensia*, the only species cultivated. It is rather a tender plant thriving in the south-east and other similarly mild regions but needing winter protection in most parts of the country. This fact, combined with its excess of leaves in proportion to bloom, will always prevent it from becoming popular but it is none the less an interesting plant worthy of consideration in districts in which it is known to succeed. Plant in good, rich, porous soil and increase by careful division in spring. The flowers are produced in May and June.

NEPETA (*Catmint*). *N. Faasenii* is a favourite plant for edging. It makes a dense mass of slender stems set with small, grey leaves and terminated by spikes of lavender flowers; the whole plant has a distinct mint-like fragrance when crushed. It is in bloom throughout the summer and early autumn and its one fault is that, like many other free flowering perennials, it is inclined to die out in winter, particularly if the soil is very rich and poorly drained. It is seen at its best in rather light, poor soils in sunny positions. One form known as Six Hills Giant, is larger and looser in all its parts. These features are also characteristic of *N. macrantha*, a plant which requires identical treatment. Plant in spring and increase by careful division at that time or by cuttings of firm, young growth taken at practically any time in spring or summer.

OENOTHERA (*Evening Primrose*). The true Evening Primrose, *O. biennis*, is, as its name implies, a biennial and therefore not for treatment in this chapter, but there are some excellent perennial kinds, notably *O. fruticosa* and its varieties such as *Youngii* and *major*. All are bushy, branching plants, $1\frac{1}{2}$-2 ft. high, with innumerable golden yellow flowers each as big as half-a-crown throughout July and August. These are plants for full sun and well-drained soil. In fact in a dry season they are likely to be the best plants in the border. Plant in spring for preference and increase by careful division at that time.

OSTROWSKIA. *O. magnifica* is a very beautiful and an uncommonly striking plant but it is also a difficult one to grow and I do not recommend it to beginners. It looks like an immense campanula, 6 ft. or more high branching out at the top to carry numerous saucer shaped flowers on the same ample scale. To do it well it must be given a sunny—perhaps I should say sun-baked—position, in very well-drained soil; yet it must have plenty of moisture in spring and early summer while it is making its growth. It often pays to cover the roots with framelights during August and September to ensure ripening. Spring is the best planting time. Old roots can be divided then but it is better to leave them alone and rely for increase on seed sown as soon as ripe and germinated in sandy soil in greenhouse or frame.

PAEONIA (*Peony*). There are two quite distinct classes of Peony, the herbaceous ones with which we are interested in this chapter and the tree peony which is dealt with in the chapter on trees and shrubs. The herbaceous peonies are in the main derived from two sources, the European species *P. officinalis*, and the Chinese one, *P. albiflora*. Both are hardy plants not in the least difficult to grow in ordinary soil and sunny positions, though they all dislike root disturbance and sometimes take quite a few years to get fully established after a shift. For this reason they should be given permanent places where they need not be disturbed even when other plants have to be lifted and divided. Plant in spring or early autumn, just covering the crowns with soil. Propagation can be effected at either season by carefully dividing the roots, but a sharp knife will be required to cut through the hard, fleshy crowns. There are a great many varieties, some with single flowers, others fully double and yet others with an outer ring of broad petals as in a normal

167

single flower, containing a central ball of narrow petal segments often in a contrasting colour. Full details of these are to be found in any nursery catalogue. All flower in May and June and are about 3 ft. in height and often rather more through.

PAMPAS GRASS. One of the few ornamental grasses which everyone knows is the pampas grass, *Cortaderia argentea,* which delights in light but fairly rich soils and warm, sunny places. It can be planted at the back of the herbaceous border but looks better grown in a group by itself in a prominent spot such as a circular bed on the lawn. It can be increased by division in spring but clumps should not be pulled apart too murderously or they may be very slow in recovering. Allow the leaves to remain all winter on established plants as they serve as a protection to the crowns, but withered leaves can be removed in the spring.

PAPAVER (*Poppy*). A great many poppies are annuals and are dealt with in the chapter on those plants but there are in addition perennial kinds of which the oriental poppy (*P. orientale*) is the most important. This is a bold plant with very large scarlet and black blooms on 2-ft. stems in June. Its one fault is that it is apt to sprawl about, particularly after flowering, when it gets rather untidy. There are many named varieties, some scarlet and black like the type but more vivid in colour or larger in bloom (e.g. Lord Lambourne); others soft pink, as Mrs. Perry; vivid cerise as Mrs. Stobart or Ethel Swete; deep crimson as Mahony. All grow freely in any ordinary soil and full sun. They will also grow in places too dry and hot for many other perennials. Plant in spring and propagate either by seed sown outdoors in May–June or by root cuttings taken in winter. Named varieties do not come true from seed and root cuttings must be employed.

PENSTEMON. The majority of penstemons are partially tender plants mainly used for summer bedding but a few are hardy enough to be grown outdoors throughout the year, some in the rock garden and others in the herbaceous border. Of the last group the best is *P. isophyllus.* This makes slender spikes of narrowly trumpet shaped salmon-scarlet flowers in July and August the whole plant being about 3 ft. high. It delights in loamy soils, good drainage and plenty of sunshine. Plant in spring and propagate by cuttings of non-flowering shoots taken at practically any time obtainable. These cuttings should be rooted in sandy soil under a hand light.

PHLOX. In addition to the true herbaceous phlox discussed here there are many rock garden species to be found in Chapter VIII. Most important of the herbaceous kinds is *P. decussata*, which flowers from July to September and has given rise to a vast number of varieties. Typically this is a plant 3 ft. high, but there are dwarfer forms, such as Jules Sandeau and Mia Ruys, which barely attain 2 ft. All have big trusses of very fragrant blooms. Colours range from white, through pale pink and soft lavender to scarlet, crimson and purple. The flowering season extends from July to September.

Phloxes grow best in rather rich, loamy soils with plenty of moisture during the growing season. They will succeed in either full sun or slight shade. They can be planted in spring or autumn and increased by division at either season or by root cuttings in winter. The latter are particularly recommended when plants become infested with eelworms, minute pests which cause the foliage to become distorted or even, in severe cases, thread-like.

PHORMIUM (*New Zealand Flax*). *Phormium tenax* is a plant of the largest size. Its stiff, sword-like leaves are themselves as high as a man and form a clump which may easily be 6 or 8 ft. through. From this spear up in summer to a height of 10 or 12 ft. several stout stems branching towards the top to carry red and yellow flowers which, at that distance, are too small to be really effective. It is the tropical luxuriance of the plant which makes it so valuable in the right place. This should be sheltered and warm, in soil well drained but rich, so that the plant develops its full proportions. Plant in spring. Division can be carried out at the same season but it is better to rely on seedlings which can be raised in frame or greenhouse in spring. There is also a reddish-bronze leaved variety named *atropurpurea*.

PHYGELIUS (*Cape Figwort*). This is a handsome plant for a very sunny, warm position in rather dry soil. It makes numerous stems 2–3 ft. high, branching out to carry many tubular, scarlet flowers, curved and down-hanging in a rather curious fashion. This plant never fails to attract attention and it is surprising that it is not more widely grown as it is not difficult in the right situation. Plant in spring and increase by division at the same season.

PHYSALIS (*Cape Gooseberry*). Cape gooseberries are more useful as plants for cutting than for the herbaceous border as they are untidy in growth and not very attractive until the autumn when their seed vessels develop into the blown-out, brightly-coloured lanterns which are so familiar as Christmas decorations. The cultivated species is *P. Alkekengii* which also masquerades as *P. Bunyardii* and *P. Franchettii*. There is also a variety with particularly large lanterns which is usually sold as *P. Franchettii grandiflora.* Physalis should be grown in ordinary soil and sunny, sheltered positions. They can be planted in spring and divided at that season. It is a good plan to stick some bushy twigs around them in May as support for their rather weak stems. When planting spread out the thick roots and cover them with a couple of inches of good soil.

PHYSOSTEGIA (*Dragon's Head or Obedient Plant*). The physostegias got their name of Obedient Plant because the long, tubular, pink flowers which are carried in a narrow spike, appear to be jointed at the stalk and will stay in whatever position they are set. The best kind is a form of *P. virginiana* (syn. *Dracocephalum virginianum*) named Vivid.

P. *virginiana* itself is a rather tall, straggling plant with flower spikes diminished in effectiveness by the general leafiness of the plant, but in Vivid the stems are reduced and the flower spikes increased in size, the result being a decorative plant about 18 in. high, which is as bright as anything to be found in the September border. The colour of the flowers, too, is a deeper pink than those of the type. All physostegias grow very readily in ordinary soil in sunny or partially shaded positions. They can be planted in autumn or spring and increased by division at either season.

PINK. The fragrant garden pink is a dianthus which has been highly developed over the centuries. There are many 'named' varieties of it, such as the white flowered Mrs. Sinkins and Her Majesty, pink flowered Inchmary, and rosy-red Glory. The laced pinks are distinguished by a zone of deeper colour round the edges of the petals. Numerous hybrids have also been raised, notably the long flowering race known as All-woodii which runs to both single and double flowered forms and has a colour range from white and palest pink to crimson, many varieties being enlivened by eyes or zones of a deeper shade than the rest of the bloom.

Most of these pinks are not fussy about soil and will grow rapidly and flower freely without special attention. But some of the choicer varieties tend to winter badly especially on cold and heavy soils and need to be frequently renewed from cuttings to keep them in full vigour. These may be planted in slightly raised beds of good but not too rich soil, containing a fair quantity of sand to ensure quick drainage in wet weather—for wet is always more harmful to pinks than cold.

All should be planted in spring or early autumn and be raised from cuttings or pipings (cuttings pulled out at a joint instead of being cut), inserted in sandy soil in a frame or sheltered border outdoors in June or July.

PLATYCODON (*Balloon Flower*). These are very attractive plants which deserve to be better known. They suggest dwarf campanulas and are in fact sometimes included in that family. *Platycodon grandiflorum* is 1 ft. to 18 in. high, compact, with widely bell-shaped flowers, deep blue in the type and white in the form *album*. The flower buds are particularly striking as they are inflated like small balloons or Chinese lanterns. The plant does well in well-drained soil and sunny position, is in bloom in July and August and should be planted in spring. It can be increased by very careful division at that time or, better, by seed sown in frame or greenhouse in March. There is also a variety named *P. Mariesii* which is dwarfer, more compact and has deeper blue flowers.

PLUMBAGO (*Leadwort*). The best-known plumbago is the greenhouse climber with clusters of pale-blue flowers. There are in addition two plants for the herbaceous border commonly known in gardens as plumbago though their correct name is Ceratostigma under which they may appear in some catalogues. One, *P. Larpentiae* (*C. plumbaginoides*) is a true herbaceous plant dying down to ground level each winter. It makes a plant 1 ft. high and considerably more through and its stems are terminated by clear blue flowers from August to October. The other species, *C. Willmottianum*, is a much more bushy plant, in fact a dwarf shrub 2 or 3 ft. high and only partially dying down in winter. The flowers are a similar azure blue. Both should be grown in well-drained, rather light soil and a warm, sunny position. Plant in spring, preferably from pots, and increase by cuttings of firm, young shoots inserted in sandy soil under a hand light in summer.

PODOPHYLLUM. It is only occasionally that one meets a podophyllum outside the gardens of collectors yet these are attractive, unusual and useful plants which, so far from being difficult to grow, will thrive in shady places where many other plants would fail. They like soils with plenty of humus (peat or leaf mould) and plenty of moisture without actually approaching the conditions of the bog garden. The best is *P. emodi*, about 15 in. high with broad, spreading leaves, white but not very showy flowers followed by extremely showy, scarlet fruits almost as big as tomatoes. Plant in spring and divide, when necessary, at planting time.

POLEMONIUM (*Jacob's Ladder*). These plants, so common in cottage gardens, seem to be losing popularity. They are certainly not very striking but they are pretty in a quiet way and have the merit of thriving in any soil in sun or partial shade. They make compact tufts of fern-like foliage from which arise straight 2-ft. stems terminated by spikes of blue flowers. The best known is *P. cœruleum* but a better plant with brighter flowers is *P. Richardsonii*. Both are in bloom from about mid-summer until August and can be planted in spring or autumn and divided at either season.

POLYGONATUM (*Solomon's Seal*). These well-known plants are ideal subjects for positions too shady for most perennials. They will even thrive in quite close woodland and few are particular as regards soil. *Polygonatum multiflorum*, the best species, makes 3-ft. arching stems with leaves suggesting those of the lily of the valley and pendent, creamy white, tubular flowers in May and June. Plant this and other kinds in spring or autumn and leave alone for as long as possible as they improve with time. Propagation is readily effected by division when planting.

POLYGONUM (*Knot Weed*). This is one of those unfortunate families which contain more weeds than useful garden plants and the amateur is apt to get disgusted by trying the wrong species before he gets hold of the really useful ones. For the herbaceous border there is really only one worth planting, *P. campanulatum*, a really beautiful plant making a rounded bush 3 ft. high and as much through, with deeply veined, grassy green leaves, reddish stems and masses of tiny, pale pink flowers in August and September. There is no better plant at its own season and it will grow as well under trees as in full sun, nor is it at all particular regarding soil, but it must have plenty of moisture. Plant in spring or autumn and propagate by division, preferably in spring.

POTENTILLA (*Cinquefoil*). Another family containing an unfortunate percentage of weeds but not lacking in good garden material. There are many hybrids of *P. atrosanguinea*, mostly with double or semi-double flowers in various shades of scarlet, crimson and yellow. One form which almost all nurseries offer is Gibson's Scarlet, a truly magnificent plant, almost prostrate in habit and with the most vivid single scarlet flowers imaginable. Most of the hybrid potentillas are taller than this, often a couple of feet high and rather straggling. All should be grown in full sun and will succeed in any soils, even those too dry for most perennials. Plant in spring or autumn and divide when necessary at either season.

POTERIUM (*Burnet*). These are dainty plants making low mounds of deeply divided leaves from which ascend in August and September slender stems terminated by bottle-brush spikes of feathery flowers. These are white in *P. canadensis* and soft pink in *P. obtusum*. Both kinds are readily grown in a sunny place and in ordinary soil. Plant in spring or autumn and increase by division in spring.

PRIMULA.—*See* p. 222.

PULMONARIA (*Lungwort*). These have two outstanding merits—they flower very early in the year and will succeed in shady places. They are low growing plants, seldom exceeding 1 ft. in height and therefore suitable for the front row of the border. Some are, perhaps, a little too leafy for the rather small flowers, carried in clusters on short stems in March and April. The two best kinds are *P. angustifolia azurea*, sometimes known as the Blue Cowslip though it really has very little resemblance to a Cowslip, and *P. rubra*. The first has gentian blue flowers while the other is brick red. Neither is in the least particular as to soil. Plant in spring, immediately after flowering, or in early autumn, and increase by division in spring or autumn.

PYRETHRUM. Strictly speaking from a botanist's standpoint these plants are merely a species of chrysanthemum but they will always be known as pyrethrums in gardens. They are showy flowers, particularly serviceable for cutting on account of their long, stiff stems and the way in which they last in water. All make pleasant looking clumps of fine, ferny foliage and have showy, daisy flowers in May and June. There are fully double forms which rather resemble small, double chrysanthemums, and also natural, single flowered types. Most catalogues offer a great many named varieties in shades varying from white and palest pink to deep crimson. All transplant rather badly in autumn except on the lightest and best-drained soils. They are best moved either in spring or in summer as soon as possible after flowering, but if the latter season is chosen they must be well watered for the first few weeks. They can be divided either in spring or summer and succeed best in rather light, loamy soils and sunny positions. Where drainage is bad they can often be grown well by raising the beds a little above ground level or planting along the summit of ridges and on shallow mounds.

RANUNCULUS (*Buttercup*). The buttercup family has not only given us beautiful, if infuriating, weeds; it has also provided our gardens with several delightful and quite innocuous plants, notably the Turban and French ranunculi which I have described in Chapter XI. Here I want to call attention to a beautiful perennial for the herbaceous border, *R. aconitifolius*, often known by the pleasant name 'Fair Maids of France' and to its double flowered form even more appropriately called 'White Bachelor's Button'. Both are freely branched plants a couple of feet in height, the first with single white flowers, the second, also white, with each bloom converted into a perfect globe of petals. Both thrive in damp, loamy soils but can be grown in almost any soil that does not dry out too quickly in summer. They flower in early summer and the plants are readily increased by division in the spring.

RED-HOT POKER.—*See* KNIPHOFIA p. 162.

RHEUM (*Rhubarb*). The common rhubarb is, of course, a plant for the vegetable plot alone but it has close relatives with foliage and flowers of such beauty that they are welcome inhabitants of the ornamental garden where they may be planted in big beds and borders, by the waterside and in thin woodland. Typical of these is *Rheum palmatum* with immense, deeply divided leaves and the typical creamy white flowers of the rhubarb but on 10-ft. stems. There is a variety of it named *rubrum* in which these flowers are crimson and another, Bowles' variety, in which these red flowers are coupled with leaves green above and red beneath. All will grow readily in any fairly rich soil and can be increased by careful division in spring.

RODGERSIA. This is another family of plants grown quite as much for beauty of foliage as of flower and which is happy in damp soils though it can also be grown successfully in the ordinary border. *Rodgersia pinnata* is the best loved and most planted species. It has deeply divided leaves a little like those of a horse chestnut in shape and deep green in colour. The flower stems are close on 3 ft. high, terminating in dense plumes of small rose pink flowers strongly resembling those of an astilbe. There is a variety with even deeper coloured flowers and bronze leaves. *R. aesculifolia* and *R. podophylla* both have white flowers. All bloom about mid-summer and like best a cool, partly shaded position. Division in March provides a safe means of increase.

ROMNEYA (*Californian Tree Poppy*). Two species and their hybrids are cultivated but they are so much alike in all but botanical details that the gardener will probably regard them as identical. One is named *R. Coulteri* and the other *R. trichocalyx*. Both are extremely beautiful and not difficult to grow once established but they hate root disturbance. They have enormous, pure white, poppy-like flowers, each with a big bunch of golden anthers in the centre, and they are carried on tall, half woody stems clothed with grey-green foliage. Height averages 5 ft. and the plants are in bloom from June to September. Romneyas thrive in sunny, warm positions and poorish soils; in fact I have seen them doing well in a gravel path. Propagation is best effected by root cuttings taken in winter and inserted singly in small pots. The young plants are then potted on carefully until they reach 4 in. pots, from which they are transferred in spring with the minimum amount of root disturbance to their permanent flowering positions. Dead or damaged growth should be cut out each spring.

RUDBECKIA (*Cone Flower*). These are easily grown plants of the daisy family, mostly tall, back row subjects, though one species, variously known as *R. Newmannii* or *R. speciosa*, is only 2 ft. high and can be used as a front line plant. All are extremely showy and in bloom during late summer or early autumn. The best are Golden Glow, 7 ft. high with fully double, golden yellow flowers in great profusion; *R. speciosa* which has single, rather starry, deep golden blooms with black centres and Herbstonne, 6 ft. high with clear yellow single flowers each with an upstanding pale green cone. All will grow in any ordinary soil and sunny position. They can be planted and divided in spring or autumn. For the plant sometimes known as *R. purpurea* see Echinacea p. 153.

SALVIA (*Sage*). A good many of the sages are half hardy plants useful for bedding out or growing in the greenhouse and one is, of course, the familiar herb. But there are also a few good kinds for the herbaceous border, notably *S. superba* (*virgata nemorosa*,) a grand plant, 3 ft. high with masses of erect stems clothed for fully half their length with small Oxford blue flowers set off by purple bracts; *uliginosa*, twice as high and considerably more open in habit with rather small spikes of sky blue flowers, and *patens*, which is about as true a blue as anything in the garden but unfortunately requires winter protection in most districts. It makes tubers, not unlike those of a dahlia, and these can be lifted and stored dry in a cupboard from October to April. It is in flower throughout the summer whereas the other two are for August and September only. All will grow in any ordinary soil and sunny position and should be planted and, if desired, propagated by division in spring or autumn (*S. patens* in spring only).

SANTOLINA (*Lavender-cotton*). These plants are grown principally for their foliage which is very fine and intensely silver grey. The flowers are little yellow balls like those of the tansy and are not particularly showy. Two kinds are commonly planted, *S. Chamaecyparissus* and a dwarf form of the same plant usually sold as *S. nana compacta*. They differ solely in height, the former being 2 ft., the latter 9 in. Both are seen to best advantage in rather light, well-drained soils and sunny positions. Plant in spring and propagate by cuttings in spring or early summer.

SAPONARIA (*Soapwort*). Species of saponaria will be found in both Chapters VI. and VIII. Here I want to call attention to *S.*

officinalis, the common perennial soapwort or 'Bouncing Bet', in its two double flowered forms, one pink and the other white. Both have heads of quite big and showy, fully double flowers on 18-in. stems and though they may be just a little too coarse to be reckoned as really choice plants nevertheless it is high time they enjoyed renewed popularity. They were certainly more appreciated by our great grandparents who did not despise simple, easily grown flowers which have no special requirements regarding soil or position and can be as readily raised from seed as from division. These soapworts flower in August and September.

SAXIFRAGA (*Saxifrage*). Most of the saxifrages are rock plants but one group, often separated under the generic name *Megasea* or *Bergenia*, is for the herbaceous border. They are all plants with very large, undivided leaves and clusters of pink flowers early in the year. They are worth growing for their foliage alone quite apart from their useful bloom. Moreover they have the merit of thriving in shady as well as sunny places and are first class town plants. There are a number of species and varieties, many of them very much alike though differing in the precise shade of the flowers or size of the leaves. All may be planted and divided either in spring, immediately after flowering, or in early autumn.

SCABIOSA (*Scabious*). The most important of the hardy perennial species from the gardener's standpoint is *Scabiosa caucasica*, a plant notable for its exceptionally long flowering season and its value as a cut flower. The so-called yellow perennial scabious I have described under Cephalaria. The wild type of *S. caucasica* has pale blue flowers often marred by a few faulty petals but this drawback has been entirely bred out so that now many excellent forms are available, ranging from white and palest silver to deep purple, and all with perfect flowers. All bloom from early July until October and average 3 ft. in height. They do not make a very great display at any one time and are, in consequence, more useful for cutting than for border display. They like a well-drained soil and sunny position and resent autumn root disturbance. Lime is beneficial but not essential. Do not plant and divide in autumn but only in spring or, better still, propagate by cuttings of young growths severed close to the crown in April and rooted in sandy soil in a frame. Seed germinates fairly easily in a pan of well-drained soil in March or April but seedlings differ from their parents in many respects.

SCHIZOSTYLIS (*Kaffir Lily*). Only one species is grown, *S. coccinea*, and this is invaluable because it flowers in October and November when practically everything else in the border is over. It has spikes of scarlet flowers not unlike miniature gladioli and there is a delightful pale pink variety known as Mrs. Hegarty. Unfortunately both are a little tender; they need a warm, sunny position and well-drained, rather light soil. Plant in spring and increase by division at that season.

SEDUM (*Stonecrop*). In this immense family only two species are important for the herbaceous border. These are *S. spectabile*, one of the best autumn flowers with flattish heads of small, bright pink bloom on stiff, 18-in. stems; and *S. maximum*, rather taller with beetroot red foliage and similar heads of dull purple flowers. Both are in bloom during September and October, are easily grown in any ordinary soil, like sun, are resistant to drought and may be planted in spring or autumn. Propagation is by division at either season.

SENECIO (*Groundsel*). A family mainly composed of weeds, reckoning amongst their number the ubiquitous groundsel and poisonous ragwort. Nevertheless there are one or two useful kinds for the garden, notably *S. clivorum*, a bold plant 4–5 ft. high with big, roundish leaves and heads of large, orange yellow daisy-like flowers in August and September. It is easily grown in any soil and situation and does particularly well in damp places. Plant it in spring or autumn and increase by division at either season. This plant is correctly *Ligularia clivorum*.

SIDALCEA. These are plants which have been wonderfully improved by breeders. The species tend to be rather weedy in habit and lacking in variety of colour, but garden forms now have a wide range from white and palest pink to rosy crimson. The habit of the best of these garden sidalceas leaves little to be desired, for they make compact plants throwing up slender spikes of bloom 3–5 ft. in height. Typical varieties are Sussex Beauty, pale pink; Rose Queen, rose pink and Crimson King. All flower from July to August and do well in all soils, particularly those that are well drained. They like sun, should be planted in spring and may be divided at the same season.

SILPHIUM. The silphiums are rather coarse perennials with big, yellow, daisy flowers in late summer. They grow 4 or 5 ft. high, will thrive in almost any soil and do not mind either sun or light shade. One of the best is *S. perfoliatum*. Division in spring or autumn will provide all the fresh stock necessary.

SMILACINA. *S. racemosa* is a good hardy plant for a shady place. It has bright green, shiny leaves, plumed, creamy white flowers and a general appearance of elegance. It grows 2–3 ft. high, likes cool soils as well as cool spots and is happiest in a moist, rather rich soil—in fact it can be planted in the bog garden as long as it is safe from inundation during wet seasons. As it creeps about underground in a moderate manner it is especially easy to increase by division, which should be done in spring, also the best planting season.

SOLIDAGO (*Golden Rod*). Many people regard the common golden rod as a weedy plant not worthy of a place in the garden but at its season, August–September, there is nothing to beat it for display and it makes a fine foil for the blue Michaelmas daisies. In addition to the common golden rod, *Solidago officinalis*, there are now quite a number of named forms, some, such as Peter Pan, comparatively dwarf and compact in habit, others, such as Golden Wings, even bigger and more impressive than the type. All have the merit of thriving everywhere, even in soils too poor for many plants and they flower equally well in sun or partial shade. Planting and division can be carried out in either spring or autumn; and these are plants which pay for frequent lifting and division.

SPIRAEA (*Goat's Beard*). There is a good deal of confusion in the minds of gardeners between these plants and astilbes which are closely allied but botanically distinct. Most of them are shrubby plants to be found in the section of this book dealing with such subjects. Those suitable for the herbaceous border are *S. Aruncus*, the true Goat's Beard, a magnificent plant 6–7 ft. high with huge plumes of creamy flowers at mid-summer; *S. Filipendula plena*, the Double Dropwort with ferny foliage and loose plumes of small white pom-pon flowers; *S. lobata venusta magnifica* which is as big as the Goat's Beard but has carmine instead of creamy flowers; and *S. palmata* which has the colour of the last but a more compact flower cluster and 2-ft. stems. The first and last two do best in rather moist soils though they will grow practically anywhere. By way of contrast *S. Filipendula plena* has a preference for dry places. Incidentally this plant is correctly named *Filipendula hexapetala plena*. All can be planted and divided in spring or autumn.

STACHYS. One kind, *S. lanata*, is frequently grown in gardens for its grey, densely woolly foliage. It is often known as Lamb's Ears and the leaves certainly are as soft and hairy as any animal's coat. The flowers are nothing to look at and it is solely for its foliage that the plant is grown. It will thrive anywhere, in rich or poor soil, sun or shade and can be planted and divided at practically any time of the year.

STATICE (*Sea Lavender*). The statice is known as Sea Lavender because one species with lavender coloured flowers does really grow so close to the water's edge that the tide often washes over it. The best perennial kind for the border is *S. latifolia,* a grand plant for cutting because its masses of tiny lavender flowers will last for months if cut and dried. *S. incana* is a rather dwarfer plant with bigger, whitish-pink flowers. Both are in bloom in August and September and will grow in most soils though they must have an open, sunny situation. Plant in spring and increase by seed in spring or by root cuttings taken in winter.

STOKESIA. The only species grown, *S. cyanea,* looks very much like a small, annual aster when in bloom and is useful because of its late season. It is 2 ft. high, perfectly hardy and perennial and easily grown in any ordinary soil and sunny place. Increase it by division in spring, which is also the best season for planting.

SWEET WILLIAM.—*See* p. 127.

THALICTRUM (*Meadow Rue*). Very graceful plants mostly with finely divided foliage not unlike maidenhair fern in some species. The majority, such as *T. aquilegifolium, T. adiantifolium, T. minus* and *T. glaucum,* are easy to grow in any ordinary soil and sunny or half shady position but the most beautiful of all, *T. dipterocarpum,* is a trifle more exacting. It needs a deep, well-drained but not dry soil and should be renewed fairly frequently from seed. It grows 4–6 ft. high, is sparse and open in habit and has the daintiest imaginable violet coloured flowers, each with a tassel of yellow stamens, hanging on thin, wiry stems in large, loose sprays. It is a plant deserving every care and attention and is unrivalled for cutting. There is also a form with fully double flowers named Hewitt's Double, which is equally desirable but cannot be raised from seed. Roots may be carefully divided in spring. Other kinds can be planted and divided in spring or autumn. All flower in July.

THERMOPSIS. *Thermopsis montana* has had its thunder stolen by the magnificent garden lupins. With its abundant divided leaves and short spikes of yellow pea flowers it is difficult to persuade people that it is not an inferior lupin of some kind yet it is a pretty enough plant with the unspoiled grace of the wilding and a useful habit of thriving in dry, poor places once it gets established. It likes best light, sandy soils and sunny places. Old plants can be divided in spring but as they are rather slow to recover from a shift it is, perhaps, better to rely on seedlings for propagation. These can be produced readily enough either in a frame in March–April or outdoors in May–June.

TIARELLA (*The Foam Flower*). Foam flower is an appropriate name for *Tiarella cordifolia* far when it is in flower little can be seen of it except low, foaming masses of tiny white flowers, the effect being very much that of a white and unusually fine London Pride. The rounded leaves make neat, low clumps and are attractive for months after the spring flower display is over. The Foam Flower likes ordinary, loamy soils and shady places. It can be planted and, if desired, divided in March.

TRADESCANTIA (*Spiderwort*). There is only one hardy kind suitable for the herbaceous border and that is *T. virginana*, a plant remarkable for the fact that each bloom consists of three petals only. The flowers are as large as half crowns, violet blue in colour and produced a few at a time in constant succession from June to September. The foliage is grassy and the whole plant a couple of feet in height. A number of garden forms have been raised, some, such as J. C. Weguelin, with flowers of a clearer, richer shade of blue. All grow readily in sun or shade and in ordinary soil. Planting and division can be carried out equally well in spring or autumn.

TRITOMA.—*See* KNIPHOFIA p. 162.

TROLLIUS (*Globe Flower*). Plants for damp places which will thrive in either sun or partial shade. The flowers resemble enormous, globular buttercups and appear in May with sometimes a second crop in July or early August. There are numerous named varieties all in various shades of yellow or orange, typical kinds being Canary Bird, Fire Globe and Goldquelle. Most are about 2 ft. in height, but *T. pumila* is only 9 in. while *T. Ledebouri* may reach 3 ft. Plant in spring or autumn and increase by division, preferably in spring.

TROPAEOLUM (*Nasturtium*). The common 'nasturtiums' are annuals which I have dealt with on p. 113. The genus also includes some excellent perennials, several of them half-hardy (see p. 503) but a few quite hardy. The loveliest of them is *Tropaeolum speciosum*, well named the Flame Flower. It is a vigorous climber with bright green leaves and small 'nasturtiums' in the brightest imaginable shade of scarlet. It does well in the north and, as a rule, badly in the south apparently because it likes a cool, moist atmosphere better than a hot, dry one. A possible method of growing it is to plant its couch-grass-like roots in rich, leafy soil at the foot of an evergreen shrub, such as a holly, and allow it to ramble up into the branches above. It can be trained on walls with a northerly aspect or, indeed anywhere except in a hot, dry exposure.

Very different is *T. polyphyllum*, a sprawling plant with blue grey leaves and wreaths of yellow flowers. This loves sun and warmth and should be planted 5 or 6 in. deep in light, sandy loam.

The Flame Flower can be increased by spring division of its mat-forming roots, but seed sown in frame or greenhouse in spring provides the only satisfactory method of propagating *T. polyphyllum*, for a well-established plant is far too valuable to be disturbed.

VERATRUM. Though these are plants for the collector rather than the general gardener, *Veratrum nigrum* might be more widely welcomed. It has big, oval, glossy, pleated leaves which certainly look very handsome. The tall, stiffly branched flower spikes are strange rather than beautiful for the small flowers are such a deep shade of purple as to appear black at a short distance. The plant thrives in ordinary soils but is often spoiled by heavy slug attacks. It can be planted and, if desired, carefully divided, in spring.

VERBASCUM (*Mullein*). A good many of the mulleins are biennial plants needing to be renewed from seed every year. There are, however, true perennial forms as well, such as *V. vernale*, *V. densiflorum* and various garden hybrids such as Cotswold Beauty, Cotswold Queen and Gainsborough. These are mostly rather tall plants for the middle or back of the border with slender spires of yellow or bronzy flowers. One species, *V. phoeniceum*, is dwarfer, 2–3 ft. with flowers in shades of purple or violet. All prefer sunny positions and rather poor, dryish soils but will grow practically anywhere. They flower in June and July, can be planted in spring or autumn and are best raised from seed or, with the named varieties, by root cuttings taken in winter.

VERBENA. Almost all verbenas are half-hardy plants suitable for bedding out in summer or for greenhouse culture but there is one good, hardy perennial amongst their number, *V. venosa*. This makes a bushy plant about 1 ft. high with small, claret purple flowers from midsummer until autumn. It needs a sunny position and well-drained soil, should be planted in spring and divided then if necessary.

VERONICA (*Speedwell*). This enormous family contains much useful material for the shrubbery and rock garden as well as for the herbaceous border. There is a great deal of variety even in the herbaceous species which range in height from the 12 in. of *V. spicata* to the 6 ft. of *V. virginica* and in colour from the Wedgwood blue of *V. gentianoides* to the intense purple of *V. japonica*. One of the best is the plant variously known as *V. longifolia subsessilis* and *Hendersonii*. This flowers in August and has substantial, 18-in. spikes of royal blue flowers. *V. virginica* is much smaller in bloom though a far taller plant, more branching and of a rather ineffective silvery white. The *V. spicata* forms vary in colour from pink to violet and flower, like most of the rest of the family, in July and August but *V. gentianoides*

181

is in bloom by May and continues into June. All grow in any ordinary soil and sunny positions. Plant and divide in spring or autumn.

VIOLA. The bedding viola is very closely allied to the pansy, in fact botanically the pansy is a species of viola. But the viola differs in important garden features, notably its more compact, tufted habit which makes it a more permanent, and a more satisfactory bedding plant, its longer flowering season and the prevalence of self colours or one colour blending into another rather than the strong and sharply defined contrasts characteristic of pansies.

Violas can be raised from seed and a few varieties come reasonably true to colour and type in this way but usually there is considerable variation and the usual method of increasing selected varieties is by cuttings taken in August or September. A few sturdy plants are cut back with sharp scissors to within a few inches of the roots and are top dressed lightly with fine soil, sand and peat in about equal parts. In a few weeks new shoots will come sprouting from the roots through this top dressing and can be pulled out, often with a few white rootlets attached. Dibbled into similar rather sandy and peaty soil in a shaded frame and kept well watered they will make further roots in a few weeks and be ready for planting out the following spring.

Violas succeed best in moderately rich, rather moist soils and partially shaded positions. If faded flowers are picked off and plants are well supplied with water during dry weather they will flower from May to August or even later. There are innumerable varieties to be found in the lists of specialists, also a few beautiful species most of which are more at home in the rock garden than the border (see p. 236).

The sweet violet is derived from the wild *Viola odorata*. There are a great many varieties differing in the size, form and colours of their flowers. Double flowered forms (Parma violets) are rather weaker than the singles. All can be grown in the open, winter and summer, but for winter flowers the plants require frame protection from October to March. Small rooted pieces are planted in March or April in rich soil and slightly shady positions, keep them clear of runners and free of red spider during the summer and lift with plenty of soil at the end of September and place in a frame. Protection will probably not be required until the end of October and advantage should be taken of mild winter days to open the frame and admit air. Summer planting distances for singles are 1 ft. by 18 in; for doubles 9 in. by 1 ft. In the frames the plants can just touch one another. Propagation is by division in March or April or by cuttings prepared in August and September from runners and inserted in sandy soil in a frame.

CHAPTER VIII

Rock Gardens and Rock Plants

ERE WE have yet another example of the gardener's genius for
inventing vague and undefinable terms. For it is quite impossible to give any exact meaning to either 'rock garden' or 'rock
plant'. To one person any heap of soil bestrewn with stones is a rock
garden; to another it is rank heresy to apply the term to anything less
than a carefully conceived and painstakingly made structure in which
the soil has been specially prepared to meet the requirements of various
mountain plants and each rock has been placed as it might have been
expected to be found naturally 'growing' on a mountain side. And if
at this point some reader feels like saying that at least a rock plant can be
defined as a plant that in nature grows on rocks, let him consider that
there are good rock plants from woodland homes (cyclamens and some
anemones, for example) others from the stream side (*Nierembergia rivularis* and some primulas come to mind at once) and a great number from
meadows, alpine or otherwise and in neither case necessarily rocky. I
have even seen rock gardens planted with geraniums and marguerites,
geums, gaillardias and 'bedding' violas but I certainly would not say
that any of these were good rock plants. So one appears to be left with
the rather unsatisfactory definitions that a rock garden is any part of the
garden in which rocks play a prominent part and that a rock plant is
any plant which looks at home in such a setting—and that, of course,
is a matter of opinion.

DRY WALL GARDENING. This variation on ordinary rock gardening
has far greater possibilities than are generally realised. The 'dry' wall is
one made without mortar or cement. In many upland districts such
walls are used by farmers in place of hedges but these are usually made
by building the stones one on top of another with no matrix of any
kind. In the garden the dry wall must be built with soil packed firmly
between the stones, at any rate if plants are to be grown on it. To be
really satisfactory for a wide range of rock plants it is also necessary
that the wall should have a good core of soil or be used to retain a
terrace of soil into which the plants can root. A good scheme with walls
that are not used in the latter way is to make them double with a space
of a foot or more between and to pack this space with good soil of the
type recommended for the rock garden itself. It will then be possible to
plant alpines of many kinds in the crevices between the stones on both

183

faces of the wall and to establish still more, possibly, including some good trailing kinds such as aubrietia, yellow alyssum, arabis and helianthemum along the top.

When building dry walls always start by excavating a few inches to accommodate a foundation layer of carefully chosen and rather big stones well bedded down into the soil. Build up on these in courses similar to those in an ordinary wall and copy this also in the 'bonding' of the stones so that the vertical crevices do not come in line. In this way the stones will bind together and the wall will have considerable strength even though it is not mortared.

Almost any stones, or even bricks, can be used for dry wall building but quarried sandstone and limestone in pieces about twice to three times the size of ordinary bricks are ideal. It is not, of course, essential that all the stones are of one size or shape nor even that they shall be squared or 'dressed' though this does make the task of building much easier.

MAKING A ROCK GARDEN. Though I have said that any heap of soil into which stones have been stuck at random is, to some people, a rock garden, yet I must add that it is scarcely likely to prove a very satisfactory one. The selection of plants which can be grown in it is likely to be limited to the sturdiest and most indestructible.

If the object of building a rock garden at all is to enjoy a wide range of the astonishingly varied plants that we agree to call 'rock plants' (and one of the merits of this form of gardening is that it does enable one to enjoy so much variety in little space) then I strongly advise that considerable pains be taken in the preliminary work. In the first place it will be wise to choose an open spot clear of the overhang of trees and to make quite certain that drainage is good. If there is any doubt on this point, excavate all the soil from the proposed site to a depth of at least 18 in., put in a good layer of clinkers or brick ends and then, before returning the soil, make a drain leading to a soakaway, ditch or other suitable outlet. If there has to be considerable excavation and building up to get the contours desired for the finished garden remove the top soil before starting on this work and replace it afterwards so that there is an even depth of fertile soil all over.

The soil itself is almost certain to need some improvement—but in texture rather than in plant foods. Peat of the granulated type, coarse sand, and stone chippings are the ingredients which will help to make an ordinary garden soil suitable for choice rock plants. The proportions may be varied indefinitely to suit particular groups of plants but a good foundation mixture on which to base these variations is one very like the Innes potting compost (see p. 422), namely about three parts of good soil to one of sand and one of peat. For plants that need specially good drainage a further part may be added of limestone or sandstone chippings passed through a 1-in. mesh sieve. If the natural soil of the garden is known to be poor it may be advisable to replace half the peat with well-rotted dung or old mushroom bed compost.

MORAINE AND SCREE. A special feature of some well-made rock gardens is a moraine or scree. The names are practically synonymous except that provision should be made to water the moraine from below ground whereas the scree lacks this refinement. In both cases the soil mixture is even more stony than usual, the proportions often being as much as ten parts of stone chippings to one of soil, one of peat and one of sand. There must be at least 2 ft. depth of this compost for the diet is Spartan and plant roots will need to roam far and wide in it to get the nourishment they need. It is also an advantage if the moraine can be on a slight slope but this is not so necessary for the unwatered scree. The moraine water is supplied from a pipe laid a foot beneath the surface at the top of the slope. This pipe must be drilled with a few very small holes and connected to a water supply with a tap so that the flow of water can be very carefully regulated or cut off entirely. In practice, it will be used only in early summer during the comparatively brief period at which the plants are making their growth. Moraine and scree are invaluable for cultivating many of the more difficult rock plants, particularly those which really are high mountaineers and so accustomed to excessively stony soils and the abundant moisture provided by melting snow.

CHOICE OF ROCKS. Many show gardens are made with naturally weather-worn stone dug out of hillsides but this is necessarily expensive and carriage often adds greatly to the initial cost. There is no reason why good rock gardens should not be made from stone quarried in the ordinary way provided it is not so hard that it will not weather easily. If a good limestone or sandstone of this type can be purchased cheaply near the site it should certainly be considered. In any case try to get at least a few really big pieces included because some bold spurs do add greatly to the effect of the rock garden. Though these can be built with several stones one upon another a better effect is obtained if the component parts are not too small and numerous.

Always build from the bottom up and be careful to have the majority of the stones well bedded in the soil. The aim should be to give the garden, directly it is well clothed with plants, a natural appearance as if it really belonged to the site and this it can never have if many of the rocks are perched on the surface of the soil instead of emerging from it.

Many rock gardens are built on the model of the natural outcrop, examples of which may be seen on almost any hillside. It will be noted that such outcrops generally have a definite angle of emergence which is common to the whole formation, this being due to the strata tilt which the rock follows far back into the earth. One advantage of following this pattern is that it does give unity to the whole design, but care must be taken that this unity does not degenerate into monotony. All kinds of variations can be introduced by varying the spacing of the outcrops, making some bigger than others, changing their outline while retaining the same main angles, and constantly varying the slope and contour of the ground. While building always bear in mind the plants for which the rock garden is being made and leave a variety of suitable homes for them, some flat and wide for the carpeters, others steep and craggy for those plants that like to grow out of crevices and in deep fissures.

For the same reason see that every nook and cranny is filled with soil so that plants may be able to find roothold even between the largest boulders. Ram soil behind every rock so that there are no pockets to cause trouble and provide homes for mice and other vermin.

Avoid unnecessary use of concrete. When it must be employed to cement together rocks which would otherwise be insecure, tint it to simulate the rock itself and, if possible, arrange matters so that plants will soon completely hide the joint.

PLANTING ROCK PLANTS. Nurserymen grow almost all their saleable stocks of rock plants in small pots and this enables them to be moved with little or no root disturbance. In consequence it is possible to plant at almost any time of the year, except when the soil is frozen or very wet. In the case of seedlings it is usually wise to get these permanently planted as soon as they are of reasonable size while with other plants not in pots it is usually best to plant either in March–April or, if this is their flowering season, directly it is over.

If roots are bound into a tight pot ball it will be wise to loosen them a little with the fingers before planting. In all cases a little of the new soil should be worked among the roots. Plant firmly and water in if the weather is dry.

When planting in dry walls and in crevices between boulders it is wise to begin with very small plants or else to build them into position as the wall or rock garden is made. It is impossible to push the roots of a big plant into a narrow place without damaging them.

PROPAGATION. Many rock plants can be raised from seed and the best time for sowing this is almost always as soon as it is ripe. Unfortunately purchased seed can scarcely ever be got quickly enough for this and then it is, as a rule, best to wait until March or April when seed will usually germinate fairly readily in a frame or unheated greenhouse. Ordinary seed composts (see p. 421) can be used but very small seeds should have practically no covering.

Seedlings are potted singly before they get overcrowded in the seed pans. Subsequently they are grown on in a frame till planting time, but lights are only used as protection from excessive rain and frost so severe that it would freeze the soil in the pots solid. Always treat rock plants as what the great majority are—thoroughly hardy plants.

A good many alpines can be divided just like herbaceous perennials and this, too, can be done in spring, or immediately after flowering in the case of spring flowering plants. Avoid pulling the plants apart too drastically and, after replanting, always keep the plants well watered for a few weeks if the weather is dry.

Cuttings provide a method of increasing many shrubby plants that cannot be divided and some herbaceous rock plants are also more satisfactory from cuttings than from divisions. Firm young growths secured in early summer generally provide the best material and the cuttings should be rooted quickly in pure silver sand or very sandy soil under a handlight or in a close but not heated frame. Cuttings prepared from pieces of root and treated in the same way as those of herbaceous plants (see p. 137) are effective in a few instances, e.g. morisia, while leaf cuttings may be used in the case of ramondas and haberleas.

PROTECTION. While very few rock plants are in any way tender in the sense that cold will kill them, many suffer from the dampness of our winters. This is particularly true of those with very downy foliage, e.g. androsaces and *Asperula suberosa*. These may be protected from October to April by panes of glass supported on bent wires or notched sticks so that they are held well above the foliage with the sides open for free circulation of air. Some choice and early flowering alpines are seen at their best when grown in pots or pans plunged to their rims in a sand or peat box for the greater part of the year and stood outdoors during the summer.

AN ALPHABETICAL LIST OF ROCK PLANTS

ACAENA. A rather large family of lowly plants, chiefly useful for growing in the crevices of crazy paving though they also make a good carpet in the rock garden and can be used to cover the ground round early bulbs such as crocuses. The thin stems creep along the ground and root as they go. The leaves are small and sometimes finely divided. The flowers are like tiny burrs, curious rather than beautiful.

Acaenas will grow in any ordinary soil and sunny or partially shady position. They can be increased by division at any time. Amongst the best kinds are *Buchananii*, with grey-green leaves; *microphylla*, which has bronzy foliage, very deeply divided; and *novae-zelandiae*, with green foliage.

ACANTHOLIMON (*Prickly Thrift*). These compact, tufted plants have neat rosettes of narrow, spiky leaves and flowers in small heads on 3 to 6 in. stems in June and July. They are in consequence useful to give a succession after the earlier flowering rock plants.

Prickly thrift likes a sunny place and well-drained, gritty soil. It can be increased by careful division in spring, though seed sown in pans in a frame or greenhouse in March is preferable. The best kind is *A. glumaceum* which has bright, rose-coloured flowers.

ACHILLEA (*Yarrow, Milfoil*). This is one of the big families of the garden world and includes weeds, excellent herbaceous plants (see p. 139) as well as a number of useful rock plants. As a family achilleas are noted for their hardiness and the ease with which they can be grown in practically any soil and situation. They are mostly trailing plants and some are a little apt to spread quickly and over-run smaller subjects. Propagation is easily effected by careful division in the spring.

Excellent kinds are *A. Clavennae*, with silvery leaves and showy heads of white flowers on 6-in. stems in early summer; *A. Lewisii*, a neat and showy kind with clusters of pale yellow flowers throughout the summer; Edward VII, a garden seedling very similar to the last named, and *A. tomentosa*, which looks much like our native yarrow, except that it is smaller, neater and has golden yellow instead of white flowers.

AETHIONEMA. These are all very lovely plants, bushy in habit, with neat spikes of pink flowers in spring and early summer. They are related to the candytufts (iberis) but are choicer and more refined. Grow them in good, well-drained soil and full sun. They make ideal plants for a dry wall or a crevice in the rock garden and, once established, should be left alone for they do not like disturbance. Propagate by seed sown in a frame or greenhouse in spring or by cuttings of firm, young growths inserted in very sandy soil under a bell glass in July.

All kinds are lovely, but three of the best are *A. grandiflorum* which is 1 ft. high, often considerably more through, and has clear pink flowers; *A. pulchellum* which is a little dwarfer, laxer in habit but similar in colour, and Warley Rose (*warleyense*) which is particularly neat and bushy in habit and has deep rose flowers.

AJUGA (*Bugle*). One ajuga is an attractive British wild plant known as Bugle. This has produced at least two varieties that are worth a place in the rougher parts of the rock garden. They are *A. reptans atropurpurea*, with deep purple foliage and the other *A. reptans tricolor*, with green, white and rose-tinted foliage. Both produce 6-in. spikes of purplish blue flowers in May and June. *A. genevensis Brockbankii* has much clearer and brighter blue flowers and green leaves; all will grow in any soil and situation and may be propagated by division in spring or autumn.

ALYSSUM (*Gold Dust*). These are not on the whole very choice plants judged by the standards of the rock garden enthusiast but there is none that makes a better display. *A. saxatile* is the familiar golden yellow species which comes into bloom in spring at the same time as aubrieta and arabis and contrasts so admirably with them. It grows easily and spreads rapidly but does need good drainage if it is to prove permanent. It is seen to best advantage in a dry wall or planted in a sunny crevice or ledge in the rock garden. There are numerous forms, including one with double flowers and another with lemon yellow flowers. There are many other species but none quite rivalling *A. saxatile* in display. One of the best is *A. spinosum*, which forms a small, compact, definitely spiny bush covered with white flowers in early summer.

Increase by seed sown in a greenhouse or frame in spring or by cuttings of firm, young growths rooted in sandy soil under a bell glass in spring or early summer.

ANDROSACE. These are real rock plants and amongst them are numbered some of the most beautiful and difficult of the high alpine flora. For example there is *A. imbricata*, a plant about which the experts talk with bated breath. If you can grow it there is no alpine with which you cannot succeed for it needs the hottest and driest of places in deep, sandy soil and usually disappears the first winter.

Fortunately there are other species which are, by comparison, easy and very beautiful. Of these *A. sarmentosa* is a tufted Himalayan alpine with rosettes of downy, grey-green leaves which slowly spread into a wide clump from which, in May and June, stand up thin, 4-in. stems, ending in clusters of clear pink, confetti-like flowers. It will grow in any open, well-drained soil and sunny position but may with advantage be protected in winter by a sheet of glass. There are several varieties varying slightly in flower colour and all equally easy to grow.

Then there is *A. lanuginosa*, looser and trailing in habit and flowering from July to August. It thrives under similar conditions and also has pink flowers. There is a pretty variety named *Leichtlinii,* in which the flowers are white with a deep rose centre.

All these androsaces can be increased by careful division in spring. Seed can be sown in a frame or greenhouse in spring and will reproduce the species true to type, but not always the varieties.

Those who want to try their hand at the more difficult androsaces should plant them in the scree or moraine (see p. 185) in the stoniest of mixtures and be particularly careful about winter protection from rain. Alternatively they can be grown in very well-drained pans filled with a scree mixture and housed in the alpine frame or greenhouse.

ANEMONE (*Windflower*). One of the great families of the plant world in which are included many excellent herbaceous plants (see p. 141) and bulbs (see p. 337). There are, in addition, some good rock garden kinds, notably *A. apennina* which forms wide, mounded clumps of foliage above which stand in early spring the fragile, sky-blue flowers. *A. blanda* is much like it in appearance but several weeks earlier in flower. Both will grow in any ordinary soil and like partial shade. *A. angulosa, A. Hepatica* and *A. nemorosa* can also be planted in shady parts of the rock garden but are not true rock plants. Propagate all these by careful division immediately after flowering.

Genuine mountaineers are *A. sulphurea* and *A. alpina.* According to some authorities the former is merely a variety of the latter, the one having pale yellow flowers and the other pure white flowers. Both are difficult to grow, the best method being to sow seed where the plants are required or obtain small seedlings and establish these in spring in a very well-drained bed of light soil containing plenty of peat or leaf mould. They bloom in June.

A. Pulsatilla, the Pasque Flower, is a beautiful native plant found on the Chilterns and in other similar places. It likes sun and sharp drainage, makes a biggish clump of silky leaves, and opens its showy pale violet flowers at Easter. There is a pink form. Seed germinates readily in a frame in spring or plants can be divided carefully in March.

ANTENNARIA. Not a very important genus but it contains one pretty rock plant, *A. dioica.* This makes a close carpet of grey-green leaves and produces in early summer an abundance of small white flowers on 3-in. stems. There is a variety known as *tomentosa* in which the hairiness of the leaves is more pronounced, and another more valuable named *rosea* which has pink flowers. All are easily grown in ordinary lightish soil and a sunny place. They can be increased by division in the spring.

ANTHEMIS (*Chamomile*). There are a lot of weeds in this family and the novice should be rather wary about buying any anthemis which he has not seen and about which he has no reliable information. About the best of the lot for the rock garden is *A. ageratifolia Aizoon*, which usually passes in catalogues simply as *Achillea ageratifolia*. It is a low-growing plant with small, silvery, deeply divided leaves and pure white, daisy flowers carried with the utmost profusion in early summer. It will grow in any well-drained soil and open place but is most attractive if planted in rather poor soil, in fact almost moraine conditions, as it will then remain dwarf and compact. Propagate by division in spring.

ANTHYLLIS (*Kidney Vetch*). A small race of pea-flowered plants of which one, *A. Vulneraria* is a pretty English wild flower commonly known as Ladies' Fingers. This is showy but not choice enough to be admitted to the garden. However, *A. montana*, an alpine species, is well worth planting on a sunny ledge. It will quickly make quite a wide carpet of small leaves densely covered with silvery hairs. On these sit closely the rather large, deep red flowers. The plant is at its best in June. It does well in a rather limy, well-drained soil. Seed provides the easiest means of increase.

ANTIRRHINUM. Of course far and away the showiest antirrhinums are the so-called annuals which I have described elsewhere (see p. 90) but there are a couple of useful rock plants in the family, *A. Asarina* and *A. glutinosum*. Both are a little tender and should have a very sunny position and perfect drainage. Otherwise they are not difficult to grow in ordinary soil. Both trail about though not very widely and both have typical snapdragon-like flowers, but much smaller than those of the bedding kinds. In *A. Asarina* they are white marked with yellow and in *A. glutinosum* yellowish white. They flower most of the summer. It is wise to root a few cuttings in a pot of sandy soil each August just in case the parent plants fail to survive the winter.

AQUILEGIA (*Columbine*). Many aquilegias are herbaceous plants and these have been described on p. 142. For the rock garden there are several outstanding species. *A. glandulosa*, with very large blue and white flowers on 1-ft. stems, is rather difficult to establish though once growing it usually does well in deep, rather light but not dry soil. The secret appears to be to start with really small plants which should be put out from pots in March or April. *A. caerulea*, a really delightful plant with very big, pale blue and white flowers is just as easy to grow as an ordinary border columbine and requires similar treatment. It grows just over 1 ft. in height so is quite at home in the rock garden.

Seed sown outdoors in May will give flowering plants the following year.

ARABIS (*Rock Cress*). Though there are quite a number of species of arabis there is only one which immediately leaps to mind when the name is mentioned. This is *A. albida*, the remarkable white-flowered, trailing plant which, together with aubrieta and alyssum, fills every rock garden and dry wall with bloom in April and May. Though it grows very vigorously and spreads quickly it seldom becomes a nuisance and it has no underground stems to sprout up in unexpected places. It will grow anywhere but is seen to best advantage in not too rich soil and a fully sunny situation. The double flowered form, *flore pleno*, is if anything even better than the single kind and quite as easy to grow. Old plants can be carefully divided after flowering but a better method of propagation is by cuttings made from the young growths and rooted in sandy soil in a frame or under a hand light. Single arabis can also be raised quickly from seed sown in a frame in March or outdoors in April and May.

ARENARIA (*Sandwort*). These are mainly dwarf plants, grown for their close carpets of tiny green leaves, but *A. montana* is a trailer of looser habit with big white flowers, like those of a refined stitchwort, in May and June. It will grow in any ordinary soil and sunny position. *A. balearica*, the best of the carpeters, is also most attractive when smothered with its tiny, white blooms on thread-like stems no more than $\frac{1}{2}$ in. high. This is a grand plant to use as a ground cover over choice rock garden bulbs such as crocuses and miniature daffodils. It likes cool, moist but not stagnant places and spreads very rapidly.

Other useful kinds are *A. caespitosa* and its golden-leaved form *aurea*, both mounded, moss-like plants useful for crazy pavements in sun or shade and *A. purpurascens*, which is a coarser edition of *A. balearica* with pinkish lilac flowers. It needs the same treatment. All may be increased by careful division.

ARMERIA (*Thrift*). There are thrifts sufficiently robust to be planted in the herbaceous border (see p. 143) but the common type is a true rock plant which can be found wild on cliffs in many parts of this country. It is an attractive, tufted plant with narrow, grassy leaves and globular heads of small pink flowers on 6-in. stems. Its botanical name is *Armeria maritima* and from the garden standpoint it is surpassed by its more highly coloured varieties such as Vindictive (crimson) and *Laucheana* (deep rose). All will grow easily in well-drained soil and a sunny place. *A. caespitosa* needs more care for it is a true alpine from fairly high levels and must have perfect drainage. It does well in full sun in the scree or in a vertical crevice where it will form a slowly spreading and very close tussock of foliage on which sit the pale pink flowers.

All these thrifts flower in May and June. Increase by cuttings in very sandy soil in spring or, in the case of the species, by seed sown in a frame in March or April.

ARTEMISIA. In addition to border species there are some useful artemisias for the rock garden, all easily grown plants in any sunny place and poorish, well-drained soil, and all with silver or grey leaves, often beautifully dissected like those of a fern. Names are numerous and not always very reliable. *A. frigida Ludoviciana* (this is rather big for the rock garden), *Stelleriana* and *pedemontana* are a few worth collecting. There are also some species from the higher Alps which are much more difficult to grow and best suited to the moraine. All can be increased by careful division in spring. Flowers are insignificant.

ASPERULA (*Woodruff*). A very variable family, containing a good many weeds besides some really lovely gems for the rock garden. Outstanding amongst the latter is *A. suberosa*, which makes dense tufts of very slender stems and tiny leaves all densely clothed with grey-green silken down, and suddenly, in early June, becoming completely covered with tiny, tubular, soft pink flowers. The whole plant grows no more than 4 in. high. It must have full sun and perfect drainage and in winter it is advisable to protect its downy growth with a pane of glass supported well above it so that there is free circulation of air beneath.

Less exciting but easier to manage are *A. Gussonii* and *A. hirta*, both with pink flowers throughout the early summer, and the native British *A. odorata*, white flowered but chiefly remarkable for the hay-like perfume of its leaves. All will grow in any porous soil and open place.

Propagate by seed in a frame in spring or by very careful division at the same time (but this is not possible with *A. suberosa* because of its solitary main root).

ASTER. Most of the perennial asters are herbaceous plants (see p. 143) but there are some rock plants in the family, notably *A. alpinus*, *A. Farreri* and *A. subcaeruleus*. *A. alpinus* is low growing and compact with lavender blue, daisy-flowers solitary on 6-in. stems in May and June. There are several forms, including one that is nearly pink, another that is pure white and a third that is deep blue. *A. Farreri* is a bigger plant, at least 1 ft. and sometimes more in height with big, rather ragged flowers each with a striking orange centre to set off the violet-blue ray petals. *A. subcaeruleus* might be described as a big *A. alpinus* with

M 192

bluish-mauve flowers. *A. acris nanus*, which makes 1-ft. high bushlings of thin stems and narrow leaves simply smothered in late summer with small blue daisies, is another which may be admitted to the rock garden.

All grow readily in quite ordinary soil and an open situation and require no special care. They can be increased quite readily by division in spring. Seed sown in a frame in March or April usually germinates easily but may not reproduce the various forms of the species entirely true to type.

ASTILBE *(Spiraea)*. There are only two astilbes which need concern the rock gardener but both are very lovely plants. One is *A. simplicifolia* and the other *A. crispa*, a hybrid from the first named. Both are real miniature 'spiraeas' with the same fluffy flower plumes as the big, herbaceous border species but diminished to the scale of rock plants. Neither exceeds 6 in. in height. *A. simplicifolia* is pink or white; *crispa* is various shades of salmon pink. Both like rather damp, cool spots and are ideal for massing in valleys between the spurs and outcrops. Increase by careful division in spring or by seed sown in pans of rather peaty soil in March and germinated in a cool greenhouse or frame.

AUBRIETA *(Purple Rock Cress)*. This plant should need no introduction for it is the best known of all rock plants. It is the aubrieta which makes those great drifts of purple and lavender in the spring rock garden at the time the white arabis and yellow alyssum are in bloom. Thanks to hybridisation and selection the colour range has been greatly widened and there are now pink and even purplish-crimson aubrietas to brighten the garden. All the same, there are none, in my opinion, to beat some of the old purple varieties, such as the well-known Dr. Mules which is easy to grow, exceptionally free flowering and always reliable. The same cannot be said for some of the later seedlings which though big and showy in bloom are sometimes stingy with their flowers.

Aubrietas love sun and do best in rather limy soils. They are seen at their best planted at the top of a cliff or ledge or on a dry wall down which they can cascade.

Seed sown in fine soil in a frame or greenhouse in spring germinates readily but the seedlings seldom come true to colour. In consequence 'named' varieties must be increased by cuttings which are not always too easy to root. They should be prepared from young, non-flowering shoots taken in June. Root them in very sandy soil in a frame which should be kept closed for the first week or so but must be ventilated freely as soon as the cuttings are rooted or many may damp off.

Rock Gardens and Rock Plants

AURICULA.—*See* pp. 224 and 492.

BELLIUM (*False Daisy*). The species grown in rock gardens, *Bellium bellidioides*, is exactly like a lawn daisy but without that plant's incurable habit of running about all over the place and coming up where not wanted. It is free flowering, pretty and capable of flowering from May to September. It requires no special care and will grow in sun or partial shade. Propagate by division in spring or early autumn.

B. minutum, also known as *B. rotundifolium*, is similar but smaller and needs a little more care if it is not to be smothered by more robust plants. Give it good soil on a ledge by itself in full sun. Otherwise treatment is as for the commoner kind.

CALAMINTHA (*Calamint*). These are not very choice plants as alpines go but they are useful 'bread and butter' alpines which have the merit of growing almost anywhere and never failing to give a good display. The two kinds usually seen are *C. alpina* and *C. grandiflora* and of these the second is the better. It has 6-in. spikes of rosy purple flowers, at their best in June and July, and it makes a grand display when in full bloom. *C. alpina* is a duller violet purple and more spreading in habit.

Plant in a sunny place and open, gritty soil. Propagation is by seed in a frame or greenhouse or by careful division, both in spring.

CALANDRINIA (*Rock Purslane*). These, to be satisfactory, need drier, better drained soil and more warmth than most English rock gardens can offer. They should be planted in the scree or in a really sunny crevice between vertical rocks. They are worth a little trouble for at their best they are brilliant plants, the best being *C. umbellata*, with loose clusters of vivid magenta flowers all the summer. It is about 6 in. high. Raise it from seed which should be sown in very sandy soil in a cool greenhouse in March, the seedlings being planted out while they are still quite small.

CALCEOLARIA. While most of the calceolarias are greenhouse or bedding plants one delightful species, *C. polyrrhiza*, is well fitted for planting in the rock garden where it will enliven the damper, and even shadier, spots with its mats of broad leaves from which ascend in early summer, 6-in. stems ending in one, or sometimes two, big, baggy, yellow flowers. Given moisture and a rather humus-rich soil it is perfectly easy to grow. It can be taken up and divided in spring when extra plants are required.

CAMPANULA (*Bellflower*). This is one of the big families of the rock garden world. Species and varieties run into hundreds and there are certainly several dozens which are worth a place in any rock garden.

195

They do not lend themselves to easy generalisation regarding culture and there are numbered amongst them difficult as well as easily managed plants. The expert will take delight in trying his skill on *C. Allionii*, which will thrive in the moraine in the grittiest of soils but with plenty of moisture beneath. The blue flowers look something like Canterbury bells sitting singly on a carpet of foliage. Then there is *C. excisa*, a plant from the high alps and a good thing for the alpine house or frame in the grittiest of soils. A third species which is always being talked about by connoisseurs is *C. Zoysii*, with flowers curiously puckered at the mouth. It would not be so difficult to grow if only slugs would leave it alone. Zinc collars a couple of inches high round each plant are said to be the best protection but are unsightly.

There are a lot more of this 'difficult' type but the ordinary gardener will probably be content to plant such 'easy' kinds as *caespitosa* (syn. *Bellardii* and *pumila*), *Portenschlagiana* (syn. *muralis*), *Elatines* and its varieties *garganica, carpatica, Tommasiniana, Raddeana, pulla, pulloides, Stansfieldii* and a lot more which will grow in any reasonable soil and open position. In fact quite a lot of these will even tolerate a fair degree of shade, though, contrary to popular belief, very few campanulas are real shade lovers. Many of these are trailing plants which should be placed where they can spread for 1 ft. or so in all directions, but *Raddeana*, and *Tommasiniana* make compact little bushes, branching freely but not spreading far.

Blue is the typical colour of the campanula family but there are a great many variations of it from palest lavender to deep violet, with a few excursions into mauvy pink and a great number of albinos. They flower for the most part in early summer, though some continue until the autumn or give a second display in the autumn. *C. muralis*, one of the finest for dry walls or rock gardens, is notable amongst these.

All campanulas can be increased rapidly from seed but as this is very small it should be sown in the finest possible seed compost and either be covered very lightly or else simply have a sheet of brown paper and a pane of glass over each pan. Sow home saved seed as soon as harvested; purchased seed must usually be sown in March. Germinate in an unheated greenhouse or frame. Seed will not as a rule reproduce selected colour forms true to type and these, together with double-flowered campanulas (which may produce no seed), can be increased by division in spring, a method which can be applied to any other kinds though it is not so rapid and cheap as seed.

CERASTIUM (*Snow in Summer*). This is a plant which really should not be allowed in the rock garden proper for, though beautiful, it is a rampant weed which is quite capable of annexing the whole garden if given a chance. Nevertheless in the right place it is undeniably useful. There is no better plant for covering a difficult wall or bank. It will grow anywhere, even in the poorest and driest of soils and will soon cover the ground for yards with soft masses of grey-green leaves which disappear in early summer beneath a cloud of big white 'stitchwort' flowers. It is a pity that so attractive a plant should be such a nuisance.

There are two species commonly planted, *C. tomentosum* and *C. Biebersteinii*. It is said that the latter is both more showy and less invasive than the former but I am not prepared to answer for this. Perhaps the plants which have been sold to me as *C. Biebersteinii* were really *C. tomentosum*. Both can be increased by division at practically any time.

CHEIRANTHUS (*Wallflower*). The popular bedding wallflower is not a suitable plant for the rock garden, nor should the Siberian wallflower, *C. Allionii*, be admitted. But there are some smaller and more permanent members of the family which are well worth including. One of the best is a hybrid called Harpur Crewe, a compact, foot high bushling glowing in late spring with short spikes of fully double yellow 'wallflowers'. *C. mutabilis*, which is also like a half size wallflower but with single blooms which open creamy white, later change to yellow and finally fade to a quite attractive purple is another which should be planted. Pamela Pursehouse suggests *C. Allionii* on a reduced and neater scale.

All these rock wallflowers will grow in ordinary soil and sunny places. The singles can be raised from seed treated like that of ordinary wallflowers, the doubles should be increased by cuttings of firm, young shoots struck in a frame or under a handlight any time during the summer.

CHRYSOGONUM. The only species grown is *C. virginianum*, a very showy little plant, 6 or 8 in. high, freely branched and producing all summer and well on into the autumn bold, starry, golden-yellow flowers. There is no need to make any special preparations for it either as regards soil or position. Increase is by division in spring.

CODONOPSIS. Trailing or twining plants of which a good number have been listed from time to time, though only one, *C. clematidea*, ever appears to have been widely planted. This suffers from the rather unexciting pale blue of its bell-shaped flowers. Otherwise it is an attractive plant 1 ft. or more in height flowering freely in July and August when flowers are particularly welcome in the rock garden. It grows readily enough in any ordinary, well-drained soil and sunny place and can be increased by division in spring.

COLCHICUM.—*See* p. 340.

CONVOLVULUS. No doubt this family suffers from having produced one of our most troublesome weeds, the all too familiar bindweed. All the same there are excellent species for the garden which are not at all weedy; in fact if they have a fault it is that they are rather too difficult to keep.

C. mauritanicus is a glorious trailer, soon covering several square feet of ground and producing generous numbers of widely open, trumpet flowers in a grand shade of clear, soft blue. It is in bloom most of the summer and is at home in a warm, sunny place where it can cascade over rocks or down a wall. Perfect drainage is part of the secret of success but it is not really quite hardy and it is advisable to strike a few cuttings annually in a frame in July or August just in case the parent plant should disappear in winter.

The same remarks regarding lack of hardiness apply to *C. Cneorum*, though in other respects it is very different; a compact bush 1 ft. or more high and as much through with narrow, silvery leaves and pale pink, saucer-shaped flowers. It also needs a sunny place and good drainage.

Propagation of either plant is best effected by summer cuttings in sandy soil in a frame or under a hand light.

COREOPSIS. This genus, so well known for the showy border plants and annuals with which it has enriched our gardens, has also given us one charming little rock plant, *C. rosea*. This delights in damp spots (another novelty for the family) and it has innumerable small pink daisies on fragile, 9-in. stems in June and July. It can be increased by division in the spring.

CORYDALIS. You can see *C. lutea* growing in practically any cottage garden and a very pretty plant it is, though a bit of a nuisance in the rock garden because of its habit of spreading far and wide by means of self-sown seedlings. Individually it is a delightful plant, 1 ft. high with fern-like, grey-green leaves and little clusters of bright yellow, tubular flowers at their best in May and June but continuing spasmodically most of the summer.

A choicer plant for the garden is the Chinese species, *C. cheilanthifolia*, with showier clusters of flowers and a far less invasive habit. It has the same long flowering season.

Both can be increased very readily by seed sown in a frame in March or outdoors in April and May. They are not particular as regards soil and will grow in either sun or partial shade. *C. thalictrifolia*, which is much like *C. cheilanthifolia* in appearance and culture, may require a little protection in winter as it is not quite hardy.

COTONEASTER.—*See* p. 271.

COTULA. Two species are grown, mainly as crevice plants in crazy paving. They have the merit of keeping very close to the ground and withstanding a considerable amount of wear. Neither has any beauty of flower but both have attractive, ferny leaves. The names of these two species are *C. squalida*, in which the leaves are entirely green, and *C. acaenifolia*, in which they are more or less flushed with bronze. Both will grow in any soil and can be increased with the utmost ease by division at any time.

COTYLEDON (*Pennywort*). The true pennywort is a native plant, *C. Umbilicus*, with thick, circular leaves and narrow spikes of greenish-yellow flowers. It is not worth planting in the garden though it is attractive in a subdued manner when naturalised on an old wall.

Very different is *C. simplicifolia*, a really cheerful plant with a long flowering season. The small flowers are carried on arching stems 6 in. high, and they are bright yellow, well set off by the shining pale green foliage. It is a plant that grows easily, without special requirements, though it likes a sunny place. It will withstand a good deal of heat and drought and looks its best on a dry wall or in a sunny crevice. It can be increased by careful division in spring.

CREPIS. Most species of crepis are weeds and all have flowers like small dandelions. In one species, *C. aurea*, these are bright bronze-red and very showy. In good soil the plant is too leafy and rampant but established in poor, sandy soil it is curbed satisfactorily and encouraged to bloom with the greatest freedom, which it will continue to do most of the summer. It is a plant which it would be difficult to kill. Propagation, by division, can be carried out at almost any time.

CROCUS.—*See* p. 341.

CYCLAMEN.—*See* p. 342.

CYPRIPEDIUM (*Lady's Slipper*). The best-known cypripediums are greenhouse plants and amongst the most popular of orchids. There are, however, several quite hardy kinds which will grow well in the rock garden, particularly in the damper spots. They like lime-free, peaty soil and should be planted carefully from pots in spring, thereafter being left undisturbed for as long as possible.

Two of the best species are *C. spectabile*, a really grand North American orchid, with fine rose and white flowers of the typical Lady's Slipper shape and *C. Calceolus*, a rare native with curious but distinctly handsome chocolate and yellow blooms. Both are 1 ft. or a little more in height.

Propagate by careful division at planting time.

CYTISUS.—*See* p. 274.

DAPHNE (*Garland Flower*). Apart from the truly shrubby daphnes which are described elsewhere (see p. 275) there are several dwarf kinds to be planted in the rock garden. Of these, the showiest is *D. Cneorum*, which makes a low, dense bush of wiry stems and narrow leaves, each stem terminated in early June by a cluster of small, deliciously scented brilliantly pink flowers. It is one of the outstanding glories of the rock garden but not, unfortunately, one of the easiest to grow. In some places it thrives like a weed, in others it soon fades away. The secret seems to be a good, deep, loamy soil containing some lime. The position can be in full sun or slight shade but the plants flower most freely in sun.

Very different is *D. Blagayana*, which trails about rather ineffectively and then surprisingly produces terminal clusters of lovely, waxy white flowers which are if anything even more fragrant than those of *D. Cneorum*. It delights in warm, sunny places but is not difficult in rather stony soil.

A third, but more difficult, species is *D. petraea* (syn. *D. rupestris*) which forms a close, dense hummock of growth only a few inches high. This disappears completely in spring beneath the big, deep rose, deliciously fragrant blooms. It is a plant for the scree or moraine or it can be grown successfully in pans of gritty soil in the alpine house.

Plant all these daphnes from pots with as little root disturbance as possible. The first two can be increased by cuttings in summer rooted in sand beneath a bell glass. *D. rupestris* is sometimes grafted on to one of the other kinds, a very undesirable policy. It is better to detach pieces from the parent clump in the spring and start them into growth in almost pure sand with just a little leaf mould and loam.

DELPHINIUM (*Larkspur*). Of course the familiar, hybrid delphiniums with their giant spikes of bloom are quite out of place in the rock garden but there are two or three species which, though not actually alpine plants can be included in the rock garden.

The best is *D. nudicaule*, a showy plant with 1-ft. high stems terminating in short spikes of terra-cotta-red flowers. It has a habit of disappearing in the winter unless planted in very well-drained soil and sheltered position but it can be raised easily enough from seed sown in a pan of sandy soil in a frame in March.

D. cinereum is like a dwarf blue garden delphinium and a perfect miniature for the rock garden. Unlike the last it grows in quite ordinary soil and is usually as permanent as can be desired.

D. formosum, which is rather bigger but still in proportion for a fair-sized rock garden, thrives under similar conditions. The flowers are big and a grand cornflower blue.

Plant all these in as sunny a place as possible and well-drained soil. Seed sown in a frame in spring or as soon as ripe in summer provides the best method of increase.

DIANTHUS (*Pink*). Here is another 'big' family; big, that is to say, in numbers and also in importance. Species are very numerous and many have given rise to almost equally numerous varieties and forms. The family has its representatives in the herbaceous border and in the greenhouse. The carnation represents the peak of its man-made development. But the rock gardener is only interested in unimproved species and the simpler garden variations upon them. Dianthus has plenty to give him, and much of it is as easy to grow as it is beautiful to behold.

Dianthus deltoides is a miniature 'pink' which sprawls about in lush green mats and produces without fail each May myriads of bright rose flowers. There are garden forms in which the colour deepens to near-crimson.

Then there is the Cheddar pink, *D. caesius* which is found on limestone rocks in the famous Somersetshire gorge and is a grand plant for the dry wall or a sunny crevice. Imagine a garden pink reduced to quarter scale but with fine, single flowers of a soft, gleaming rose and you have a fair idea of it. These are both very easy to grow in any sunny place.

A little more exacting but still quite practicable for the beginner are *D. alpinus* and *D. neglectus*, both tufted plants but the second making particularly close hummocks of narrow leaves. It has big, short-stemmed flowers, glowing rose on top and shiny buff beneath. *D. alpinus* is a little taller with flowers that are clear rose throughout save for a darker central 'eye'. Both will grow in any gritty soil but are seen at their best in the moraine, and, of course, full sun which is really essential for the whole race.

Others that may go with these in the moraine and are sure to please are *D. microlepis,* white flowered and no more than 2 in. high; *D. glacialis,* no bigger and pink, and *D. Freynii,* which is either white or pink and even more dwarf and mat-forming.

D. superbus returns us to the realm of garden 'pinks' which it much resembles in habit though it is rather soft and weak. Still the deeply fringed lilac flowers are very beautiful and have the true pink fragrance into the bargain.

In addition to these and many more excellent species there are hundreds of hybrids combining the charms of the species in as many new ways. Most of these are easy to grow though a few prove a little impermanent particularly if the soil lies damp and cold in winter.

All dianthuses can be raised from seed sown in frames in March or as soon as ripe in summer but hybrids are unlikely to come true by this means. Early summer cuttings may be taken in their case and also, if more convenient, for the species, while some of the more mat-forming kinds can be divided with care in the spring.

DODECATHEON (*American Cowslip*). One more often sees these charming plants at shows than in private gardens and they are undoubtedly difficult to get going satisfactorily. From the cultural standpoint they fall into two groups, the 'easier' kinds, of which *D. Meadia* is the type, all of which should be planted in damp, peaty soil near the water's edge and left to increase until undeniably overcrowded; and the more difficult species from high mountain levels which should be planted in the moraine in a not too stony but porous compost with an underground supply of water all the summer. Of these *D. pauciflorum* and *D. pubescens* are good examples.

All have cyclamen-like flowers hanging on slender stems 6 in. or more in height. In *D. Meadia* they are in various shades of rosy-purple and lilac and there is also a good white.

Division is not very desirable and seed sown in sandy peat in the spring is the best method of increase. Spring is also the best planting time.

DRABA. In my opinion these get more praise than they are really worth. They are, on the whole, somewhat insignificant plants, neat and mossy in habit and useful for planting in crevices but not of outstanding beauty.

D. bruniifolia, which makes compact tufts not unlike those of a cushion saxifrage, with small yellow flowers in May is typical. *D. dedeana* and its variety *Mawii,* both with innumerable heads of tiny, white flowers are pretty and neat. *D. pyrenaica* is pink and would be more useful if it were a little easier to grow. As it is it really requires moraine treatment or a pan of very gritty soil in the alpine house, a position it may share with *D. imbricata*.

Many of the commoner species including the others I have named can be grown in quite ordinary, porous soil and a sunny place. All should be increased by careful division in spring, which is also the best planting season.

DRYAS. There are several very lovely trailing species of which the best known is *D. octopetala*. This makes wide carpets of dark green, leathery leaves on which lie the widely open, white flowers, rather like dog roses. It is at the height of its splendour towards the end of June just at the time when the rock garden is tending to get dull. Plant it in full sun and open-textured soil and then leave it alone, for it takes a good time to recover from root disturbance. It can be raised from seed sown in a pan of sandy soil in spring, and it is a good plan to get the seedlings established in their flowering quarters while still quite young, before their woody roots penetrate too far and wide. Cuttings can also be rooted in sand under a handlight during August.

Other kinds are *D. Suendermanni*, with yellow buds opening to flowers, and *D. integrifolia*, which is smaller than *octopetala* in all its parts but otherwise similar.

EDRAIANTHUS. These are closely allied to campanulas and have often been confused with wahlenbergias; in fact it is quite likely that some of them will be offered in catalogues as wahlenbergia. There is really only one species which need concern the amateur, namely *E. graminifolius*, a flopping plant with very fragile stems, narrow leaves and big, bell-shaped, blue flowers most of the summer. It needs more care than most campanulas and is fully at home in the moraine though it can also be grown in deep, cool, gritty soil in any sunny place. Plant in spring and raise from seed sown in spring (or as soon as ripe) in a frame.

EPILOBIUM (*Willow Herb*). The true willow herbs are native weeds, very beautiful but not to be permitted in the garden. There is, however, an alpine epilobium, usually sold as *E. Dodonaei*, though its true name is *E. Fleischeri*, which is quite a pretty, inoffensive plant with slender, bronzy stems and leaves and small pale pink flowers in late summer. The whole plant is perhaps 6 or 8 in. high (less if the soil is very gritty) and it can be grown in any decently drained soil and open place. Seed is the simplest method of increase and can be sown in a frame in spring.

ERANTHIS.—*See* p. 346.

ERICA.—*See* p. 277.

ERINUS. This is a small family of small plants but it certainly must not be overlooked on either count. *E. alpinus* is the species that matters. It is a dainty little plant with 2 in. spikes of pale magenta flowers in spring and early summer. It is surpassed by several of its varieties of which quite the best is Dr. Hanele. This is similar in all respects except that the flowers are a really telling shade of carmine. The plant likes dry walls or may be used to clothe crevices between large boulders. Seed of the type can be sown where the plants are to grow but Dr. Hanele will not reproduce true to colour from seed and must be propagated by careful division in March or April.

ERITRICHIUM. Every writer agrees in describing *E. nanum* as the king of alpines but I am prepared to wager that many have never seen it. Certainly that is my own position. This is because it is a plant of exceptional difficulty in cultivation and even when a specimen can be induced to survive for a few months it has no chance to reproduce its alpine form. Only those who have been fortunate enough to visit the high granitic Alps in early summer can have any idea of its true worth. It makes close hummocks of silk-coated leaves from which sprout, as soon as the snows melt, tiny stems terminated by clusters of forget-me-not flowers. So far there is nothing in the description to suggest exceptional beauty but it is in the peculiar intensity of the blue that the real charm of this plant lies. It is described as purer and even more brilliant than that of the best gentian and a marvellous contrast to the dark granite rocks in which it is found.

If anyone is fortunate enough to obtain a plant in this country it should be tried in granite scree or, better still, in an exceptionally stony mixture, entirely lime free, in a pan to be kept throughout the year in the alpine frame or house. But really there is very little use in writing cultural notes about a plant of which even the experts despair.

ERODIUM (*Heron's Bill*). This brings us back to the realm of eminently possible alpines, in fact a good many of them are so easy to grow that unless one takes care they become weeds. All the same there are some good things in the family, notably the charming carpeter known variously as *E. Reichardii roseum* and *E. chamaedryoides roseum.* It will soon cover a square foot or more of ground with a mat of neat, rounded leaves freely speckled from spring to autumn with small soft rose flowers, almost stemless. It will grow practically anywhere and loves a sunny ledge. It is the simplest thing in the world to increase it by division in the spring.

Others needing similar treatment are *E. guttatum*, with white, purple-stained flowers, *F. macradenum*, in which each pink flower has a maroon blotch to liven it up; *E. corsicum*, pink, veined red; and *E. chrysanthum*, with deeply divided, silvery leaves and sulphur yellow flowers.

ERYSIMUM. These are wallflower-like plants, mostly too big for the rock garden, though one or two can be included with safety. The best are *E. mutabile* which makes a small, greyish bush with blooms varying in colour from yellow to violet on the same plant, and *E. pumilum*, which is yellow flowered and no more than 4 in. high. The first grows under exactly the same conditions as Cheiranthus (see p. 97) while *E. pumilum* should be planted in the moraine.

ERYTHRONIUM.—*See* p. 348.

EUPHORBIA (*Spurge*). A family that has produced a surprising number of weeds but has also given us a few excellent, though little known, garden plants. Most of these are too big for the rock garden though *E. Cyparissias*, *E. Myrsinites* and a few others are useful in the right kind of place. They will withstand drought and *E. Cyparissias* in particular gives its best colour when well baked. It has very fine, almost ferny-looking foliage, pale green at first but becoming coppery-red in autumn. The greenish-yellow 'flowers' are in loose sprays in summer. Unfortunately it is very invasive. All species can be increased by division in spring.

FRANKENIA. The one species grown, *F. laevis*, is a fragile plant with trailing stems and small, pale pink flowers in the early summer. It can be used as a carpet for choice bulbs, is not faddy regarding soil but likes best a fairly sunny place. When further plants are required, detach a few rooted fragments in spring.

FRITILLARIA.—*See* p. 348.

FUCHSIA. One species only is suitable for the rock garden, the rest being comparatively large shrubs, described on p. 281. This is a completely prostrate plant, known as *F. procumbens*. The flowers are small, yellow and not particularly showy but they are followed by bright, scarlet berries which remain for a long time. It is not very hardy so should be planted in a warm, sunny, sheltered spot in rather light, sandy soil. New plants can be raised from seed saved from the ripe berries or rooted fragments can be detached in spring from the parent plant. Plant in spring or autumn.

GALANTHUS.—*See* p. 349.

GALAX. The solitary species grown, *G. aphylla*, is a tufted plant with glossy green leaves which take on grand autumn colours. The white flowers are produced in fluffy spikes roughly 1 ft. high and are at their best in June. The plant likes a little shade and a cool, deep soil with plenty of leaf mould or peat; in fact it is a woodlander rather than a true rock plant. When necessary, divide in spring.

GALIUM (*Bedstraw*). A big family of weeds, containing just a few fairly good plants for the rock garden. They almost all tend to sprawl and cover too much ground but there are exceptions such as *G. olympicum*, which is neat and tufted with clusters of tiny ivory-white flowers. *G. purpureum* and *G. rubrum*, sometimes recommended, are not troublesome but the flowers are rather a dull purple and red respectively. All like sun and stony soils and *G. olympicum* can be planted in the moraine. Raise from seeds in spring or by careful division after flowering.

GENTIANA (*Gentian*). Here we come back to one of the big and important rock garden families, one which ranks with Primula and Saxifraga for the wealth of wonderful material with which it has provided our gardens. It is almost impossible to generalise about a family with such an extended range and with so many varied requirements and certainly impossible to do it justice in the space available.

Everyone knows the Gentianella, *G. acaulis*. The diminutive 'ella' does not, as might be supposed, indicate that this is small as rock garden gentians go for it is used in contrast to the large, yellow flowered herbaceous gentian (*G. lutea*). The 2-in. long, rich blue trumpet flowers of the Gentianella are one of the outstanding sights of the rock garden in spring. In some places it thrives so readily that it is grown in borders and beds without special treatment. In others it grows freely but refuses to flower, though often this difficulty can be overcome by importing a little soil from another garden in which it does bloom. Contrary to the general rule with rock garden plants this gentian likes a rich soil and may even have some well-rotted farmyard manure dug in prior to planting. It also likes lime and I have seen it doing well in a garden on the North Downs where there was no more than 3 or 4 in. of soil over pure chalk. All the same this is not the ideal site for it but rather a deep, cool, well-fed soil of the sort one might expect would suit roses.

G. verna is a very different plant, much smaller in all its parts, with narrow starry-tipped trumpets no more than 1 in. long but of an exceptionally pure blue. It flowers in April and likes an open, rather spongy soil with plenty of sand and peat ensuring good drainage in winter but plenty of moisture in summer. There are a number of varieties of it and species closely allied to it of which G. *bavarica* is one of the most beautiful.

Then there are those two autumn beauties G. *Farreri* and G. *sino-ornata* and a hybrid between them, G. *Macauleyi*. These have flowers almost as large as those of the gentianella, clear sky-blue in colour streaked outside with white, most noticeable in the case of G. *Farreri.* This particular species is difficult in many places though it does well in the cool, damp atmosphere of Scotland. G. *sino-ornata* and G. *Macauleyi* are much easier and seldom fail to give a good display if planted in a deep mixture of about equal parts of lime-free loam, peat and coarse sand. They will soon carpet the ground and rooted pieces can be plucked from this mass in spring or early summer to be dibbled in elsewhere and grow into fresh plants.

Then again the family branches out into such ramifications as exemplified by G. *asclepiadea*, the willow gentian, with arching stems 18 in. high and rather dark purple flowers almost all the way up. It is a woodlander, thriving in thin shade and cool, leafy soils.

Useful summer flowering kinds are G. *Freyniana* and G. *septemfida*, with trailing stems and terminal clusters of the typical blue trumpet flowers of the family but neither so big as those of the Gentianella nor so blue as those of G. *verna.* They are comparatively easy plants, thriving in most reasonably prepared rock garden soils.

Where possible, with the exception of the autumn flowering species, seed should be used for propagation, but G. *acaulis* usually divides readily enough after flowering and division can be used for other kinds as well.

GERANIUM (*Cranesbill*). Most people immediately think of scarlet bedding 'geraniums' when you mention this name, though in fact these plants have no true right to the name at all. Bedding 'geraniums' are in fact pelargoniums and are described on p. 488. All the true geraniums are hardy plants, some big enough for the herbaceous border (see p. 156) while others are pleasant, easily grown rock plants.

Typical of these last are G. *sanguineum*, which really deserves the name for the flowers are a rich, blood red; the very distinct form of it known as G. *lancastriense*, frequently included in lists of the 'best' rock plants, and a neat, prostrate plant with masses of warm pink flowers all through the summer; and the unfortunately named G. *Pylzowianum*, with thin, floppy stems and showers of astonishingly big rose-pink flowers.

All grow readily in any reasonably drained soil and sunny place; in fact *G. sanguineum* and its forms can be planted as edgings to the herbaceous border. All can be divided in spring or can be raised from seed sown in spring in a frame.

GEUM (*Avens*). The best-known geums are border plants but there are some smaller growing and very showy species which make excellent rock garden specimens. *G. montanum*, with big, single, bright yellow flowers is perhaps the best, but *G. reptans*, a trailer also with yellow flowers is good if it can be obtained true to type. As often as not, however, other, inferior species are supplied under its name.

Then there is the Water Avens, *G. rivale*, with nodding heads of old-rose flowers. This is a plant for the streamside in dampish soil, whereas the others like gritty, open soil in a sunny, even dry position. All come into the category of 'easy' alpines; they spread rapidly and can be raised from seed or division in spring.

GLOBULARIA. These are not very striking plants but they are attractive in a quiet way and have the merit of being very easy to grow. The fluffy flower heads have somewhat the appearance of ageratum and are a similar soft, blue-mauve in colour. There are several species not differing greatly in appearance and all about 6 in. in height. Perhaps the best are *G. cordifolia* and *G. nudicaulis*. Plant in any ordinary soil and sunny place and increase, as necessary, by division at planting time.

GYPSOPHILA. The big, white gypsophila is a herbaceous plant which I have described on p. 157 and there is another popular species which is an annual, to be found on p. 105. Here I am only concerned with two or three dwarf, trailing perennials which grow well in rather dry sunny places and are seen to good advantage in the face of a wall or in vertical crevices. *G. repens* is the best of this set. It has masses of small white flowers in summer and there is an even prettier variety named *rosea* with pink flowers. There is absolutely no difficulty about its cultivation and it can be increased readily from seed or by cuttings in summer struck in sand in frame or handlight. *G. monstrosa*, a slightly bigger plant in the style of *G. repens*, needs identical treatment.

HABERLEA. This is one of those rare families of rock plants which do best in the shade. Haberleas make flat rosettes of leathery, dark green leaves. They are happiest when planted almost vertically so that moisture does not settle in these rosettes. A cliff face with a northerly aspect is ideal if there are plenty of fissures in it connected with a good bulk of rather leafy soil behind, for the haberlea, though it resents too much moisture on its leaves, likes a reasonable amount at its roots. The flowers, which appear in June, are like tiny Gloxinias carried in loose sprays on 6 or 8 in. stems. They are a bluish-lilac in the most familiar species, *H. rhodopensis*, but there is also a beautiful, rather rare kind, known as *H. virginale*, with pure white blooms. All can be increased by leaf cuttings in a frame or under a handlight in early summer, or by seed on the surface of peaty soil in the greenhouse in spring.

HELIANTHEMUM (*Sun Rose*). These are amongst the most vividly coloured of rock plants. Most are low-growing, rather sprawling shrubby plants with single or, in a few cases, double flowers borne in great profusion during late May and June. Most of the varieties grown are garden seedlings with 'fancy' names such as Jubilee, double yellow; Chamaecistus, single, wine red; Rhodanthe carneum, single pink; Mrs. Earle, double crimson and so on. All delight in sunny places and light, well-drained soils and benefit from a light trimming up with shears or scissors immediately after flowering. They can be increased by cuttings stuck in sand in a close frame in July.

HELICHRYSUM. This name will be most familiar to readers as belonging to the 'everlasting' annuals but the perennials should not be overlooked. I think the best is *H. bellidioides*, with rather rapidly spreading tussocks of stiffly erect, 4-in. stems terminated in early summer by the daintiest imaginable white 'everlastings'. It grows readily and spreads quickly in any light, sandy soil and warm, sunny place and when new plants are needed the old ones can be lifted and pulled to pieces in April.

HELXINE. In cool shady places in the garden (and sometimes under the greenhouse staging into the bargain) one may perhaps see wide spreading carpets of little, roundish, bright green leaves that are sometimes vaguely, and quite erroneously, referred to as 'moss'. This is *Helxine Soleirollii* a plant of the easiest culture provided it is never baked or dried nor exposed for long to very severe frost. It can be increased at any time by division.

HEPATICA.—*See* ANEMONE, p. 190.

HERNIARIA. Another of the dwarf carpeting plants useful in the rock garden to give a cover of tiny leaves to the soil under choice bulbs. It will grow in any ordinary soil and open place and can be increased by division in spring. *H. glabra* is the only species grown.

HIERACIUM (*Hawkweed*). There are a great many Hawkweeds and though I do not know one that is not showy in flower there are few I would care to admit to the garden. To be plain most Hawkweeds are weeds that soon take up much more room than can be spared. Even the best of them, such as *H. aurantiacum*, with vivid orange-red, dandelion blooms or *H. villosum*, with smaller but yellow flowers and leaves whitened by silky hairs, must be placed with some care or they will soon over-run less vigorous plants. They are ideal for sun-baked places and poor, dry soils, which tend to keep them within bounds.

Frequent division is an advantage with such rampant plants and they will recover from this in either spring or autumn with the greatest alacrity.

HUTCHINSIA. These are lowly little crucifers with masses of tiny white flowers in spring. *H. alpina* is the kind usually grown and it is pretty enough in its way, though a little lost amongst the showy alpines of its season. Being very small it makes a useful carpeting plant over bulbs and it will grow in any soil in either sun or partial shade. Pull the old plants to pieces in spring when you want to make some new plantations.

HYPERICUM (*St. John's Wort*). There is a sharp division in this family between the big, shrubby plants which I have described in Chapter IX and the small, often trailing species whose proper place is the rock garden. There are a lot of these, of very unequal merit. In some, the flowers are too small to be really effective but this does not apply to such grand plants as *H. repens*, *H. reptans*, *H. fragile*, *H. nummularium*, *H. Coris* and *H. polyphyllum*, all of which are showy, dwarf and more or less spreading (*H. reptans* is a true trailer) nor to the more erect and bush-like *H. olympicum* which is a good foot in height. All have golden flowers, very bright and luminous and all grow in any decent soil and open place. Seed germinates readily in a frame in spring or old plants can be carefully divided at that season.

IBERIS (*Candytuft*). When choosing candytufts for the rock garden be careful not to get confused with the annual kinds which, though attractive enough, will only last one season and must be renewed each spring from seed. These species I have described on p. 107. The real rock garden species are true perennials which will continue for many years without renewal. They are very fine plants indeed; common, perhaps, but making a really big display worthy to be compared with that of aubrietas, golden alyssum and arabis.

The three best species are *I. saxatilis*, *I. corifolia* and *I. semper-virens*. The first is a compact, low growing plant with very dark, glossy leaves and innumerable thimble-shaped heads of shining white flowers in May and early June. It will grow anywhere but to see it at its brightest and most compact it should be given rather poor, stony soil and a fully sunny position.

I. corifolia is a much bigger plant, spreading in time over a square yard of rock garden or wall and with 9 to 12 in. high stems set with evergreen foliage and terminated in spring and early summer by bold spikes of showy white flowers. Personally I think there is no better white-flowered alpine at this season. There are plenty of varieties on the market with names such as Snow Queen, Snowflake, etc., differing in minor details and all desirable. Moreover all will grow anywhere and will put up with the poorest of soils but they do like sun and warmth.

I. sempervirens is intermediate between the other two in size and as easy to grow as *I. corifolia* under exactly the same conditions. There is a more compact variety named Little Gem.

In a rather different style is *I. gibraltarica,* a loose, bushy plant with rather drawn out spikes of flowers which fall between pink and lilac and are not, in my opinion, very effective. Moreover the growth is soft and liable to be killed in winter but it usually does well in a sheltered place and rather sandy soil.

All perennial candytufts can be raised from seed but selected forms which might vary from the seed can be increased by cuttings of firm, non-flowering shoots rooted in sandy soil in a frame in early summer.

INULA. Most of these plants are coarse perennials for the herbaceous border or woodland but *I. acaulis,* a mat-forming species with big, daisy blooms, of a bright golden colour, is worth planting in sunny places in the alpine garden. It likes good drainage and a light soil, and can be increased by careful division in spring. It flowers in June and July.

IRIS. It is inevitable that a very big and varied family such as this should be spread about in different sections of this book. Those who are interested in the big flag irises will find them on p. 160, while the bulbous-rooted irises, many of which are small enough to be grown in the rock garden, are dealt with separately on p. 253.

This leaves a few non-bulbous but dwarf species to be accounted for, notably *I. pumila* or, more correctly, *I. Chamaeiris.* This averages 8 in. in height and is exactly like a miniature flag iris in all respects. Most catalogues offer numerous named varieties, differing slightly in height but far more in colour. The range includes purple, mauve, lilac, yellow and white. All do best in freely-drained or even rather dryish soils and full sun and all like lime. There is no reason why they should not be used at the front of the herbaceous border as well as in the rock garden.

Transplant immediately after flowering and increase by division of the rhizomes at this period.

KNIPHOFIA (*Red Hot Poker*). These are almost entirely border plants, many of them giants of 6 ft. and over. Nevertheless there are a few very dainty species which can be introduced with care in the rock garden. One of the smallest and best is *K. rufa*, with tufts of grassy foliage and miniature yellow, red-tipped pokers on 18-in. stems. Like a good many more of the species it is not too hardy in this country and misses its native South African sun. It should have light, sandy but rather rich soil, perfect drainage and a sheltered position. *K. Galpinii*, with orange torches on 2-ft. stems is another worth planting, while a whole race of dwarf hybrids, some of doubtful hardiness, has made its appearance.

To be successful with these plants see that they get plenty of water while they are forming their flower spikes and the best possible drainage in winter. Increase by careful division at planting time.

LAMIUM (*Dead Nettle*). These are really weeds and not to be tolerated in select parts of the rock garden but the variegated Dead Nettle, *L. maculatum* is sometimes useful to clothe rough places or heaps of stones in odd corners; in fact it is a typical 'rockery' as opposed to 'rock garden' plant which will put up with any rough treatment. Its beauty, such as it is, lies in the small, nettle-shaped leaves, darkish green except for a central stripe of pale cream. Old plants can be pulled to pieces and replanted at practically any season.

LEONTOPODIUM (*Edelweiss*). *L. alpinum* is the plant which every tourist brings back as a memento from the Alps. It has acquired a reputation out of all proportion to its genuine merit. All the same it is a reasonably attractive plant, not difficult to grow in a porous, gritty compost and producing each June 6-in. spikes terminated by curious white woolly flowers shaped rather like a starfish. The leaves are also densely silvered with white hairs which tend to collect moisture in winter, so that it is a kindly act to protect the plants with a sheet of glass from October to March.

Edelweiss can be propagated by seed or division in spring.

LEWISIA. With these we return to plants of really outstanding beauty. The lewisias all have big, widely open flowers mostly in unusual shades of orange and salmon. They are not too easy to grow as most of them come from warm, semi-desert regions and find our climate too damp and dull for their liking. They should be planted in stony mixtures such as those of scree or moraine and, once established, should be left severely alone as they do not quickly recover from root disturbance.

L. Tweedyi and *L. Howellii* are two of the best, the first seldom above 4 in. in height with very big soft apricot flowers; the second nearly 1 ft. in height and with smaller but still ample blooms of a rather deeper shade. Seed, when available, can be sown in spring in a pan of very sandy soil in a warm greenhouse but as a rule one must increase by the most careful possible division, also in spring.

LINARIA (*Toadflax*). This is a family which contains a great many weeds and only a few worthwhile garden plants but fortunately the few really are worth having. The best for the rock garden are the several forms of *L. alpina*, a tiny, slender plant with narrow, grey-green leaves and spikes of hooded flowers which look for all the world like antirrhinums seen through the wrong end of a pair of opera glasses. There are pink, white, purple and prawn coloured varieties and all grow readily from seed sown in gritty soil in spring. Give them a sunny place in light soil full of small stone chips; in fact they are excellent beginner's plants for the scree. They flower from May to August.

A very different plant is *L. pallida*, which is exactly like our own native Kenilworth Ivy on a slightly larger scale. It is a useful, if rather weedy plant for a sunny or shady position and will grow in walls with a minimum amount of soil as well as in more ordinary places. The pale lilac flowers continue all the summer. *L. aequitriloba* is just like it but only half the size and just right for planting in the crevices between paving slabs. Both can be increased by division at any time.

LINUM (*Flax*). This is a family which has given us one of the most important of economic plants, the flax from which linen fibre and linseed are obtained. The gardener has to thank it for one brilliant annual which I have described on p. 110 and several charming rock plants of which the best is *L. arboreum*. This is a miniature shrub 1 ft. or more high, freely branched with saucer-shaped yellow flowers which continue to appear most of the summer.

L. flavum is often offered in its place. It is rather similar in appearance but with softer non-shrubby growth. Like *L. arboreum*, it is in bloom all the summer.

For colour contrast there is *L. perenne*, with slender, wiry stems 18 in. high, terminating in loose clusters of fragile, sky-blue flowers at their best in June and July. Similar, but of a more intense blue, is *L. narbonnense*, while a more spreading plant with palest pink flowers is *L. salsoloides*.

All like gritty, well-drained soils and sunny places but *L. perenne* is so easy that it will usually grow anywhere. All can be raised from seed sown in a frame in spring.

LITHOSPERMUM. This is one of the names which experienced rock gardeners always mention with enthusiasm. The reason is that the family contains some of the best shades of blue to be seen in the rockery and also, perhaps, because the best species are not always very easy to grow well. Nevertheless lithospermums are certainly not plants to be left to the connoisseur. All that most need is good drainage, plenty of sun and a loamy soil. Those, such as *L. prostratum*, which are sometimes difficult, are quite likely to succeed in such a soil and place in the beginner's garden and fail under apparently identical conditions with the expert—no one quite knows why. So why not try your luck?

L. prostratum is certainly the star of the family and a grand plant established in crevices between large boulders or in the face of a sunny wall. It is really a spreading, evergreen shrub, usually no more than 8 in. high, but covering maybe a square yard of ground. It has narrow, stiff, dark green leaves and clusters of forget-me-not like flowers which are a real gentian blue in the best forms, such as Heavenly Blue. It is at its best in May and June. Other kinds which would be regarded as first rate were they not a little overshadowed by *L. prostratum* are *L. graminifolium*, with tufted bright green leaves and deep blue flowers; *L. intermedium* and *L. Froebellii*, which are rather similar to the last, and *L. rosmarinifolium* which, as its name implies, has rosemary-like leaves, the flowers being blue and white.

All can be increased by seed but the best forms should be kept true by cuttings rooted in sand in summer.

LYCHNIS (*Campion*). Everyone knows the red and white campions to be found in any English hedgerow in summer and these give a very fair idea of the style of the whole family. The rock garden campions are, of course, much smaller and incidentally they have bigger flowers so that the whole effect is more showy.

Outstanding amongst them is *L. Haageana*, a startlingly vivid plant with coppery-scarlet flowers as big as florins, carried on 12 in. stems. The plant would be grown much more widely were it more permanent but it has an unfortunate tendency to disappear in winter. The secret of success is to grow it in rather dry, well-drained soil, in fact something approaching the conditions of moraine or scree and to renew frequently from seed. Full sun is essential. The plant flowers all the summer.

Far smaller is *L. Lagascae*, 4 or 5 in. in height, loosely tufted with pale carmine flowers in May and June. The conditions should be as for *L. Haageana*.

Seed may be sown in sandy soil in frame or greenhouse either in spring or as soon as ripe.

LYSIMACHIA (*Loosestrife*). The only Loosestrife which will interest rock gardeners is our native Creeping Jenny, *L. Nummularia*. No doubt this would get far more praise if it came from the Himalaya or Andes. In point of fact it is often regarded as a weed and it certainly will grow almost anywhere, even in damp, shady places, where little else would grow. It makes carpets of trailing, pale green growths set with bright buttercup yellow flowers. There is a form with yellowish leaves which some like, though personally I find it sickly looking. The flowers continue in succession all summer. To increase this plant it is only necessary to lift a root and pull it to pieces at practically any time.

MAZUS. There are only two species commonly grown, *M. Pumilio* and *M. reptans*. Both are dwarf, carpet-forming plants, with small, hooded blue and white flowers. They grow readily and can be used as edgings to beds and borders, but their real home is the rock garden in rather leafy or peaty soil and sunny position. Both flower throughout the summer.

MECONOPSIS (*Himalayan Poppy*). A chapter not a paragraph is required in which to deal with the many species of Meconopsis and I can do no more than touch the fringe of the subject. This is one of the 'big' families both in the number of its species and their importance in the garden. Many are rather difficult plants to grow and most succeed best in deep, cool soils rich in humus yet porous and open, conditions which can be secured by working in plenty of granulated peat and flaky leaf mould. Partial shade suits many of them and for this reason they are often seen to better advantage in the open shrubbery or thin woodland than in the rock garden despite the fact that they are generally regarded as rock plants.

One of the most beautiful and widely grown is *M. betonicifolia*, better known to the public as *M. Baileyi*, the blue Himalayan poppy. It will grow 3 or 4 ft. high in favourable conditions, each stem carrying numerous widely open poppy flowers which are sky-blue in the best forms with a golden cluster of anthers in the centre. Unfortunately it is a variable plant from seed and seed is the only satisfactory method of propagation, as is the case with most Meconopses. Often seedlings turn out to have blooms of a poor shade of amethyst and these should be discarded.

M. horridula and *M. napaulensis* (syn. *Wallichii*) are two other lovely blue-flowered Himalayan poppies, the first 3 ft. and the second 6 ft. in height, while *M. quintuplinerva* has flowers like large harebells on slender, 12-in. stems. *M. paniculata*, another giant of 5 or 6 ft. has long spikes of pale yellow blooms. *M. integrifolia*, also yellow, is seldom over a foot in height but the flowers are very large and showy.

Any good catalogue of alpine plants may list a dozen further species all worth growing, but I have no space to mention any more except the Welsh poppy *M. cambrica* which is rather like a dwarf Iceland poppy with single or double flowers in various shades of yellow and orange. It will often naturalise itself in cool, shady places.

All species can be raised from seed sown directly it is ripe on the surface of fine, peaty soil in a well-drained pan. Seedlings must be transferred to flowering quarters while still small as later they transplant very badly. Many of the species die after flowering, so regular renewal from seed is a wise precaution.

MENTHA (*Mint*). Most mints have no business in the rock garden, but one, *M. Requienii*, is always welcome because of its almost excessively neat, carpeting habit, tiny purple flowers and refreshing mint perfume when bruised or even lightly brushed. It likes, and deserves, a cool, rather moist but sheltered position and can be increased by careful division in April.

MIMULUS (*Musk*). The true Musk is an annual which I have described on p. 113 and there are also perennial species suitable for the border. Here I wish to call attention to the dwarf perennial kinds of which the brilliant hybrid Whitecroft Scarlet may be taken as a sample. These are dwarf, rapidly spreading plants averaging 4 or 5 in. in height with the big, showy, hooded flowers typical of the family. Whitecroft Scarlet, as its name implies, is scarlet and an exceptionally brilliant shade at that. All are suitable for cool, damp places in the rock garden and, if there is a stream or pool attached to the rock garden, they can be planted alongside it with advantage. They bloom most of the summer.

MORISIA. There is only one species of morisia and this is *M. monanthos* often known as *M. hypogaea*, a very neat plant which makes a rosette of dark green, deeply-slashed leaves in the centre of which nestles in spring a cluster of small but very bright yellow flowers. The whole plant grows closely to the ground or presses itself flat against the rocks if it is planted in a crevice, the ideal spot for it. It will stand any amount of sun and heat and likes a deep, open soil. It can be propagated by seed in spring or by cutting up some of the thicker roots into 1-in. long pieces in January, strewing these thinly in a seed pan filled with sandy soil, covering with ½-in. similar soil and placing in greenhouse or frame.

MYOSOTIS (*Forget-me-not*). The common Forget-me-not is a plant for bedding schemes rather than for the rock garden but there are some good alpine species, particularly *M. alpestris*, which is exactly like the common Forget-me-not but on a smaller scale and with a neater, more tufted habit. The flowers are bright blue with a small yellow eye. It should be grown in gritty soil and a sunny position and may be increased from seed, though specially selected forms, such as the very fine Ruth Fischer, should be kept true by careful division in spring. *M. rupicola*, a Forget-me-not reduced to 2 in. stature, should be grown in the scree.

NERTERA. *N. depressa*, the only species grown, is a quite prostrate plant with very slender, trailing stems and the neatest of circular leaves. On this almost moss-like carpet of pea-green lie in late summer a profusion of small, globular, coral red berries. The plant is so different from anything else that it is well worth a place in the rock garden despite the fact that it is a little tender and may need the protection of a handlight in winter. It should be grown in a rather richer soil than usual, moist and containing plenty of leaf mould or peat and it is an advantage if the position is partially shaded. Division in April provides a ready means of increase.

NIEREMBERGIA. The two species usually grown in rock gardens are very different in character. One, *N. rivularis*, is a trailing plant with widely opened, white flowers which continue to appear most of the summer. It likes plenty of moisture and yet must have good drainage, a paradox which can be resolved by planting it in sandy soil near a stream or in the moraine with an underflow of water all the summer. The other kind, *N. caerulea*, often wrongly known as *hippomanica*, is bushy and branching with innumerable slender stems and masses of cup-shaped lavender flowers, also produced throughout the summer. It likes a warm, sheltered place and gritty soil but not the abundant moisture required by its cousin. Some protection may be required in winter. Increase by careful division in spring.

OENOTHERA (*Evening Primrose*). There are Evening Primroses for the herbaceous border, woodland and shrubbery and, in addition, there are a few dwarf forms which make delightful plants for the sunny rock garden. One of the best is *O. missouriensis*, a sturdy, trailing plant with grey-green leaves covered with silken hairs and very large, canary-yellow flowers from July to October. The plant can stand any amount of warmth and is happiest in the lighter, grittier types of soil. Another lovely dwarf species is *O. mexicana*. The flowers are soft pink and the plant neat and dwarf. It requires similar treatment to *O. missouriensis* but may need winter protection with a handlight freely ventilated. *O. teraxacifolia* with white flowers and dandelion-like leaves, and *O. caespitosa*, blush white and spreading, are other desirable kinds.

All the rock garden Oenotheras are best increased by seed sown in sandy soil in frame or greenhouse in spring.

OMPHALODES. This genus contains one of that small, select group of plants which the connoisseur mentions with bated breath. This is *O. Luciliae*, a plant which to the uninitiated looks much like a neat Forget-me-not, with blue-grey foliage and the usual Forget-me-not blue flowers. It does in fact belong to the Forget-me-not family but is far more difficult to grow, requiring perfect drainage and yet an abundant supply of moisture in summer—in brief this is a plant for the moraine or alpine house and not a beginner's subject at that. Moreover slugs love it.

In quite a different category is *O. verna*, often known as the creeping forget-me-not, or Blue Eyed Mary and a lovely, sprawling thing with loose sprays of small blue flowers in April and May. It will grow anywhere, even in the herbaceous border, and in the rock garden the only point to observe is that, if not carefully placed, it may overrun some less vigorous plants. It is as happy in shade as in sun and can be increased by division in spring. *O. cappadocica* needs similar treatment, is neater in habit and flowers in early summer.

ONONIS. This is the family which has given us the Rest Harrow of British commons. No one, of course, would wish to grow this in the garden, pretty as it is. But there are one or two other species of ononis worthy of inclusion in the rock garden, notably *O. rotundifolia*, a bushy plant 1 ft. or rather more in height with abundant bright pink flowers all the summer through. It loves sun and warmth, is not particular as regards soil and can be increased by seeds sown singly in small pots in spring. Transplant the seedlings, when big enough, with as little root disturbance as possible.

ONOSMA. Onosma belongs to the same family as the Comfrey of British lanes and looks rather like a Comfrey on a very much reduced scale. It has the same arching stems terminated by several drooping, tubular flowers which give one species its popular name Golden Drop. But the Onosmas are mostly below a foot in height and they are neat in habit, not leafy and gross like Comfrey; in fact they are ideal plants for the dry wall or a crevice between boulders in the rock garden. The best-known and in some ways the most useful is *O. tauricum* (syn. *echioides*), with golden yellow flowers in June. *O. albo-roseum* is a little more difficult to grow, needing especially good drainage and it has even more markedly silvered foliage to set off its pink and white flowers. All kinds may be increased by seed sown in pans of sandy soil in greenhouse or frame in March, or as soon as ripe, while cuttings of firm young shoots will usually root in sandy soil under a handlight.

ORIGANUM (*Marjoram*). The common marjoram is suited only to the herb garden, but *O. pulchellum* is an attractive, bushy plant with sprays of tiny pink, hop-like flowers in summer. It grows about 9 in. in height, likes sun and is not fussy about soil. Cuttings can be struck in sandy soil under a bell glass in summer or seed sown in a frame in spring.

OROBUS. These are small, bushy, pea-flowered plants, most of which are too weedy to be worth planting. *O. vernus*, however, is quite attractive in an unexciting manner and useful in poor soils and dry places where it will make a leafy plant 1 ft. high, covered in early summer with rather pale, pink flowers like dainty vetches. Seed germinates readily in a frame or even outdoors in spring and old plants can be carefully divided at the same season.

OTHONNOPSIS. These are not really rock plants at all but as they are dwarf and spreading they can be used to fill certain positions in the rock garden with good effect. Their yellow, daisy flowers look very bright against the fleshy grey foliage and are produced with the utmost freedom throughout the summer. The great merit of the Othonnopsis, however, is the fact that it will stand almost unlimited drought and heat and its drawback, that it is on the border-line of hardiness and so may need protection in winter. Cuttings of young shoots can be rooted in sandy soil under a bell glass in July or August. The two best kinds are *O. cheirifolia* and *O. rotundifolia*.

OURISIA. Only one species is grown to any extent, namely *O. coccinea* and this is another plant which may need winter protection. It is at its best in deep, spongy, rather moist, but never stagnant, soil. It makes low, spreading masses of bright green leaves from which sprout up all summer 9-in. stems carrying vivid, scarlet trumpets. Seed provides the most satisfactory method of propagation.

OXALIS (*Wood Sorrel*). The native Wood Sorrel, pretty plant though it is, is far too invasive for the rock garden, but there are two very fine foreign species which are real gems. They are *O. enneaphylla* and *O. adenophylla*. Both like sunny places and gritty, well-drained soils and both flower in early summer. *O. enneaphylla* has pure white flowers, though there is a pale pink form, while *O. adenophylla* is lilac pink.

Another point of difference between them is that whereas *O. ennea-phylla* slowly spreads by means of underground rhizomes and little bulbs, *O. adenophylla* 'stays put', having a solitary corm which does not split up. In consequence whereas *O. enneaphylla* can be increased by division of corms in spring, *O. adenophylla* must be propagated by seed sown in very sandy soil in a greenhouse in March. Both are prostrate plants. *O. floribunda* is much looser and more lush in habit, with abundant, pale green, shamrock leaves and fine sprays of gleaming rose-pink flowers all the summer. Grow it in poor, stony soil and a hot, sheltered place and, when you want more plants, divide the old ones in spring.

PAPAVER (*Poppy*). Most of the rock garden 'poppies' do not belong here but come under the heading Meconopsis (see p. 215). There are, however, a few true poppies small enough for the rock garden and the best of these is a real mountaineer, *P. alpinum*. It suggests an Iceland poppy reduced to 6 in. in height, with genuine miniature poppy flowers in various shades of yellow, orange and pale pink, together with a good white. Like most poppies it delights in sun and good drainage and will thrive in the grittiest soils; in fact I recommend it to the beginner with a scree. It is readily raised from seed which, being very small, should be sown on the surface of fine, sandy soil and germinated in a frame in April. Transplant the seedlings to their flowering quarters while still small for later they resent root disturbance; or, if you prefer, sow directly where the plants are to flower and so cut out the risk inseparable from transplantation.

PAROCHETUS. The only species that is grown in gardens is *P. communis*, a rather rampant trailer which makes lush masses of three-parted leaves amongst which appear, all summer through, sky-blue flowers. It really is a very pretty plant, but rather a nuisance because it grows too fast in the summer, smothering other plants in its way and then in winter, not being quite hardy, is apt to die out completely. Give it a sheltered place and pot up a few pieces each autumn so that they can be overwintered in a frame. Then there will be no danger of losing it. The plant can be increased by division at practically any time, is not fussy about soil and likes sun.

PENSTEMON. This large family hovers on the borderline of hardiness, a characteristic which limits its usefulness in the rock garden. All the same there are some excellent rock plants in the family, three of the best being *P. Davidsonii*, dwarf, spreading and small-leaved and with glowing magenta flowers; *P. heterophyllus*, 1 ft. or rather more in height with slender spikes of flowers which are sky blue in the best forms and a rather dingy amethyst in the worst, and *P. Scouleri*, similar in height to the last and with blue-lilac flowers. The first and last flower in early summer while *P. heterophyllus* flowers most of the summer. All are plants for sunny places and porous soils. *P. Davidsonii* looks its best on a ledge and will stand any amount of heat. All can be increased by cuttings of firm, young growth struck in very sandy soil under a hand-light in late summer. They can also be raised from seed sown in the greenhouse in March, but colour is apt to be variable.

PHLOX. The family which has given us the gorgeous summer Phloxes of the herbaceous border has also provided a great deal of useful material for the rock garden, especially *P. subulata* and the numerous forms and hybrids usually grouped under this name. These are all loosely mat-forming plants, most of which spread fairly rapidly and can be planted either on the flat or in crevices between boulders or on the face of a dry wall. They delight in sun and prefer light soils but are not really particular on this count. Some of the best forms, such as the white-flowered *Nelsonii*, are exceptionally compact, whereas others, such as the pale mauve G. F. Wilson, are distinctly sprawling. Heights vary from 3 to 8 in. All bloom in late spring and early summer. Colours include lilac, mauve, pink, carmine and white.

Very similar to the last and often confused with it is *P. Douglasii* which requires identical treatment. The blooms are lilac. A taller plant but still suitable for the rock garden is *P. divaricata*, of which the best variety is named *Laphamii*. In habit this is more like a border phlox, erect and tufted, with 12-in. stems ending in loose heads of lavender flowers in early summer.

The *subulata* and *Douglasii* varieties can be increased by cuttings in sandy soil outdoors or under a handlight in early summer. *P. divaricata* and varieties can be divided in spring.

PHYTEUMA. These very curious looking plants belong to the Campanula family though one would hardly guess it by looking at them. They make tufts or rosettes of leaves from the centres of which appear in early summer circular heads of small, beaked flowers. The best for the rock garden is *P. comosum*, which is not more than 3 in. high and has deep blue flowers. It would not be difficult to grow were slugs not so fond of it. Give it a sunny place and open soil with plenty of lime and either surround it with a zinc collar or be generous with slug killer. It can be increased by seed sown in frame or greenhouse as soon as ripe.

PLUMBAGO.—*See* p. 171.

POLYGALA (*Milkwort*). The common Milkwort is a minute but decidedly attractive weed of meadows, particularly hillside meadows. It is scarcely a plant for the garden but it has an alpine cousin that is much more showy and well worth inclusion. This is *P. Chamaebuxus*, a dwarf, spreading, shrubby plant with small, evergreen leaves and abundant yellow, white and pink or crimson flowers most of the spring and summer. It is happiest in a mixture of about equal parts sand, peat and lime-free loam in sun or shade and it can be increased by careful division in the spring.

POLYGONUM (*Knot Weed*). This vast family has been generous in producing weeds or plants which, however beautiful, behave like weeds in the garden. Every new polygonum should be examined with care before it is admitted but no qualms need be felt about either *P. affine* or *P. vaccinifolium*, both low-growing plants which soon make wide carpets of evergreen leaves, which in the case of *P. affine* become delightfully tinted with bronze and crimson in the autumn, and from which spring in late summer a multitude of short, neat spikes of rose-pink flowers. In effect the two are rather similar except that *P. vaccinifolium* is far smaller and neater in all its parts than *P. affine*. Both will grow in any ordinary soil and sunny place. *P. affine* can be increased by division in spring; *P. vaccinifolium* by cuttings of young growth rooted in sandy peat under a handlight in summer.

POTENTILLA (*Cinquefoil*). Another family which has produced far more weeds than good garden plants but nevertheless has given us gold amongst the dross. One of the loveliest species for the rock garden, and incidentally one of the best twelve plants for the beginner, is *P. nitida*, a very dwarf, carpet forming species with small, silvery leaves and almost stemless, pink flowers from June to August. There is a white form but this is not so pretty. Other useful potentillas are *nepalensis*, which has an important form named Miss Willmott, producing masses of cherry-red flowers on 1-ft. high stems from mid-summer to autumn; *alba*, low-growing, spreading and white flowered, and *P. Tonguei*, prostrate with almost stemless, apricot flowers. All these potentillas will grow in any decent soil and sunny place and can be divided at practically any time.

PRIMULA (*Primrose*). This is another of those families about which the experts write volumes and yet leave something unsaid. It contains hundreds of species and probably still more garden varieties, and these vary very greatly in their appearance and requirements. Some are natives of meadows, others grow in woodlands, yet others by the sides of streams or in bogs, while many are found high up on the mountainsides often growing out of apparently barren rocks with no visible root hold till one realises that they are established in a deep crevice filled with rich soil mainly composed of decayed vegetation.

It will be realised that it is extremely difficult to give useful information about so great a family in the space of a mere page or so. There is danger that in condensing and generalising the final impression left may be misleading and I would certainly advise anyone who intends to embark seriously on the culture of the choicer primulas to study the subject in specialised volumes before expending a lot of money.

Broadly the family from the standpoint of culture can be split up into three groups: (1) those that thrive in ordinary, loamy soils and cool positions as, for example, those partly shaded by trees or buildings; (2) bog or stream-side types which like deep, rich, porous soils abundantly supplied with moisture and (3) alpine types which should be planted in positions containing plenty of leaf mould or peat with abundant stone chippings and coarse sand to keep the soil open. These last like to be in full sun as long as this does not imply excessive dryness in summer, but rather than risk that evil it is better to place them where they are at least shaded from the hottest mid-day sun by boulders or neighbouring plants.

The first group contains the primrose and polyanthus and, provided the soil is well drained, the conditions outlined for it will also suit some choicer subjects such as *P. denticulata*, with globular heads of mauve, purple or white flowers on 9-in. stems in April; *P. cashmiriana*, which many consider to be a form of the last and is distinguished from it by slightly smaller, more graceful heads of flowers and mealy stems; *P. capitata*, a truly delightful plant with little cartwheels of cowslip flowers, the colour of violets; *P. Mooreana*, an important form of the last, with bigger heads and a heavier powdering of meal; *P. Juliae*, a mat-forming species with glossy, rounded leaves and claret coloured, almost stemless primrose flowers; *P. Juliana*, a name given to a race of hybrids between the last named and our native primrose, intermediate in many respects and with flowers in all shades of rose, claret and ruby, and *P. Sieboldii*, with tuffets of ferny leaves quite unlike those of any other primrose and clusters of rose-pink flowers. This last is just a little tender and may need protection under a handlight in winter.

In Group 2 the most notable species are *P. japonica*, *P. pulverulenta*, *P. Florindae* and *P. rosea*, but there are a great many more almost as beautiful and also hosts of hybrids and colour forms carrying 'fancy' names such as Bartley Strain, Lissadel Hybrid, Red Hugh, Aileen Aroon, etc. *P. japonica* and *P. pulverulenta* are very similar in appearance, making bold clumps of primrose leaves from which stand up stiffly in early summer 2-ft. stems with tier upon tier of brilliant magenta flowers. *P. pulverulenta* is white with meal, whereas *P. japonica* is plain green. *P. Florindae* is the giant cowslip of Tibet, an astonishing plant with the robustness of a cabbage, broad leaves 6 in. across and 1 ft. long, and stout, 3 or 4-ft. stems terminated by wide clusters of big, pendent, clear yellow blooms which have the fragrance of cowslips. Rather smaller but otherwise similar is *P. sikkimensis* from the uplands of Western China while *P. secundiflora* has nodding heads of wine-red blooms. *P. rosea* is, in marked contrast to all the foregoing, a dwarf plant seldom more than 6 in. high with flower stems which appear in April before the leaves and carry small heads of the most brilliantly carmine flowers imaginable. A good drift of this near the pool or stream-side is one of the outstanding sights of the rock garden in spring. Others to note here are *P. Cockburniana*, like a coppery-orange *P. japonica*; *P. microdonta*, in the style of *P. sikkimensis* but pale primrose-yellow, and *P. Bulleyana* with tiers of orange-yellow flowers.

Coming to the truly alpine species in Group 3, we must take account of *P. Auricula* in all its innumerable forms; *P. marginata*, with similarly leathery leaves and clusters of bluish lilac flowers on 6-in. stems; *P. pubescens*, a race of hybrids of which the best form, Mrs. Wilson, is not unlike *P. marginata*; *P. hirsuta*, like a neat tawny-leaved auricula in various shades of pink or mauve; *P. Winteri*, which again rather resembles *marginata* but blooms in mid-winter or early spring and so needs a specially sheltered place, and *P. glaucescens*, with rosettes of milky green leaves and neat clusters of purplish flowers on 4-in. stems. This is one of the few truly alpine primulas that appreciate a little shade from a boulder or spur.

I have only given the briefest of selections in the above lists and many more equally attractive species and varieties will be found in any good catalogue. All should be propagated when possible from seed, which germinates readily enough if sown as soon as it is ripe in gritty soil with some granulated peat to hold moisture. Seed is very small so should be given the lightest of coverings. Old clumps which have made numerous crowns can be lifted and divided in spring or immediately after flowering but this is not such a good method of propagation as seed except in the case of selected forms which will not breed true from seed.

For polyanthus see page 119 and primrose page 120.

RAMONDA. The rock gardener owes the ramondas a double debt of gratitude for they are both very beautiful and shade lovers—and it is none too easy to find good rock plants for the shady spots that almost inevitably occur even in the best made rock gardens.

Ramonda pyrenaica is the species most widely planted and is typical of the genus. It makes a big, flat rosette of dark, leathery, wrinkled leaves from the centre of which, in May, appear several ascending stems 6 or 8 in. high each ending in a small spray of blue-lilac, yellow-centred flowers. There are several forms, one with white and one with soft pink flowers while there are also two or three quite distinct species of which the best is *R. Nathaliae* because it is neater, freer flowering and bluer than even the best forms of *R. pyrenaica.* Unfortunately it is also a good deal more difficult to purchase.

Plant all these ramondas on their sides in vertical crevices but always where they have a deep root run into cool, leafy or peaty soil containing enough sand to keep it open at all times yet not enough to make it dry and harsh.

Ramondas can be raised from seed sown on the surface of sandy peat or a fine compost containing plenty of sand and peat, but as seedlings may prove variable specially fine forms should be kept true by raising them exclusively from leaves detached carefully in early summer and pushed a little way into a similar compost to that used for seed raising. Keep in a cool, shaded frame or greenhouse when each leaf will in time make a new plant.

RANUNCULUS (*Buttercup*). Do not get the idea that because the common buttercup of our meadows is a ranunculus, there are no species worth growing in the garden. On the contrary, there are several excellent ornamental plants in the family including border plants and very showy tuberous-rooted, double-flowered ranunculuses which are described on p. 362. For the rock garden there is a choice species named *R. alpestris,* which is best planted in the moraine, as it needs a very gritty soil with abundant moisture in summer. It keeps close to the ground and has small, white flowers about mid-summer. Much easier is the grass-leaved buttercup, *R. gramineus,* with narrow leaves and branching sprays of typical buttercup flowers, though the plant has none of the buttercup's inclination to ramble further than it should. This species will grow in any ordinary soil and looks grand in a dry wall. All rock garden buttercups can be increased by division in spring.

RAOULIA. These are carpeting plants of the greatest merit, the best species being *R. australis,* which has very tiny, silvery leaves and keeps absolutely flat to the ground. It is ideal cover for the choicer and smallest rock garden bulbs such as snowdrops, miniature narcissi and crocuses. It likes gritty, well-drained soils and sheltered, sunny positions and can be increased by lifting a portion of the mat in spring and pulling it to pieces.

RHODOHYPOXIS. These are very beautiful but rather difficult plants which should be grown in a compost of equal parts lime-free loam, coarse lime-free grit and granulated peat. *R. Baurii* is typical of the family and one of the best. It makes compact little tufts of grassy leaves, spangled all the summer with carmine flowers looking like tiny butterflies. Increase this and other kinds by seed sown in sandy peat in the greenhouse or frame in spring.

ROSA (*Rose*). There is really only one rose which belongs to the rock garden, namely that exquisite miniature, *R. Roulettii*. Imagine a pink polyantha rose reduced to 6 in. in height with all its parts in perfect proportion, and you have an excellent idea of its charm. It will grow in any ordinary soil and sunny place and can be increased by cuttings of firm, young growth inserted in a frame in the late summer or autumn.

ROSCOEA. A deep, cool, moist yet porous soil is required to grow roscoea well. They are worth a little trouble for they are very unusual in appearance and distinctly beautiful, with hooded flowers packed closely together on erect stems, varying from 6 in. in the dwarf species *R. alpina*, to 12 in. in the case of the best kind, *R. cautleoides*. The first is pink, the second pale yellow. Both can be increased by careful division in spring, though seed sown in a frame at the same season is really a better method.

ROSMARINUS (*Rosemary*). The common Rosemary is, of course, a shrub, far too big for the ordinary rockery, but there is a miniature form named *R. officinalis prostratus*, which spreads slowly along the ground, never exceeds 3 in. in height, and has the typical fragrant foliage and pale blue flowers of Rosemary. It will grow in any ordinary soil and sunny place and can be increased by summer cuttings in sandy soil under a bell glass.

SANGUINARIA (*Bloodroot*). The only species that is grown is *S. canadensis*, a trailing plant with grey-green leaves and widely opened, white flowers. It is a member of the poppy family but unlike most of its kith and kin it inhabits moist, shady places and delights in cool, leafy soils. It is a good plant to place near a stream-side or in the better drained portions of the bog garden. It flowers in spring and can be propagated by division immediately after flowering.

SAPONARIA (*Soapwort*). The common Soapwort is a herbaceous plant (see p. 175), while there is one annual species (see p. 121). For the rock garden there is a trailing kind named *S. ocymoides*, which will soor cover a square yard of ground with rather lush masses of soft, green leaves and clouds of rose-pink flowers during June and July. It is a real beginner's plant in the sense that it will grow anywhere and give no trouble beyond, possibly, over-running some smaller and choicer plants in its way. It can be raised quickly and easily from seed sown in a frame in March or outdoors in May that no other method of propagation need be considered.

SARRACENIA. These are interesting rather than beautiful plants, the interest lying in the fact that they are carnivorous. Each plant in addition to producing ordinary leaves has several pitcher-shaped leaves which serve as traps to insects, which are then digested. The sarracenias are bog plants, needing to be planted in damp, peaty soils. The best kinds are S. *flava*, with yellowish-green pitchers, and S. *purpurea*, with pitchers which are green at first but later become red. Careful division in May provides the best method of propagation.

SAXIFRAGA (*Saxifrage*). This vast family of plants should really, from the garden standpoint, be regarded as a collection of quite separate groups of plants, each with its own particular characteristics and requirements. Even the botanists agree that the name has been stretched to cover plants very distinct in type and it is customary to sub-divide the genus into as many as seventeen sections. Some of these are of no great significance from the garden standpoint but there are at least eight groups with which the gardener should be familiar. These are as follows:

(1) Megasea Saxifrages, with big, leathery leaves and showy heads of pink flowers in spring. They are herbaceous plants with which I have already dealt on p. 227.

(2) Mossy Saxifrages, with soft cushions of growth and flowers carried on slender stems in April and May. These all like cool positions and may be grown in shady places and ordinary soils provided they do not dry out quickly in hot weather. It is an advantage to add leaf mould or peat and perhaps a little well-rotted manure before planting, particularly if the soil is by nature inclined to be poor or dry.

(3) Silver Saxifrages, many of which make compact, flat rosettes of stiff leaves often heavily silvered. From these arise, in May or June, plumes of flowers often a couple of feet in height. These are all true alpines, delighting in light, gritty soils and full sun. Many are seen to best advantage when planted on their sides in vertical crevices or on well-made, dry walls with an ample core of good rock garden compost.

(4) Cushion Saxifrages, which are also true alpines but on the average very much smaller and more compact than the Silver Saxifrages; as their name implies they make compact cushions of growth but firm and sometimes almost spiky, not soft like those of the Mossy Saxifrages. These, too, need true alpine conditions with quick drainage coupled with an ample water supply in spring and summer. The choicest are plants for the moraine. Almost all flower very early, some starting in February in a favourable season.

(5) A small group which has no popular name so must be known by its botanical title, Engleria. These are rather like small, neat Silver Saxifrages with very compact rosettes. Their flowers are often insignificant but in some species the flower stems are adorned with brightly coloured bracts, quite as showy as any blooms. They need exactly the same conditions as Cushion Saxifrages.

(6) Another group without a popular name which I will call Oppositifolia after its best-known species. These are prostrate, mat-forming plants which appreciate very gritty soils but a little shade from the mid-day sun. They are good subjects for the moraine and flower in March–April.

(7) The London Pride group, well typified by the popular species whose name I have used to describe the section. There are neater forms, however, than the London Pride itself. All are easily grown in any ordinary soil and sunny or partially shaded position. They flower in May and June.

(8) A group known botanically as Trachyphyllum, of small tufted or trailing plants mostly with narrow little leaves and sprays of starry flowers. They like cool, moist but open soils and partially shaded places. Most flower in late summer.

One could multiply examples in each group almost indefinitely and I must confine myself here to a few only of the best or most widely planted.

Mossy Saxifrages are now chiefly represented in gardens by hybrids which pass under 'fancy' names, such as Pompadour (crimson), James Bremner (white), General Joffre (red), Bathoniensis (rose pink), and so on. Catalogues should be consulted for these for many nurserymen have their own specialities. All can be multiplied indefinitely simply by sowing seed in fine, sandy soil in greenhouse or frame in spring.

There are also a few species or sub-species of the mossy group which are worth planting, notably *S. Whitlavii compacta*, really a form of *S. hypnoides*, which is exceptionally close growing and moss-like with small, white flowers in great profusion. *S. sanguinea superba*, which is looser in habit and has large, bright crimson flowers on 4-in. stems; *S. moschata*, often wrongly sold as *S. muscoides*, which is almost as close as the last, and has creamy flowers; its pink-flowered form, Wild Rose; *S. Wallacei*, rather loose in growth with white flowers; *S. cuneata*, with loose, spreading rosettes and big white flowers in sprays, and *S. ceratophylla*, known as the Stag's Horn Saxifrage because the leaves look like tiny stag's horns. The flowers are large and white.

All these Mossy Saxifrages can be increased by division after flowering. It is often advisable to divide and replant every second or third year to prevent the plants becoming starved and brown at the centre.

Not a true mossy saxifrage but rather like one in appearance and thriving under similar conditions is our own British meadow saxifrage, *S. granulata*. The flowers on 6-in. stems are white and there is a very fine double-flowered form.

The four outstanding Silver Saxifrages are *Aizoon, Cotyledon, lingulata* and *longifolia*. Each has given rise to numerous garden varieties, often more beautiful than the species itself. *S. Aizoon*, for example, which has small rosettes multiplying rapidly and soon covering quite a considerable area of ground, is white flowered, but has pink and yellow flowered varieties. Personally I like the pink form best of all. There is also a variety, named *baldensis*, in which everything is reduced in size so giving almost the effect of a Cushion Saxifrage.

S. Cotyledon is a much bigger plant with rosettes often as large as a tea plate and plume-like sprays of white flowers on 18-in. stems. One of the best forms is *caterhamensis* in which the flower sprays are almost twice as big as normal and the flowers are heavily spotted with red.

S. lingulata has narrower leaves than the last and arching plumes of flowers which are especially graceful. The flowers are white. There is an unusually fine form named *Albertii* which is bigger and broader in leaf and has specially fine flower trusses.

S. longifolia itself is a difficult plant as it dies after flowering and in any case needs very good drainage and a deep root run, but it has a form named Tumbling Waters which is as easy to grow as *S. Cotyledon* and produces enormous plumes of white flowers from stiff, densely-silvered rosettes of leaves.

Another Silver Saxifrage worth noting is *cochlearis*, which makes a firm, dome-like mound of tiny silver leaves. It is so small that it might be mistaken for a cushion saxifrage and it has an even more compact, huddled form named *minor*.

All these can be propagated by careful division or by seed sown in greenhouse or frame in spring.

The Cushion Saxifrages have been very highly developed, with the result that catalogues teem with fancy or pseudo-botanic names such as Arco-Valleyi, with cherry pink flowers; Boydii, golden yellow; Myra, lilac pink; Irvingii, pale pink; Elizabethae, yellow; Haagii, bright yellow and Jenkinsae, rose-blossom pink. There are, in addition, some true species, such as *apiculata*, primrose yellow and especially easy to grow; *Burseriana*, with slender red stems and flowers like white cherry blossom, and *lilacina*, which is absolutely prostrate with almost stemless lilac flowers. All may be carefully divided after flowering.

Far and away the best Engleria is *S. Grisebachii*. This makes numerous very compact silver rosettes, each of which erupts in spring into a short, arching stem clothed throughout in crimson plush bracts. It needs exactly the same treatment as any of the choice Cushion Saxifrages.

The best of the Oppositifolia group is *S. oppositifolia* itself. It sprawls about this way and that with slender stems closely clad with tiny leaves and bearing heather-red flowers in March and April. There are a good many varieties, some with bigger blooms, one white, another purplish crimson. All can be increased by careful division after flowering.

The member of the London Pride group which I like best is the dainty variety known as *S. umbrosa primuloides*. Imagine a London Pride reduced to 6 in. stature very neat in growth and with flowers in an extra warm shade of pink and you have it exactly. It blooms in May and can be pulled to pieces and re-planted at almost any time. Another useful plant in this group is *S. Geum*, with stout, roundish leaves and similar loose clusters of pink flowers on 9-in. stems in May.

Lastly the Trachyphyllum group contains such dainty, rather fragile looking plants as *S. aizoides* with dark green leaves and golden flowers; its form *atrorubens* in which the flowers are mahogany-red; and *S. aspera*, low-growing, almost bushy in appearance with straw-coloured flowers.

SCABIOSA (*Scabious*). The best-known varieties of scabious are either plants to be treated as annuals (see p. 122) or herbaceous perennials (see p. 176). There are, however, in addition one or two dwarf species which make pretty rock garden plants, notably *S. pterocephala* and *S. graminifolia*. The first forms a cushion of soft, grey-green leaves, the second makes tufts of very narrow, silvery-grey leaves and both produce a profusion of small, mauve, scabious blooms throughout the greater part of the summer. Both will grow in any ordinary soil and sunny place and look especially well in the dry wall or planted between big boulders. They can be increased by division or by seed in the spring.

SCHIZOCODON (*Japanese Moonwort*). The only species of schizocodon at all widely grown is *soldanelloides,* a good name as the plant does resemble a soldanella. It is a small plant, tufted in habit with shining, evergreen leaves and pale pink, fringed flowers on 6-in. stems in spring. It is not an easy plant to grow as it needs plenty of moisture and yet good drainage. Plant in a mixture of sand, leaf mould or peat with a little loam and give it a cool, partially shaded position but not where it will catch the drip of overhanging trees. Propagate it when necessary by very careful division in spring or, when seed is available, by sowing this in sandy peat in greenhouse or frame.

SCUTELLARIA (*Skullcap*). These are for the most part small and not very attractive plants but *S. alpina* is reasonably neat in growth and free with its small, blue-purple flowers which have the merit of coming in the latter half of the summer when colour is scarce in the rock garden. It will grow practically anywhere provided the position is open and the soil porous and it can be increased by seed or division in the spring. *S. indica japonica,* requiring similar treatment, is also worth planting for its abundant short spikes of violet-purple flowers.

SEDUM (*Stonecrop*). This is a family of the very first merit for the rock garden, though it is not devoid of weeds. Nevertheless most of the sedums are really bright and cheerful plants with the merit of growing in the hottest situations and with the minimum amount of soil. There is great diversity in the family, from the tiny, chubby-leaved forms typified by our own natives, *S. album, S. acre* and *S. dasyphyllum,* the first with white, the second with yellow, and the third with pinkish flowers, to the big, flat-leaved types such as *S. spectabile* and *S. maximum,* plants more suited to the herbaceous border than the rock garden on account of their size.

There are a great many species and varieties of which I can give no more than a brief selection here. Those which I would recommend to the beginner are *S. Ewersii,* 6 in. high, with grey-green leaves and purplish flowers; *glaucum* (*hispanicum*), with very tiny, pale, grey-green leaves and pink-tinged flowers, the whole plant being no more than 2 in. high; *kamtschaticum,* quick-growing and carpet-forming, with shining dark green leaves and orange yellow flowers; a form of the last known as *variegatum,* in which the leaves are blotched with yellow; *lydium,* which is like *glaucum* except that the leaves turn bronze when the plant is grown in a dry, warm place; *pulchellum,* trailing, with rosy-purple flowers and one of the few sedums which likes a cool, shady, slightly moist place; *reflexum,* with sprawling stems densely set with narrow, grey-green leaves and terminating in crozier-heads of yellow

231

flowers; *spurium*, with glossy foliage and pinkish-white flowers and *spathulifolium*, which I have kept to the last because it is in my opinion the best of all, particularly in its colour form, *atro-purpureum*. It is quite prostrate, spreads quickly, has fleshy, spoon-shaped leaves, which are grey-green in the type, purplish crimson in the colour form, while the flowers are bright yellow in both plants.

Almost all these sedums flower around mid-summer and all can be increased by careful division in spring. There is in addition a charming pale blue flowered sedum named *caeruleum*, which is an annual and should be sown in spring where it is to grow, and another, named *pilosum*, which looks like a sempervivum, has soft pink flowers, is a biennial and so, like the last, should be re-sown each year though as soon as the seed is ripe rather than in spring.

SEMPERVIVUM (*House Leek*). House Leeks are amongst the hardest wearing and most long suffering of all rock plants. They will grow practically anywhere and it is no uncommon thing to see *Sempervivum tectorum* happily growing on old roofs with apparently no soil whatever, though closer examination will always reveal a thin covering of drifted grit and old leaves caught in an angle of the tiles. They are admirable plants for walls, ledges in the rock garden or other hot and dry positions where there is little soil. Nevertheless to get them started it is wise to prepare a mixture of rather rich soil even, possibly, with some old, dry cow manure crumbled into it, and spread this an inch or so thick over the stones which are to be covered. Later, when firmly rooted, the Sempervivum will be able to look after itself. All can be most readily increased by division at practically any time of the year though spring is the most favourable season. All make stiff rosettes of succulent leaves which gradually spread into wide masses. From these appear curious, stiff flower stems in late summer terminated by big, flattish clusters of starry and usually pink or purplish flowers which, though not so effective as the leaves, are nevertheless arresting by virtue of their unusual appearance.

There are a great many species, of which a few of the best are *arachnoideum*, with small, purplish rosettes covered all over with white, cobweb-like filaments; *Boutignyanum*, with massive, bronzy-red rosettes; *calcareum*, also with rather big rosettes, blue-green in colour and red tipped; *Doellianum*, rather like the first named but smaller; *globiferum*, often known as the Hen-and-Chickens House Leek because of its habit of throwing out a number of stems from the main rosette, each stem terminated by another smaller rosette; *Greenii*, bright green tipped with red; *Laggeri*, the best of the cobweb House Leeks, being both bigger and more webbed than *arachnoideum; Reginae-Amaliae,* purplish brown in leaf and yellow flowered; *tectorum,* the common House Leek, pale green tipped with reddish-brown, and *triste,* in which the reddish-brown leaves have an almost metallic sheen.

SHORTIA. These are not really rock plants at all but woodlanders, though they are so small and neat and need such special care that they are almost invariably planted in the rock garden. They should be given a partially shaded place in a deep bed of leaf mould containing a little sand and scarcely any soil. The two best are *S. galacifolia* and *S. uniflora,* both with shining green leaves and pale pink flowers on 4 in. stems in spring, but the colour is a shade warmer in *uniflora* than in *galacifolia.* Both can be increased by careful division in spring.

SILENE. There is a silene for the annual border (see p. 122) as well as those described here for the rock garden. Some of these latter are disappointing plants, notably *S. acaulis,* which makes cushions of narrow green leaves and should produce numerous pink flowers in early summer but often fails to do so for no apparent reason. A better plant is *S. alpestris* which makes loose tufts of shining leaves and has abundant starry, white flowers on 6-in. stems in June, July and, often enough, August into the bargain. *S. Schafta* is a little loose and untidy in habit but has the merit of flowering from July to October. The blooms are a rather harsh rose pink. All will grow in ordinary rock garden soil and sunny position and all can be increased by division in spring. *S. Schafta* is also very easily raised from seed sown in a frame, or even outdoors, in spring or as soon as ripe.

SISYRINCHIUM. Some of the Sisyrinchiums are disappointing plants but the family includes a few real gems, notably *S. grandiflorum,* with narrow, rush-like leaves and very slender flower stems 9 in. high, terminated by drooping, amethyst flowers which have the texture and sheen of satin. There is a pure white form which is equally beautiful. Both flower in early spring and are so fragile that they merit the protection of a pane of glass. They should be planted in deep, peaty soil with plenty of coarse sand and stone chips. More robust are *S. angustifolium,* often known as the Blue-Eyed Grass and really very like grass with starry, blue flowers in early summer; and *S. Bermudiana,* which is very similar but rather larger and paler. *S. striatum* should be avoided as it is ugly. These 'easy' kinds grow in ordinary well-drained soil and open position. Propagation in all cases can be by division after flowering or by seed sown in frame or greenhouse in spring.

SOLDANELLA. In the Alps one may see the violet-blue, fringed flowers of the soldanellas forcing their way through the snow before it is fully melted, yet in our gardens they sometimes need the protection of a pane of glass in late winter and early spring. This is not because they lack hardiness but because they will flower so early that their fragile blooms get prematurely spoiled by rain, mud splashes and alternating frost and thaw. These are good plants for the moraine or for any very porous soil and open position. The two species commonly grown, *S. alpina* and *S. montana*, are much alike in appearance except that the last named is considerably larger (6 in. high against 3 in.) and blue-lilac rather than violet. Both can be increased by very careful division in spring or by seed sown in sandy soil and germinated in a frame in spring.

STACHYS (*Woundwort*). These plants, so closely related to the Dead Nettles, are for the most part weeds, but there is one delightful species for the rock garden which in a warm, sunny place will form close carpets of tiny leaves on which sit all summer small, pale pink, practically stemless, flowers. This is *S. corsica*, and because it comes from Corsica it is just a little tender, particularly if the weather happens to be wet and cold alternately. Give it good drainage and place a pane of glass over it from November to April. It can be propagated by division in spring.

SYNTHYRIS. *S. reniformis* is not a very well-known plant but it would almost be worth planting for its leaves alone, they are so exceptionally bright and shining. It is quite a tiny plant, seldom more than 4 in. high, running about readily in any ordinary soil and sunny or shaded place, and producing numerous fluffy spikes of blue flowers in early summer. This is one of those easily managed rock plants that require no particular precautions and can be increased by division in spring.

THYMUS (*Thyme*). The common thyme is not, of course, a plant for the rock garden but rather for the herb garden. There are, however, a number of smaller species which make very good rock plants. Of these one of the best is *T. Serpyllum*, a carpet-forming species with tiny, fragrant leaves and sheets of small, reddish purple flowers in early summer. It has a number of garden varieties, such as *coccineus*, with brighter red flowers; *albus*, white flowered; and *lanuginosus*, with leaves so hairy that the whole plant has a silvered appearance. Another fine variety is *T. citriodorus*, with lemon-scented leaves. There are variegated forms of this, some silvery, others golden. *T. Herba-barona* has leaves which smell of caraway. All will grow in any ordinary soil and sunny position. They are excellent for forming a carpet over choice bulbs. A bigger plant, rather like a neat, very erect and compact form of the common Thyme, is *T. nitidus*. This makes a little bush 6 or 8 in. high, smothered in rosy-purple flowers in June. The mat-forming kinds can be increased by division at almost any time, *T. nitidus* by seed in spring or cuttings of firm young growths in a frame in summer.

TRILLIUM. These very beautiful plants are woodlanders rather than rock plants but they are frequently planted in shady parts of the rock garden. They need deep, cool, peaty or leafy soil but otherwise are not difficult to grow. All grow to a height of about 1 ft. or 18 in., have broad, three-parted leaves and showy, three-petalled flowers. Good kinds are *T. grandiflorum*, which is pure white; *T. sessile*, purple; and *T. erectum*, reddish purple. All bloom in April and May. Increase by very careful division in March.

TUNICA. The only species of importance is *T. Saxifraga*, a very dainty plant which might easily be mistaken for an alpine Gypsophila for it has similar thin, wiry stems, narrow leaves and loose sprays of pale pink, starry flowers. This is an admirable plant for a wall or a sunny crevice in the rock garden. It is not fussy regarding soil and can very readily be raised from seed sown in greenhouse or frame in spring.

VERBENA. There are only one or two verbenas which have any place in the rock garden and of these the best is not a true rock plant, nor is it quite hardy. Nevertheless it keeps so close to the ground and makes such a brilliant display with its clusters of scarlet flowers that it is well worth planting in any sunny place and well-drained soil. Its name is *V. chamaedrioides* (sometimes written *chamaedrifolia*). Cuttings of non-flowering shoots will root very readily in sandy soil in a frame in August or September and it is always wise to strike a few in this manner every year just in case the parent plant is killed by a hard winter.

VERONICA. This very large family contains shrubs for the shrub border and herbaceous plants for the herbaceous border besides a number of excellent dwarf kinds for the rock garden. So varied, indeed, is the group that some botanists have split it up into two separate genera, giving the name Hebe to many of the shrubby kinds.

The rock garden varieties are either trailing plants or neat little shrubs some of which ape other families of plants. All will grow in any ordinary soil and open place. Typical is *V. rupestris*, which also appears in some lists under the name *V. Teucrium dubia*. It will soon form a mat almost a yard wide with small, dark green leaves and little spikes of bright blue flowers throughout May and June. There are pink and white varieties, neither so good as the type. Rather similar is *V. Teucrium Trehane* with golden leaves and blue flowers.

V. filiformis carries the free-growing habit of the family to an extreme, making such enormous carpets of growth that it smothers everything else in its way. Nevertheless it is a pretty plant for a rough corner with mounds of soft green leaves, thread-like stems and abundant, pale blue flowers in May and June. It will grow in sun or shade. *V. catarractae* is a much neater plant with small, shining, evergreen leaves and pale lilac flowers.

Other good kinds are *V. incana*, with silver-grey leaves and 10 in. spikes of Oxford blue flowers in early summer; *V. cupressoides*, a compact bush which looks just like a small conifer until it bursts out into washy blue flowers in May; *V. Bidwillii*, an even smaller bush, 4 in. in height, with white flowers in July; *V. lycopodioides* and *V. Hectori*, quaintly congested masses of tiny, bronze leaves, and *V. saxatilis*, prostrate, evergreen with blue, red-ringed flowers in May. The trailing kinds can be increased by careful division in spring; the shrubby ones by cuttings of firm, young growth in sand under a bell glass in summer.

Vinca (*Periwinkle*). *V. major*, the large, English Periwinkle is a little too rampant for the ordinary rock garden though it is useful for a rough corner, particularly as it will grow in shade. *V. minor* is a neater version with the same trailing stems set with glossy, privet-like leaves and ending in clusters of showy blue flowers. Both plants will grow in any soil and practically any position. They flower from January to April and can be increased by division after flowering.

Viola. The highly developed garden violas have no place in the rockery, their proper position being beds and borders of more formal character, but some of the species are first class rock plants. One of the best is *V. gracilis* which in habit is rather like a good, mat-forming, bedding viola with very narrow leaves. It has small, exceptionally graceful and very rich purple flowers from April to July. There is a pale yellow form which is not so attractive and a number of garden varieties in various shades of yellow and blue. More vigorous is *V. cornuta* which makes big, loose mounds of thin stems and has spurred flowers rather like those of a very large violet. The normal colour is mauve but there are many varieties including a good white and a deep purple. *V. bosniaca*, with very tiny, rosy-lilac flowers like miniature pansies is also charming but needs more care and a well-drained soil.

All can be raised from seed sown in spring in a frame but selected forms must be kept true to type by division in spring or by cuttings of basal, non-flowering shoots taken in August or September, like those of bedding violas. Most may also be divided carefully in spring.

WAHLENBERGIA. The uninitiated might be pardoned for mistaking the wahlenbergias for campanulas, to which they are closely allied. They are for the most part fragile, sprawling plants with big, blue, bell-shaped flowers in late spring or early summer. One of the best is *W. serpyllifolia major*, in which the flowers are very large and purple rather than blue. *W. vincaeflora* and *W. graminifolium* are others worth noting. All should be grown in well-drained, peaty soil and a sunny position. In fact they are good plants for the moraine. Increase by seed or very careful division in spring.

ZAUSCHNERIA. The only species widely grown is *Z. californica*, a brilliant, half-shrubby plant with tubular, scarlet flowers in September and October. It would be more valuable if it were a little hardier. In point of fact it is often lost in winter. Grow it in rather poor, sandy soil and a hot, sunny position. It is first class on a wall or in a narrow, south-facing crevice between boulders. The plants are a little bushy in habit and about a foot in height. They can be increased by cuttings of non-flowering shoots struck in sand under a bell glass in August or by seed sown in the greenhouse in March. *Z. cana* is at least equally attractive and deserves to be better known as it is similar in flower but has narrow greyish leaves. *Z. latifolia* has broader leaves than those of *Z. californica*.

CHAPTER IX
Trees and Shrubs

IN THIS section I only include trees and shrubs sufficiently hardy to be grown outdoors in most parts of the country. In themselves they are a sufficiently imposing collection and one which might easily fill several volumes each the size of this. Obviously, therefore, in this chapter very severe compression and selection are essential and in this preliminary consideration it is necessary to group the bewildering wealth of material in the broadest and simplest possible manner.

An obvious first division can be made by separating evergreen from deciduous (leaf-losing) varieties. This is quite an arbitrary division and one which cuts right through some families, berberis for example, which have both evergreen and deciduous species. Nevertheless it is a useful distinction whether one is considering culture or ornamental use.

Trees and shrubs may also be divided into conifers (cone bearers) and broad-leaved types, or may be regarded as lime haters as opposed to lime tolerators. These are not sub-divisions of the first grouping, for there are both evergreen and deciduous conifers as well as evergreen and deciduous broad-leaved trees and shrubs, while lime-hating and lime-tolerating kinds are to be found in all the other divisions. Nevertheless the gardener must learn to recognise these distinctions if he is to begin to understand the needs of trees and shrubs in any kind of ordered manner, for each has a distinct bearing on culture.

Taking the evergreen v. deciduous division first, the cultural distinction resolves itself largely into a question of the time at which they are planted and, to a lesser degree, the time at which they are pruned. With a small number of exceptions, of which magnolias are the most important, deciduous shrubs are most safely planted directly they have lost most of their leaves in the autumn, but before the soil has become very wet and cold—roughly from the end of October to the end of November. Work can continue during any mild and fairly dry weather throughout the winter until about the last week in March but the later it is left the more risk there is likely to be especially if the spring happens to be hot and dry.

Evergreens, by contrast, with the notable exception of evergreen conifers, do not transplant very satisfactorily during this period because their roots then recover too slowly and are unable to keep pace with the demands of the leaves which are constantly evaporating water even in mid-winter. This peculiarity not unnaturally makes evergreens as a class a little more difficult to transplant than deciduous trees and shrubs. As a consequence it pays to purchase some kinds in (or recently tapped out of) pots so that they suffer the minimum amount of root disturbance. Nevertheless most kinds can be transplanted from the open ground either in late spring or early autumn (April–May and September–October) in an average season. At these periods roots are still sufficiently active to take hold of the soil reasonably quickly whereas the weather is not, as a rule, so warm that leaves are losing an excessive amount of water. The danger of death can be lessened by lifting the trees or shrubs with a good ball of roots and soil, replanting firmly and with as little delay as possible and watering freely for the first few weeks. If the weather turns hot after spring planting it may pay to syringe leaves daily with tepid water and perhaps even to shade them with a screen of sacking, hurdles or evergreen boughs. After autumn planting a similar screen may prove of value to keep off cold, drying winds.

Conifers all have comparatively narrow and often very small leaves which do not give off moisture anything like so rapidly as those of broad-leaved trees and shrubs. For this reason the objections to the transplanting of other evergreens in the October–March period do not apply to evergreen conifers most of which can be moved during mild weather and when the soil is in good working condition throughout this period. All the same a few conifers prove difficult to transplant at any time, apparently because they resent root breakage, and these must either be established while still quite young and small or else be purchased in pots. The popular hedging plant *Cupressus macrocarpa* is an example.

The distinction between lime-hating and lime-tolerating shrubs is one about which the amateur is likely to hear a lot yet in many ways it is the most unsatisfactory of these loose divisions and the least understood. Some varieties which were once supposed to dislike lime have proved, on closer investigation, to be distinctly tolerant and much more work of this character remains to be done. Nevertheless it is broadly true that the majority of shrubs belonging to the heather family (*Ericaceae*) are happiest in soils that contain no free lime i.e. have a *p*H below 7 (see p. 27). The heather family includes not only the heathers themselves but also the rhododendrons and numerous less important genera such as pieris, andromeda and kalmia. Obviously when preparing ground for these it is wise to avoid all use of lime and, so far as possible, to choose land that is itself inclined to be acid. Leaf mould, peat, old mushroom bed or cucumber compost and similar humus-rich dressings can be used to decrease the *p*H of soils that have too much lime to be satisfactory for these shrubs.

Soil Preparation. This brings us to the general methods to be employed when preparing ground for either trees or shrubs. The guiding principle in all cases must be thoroughness, for the first cultivation is also likely to be the last at any rate so far as any deep stirring of the soil is concerned. Once planted many trees and shrubs will form roots quite close to the surface making it impossible to do more than hoe or prick the top soil very lightly with a fork.

Dung can be used to enrich poor soils and improve the texture of both light and heavy ones. Dressings in excess of 1 cwt. to 10 sq. yd. will seldom be desirable as too much manure may cause excessive growth, probably at the expense of flowers or fruits. Of concentrated fertilisers those that are slow in action are most valuable, notably coarse bone meal and hoof and horn meal which may be worked in at normal rates while breaking down the surface in preparation for planting. Preliminary digging should be completed at least a month before planting time to give the ground an adequate chance to settle.

Planting. This does not differ in any material respect from the planting of fruit and I therefore advise the reader to turn to pp. 641–2 and study what I have said there. When dealing with shrubs supplied in pots it is usually advisable to loosen the ball of soil a little so that roots can be spread out in the new soil, but great care must be taken not to break roots while doing this.

Pruning after planting is by no means always essential but it is usually desirable with trees and shrubs which are required to make strong growth from the outset, e.g. those required for hedges and windbreaks. Without such pruning the strength of the plant is liable to be dissipated the first year and weak shoots will result. The only course then is to prune more severely the following year with consequent waste of time. An exception must be made in the case of conifers which should not be pruned after planting as this may spoil their natural habit.

Spacing is very important as in my experience most beginners err on the side of planting much too closely. It is difficult to suggest any rule of thumb on this matter if the full spread of the specimen is not known (if it is known the problem is simple as the minimum spacing should be three quarters the ultimate spread) but perhaps as good a guide as any is to allow between plants at least two thirds of their normal height when full grown, a figure which is given in most nursery

Taking a 'heel cutting' of a deciduous barberry

The 'heel cutting' is prepared for insertion by trimming off the ragged end

A root cutting is prepared from a lifted plant of anchusa

Removing from a lupin a young shoot which can be prepared as a cutting

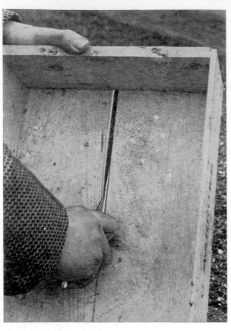

Preparing a seed box. The slit in the bottom is widened to ensure good drainage

The slit is covered with pieces of broken pot to prevent soil from washing through

The seed box is nearly filled with soil which is firmed, specially around the sides

The surface of the soil is made smooth with the bottom of a flower pot

Pricking out seedlings an inch or so apart in a box and soil similar to that in which they were raised

Watering seedlings by partial immersion in a cistern of water

Dividing a herbaceous plant by the leverage of two border forks

With some roots, such as those of dahlia, a knife is necessary for successful division

Many perennial roots can be pulled apart by hand as in the case of this helenium

Preparing a border carnation layer by slitting the stem through a joint

The prepared carnation layer is half buried in soil and made secure to a stick

A shrub layered by bending pliable branches to the ground and either pegging or weighting them there

Disbudding a chrysanthemum by removing all shoots or buds from around the central bud

The effect of disbudding a chrysanthemum. Only one flower is developing per stem

An undisbudded rose stem

The rose stem after disbudding

A bush rose before pruning

An old, worn out branch is sawn off

The bush rose after moderate pruning. Three young branches have been retained and shortened to four or five growth buds each

Aerating an over-hardened lawn by per-
forating the surface

Removing leaves and moss from a lawn with
a spring-toothed rake

Renovation of the lawn. Fertiliser and compost top-dressing are applied
and worked in with the back of a rake

catalogues. Note that these are minimum spacings which can usually be increased with advantage, particularly if it is desired that the various trees and shrubs should display their individual shape and not eventually merge into one more or less continuous mass.

This consideration of spacing naturally links up with the method of grouping employed. Frequently trees are employed as isolated specimens and then the more room they can be allowed, within reason, the better. Shrubs are sometimes planted in the same way, particularly big shrubs such as lilacs and viburnums. More often where it is desired to make a special display of one kind of shrub a small group is planted in a bed by itself on a lawn or in some similar position which will give it due prominence.

Shrub borders, which have displaced the old time shrubberies, should be planned and planted in much the same way as herbaceous borders except that far more single specimens will be used and fewer and smaller groups. There should be the same care in associating types of varied habit, colour and flowering time, in avoiding set lines and in obtaining a pleasingly varied contour by letting some of the taller varieties come towards the front and setting some of the dwarfer kinds towards the back. Avoid the use of too many evergreens or the result may be heavy and displeasing, but ignore this rule when planting solely for some particular display, as, for example, when making a border of rhododendrons. It will usually pay handsomely to include a fair proportion of berry-bearing shrubs in the mixed border to carry colour well on into the winter. A similar object can be achieved by planting some shrubs which assume brilliant foliage colour in the autumn and also varieties with coloured barks such as some of the willows, dogwoods and brambles.

CLIMBERS. Many of our best climbing plants are shrubs in the sense that they have perennial and more or less woody growth. Some are, in fact, shrubs in the narrower sense and will make bushy plants if placed in the open; such only display a climbing habit when planted against a wall or fence and even then may need considerable pruning to keep them in shape. Honeysuckle, clematis and jasmine are examples of the true climber, *Cotoneaster horizontalis* of the shrub which will climb if given half a chance, while *Cydonia japonica* (the 'japonica' of many gardens) and *Pyracantha coccinea* of shrubs which, with little difficulty, can be trained and pruned to fill a wall space.

The true climbers all need something to support them, be it wires, trellis work or in the case of those provided with adhesive tendrils (e.g. ivy and *Ampelopsis Veitchii*) a wall to which to cling. The more woody shrubs which can be used as climbers will frequently support themselves with no more help than that afforded by the protection of a wall and, perhaps, an occasional tie to guide them.

Apart from these matters the general observations to be made about climbers are the same as those for other shrubs. Some are evergreen, some deciduous and the same remarks about planting apply. Spacing cannot be decided by the ultimate height of the climber nor even by its maximum spread which may be a very variable factor depending much upon situation. All the same it is desirable not to overcrowd climbers and it is seldom wise to plant them closer than 6 ft. while 8 to 10 ft. might be regarded as a fair average.

PRUNING. This is by no means so essential a feature of the cultivation of trees and shrubs as many gardeners appear to imagine. Provided they have sufficient space and do not fall into ill health a great many kinds can be left severely alone for the greater part of their lifetime and will continue to grow happily and produce their flowers, fruits or ornamental foliage in season as by nature ordained. It may be good policy occasionally to remove a badly placed branch which is rubbing against another or creating an unbalanced look, but nothing in the way of systematic pruning is necessary.

Pruning is most likely to be of value in the early years, when a little discreet shoot regulation may help to build up a shapely plant and, later on, in the case of shrubs grown for some specific purpose such as to produce a few very large flowers or to fill a special position. Then one must learn to achieve this object with the minimum amount of interference with the natural processes of the shrub.

Evergreen shrubs can be pruned with greatest safety in April or May but if they are in flower then, pruning should be delayed until the flowers fade. As a rule pruning is only wise when the shrubs have to be shaped for some particular purpose as, for example, to form a hedge or to cover a wall. Pruning should be restricted to the minimum necessary to fulfil this purpose.

Deciduous shrubs which flower before mid-summer should be pruned immediately after flowering while those that flower after mid-summer should be pruned in February if quite hardy, or in early April if the young growth is inclined to be tender e.g. *Buddleia variabilis* and *Hydrangea paniculata*.

As regards the early flowering group a fairly safe general rule is to shorten each stem that has just been carrying flowers to a point from which a young shoot is starting. This will have the rest of the summer to grow and ripen in readiness to flower the following spring.

The later flowering shrubs can generally be thinned by the removal of some of the oldest stems, particularly those that are not carrying much new growth, while the younger and stronger branches can often be shortened a little without seriously interfering with the floral display. In one or two cases, notably *Buddleia variabilis* and *Hydrangea paniculata*, all branches can be shortened to within a few inches of ground level as the result will be a few very strong new growths each of which will produce a flower truss of extra size. Note, however, that even in these cases hard pruning, or even any pruning at all, is not essential as more numerous if smaller flower trusses will be carried if the bushes are allowed to grow unrestricted.

Deciduous hedges can have a thorough shaping in February or March and may have one or two light trimmings during the summer. Evergreen hedges may get their main clipping in early May with subsequent occasional trimming until mid-September.

Climbers fall into much the same groups as shrubs, the early flowering kinds being thinned and shortened a little after flowering, whereas the summer blooming kinds are dealt with in February. True climbers tend to be spoiled by much pruning though the large-flowered clematises, particularly those of the 'Jackmanii' type, can be cut back quite hard with the result that they produce still bigger, though fewer, blooms.

Shrubby climbers which are made to cover a wall by training and pruning need the most careful attention. Very often the problem of restricting growth without unduly reducing the flower display can be solved by shortening to 6 or 8 in. all side growths directly they commence to get really hard and woody at the base (usually some time between June and August). If they are berry-bearing kinds take care not to remove the young berries while doing this work.

PROPAGATION. Trees and shrubs are increased by division, cuttings, layering and grafting (including budding) and seeds. I will deal with these in order.

Division is the least general method and yet the simplest. Unfortunately it is only possible with those shrubs or trees which produce numerous shoots or suckers direct from the roots, e.g. *Berberis Aquifolium*, *Rhus Cotinus* and lilac (but if lilac is grafted the suckers will have the character of the stock not of the variety grafted on it). All that is necessary is to lift the shrub or tree at the normal planting season and pull off some of the stems complete with roots; or, if it is too big and old for this, to dig out some of the suckers with roots attached but without unduly disturbing the parent plant.

251

Cuttings are of two main kinds; summer cuttings made from half-grown shoots commencing to get hard and woody at the base, and autumn cuttings made from fully-grown shoots of the same year.

Summer cuttings must always be rooted fairly quickly and for this purpose a bell glass, handlight or propagating box is an almost essential accessory. Very sandy soil, or even, in some cases, pure silver sand, is used as the rooting medium and the cuttings are watered fairly freely, shaded from strong sunshine and only ventilated for a few minutes daily until they are rooted, a state which they will indicate by immediately beginning to grow.

Autumn cuttings can be allowed to root slowly over a period of months and can often be handled outdoors without protection, though the covering of a bell glass or handlight is a help with the more difficult kinds. In this case no watering is likely to be necessary after the initial watering-in and the bell glasses can be left in position from the time the cuttings are inserted in September–November until the following April when they will probably be rooted and commencing to grow.

Summer cuttings should be potted in ordinary potting soil as soon as rooted and then accommodated in a frame for the next few weeks while being hardened off. Subsequently they can be potted on or planted out. Autumn cuttings are usually left undisturbed till the following autumn when they may be transplanted to a nursery bed or their permanent quarters.

Layering means that the shoots are rooted first and removed afterwards. It has the merit of being particularly safe and easy and therefore I specially recommend it to the beginner. Well-grown young stems are best, though older branches can sometimes be rooted successfully. Autumn is the best season, spring the second best, though really layering can be practised at any time because, even if the shoots do not commence to root at once, no harm will be done.

The method is to bend the shoot down so that it touches the soil at a point a little behind its tip (occasionally the tip itself may be used) and either peg it there or weight it in position with a heavy stone. A little soil can first be drawn over the shoot, still further to encourage it to root. With the same object it may be given a sharp twist to rupture the bark where it will be buried and then be bent sharply upwards to restrict, but not stop, the flow of sap. Layers pegged down in the autumn should be well-rooted by the following autumn when they can be severed from the parent and lifted for planting on their own.

Air Layering is another form of layering and is done without bringing the shoots to ground level. An incision is made in the branch or stem to be layered and the cut surfaces dusted with hormone rooting powder. Sphagnum moss is then placed around the cut and enclosed in a sleeve of polythene film, tightly tied at each end. Roots are formed into the moss and when there are plenty of these the layer is severed and after removal of the polythene is potted or planted. Air layering can be done at any time but is usually most effective in spring and early summer.

Grafting and budding are used to propagate some choice garden varieties of highly developed shrubs such as lilacs and rhododendrons and are common methods of increasing ornamental apples, cherries and plums. The systems employed are closely similar to those used for fruit trees (see p. 637) and as a rule seedlings or suckers of the common form of the shrub or tree to be increased are used as stocks e.g. common lilac suckers for choice lilacs, seedling *Rhododendron ponticum* for the big-flowered, hybrid rhododendrons, seedling crab apples for ornamental crabs, and so on. Occasionally it is found necessary to graft or bud in the greenhouse, the stocks being potted and brought inside for this purpose and subsequently placed in a propagating frame until a union has been made.

Seeds are not much used by amateurs as a method of propagation probably because of the long time that must elapse before a specimen is obtained of reasonable size for the shrub border. Nevertheless there are a good many shrubs which can be raised quite readily from seeds sown in a frame in spring or even indoors in a sheltered place in spring. All the deciduous barberries (berberis) come into this class and so do most of the cotoneasters and rose species as distinct from the highly developed garden roses. Here it should be noted that though most species of any kind can be raised reasonably true to type from seed hybrids always show a degree of variation when increased by this means.

Seed should be sown in the same type of soil as that favoured by the shrub or tree i.e. peaty soil for peat lovers, ordinary loamy soil for the great majority that will grow anywhere and so on. If to be raised in pots or pans these must be very well drained. Outdoor seed beds should be thoroughly cleaned of weeds first as germination may in some cases be slow and irregular. March is usually the most favourable month for sowing but it often pays to place berries or heps, as soon as ripe in the autumn, in shallow sand-filled boxes and place these outdoors to be frozen and thawed a few times during the winter. This hastens the decay of the flesh and has some action on the seed itself which tends to hasten germination. Then in March sand and berries together can be rubbed between the palms to separate the seeds after which the whole mass can be 'sown' in drills about 1 in. deep. As regards depth for other seeds a good general rule is to cover them with soil to twice their own depth e.g. $\frac{1}{4}$ in. diameter seeds in $\frac{1}{2}$ in. deep drills and so on.

Leave the seedlings undisturbed till they are several inches high and then transplant them at the normal planting season for the species placing them a few inches apart each way in a bed of well-broken soil. Here they can grow on for at least a further year by which time they may be large enough to go to their permanent quarters or if not should be shifted to another similar bed but given a little more room.

CHOICE AND CARE OF HEDGES

Appropriately selected and well cared for hedges can add greatly to the attractiveness of almost all gardens. The choice of suitable hedge plants is great and there is certainly no reason for the monotonous repetition of any one subject, however good. And I should be far from denying that privet is a good hedge plant. It has the merits of neatness, hardiness and adaptability in a very marked degree and it withstands clipping well. Moreover the broad-leaved green privet (*Ligustrum ovalifolium*) has a good appearance and its golden leaved form must certainly be reckoned amongst the brightest of variegated shrubs. But because of these qualities both have been over-planted to a degree which makes many discriminating gardeners desire to plant almost any hedge shrub rather than either of the popular privets.

Lonicera nitida is one of the most favoured substitutes—so much so that there is danger of its becoming as common as privet. It is exceptionally neat in leaf but apt to be a little straggly in habit unless it is pruned fairly severely. For a small hedge, say up to $4\frac{1}{2}$ ft. in height, it is difficult to beat amongst moderately priced shrubs.

Those who are prepared to pay more for something of greater quality should consider yew or holly, both rather out of favour but unsurpassed for appearance and permanence. They are often referred to as slow-growing but this is not so in reasonably rich soil.

For large hedges and windbreaks some of the cypresses are excellent, notably *Chamaecyparis Lawsoniana* and its numerous forms, and *C. macrocarpa*. The last is exceptionally quick growing and does not rob the soil as much as most hedge shrubs but it suffers the drawback of lack of hardiness. Far better is the hybrid between this and *Chamaecyparis nootkatensis* known as *Cupressocyparis leylandii*. This is very fast growing and quite hardy. *Thuya plicata* and *T. occidentalis* are rather like *Cupressus Lawsoniana* in appearance and are both hardy and reasonably quick growing.

Cherry laurel, Portugal laurel and aucuba both 'spotted' and plain green all make fine boundaries or screens but are not desirable where small, closely trimmed hedges are required.

Beech and hornbeam are remarkable in that, though both large trees when left to grow naturally, they will submit to drastic pruning and make fine hedges no more than 18 to 24 in. through and anything from 4 to 20 ft. in height. Moreover, though deciduous, they will retain their dead leaves all winter when hard pruned and then make fine windbreaks besides providing a pleasant variation in colour from the evergreens.

Cherry plum (*Prunus cerasifera*) and quickthorn (*Crataegus monogyna* and *C.Oxyacantha*) are useful for outer boundaries to large estates but are scarcely choice enough for small gardens. Many better flowering or berry bearing shrubs are available, notably *Berberis Darwinii*, *B. stenophylla*, *Cotoneaster Simonsii*, *Escallonia rubra* and some of the hybrids of this shrub, lavender or rosemary for a small hedge, our native sweet briar (*Rosa rubiginosa*) and vigorous hybrid polyantha roses such as Else Poulsen and Karen Poulsen. Rambler roses can also be used for making wide, rather informal hedges. In seaside districts tamarix makes a delightful hedge while *Atriplex Halimus*, though rather untidy, has good silver grey foliage.

PREPARATION OF THE GROUND. This is often scamped with the result that the hedge is hampered from the outset. A strip of ground at least a yard wide should be dug as deeply as the nature of the soil allows and be well manured with dung or, failing this, with generous quantities of such artificials as bone meal and hoof and horn meal. A month or more should be allowed for the soil to settle before planting commences.

PLANTING. The two commonest faults are to crowd roots into narrow, carelessly dug holes and to space the shrubs too far apart. It is usually best to dig out a trench 15 to 18 in. wide and 9 to 12 in. deep along the whole length of the proposed hedge site. Then the plants can be properly spaced 9 to 12 in. apart for privet and quick; 12 to 15 in. for *Lonicera nitida*, beech, hornbeam and cherry plum; 15 to 18 in. for yew and holly, and 2 to 2½ ft. for cupressus and thuya. Moreover there will be plenty of room to spread the roots properly and cover the uppermost with 2 or 3 in. of soil. Make this really firm around and over the roots and, if possible, stake the newly planted shrubs or tie them to horizontally trained wires to that they may not be disturbed by wind.

SUBSEQUENT CARE. Hedges are usually grossly neglected after planting, except for pruning or clipping. They are seldom fed yet they need this almost more than most other shrubs because of the keen competition between their rather closely placed roots. It is wise to give the hedge an annual spring mulch of rotted dung, vegetable compost or hop manure and this may be supplemented occasionally by a 'complete' artificial containing nitrogen, phosphorus and potash. Pruning should be done as described on p. 250.

TREES AND SHRUBS ALPHABETICALLY ARRANGED

ABELIA. These are not very brilliant or showy shrubs and on that account will probably never be very popular with the multitude but the best species such as *A. grandiflora* and *A. Schumanii* are graceful and refined and will always appeal to connoisseurs. The first is evergreen with small white flowers from July to October, the second deciduous with pale pink flowers from about June to October. Both are about 5 ft. high and as much through. *A. Schumanii* is just a little tender so should be given a rather sheltered position at any rate in cold districts. Ordinary soils and no pruning. Propagate both kinds by cuttings in July–August under a bell glass in the greenhouse.

ABUTILON. Most of these I have dealt with under Greenhouse Plants (see p. 433) but one kind, *A. vitifolium*, is a beautiful, hardy, deciduous shrub for a sunny sheltered position outdoors. It has an open habit, will grow 12 ft. high and 10 ft. through, but is often less, and has soft, grey-green leaves and pale lavender, mallow-flowers in June and July. It likes well-drained soil and needs no pruning as a rule though overgrown branches can be shortened in March. Propagate by seed sown in a greenhouse in spring or by cuttings under a bell glass in the greenhouse in summer.

ACER (*Maple*). The maples are deciduous trees many of great size though the numerous forms of the 'Japanese' maples, *A. japonicum* and *A. palmatum*, are seldom above 12 ft. in height and are often almost shrub-like. The common sycamore is an acer, its botanical name being *A. pseudo-platanus*, and it has several garden varieties with coloured leaves such as *brilliantissimum*, young leaves pink; *Leopoldii*, leaves blotched with salmon and pink, and *purpureum*, leaves reddish purple. *A. platanoides*, the Norway maple, is a similar tree of large size with several coloured leaved forms. The true sugar maple, *A. saccharum*, does not grow very well in this country. *A. Negundo* is a tree of medium size with bright green stems and leaves. It is chiefly represented in gardens by a form, *variegatum*, in which the leaves are blotched with white. Yet another group of acers has the additional attraction of bark which is handsomely marked. Notable amongst these is *A. griseum* with bark which peels like that of a plane tree revealing a highly polished bronzy surface beneath. It is a tree of medium size. The Japanese maples all have brightly-coloured leaves, often deeply and repeatedly divided.

All the acer species should be raised from seed while the garden forms must be increased by grafting or budding on to seedlings of the same species. They thrive in ordinary soils and, for the most part, open positions but the Japanese varieties, being less hardy, should be given a sunny and sheltered spot.

AEGLE (*Hardy Orange*). *Aegle sepiaria* is an evergreen flowering shrub (in some cases almost a small tree) with angular, heavily-spined branches and a dense, bushy habit which would make it a good subject for an impenetrable hedge were it a little easier to buy. As it is one seldom sees more than an isolated bush or two in the garden of some connoisseur by whom it is valued for its unusual appearance, abundant white flowers in May and occasional crops of small, orange-like fruits. It likes a warm, sunny position and well-drained soil. Propagate by cuttings of firm young shoots in a warm propagating frame in July–August. This plant is correctly *Poncirus trifoliata*.

AESCULUS (*Horse Chestnut*). Trees for the most part of large size—too large, in fact, for many modern gardens, though they are very beautiful for planting in open, spacious places. The showy spikes of white flowers of the common horse chestnut, produced in late spring, are too well known to need description. Besides this species known as *A. Hippocastanum*, there is the so-called red Horse Chestnut, *A. carnea*, which is a rather smaller tree with deep rose flowers, and several other less well-known kinds of which one of the best is *A. parviflora*. This is not much more than a large shrub 10 ft. high and 12 ft. through with white flower spikes in July and August. All can be raised from the seeds or 'conkers'. They are not fussy about soil or position and need no regular pruning.

AILANTHUS (*Tree of Heaven*). Only one species is commonly planted, and this is *Ailanthus glandulosa*, a tree of considerable size with large, divided leaves like those of an ash but at least twice as big. This makes a handsome specimen with an ultimate height and spread of something like 60 and 40 ft. respectively. It will grow in ordinary soil. Pruning is not in the least essential but, if desired, branches can be cut back each February fairly severely, the result being a considerable loss in beauty of habit but a gain in the size of individual leaves. Increase by digging up rooted suckers in autumn or by inserting in February in a frame filled with sandy soil, cuttings made from short pieces of root.

ALNUS (*Alder*). The alders are deciduous trees of medium size most of which thrive in damp places but are not of the first merit for garden planting. *Alnus glutinosa*, the common British alder, is worth planting in wild boggy places and near streams for its long, dull purple catkins in late winter. A better tree is *A. incana* with similar catkins and leaves which are grey beneath. Both can be increased by seed sown outdoors in March or by cuttings of current year's wood inserted outdoors in moist soil in autumn.

ALEXANDRIAN LAUREL.—*See* DANAË (p. 275).

AMELANCHIER (*Snowy Mespilus*). The amelanchiers are all very beautiful deciduous trees of small to medium size and with very abundant white flowers in April and early May. They might well be planted more freely in gardens as they will grow in any ordinary soil and are a pleasant change from more hackneyed kinds. The best are *A. canadensis*, about 25 ft. high and as much through, with leaves which are bronze when young; and *A. vulgaris* which is smaller, sometimes shrubby rather than tree-like, with leaves which are distinctly white when young. Neither requires pruning. Both can be increased by layers, rooted suckers removed in autumn, or seeds sown in a frame in spring. Seeds, however, sometimes take a year or more to germinate.

ANDROMEDA (*Bog Rosemary*). Many of the shrubs which were once known by this name have been transferred to other genera such as Pieris and Zenobia under which names they should be sought. The sole garden survivor is *A. polifolia*, a pretty, dwarf evergreen with pale pink, heather-like flowers in May. It likes a moist, peaty soil devoid of lime. No pruning is desirable. Seeds can be germinated in sandy peat in greenhouse or frame in spring or by cuttings prepared in August from the tips of branches and rooted in similar compost under a bell glass.

ARBUTUS (*Strawberry Tree*). The true strawberry tree is *Arbutus Unedo* and it gets its popular name from the red, rather vaguely strawberry-like fruits which hang on the tree all summer and only colour up in the autumn, at which season the small white or pale pink, bell-shaped flowers also open. It has evergreen, laurel-like leaves and makes a big, freely-branched shrub or small tree anything from 12 to 24 ft. high and at least as much through. It will thrive in most soils though it has a preference for peaty ones. This feature is even more marked in some of the other species such as *A. Menziesii*. This is less beautiful in flower and fruit but has notably handsome, evergreen leaves and reddish bark which peels like that of a plane tree. All kinds can be increased by seeds in spring or by layering in spring or autumn.

ARTEMISIA (*Wormwood, Southernwood*). Many of the artemisias are plants for the herbaceous border or rock garden (see pp. 143, 193) but one, *A. Abrotanum*, is a shrub with a height and spread of about 3 ft. and finely divided, grey leaves which are strongly aromatic when bruised. It likes a warm, sunny place and well-drained soil and can be increased by cuttings struck in sandy soil under a bell glass in August or September.

ARUNDINARIA.—*See* BAMBOO (p. 260).

ASH.—*See* FRAXINUS (p. 281).

ATRIPLEX. The only species planted is *Atriplex Halimus*, a rather loose untidy shrub 7 or 8 ft. high and at least as much through with silver-grey, evergreen leaves. It is specially useful for planting near the sea as it will withstand salt spray and thrive in the sandiest and poorest of soils. It is frequently used as a windbreak to seaside gardens. Inland it is occasionally injured by frost. Increase is by cuttings of firm young growth inserted in a frame or under a bell glass in late summer or early autumn. It can be pruned in May as much as is necessary to maintain shape.

AUCUBA. *A. japonica* was once a favourite evergreen shrub for hedge making. It is far less popular now, no doubt because of the room it takes up, for it is a big, freely-branched bush up to 10 ft. high and through, though capable of being restricted to half those dimensions. It has big, glossy, evergreen leaves, plain green in one type but more commonly heavily spotted and blotched with pale yellow (hence the name 'Spotted laurel' sometimes applied). There are two sexes and if both are planted the female bushes will produce showy scarlet berries in autumn. Aucubas will grow in any soil, and sunny or shady position. They are a little liable to be damaged by hard spring frosts and cold winds but otherwise are quite hardy. Propagation is usually by cuttings of firm young shoots inserted in a frame in September or October.

AZALEA. Strictly speaking the shrubs known in gardens as azaleas are rhododendrons but to simplify matters for the ordinary reader I have retained the common name. The family is a big and varied one, including evergreen as well as deciduous species. Almost all are very showy, with bold trusses of brightly-coloured flowers in late spring. All like peaty, lime-free soils and do best in partially shaded positions though they can also be grown successfully in full sun.

Most popular are the innumerable hybrids usually grouped under the names *mollis* and *sinensis*. These vary from 4 to 8 ft. in height, are as much or a little more through and deciduous. They have specially fine clusters of large flowers in many shades of pink, salmon, orange and red. Closely allied to these are the Ghent hybrids and the 'rustica flore pleno' varieties, the first with clusters of very fragrant tubular, single flowers and the second with similar but double flowers in a variety of colours.

Then there are the dwarf hybrids, often known as Kurume azaleas, with little rounded, evergreen leaves and clusters of small pink, rose or scarlet flowers, the whole bush being little over a foot high and perhaps 2 or 3 ft. through. *Hinomayo*, salmon-pink and *Hinodegiri*, bright scarlet are well-known varieties of this type. These and others of the same class are often planted in the rock gardens. Very similar are *A. amoena* and its varieties, all low growing, very spreading and with masses of vivid magenta or crimson flowers of small size.

All azaleas can be increased by layering in peaty soil in spring or autumn. None requires any regular pruning. The deciduous kinds should be planted in autumn, the evergreens in spring. The dwarf kinds can often be obtained in pots, which makes transplanting a particularly easy task as root disturbance can be kept to a minimum.

BAMBOO. The plants familiarly known as bamboos in gardens belong to several different families of which the two most important are arundinaria and phyllostachys. The commonest is *Arundinaria japonica*, frequently wrongly named *Bambusa Metake*. It is an excellent plant, vigorous, hardy and thriving in any fairly rich and not too dry soil. It will soon attain a height of 10 or 12 ft. and, like others of its kind, will spread into a very large clump by means of underground stems. Even bigger is *A. fastuosa* which, under favourable conditions, may attain a height of 25 ft. For the smaller garden *A. nitida* is preferable. This averages 8 ft. in height and has slender, arching canes and comparatively small leaves. Of the second genus two of the best are *Phyllostachys flexuosa*, moderate in growth and graceful in habit and *P. nigra* in which the young canes are almost black.

All these bamboos, including those varieties described as quite hardy, appreciate some shelter from cold winds which are apt to disfigure their foliage. They will thrive in sun or shade and prefer fairly moist soils.

All can be increased by careful division in April–May which is also the best planting time.

BAMBUSA.—*See* BAMBOO (p. 260).

BAY.—*See* LAURUS (p. 290).

BERBERIS (*Barberry*). This is a very big and also a very important family of shrubs. It includes both evergreen and deciduous kinds some of which are grown mainly for their flowers, others for their berries and yet others for foliage. All will grow in a wide range of soils. The evergreens with big, divided leaves, of which *B. aquifolium* may be taken as the type, are often considered as a separate genus under the name Mahonia. They are, in general, a little less hardy than the small-leaved evergreen and deciduous types and succeed best in sheltered or even partially shaded positions, whereas the others prefer open, sunny places.

All barberries can be raised from seeds sown in a frame or sheltered place outdoors in spring but it takes some years to obtain flowering bushes in this way. Some of the big-leaved evergreens make several shoots direct from the roots and can be carefully divided in spring or autumn. More commonly cuttings of firm young shoots must be inserted in sandy soil under a bell glass, in July–August for the deciduous kinds, August–September for the evergreens. Seeds of most kinds germinate readily in a frame in March but will take a few years to grow into sizeable bushes.

Species and varieties are very numerous. Here are a few of the best.

A. Deciduous kinds with scarlet or coral berries in autumn: *Berberis aggregata* 4 to 5 ft.; *polyantha*, 7 to 8 ft.; *Thunbergii*, 5 to 6 ft. (with beautiful scarlet and orange autumn foliage tints as an additional attraction); *Thunbergii atropurpurea* (similar in every respect except that the leaves are purple from the outset); *vulgaris*, 8 to 10 ft., and *Wilsonae*, 3 to 4 ft.

B. Evergreen kinds with small to medium leaves and yellow or orange flowers in May–June: *buxifolia*, 6 to 8 ft. (deciduous in a hard winter); *Darwinii*, 8 to 10 ft., a grand shrub and excellent for hedge making as well as for border planting; *Gagnepainii*, 5 to 6 ft.; *pruinosa*, 5 to 6 ft., berries heavily covered with a whitish bloom; *Sargentiana*, 6 to 7 ft., very long, sharp thorns; *stenophylla*, 8 to 10 ft., useful for the same purposes as *Darwinii*, and *verruculosa*, like a small edition of *Darwinii* not above 5 ft. in height.

C. Evergreen kinds with big divided leaves and clusters of yellow flowers in winter or early spring: *Aquifolium*, 3 to 4 ft.; *japonica*, 6 to 8 ft.

with very large flowers carried on long slender spikes radiating like the spokes of a cartwheel, and *Bealei*, like the last but still finer in bloom.

BETULA (*Birch*). The graceful silver birch, *Betula verrucosa*, needs no introduction. It is one of the few forest trees which may be admitted to the ordinary garden. Other good kinds are the Paper Birch, *B. papyrifera*, which has a stouter and even whiter trunk than the silver birch, and *B. nigra*, with rough, blackish bark in marked contrast to the others. Both these are rather too big for many gardens, often attaining a height of 40 ft. All are deciduous, will grow in ordinary soils and situations, need no pruning and can be increased by seed sown outdoors in March or as soon as ripe.

BIRCH.—*See* BETULA above.

BOX.—*See* BUXUS below.

BROOM.—*See* CYTISUS (p. 274) and GENISTA (p. 282).

BUDDLEIA. *Buddleia variabilis* is a popular deciduous shrub 10 or 12 ft. high and as much through, producing from July to September long, tapering spikes of pale purple, fragrant flowers which are a great attraction to butterflies. It has several fine varieties, notably *magnifica*, deep purple, and *Veitchiana*, pale purple but extra large. All are very easily grown in any ordinary soil and sunny place, but cold spots and frost pockets should be avoided as the young shoots are a little tender. Very severe pruning can be carried out each March if desired, even to within a foot of soil level, and the result will be the production of fewer but larger flower spikes.

B. alternifolia is similar in height and spread but lighter and more arching in habit with the small purple flowers produced in June in little clusters all along the stems instead of being gathered into big spikes. No pruning is required.

B. globosa is semi-evergreen 12 to 15 ft. high, scarcely as much through, with, in June, small orange flowers gathered into compact balls each about an inch in diameter. Like *B. variabilis* its young growth is rather tender.

All can be increased by cuttings of firm shoots taken in October and rooted in a frame or sheltered place outdoors.

BUXUS (*Box*). The familiar British box, with its densely-branched habit and multitude of little, rounded leaves is one of the best hardy evergreens for clipping. It has been a favourite with gardeners for centuries for making complicated topiary specimens representing peacocks, bears and many other fantastic shapes. It is less popular for hedge making but a form of it which keeps dwarf is used for edgings in many gardens and can be clipped to a height and breadth of a few inches. All kinds will grow in ordinary soils in sun or shade.

The common box is increased by cuttings of firm shoots 4 to 6 in. long inserted in sandy soil outdoors or in a frame in autumn. The edging box can be divided in March or April and the divisions should be re-planted a few inches apart to form a continuous line. Clipping of all kinds can be continued from May to September but any hard cutting should be done at the beginning of this period.

CALLUNA (*Heather or Ling*). It must be a little disconcerting to the beginner to discover that, though the common heather which covers so much of the English and Scottish countryside is botanically calluna, all other heathers despite their obvious similarities belong to quite a different genus with the name erica. However, there it is and one must make the best of it. *C. vulgaris* is the solitary representative of its family and is a dwarf, evergreen shrub so familiar that it needs no description. There are, however, numerous forms of it, some with white flowers, others crimson; one with golden instead of green foliage; by contrast one with silvery leaves, a fifth which has double flowers, a sixth that is extremely dwarf, and so on to fill quite a long list. All grow in poor, peaty soils, show a marked dislike for lime, and flower in August and September. All can be increased by cuttings of short, non-flowering shoots taken in July and rooted in sandy peat under a bell glass. An easier method for beginners is to cut back the old plant fairly severely in spring, mound it up with sandy peat and leave it to form its new shoots in this soil. It can then be lifted and carefully divided the following October or March which, incidentally, are the best planting months.

CAMELLIA. The common camellia is frequently regarded as a greenhouse plant and does in fact succeed well in a cool greenhouse (see p. 447). Nevertheless it is also sufficiently hardy to be grown outdoors in many parts of the country including the London area. It should have a sheltered or even partly shaded position in ordinary, loamy soil and requires no special treatment and no pruning. It will make a shapely evergreen shrub or small tree up to 30 ft. high, though plants 12 ft. high and as much through are more common. Flowers, which may be single or double, pink, red or white, are produced in April and May.

Increase by cuttings of firm, young shoots rooted in sandy soil in a propagating box within the greenhouse in early summer.

CAMPSIS.—*See* TECOMA (p. 317).

CARPINUS (*Hornbeam*). The chief garden value of the hornbeam, *Carpinus Betulus*, is as a hedge shrub for which purpose it rivals, and closely resembles, beech. Though deciduous it will, like the beech, retain its brown autumn foliage throughout the winter when clipped to form a hedge. It has the merit of thriving in practically all soils, even those that are comparatively poor, and of standing any amount of wind. In fact it is an ideal plant with which to form an outer windbreak to the exposed garden. For this purpose plant young hornbeams 1 ft. apart in autumn or late winter and prune them each February to make a narrow hedge. In addition to winter pruning the hedge can be clipped occasionally, but not too severely, in summer. Planted as an individual specimen, the hornbeam makes a big, rounded tree 50 ft. or more in height and with corresponding branch spread. It is raised from seeds sown outdoors in spring.

CARYOPTERIS. Several species are widely grown in the milder parts of the country and are attractive, deciduous shrubs 3 to 5 ft. in height. They make numerous, rather soft stems, with small leaves closely covered with hairs but their great value is that they carry their spikes of bright blue flowers in September and even October, when colour is scarce in the shrub border. The best kinds are *C. Mastacanthus, C. tangutica* and *C. clandonensis*; the last a hybrid of exceptional beauty. Some are inclined to be killed back by frost each winter with the result that they never make more than small shrubs, but *C. clandonensis* usually behaves in a thoroughly reliable manner. The only pruning necessary is to remove dead or damaged wood in April. Cuttings of firm, young growth root readily in a greenhouse propagating frame in summer.

CASTANEA (*Chestnut*). The castaneas are the true chestnuts in contrast to Aesculus, the horse chestnuts. The best as an ornamental tree is undoubtedly the Sweet Chestnut, *C. sativa*. This is very big, sometimes 100 ft. high and with branches spreading 50 or 60 ft. It has big, shining, deciduous leaves, small white flowers in long 'rats' tails' in June, followed by the familiar nuts, each in a large, spiky, green 'case'. Incidentally, the bark of this tree, with spiral furrows on old specimens, is notably handsome.

The sweet chestnut thrives in ordinary soils and will survive in many that are too dry and sandy for most other trees. It grows quickly from seed, which can be sown outdoors in spring. No pruning is required.

CATALPA (*Indian Bean*). *C. bignonioides* deserves to be better known for it is a quick-growing tree with very handsome foliage and, under

264

favourable conditions, showy spikes of white, purple-spotted flowers which are a little like those of the horse chestnut. These appear in August. The Indian bean will usually thrive well in town gardens and there are good specimens in most of the London parks. It makes a tree 30 to 40 ft. high and rather more through. Pruning is not essential but, if desired, branches can be cut hard back each March with the result that a much smaller tree is maintained but the individual leaves are considerably bigger. They are rounded, pale green and up to 1 ft. in diameter. The two drawbacks are that it comes into leaf rather late, often not until the end of May, and the young shoots are occasionally injured by late frosts. For the latter reason it should not be planted in frost pockets. It can be increased by seeds sown in a warm greenhouse in spring or by cuttings of firm young shoots in July in a greenhouse propagating box.

CEANOTHUS. There are both evergreen and deciduous species of ceanothus and while most of the former flower in May and early June, the latter bloom towards the end of the summer. Many of the evergreen kinds are a little tender, needing the protection of a sunny wall in most parts of the country. The hardiest is *C. thyrsiflorus*, with thimble-like clusters of pale blue flowers. In the open it will make a shrub 15 ft. high and almost as much through, but it is more commonly seen as a wall-trained tree, in which position it is very beautiful. Even better is *C. rigidus*, with brighter blue flower clusters, but this is considerably less hardy and really does need a sheltered position. *C. Veitchianus*, which is probably a hybrid between the last two, is intermediate between them both in brightness of colour and in hardiness.

Of the deciduous kinds the most important are the hybrids from *C. azureus* which have fancy names such as Gloire de Versailles (bright blue), Indigo (deep blue) and Perle Rose (pink). The flowers are individually small but produced in rather big, loose clusters.

All will grow in ordinary well-drained soils and sunny positions. The evergreens need no regular pruning unless grown against walls, when side growths should be shortened to a few inches immediately after flowering. The deciduous kinds can, if desired, be pruned hard back each March like *Buddleia variabilis* (see p. 262), when they will make fewer stems but with bigger flower trusses. Alternatively they can be left unpruned in which case they will form loose specimens 7 to 10 ft. high and as much through. Propagation of all kinds is by cuttings of firm, young growths rooted during July and August in sand in a propagating box within the greenhouse, preferably with gentle bottom heat.

CEDAR.—*See* CEDRUS below.

CEDRUS (*Cedar*). All the cedars are evergreen, cone-bearing trees of the largest size and consequently quite unsuitable for small gardens, though they are admirable where there is space for specimens 80 to 100 ft. high with branches spreading 40 or 50 ft. in all directions. There are three valuable species, *C. libani*, the famous cedar of Lebanon, distinguished by a flat-topped habit with horizontally held branches; *C. atlantica*, the Mount Atlas cedar, which is more conical when young though it becomes flat-topped with age, and *C. Deodara*, the deodar of the Himalayas which has a slightly weeping habit when young. This last is the least hardy of the three but is very beautiful. The Mt. Atlas cedar has a particularly attractive form named *glauca*, in which the young leaves are blue-grey.

All should be grown in good, loamy soils with first class drainage. Some protection, such as that afforded by neighbouring trees, is advisable when young but later these should be removed so that the cedars can stand alone. No pruning should be attempted at any time. Increase is by seeds sown in a frame in spring, but propagation of cedars is hardly a task for amateurs.

CELASTRUS. *C. articulatus* is a very vigorous deciduous climber with insignificant, greenish flowers followed by striking golden and scarlet 'berries' in the autumn. This deserves to be better known for it is easily grown in ordinary soil and sunny position and is one of the brightest climbers in the autumn and early winter. It can be used to cover a shed or outhouse or allowed to ramble up into the branches of a dead tree. No pruning is necessary. Increase is readily effected by layering in autumn.

CERCIS. *C. Siliquastrum* is well known as the Judas tree, the legend being that it was on this tree that Judas hanged himself. It is a beautiful deciduous tree of freely branching habit, about 20 ft. high and as much through, with elegant, rounded leaves and clusters of magenta, pea-type flowers in May. It likes a warm, sheltered, sunny position and ordinary, well-drained soil. No pruning is required. Propagation is by seeds sown in a slightly heated greenhouse or frame in spring. The Judas tree transplants badly when old so it is advisable to start with quite small specimens, preferably tapped out of pots. These should be planted in May.

CHERRIES.—*See* PRUNUS (p. 301).

CHESTNUT.—*See* AESCULUS (p. 257) *and* CASTANEA (p. 264).

CHIMONANTHUS (*Winter Sweet*). *C. fragrans* flowers in mid-winter but nevertheless one might easily pass it by were it not for its exquisite fragrance, for the flowers are a very pale yellowish green with petals so thin that one can almost see through them. However, this deciduous shrub is well worth growing for its perfume alone. It is quite hardy but should have a sunny, sheltered position to protect its blossoms. Grow it in any ordinary soil and if it is trained against a wall (which is a popular method) shorten the side growths and remove any weak shoots in spring as soon as flowering is over. Propagate by layers in autumn. Full grown specimens are 8 or 9 ft. high and about the same in spread.

CHOISYA. The only species grown is *C. ternata*, a very beautiful evergreen shrub with white, fragrant flowers not unlike orange blossom. This choisya makes a dense, rounded specimen 5 or 6 ft. high and rather more through. It is at its best in May but will sometimes flower spamodically all the summer. It should be given a fairly sheltered, sunny position in good, well-drained soil. No pruning is required. Cuttings of firm root in an unheated frame in early autumn.

CISTUS (*Rock Rose*). All rock roses are evergreen shrubs, most of them of medium or small size, with compact habit and great freedom in flowering. They have, in fact, all the qualities required for the small garden with the one exception of hardiness. Few will survive really hard winters in the North and East, though many are satisfactory in the South and West. Amongst the hardiest are *C. laurifolius*, 5 to 6 ft. high, rather more through, with white flowers; *C. cyprius*, similar in habit with white flowers each with a central blotch of blood red; Silver Pink, a delightful hybrid no more than 3 ft. high, with rose pink flowers and *C. ladaniferus*, with very dark green, sticky leaves and white, red-blotched flowers. In some ways the most beautiful of all is *C. purpureus*, with bright rose, red-blotched flowers 3 in. in diameter. Unfortunately it needs a distinctly sheltered position.

All bloom in early summer and succeed in ordinary soils with preference to those that are well-drained even to the point of dryness. They are unsurpassed for dry, sunny banks and usually succeed particularly well near the sea. No pruning is needed. All can be raised from cuttings of firm young shoots struck in late summer under a bell glass or in a propagating box within a greenhouse.

CLEMATIS. This is an immense genus of plants, mostly climbers though a few are herbaceous (see p. 150). A great number of hybrids and garden forms have been raised, often with very large flowers in bright and

varied colours produced over a long period. Typical examples are
C. Jackmanii superba, with rich purple flowers in early summer;
Nelly Moser, with mauve flowers each with a band of red down
the centre of the petal, blooming in late summer; Comtesse de
Bouchaud, with double pink flowers in mid-summer, and *C. Henryi*,
with huge white flowers in late summer. Equally attractive, though
rather less popular, are the small-flowering kinds such as *C. montana*,
with innumerable white flowers in May and early June; its pale pink
form *rubens*, and the late-flowering *C. flammula*, with masses of tiny,
white, fragrant flowers. One of the first to flower is *C. Armandii*,
which, unlike most of the others, is evergreen. The white flowers are
of medium size and produced in April, but the plant is a little tender
and prefers a wall facing south or west. There are a great many other
beautiful species and varieties to be found fully described in the
catalogues of nurserymen.

All clematises thrive in chalky soils but will grow in ordinary soils
provided they are moderately well drained without being really dry.
They like best to have their roots in the shade and their leaves and
flowers in the sun, opposites which can be reconciled by planting in a
sunny place but near an evergreen shrub which will throw shade over
the base of the plant. The growths are very slender and brittle and
should be given good support into which to ramble, for example the
trunk of a dead tree or a well-made trellis.

Regular pruning is not essential but flowers of extra size can be
obtained in some varieties, notably those of the *C. Jackmanii* type,
by cutting fairly hard back every February. In other cases thinning and
shortening sufficient to keep the plants within bounds can be carried
out without harm, in late winter in the case of summer flowering kinds,
or immediately after flowering in the case of those varieties which
finish blooming by early June.

Nurserymen frequently propagate clematises by grafting in the
greenhouse in the spring, using seedlings of the wild British clematis as
stocks. This is an unsatisfactory method and if plants of this type are
purchased they should be planted rather deeply so that the point of
union is buried an inch or so below the surface enabling the scion to
make roots of its own. The amateur should increase his plants by
layering vigorous young shoots in autumn or spring.

CLERODENDRUM. The value of the hardy clerodendrums (there are also
tender kinds described on p. 453) is that they flower very late in the
summer. Their drawback is that most have foliage that is distinctly
unpleasant in odour when bruised. The best is *C. trichotomum*, almost

a tree in habit, 10 ft. or more high, as much through, loosely branched, deciduous and with numerous white flowers in August and September. It will grow in any ordinary soil and is moderately hardy but prefers a sheltered position. *C. Fargesii* is rather similar. No pruning is needed in either case. The simplest method of increase is by removing rooted suckers in the autumn.

COLLETIA. There is a species which was known as *C. horrida* and it is a pity that the name has been changed to *C. infausta*, for 'horrid' is a fine description of the immense, green spines produced all over the plant and serving it instead of leaves. This, and its relation *C. cruciata*, with flattish, triangular spines, equally injuring to the flesh, are oddities worth growing for the questions they arouse and also for the numerous white, bell-like flowers produced along the spines in autumn. They will grow in any well-drained soil and sunny, sheltered position, will eventually reach a height of 7 or 8 ft. and can be raised from short cuttings struck in a frame in autumn.

COLUTEA (*Bladder Senna*). These are showy, deciduous shrubs with clusters of small, pea-type flowers followed by inflated seed vessels which look like small bladders. They have the merit of thriving in poor, stony soils and hot, dry places and are amongst the easiest of shrubs to grow. One of the showiest is *C. arborescens*. This may eventually grow 10 ft. high and 7 or 8 ft. through, but can be kept considerably smaller by judicious thinning out each February. The flowers are yellow and continue throughout the summer.

Increase by seeds sown in a frame in March or by cuttings of firm, young growth taken in July and rooted in a propagating frame with gentle bottom heat.

CONVOLVULUS. The only truly shrubby species is *C. Cneorum*, a delightful plant a couple of feet high and through, very branching, with silvery leaves and blush-white flowers throughout most of the summer. It is none too hardy and should have a light, well-drained soil and sunny, sheltered position. Increase it by cuttings treated like those of colutea (see above). This is a good dwarf shrub for the rock garden.

CORNUS. From the gardener's standpoint this family splits up into three distinct groups, one composed of those species grown mainly for the beauty of their bark in winter, another of those grown principally for the foliage effects and a third consisting of those cultivated for their flowers, though in the last it is often the bracts surrounding the flowers rather than the flowers themselves that make the real show.

Taking these in order, the best of the bark species is *C. alba.* This is deciduous, grows 6 to 8 ft. high, makes numerous strong shoots from the base, and is seen to best advantage if hard pruned each spring. The bark is red and most highly coloured on year-old wood. This easily-grown shrub delights in moist places and is an ideal plant for the stream or lake side.

Of the foliage varieties, *C. sanguinea,* the common dogwood, is sometimes worth a place for its fine autumn colour but the best is really a variety of *C. alba* named *Spæthii,* which has leaves heavily variegated with yellow. It is a very bright shrub, well worth including in every shrub border, and one which will grow in ordinary or moist soils. It need not be pruned if a large specimen is required.

Of the species grown for genuine flowers, *C. mas* is, perhaps, the best. It is a small, deciduous tree 15 or 20 ft. high and as much through, branching freely and with numerous small yellow flowers produced in February and March on the bare branches. They are followed by bright orange fruits, hence the popular name, 'Cornelian cherry'. By contrast a very typical example of the type grown for the bracts surrounding the flowers is *C. Kousa.* This is a small tree, about the size of *C. mas,* with inconspicuous clusters of flowers, each surrounded by four large, creamy-white bracts which look like petals. They are at their best in May and June. Rather similar are *C. florida,* also with white bracts and *C. Nuttallii,* in which the bracts are at first cream but later become pink. All these flowering kinds need good loamy soils and rather sheltered positions.

C. alba and *C. sanguinea* can be increased very easily by cuttings of well-ripened wood taken in October and November and rooted outdoors in ordinary soil. Other kinds should be layered in the autumn or raised from seed sown in a frame or unheated greenhouse in March.

CORYLOPSIS. These are not very brilliant shrubs but they have the merit of flowering early. *C. spicata,* the species most usually seen, is generally in bloom by the end of March, while *C. pauciflora* may even be a week or so earlier. Both have little hanging tassels of pale yellow flowers along the length of the previous year's growth. They are deciduous shrubs 4 to 6 ft. high and more through, thriving in ordinary soils and sheltered positions. No pruning is required. They can be increased by cuttings of well-ripened growth in autumn, rooted under a hand light in a frame.

CORYLUS (*Hazel, Filbert*). Though the common hazel is not a shrub for the ornamental garden it has several forms which are worth planting both for their foliage and catkins. The handsomest of these is *C.*

maxima atropurpurea, with deep purple foliage. Left to itself it will make a dense shrub 12 to 15 ft. high and as much in diameter but it can be kept a good deal smaller by pruning each spring immediately the catkins fade. It will grow in any ordinary soil and sunny or shady position and can be increased by layering in autumn or removal of rooted suckers at the same time.

COTONEASTER. There are a great many cotoneasters and almost all are useful shrubs or trees for the garden. There are both deciduous and evergreen kinds and they range in stature from the absolutely prostrate *C. humifusa* to the 25 ft. high *C. frigida.* Most are grown principally for their scarlet or crimson berries which make a fine display in the autumn but some are also very attractive in flower and almost all have good foliage. All will grow in ordinary soils and sunny or, in many cases, slightly shaded positions. A few make fairly good hedge shrubs and some are first class for the rock garden. All can be increased by seed sown in a frame or even outdoors in a sheltered position in March but some varieties do not breed entirely true from seed. This is particularly true of some of the dwarf forms of larger species.

Here are a few of the best roughly in order of size, the largest first: *C. frigida,* deciduous, 15 to 25 ft. high and a little less through, with flattish clusters of white flowers followed by scarlet berries; *C. Henryana,* 12 ft. high and through with narrow, evergreen leaves, white flowers and deep crimson berries; *C. buxifolia,* evergreen, 10 ft. high and through with small clusters of white flowers followed by red berries; *C. Franchetii,* 8 ft. high and rather more through, with narrow, evergreen leaves and good clusters of whitish flowers followed by vivid scarlet berries; *C. Simonsii,* 8 to 10 ft. high, 6 to 7 ft. through, partially evergreen with neat, box-like leaves, small white flowers and scarlet berries (this is a good kind for hedge making, either alone or mixed with privet, hawthorn, etc.); *C. Dielsiana,* 8 ft. high and through with small clusters of whitish flowers and scarlet berries; *C. microphylla,* with narrow, dark green, evergreen leaves and making a stiff, densely-branched bush 3 ft. high and 4 or 5 ft. through or, against a wall, climbing to a height of 8 or 10 ft., with solitary white flowers followed by deep red fruits; *C. horizontalis,* which is so called because its branches are spread out flat in herring-bone fashion enabling it to spread widely over the ground or climb against a wall, in either of which positions it will display its deciduous, box-like leaves, solitary, pinkish flowers and red berries; *C. adpressa,* like a miniature version of the last named, no more than 1 ft. high, though often 4 or 5 ft. in diameter; *C. thymaefolia,* which is really a dwarf form of *C. microphylla,* similar in habit but practically prostrate, and *C. humifusa*, which will mould itself to every contour of rock and soil and produce abundant coral red berries in autumn.

CRATAEGUS (*Thorn*). The common hawthorn or quick is a species of crataegus or, to be exact, two species for botanists distinguish between *C. monogyna* and *C. Oxyacantha* though to the layman both are equally hawthorns. The best thorns for garden display are the double-flowered varieties of *C. Oxyacantha*, known usually as Double Scarlet and Double Pink, according to the colour of their flowers. There is also a double white form, less frequently seen. These all make densely-branched trees up to 20 ft. in height with corresponding branch spread, but the common species can be planted close together and pruned hard to form hedges and are still favourites with farmers for this purpose. For hedgemaking seedlings should be planted not more than 1 ft. apart and preferably 9 in.

Other ornamental kinds are the Glastonbury thorn, a variety of *Crataegus monogyna*, which opens its white flowers in winter or at latest by early April; the scarlet haw, *C. coccinea*, rather like the hawthorn in habit and with similar clusters of white flowers in May but followed by very big red berries, and the cockspur thorn, *C. Crus-galli*, a small tree with white flowers, large red berries and enormous thorns. All these will grow in ordinary soils and open positions and are amongst the hardiest of ornamental trees. No pruning is required, though badly placed or overcrowded branches can be removed in winter.

Propagation is in most cases effected by seed sown 1 in. deep outdoors in March, but double-flowered thorns must be grafted in spring or budded in summer on to seedlings of the common hawthorn.

CRYPTOMERIA. *C. japonica* is one of the most beautiful of evergreen, cone-bearing trees but unfortunately it is just a little tender in its young state. The foliage is feathery and the tree makes a particularly compact, cone-shaped specimen up to 70 ft. in height though as a rule it is rather smaller. Even more graceful is the form known as *elegans*, in which the effect is even finer and softer. These trees succeed best in deep, rather rich soils with plenty of moisture during the spring and summer. No pruning is required. Propagation is by seeds sown in a frame in March.

CUPRESSUS (*Cypress*). This is another genus of evergreen, cone-bearing trees, this time a very big one containing a large number of species and even more varieties some of which are amongst the most useful of their kind in gardens. One species alone, *C. Lawsoniana*, has provided a whole string of excellent varieties, some, such as *Stewartii*, with golden leaves, others, such as *erecta viridis*, very upright in habit, emerald green in colour, others with blue-green foliage (*Allumii*, Triomphe de Boskoop and *Fletcheri*). Many of these are fast-growing trees eventually 60 ft. or more high and 20 ft. through but there are also very dwarf forms which can be grown in the rock garden, such as *nana*, while *Fletcheri* seldom exceeds 6 ft. and *Allumii* and *erecta viridis* stop at about 30 ft. The common types make excellent hedges or windbreaks as they are quick growing, hardy and not particular about soil or situation.

Another cypress which is much used for hedge planting is *C. macrocarpa*. This is more graceful in appearance than *C. Lawsoniana* but less hardy and particularly liable to be damaged by cold winds in spring. Moreover it has not a very good root hold and may be blown out in wind-swept localities. It is even quicker growing than *C. Lawsoniana* but transplants so badly when old that young plants should always be purchased, in pots if possible as they can be moved from these with the least possible injury to the roots.

A third species which is gaining in popularity as it has the elegance of *C. macrocarpa* combined with some of the hardiness of *Lawsoniana*, is *C. arizonica conica*. This has blue-green foliage and makes a graceful, narrowly cone-shaped tree 30 or 40 ft. high.

Another group of cypresses frequently passes under the name 'retinospora' in gardens. Of these the two most important are *C. obtusa*, a rather broad, spreading tree of medium size and *C. pisifera*, which is rather similar in habit. Both are most frequently represented in gardens by their numerous varieties, many of which are excellent shrubs of quite modest proportions. Two of the most beautiful are *C. pisifera plumosa* and *C. pisifera squarrosa*, both with fine, ferny foliage, grey-green in colour. There are also forms which are yellowish or yellow-tipped.

All these cypresses will grow in ordinary soils and open or partially shady positions. Pruning is not essential but most will submit to very severe pruning if carried out early in May. They can, in addition, be clipped during the summer though this should only be done when they are used as hedge plants as it spoils their natural habit.

The best method of increase is by seeds sown in a slightly heated greenhouse in March but selected forms of species which do not reproduce true to type from seed must either be grafted on to seedlings of the parent species or be raised from cuttings struck in sandy peat under a bell glass in September.

CYDONIA (*Quince*). Far and away the best-known ornamental species is *C. japonica*, the scarlet flowers of which are a familiar sight very early in spring. This is a fine shrub to plant against a sunny wall up which it can be trained and it will also make a bushy specimen 7 or 8 ft. high and as much through in the open. There are numerous forms of it some with white, others with salmon and yet others with crimson flowers. Another useful species is *C. Maulei*, a branching, spiny shrub only 2 or 3 ft. high but often 8 or 10 ft. through, with scarlet or blood-red flowers from April to June. Both are deciduous and have large apple-like fruits which have the true quince perfume and can be used to make quince jelly. They will thrive in any ordinary soil, prefer sunny positions, and can be increased by layers or rooted suckers

CYTISUS (*Broom*). Because of their bright green branches many people regard brooms as evergreen, though in fact they are deciduous; many, in fact, are leafless practically all the year, the green stems performing the functions of leaves. These are amongst the most free-flowering and brilliant of hardy shrubs. A great number of valuable hybrids have been produced, mostly derived from *C. scoparius*, an open, loose-habited shrub 5 or 6 ft. high and about the same in diameter. It blooms in late May and early June, the type having yellow, pea-like flowers but the forms and hybrids derived from it are in all shades of yellow, crimson, maroon and reddish pink, with many combinations of these shades.

Other good species are *C. praecox*, with sulphur yellow flowers early in May; *C. albus*, which is taller and looser than *C. scoparius* and has small pure white flowers; *C. Ardoinii*, a prostrate shrub for the rock garden with yellow flowers in April and May, and the equally golden *C. Beanii*, which is, however, just a little less prostrate than the last though still a rock garden kind. The mauve-pink *C. Dallimorei* is really a hybrid of *C. scoparius*.

All these brooms delight in sunny places and light, well-drained soils. Contrary to popular belief they do not like lime and thrive best in slightly acid soils. They transplant badly and so should be purchased while young in pots from which they can be planted with a minimum of disturbance. Plant in November or March, making very firm and staking the larger kinds firmly as they are very liable to be disturbed by winds.

The species can be increased by seeds sown outdoors in March–April, but selected varieties and hybrids must be raised from cuttings which are rather difficult to handle. Prepare them in August from firm young side growths removed with a heel of older wood, and root in very sandy soil under a bell glass.

The larger kinds benefit from an annual pruning immediately after flowering. The flowering stems can then be shortened to 1 in. or so each.

DABOËCIA. Only one species is grown. This is *D. polifolia*, a compact, evergreen shrub which looks very much like a heather and is, in fact, popularly known as St. Dabeoc's heath. The ordinary form has heather-purple flowers but there is also a beautiful pure white form and a curious variety, named *bicolor*, in which some flowers are white, some purple and some combine both colours. All bloom from mid-summer to autumn. They require precisely the same conditions as the ordinary heathers (see Erica, p. 277).

DANAË (*Alexandrian Laurel*). *D. Laurus* is the only species grown in gardens. It is a graceful, evergreen shrub about 3 ft. high with narrow, pointed 'leaves' (these are really flattened stems). It makes an excellent foliage subject both for the garden and for cutting and it has the merit of thriving in shady places and moist soils. The flowers are insignificant. No pruning is necessary but branches can be cut for foliage at practically any time of the year without damaging the shrub. It can be increased by careful division in April, which is also the best planting time. This shrub is sometimes known as *Ruscus racemosus*.

DAPHNE. There are both evergreen and deciduous species in this family and they vary greatly in size. Almost all are beautiful shrubs, many with intensely fragrant flowers, but some are a little too tender to be reliable outdoors in all parts of the country. One of the best is *D. Mezereum*, a deciduous shrub about 4 ft. high and through with a stiff, erect habit and small, very fragrant, wine-red flowers produced along the bare branches as early as February in a favourable season. There is also a pure white form. In both cases bright red berries follow the flowers. *D. Mezereum* thrives in rather rich, loamy soils with plenty of moisture during spring and summer, and is a little apt to die off suddenly for no apparent reason.

Another fine kind is *D. Cneorum*, a small, evergreen shrub 1 ft. in height but often a yard through, with narrow leaves and terminal clusters of bright rose, exquisitely fragrant flowers in May. It does well in light, peaty soils and sunny positions and is first class for the rock garden. Even more prostrate is *D. Blagayana*, which sprawls on the ground and has clusters of creamy white, fragrant blooms in March and April. It does best in rather stony, well-drained soils and if the branches are held down to the soil with small stones they will form roots and so increase in vigour.

D. Cneorum and *D. Blagayana* can be increased by layering in autumn or spring; *D. Meȥereum* by seeds sown in a frame or outdoors as soon as ripe. No pruning is necessary with any of these.

DESFONTAINEA.—*See* p. 462.

DEUTZIA. These are deciduous shrubs of vigorous growth which produce small but abundant white or rose-coloured flowers mostly in early summer. The best-known and in many ways the most beautiful is *D. scabra*, which grows 7 to 10 ft. high and nearly as much through, is stiffly erect in habit and has graceful clusters of white, pink-tinged flowers just after mid-summer. There are several fine double-flowered forms or hybrids which are even more attractive than the type, two of the best being *Watereri*, in which the flowers are almost purple and Pride of Rochester, double-flowered and pure white. All thrive in warm, sunny places and ordinary soils and require little pruning though old branches can be cut out in March. It is generally sufficient to do this every second or third year. Propagate by cuttings of firm young shoots rooted in July in a propagating frame, preferably with gentle bottom heat.

DIERVILLA. To many gardeners the Diervillas are still more familiar under the old name Weigela. All are beautiful, deciduous shrubs with bell-shaped flowers very freely produced. The two best are *D. florida* (often known as *W. rosea*) 6 or 7 ft. high and a little more in diameter, with arching branches and deep rose flowers in May and June, and *D. floribunda*, which is similar in height but more erect in habit and with deeper, reddish blooms in June. There are numerous good garden varieties of which two of the most popular are Eva Rathke, which is almost crimson and seldom above 5 ft. high and Abel Carrière, rose-pink, vigorous and arching.

All thrive in ordinary soils and open positions while the more vigorous kinds may be trained against fences and walls. Pruning is not essential but if desired flowering branches can be cut back as far as non-flowering side shoots immediately the blooms fade. Increase by cuttings of firm young shoots under a bell glass in summer or by riper shoots in early autumn in a sheltered place out of doors.

ELAEAGNUS. There are both deciduous and evergreen shrubs in this family but the latter are the more important from the gardener's standpoint. Easily the best is a showy variety of *E. pungens* known as *aureo-variegata*, or *medio-picta*. This is one of the best variegated evergreen foliage shrubs. It makes a dense bush 10 ft. or more high and quite as much through, with shining, bright green leaves each with a broad, central band of pale gold. It grows well in all ordinary soils and sunny places and is perfectly hardy. *E. argentea* is an attractive deciduous species. The flowers are small, silvery and though not very showy have an extremely pleasant fragrance while the silvery leaves are very handsome.

No pruning is required in either case. Propagation in the case of *E. pungens* is by cuttings of firm, young growths taken in September and rooted in sandy soil under a bell glass or an unheated frame. *E. argentea* can usually be increased by rooted suckers detached in autumn.

EMBOTHRIUM. *E. coccineum* is a very handsome evergreen shrub which would be planted far more widely if it were a little hardier. As it is it is seldom seen outside Cornwall, Devon and a few of the western counties where it does well in sunny, sheltered positions. It makes a big shrub or small tree up to 25 ft. in height and as much through, with handsome, glossy green leaves and clusters of narrowly tubular, scarlet flowers produced with great freedom in May. So brilliant is this shrub when in flower that it has been called the 'fire bush'. Plant it in good, well-drained soil and leave it alone; it needs no pruning. It can be increased by cuttings of firm, young shoots in summer in a propagating frame with gentle bottom heat or occasionally by means of rooted suckers detached in spring.

ENKIANTHUS. These are shrubs belonging to the heather family and like their relatives need lime-free and preferably peaty soils. Unlike heathers, however, they prefer moist soils, particularly in summer. The best kind is *E. campanulatus*, a deciduous shrub as a rule about 5 ft. high and through. The flowers are small, bell-shaped, cream with a flush of orange and produced in May. The foliage takes on grand autumn tints. This refined shrub should be planted in a sheltered position, such as thin woodland, as it is liable to be damaged by late spring frosts. No pruning is needed. Increase is by seed sown in sandy peat in a frame in March.

ERICA (*Heather, Heath*). The value of heathers in gardens is greatly enhanced by the fact that hardy species are available to flower almost throughout the year. All heathers are evergreen and all have small, bell-shaped flowers. In other respects they vary greatly, some being dwarf, spreading shrubs less than 1 ft. high, while others are erect and almost tree-like, up to 8 ft. in height, with corresponding branch spread. Almost all dislike lime and succeed best in light peaty soils, but *E. carnea*, a dwarf species with pink or white flowers from January to April, will succeed in almost any well-drained soil, even those containing lime. There are numerous varieties of this heather, some with much deeper coloured flowers than the type.

Other good species are *E. cinerea*, the twisted heather, about 1 ft. high, and producing its purple flowers from July to September (there is a white and an almost scarlet form); *E. darleyensis*, a hybrid from *E. carnea*, which is similar in character but nearly 2 ft. high; *E. mediterranea*, a handsome shrub 6 or 7 ft. high with rosy red or white flowers from March to May; *E. tetralix*, about 1 ft. high flowering from June to October and either heather-pink or white; *E. ciliaris*, the Dorset heath, pink-flowered and sprawling in habit, and *E. vagans*, the Cornish heath, which blooms from July to October and has pale purple or white flowers. There are numerous garden varieties of almost all these heathers, differing chiefly in the colour of their flowers which are often much brighter or richer than those of the wild species. The common heather of English commons is *Calluna vulgaris* (see p. 263).

Heathers can be grown mixed with other shrubs or plants in the shrubbery or rock garden, but are probably seen to best advantage if kept in beds by themselves or planted to form a heather garden. Rich soil is a distinct drawback. Regular pruning is as a rule unnecessary but if the plants become straggly they can be pruned fairly severely in spring or, in the case of spring flowering kinds, immediately the flowers fade.

Propagation is usually by short cuttings of young growth rooted in pure sand or sandy peat in July–August under a bell glass or in a propagating frame, but in the case of the dwarfer kinds it is often possible to work sandy soil around and over the branches in spring so layering them and encouraging them to form roots so that later on the whole plant can be lifted and divided. *See also* DABOËCIA (p. 275).

ESCALLONIA. Some of these very handsome evergreen shrubs are a little tender to be planted fully in the open in all parts of the country, though most succeed in the south and west. Two of the most popular are *E. macrantha*, with deep green, glossy leaves and clusters of bright rose flowers in June and July, and *E. langleyensis*, which has rather smaller leaves but even brighter carmine flowers in June and July. Both grow about 8 ft. high and through but *E. langleyensis* has a more graceful, arching habit, *E. macrantha* being more stiffly erect and, in consequence, popular for hedge making in mild districts. *E. macrantha* is fully evergreen whereas *E. langleyensis* often loses many of its leaves in a cold winter. Nevertheless the latter is really the hardier of the two and can be planted in the open in places where *E. macrantha* would need the shelter of a south or west wall. The hardiest of all is *E.*

Philippiana, with white flowers in early summer, but this is deciduous. It will grow 8 ft. high.

All escallonias grow in ordinary soils and sunny positions. Regular pruning is unnecessary though hedges or trained plants can be pruned after flowering. Cuttings of firm young growth will usually root readily in a propagating frame in July–August, especially if given a little bottom heat.

EUCRYPHIA. The best eucryphia for the garden is *E. glutinosa* (*pinnatifolia*). This is a very beautiful shrub or small tree which is deciduous or, in a mild winter, partially evergreen. The foliage is deep green and shining and the flowers, which are pure white, are rather like dog roses and are produced with great freedom in July and August. It thrives in cool, leafy or peaty soils though good specimens are to be seen in quite ordinary, lime-free soils. The principal difficulty with it is that it transplants badly. In consequence a start should be made with very small specimens or, better still, it should be purchased in pots and planted from these with a minimum amount of root disturbance. March and April are the best months for planting. Seed provides practically the only method of increase though layering in autumn can be tried.

EUONYMUS. This genus has provided one of the very best evergreen shrubs for hedge-making near the sea. Its name is *E. japonica*, and it is a densely-branched shrub or small tree which will sometimes grow 20 ft. or more high but is more often seen at half that height and can be kept still smaller by regular clipping. The foliage is dark green, leathery and handsome and there are several forms variegated to a greater or lesser degree with white or yellow. All thrive in ordinary or poor soil and will put up with any amount of salt spray. For hedge making young plants should be spaced 18 in. apart.

Very distinct from this is *E. radicans*, a creeping, evergreen shrub which can be used as an edging or may be planted against a wall to grow vertically up it like a climber. It has small, glossy, evergreen leaves heavily marked with white in the variety *variegata*. It will grow in any ordinary soil and sunny or shady position.

For further contrast there are several deciduous species of which the two best are *E. europaeus* and *E. latifolius*, both grown mainly for their orange and rosy-red fruits, freely produced in the autumn. The first named is the 'spindle tree' of British hedgerows. Both are small trees 10 to 15 ft. high and with a similar spread with a loosely branching habit and leaves which usually take on fine autumn tints before falling.

The deciduous species require no regular pruning; the evergreens can be pruned hard in May and trimmed at any time from then until the end of September. Propagation of the deciduous kinds is generally by seeds sown outdoors or in a frame in March; of the evergreen kinds by cuttings of firm shoots rooted in late summer in a frame. *E. radicans* can be divided in spring.

EXOCHORDA. These are deciduous shrubs of which the most popular is *E. grandiflora*, a very bushy plant 8 ft. or so high and rather more through, with numerous pure white flowers in short spikes along the arching branches in May. A bush in full flower is a very fine sight and the shrub deserves to be more widely planted. It is quite hardy, thrives in ordinary soil and likes a sunny place. No pruning is needed though flowering branches can be shortened to side growths after the flowers fade. It can often be increased by suckers removed with roots in autumn but failing this cuttings of young growth will strike in June in a propagating frame with bottom heat.

FABIANA. The only species grown, *F. imbricata*, is often mistaken for a giant heather, though in fact it has no connection, even remote, with the family, and is related to the potato. It is an evergreen shrub 7 or 8 ft. high, 4 or 5 ft. through, erect in habit with tiny, pointed leaves and masses of small, tubular, white flowers in early summer. Its one fault is that it is a little tender and must be given a sheltered position. It likes well-drained soils, needs no pruning and can be increased by cuttings of firm young growth in August in a frame with gentle bottom heat.

FATSIA. *F. japonica* is sometimes mistaken for a fig with its big, leathery leaves which are certainly a little like those of a fig tree. They are deeply divided into a number of lobes and are often over 1 ft. in diameter. The spherical clusters of creamy white flowers are produced in stiffly-branched sprays in late summer. This plant is frequently cultivated in pots in cool greenhouses but it is hardy enough to be grown in the open in most parts of the country in a sheltered, sunny or half shady position. Plant in ordinary soil; increase by cuttings of young growth in a propagating frame with bottom heat in spring or summer. Pruning is unnecessary. This shrub is often known as *Aralia japonica*.

FORSYTHIA. There is no better yellow-flowered shrub than *Forsythia spectabilis*. It is deciduous and makes a big, broad bush with many long whippy shoots and the bright golden yellow flowers are borne along the length of the year-old branches in March and April. It will grow in any ordinary soil and sunny or partially shady position.

Though pruning is not essential specimens of moderate size with extra fine blooms can be obtained by cutting the flowering branches back to young side shoots immediately the flowers fade. Another good forsythia is *F. suspensa*. This has paler yellow flowers and a looser, more arching habit, which makes it suitable for training against walls. When grown in this way it can be pruned hard after flowering. Like *F. spectabilis* it is easily managed in sun or shade. There are, incidentally, two very distinctive forms of *F. suspensa, Fortunei* and *Sieboldii*, the latter considerably more rambling than the former and consequently more suitable for wall training. All kinds can be increased readily by cuttings of well-ripened growth inserted outdoors in autumn.

FRAXINUS (*Ash*). Botanically the numerous species of ash are classified as Fraxinus. All are deciduous and most are trees of large size, though a few are big bushes. The two most important from the garden standpoint are the common ash, *F. excelsior*, which has a number of good varieties including a beautiful weeping form, and the flowering ash, also known as manna ash, *F. Ornus*. Both will grow in any ordinary soil and open position. The common ash may eventually attain a height of 100 ft. with a branch spread of 50 or 60 ft., while the flowering ash is considerably smaller, seldom over 50 ft. in height, rounded in habit and with a spread of 25 or 30 ft. It is a most useful ornamental tree with clusters of whitish flowers produced very freely in May. The common ash is too big and too quick-growing for ordinary gardens, but the weeping form of it is often worth planting and will make an excellent natural arbour as its branches come right down to ground level. No pruning is needed for any of these. Propagation is by seeds or, in the case of selected forms such as the weeping ash, by grafting in spring on to seedlings of the common form.

FUCHSIA. Most of the fuchsias are too tender to be grown outside except in the mildest parts of the country, but a few species, notably *F. magellanica riccartonii* with medium sized scarlet and purple flowers and *F. magellanica gracilis*, which is more arching and spreading in habit, can be grown in the open in many districts and, even when severely cut by winter or spring frost, will usually throw up new shoots from the base to make a good display in late summer.

Give these 'hardy' fuchsias as sunny and sheltered a position as possible in fairly rich but well-drained soil. Cover the base of the plants in winter with bracken or dried straw as a protection. Prune away all frost-damaged growth in April. Increase by cuttings of young growth rooted in a propagating frame in a greenhouse in spring.

For the greenhouse kinds, see p. 469.

GARRYA. Far and away the most important species is *G. elliptica*, a rounded, evergreen shrub, 8 to 10 ft. high and as much through and remarkable for its long, silvery-green catkins produced in mid-winter. There are two sexes, one bearing male and the other female catkins; the former is the more ornamental on account of the yellow stamens. It is reasonably hardy but should be given a fairly sheltered and sunny position. It will grow in any ordinary soil, even those which are rather dry and poor and no pruning is needed. Propagation is by cuttings of firm young shoots taken in August and rooted in a propagating frame in a greenhouse, preferably with some bottom heat.

GAULTHERIA. These are evergreen shrubs for peaty soils and most of them will not grow satisfactorily where there is much lime. The two most useful are very distinct in appearance. One, *G. procumbens*, is completely prostrate with small, rounded leaves and little pinkish-white flowers in summer soon followed by showy red berries. It is a good shrub for the rock garden or for clothing banks especially in moist, partially shaded places. The other, *G. Shallon*, is a dense, branching shrub 4 or 5 ft. in height and rather more through with leathery leaves and short clusters of pinkish-white flowers in May and June. It will grow in dense shade but its usefulness is somewhat limited by the fact that it also needs abundant moisture coupled with a porous soil, a rather awkward combination. Neither requires any pruning; both can be increased by seeds sown in sandy peat in a frame in spring.

GENISTA (*Broom*). The garden brooms are divided by botanists into two distinct families, genista and cytisus (see p. 274). Some of the showiest of the genistas are greenhouse plants (see p. 469) but there are several useful hardy species, such as *G. hispanica*, popularly known as the Spanish Gorse, a compact, spiny bush 18 in. high and 2 or 3 ft. broad with very numerous, golden-yellow flowers in May and June, and *G. tinctoria*, a wild British shrub of semi-prostrate habit and with the typical yellow broom-flowers in July. This latter has several varieties of which the double-flowered one is the most useful for garden planting. All genistas revel in warmth and sunshine and will usually grow in the poorest of soils. They require no special treatment and can be raised from seed sown in spring either outdoors or in a frame. *G. tinctoria* is popularly known as Dyer's Greenweed, and was at one time an important source of yellow dye.

GINKGO (*Maidenhair Tree*). *G. biloba* is one of the most beautiful and distinctive of all cone-bearing trees. It grows to a great height (over 100 ft. in time), is not very spreading and has leaves which are very much the shape of the leaflets of a maidenhair fern but a couple of inches in diameter. Though the tree is rare in British gardens it is not difficult to grow if planted in good soil and given a sheltered, sunny position. When young it may be cut by spring frosts but as it matures it is perfectly hardy. No pruning should be attempted at any time. Seed, which can be sown in a cool greenhouse in spring, provides the only method of propagation.

HAMAMELIS (*Witch Hazel*). These are large shrubs or small trees, all deciduous and all flowering in mid-winter. The flowers themselves are curious rather than showy, rather ragged little clusters of narrow, strap-shaped, yellow petals all along the length of the bare twigs. They make up in numbers what they lack in individual brilliance and altogether make a very pleasant picture on a dull January or February day. They also have a very attractive scent. The best species is *H. mollis*, in which the flowers are bright yellow (in some other species they are rather dull or pale). It likes a good, loamy soil and will grow in any sunny position. No regular pruning is necessary. Nurserymen usually increase by grafting in spring on seedlings of *H. virginiana*, but rooted suckers can sometimes be detached in autumn from old specimens.

HAWTHORN.—*See* CRATAEGUS (p. 272).

HAZEL.—*See* CORYLUS (p. 270).

HEATHER.—*See* CALLUNA (p. 263) and ERICA (p. 277).

HEDERA (*Ivy*). The botanical name of the common ivy is *Hedera Helix*. It is the only species of importance to the gardener but it has produced so many varieties, that whole books have been written about it. These varieties differ in size and shape of leaf and also in leaf colour, some being plain green and others very heavily variegated with silver or gold. Among the most beautiful are *colchica dentata*, with very large leaves almost triangular in outline; *Regneriana*, with enormous leaves rather heavily blotched with pale gold; *Cavendishii*, neat and variegated with cream, and *palmata*, green and deeply indented. All are self cling-ing and will grow in sun or shade in any soil and they are among the very best climbers for clothing a wall or an old tree stump. Contrary to popular belief ivies do no damage to buildings; in fact they tend to preserve masonry by protecting it from the weather.

It often pays to clip ivy closely with shears in April and then brush out dirt and dead leaves with a besom. Apart from this no attention is required once planted. Propagation is by cuttings of firm growth rooted under a bell glass in early autumn. An interesting point is that if cuttings are prepared from the bushy top of an old plant that has commenced to flower and fruit, these will produce plants of bush-like instead of climbing habit. Such ivies make handsome evergreen shrubs of rounded shape with a height and diameter of 6 or 7 ft.

HELIANTHEMUM (*Sun Rose*). Most of the helianthemums are rock plants rather than shrubs and will be found on p. 209. There are, however, a few species suitable for the front of the shrub border, notably *H. ocymoides*, a bush 2 or 3 ft. high, with very numerous, golden-yellow flowers blotched with purple. It is in bloom during May and June and, like the rock garden kinds, delights in a sunny, well-drained spot and rather light soil. Increase by seeds in a greenhouse in spring or by short cuttings of young growth under a hand light in July or August.

HIBISCUS. This is a family with a very wide range, both geographically and in style. There are gorgeous, tree-like species from the tropics, one of which I have described on p. 106, and also small annuals for the herbaceous border included on p. 473. One outstanding hardy shrub or small tree to be noted here is *H. syriacus*. This is deciduous, freely-branched, 8 or 10 ft. high, though rather slow-growing, and one of the best late-flowering shrubs. In the type the flowers are single, like those of the mallow in shape and white, blue, purple or red in colour, but there are a great many garden forms, some with large double, or semi-double flowers of great beauty. All are at their best in September and continue to bloom well on into October if the weather is favourable. They should be planted in a sunny, sheltered position in rather rich, well-drained soil. No regular pruning is required, but overgrown plants can be reduced in April. Propagation in nurseries is often by grafting, but amateurs should try layering in autumn.

HIPPOPHAË (*Sea Buckthorn*). The true sea buckthorn, *H. rhamnoides*, is a very beautiful British tree with narrow, silvery, deciduous leaves and masses of small, vivid orange berries in late summer and early autumn. It seldom exceeds a height of 15 ft. and is usually densely branched and twisted. As its popular name suggests, it likes coastal districts and will put up with the worst sea gales, but it will also thrive in inland gardens providing it is given reasonably good soil and first class drainage. There are two separate sexes, one bearing male and the other female flowers and only the females will produce berries after pollination from a male. In consequence one male should be included for every five or six females, not too far removed, as pollination is by wind. Pruning is unnecessary. Seeds can be used for propagation but there can then be no certainty about sex, whereas if plants are increased by layers in autumn they will be of the same sex as their parents.

HONEYSUCKLE.—*See* LONICERA (p. 293).

HOLLY.—*See* ILEX (p. 286).

HORNBEAM.—*See* CARPINUS (p. 264).

HORSE CHESTNUT.—*See* AESCULUS (p. 257).

HYDRANGEA. For the really cold garden there is really only one hydrangea that is fully reliable for outdoor planting and that is *H. paniculata grandiflora*. This is perfectly hardy and makes many strong growths, terminated in late summer by enormous, cone-shaped clusters of creamy-white flowers. It is a really magnificent shrub, seen at its best when planted in rich soil and hard pruned early each April. By this method it will not exceed a height of 4 ft.

The hydrangras so familiar in greenhouses are varieties of *H. macrophylla* and closely related species and many are unreliable out-doors except in the south and west. It is not that they are obviously damaged by frost but the terminal buds are so injured that few or no flowers are produced unless the position is very sheltered. However, in some favoured places they do make magnificent shrubs up to 12 ft. high and 14 or 15 ft. through, covered with their large, dome-shaped heads of flowers in July. However, there are some varieties that flower even when all terminal buds have been destroyed and these are to be pre-ferred for outdoor planting. Blue flowers are only produced in acid soils and then only from certain varieties of which General Vicomte de Vibraye is one of the best. In neutral or alkaline soils it is best to plant the strongly pink or reddish varieties such as Parsifal. Mariesii and Bluewave are very distinct forms in which only the outer flowers in each cluster are big and showy the rest being small and closely clus-tered. All those named are suitable for outdoor planting in sheltered places. No pruning is required by any of these forms of *H. macrophylla*, except to remove dead growth each spring.

There are also a number of rare species which are much sought after by connoisseurs but are too difficult or insufficiently showy for ordinary growers. Typical examples are *H. Sargentiana*, a sparse-looking bush 6 ft. high with hairy stems and enormous heads of dull pink flowers in July, and *H. petiolaris*, a self-clinging climber for a sheltered wall with flat clusters of white flowers in June.

All hydrangeas can be increased by cuttings of firm young growth in August as described on p. 252.

Hypericum. Some of the best shrubs for the beginner are in this genus, such as the easily grown *H. patulum*, a twiggy bush 4 ft. high and as much in diameter, with big, yellow, saucer-shaped flowers all the summer. It has two fine forms, *Henryi* and *Forrestii* both with flowers of increased size. All will thrive in any ordinary soil and sunny or shaded position. Then there is a hybrid from *H. patulum* named *H. Moserianum*, which is little over a foot in height and tends to die down in winter, though it shoots up from the base each spring. It has similar, yellow flowers all the summer. *H. calycinum*, known as rose of sharon, is, unlike those already mentioned, evergreen. The flowers are 3 or 4 in. across, golden yellow, with a central tuft of golden stamens. The habit is sprawling and it is one of the best carpeting shrubs for banks and beneath trees.

None of these hypericums requires pruning except for the removal of dead growth in spring and all can be increased by cuttings prepared from firm growth in August and rooted in a propagating frame. *Hypericum calycinum* usually roots as it grows and can be increased by division in April.

Ilex (*Holly*). There is no better ornamental evergreen shrub or tree than the holly, *Ilex Aquifolium*. Its principal drawback is that it grows rather slowly and is a little difficult to propagate. Seed germinates readily enough either in a frame or outdoors in spring but seedlings cannot be guaranteed to reproduce the particular features of their parents such as size and colour of leaf or freedom of fruiting. On this last point it should be noted that hollies produce male and female flowers on separate plants. It is the females which produce the berries but only after fertilisation with pollen from males, so at least one male bush should be planted for every five or six females and preferably within 40 or 50 ft. of them.

There are a great number of garden varieties, some, such as Silver Queen and Silver Milkmaid with silver variegated leaves, others, such as Golden Queen and Golden Milkmaid, with yellow markings and yet others, of which *camelliaefolia* is the best, with green leaves of very great size. Golden Queen and Silver Queen are both males and so cannot produce berries, but Silver Milkmaid and Golden Milkmaid are to be obtained in both male and female types. *Camelliaefolia* is also female.

An interesting form is the hedgehog holly *(ferox)*, which has small leaves armed with spikes on the surface as well as along the edge. There are golden and silver forms of this also.

All these hollies are completely hardy. They grow best on deep, rather rich, loamy soils and will thrive in sun or partial shade. Most make excellent hedge shrubs if planted about 2 ft. apart and may then be pruned to shape in May or lightly cut at any time during the summer. When grown as specimens no pruning is necessary.

Propagation of selected forms is usually by grafting in spring on to seedlings of the common holly but amateurs should try cuttings of short side growths taken in early summer with a heel of older wood. These may be rooted in a propagating frame with gentle bottom heat, or even outdoors under a bell glass after preliminary treatment with one of the root-forming hormones.

INDIGOFERA. The indigo of commerce belongs to this family but is a sub-tropical plant for greenhouse culture. There are, however, some hardy kinds such as *I. Gerardiana,* and *I. decora,* both deciduous shrubs flowering in late summer. The first is 3–4 ft. high, sometimes more, the second not above half this height. The flowers are of the pea type in loose spikes, rosy-purple in *I. Gerardiana,* crimson and pink in *I. decora.* Both like warm sunny positions and good but rather light soils. Propagation is by cuttings rooted in summer in a propagating frame with some bottom heat.

IVY.—*See* HEDERA (p. 283).

JASMINUM (*Jasmine*). The two most popular jasmines are the summer-flowering species, *J. officinale* which has white, fragrant blooms from late June to September, and the winter-flowering *J. nudiflorum,* which opens its bright yellow flowers from December to February. Both are deciduous and both are hardy. *J. officinale* likes a warm, sunny position, while *J. nudiflorum* will grow in either sun or shade and is in fact one of the best climbers for a north-facing wall or fence. Though regular pruning is not desirable, overgrown shoots can be cut back in spring. These jasmines are not fussy about soil and will usually thrive in town as well as in country gardens. Increase is by layering in spring or autumn or by cuttings of firm shoots in late summer under a bell glass.

JUGLANS (*Walnut*). The walnut, *Juglans regia,* is sometimes planted for ornament and makes a very handsome specimen tree, slow in growth but eventually attaining a height of 50 ft. or more with a spread of 30 or 40 ft. Cultivation is as described in the Fruit Section, see p. 741.

JUNIPERUS (*Juniper*). The junipers are evergreen, cone-bearing trees, some of which are of great ornamental merit. The three most important as garden plants are *J. communis,* normally a spreading shrub or small tree 10 to 15 ft. in height but with numerous forms, some of which are quite erect; *J. sabina*, popularly known as savin, which is seldom more than 7 or 8 ft. high with spreading branches, and *J. virginiana*, sometimes called the red cedar, which is a tree 40 ft. or more high with branches spreading 20 or 30 ft. and a conical outline. This last is a very handsome specimen tree which succeeds in all parts of the country and thrives particularly well on chalky soils. Of the numerous varieties of *J. communis* the most important are *compressa*, which is so slow-growing that after 10 or 12 years it may be no more than 1 ft. in height and a perfect, compact column of tiny, spiny leaves, and *fastigiata*, known as the Irish juniper, which has the same erect habit as the last but soon reaches a height of 10 ft. with a spread of perhaps 2 ft. It makes a striking specimen and may be used most effectively to form an avenue.

All the junipers are easy to grow, thriving in most soils and requiring no special attention. Pruning is not required but the erect forms should be circled with several bands of string in winter to prevent their branches being pulled out of shape by snow. Increase is by seed which may be very slow in germination, or by cuttings of firm shoots in August–September, rooted under a hand light.

KALMIA. These evergreen shrubs belong to the heather family and like most of their tribe succeed best in rather acid soils and strongly object to lime. A deep, peaty soil with plenty of moisture in summer is ideal. The most striking species is *K. latifolia*, sometimes known as the calico bush. It makes a rounded shrub 8 or 10 ft. high and rather more through, with leathery, dark green leaves and large clusters of pink, lantern-shaped flowers. The shrub is at its best in late June and is then very beautiful. No pruning should be attempted. Propagation is rather tricky for the amateur but layering can be tried in spring.

KERRIA. The only species cultivated is *K. japonica* and this is almost invariably seen in its double-flowered form. It is a loose, rather straggling, deciduous shrub which is generally grown as a climber and trained against a wall or fence. It is very handsome in such a position when covered in April and May by its large, golden-yellow blooms. This shrub will grow anywhere, even in quite dense shade, but its young growth may be cut by frost if in a very exposed position. It can be pruned when the blooms fade, the flowering growths being cut back to young, non-flowering side shoots. Propagation is by layering in autumn or by young shoots prepared as cuttings in May or June and rooted in the greenhouse in a propagating frame with a little bottom heat.

LABURNUM. The common laburnum is one of the most useful and beautiful ornamental trees for the garden. It succeeds everywhere, grows fairly rapidly and flowers while quite young. A drawback is that it is not usually a very long-lived tree and is sometimes liable to die suddenly without apparent cause. Also the seeds are poisonous and as they are usually produced in great numbers the laburnum is not a very good tree to have in a garden in which young children play. The ordinary variety is surpassed in beauty of flower by the hybrid known as *L. Vossii*, but this is taller and more angular in habit often growing to a height of 30 ft. against the 20 ft. of *L. vulgare*, and this may be a drawback in small gardens. Nevertheless the very long trails of golden flowers are undeniably beautiful.

A curious member of the family is *L. Adamii*, which produces flowers of three different colours and growth of two different types. It is what is known as a graft hybrid, a very rare occurrence, and it contains the tissues of two different plants, the common laburnum and the purple-flowered broom. In general appearance it is a tree resembling an ordinary laburnum but with tufts of thin, broom-like growth here and there along the branches. Some of the flowers are in trails and yellow like those of the laburnum, others are in similar trails but yellow and purple while yet others are carried along the thin branches like those of broom and are purple. It is worth planting as an oddity as well as for ornament.

No laburnum requires pruning, though misplaced branches can be removed in winter. Seed sown outdoors in spring provides the readiest method of increasing the common type of laburnum, but *L. Adamii* and *L. Vossii* must be increased by grafting in spring on seedlings of common laburnum.

LARCH.—*See* LARIX below.

LARIX (*Larch*). Botanically the correct name of the larch is larix, the common British species being *L. europaea*. It is a familiar cone-bearing tree of the largest size, specimens being known which are well over 100 ft. in height and with an almost equal branch spread. Because of its size and quick growth it is unsuitable for small gardens. Unlike most cone-bearing trees it is deciduous and on this account is particularly beautiful in the spring when it is getting its new foliage, which is a very light green. Equally attractive and also deciduous is the Japanese Larch, *L. leptolepis*, which is similar in general appearance but has stouter branches. Both these larches thrive in a great variety of soils and require no special treatment. Pruning is undesirable. Propagation is almost invariably by seeds, which will germinate readily outdoors in spring if sown in peaty soil.

LAURUS. *L. nobilis* is the true laurel of classical times but not what is commonly meant by laurel by present-day gardeners, who use the term loosely for the Cherry laurel, *Prunus Laurocerasus* (see p. 302). *L. nobilis* is usually called bay, and is most familiar as a shrub for clipping into topiary specimens to be grown in tubs or large pots. It has fragrant foliage, sometimes used for flavouring soups and sauces, is an evergreen, stands clipping well and will put up with the grime of city gardens. It would be even more useful were it a little hardier. In exposed places it may be somewhat severely damaged during cold winters and if grown in pots or tubs it is wise to move these to a sheltered spot in November. In other respects it is easy to grow in any good loamy soil and sunny or partially shady position. It can be pruned severely in May and clipped at any time from then until mid-September. Propagation is by cuttings of firm growth in a frame or under a bell glass in August–September.

LAVATERA. Some of the best lavateras are annuals (see p. 108) but there are in addition some shrubby or sub-shrubby kinds of which the most attractive is *L. Olbia*. This makes a big, loosely-branched bush about 10 ft. high and nearly as much in diameter, with large, soft leaves and numerous big rose-pink flowers of the typical mallow type. It is in bloom in the late summer and is a handsome plant for the back of the shrubbery or herbaceous border. This tree mallow likes light, well-drained soils and warm, sunny places and is seldom very long lived. It may be cut back considerably by frost in winter but usually breaks out again in spring in time to make a big bush once more before the flowers open. Dead or damaged shoots should be removed each April. Propagation is by seed sown in a warm greenhouse in March.

LAVANDULA (*Lavender*). The garden lavenders are almost all forms of *L. spica*, an evergreen shrub of rounded habit about 3 ft. high and usually slightly more in diameter. The fragrant flowers are too well known to need description. The garden varieties differ chiefly in size and depth of colour. For example Munstead variety is comparatively dwarf, with deep purple flowers, Folgate variety is intermediate in height and paler in colour while Grappenhall is 4 ft. or more in height and normal in colour. All like well-drained, rather light soils and warm, sunny positions. If desired they can be grown as small hedges, in which case they should be clipped in March or early April to keep them trim. The so-called Dutch lavender is *L. vera*. It is more spreading and shorter than *L. spica* and is the kind grown around Mitcham for lavender oil. The flowering season of all is July and August and if flowers are required for drying they should be cut just before they are fully open, tied in small bundles and suspended head downwards in a cool, airy place not in direct sunshine. Propagation is by cuttings of non-flowering shoots taken in August and rooted under a bell glass or in a frame, or by firmer cuttings taken in September–October and inserted outdoors in a sheltered place.

LEPTOSPERMUM. Only one species *L. scoparium* is grown and even this is confined chiefly to the gardens of specialists as it is a little difficult to manage. It is extremely beautiful, particularly in its variety *Nichollsii*. Both species and variety make a freely-branched bush of rather wiry stems, eventually 7 or 8 ft. high and 6 or 7 ft. in diameter, with narrow, heather-like leaves and small flowers produced all up the stems in May. The type is white, the variety *Nichollsii* a glowing carmine. These shrubs dislike lime and require a sheltered position such as in thin woodland. Propagation is by cuttings of firm young side shoots taken in July–August, and rooted in very sandy soil under a bell glass.

LEYCESTERIA. The only species grown, *L. formosa*, is half way between a herbaceous plant and a shrub. It makes long, semi-woody stems from the upper part of which, in late summer, hang short trails of dull purplish flowers surrounded by claret coloured bracts. It is not a very showy plant but worth growing because it will thrive in shady places, even beneath big trees. It does best in rich, rather moist soil and can be pruned hard each March if desired, treatment which will encourage it to produce new growth of exceptional length. The average height is 7 ft. This shrub is readily increased by division in autumn or by seed sown in a sheltered place outdoors in spring.

LIGUSTRUM (*Privet*). The common hedge privet is a species of ligustrum named *ovalifolium*. This must not be confused with the wild British privet, *L. vulgare*, which has smaller, narrower leaves and is not nearly so effective. Both shrubs are liable to lose their leaves in a really hard winter but as a rule *L. ovalifolium* retains its foliage for a longer period. It is, despite over-planting, still one of the best hedge shrubs, particularly for the town garden for it will stand any amount of ill treatment and grow anywhere, in sun or shade, light soil or heavy. Moreover its golden leaved form is really bright and attractive. For hedge making young plants should be used and placed no more than 1 ft. apart. They can be clipped at any time from May to September.

Other species worth noting are *L. Prattii*, a stiff, bushy evergreen with small, rounded leaves, a good deal firmer than those of the common privet, and *L. lucidum*, a tall, evergreen shrub or small tree worth growing for its large handsome foliage and sprays of small white flowers in August and September. When in bloom it has rather the appearance of Lilac.

All these privets can be increased by cuttings of well-ripened shoots taken in early autumn and rooted in sandy soil in a frame or shady position outdoors.

LILAC.—*See* SYRINGA (p. 315).

LIME.—*See* TILIA (p. 319).

LIPPIA *(Lemon-scented Verbena)*. The correct name of the popular lemon scented verbena is *Lippia citriodora*. It is a deciduous shrub or, in some cases, a small tree but as it is on the borderline of hardiness in this country it is grown in most districts as a wall-trained shrub. It delights in warm, sunny positions and is ideal for a south-facing wall, though it can be planted fully in the open in Devon, Cornwall and some other mild districts. The flowers are small, purplish, not very striking and produced in August. The plant is grown mainly for its fragrant leaves which can be used in the preparation of perfume, pot pourri, etc. Plant in light, moderately rich soil, which must be well drained. The only pruning necessary is the removal in March of growth which has been damaged by frost during the winter. Propagate by cuttings of firm young side shoots taken in July and rooted in a propagating frame, preferably with a little bottom heat.

LIQUIDAMBAR. The most important member of this small family of deciduous trees is *L. Styraciflua*, popularly known as the Sweet Gum because of the fragrant resin which it produces. It is a handsome, North American tree which may eventually grow to a height of 60 or 70 ft. with a spread of at least 40 ft. It has maple-like leaves which glow with colour in the autumn. In this country it is not always successful but it does thrive in some moist, rich soils and is worth trying where such conditions exist. No pruning is required. Propagation in this case is scarcely a matter for the amateur but if seed can be obtained it should be sown in a slightly heated greenhouse or frame in March. Young plants should be protected from late spring frosts.

LIRIODENDRON. Here again is a small genus of trees of which one North American member only is of importance in British gardens. This is *L. Tulipifera*, the true Tulip Tree, though the name is often wrongly applied to various species of Magnolia. The family is related to the Magnolia and has somewhat similar requirements, certainly a similar dislike of root disturbance at any stage. If possible young plants should be obtained in pots in May and planted in good, loamy soil with as little injury to the roots as possible. The tulip tree will eventually reach a great size, possibly over 80 ft. in height with corresponding branch spread. The flowers, which are mainly greenish white, are shaped like tulips and open about midsummer. The leaves have a rather curious shape, as though the ends had been cut off. No pruning should be attempted. Seed provides practically the only method of propagation but usually germinates badly even when sown as soon as ripe in a slightly heated greenhouse.

LONICERA (*Honeysuckle*). This is the genus to which the honeysuckles belong but it contains many species which have little outward resemblance to the familiar honeysuckle of British hedgerows. This latter plant is *L. Periclymenum.* It is a beautiful and vigorous twiner but is surpassed for garden purposes by two of its forms, known respectively as Early Dutch and Late Dutch. These have larger and showier clusters of flowers, the early form flowering in June and July, the late in July and August and both sharing the fragrance of the common honeysuckle. Another climbing species is the Japanese honeysuckle, *Lonicera japonica.* It is as vigorous as the British variety, similar in habit with flowers which are white at first but become yellow as they age. In gardens it is most familiar in its variegated form, *aureo-reticulata,* in which each leaf is netted with gold.

Then there are several good shrubby honeysuckles, some of which flower in mid-winter or early spring. One of the best of these is *L. fragrantissima,* a deciduous bush of loose habit, 6 ft. high and rather more through, with small, creamy white, highly fragrant flowers produced from December to March. It needs a sheltered position to protect its blooms. *L. Standishii* is very similar.

In contrast to these kinds grown for their flowers are the honeysuckles used for hedge making and to form topiary specimens. The most famous of these is *Lonicera nitida,* an evergreen shrub of densely branched habit with small, rounded leaves not unlike those of a Box. It makes an ideal hedge where the height is not to exceed 5 ft. It will grow taller but then becomes rather weak and is apt to sag. Of stiffer habit is *L. yunnanensis* and as this becomes more widely propagated it may rival *L. nitida* in popularity. These hedge-making honeysuckles should be planted 15 in. apart. Like most evergreen hedge plants, they can be clipped at any time from May to September.

Climbing honeysuckles require no regular pruning but when overgrown some of the oldest vines can be cut out in March. Propagation in their case is simply effected by layers in spring or autumn. The shrubby flowering kinds can be increased by cuttings of firm young growth in July in a propagating frame. The hedge honeysuckles can also be raised from cuttings but of riper growth taken in September and rooted in an unheated frame outdoors. Where only a few plants are needed it is often possible to get them by dividing old plants in spring.

LUPINUS (*Lupin*). The botanical name of the tree lupin is *Lupinus arboreus* and it is more commonly grown as a herbaceous plant than in the shrubbery. Nevertheless it is an evergreen shrub though rather soft wooded and which in a well-drained soil and fairly sheltered, sunny position will make a big bush 5 or 6 ft. high and fully as much through. The flower spikes are produced freely in June and are shorter than those of the familiar herbaceous lupin; normally pale yellow though there are white and bluish forms. Tree lupins can readily be raised from cuttings struck in sandy soil in a frame in spring or from seed sown in a frame or outdoors in March–April. No pruning is required.

MAGNOLIA. Popularly magnolias are sometimes known as tulip trees though this name really belongs to Liriodendron (see page 292). Magnolias are mostly deciduous though there are a few evergreen species. Some make quite big trees but the majority of the popular garden varieties are large bushes or small trees. All like warm sheltered positions and deep well-drained loamy soils containing a fair quantity of peat or leaf mould and no free lime. All are difficult to transplant. May is the most favourable month and small plants should be obtained, preferably in pots, from which they should be transplanted with a minimum of root disturbance. Keep really well watered for the first few months. Pruning is as a rule quite unnecessary except in the case of wall trained specimens which can be thinned and shortened a little to keep them shapely, in March in the case of the deciduous kinds, early May for the evergreens. Propagation is most simply effected by layering in autumn, though grafting in spring in a greenhouse on to seedlings of *Magnolia denudata (conspicua)* and seed sown in a greenhouse in spring are also used.

Amongst the best kinds are *M. denudata*, the common Yulan, a small deciduous tree of spreading habit, with big white flowers in April and May; *M. Soulangeana*, a hybrid from the last, similar in habit but with fine, rounded, purple-tinted flowers; *M. stellata*, with small pure white blooms, very freely produced in April and May on a compact bush 10 or 12 ft. high and as much through; and *M. grandiflora*, the best evergreen kind, which has large, laurel-like leaves and, in late summer, fragrant white flowers rather like water lilies. *M. grandiflora* is happiest on a sunny wall but it can be grown in the open in a sheltered place.

METASEQUOIA. This interesting and beautiful cone-bearing tree closely resembles the swamp cypress (taxodium) in appearance but, unlike that tree seems to thrive in almost any soil or place, wet or dry. It is deciduous and in some places the fine, ferny foliage colours well in the autumn. There is only one species *M. glyptostroboides* and as this was only introduced from China in 1947 it is too early to decide exactly how useful it is going to be in our climate. First impressions are, however, that it will be a valuable ornamental tree where there is space for its full development—probably to an eventual height of 80 ft. or more with corresponding branch spread. It is easily raised from seed sown in sandy soil in a cool greenhouse or frame in spring or from cuttings of firm young growth taken in July or August and rooted in sandy soil in a propagating frame.

MOCK ORANGE.—*See* PHILADELPHUS (p. 297).

MOUNTAIN ASH.—*See* PYRUS AUCUPARIA (page 306).

MYRTUS (*Myrtle*). This beautiful evergreen shrub is a native of the Mediterranean and just a little too tender to be entirely reliable outdoors in this country. The common species is *M. communis,* and it thrives well in the S.W. and W. and in mild districts elsewhere or can be grown in the shelter of a sunny wall. It makes a neat, rounded shrub 8 or 10 ft. high when full grown and 6 or 7 ft. through, with dark, shining, fragrant leaves and small, white, scented flowers in July and August. It grows best in good, well-drained, loamy soils. No pruning is required. Propagation is by cuttings of firm young growth rooted in very sandy soil in July in a propagating box, preferably with gentle bottom heat.

OAK.—*See* QUERCUS (p. 306).

OLEARIA. This family of evergreen shrubs contains numerous good plants which are a little too tender to be grown out-of-doors with safety. There are exceptions, however, notably in *O. Haastii,* a grand shrub 6 or 7 ft. high and at least as much through, with small, oval leaves and very abundant white, daisy-like flowers in July and August. It often grows well in town gardens, likes sunny places and is not particular regarding soil. Rather smaller but similar in general habit is *O. Gunniana,* which has white, daisy flowers in the type but has produced numerous forms with variously coloured flowers including pink and blue. It is, unfortunately, considerably less hardy than *O. Haastii* and frequently killed to the ground in winter. A third good species is *O. macrodonta*, with much bigger greyish, holly-like leaves and less numerous, silvery-white flowers. It will reach a height of 20 ft. in favourable places and is sometimes used for hedge making in Devon, Cornwall and other mild districts. All these Olearias can be increased by cuttings of firm young shoots inserted in sandy soil in a propagating frame in July, preferably with bottom heat. Pruning is unnecessary except for hedges, which can be trimmed in May.

OSMANTHUS. Another family of evergreen shrubs or small trees. The best is *O. Delavayi*, which is a stiffly branched, rather spreading shrub, seldom much above 5 ft. in height though often 8 or 9 ft. through, with small, very dark green leaves and clusters of little tubular, white flowers in April. These blooms, though not very showy, are intensely fragrant. Also occasionally planted is *O. Aquifolium*, a bigger bush grown mainly for its holly-like leaves. It is less hardy than *O. Delavayi*. Both species thrive in sunny, sheltered positions and like ordinary, well-drained soils. No pruning is required. Cuttings prepared from firm young growths and rooted in a propagating frame in a greenhouse in July provide the readiest method of increase, though layering may also be tried.

PAEONIA (*Peony*). The herbaceous peony has become such a popular plant and is so easily grown practically anywhere that a good many gardeners forget altogether that there are other kinds, including shrubby or even tree-like species. Of these the best is *Paeonia suffruticosa* (*Moutan*), known as the tree peony, though it is in fact seldom above 5 ft. in height in this country. It is deciduous, freely branched, and produces abundant, large, very showy flowers in May and June. There are single and double flowered forms and the best varieties are quite as effective in bloom as the finest herbaceous peonies. These shrubby varieties are a little more exacting to grow. They need a very sheltered position and good, loamy, well-drained soil. They should not be planted in low lying places where frost is likely to be severe in spring as the young growth is distinctly tender. No pruning is required. The best method of propagating is by layers in autumn or spring. Commercially grafting is practised on a large scale, the herbaceous peony being used as a stock but grafted plants are seldom so satisfactory as those produced by layers.

PASSIFLORA (*Passion Flower*). The only passion flower hardy enough to be grown outdoors in this country is *P. caerulea*. Even this requires a very sunny, sheltered position and is more suitable for the South and

West than for colder North and East districts. It is a vigorous climber with big, pale blue, curiously formed flowers produced spasmodically throughout the summer. The colour is rather indeterminate and many prefer the pure white variety, Constance Elliott. Grow in ordinary, well-drained soil and train against a sunny wall. Do not attempt any pruning beyond the removal of frost-damaged growth in the spring. Propagate when necessary by layering in autumn.

PEAR, ORNAMENTAL.—*See* PYRUS (p. 306).

PERNETTYA. Another genus with only one species of interest to the gardener. This is *P. mucronata,* a most attractive evergreen belonging to the heather family. Small white flowers in May are followed by very showy berries in a variety of colours including pink, puce, crimson, purple and white. Height varies from 3 to 5 ft. and the shrub spreads over a considerable area by underground shoots. Incidentally, this habit makes it easy to propagate it by division in April or May, which is the best planting time. Like most of the heather family, this shrub requires a lime-free soil and succeeds best in a deep, rather moist peat and a sheltered position. No pruning should be attempted.

PEROWSKIA. Here again one species only is grown, a very beautiful semi-shrub named *P. atriplicifolia* which would, no doubt, be planted more widely were it a little hardier. It has grey-green stems and leaves and small, violet blue flowers carried in loose, branching spikes in late summer and each year it throws up many 4 or 5 ft. long stems from the base. When in bloom it has a slight resemblance to a very large and loose lavender. It should be planted in light, well-drained soils and sunny, sheltered positions. It is advisable to prune fairly severely at the end of each March, cutting back to about 1 ft. of growth of the previous year. Propagation is by short cuttings of non-flowering side growths taken in July and rooted under a bell glass in very sandy soil.

PHILADELPHUS. (*Mock Orange*). There has for years been a terrible muddle over the popular naming of this plant for almost every amateur gardener calls it syringa, despite the fact that this is the correct botanical name of the familiar lilac. Mock Orange is, in fact, a far more suitable name from every standpoint for the large, white, widely opened flowers, which are frequently heavily scented, do resemble the blossom of the orange.

Some of the best deciduous shrubs for the small garden are to be found in this genus. Most are quite hardy and not at all fussy as regards soil or situation. All can be pruned after flowering, if it is desired to restrict size, the method being to cut back the flowering shoots as far as good, non-flowering side growths. The simplest method of propagation is by cuttings of young growth taken in June or July and rooted in sand in a propagating frame with bottom heat, but riper and longer cuttings can be tried in a frame in the autumn.

This is a large family with many species and varieties, most of them useful. Amongst the best are the following: *P. coronarius*, 10 to 12 ft. high and more through, with creamy white, very fragrant flowers in early June; *P. grandiflorus*, a still more vigorous shrub with pure white flowers which are very showy but unfortunately scentless; *P. Lemoinei*, a hybrid from *P. coronarius*, and a neat bush 6 or 7 ft. high and wide with big clusters of pure white, scented flowers, and *P. microphyllus*, the other parent of *P. Lemoinei* and the most modest in stature of all the species, seldom exceeding a height and width of 4 ft. In addition there is a varied assortment of hybrids with 'fancy' names and big, frequently double flowers of which my choice would be Virginal, a really magnificent shrub of medium size with big clusters of fine, double white, scented flowers.

PHLOMIS (*Jerusalem Sage*). The Jerusalem Sage is a bushy, evergreen shrub, but with rather soft stems which may be killed back by frost in winter. Its full botanic name is *Phlomis fruticosa*, and it is a good plant for a rather dry, sunny position in poorish, well-drained soil. The leaves are large, downy and a little like those of the common sage, while the yellow, hooded flowers are carried in big, showy clusters in August and September, when colour is particularly welcome. A good specimen will be 4 ft high and 5 or 6 ft. through. Regular spring pruning is desirable to correct the normally rather straggly habit. Propagation is by cuttings of firm side growths taken in August and rooted in sandy soil in a frame.

PHYLLOSTACHYS.—*See* BAMBOO (p. 260).

PICEA (*Spruce*). Evergreen cone-bearing trees mostly of considerable size, and of neat, conical shape. Typical of the genus is *P. excelsa*, the common spruce, which provides the Christmas trees for our winter parties. This will eventually grow to a height of 100 ft. or even more, but it has several forms of which one, known as *clanbrasiliana*, grows so slowly that after many years it is only 2 or 3 ft. in height. *Pygmaea* and *dumosa* are rather similar. A choicer tree for the garden is *P. pungens*. This has stiffer, more horizontal branches than the common spruce and though the type is green, it has produced several beautiful forms with blue-grey foliage, the colour being most marked when the leaves are young. One of the best of these is *P. pungens glauca*. This is a highly ornamental tree for planting as an individual specimen on a large lawn or in a similar prominent position.

All spruces will grow in any ordinary soil and open position, but they like best a soil that is well supplied with moisture in summer, for which reason they do better in the West of England than in the East. They should not be pruned at any time. Propagation is by seeds sown in peaty soil in spring or, in the case of selected forms, by grafting on to seedlings of the type species.

PIERIS. Those kinds which are of value in the garden are very handsome, evergreen shrubs with clusters of small, heather-like white flowers in spring. Two of the most outstanding are *P. floribunda,* which is 4 or 5 ft. high, 5 or 6 ft. through and is often in bloom by March, and *P. japonica,* which is about twice as big and in bloom at the same time. Of the two, *P. japonica* is the less hardy and should be given as sheltered a position as possible. Both thrive in peaty soil of the type which suits rhododendrons and heathers, to which they are related. They like plenty of moisture during the summer, should not be pruned and may be increased by layering in autumn or spring.

PINE (*Pinus*). There are a great many species of pine almost all of which have some value in the garden though most grow too rapidly to be serviceable where space is at all restricted. Very typical of the family is the native Scotch pine, *Pinus sylvestris,* which will reach a height of 80 ft. or more and, though neatly cone-shaped at first, usually becomes curiously contorted with age when the trunk is often bare for 40 or 50 ft. with a one-sided head of branches at the top. Two frequently planted species are the Corsican pine, *P. Laricio,* and its variety, the Austrian pine, *P. Laricio nigricans* often listed as *P. austriaca.* Both are fully as big as the Scotch pine but the Austrian variety has longer individual leaves and a more spreading habit. The Weymouth pine, *P. Strobus,* is seldom over 60 ft. in height and an attractive species as is *P. excelsa* with very long, greyish green needles. But the most beautiful of all is *P. Montezumae,* with leaves as much as 12 in. in length. Unfortunately it is too tender to be grown in any but the mildest parts of the country. *P. insignis* also needs a mild climate but is distinctly hardier. One of the smallest kinds is *Pinus montana pumilio,* which is often no more than 5 ft. high, though it may spread over an area of 10 or 12 ft.

All these pines will grow in a great variety of soils though they have a preference for those that are light and well drained. No pruning should be attempted at any time. Where possible trees should be planted while still very young, as most kinds tend to resent movement later on.

Propagation should always be by seeds sown in sandy soil either out-doors or in a frame in spring.

PITTOSPORUM. There are some extremely beautiful evergreen foliaged shrubs and small trees in this genus but unfortunately most of them are a little too tender to be grown outdoors in this country except in the mildest districts. One of the most reliable is *P. tenuifolium*, which has black stems and shining, bright green leaves. It is very popular with florists for cutting and mixing with flowers, and in the garden will make a shapely shrub 10 ft. or more high and as much in diameter. It has a good variety, named *Mayii*, in which the leaf margins are waved. Neither is fussy about soil but should have a warm, sheltered position. No pruning is required, but overgrown bushes can be cut back in May. Propagation is by cuttings of firm young shoots taken in mid-summer and rooted in a propagating frame with some artificial heat. *P. Tobira*, with bigger, dark green leaves and fragrant white flowers, needs even more protection.

PLATANUS (*Plane*). The London plane, *Platanus acerifolia*, is a great favourite with town planning authorities. It has the merit of thriving anywhere, even in the most heavily grime-laden atmosphere, but it grows too quickly for the small garden, soon making a big tree, 50 or 60 ft. in height with corresponding branch spread. Though it can be pruned severely this usually spoils its shape. A peculiarity is the peeling bark, which gives the trunk a piebald and rather attractive appearance. Curiously enough although the mature tree is absolutely hardy, young plants are a little tender and occasionally severely cut by late spring frosts. Propagation is by cuttings of well-ripened young stems pulled off with a heel of wood in autumn and rooted in a frame or under a hand light.

PLUMS, ORNAMENTAL.—*See* PRUNUS (p. 301).

POLYGONUM. The only important species for consideration in this section is *P. baldschuanicum*, popularly known as the Russian vine. This is one of the most vigorous and quick growing climbers ever to be introduced to English gardens and a grand subject for covering un-sightly outhouses, tree stumps, fences, etc. It needs plenty of space, however, and can become a nuisance in the wrong place. It will soon make vines 20 ft. or more in length, spreading in all directions or climb-ing upwards, according to their position. The plant makes a mass of twining shoots and smothers itself in late summer beneath a cloud of small white or pink-tinged blossoms. If necessary it can be cut back hard each February or it may be allowed to grow without pruning if space permits. Fairly long cuttings of firm growth taken with a heel of older wood in October usually root readily in a frame.

POPULUS *(Poplar)*. There are many kinds planted for ornament but all are too big and quick growing for any but the larger gardens. The well known Lombardy poplar, *Populus nigra italica,* so popular as a roadside tree in France, is occasionally planted as a screen in English gardens, but unless very severely pruned is apt to become a nuisance, particularly as it sends its roots far and wide. It will reach a height of 100 ft. with a spread of no more than 10 or 15 ft.

The common aspen, *Populus tremula,* is so called because its thin leaves are constantly on the move even in the lightest breeze. It is an elegant tree 40 to 50 ft. high and as much in diameter. Another ornamental species is *P. alba,* the white poplar, with leaves that are greyish-green above and almost pure white beneath. This looks particularly attractive on a windy day. It has the added merit of being comparatively small, seldom exceeding 40 ft. in height or 30 ft. in breadth. The balsam poplars are also worthy of attention because of their fragrant winter buds and young leaves. The best is *P. balsamifera,* a tree of great size and rapid growth.

All poplars are deciduous, none requires regular pruning and all can be increased by seeds sown outdoors in spring. They will grow in most soils but prefer those that are fairly rich and not liable to dry out severely.

POTENTILLA. In addition to the herbaceous and alpine plants and numerous weeds which make up the greater part of this genus there are a few good shrubs of which easily the best is *P. fruticosa.* This is rounded and well branched, seldom over 3 ft. in height and about as much through, with little divided leaves and a constant succession of bright yellow flowers throughout the summer. There are several forms, of which the two most striking are *Veitchii,* in which the flowers are white, and *Vilmoriniana,* which has silvery leaves and creamy-white flowers.

All should be planted in good soils and sunny but not dry positions. Pruning is not necessary. Seed usually germinates readily if sown in a frame in spring, or cuttings of firm young shoots may be rooted under a bell glass in late summer.

PRIVET.—*See* LIGUSTRUM (p. 291).

PRUNUS. This vast genus includes many of the most highly ornamental trees and shrubs grown in British gardens. Popularly the family is split up into numerous groups under such sub-headings as Cherries, Plums, Apricots, Almonds, etc. but on the whole it is less confusing to describe them under the one heading, 'prunus', than to attempt to deal with the groups separately.

Almost all kinds are hardy and easily grown in a great variety of soils but a few flower so very early that it is desirable to give them a sheltered position, with the sole object of giving their blooms a fair chance of survival. Most are deciduous but the family does include evergreen species, of which the two most important are the cherry laurel, *P. Laurocerasus*, and the Portugal laurel *P. lusitanica*. Pruning is on the whole undesirable, at any rate with the deciduous kinds, but the cherry laurel will stand any amount of cutting about, provided it is done in late April or early May. In the case of the early flowering, deciduous kinds, any pruning that is essential to maintain shape should be done immediately the flowers fall.

Propagation of the deciduous kinds is as a rule by budding or grafting and plum or cherry stocks are commonly employed. The evergreens can be increased by cuttings of well-ripened young growth taken in early autumn and rooted in a frame or under a bell glass.

One of the first of the genus to bloom is *P. cerasifera Pissardii*, more familiar to most gardeners simply as *P. Pissardii*, or the 'purple plum'. Its small, pale pink flowers commence to open in March slightly ahead of the leaves. The foliage is purple and ornamental in itself. Even better is *P. Blireana*, in which the flowers are fully double, considerably larger and a bright pink instead of the rather washy pink of the common purple plum.

These early flowering plums are followed very shortly by the almond, *P. Amygdalus*. This has large, bright pink flowers all along the bare stems and is one of the most beautiful of spring flowering trees. There are numerous forms of which the finest is *Pollardii*, with flowers of great size and extra bright colour.

The peach, *P. Persica*, resembles the almond in many respects but flowers about a fortnight later. For ornament the double-flowered forms are usually planted, such as Clara Meyer, which has big, rose-pink flowers. There is also a grand variety, named Russel's Red, which has double carmine flowers.

Not unlike *P. Blireana* but less hardy and, in consequence more satisfactory against a sunny wall than planted in the open, is *P. triloba flore pleno*. This is a fine shrub for forcing in pots in the greenhouse and its long sprays of double pink bloom can be had soon after the New Year with very little heat. Outdoors it generally starts to bloom about the end of March at approximately the same time as the almond.

The so-called Japanese cherries are derived from two species, *P. serrulata* and *P. Lannesiana*. The colour range is from white to rose;

the flowers themselves are single, semi-double or fully double, according to variety and for the most part are very large and borne in marvellous profusion in April. There is also great variation in habit, from the completely erect Ama-no-gawa, which looks like the Lombardy poplar in habit, to the spreading *Veitchiana* (Fugenzo) and weeping *pendula* (Shidare-Sakura).

These Japanese cherries are fairly big trees, up to 30 ft. in height. The so-called dwarf cherry, *P. Cerasus*, from which the Morello cherry of the fruit garden is obtained, seldom exceeds a height of 15 ft. and is a good tree for the small garden. Its best ornamental variety is *flore pleno* (also known as *Rhexii*) in which the flowers are pure white and fully double.

Not to be confused with the last named is the double white form of the wild British cherry or gean, *P. avium*. This makes a very much larger tree, sometimes reaching a height of 60 ft. with corresponding branch spread.

P. subhirtella is a small flowered cherry which flowers in April but it is chiefly remarkable for its form '*autumnalis*', which gives one crop of flowers in November and then blooms again in March-April. The only drawback to this tree is that the small pink blooms are rather apt to be destroyed prematurely by frost.

The bird cherry, *P. Padus*, is taller than most so far mentioned, sometimes attaining a height of 50 ft. with long, narrow trails of small white flowers in May. By comparison with some of the Japanese cherries this is not a showy tree, but none the less attractive. There are numerous forms of which one of the best is *Watereri*, with flower trails of extra length.

P. serrula is grown principally for its bark, which is smooth and shining, like highly polished bronze and in my opinion it is the most handsome of all bark trees for the garden of moderate size.

The cherry laurel *P. Laurocerasus* has numerous forms, some of which are a great improvement on the type, though for some reason or other it is almost always this that is seen. Outstanding kinds are *colchica*, with leaves 6 or 7 in. long, and *magnoliaefolia*, in which the leaves may be as much as 1 ft. in length.

The Portugal laurel makes a big, rounded shrub, often 20 ft. high and as much through, with reddish shoots and oval leaves a little like those of the bay tree. It is a fine shrub to form a screen or shelter belt but is rather 'hungry' and exhausts the soil for a considerable distance.

PSEUDOTSUGA (*Douglas Fir*). In its home, North America, specimens of *P. taxifolia* (*Douglasii*) occur much over 200 feet in height. It is a very handsome cone-bearing tree, conical in habit with wide, spreading, horizontal branches. There are several forms including one named *glauca* with blue-grey foliage. Obviously on account of its size the Douglas fir is only suitable for planting in the largest gardens. Even then it is not always a satisfactory tree as it needs plenty of moisture during the growing season; in consequence it is most likely to succeed in the west and north where rainfall is high. It should not be pruned for fear of spoiling its shape. Propagation is by seeds sown in a frame in spring.

PYRACANTHA (*Fire Thorn*). One of the most popular evergreen climbers in British gardens is *P. coccinea*. This has dark green, shining leaves, and flattish clusters of white flowers in early June, both of which are quite attractive, but the plant becomes really spectacular in late summer when covered with crops of small, vivid red berries. Even better is the variety *Lalandii*, in which the berries are a little larger and orange red. Left to its own devices this shrub would make a bushy specimen 12 or 15 ft. high and rather more through but when planted against a wall it shapes itself quite readily to this and requires only a little pruning of side growths each summer to keep it in shape. There are other good species, notably *P. angustifolia*, which is similar in habit but has orange yellow berries. Unfortunately it is less hardy and requires a sheltered, sunny wall whereas *P. coccinea* and *Lalandii* will succeed practically anywhere, on north walls as well as south. For cultivation in the open as a bush the scarlet berried *P. Rogersiana* is recommended because of its graceful arching habit.

Propagation in all cases is by seeds sown in a frame or unheated greenhouse in spring or by cuttings of firm young side shoots pulled off with a heel in late summer and rooted under a bell glass.

PYRUS. This shares, with Prunus, the honour of having provided the gardener with more useful material than any other genus of ornamental trees or shrubs. Also like prunus, it consists of a number of distinct groups of plants to which separate names may be given such as apples, whitebeams, pears, service trees, and chokeberries, but I think it is simpler to treat them under the one heading because this is where they will be found in most nursery catalogues.

Most species are deciduous, hardy and of moderate size; in fact the familiar apple and pear of the fruit garden may be taken as very typical of the family. Few are fussy about soil, though a good, well-drained, loamy soil is ideal. Many of them do well on chalk formations provided the top soil has been well broken up and reasonably enriched. Regular pruning is, as a rule, unnecessary after the early years but at the outset pruning can follow the lines recommended for young fruit trees (see page 659).

In the case of the species seed offers an easy method of propagation and can be sown in a frame or outdoors in March. Selected garden varieties do not breed true from seed and must be propagated by grafting or budding in the same manner as apples or pears (see page 635). As a rule seedlings of the most nearly related species are used as stocks.

One of the most important species in this huge genus is *P. Malus,* the wild crab apple of British woods. The type is scarcely worth planting in gardens as there are so many better forms, notably the handsome fruiting crabs such as John Downie, with egg shaped, orange and scarlet fruits; Dartmouth crab, which has globular plum purple 'apples' and Cheal's Scarlet, in which the fruits are purplish red and like large cherries. In all cases the flowers are white or pale pink like those of ordinary apples. All make shapely trees 25 to 30 ft. in height and as much in diameter.

Nearly allied to these 'crabs' is *Pyrus Neidwetzkyana,* an apple-like tree with red tinged leaves and shoots, carmine flowers and small, purplish-red fruits. An attractive tree itself it has been surpassed for garden ornament by some of the seedlings raised from it, such as *P. Eleyi, P. aldenhamensis* and *P. Lemoinei.* These all resemble *P. Neidwetzkyana* in the reddish-purple colour of their flowers and fruits but are superior in size and freedom.

Then there is the Siberian crab, *Pyrus baccata,* which sometimes reaches a height of 40 ft. and has white flowers in April followed by round, cherry-like fruits which are red in the ordinary variety though there is a form in which they are yellow.

Yet another species of the apple type is *P. floribunda,* sometimes known as the Japanese crab. The flowers are small but make up in numbers what they lack in size. They are deep red in bud, pink when fully open and the tree is at its loveliest in the half-and-half stage. It is comparatively slow growing, very freely branched and makes a spreading tree about 20 ft. high and 15 ft. through.

A hybrid which has been widely planted is *P. purpurea.* It is intermediate in habit between *P. Neidwetzkyana* and *P. floribunda* with flowers of the brilliant purple red colour of the former but small and freely produced like those of floribunda.

P. coronaria, the American crab, has big, blush pink flowers which are fragrant and open quite late in May, so missing the spring frosts. Rather similar is *P. ioensis* which has a really lovely double-flowered variety often wrongly described as *P. coronaria flore pleno.* The pink flowers are as big as those of the best Japanese cherries. *P. spectabilis* also has an excellent double flowered form and both single and double are worth planting. The flowers are red in bud, blush pink when open.

This by no means exhausts the list of desirable 'crab apples' for the garden but at least it includes a representative selection of them.

One of the most valuable is the Mountain Ash, *P. Aucuparia*, a graceful, deciduous tree, growing rapidly to a height of 30 ft., and sometimes considerably more, with an eventual branch spread of 20 to 25 ft. The small white flowers carried in big, flat clusters in early summer are followed by the familiar bright scarlet fruits persisting well into the winter. It is completely hardy. In many districts it is known as 'rowan'.

The 'service tree', *P. Sorbus*, makes a tree similar in size to the mountain ash but rather more spreading, with clusters of white flowers in May followed by dull, brownish red fruits like tiny apples. Closely allied to it is *P. aria*, the common whitebeam, a tree 30 or 40 ft. high and as much through, with leaves that are bright green above, white beneath. The flowers are rather dull white carried in clusters in May and are followed by small, bright red fruits rather like large hawthorn berries. It is an ornamental tree, thriving particularly well on chalky soils. *P. intermedia*, the Swedish whitebeam is rather similar but the undersides of the leaves are grey and in my opinion less ornamental.

The pear section of the genus is not so important from the ornamental standpoint, but the willow-leaved pear, *Pyrus salicifolia*, makes an attractive, semi-weeping, grey-leaved tree, 20 ft. or so in height, with white flowers in April.

QUERCUS (*Oak*). The common British oak is a grand tree for parklands but rather too big for the ordinary garden. Its botanical name is *Quercus pedunculata*. There are many exotic species which will thrive in this country of which perhaps the two best for the ordinary garden are *Q. Ilex* and *Q. coccinea*. The first is familiar as the Holm Oak, an evergreen tree of considerable size which can, however, be restricted by means of frequent clipping to form a hedge or windbreak. It does well in seaside localities and the milder parts of the country and delights in light, well-drained soils. *Q. coccinea* is known as the scarlet oak because of the vivid autumn colours assumed by its large leaves. It is deciduous and will eventually reach a height of 50 or 60 ft. with a branch spread of 40 or 50 ft. With the exception of the holm oak all kinds thrive best in good loamy soils and open positions. They make fine individual specimens, should not be pruned except to remove misplaced or diseased branches and are best increased by the acorns collected in autumn and sown 2 in. deep outdoors in spring.

RHODODENDRON. This is one of the biggest genera of evergreen shrubs.

From the botanist's standpoint the family also includes deciduous species but these I have dealt with separately under the heading Azalea (see p. 259) as this is the name by which they are commonly known in gardens.

Whole books have been devoted to the rhododendron alone and several world famous plant collectors have spent years of their lives collecting new species in various parts of the world, but particularly the mountain ranges between India, China and Tibet. Added to this a vast amount of hybridisation has been carried out in nurseries in this country, on the Continent and in America. Small wonder, then, that there are rhododendrons of every conceivable type, size and colour from small, spreading shrubs with tiny leaves and neat clusters of flowers, to large trees with leaves in some cases 1 ft. long and magnificent, funnel shaped flowers borne in heavy trusses.

Rhododendrons thrive in a great variety of soils provided they contain no free lime but they like best a reasonably well drained, peaty soil, or a mixture of peat and lime-free loam. Very dry soils are not good. Most kinds will grow in full sun though almost all are happiest in partial shade. They do not stand up very well to cold winds and this is particularly true of some of the new Himalayan species and also some of the continental hybrids. Many of these can be grown in thin woodland in districts which would be too cold were they planted fully in the open.

No regular pruning is desirable but faded flower trusses should be removed when possible. Bushes which have become overgrown can be cut back severely in May but this means a sacrifice of one year's flowering.

New plants can be raised from seed, cuttings, layers and grafts. Hybrids will not breed true to type from seed and the seed in any case is small and a little difficult to handle. It should be sown on fine, sandy peat in a cool greenhouse or frame in spring and given the lightest of covering with silver sand only. Grafting is done in spring, usually under glass, but is a task for the expert rather than the amateur. Layering in the spring or autumn is one of the most satisfactory methods of increase for private gardeners. Cuttings of firm young side growths can be rooted in sandy peat in a frame with gentle bottom heat in July or August, but this method is not likely to be very satisfactory with hybrids or large growing species though it answers quite well with the small, rock garden species.

As I have already said, hybrids provide the best material for ordinary garden display. These for the most part make fine rounded bushes up to 15 ft. in height and diameter. They have large, dark green leaves and magnificent trusses of showy flowers in a great variety of colours including white, pink, scarlet, crimson, mauve, pale yellow and apricot. The best of these hybrids have been given fancy names such as Pink Pearl, Alice, John Waterer, Brittania, Cynthia, Countess of Athlone and White Pearl but I will make no attempt to list them as there are literally hundreds of equal merit and descriptions can be found in any good nursery catalogue.

Turning to the species and considering them roughly in order of size, the following are amongst the most useful.

R. hippophaeoides is a grand, low growing shrub for the rock garden, 1 ft. in height but 5 or 6 ft. through, with small, lavender flowers in May.

R. intricatum is similar in habit with violet-purple flowers at the same time of year. It is very slow growing and therefore suitable for the small garden.

R. praecox grows 3 or 4 ft. in height and breadth and opens its pink flowers in April. It is more tolerant of lime than many species.

R. Augustinii is very variable in height, ranging from 4 to 10 ft. with corresponding spread. The flowers may be white, pink or mauve. The best forms are very pleasing and well worth growing.

R. racemosum has small but attractive soft pink flowers and makes an erect bush 5 or 6 ft. high and 3 or 4 ft. through. It is in bloom in April in a favourable season.

R. ponticum is the common species which has been planted as game cover in many parts of the country and become so thoroughly established that it is looked upon almost as a native shrub. It will reach a height of 15 ft. with a spread of 20 to 30 ft. when well grown. The flowers vary in colour from mauve pink to rose and make a brave show in late May and early June.

R. Thomsonii is valuable for its earliness and the brilliant blood red of its flowers which commence to open in March. It needs a sheltered position and will make a fine bush up to 12 ft. high and 15 to 20 ft. through. This species together with *R. Fortunei*, which is similar in height and spread and has fragrant, blush pink flowers in May, have been used to produce a number of beautiful hybrids which flower earlier than the ordinary *ponticum* hybrids.

Hybrids which bloom after the *ponticum* kinds have been obtained from *R. discolor*, a species which may eventually reach 15 ft. in height. Its flowers are white or pink-tinged, open in June and continue into July.

R. Falconeri is tree like, sometimes 30 ft. high, with a similar branch spread and large, creamy white, fragrant flowers in May. It is distinctly tender and therefore only suitable for the milder parts of the country.

The leaves are very handsome, large, dark green above, rust coloured beneath. Not unlike this is *R. grande,* which also has white flowers and grows well in Devon, Cornwall and some other mild areas.

R. arboreum is a fine tree up to 40 ft. high. The flowers are blood red but there are many forms varying from white to crimson. Like the other tree rhododendrons, it needs a sheltered place.

RHUS. There are two outstandingly good species of Rhus for the ordinary garden. One is *R. Cotinus,* sometimes known as the Wig Tree or Smoke Plant because of the very curious 'flowers' made up of a large number of silk-like hairs in a tangled mass which give somewhat the impression of smoke or hair. A good bush will be covered with these 'flowers' in July and August, at first of a pale, pinkish brown colouring, later turning grey. The leaves themselves take on magnificent autumn colouring before they fall in November and there is a form, known as *atropurpureus* with leaves which are purple throughout the summer. The bush will eventually have a height and spread of 10 ft. but can be kept considerably smaller by pruning each February. The other highly ornamental species is *R. typhina,* known as the Stag's Horn Sumach because of the branched, stiffly erect columns of small, reddish purple flowers. It is a small tree with long leaves made up of numerous segments and these rival the foliage of *R. Cotinus* in the brilliance of their autumn colours. *R. cotinoides* is, as its name implies, very much like *R. Cotinus* and has similar virtues.

All species will thrive in any ordinary soil and open position and can usually be propagated by digging up rooted suckers in the autumn. Ordinary cuttings can also be rooted in the summer under a hand light or root cuttings can be taken in winter and started in a frame.

RIBES. The red, black and white currants of the fruit garden belong to this genus, which has also produced a few species of value in the ornamental garden, notably *R. sanguineum,* sometimes known as the American currant or the flowering currant. In habit this looks a little like a large black currant with similar, short, hanging trails of flowers in April, but bright rose instead of pale, greenish-yellow. There are even better forms, notably *atrosanguineum* and King Edward VII, both of which have deep magenta flowers.

These are all very easily grown shrubs which will thrive in any soils and sunny or partially shaded positions. They succeed well in town gardens and though regular pruning is not essential, if they get too big they can be cut back without harm immediately after flowering. Propagation is by cuttings of well grown young stems taken in October and rooted in a frame or sheltered position outdoors.

ROBINIA (*False Acacia*). Some years ago the false acacia, *R. Pseudo-acacia*, was one of the most freely planted of road trees in this country and was a favourite ornament for small front gardens. Usually the variety *inermis*, was planted. This has much shorter branches than the type and makes a mop-headed specimen instead of a fine, spreading tree up to 60 ft. in height with a branch spread of 30 or 40 ft. as in the case of the common type. The foliage of both type and variety is graceful. The mop-headed form seldom flowers but the type when established produces with great freedom in early summer Laburnum-like trails of fragrant white flowers. It is a good tree which has been neglected in recent years and should be planted again. Another species worth noting is *R. hispida*, the rose acacia, which is a deciduous shrub no more than 7 or 8 ft. high but rather spreading and producing suckers freely. It has deep rose flowers in June.

Both kinds will thrive in quite poor soils and like sunny places. The rose acacia can always be increased by suckers and the false acacia is also sometimes propagated in this manner. Seed can also be sown in a warm greenhouse in spring.

ROMNEYA. (*Californian Tree Poppy*) Plants which stand between true herbaceous plants and shrubs. They make many strong growths each year which become woody and permanent at the base though the upper parts may die back in winter. Two species are grown, *R. Coulteri*, and *R. trichocalyx*, both very similar from the garden standpoint, with grey-green leaves and stems and enormous white, poppy-like flowers each with a showy central cluster of golden yellow stamens. These flowers are at their best in late summer. There is also a hybrid between the two species which, by some authorities, is regarded as an even better garden plant.

The romneyas are plants for very well drained soils and warm, sunny positions. They transplant badly and so should be established from pots while still quite young. All damaged growth should be removed each spring. Propagation is by root cuttings taken in January and inserted singly in small pots.

ROSA.—*See* Chapter X.

ROSMARINUS (*Rosemary*). The common rosemary, *Rosmarinus officinalis*, is too well known to need much description. It is a beautiful ever-green shrub, occasionally 6 ft. high and as much through, though usually rather less, with grey-blue flowers in May. It does well in all soils except those that are very heavy and badly drained and it likes warm, sunny positions. No regular pruning is required but the fragrant young shoots can be cut in moderation at any time during the summer for drying and the various domestic uses to which they are put. Propagation is by cuttings of non-flowering side-shoots taken in late summer and rooted under a bell glass.

RUBUS. This is the family to which the fruit garden brambles and raspberries belong. From time to time various species have been recommended as ornamental plants for the shrubbery but a great many of them are too vigorous and straggly to be really satisfactory except in big gardens. Almost all are hardy and easily grown in practically any soil and a good many can be increased readily by rooted suckers removed in the autumn or by digging up old plants and dividing them. In some cases layering is easily effected in spring or autumn. Most can be pruned hard in late winter without suffering any injury and this is one method of preventing them from occupying too much space.

Two of the most beautiful are *R. deliciosus,* which may attain a height of 8 ft. with an even greater spread, and has large, white flowers in May, and *R. Giraldianus* which is much like a blackberry in habit, and has stems which look as if they had been whitewashed. A third very attractive shrub is *R. ulmifolius bellidiflorus,* which again is just like a bramble in habit. The flowers are a warm pink and fully double. It is a grand shrub for shady places.

RUSCUS (*Butcher's Broom*). The common Butcher's broom, *R. aculeatus,* is an evergreen shrub 2 or 3 ft. high and spreading to a considerable extent by means of suckers. In autumn it produces round, scarlet berries which persist all the winter. Flowers of different sexes are produced on different plants so if berries are required it is necessary to plant mainly females but to include at least one male to every six or seven of these. This is one of the best shrubs for growing in densely shaded places. It will grow in town gardens and woods, is not at all fussy about soil and can be increased by division in spring or autumn. The stems are often cut in autumn and dyed or gilded for use as winter decorations.

For the shrub sometimes known as *Ruscus racemosus* see *Danaë Laurus* (p. 275).

SALIX (*Willow*). There are a great many kinds of willow ranging from completely prostrate plants suitable for the rock garden to large trees which should be planted as isolated specimens if they are to be seen at their best. Fortunately for the novice, out of this multiplicity of types there are relatively few varieties of real importance for garden decoration. Far and away the best of the lot is the familiar weeping willow, *Salix babylonica.* This magnificent tree will eventually reach a height of 40 or 50 ft. with a similar branch spread. It is easily the most graceful of weeping trees with long, whip-like branchlets which touch the ground. It is at its best in the spring when the young leaves are a particularly tender shade of yellowish green and the young wood also has a yellowish tinge. This is a tree for moist soils and one which is undoubtedly seen to best advantage by the pool or streamside though it will often thrive far removed from water.

Salix alba, the white willow, is even taller than the weeping willow but not quite so spreading. It thrives in similar places. *Salix vitellina*, though also a tree of considerable size if left to its own devices, is more often cut back so severely each year that it never exceeds the dimensions of a large shrub. The object of this severe pruning is to get the maximum annual development of young shoots or 'osiers', for the bark of these is a bright yellow, and very decorative in winter. There is also a variety named *britzensis* in which the bark is red. The two should be planted together for contrast. A weeping form of *S. vitellina*, named *pendula*, has the habit of *S. babylonica* combined with the bright yellow bark of *S. vitellina*, and is exceptionally beautiful. All thrive under the moist conditions advised for the other species.

All willows can be increased very readily by cuttings of fully ripened shoots taken in autumn or early winter and inserted in moist soil outdoors. The hard pruning of those willows grown for bark effects should be carried out in March and may be practically to ground level. Other willows need no regular pruning.

SAMBUCUS (*Elder*). The common elder, *Sambucus nigra*, though a pretty hedgerow shrub, is not sufficiently choice for inclusion in the garden, but it has a golden leaved form, *foliis aureis*, which is amongst the best variegated shrubs. It is similar in habit to the common form, deciduous, 15 ft. high and rather more through and it thrives in most soils and places including those that are moist and shady. It is actually improved by rather hard pruning each spring which increases the size of the leaves and keeps the shrub a moderate height. There is also a variety named *laciniata* in which the leaves are the normal green but deeply and handsomely cut. It will thrive under similar conditions. Both should be increased by cuttings of fully ripened shoots taken in the autumn and rooted outdoors.

SANTOLINA (*Lavender Cotton*). The lavender cottons are only half shrubby and are as frequently seen in the herbaceous border as in the shrubbery. The best is *S. Chamaecyparissus*, also known as *S. incana*, a grey-leaved bush usually under 2 ft. in height but spreading to as much as 3 ft. It is worth growing for its foliage alone but also has considerable beauty when covered in July with its globular, golden yellow flowers rather like daisies without the ray petals. It likes well-drained, even poorish soils and sunny places and can be trimmed in March if it becomes straggly. Propagation is by cuttings of half ripe shoots taken in July and rooted under a bell glass or in a propagating box with gentle bottom heat.

SCHIZOPHRAGMA. One species, *S. hydrangeoides,* is an interesting climbing plant with flattish heads of yellowish-white flowers not unlike those of a rather poor form of hydrangea. These are at their best in July. This is a plant which clings by means of aerial roots like those of an ivy and in a congenial position it will reach a considerable height. Plant it in good, rich, rather moist soil and a sheltered position where it can climb up a wall or tree trunk and then leave it alone. It can be increased by layering young shoots in spring or autumn.

SCIADOPITYS (*Umbrella Pine*). A particularly interesting and beautiful evergreen cone-bearing tree which is seldom seen in British gardens for no very obvious reason. It is perfectly hardy, slow growing and unlikely to exceed 20 ft. in height in this country though in its native Japan it reaches 100 ft. The habit is pyramidal and compact. Plant in lime-free soil similar to that in which rhododendrons would thrive. Seed sown in a greenhouse in spring affords practically the only method of propagation for the amateur. *S. verticillata* is the only species grown.

SEQUOIA (*Wellingtonia*). This is another evergreen, cone-bearing tree but very different from the umbrella pine in its rapid growth and great size. Specimens of *S. gigantea* over 300 ft. in height have been reported in California and even in our less congenial climate this tree will grow over a hundred feet, making a very shapely pyramid not exceeding 30 ft. in width. It is rather tender when young but quite hardy later. It likes rich, loamy and rather moist but not badly drained soils and should always be planted as an individual specimen with plenty of room so that its full beauty can be displayed. No pruning should be attempted at any time. Propagation is by seeds sown in the greenhouse in spring. *S. sempervirens,* the redwood of California, is similar in size though often less dense and leafy in habit. It requires identical treatment.

SERVICE TREE.—*See* PYRUS (p. 306).

SKIMMIA. Small evergreen shrubs grown principally for their foliage and scarlet berries though they have considerable beauty in flower as well. The best known is *S. japonica,* 4 to 5 ft. high and a little more in diameter, densely branched, with dark green leaves and heads of small, fragrant white flowers in early summer. The flowers are of two sexes and these are borne on separate bushes. Only the females produce scarlet berries and then only when pollinated from males of the same species. One male should be planted for this purpose to every five or six females. *S. Fortunei* is similar though seldom above half the size and with darker red berries. It has the advantage of carrying flowers of both sexes on every bush so that there is no need to plant special pollinators. Both thrive in good rather moist soils and like partial shade. No pruning is required. The simplest method of increase is by layering in spring or autumn.

SOLANUM. The family which has given us the potato has also provided gardens with two of their loveliest, though unfortunately certainly not their hardiest, climbers. These are *S. crispum*, with purplish mauve flowers borne all through the summer, and *S. jasminoides*, which has a similarly extended season but is pure white. Of the two *S. crispum* is the hardier but even so should be given a particularly sheltered and sunny wall. Both will easily reach a height of 20 ft. but may be kept smaller by judicious pruning each spring. They like well-drained soils but these need not be rich. Increase by layering in spring or autumn.

SNOWBERRY.—*See* SYMPHORICARPOS (p. 315).

SOUTHERNWOOD.—*See* ARTEMISIA (p. 259).

SPARTIUM (*Spanish Broom*). Only one species is grown in gardens. This is *S. junceum*, a quick growing shrub soon reaching a height of 10 ft. or thereabouts with a somewhat smaller spread and a rather loose, leggy habit. It makes ample amends for this fault by producing from July to September innumerable spikes of bright yellow, pea-type flowers which have a very pleasant fragrance. It is one of the few shrubs well worth planting especially for cutting and it also makes a good display in the shrub border. The shoots are bright green which gives the shrub an evergreen appearance though in fact it is deciduous and has very few leaves at any time of the year. It thrives in light soils and sunny places and can be readily raised from seed sown in spring. It is wise to grow the seedlings on singly in pots until they are planted out as they resent root disturbance.

SPIRAEA. In addition to the herbaceous spiraeas (see p. 178), there are a number of excellent shrubby kinds. All are deciduous and most are hardy and easily grown in a variety of soils and situations. From both the cultural and decorative points of view they may conveniently be considered in two groups, one composed of early flowering kinds and the others of species and varieties that flower in summer. Of the first group excellent examples are *S. arguta*, with small white flowers all down the thin, arching twigs in April and early May; *S. Thunbergii,* which is very similar but a little earlier; and *S. Van Houttei,* which has small clusters of white flowers in early June. All these vary from about 5 to 7 ft. in height and are a little more in breadth. They may with advantage be thinned out annually immediately after flowering, some of the older branches being cut out to make room for younger wood.

In the later flowering group there is greater variety in habit and colour. *Spiraeas Douglasii, Menziesii triumphans,* and *salicifolia* all make thickets of long, erect shoots, terminated about mid-summer by short, fluffy looking spikes of pink flowers. They average 6 ft. in height and spread indefinitely. They can usually be increased by division in autumn as they produce a lot of suckers. Little pruning is needed.

S. discolor, also known as *S. ariæfolia,* flowers at the same time but is more graceful, with slightly arching shoots 10 to 12 ft. high terminated by fine plumes of creamy white flowers. It repays rather hard pruning each February. *S. Lindleyana* and *S. Aitchisonii* are rather like it in bloom but still bigger and really are small trees.

S. japonica is one of the smallest of the late flowering group, seldom above 4 ft. and often less and with a pleasing rounded habit. The flowers are produced all summer in flattish heads, rosy red in the type but a really brilliant carmine in the fine variety Anthony Waterer. Fairly severe spring thinning of old wood, followed by shortening of the younger growth, is desirable to keep these shrubs in full vigour.

Where suckers are not available, cuttings of fairly ripe wood may be rooted under bell glasses in September. *Spirea Lindleyana* and *Aitchisonii* may also be increased by root cuttings in winter.

SPRUCE.—*See* PICEA (p. 298).

SYMPHORICARPOS (*Snowberry*). The common snowberry, *Symphoricarpos racemosus,* is a branching, very twiggy, deciduous shrub well worth growing for its abundant crops of pure white berries in autumn. It has the added merit that it will grow practically anywhere, in sun or shade, good soil or poor, and needs no attention. It makes quite a good hedge, especially if mixed with something of stiffer habit such as hawthorn or Myrobalan plum. It reaches a height of 8 or 9 ft. and spreads indefinitely by suckers, which also provide a ready means of increase.

S. orbiculatus, the Coral Berry, is so called because the berries are rosy red. It is a smaller shrub and not so hardy, only producing good crops of berries in a warm, sunny place.

SYRINGA (*Lilac*). *Syringa* is the correct botanical name of the lilacs. In gardens it is often applied to the philadelphus, but this is entirely incorrect, the popular name of this genus being mock orange.

The garden lilacs are all deciduous shrubs or small trees. The most important from the decorative standpoint are *Syringa vulgaris* the common lilac, and its numerous varieties many of which have been given garden names. There are single and double flowered forms and the colour range is from white and palest mauve to a rich wine red. A few outstanding varieties are Mdme Lemoine, double white; Congo, single, reddish purple; Souvenir de L. Spath, single, deep purple; Kathleen Havemeyer, double, deep mauve; Marie Legraye, single, white; Charles X, single, purplish red; President Grevy, double, bluish lilac; Michel Buchner, double, pinkish lilac. All make fine shrubs 15 ft. or so in height and about 12 ft. in diameter. All succeed best in rather good, loamy soils and open positions.

These choice garden lilacs are often propagated by nurserymen by grafting or budding, sometimes on to common lilac and occasionally on to privet. In either case suckers, which are generally produced freely, must be removed as they will not have the same character as the rest of the bush. It is better for this reason to increase by layering in spring or autumn, or, in the case of bushes already on their own roots, by detaching suckers with roots in autumn.

The lilac species are not so important from the garden standpoint, but *Syringa persica* makes a graceful shrub 6 or 7 ft. high and as much through with fragrant, lilac coloured flowers in small sprays in May. Treatment is the same as for *S. vulgaris.*

A comparatively new race of hybrids has been produced in America between *S. Josikaea* and *S. reflexa*. These differ from the common lilacs in having looser and more lightly formed flower clusters. In the mass they are less showy but they will appeal to those who place grace before weight of bloom. Colours are mainly in shades of mauve.

None of these lilacs requires regular pruning except for the removal of faded flower heads in the case of single flowered varieties, but occasional removal of some of the oldest wood will stimulate vigour.

TAMARIX (*Tamarisk*). These shrubs or small trees all have a loose, branching habit and feathery leaves which give them a most graceful appearance. There are evergreen as well as deciduous species bu the latter group contains the most beautiful kinds. Of these one of the best is *T. pentandra* (syn. *T. hispida aestivalis*) which will eventually reach a height of 12 ft. if allowed to but can be kept very much smaller by hard annual pruning. The flowers are small, pink and carried along all the upper shoots so that a large specimen has somewhat the appearance of a very fine astilbe. It is at its best in August and September. *T. tetrandra* is rather similar in appearance but flowers in May. It can also be kept much below its full size by hard annual pruning but the work must be done immediately after flowering whereas with *T. pentandra* it should be done in February or early March. *T. anglica* is a smaller bush, seldom above 8 ft. with whitish or pink tinged flowers in late summer. It does very well by the sea and is often planted in seaside gardens to form a windbreak. *T. gallica* is similar but taller and it has more definitely pink flowers. Both can be hard pruned in February if desired.

All these tamarisks can be increased by cuttings of well ripened wood in autumn, struck outdoors in sandy soil.

TAXODIUM (*Swamp Cypress*). The only species is *Taxodium distichum* and this is one of the few deciduous cone-bearing trees. Moreover it is one of the few that will thrive in very wet places even, in fact, with its roots completely covered by a few inches of water. It has feathery foliage, not unlike that of a cypress, and it makes a shapely, pyramidal tree up to 100 ft. in height. The young leaves are a very light shade of green. They become darker with age and turn red before they fall in the autumn. Seed sown in pans of moist peat in spring provides the only method of propagation.

TAXUS (*Yew*). The common yew, one of the most famous of British evergreen trees, is botanically known as *Taxus baccata*. Left to grow unchecked it will make a broadly pyramidal tree 30 ft. or so in height and often considerably more through. It bears pruning well, however, and for this reason and also because of its dense, dark green growth, is (or was) a popular hedge subject. It is unfortunate that fewer yew hedges have been planted during the present century as it is still one of the best hedge shrubs available. There is a fine form, named *aurea*, in which the young growth is bright yellow. The variety *fastigiata*, known as the Irish yew, is erect and columnar in habit and excellent for avenue planting. This also has a form with golden young growth.

The yews thrive in most soils and do particularly well on rich loams overlying chalk. They are rather slow growing, though not so slow as some people appear to imagine. Hard pruning is best confined to May but yews can be lightly pruned at any time during the summer.

The common yew can be raised from seed sown outdoors in spring but selected forms, such as those with golden leaves, will not breed true in this way and must be increased by cuttings of firm young growth inserted in very sandy soil under a bell glass in July or August.

TECOMA. Two very showy climbers are included in this genus but neither is fully hardy except in the mildest parts of the country. Elsewhere they should be planted against sunny, sheltered walls. Both have large, trumpet shaped orange scarlet flowers in late summer. *T.*

grandiflora, which is the handsomer and also the more tender of the two, climbs by twining, whereas *T. radicans* has a few aerial roots like those of an ivy by which it can attach itself to a wall. There is also a hybrid between these two species which has inherited much of the beauty of one and the comparative hardiness of the other. It is known as *T. Tagliabuana*. The best form of this hybrid is Mme Galen. All can be increased by layering in spring or autumn. When wall space is filled, both can have all further growth cut back hard each year in early March. These plants are correctly *Campsis grandiflora* and *C. radicans*.

TEUCRIUM. The only shrubby species cultivated is *Teucrium fruticans*, an evergreen 6 or 7 ft. high and rather spreading in habit, with grey-green leaves and lavender-blue flowers in late summer. It is not very hardy and should have a warm, sunny position such as at the foot of a wall facing south. It will put up with a good deal of heat and drought and is a good plant for light soils which are liable to dry out rapidly. It can be increased by seed or by cuttings of half ripened growth rooted in July in a close frame with gentle bottom heat.

THUJA (*Arbor-Vitae*). An important genus of cone-bearing trees with many similarities to cupressus. Two of the most popular species, *T. occidentalis* and *T. plicata* (syn. *Lobbii*) are frequently used as hedge or screen plants in the same way as *C. Lawsoniana* or *C. macrocarpa*. The first named is a little apt to get thin and the foliage sometimes turns a bad colour in winter, but *T. plicata* makes a first-rate wind break or large hedge and has fine, dark green foliage. There are numerous forms of each species some with the young leaves golden (*T. occidentalis* Rheingold and *T. plicata aurea*). Left to grow unpruned these thujas will make pyramidal trees 30 or 40 ft. high in the case of *T. occidentalis*, more than twice as much in the case of *T. plicata*.

The species are best raised from seed sown in frame or greenhouse in March. Selected forms are increased by grafting in spring on to seedlings of the type species or by cuttings taken in late summer and rooted under a bell glass.

THUJOPSIS. A small group of cone bearing trees not unlike the thujas in many respects but on the whole not so useful in the garden. One species, however, *T. dolobrata*, makes a handsome specimen and is often seen as a large, rounded bush or small, broadly cone-shaped tree 15 ft. or more high and almost as much through. The foliage is dark, shining green above, blue grey beneath. It will thrive in most soils and likes a fair amount of moisture though it should not be planted in damp hollows likely to be frost pockets. In other respects culture is identical with that of thuja.

Trees and Shrubs

Tᴵʟᴵᴀ (*Lime*). The limes are all large, deciduous trees, more suitable for parks and woodlands than for garden planting. The common lime, *T. vulgaris*, will reach a height of 100 ft. or even more and a spread of 50 ft. The greenish flowers, produced with great freedom in July, have a sweet fragrance and are much sought after by bees. Incidentally this lime is often severely attacked by greenflies. A better ornamental tree is *T. euchlora* which seldom exceeds 50 ft. in height and is not subject to greenfly attack. The weeping lime, *T. petiolaris*, is also very attractive and should be planted where there is room for a large specimen. It may reach a height of 80 ft. and spread of 50 ft. All these limes will thrive in any ordinary soil.

Tᴜʟɪᴘ Tʀᴇᴇ.—*See* Lɪʀɪᴏᴅᴇɴᴅʀᴏɴ (p. 292).

Uʟᴇx (*Gorse*). The common gorse, though beautiful, is too common to be worth planting in gardens but its double flowered form, *U. europaeus flore pleno* is a very different proposition. When in full bloom in late spring no shrub is capable of making a more solid splash of golden colour. It will thrive in poor, sandy soils and dry places and makes a rounded, densely spiny bush 4 or 5 ft. high and rather more in diameter. It is apt to die out without warning particularly in rich or damp soils and, as it sets no seeds, it must be increased by cuttings of firm young side shoots in sand or sandy soil under a bell glass in July or August. No pruning is required.

Uʟᴍᴜs (*Elm*). In general the elms are much too big and they send out hungry roots much too far to make good garden trees. However, some exception may be made in the case of the weeping elm, *U. Camperdownii pendula*, which makes a very handsome specimen on a lawn, and seldom exceeds a height and spread of 20 ft. There is another variety of weeping elm, *U. montana pendula*, which is considerably bigger. *U. stricta*, the Cornish elm, is erect in habit rather like a Lombardy poplar and will reach a height of 60 or 70 ft. with a spread of little more than 20 ft. All elms like rather rich, loamy soils. No pruning is required.

Vᴇʀᴏɴɪᴄᴀ. It is a pity that many of the shrubby veronicas are on the border-line of hardiness and in consequence, only reliable for outdoor planting in the milder southern and western counties and near to the sea. This is certainly true of most of the very handsome forms or hybrids of *V. speciosa* which make rounded evergreen bushes 4 to 5 ft. high and through with showy spikes of blue, purple or crimson flowers in late summer. *V.* Autumn Glory, which is rather smaller and has deep purplish blue flowers, is hardier and will thrive in many inland gardens.

One of the loveliest of all, *V. Hulkeana*, needs the protection of a sunny wall in most places. It grows 3 or 4 ft. high, has a loose, almost

319

herbaceous habit, and produces graceful sprays of bluish-lilac flowers in early summer.

V. salicifolia, a bushy species with narrow, light green leaves, and rat-tail spikes of white flowers in July is hardier but may be damaged in cold places. The hardiest species is *V. Traversii* which is just a little too neat and formal and has rather small but very numerous spikes of whitish flowers in July.

All are evergreen, require no pruning, are not fussy about soil and can be increased by July–August cuttings in a frame.

VIBURNUM. Evergreen and deciduous shrubs are included in this genus and several species are notable for the exquisite perfume of their flowers. Of these one of the best is *V. Carlesii* which makes a well-branched bush about 4 ft. high and a little more through and bearing dome-shaped heads of white, pink tinted flowers in April. It is deciduous and reasonably hardy. *V. utile* is a little like this but evergreen, May flowering and devoid of perfume. *V. Burkwoodii,* a hybrid between the two, combines many of their good points, having the fragrance and earliness of the one and the evergreen character of the other. Another fine hybrid with *V. Carlesii* as one parent is *V. carlcephalum.* It is early flowering, white and very fragrant.

V. Opulus is the guelder rose of British hedgerows, a pretty shrub with flattish heads of white flowers followed by currant-red berries. For the garden a better shrub is the variety of this known as 'sterile' or popularly as the snowball tree because of its large, globular heads of white flowers. These are at their best in June. Guelder rose and snowball tree both make big shrubs 10 or 12 ft. high and as much through.

V. tomentosum is deciduous and has flat heads of white flowers which are better developed in the variety *Mariesii.* There is also another variety, *plicatum,* in which the flower heads are globular but smaller than those of the snowball tree. It is sometimes known as the Japanese snowball and is a very beautiful shrub. All have a rather open habit and make bushes up to 10 ft. in height and diameter.

An old favourite is *V. Tinus,* more familiar as laurustinus. It is evergreen, dense in habit, 9 or 10 ft. high and as much through with dark green leaves and flattish flower heads which are pink in bud, white when open. The laurustinus is often in bloom in January and continues well on into the spring. It is quite hardy.

Finally there is *V. rhytidophyllum,* more like a small tree than a shrub, with large handsome evergreen leaves dark green and wrinkled. The big, flat, flower heads in June are rather a dingy white and are followed by red berries which later turn black.

All these viburnums grow well in ordinary soils. The laurustinus should have a sheltered position for the sake of its winter flowers. No pruning is required. Propagation is by July–August cuttings in a frame or under a bell glass.

VIRGINIA CREEPER.—*See* VITIS below.

VITIS (*Vine*). Deciduous climbers mainly grown for their foliage. The plant commonly known as self-clinging Virginia creeper has been variously named by botanists *Vitis inconstans, Ampelopsis Veitchii* and *Parthenocissus tricuspidata*. It is a fine plant to clothe a wall and requires no support. Other vines, such as the large-leaved *V. Coignetiae* and the brilliantly coloured *V.* (*or Parthenocissus*) *Henryana*, must be given wires or trellis-work over which to ramble. All will grow in any ordinary soil and sunny or partially shaded position, and none requires any regular pruning. Propagation is easily effected by layering young shoots.

WALNUT.—*See* JUGLANS (p. 287).

WEIGELA.—*See* DIERVILLA (p. 276).

WHITEBEAM.—*See* PYRUS (p. 304).

WINTER SWEET.—*See* CHIMONANTHUS (p. 267).

WISTERIA.—All the wisterias are vigorous plants which require plenty of room if they are to do themselves full justice. The most popular species is *Wisteria sinensis* (*chinensis*) which produces its rather pale lilac-blue flowers in late May. There is a good white-flowered form. *W. floribunda* is rather similar but has more leaflets to the pinnate leaves. It has produced a number of good varieties of which one, known variously as *macrobotrys* and *multijuga* has the longest flower trails of any wisteria; they are occasionally 4 ft. in length.

All these wisterias thrive in any ordinary soil and like a sunny position. A south wall suits them to perfection. The finest flower racemes are obtained by allowing the plants to produce a number of strong growths and then shortening all subsequent side growths in two operations, first to a length of five leaves each in mid-July and later to two dormant growth buds in November. Propagation is usually by layers pegged down in early summer. Seeds will germinate in a frame or greenhouse in spring.

WITCH HAZEL.—*See* HAMAMELIS (p. 283).

YEW.—*See* TAXUS (p. 317).

Yucca. These plants give a very tropical look to the garden with their rounded masses of stiff sword-shaped leaves and tall spikes of showy, cream-coloured flowers. *Y. gloriosa* will make an almost tree-like specimen 8 or 10 ft. high and with a trunk and branches. Most kinds, however, have quite a short main stem and do not exceed 3 or 4 ft. in height except when in flower. One of the smallest and most attractive is *Y. filamentosa* so called because of the thread-like filaments which are attached to the leaves. All flower in July or August. They will grow in ordinary or even in poor, sandy soils, are first rate seaside shrubs and require no pruning. They can be increased by seed which should be germinated in a warm greenhouse in spring.

Zenobia. A very beautiful, peat loving shrub belonging to the rhododendron family is *Z. pulverulenta*. It grows 5 or 6 ft. high and rather more through, has greyish, evergreen leaves and long clusters of pendent, waxy white bell shaped flowers at midsummer. No pruning is necessary. A semi-shaded position is most favourable. Propagate by seed as for rhododendrons.

CHAPTER X

Roses

THE ROSE has been very highly developed, probably more so than any other flower. At the same time many of the original species have been retained in cultivation with the result that a great number of totally different types are available for the adornment of our gardens. Some knowledge of the characteristics of the principal types among these is a necessary preliminary to an understanding of the rose.

TYPES AND RACES. The species are themselves very numerous—about two hundred according to one authority. By no means all are of value in the garden but a considerable number have some decorative merit. Many are grown principally for their flowers, e.g. *Rosa spinosissima, Hugonis* and *alba*. Others are grown mainly for their foliage, e.g. *R. Willmottiae*; yet others for their fruits or hips, e.g. *R. Moyesii, setipoda* and *pomifera*. There is even one astonishing species which is grown for its translucent thorns. Its name is *Rosa sericea pteracantha*.

Most of these species make informal bushes and their flowers are almost always single like those of our native dog rose, though they vary in every other conceivable manner and have a most extensive range of colour, size and form. Their place is the shrub border rather than the formal rose garden but they may sometimes be used effectively in the latter as a surround or hedge.

Nevertheless it is to the hybrid roses which have been built up by crossing certain of the species that the gardener must turn for his finest material. It is only a mere handful of species that has been used in the production of these and, curiously enough, by no means always the most obviously attractive, but the result beggars description.

Undisputed queen of the rose garden to-day is the Hybrid Tea which, as might be expected, has a mixed and somewhat complicated parentage. It was developed from two earlier races both of which are still grown though to a much smaller extent than formerly. These are the Hybrid Perpetual, noted for the fine size and rich colouring of its flowers, and the Tea which is more delicate in colour and constitution but has the advantage of a longer and more continuous flowering season. The marriage produced the typical garden roses of to-day; roses with a wide colour range and a season extending from early summer to late autumn, together with considerable variation in form and fragrance.

323

Still more colour was added in the early years of the present century by a Frenchman named Pernet who crossed a hybrid tea rose with the Austrian Briar, *Rosa lutea.* The result was the race which was to become famous under the name Pernetiana. The feature of this was the introduction of rich yellow and coppery shades new to the hybrid roses but the advance was not made without handicap. There was a tendency to weak constitution inherited from the Austrian Briar and in consequence some of the earlier Pernetiana roses got a bad name. Gradually this weakness was bred out by crossing with the best hybrid teas, a process which resulted in the two races becoming so merged that it is now difficult to say where one ends and the other begins. The very name Pernetiana is dropping out and the modern novelties are almost always termed hybrid teas.

Meanwhile another race was making its appearance and being rapidly developed. This was the polyantha rose of which there may soon be almost as big a variety as of the hybrid tea. First to gain popularity were the polyantha pom-poms—dwarf roses with big clusters of small, double flowers individually not unlike those of popular ramblers such as Dorothy Perkins. They flowered continuously and were first rate for making a massed display in formal beds. Later these polyantha pom-poms were crossed with hybrid teas and a race of hybrid polyanthas was produced. These showed even greater variation than either of their parents, so great, indeed, that it became difficult to lay down any rules for their identification. One just had to take them on trust from the breeder. Some of the later additions are so much like hybrid teas that it is difficult to see why they should not be classified as such. Others more nearly approach the polyantha pom-pom type but with looser clusters of individually bigger flowers which are often single or semi-double.

All the types so far described are naturally of bush habit though they may be trained as standards or half standards by budding them on strong briar stems of suitable height. But there are also climbing roses which may either be used to clothe walls, arches, pillars and pergolas or, in certain instances, may be budded high up on extra strong briar stems and then trained downwards to form weeping standards.

Like the bush roses these climbers have been developed from a variety of parents. There are, for example, at least three distinct groups of so-called 'rambler' roses, really very vigorous climbers with big clusters of flowers and a rather short season. These are Wichuraiana ramblers, multiflora ramblers, and polyantha ramblers developed in the main from species bearing those names. They are the outstanding roses for covering large areas quickly and, in particular, for open, airy situations such as arches and pergolas. As a rule they are less happy against walls which are either too hot or too shady for their liking.

Wall climbers are provided by special forms of the ubiquitous hybrid tea rose some of which have arisen as chance sports from normal bush varieties and are, in consequence, known as 'climbing sports'. Some of these are a little unstable and show a tendency to revert to their original bush form if carelessly treated, a subject which is dealt with more fully on p. 327

There are also climbing roses belonging to the tea, noisette and Banksia types which delight in sun and warmth and are consequently excellent for walls, and an increasing number of hybrid wichuraianas such as Paul's Scarlet Climber and Chaplin's Pink Climber, which have a dual utility and can be planted in almost any position.

This by no means exhausts the story of the rose. I have said nothing about the hybrid musk race developed by the late Rev. J. H. Pemberton, mainly with the idea of enriching the rose garden with autumn bloom. Nor have I mentioned the hybrid sweetbriars connected with the name of Lord Penzance and combining the foliage fragrance of our native sweetbriar with something of the brilliance of more highly developed roses. To these must be added rugosa hybrids and older races such as damask, cabbage, moss and Bourbon, now out of favour with all but a few enthusiasts though perhaps to be taken up again in the future, to say nothing of the astonishing Mermaid, sole representative of the hybrid bracteata class, which should surely merit immediate development. But I have, perhaps, said enough to give the reader some idea why the rose is so often called the queen of flowers.

SOIL AND ITS PREPARATION. Contrary to what is often stated roses can be grown successfully on many different types of soil and not only upon the heavier loams and rich clays. I have seen highly successful rose gardens close to the sea coast in places where the soil was extremely sandy. Naturally more feeding is necessary under such conditions than on soils of better quality and greater precautions must be taken in hot weather to prevent excessive drying out. But these are measures within the scope of the ordinary gardener and, as a matter of fact, they apply with equal force to many other ornamental plants and practically all vegetables. Indeed I would say of roses what I have said elsewhere of fruits, that they may be planted with confidence in any garden which will produce reasonable crops of the commoner vegetables such as potatoes and cabbages.

Because of their permanent nature it is necessary to prepare the ground with particular thoroughness for roses. Mark well this does not simply mean that the soil must be deeply dug and well supplied with manures or fertilisers. Preparation also involves the elimination of all deep-rooting, perennial weeds such as bindweed, coltsfoot, ground elder and horsetail. If pieces of these are left in the rose beds after they have been planted, it will be extremely difficult ever to get them thoroughly clean because of the impossibility of doing anything but surface cultivation. On account of this difficulty it is often wise to delay the planting of roses on new ground or in neglected gardens until the second year, so that the first season may be devoted to cleaning the ground.

Digging should be as deep as possible but of course there is no point in going down into stone, chalk or other medium into which it would obviously be undesirable for roses to penetrate. There are places in which full trenching is not only possible but highly desirable and others where, if not quite impossible, it would be wholly unprofitable.

Dung, if available, should be used in the preparation of the ground. Nor should it be confined to the second spit of soil, as is so frequently stated. It will do far more good turned in with the top spit though, if there is enough to fork some more into the second spit as well, so much the better. The only qualification is that, for top spit use, manure must either be well rotted or applied a good three months before the roses are to be planted. Fresh manure used late may check root growth.

If no manure can be obtained, chopped turves make a very good substitute; in fact they can be used in addition to manure with excellent results. Turn them in, as far as possible grass side downwards, under about 10 in. of soil. This will ensure that they rot properly and yet are near enough to the roots to feed them when they need it most.

Whether manure, turves or both are used give, in addition, some coarsely ground bones or bone meal. A dressing of 4 oz. per sq. yd. will usually be sufficient, forked in when the beds are finally prepared for planting.

PLANTING. This is best done early in November though it is possible to plant roses from about the middle of October to the middle of March in an average season in the south. In the north it may be practicable to plant a little earlier and later but there is more likelihood that a prolonged break will be imposed by weather in the middle of the planting.

All instructions regarding the planting of shrubs apply with equal force to roses. A good many different stocks (see p. 331) are used for roses and these vary in the character of their root system. This in turn will affect the shape and size of the hole required, but if the planter takes care always to allow the roots to assume a natural position without bending and to cover the uppermost with about three inches of soil, he will not go far wrong. Usually when roses arrive from the nursery the soil mark can be seen quite clearly on the stem. It is wise to plant so that this soil mark is about an inch below the surface when planting is completed. Contrary to practice with fruit trees it is an advantage if the point of union between stock and scion can be covered with soil as it is a good thing for the rose to make roots of its own. This is never possible with standards which are budded high up but it can usually be ensured with bushes and climbers.

Plant very firmly and make certain that standards are staked at once. Climbers and ramblers should be tied to some kind of support even though most of the growth treated in this way is to be cut away within a few months. Windrocking can do as much harm to newly planted roses as to fruits.

PRUNING OF NEWLY PLANTED ROSES. This is the commonest stumbling block for the beginner. Many roses need rather severe initial pruning if they are to give the best possible results and the novice finds it goes against the grain to sacrifice so much apparently promising growth.

Hard pruning is particularly necessary in the case of newly planted roses. The reason is that after transplanting roots take some time to recover and meanwhile the supply of sap is curtailed. If it is distributed over too many shoots, all will be starved; if it is confined to a few of the most promising, growth will be strong and will, in turn, stimulate increased root activity.

The general rule is to shorten all strong shoots of bush and standard roses to about three inches and to eliminate weak shoots entirely. This pruning, like that of mature bush and standard roses, is delayed until danger of really hard and prolonged frost is over, usually about the end of March in the south and the first week in April in the north.

Rambler roses are hardier and more vigorous. In consequence they can be pruned about a month earlier and not quite so severely. It is sufficient to shorten strong growths to a foot each. Note that weeping standards are simply rambler roses budded on the top of a strong briar stem and that for our present purpose they are pruned just like any other ramblers.

Many climbers are treated in much the same manner as ramblers the first spring after planting, but one very important group of climbers known as climbing sports requires a different technique. These are not touched until the March–April period and then they are only lightly tipped to get rid of shoot ends which have suffered damage from one cause or another. The reason is that climbing sports are simply very vigorous forms of normally bush varieties: forms which have the climbing habit fairly well ingrained but nevertheless may revert to bush type once more if given any encouragement so to do.

PRUNING OF ESTABLISHED ROSES. In subsequent years the pruning of roses becomes a much more complex matter. It is not that the treatment of any particular plant is itself difficult once the method is understood but that there are so many different methods to be mastered and the uses of each understood.

First there are methods to suit the special peculiarities of the numerous classes of rose, hybrid tea, polyantha, rambler, etc. Then, within these classes, there are individual idiosyncrasies of growth to be taken into account. A third complication is added by the fact that pruning may vary according to the purpose for which the rose is grown. Thus the same variety is usually pruned harder if it is grown for exhibition or for cut flowers than if it is required solely for garden decoration. No easy generalisations are possible here and so I have set out below the appropriate methods under the headings of the principal types concerned.

Teas, Hybrid Teas and Pernetianas. For garden decoration cut back strong shoots to four or five buds, weaklier shoots more severely. For exhibition cut strong shoots to two or three buds and remove all weakly shoots. Severity of pruning may in all cases be increased for plants which fail to make satisfactory growth and conversely may be decreased for plants which grow too strongly. All pruning in March–April.

Hybrid Perpetuals. Prune as above but, as most of these are normally very vigorous varieties, the precautions for curbing vigour must usually be observed. Often it will pay to leave some strong shoots with as many as eight buds. An alternative is to leave the best of the previous year's growth unpruned and tie it down to pegs driven in conveniently for the purpose. All remaining growth, including as much as possible of the old wood, is cut out entirely. This system is known as pegging down.

Polyantha Pom-pom. Shorten the best stems by about half their length and remove the remainder. If it is desired to keep plants as dwarf and compact as possible, cut most growth to within 3 or 4 in. of the base. Do all pruning in March–April.

Hybrid Polyanthas. These are hybrids between the true polyanthas and the hybrid teas. Most do well with a moderate thinning of the older or weaker wood and shortening of young growth by about one third but some modern varieties approach very closely to the hybrid tea in character and need to be pruned more like that class

Wichuraiana, Multiflora and Polyantha Ramblers and Climbers. For the purpose of pruning these fall into two groups. One is composed of varieties which normally make a lot of strong growth right from the base each year, e.g. Dorothy Perkins, Excelsa, Blush Rambler. The other group makes comparatively little basal growth, most of the new shoots coming from the older wood at various heights above ground level, e.g. Emily Grey, Alberic Barbier, Albertine, Paul's Scarlet and Chaplin's Pink Climber.

Group one is pruned by cutting out all stems that have borne flowers and training non-flowering stems in their place.

Group two is pruned more lightly. A few of the oldest stems are removed, but those which are producing a good number of healthy young side growths are retained or at most only shortened a little. In both cases pruning should be done in late summer or early autumn as soon as possible after the plants have finished flowering.

Hybrid Tea Climbers. A few climbers are classed as hybrid teas. These must not be confused with the climbing sports derived from hybrid teas (see p. 325). The climbers referred to here have not originated from bush varieties and therefore have no tendency to revert to bush form. Prune moderately in March cutting out some of the older wood to make way for the best new growth which may itself be shortened a little to get rid of unripe or damaged ends.

Climbing Sports. Retain strong young growths at practically full length. Shorten weaker shoots by a third to two thirds and cut out wood that is producing little fresh growth. If the plants tend to get bare at the base, cut one or two good shoots back to within a foot of ground level and so force fresh growth from low down. Do all this in March-April.

Climbing Teas. Roses of the Gloire de Dijon type should be pruned in much the same manner as climbing sports with the difference that, as they usually make sufficient basal growth, it is not so necessary to cut some strong good shoots hard back. In the case of Marechal Niel most of the young growth can be retained at full length without even being tipped.

Sweetbriars. These, including the Penzance Briars, require little pruning beyond the removal of some of the older branches to make way for younger growth. This may be done in autumn or spring, whichever is more convenient. When grown as hedges this type of rose should be pruned more severely to maintain shape and may be trimmed up again immediately after flowering. It often pays to weave a few long shoots through the base of the hedge to keep it dense.

Hybrid Musks. Little pruning is required beyond a thinning out of the older wood which may be done in February or March

Provence, Damask, Moss and Bourbon. None of these old-fashioned roses requires much pruning. Old wood should be cut out and the best of the year-old wood shortened by about a third. Thinner shoots can be cut back to a half or two thirds according to the room available. All this work should be done in March.

Species. Thinning only is required, preference being given to the best young wood as in the case of sweetbriars. As with them the work can be done in autumn or spring to suit the gardeners' convenience.

SUMMER PRUNING. Heavy flowering roses of the hybrid tea and Pernetiana types often repay a fairly drastic thinning out in summer immediately after the first flush of bloom is over. This in no way replaces the ordinary spring pruning but is supplementary to it. The object is to encourage strong new growth as quickly as possible and so give the plants a chance to build up suitable wood for autumn flowering. In the case of roses grown mainly to supply cut flowers sufficient summer pruning is usually given by the mere act of cutting the flowers with good long stems.

DISBUDDING. This is really a branch of pruning. It is only necessary in the case of large flowered roses of the tea, hybrid tea, Pernetiana and hybrid perpetual types and then only if fine individual blooms rather than a good general display are the object in view. Disbudding means that only one flower bud is left per stem, all other buds being rubbed or cut out at as early a stage as possible. Usually it is best to retain the terminal bud and remove the smaller buds just below it. There are occasions, however, when this rule may be reversed, one of the side buds being retained in preference to the terminal one. This will occur if the terminal bud has been damaged in any way or if it appears to be deformed. It may also be wise with very large, full roses such as Dame Edith Helen, especially early in the summer or if the weather is very wet. The reason for this is that, under such conditions, the terminal bud often fails to open properly, commencing to decay instead, a condition known as 'balling'. Side buds are not so prone to this fault.

MULCHING. A mulch of lawn mowings spread all over the rose beds in spring and renewed from time to time throughout the summer is often of the greatest value in maintaining growth especially on thin, dry soils. It is also of value in decreasing infection by black spot disease, the spores of which may overwinter in the surface soil and be carried from it to the foliage in spring or summer. The mulch, if it is not disturbed, appears to prevent this infection passing from soil to leaves

FEEDING. Once established the best method of feeding roses is to spread a good dressing of well-rotted dung around them each March or April. This may be supplemented where necessary or be replaced when not available by a mixture of fertilisers such as that known as Tonks' Formula. This is prepared by mixing 12 oz. superphosphate of lime, 10 oz. nitrate of potash, 2 oz. sulphate of magnesium, 1 oz. sulphate of iron and 8 oz. gypsum. Crush well, mix thoroughly and apply at 4 oz. per sq. yd. in early April. Alternatively any commercial rose fertiliser may be used or a general garden fertiliser containing nitrogen, phosphates and potash.

EXHIBITING. There are classes for roses at most flower shows and at many of these the standard necessary to win prizes is very high indeed. The essentials for a prize-winning bloom are that it shall be as large and full as possible, well developed, free from blemishes such as split or double centre and deformed, spotted or faded petals, and in colour typical of its variety. To produce such blooms with any degree of certainty a few special precautions are necessary.

First the fertility of the soil must be high and manuring must be generous. Next pruning should be more severe than for garden decoration and subsequently the number of shoots per plant should be reduced considerably. The precise number retained will depend upon variety, strength, age, etc., but should seldom exceed half a dozen. Disbudding must be rigorous. In the last stages of development the opening bud may be protected with a conical rose shade held a few inches above it by a wire clip attached to a stake. The shade may be used both to keep off rain and to protect the bloom from strong sunlight which might fade or burn it. But too much shading is harmful and may spoil the colour of the flower.

The last precaution is to place a woollen tie around each bloom just before it is cut. This tie will prevent the flower opening too quickly while being taken to the show. It should be left around the bloom until the exhibitor has to leave the hall prior to judging. Such ties must always be of natural coloured wool. Any dye is liable to run and stain the petals.

PROPAGATION BY BUDDING. Most roses are increased by budding on to one or other of several different types of rootstock. The wild English dog rose is the stock most frequently used but its supremacy is being challenged by the Rugosa stock, which is cheap to raise, easy to work and encourages rapid growth for the first few years, and by the Laxa stock which is particularly suitable for the poorer types of soil.

Stocks can be raised from seed sown outdoors in March but a far better method is to take cuttings in autumn from selected plants of proved quality. The cuttings should be 9 to 12 in. long, prepared from well-ripened young stems severed just below a joint or leaf. Remove the lower leaves, if any, and line the cuttings in a straight-backed trench about four inches deep in any well-drained soil. Return the soil and make very firm. By the following autumn the cuttings should be well rooted and ready for removal to a reserve bed in which they may be planted 9 to 12 in. apart in rows at least 2½ feet apart. In this they will be budded the following summer and will grow on for a further fifteen months by which time the roses will be ready for removal to their flowering quarters.

Standard roses are best worked on strong briar stems cut from the hedgerow with as much root as possible. Do this in autumn and transplant the stems immediately to the nursery bed in which they will be budded the following summer. The stems should be from three to five feet long—seven or eight feet for weeping standards. In the spring they will probably each produce a number of shoots. Retain three only per stem as nearly as possible where the head of branches is required. Rub out all others at an early stage.

Budding is done in July and August. The 'buds' are growth buds, not flower buds. One will be found in the angle made by each leaf stalk with its shoot. By July many of these buds, especially towards the middle of shoots that have already flowered, should be fat and prominent. These are the kind of buds required.

Shoots bearing such buds are cut from the parent plant and the leaves are removed but the leaf stalks left. They are then stood upright in a jam jar containing a little water.

The stock is prepared by making a T-shaped incision in the bark and lifting the flaps of bark on each side of the downstroke of the T. The bud is cut from the shoot with a shield-shaped portion of bark about an inch in length. As cut this will enclose a thin slip of wood within the bark. This wood should be stripped out, leaving the bark and bud only. This is slipped down under the flaps of the T incision so that the inner surface of the 'shield' lies snugly against the wood of the stock. It is bound firmly in this position with soft raffia or twist.

No further treatment is necessary until the following March when the whole top growth of the stock should be cut off just above the point of budding. This will divert all the rising sap to the bud which will start into growth and so lay the foundation of a new rose plant. Sometimes buds start to grow the first summer within a few weeks of being inserted. This does not matter much, though 'shot eyes' as they are called do not always come through the first winter so well as buds which remain dormant in the normal manner.

For bush roses one bud only is inserted low down on each stock—actually below soil level if possible. A little soil may be scraped away for this purpose and should not be returned afterwards. Standard and half-standard roses are budded high up, one bud being inserted near the base of each young side shoot retained for the purpose. This means that as a rule three buds are inserted on each standard stock. In the case of rugosa standard stems the bark is sufficiently pliable to allow the buds to be put direct on to the main stem at the desired height. Again it is usual to insert three buds per stem spacing these a little above one another and equidistant round the stem.

CUTTINGS. Garden roses may be increased by cuttings in exactly the same manner as rose stocks (see p. 331). Ramblers and species succeed especially well in this way but many modern bush varieties can be propagated in the same manner with tolerable success.

SEEDS. Garden roses do not breed true to type from seed however carefully it is produced. All new roses are raised in this manner, the seed being obtained from hand made crosses between selected parents. The hips are gathered in October, placed in shallow, sand-filled trays and stood outdoors to freeze during the winter. In March the seed is separated from the now rotten pulp and is sown thinly in half-inch deep drills in well-broken soil outdoors.

CHAPTER XI

Bulbs, Corms and Tubers

THE SUBDIVISION of plants which I have adopted as a heading for this chapter has many drawbacks from the systematic writer's point of view. It has neither botanical nor cultural significance. Plants with bulbous or tuberous roots are to be found in all families and they are of very diverse types. Some are hardy, some tender. Some are bedding plants, others appear most at home in the herbaceous border; yet others are purely for greenhouse cultivation.

Why, then, adopt the classification at all? Because it is such a familiar one to the ordinary gardener and one which will always be used by nurseryman and seedman. 'Bulb' catalogues will continue to drop through our letter boxes whatever the more orderly minded may feel about the foolishness of such an arbitrary division. Accustomed by such means to regard bulbs as bulbs I think it would be confusing for the ordinary reader of a popular book such as this to find them classified in more scientific but completely unfamiliar ways. And so, in this chapter I have included all those plants which one might expect to find in a comprehensive 'bulb list' plus a few more, such as dahlias, which do not readily fit into any other category. The purely greenhouse kinds will be found in the section on greenhouse plants.

DESCRIPTION. First a very brief description of the distinctions between bulbs, corms and tubers. Bulbs are always composed of a number of scales more or less tightly packed one on top of the other. The onion and the daffodil are typical examples. These scales are frequently the thickened bases of the leaves.

A corm is solid flesh right through and is, in fact, a thickened stem. It is covered by membraneous sheaths and the presence of these is perhaps the surest means of distinguishing the corm from the tuber for this is also solid flesh throughout but without any sheath. The tuber may be either swollen stem, e.g. kohl rabi; or swollen root, e.g. dahlia.

CHARACTERISTICS. As I have already remarked, because of their very diverse origins and relationships it is not possible to generalise about the treatment of bulbs, corms and tubers in the manner one can with most other groups of plants but a few observations can be made which apply in measure to all.

The most obvious and also the most important of these is the fact that the bulb, corm or tuber is a storage organ which permits the plant to sustain quite long periods of dormancy or semi-dormancy during which it may often be entirely deprived of food and water without suffering the least injury. On the contrary there are a good many plants in each of the three groups which derive benefit from being kept quite dry for a period each year and some are best lifted and shaken free of soil during this resting period.

Nevertheless it would be a mistake to push this point too far, particularly as there is a danger, rather fostered than otherwise by nurserymen and seedsmen who find it useful for trade purposes, in encouraging the belief that *all* bulbs, corms and tubers may be lifted and dried off for quite long periods with impunity. This is not so. Many are better kept in the soil though allowed to get dry for a time while there are some which need a little moisture even during their time of greatest dormancy.

The second generalisation which might be made is less universal in application but nevertheless still applies to a substantial proportion of bulbs, corms and tubers. It is that they often have enough stored nourishment to carry first season flowers with very little extra assistance beyond a supply of moisture. Not infrequently the flowers are already formed in embryo in the bulb before it is planted. In consequence the first season's results depend very little on the skill of the gardener. It is in subsequent years that he will find out whether his methods are good or bad.

A good deal of disappointment and misunderstanding is due to failure to appreciate this point. Novices buy fine bulbs, plant them in an unsuitable environment and yet get very good blooms the following spring or summer. Subsequently results get worse and worse until eventually there are no flowers and probably, soon after, no bulbs either.

And so leaving generalities let us get down to a subject by subject discussion of the plants to be grown and their individual peculiarities.

THE BEST KINDS TO GROW

ACHIMENES. *See* p. 434.

ALLIUM. The familiar onion of the vegetable garden is an allium but here we are concerned only with its purely ornamental relatives. There are a surprising number of these and very beautiful some of them are though almost all suffer from the characteristic onion smell. However this is only noticeable when they are crushed or cut so it is no handicap to their use in the garden.

All will grow readily in any ordinary soil. They are not faddy but most prefer sun and good drainage to shade and excessive moisture. Bulbs should be purchased in early autumn and planted 3 to 4 in. deep and 6 to 18 in. apart according to the size of the full grown plants. Leave undisturbed until obviously overcrowded. Then lift in late summer, divide into single bulbs and replant.

Amongst the best kinds are *A. albo-pilosum* with showy globular heads of large lilac flowers on 2 ft. stems in June; *A. giganteum,* greyish blue, very large and 3 ft. in height; *A. Moly,* buttercup yellow, flowering in May and 1 ft. high; *A. oreophilum,* with big heads of pinkish flowers on rather short stems; *A. stipitatum,* a reddish purple giant, 4 ft. tall flowering in May, and both *A. sphaerocephalum* and *A. descendens,* very similar species with egg-shaped heads of maroon flowers on slender 2 ft. stems in July.

Alstroemeria. *See* p. 140.

Amaryllis (*Belladonna Lily*). This is one of those families about which the botanists seem to have conspired to make things as difficult as possible for the amateur. The name has been applied to quite distinct groups of plants at different times and at present is said to belong to the greenhouse plants familiar to most gardeners as hippeastrums. As there is no certainty that this latest change is to be the last I propose to stick to the familiar garden nomenclature. In consequence by 'amaryllis' I mean primarily *A. Belladonna* the lovely semi-hardy bulb known by many gardeners as the 'Belladonna Lily'. Those who seek information about the showy greenhouse kinds will find this under the heading 'hippeastrum' on p. 352.

A. Belladonna will thrive outdoors in a warm, sunny position and deep, well-drained soil. It usually does well at the foot of a wall facing south or against the outside of a greenhouse with a southerly aspect. The bulbs should be covered with 6 in. of soil except in very mild districts in which 3 in. is enough. If the natural soil is heavy it should be replaced with a lighter mixture containing plenty of sand and leaf mould. Plant in September or October and subsequently leave the bulbs alone. Mulch each May with well-rotted stable manure and peat or leaf mould mixed in equal parts. It will probably be many years before they become so overcrowded that they need to be transplanted. Meanwhile, if the position suits them, and in particular if they get enough sun to ripen the bulbs fully, they will delight you each September with a display of showy and very fragrant, trumpet-shaped, pink flowers borne several together on stiff 2 ft. stems. The flowers appear before the leaves.

ANEMONE (*Windflower*). There are so many anemones and they vary so much in character that it is small wonder if the gardener gets a little confused between them. Probably it will be the showy hybrids of the St. Brigid type that he will get to know first as anemones, though long before that he may have been familiar with our own native woodland windflower without knowing that it was also an anemone.

Some, though by no means all anemones, are tuberous rooted. These tuberous kinds, of which by far the most important to the gardener are the hybrids deriving from *A. coronaria* (St. Brigid and Du Caen belong here), like medium to light soils with plenty of leaf mould or peat, ample moisture while they are in growth but good drainage at all times. They should be planted either in October or from February to April and may be left undisturbed subsequently if the position is really well drained. Should there be any doubt about this it is better to lift the tubers in late summer when leaves turn yellow and store them away in a cool, dry place until the following spring. Plant 2 to 3 in. deep and 4 to 6 in. apart for a massed display. These plants are first rate for cutting and flowers can be had outdoors from April to June.

The season can be lengthened by planting some tubers in an unheated frame but no attempt should be made to force these with artificial heat. Plant in October and use the lights to protect the plants from severe weather but ventilate fairly freely at other times.

A. coronaria varieties can also be raised easily from seed sown outdoors in early June. Choose a sunny place and rather light, open soil. Sow very thinly in drills ¼ in. deep and leave the seedlings to flower in the seed bed the following year, after which the tubers should be lifted and replanted with the usual amount of room.

All varieties of *A. coronaria* have brightly coloured, poppy-like flowers on 9 to 12 in. stems. The St. Brigid strain has double flowers and the petals are often deeply slashed. Colours are very varied— scarlets, blues, pinks, whites and various combinations.

Other attractive tuberous rooted anemones are *A. fulgens*, with vivid scarlet flowers on 12 in. stems in May; March flowering *A. apeninna*, a low growing plant suggesting a bright blue and compact edition of our native wood anemone; *A. blanda*, which is very similar, and, of course, any good forms of the wood anemone (*A. nemorosa*) itself such as the silvery-blue *Robinsoniana,* and large-flowered *Allenii* all of which flower in April.

A. fulgens is a lover of sun and well-drained but rather rich soils. The others will grow best in light shade and open soils containing plenty of humus. All should be planted 2 in. deep and 6 to 8 in. apart in September or October.

ANTHERICUM. *See* p. 437.

ANTHOLYZA. These little known but showy plants are rather like montbretias in appearance and require similar treatment. The best is *A. paniculata,* with narrowly tubular, scarlet flowers produced in short spikes at the ends of slender, arching 3 ft. stems early in autumn. Plant in March or April in a sunny, sheltered spot and rather light soil. The foot of a south wall is a suitable place for it and here, given good drainage, it will prove reasonably permanent.

ASCLEPIAS. There is one tuberous rooted member of this genus named *A. tuberosa,* which is worth planting in the herbaceous border for its handsome, lance-shaped leaves and showy clusters of orange flowers on 2 ft. stems in late summer. It is a hardy perennial which does best in the lighter types of soil and warm, sunny positions. Plant in early spring and leave undisturbed for a number of years. It should be treated like a herbaceous perennial rather than a typical tuber.

BABIANA. These are too tender to be grown outdoors in most districts and are usually treated as cool greenhouse pot plants. But in a few favoured localities babianas may be planted in the open in sunny, sheltered positions and rather sandy soils. Plant the bulbs 3 in. deep and 6 or 8 in. apart in March or April and protect in winter with dry straw or bracken. The flowers are trumpet-shaped, brightly coloured and borne in close spikes on 6 to 12 in. stems. Blue, purple, scarlet, crimson and white are the commonest colours. The plants flower outdoors in May and June.

BEGONIA. *See* p. 440.

BRODIAEA. Another comparatively unimportant genus. Most of the species need more sun and warmth than we can easily give them but one, *B. uniflora,* is a pretty plant with starry blue flowers on 6 in. stems in April and May which will grow readily enough in any ordinary, nicely drained soil and sunny position. It makes a good edging to beds and borders or may be used effectively in the rock garden. It should be treated as a herbaceous plant rather than as a typical bulb, and planted, while starting into growth, in March or early April. This plant passes in gardens under several other names such as *Milla uniflora* and *Triteleia uniflora*. The correct name is *Ipheion uniflorum*.

BULBOCODIUM. The only species, *B. vernum*, flowers very early, often in January, has purple, funnel-shaped blooms on short stems and should be planted in warm, sheltered places and well-drained soils. It is a suitable bulb for the rock garden. Plant in September, 3 in. deep and 4 to 6 in. apart and leave undisturbed for a number of years.

CALOCHORTUS (*Butterfly Tulip; Mariposa Lily*). These very beautiful hardy bulbs are not very well known probably because they are not very easy to grow. They require better drainage and more sun and warmth than most of us can provide. In ordinary soil and places they are apt to disappear for good the first winter. However they will usually do well enough in a sunny frame and they make good pot or pan plants for the unheated greenhouse.

Plant or pot in October or November in a warm, sunny position and rather light, sandy soil with plenty of leaf mould or peat to retain moisture in summer. Cover the bulbs with 3 in. of soil (less in pots). Leave undisturbed for three or four years, then lift when foliage dies down, separate bulbs and store in a dry place until planting time. Use frame lights to protect bulbs from severe weather in winter and also to raise the temperature and dry the soil after flowering and so ripen the bulbs.

The flowers are like very delicately formed tulips on slender stems ½ to 2 ft. high according to variety. Colours are very varied and bright, including yellow, lilac, purple and rose. Some are handsomely blotched. All bloom in May–June.

CANNA. See p. 449.

CHIONODOXA (*Glory of the Snow*). These delightful hardy bulbs produce sprays of small starry blue flowers in early spring. They may be grown in the border as an edging, in beds as a groundwork for taller spring flowers such as daffodils, or in the rock garden. There are numerous varieties, the best for general cultivation being *C. Luciliae*, which combines blue and white, and *C. sardensis* which is blue almost throughout. Both are about 4 in. in height.

All are easily grown in ordinary soil and sunny position. Plant 3 in. deep and 5 or 6 in. apart in September or October. Leave undisturbed for several years, then lift in July when foliage dies down and, after cleaning off, replant in a new place.

Chionodoxas also make pretty pot plants if grown five or six in a 4 in. pot or pan in ordinary potting soil. Pot in August or September, keep in an unheated frame until November or December then bring into the cool greenhouse. Repot annually.

CLIVIA. *See* p. 455.

COLCHICUM (*Meadow Saffron, Autumn Crocus*). Superficially the colchicums bear so much resemblance to crocuses that it is usually difficult to convince people they have no connection whatsoever. The popular name 'Autumn Crocus' applied to colchicums is also very misleading for there are, in fact, true crocuses which flower at that season.

Colchicums require similar conditions to crocuses; a reasonably good soil and sunny or partially shady position. They can be established in thin woodland or under trees that are not too dense. Do not plant in pasture land as the foliage and flowers are poisonous to cattle. The bulbs should be planted in July or early August, 2 in. deep and 5 or 6 in. apart. Leave them undisturbed until overcrowded, then lift in July, separate to single bulbs and replant at once. The two best known species are *C. autumnale* and *C. speciosum*. Both are lilac pink and both have pure white forms. There are double flowered varieties of *C. autumnale* in both lilac-pink and white. In addition there are numerous other species and varieties and some very showy hybrids notable for the size of their flowers and their range of colour from soft to deep pink.

CONVALLARIA (*Lily of the valley*). One of those plants so well known under its popular name that it will probably come as a shock to many readers to realise that it has another name. The roots are rhizomes lacking sufficient substance to enable them to stand long periods without water. In consequence they should never be dried right off but should be treated more like ordinary herbaceous perennials, i.e. lifted when overcrowded, divided and replanted without delay. October is the best month for this but it can also be done in March. Just cover the points of the crowns with soil and space them 3 or 4 in. apart. The best soil is one that is cool and leafy. A little well-rotted dung can be worked in when preparing it. The position should be shady or, if in full sun, plenty of moisture must be supplied while the plants are in growth.

Outdoors flowers are produced at the end of April and early in May. Earlier blooms can be obtained by covering the bed with portable frames in January, while winter blooms can be had by forcing strong crowns in a heated greenhouse. These roots are planted close together in shallow boxes filled with coconut fibre or granulated peat instead of soil and are immediately introduced to a temperature of about 80°

but without light. Plenty of moisture must be supplied. When flower stems can be seen, light is gradually admitted to colour the leaves. The crowns are useless after forcing. An alternative method is to pot, in September, strong outdoor roots, place these in a frame until December and then bring into a cool greenhouse. The temperature may be raised to 70° when the flower spikes commence to grow, but before this, should be kept to about 55–60°. The flowers will be later than those produced by forcing but the crown will be less damaged and may be planted back in the garden.

CRINUM. Very showy plants with large, trumpet-shaped, lily-like flowers on stout stems usually about 3 ft. in height. Many of them suffer from the drawback of being on the border line of hardiness—just too tender to be grown safely outdoors and yet sufficiently hardy to tempt many gardeners to take a chance, and then probably suffer disappointment. *Crinum Powellii* with rose pink flowers in late summer is one of the best for outdoor culture and will usually succeed in the south and west if given a sunny, sheltered position. *C. longifolium*, also known as *C. capense* will also succeed under identical conditions. All other species should be treated as greenhouse plants unless there is good evidence that they will thrive outdoors in the particular garden or district under consideration.

All should be grown in rather light loamy soil. Plant the big bulbs in early autumn, covering them with at least 8 in. of soil. A good position is at the foot of a wall facing south. It is wise to cover the spot with straw or bracken from October to April as a protection against frost. Bulbs can usually be left undisturbed for a number of years and require little attention beyond weeding. Feeding is apt to cause leaf growth at the expense of flowers but may occasionally be useful, especially with old plants.

CROCUS. For the purpose of cultivation it is necessary to draw a distinction between, on the one hand, the large flowered hybrids which are used for massed displays in beds and borders and are sold either under fancy names such as Striped Beauty, King of the Purples, etc. or merely under colour and, on the other hand the usually smaller though often more beautiful species which usually pass under their botanical names such as *C. speciosus, C. Imperati, C. susianus*, etc.

The hybrids are all very easy to grow. They are not particular as to soil though a lightish but rich loam suits them best. Most of them can be naturalised in grass quite easily if the grass is not too coarse and is not cut until the crocus foliage dies down in June.

A good deal more care is necessary with many, though not all, of the species. In general these are plants for the rock garden and they are also delightful in pans or pots for the unheated greenhouse or alpine house. They like well-drained soils and sunny positions and are too fragile to rough it with coarse growing plants though they may be grown with advantage under a carpet of low-growing alpines such as *Arenaria montana* or *Thymus Serpyllum*.

The hybrids all flower in March and April but the species vary quite a lot, some starting in October, others blooming in mid-winter and yet others in spring. All are hardy but the winter flowering kinds are apt to be battered by rain and wind unless given some protection. This need be no more than a sheet of glass supported on wires or sticks a few inches above the blooms.

Autumn flowering crocuses should be planted in July or early August. The winter and spring flowering kinds may be planted in September or even October but early planting is always an advantage.

Cover the corms with about 3 in. of soil and space them 4 to 6 in. apart. They usually multiply fairly rapidly and soon form good clumps. It is unnecessary to disturb these until they become overcrowded to a degree which affects the quality or quantity of bloom. Then they should be lifted when the foliage dies down in summer, separated into single corms and replanted with the least possible delay. Incidentally this division of old plants provides the most satisfactory means of increase.

Hybrid crocuses are continually being bred by specialists so that lists of names quickly date. Little purpose would, therefore, be served by giving any. The latest favourites are to be found in any bulb merchant's catalogue. The species are not susceptible to change in this way and the following are a few of the best.

Autumn Flowering: *C. pulchellus*, lavender blue, orange-yellow throat; *C. speciosus*, violet blue with orange stigmas; *C. speciosus albus*, pure white with scarlet stigmas; *C. ʒonatus*, lilac, yellow throat.

Winter Flowering: *C. chrysanthus*, various shades of yellow; *C. Imperati*, violet within, fawn outside, orange stigmas; *C. Sieberi*, pale lilac, orange throat.

Spring Flowering: *C. biflorus*, white to lavender; *C. susianus*, rich yellow (this species is often aptly named 'Cloth of Gold'); *C. Tomasinianus*, clear bright lavender; *C. vernus*, white, lilac or purple (parent of the big-flowered garden hybrids); *C. versicolor picturatus*, white, feathered wine.

CYCLAMEN. From the garden standpoint a very sharp distinction must be made between *C. persicum* (*latifolium*) and the numerous other species. The former, though a pretty plant occasionally seen in warm, sheltered, well-drained places outdoors, is completely overshadowed by the wonderful race of garden forms raised from it. These are exclusively treated as greenhouse plants and I have dealt with them on page 460.

Here I am only concerned with the hardy or near-hardy types that can be grown with reasonable success outdoors. These are all much smaller than the greenhouse varieties, in fact some of them are quite dwarf plants which make a delightful carpet beneath the boles of large trees, beside paths or in cool rock gardens. All resent root disturbance, which makes them rather difficult to establish. Though they make big tubers which look as if they could stand a long time without moisture this is not borne out by experience. I think the prevalent habit of treating hardy cyclamens as 'bulbs' and offering them for sale as dry tubers in autumn is wrong and accounts for many disappointments. It would be far better to regard them as 'alpines' grow them in small pots and offer them for sale in spring. They could then be transferred to the ground with a minimum amount of root disturbance.

The tubers should be covered with no more than an inch of soil. The best position is one that is reasonably sheltered and a little shady. The soil should be cool and leafy with enough sand to ensure good drainage without risking severe drying out in summer. They will usually do well in cool parts of the rock garden or may be naturalised in open parts of the woodland. They do not like dense shade and must not be overgrown by coarser plants. Once established they should be left severely alone. They are unlikely to suffer from overcrowding for many years.

Seed provides the only means of increase. It should be sown in open, leafy soil in frame or greenhouse during February or March. Self sown seedlings often appear freely and clusters of these can be lifted and separated in spring.

Among the best species are *C. coum*, with crimson flowers on 3 in. stems in February-March; *C. europaeum*, similar in height and colour but not flowering till August, and with silver marbled, not dark green foliage; *C. ibericum*, which combines the flowering time and appearance of *C. coum* with the marbled foliage of *C. europaeum; C. neapolitanum* and its form 'album', the former bright pink the latter white, both 6 in. high and September flowering and both with very heavily marbled leaves; and *C. repandum* which has marbled leaves and bright crimson flowers in April-May.

DAFFODIL.—*See* NARCISSUS (p. 359).

DAHLIA. The popularity of the dahlia has grown so prodigiously that it is now almost certainly the most freely planted of all perennial summer bedding plants having annexed this position from the 'geranium'. It has several notable qualifications which fit it for this position. It flowers freely in a great variety of places and soils. Though some skill is required to produce exhibition flowers, results quite good enough for garden display can be obtained with a minimum of effort. Though a decidedly tender plant it has the convenient habit of becoming quite dormant when cold weather commences and in addition storing enough food and moisture in its large tubers to carry it through the winter without soil and in any frost-proof place. Last but not least most dahlias are refreshingly healthy. Disease is the exception rather than the rule and there are few pests which do serious damage. Earwigs and capsid bugs are the worst but the former can be trapped or kept at bay with pepper dust while capsids can be killed with summer petroleum emulsion or nicotine.

Experts recognise many different classes of dahlia but all are grown in the same way. Tubers are placed in pots, boxes or even direct on the greenhouse staging in March or April and are surrounded and almost covered with any old potting soil. This is watered, rather sparingly at first, and the temperature of the house is kept around 60°. In a very short time shoots appear and directly these are two or three inches long they are severed nearly, but not quite, at the base. The lower leaves, if any, are removed and the bottom of each cutting trimmed just below a joint.

The prepared cuttings are inserted singly in small pots, or several around the edges of bigger pots, but the first method is better. Rather fine, sandy soil is used for this purpose, mixed with plenty of peat or leaf mould. The pots are then plunged to their rims in peat or coconut fibre in a propagating frame within the greenhouse. A box about 10 in. deep with a pane of glass on top to keep it close will make an excellent 'frame' for this purpose. If the box can be stood over the hot water pipes or other heating apparatus so much the better, but this is not essential.

The cuttings are watered fairly freely and in a week or so they will form roots and start to grow again. The plants can then be removed to the greenhouse staging and after a few days, potted on singly into 4 in. pots in any ordinary potting compost. They grow very rapidly in a mild atmosphere with plenty of water and in a further week or so may be removed to a frame for hardening off. By the first week in June it should be safe to tip them carefully out of their pots and plant them outdoors.

Meanwhile the soil should have been prepared for them by thorough digging and, if it is poor, the addition of some well-rotted dung. This can be used freely for exhibition plants provided it is thoroughly dug in, as it will then serve the dual purpose of feeding the plants and holding moisture against a dry spell.

A sunny position is most favourable but dahlias can often be seen doing well in quite shady places. The principal danger is that without sufficient light they may grow excessively tall and make leaves at the expense of flowers.

Little further attention is required except secure staking for the larger growing varieties. As a rule one strong stake is driven firmly into the ground for each plant and all shoots are looped separately to this. The dwarf bedding dahlias do not need staking and a good many of the stiff growing varieties of intermediate height can also be left to support themselves but the really tall, big flowered kinds must be staked early.

When big blooms are required for exhibition it is necessary severely to restrict the number produced. As a rule the shoots are reduced to about three per plant the rest being rubbed out at an early stage. Each of these three shoots is restricted to a single flower—the terminal one. Any other flower buds are rubbed off. The plants are watered very freely whenever the soil seems dry and frequently weak liquid manure is substituted for plain water. It is surprising how much feeding dahlias will stand without showing any ill effects.

These special measures are not required when the object is simply plenty of bloom for garden display or cutting.

Dahlias generally start to bloom early in August and continue until frost puts a stop to them. This may be early in October in some places and seasons and not until late November in others. Whenever it may be the dahlias can be left outdoors until their foliage is blackened by frost. Then they must be lifted and brought into a frost-proof shed or room for a few days to give the top growth a chance to dry off. When it is well withered it is cut off an inch or so above the tubers and these are stored away in any dry, frostproof place. If it is cool and airy so much the better as this will reduce the risk of moulds growing on the roots during the winter. No soil or other covering is required and it does not matter if the store place is dark or light. The tubers are left in store until it is time to start them into growth in the spring as already described.

Those who have no convenience for starting dahlias in warmth may still grow them by planting the roots in an unheated frame in late April and then transferring them to the open ground in early June. The roots may either be planted whole or be cut up into several pieces provided each has at least one shoot.

Yet another method is to plant the tubers just as they are outdoors in early May. If they are covered with three inches of soil there will be little danger of their being damaged by frost. When the shoots first appear they can be covered at night with inverted flower pots or hand-lights if frost threatens.

Dahlias can also be raised very readily from seed but this is a method most suitable for the dwarf bedding types. The seed is sown thinly in an ordinary seed compost (see p. 421) in a warm greenhouse during February–March, in a frame during April or even in a sheltered position outdoors early in May. The seedlings are pricked off 4 in. apart in similar soil as soon as they can be handled or, alternatively, potted singly in 2½ in. flower pots. They are hardened off steadily for planting out in June.

Of the many types of dahlia the most important for the ordinary gardener are the Large Decorative, Medium Decorative, Cactus, Garden Cactus, Miniature Cactus, Single, Collerette, Show, Pompon and Dwarf Bedding. These vary in height from 18 in. in the case of the dwarf bedders to 5 or 6 ft. for some of the big types such as Decorative, Cactus, Single and Collerette. All have the wide range of brilliant colours characteristic of the dahlia and all flower freely. Apart from height they differ mainly in the formation of the flowers—double and more or less flat petalled in the decoratives, quilled in the cactus varieties, double and extremely regular in the show and pompon kinds, single in the type so named and also in many of the bedders, single with a central ring of small petals in the collerettes.

Tall kinds should be planted 3 ft. apart; those of medium height 2 to 2½ ft., dwarf bedders 18 in.

Varieties are extremely numerous and new ones are constantly taking the place of old. It is therefore useless to give lists of names which would be out of date almost as soon as printed and they should be sought in up-to-date trade lists.

DIERAMA (*Wand Flower*). The only species of importance to gardeners is *D. pulcherrima* (sometimes known as *Sparaxis pulcherrima*) an unusually graceful bulbous rooted plant which makes long, reed-like, arching stems terminated in August–September by short, one-sided spikes of hanging, funnel-shaped flowers. These are crimson in the common forms but there are white, pink and red varieties. The wand flower should be grown in light, well-drained soils and sunny positions. Plant the bulbs 3 in. deep in October and cover the soil in winter with a little dry litter as protection against frost.

ERANTHIS (*Winter Aconite*). A small family of pretty carpeting plants very suitable for naturalising in thin woodland or under deciduous shrubs. The tubers should be planted 2 in. deep and 2 to 4 in. apart in

September–October and thereafter left severely alone for as long a period as possible. They do not like disturbance and usually take a few years to settle down fully and make a carpet of golden, buttercup-like, green-ruffed flowers in February and March. The small bright green leaves are also most attractive and soon cover the ground. This plant does best in rather moist, loamy soils but it may be tried with reasonable chance of success in any garden in which trees and shrubs in variety grow well. The most important species is *E. hyemalis. E. cilicica* is very similar but not quite so easy to grow.

EREMURUS (*Fox-tail Lily*). It is a pity that these exceptionally handsome plants are being increasingly regarded, and treated, as bulbs with the result that one sees their curiously spoke-like clusters of fleshy roots offered for sale in shop windows after unknown periods of exposure to the atmosphere. This is not the way to treat fox-tail lilies if one wishes to be successful with them. They should be regarded as herbaceous perennials and transplanted in September or early October with as little delay and consequent drying as possible. Allow the roots to spread out in a wide, rather shallow hole and cover them with 3 or 4 in. of soil. Cover the whole site with a good thick layer of bracken or straw from October to April as a protection against frost or, alternatively, place a low mound of silver sand over each crown.

The best place for eremuri is a sheltered, warm spot where the soil is light and open but rather rich. An annual spring dressing of well-rotted stable manure or, failing this, a smaller quantity of hop manure, will keep them growing strongly and reduce the need for transplanting which should always be put off as long as possible. It is generally some years before the roots get fully established after a shift and the less disturbance they have the better.

Propagation can be effected by very careful division of the roots at planting time but this checks growth still more. A better plan is to raise seedlings from freshly ripened seed sown in light open soil in a frame in September. Grow the seedlings on with frame or cloche protection in winter for a couple of years and then plant them in the flowering quarters. In some very favourable places seedlings appear naturally around the parent plants.

Eremuri make bold clumps of strap-shaped leaves from which stand up in summer the stiffly erect stems terminating in long, tapering spikes of saucer-shaped flowers. In habit and dignity they are fit companions for the giant hybrid delphiniums. Amongst the best are *E. Bungei,* 4 to 5 ft. tall with yellow flowers in early July; *E. himalaicus,* which is a couple of feet or more taller, at least a month earlier and white flowered, and

E. robustus, the giant of the race with pale pink flowers in June often on stems from 7 to 10 ft. tall. There are also numerous hybrids intermediate in height and colour to the species and some of these are easier to grow.

ERYTHRONIUM (*Dog's-tooth Violet*). These very attractive plants are nothing like violets and have no connection with them so do not let the popular name mislead you. They belong to the lily family, the nodding flowers are borne singly or, at most, two or three together on slender stems and they mostly have very handsomely silver-mottled leaves. All should be planted in cool, rather moist places but not where water will stand around their roots in winter. A soil containing a good deal of peat or leaf mould is ideal and the position should be at least a little shaded. Plant the bulbs 3 in. deep and 6 to 9 in. apart in September and let them grow on for years undisturbed if they like the position.

The best-known species is *E. Dens-canis* which has several colour forms including pink, violet, purple and white. The stems are 4 to 6 in. in height and the flowers appear in March–April. *E. japonicum* is similar in habit and has clear pink flowers in April–May. *E. californicum* is a bigger plant, 9 in. high with creamy yellow blooms in April–May. *E. revolutum* is 6 in. in height, April flowering and variable in colour, one of the best forms being Pink Beauty which is a clear, pale pink.

FREESIA. *See* p. 468.

FRITILLARIA (*Crown Imperial, Fritillary*). From the garden standpoint the Crown Imperial and the smaller Fritillaries need to be considered separately as, although they belong to the same family, they have a very different appearance and different cultural requirements. The Crown Imperial, *F. imperialis*, is a big, upstanding plant which makes a bold clump of strap shaped leaves from the centre of which appear in May stout leafy stems 3 ft. high each terminated by a tuft of small leaves and a close cluster of showy, nodding, bell-shaped flowers. These may be yellow or reddish bronze according to variety. It will grow in any ordinary soil, is best accommodated in the herbaceous border and should be planted 4 to 5 in. deep and at least 18 in. apart in September–October.

Most of the fritillaries are much smaller plants. The best known is our own native Snake's-head Fritillary, *F. meleagris*, which grows freely in parts of the Thames valley and makes a great display in April–May. It will grow in any ordinary garden soil not liable to dry out too quickly in hot weather or become waterlogged in winter and may also sometimes be naturalised satisfactorily in grass. Some of the foreign species require drier and warmer positions if they are to prove permanent.

Almost all have slender flower stems 9 to 12 in. high each terminated by one or several drooping, lantern-shaped flowers. In *F. meleagris* these are either yellowish white or intricately chequered with purple on a whitish ground. The exotic species are variously coloured. All should be planted about 3 in. deep and 4 to 6 in. apart in September–October.

GALANTHUS (*Snowdrop*). Another of those plants so well known under its popular name that its botanical style hardly conveys anything to most people. The lovely British snowdrop is *G. nivalis* and it has several varieties of which the best known is that with double flowers. Some of the foreign snowdrops such as *G. byzantinus, G. Ikariae* and *G. Imperati Atkinsii*, are bigger and more showy but they usually need a little more care and are more suitable for good places in border and rock garden than for naturalising in grass and woodland. All grow in ordinary soils and, for preference, partially shaded positions. Bulbs should be planted 4 in. deep (6 in. on very light soils) and 3 to 6 in. apart in August or September. Note the depth of planting which is rather greater than usual for small bulbs. Leave undisturbed for a number of years but give an occasional light summer mulch with leaf mould or peat and a dash of hoof and horn meal and bone meal to maintain vigour. When the clumps are definitely overcrowded lift in July as soon as foliage dies down, clean off, separate to single bulbs and replant at once.

GALTONIA. This is not a very big nor a very important family but it contains one good plant for the garden. This is *G. candicans* sometimes known as *Hyacinthus candicans* and certainly rather like a hyacinth though very much larger in all its parts. The flower spike is 3 to 4 ft. in height and the creamy white, pendent flowers are in proportion. They are at their best in late July and early August. This is a perfectly hardy plant and one which may be left undisturbed for a number of years. It will grow in any ordinary soil and sunny position and is quite suitable for the herbaceous border. Plant the bulbs 6 in. deep and 12 in. apart in autumn. Lift and divide in early autumn when the bulbs get overcrowded and the quality of the flowers suffers in consequence.

GLADIOLUS. This has become the most important corm grown in the garden. Thousands of varieties have been raised and new ones appear annually. The success of the plant is all the more remarkable when we remember that it is not quite hardy and must, in consequence, be lifted annually in most localities and wintered indoors. There are not many plants which have overcome this disability and become popular with the millions. The dahlia is the other most obvious example.

The Amateur Gardener

There are a great many species of gladioli but most are of interest to the collector rather than to the ordinary gardener. To the latter it is the hybrids that are important. These may be classified roughly under four headings: large flowered, primulinus, giant primulinus and miniature. The giant primulinus has been produced by crossing varieties of the two first named and is in many respects intermediate between them. The large flowered gladioli have massive spikes of bloom 3 ft. or more high and with the blooms set close together. The primulinus varieties are much more lightly built with smaller, hooded flowers set on slender stems. Miniatures are a comparatively new race similar to the primulinus varieties in size but with open instead of hooded flowers. Usually the petals are ruffled.

In addition to these three principal types there are the forms of *G. Colvillei* which flower early in the summer and are usually grown in pots in the greenhouse. They can be potted, 4 or 5 corms in a 6-in. pot, in autumn and grown on in a slightly heated house in much the same manner as hyacinths or daffodils in pots.

The outdoor gladioli all do best in open, well-drained, but not dry soils. Those that are too heavy or too light can be improved by working in liberal quantities of peat. Manure should be used sparingly and must always be well rotted and thoroughly worked in some time in advance of planting. Bone meal at 4 oz. per sq. yd. and hoof and horn meal 2 oz. per sq. yd. may be raked into the surface prior to planting and are especially valuable on the poorer types of soil.

Planting should commence in March and may continue until mid-May. It is a good plan to plant successionally as this lengthens the flowering season. Cover the corms with 3 to 4 in. of soil and space them at least 6 in. apart—more in the case of exhibition varieties. It is customary to plant the latter in beds by themselves in straight double rows about 1 ft. apart with a 2 ft. alleyway between each pair of rows. The corms are spaced about 9 in. apart in the rows. The same general plan is used when gladioli are grown for cutting, a purpose for which they are well suited. In borders and beds it is better to avoid straight lines and space the corms more or less evenly in all directions.

Very little further attention beyond weeding is necessary in the case of gladioli grown for garden display or cutting but exhibition plants must be staked and fed. One stake is used for each flower stem and should be in position by midsummer. Make all ties with soft raffia below the lowest flower bud. Be careful not to allow the stake to rub against the flowers and damage them. Feeding is usually with weak liquid manure which may be prepared by dissolving a good compound fertiliser in water and applying it very dilute in place of ordinary water every few days from June onwards.

When cutting gladioli be careful to leave some leaves on the corm otherwise this will be starved and will be unable to form a satisfactory new corm to flower the following season.

Lift the plants in October when the foliage commences to turn yellow and hang them up in small bundles in an airy but frost-proof place such as a well-built shed or garage. When the leaves have withered completely, cut them off just above the corm, shake off any remaining soil and pull the old, withered corm from the base of the plump new one—or ones. This old corm is of no further use and should be thrown away but the new corms, if reasonably plump, will flower the following year.

There may also be some spawn or cormlets, i.e. tiny corms, clustering around the new corms. These will not flower the following year but they can be grown on to flowering size in a year or two if they are planted in good soil. The best policy is to get them planted at once in fairly deep seed boxes filled with good potting soil (see p. 422) and placed in a frame or unheated greenhouse for the winter. If kept just a little moist they will soon start into growth and may then be watered with gradually increasing freedom. By May they can be stood outdoors. When their leaves die down they should be shaken free of soil and stored until the normal planting time the following spring when they can be put outdoors just like the ordinary corms.

The sizeable corms, after autumn cleaning, should be placed in clean trays or bags and stored in a cool, airy, frost-proof place such as a spare room or well-ventilated cellar. Avoid damp, heat and frost, all of which will do much damage. Examine the corms occasionally and remove any which show signs of decay. If in any doubt it is safe to peel off the dry outer sheath from a corm to examine the flesh beneath. This should be firm and yellow. If it is soft or much pitted and scabbed it is probably damaged and diseased and expert advice should be sought.

When selecting gladiolus spikes for exhibition it is necessary to choose those that are well formed, with a good number of flowers open, none faded, and the spacing and placing of the flowers as even as possible. Sometimes plants will be found which produce flowers that are wrongly splashed and streaked with colour. This is usually due to virus disease and such plants are best destroyed.

Varieties are extremely numerous and fashions in them change rapidly. Lists of names should, in consequence, be studied in up-to-date trade catalogues.

The Amateur Gardener

GLORIOSA. *See* p. 470.

GLOXINIA. *See* p. 471.

HIPPEASTRUM. Most of the hippeastrums are tender bulbs which need to be grown in warm greenhouses, but one species, *H. pratense*, sometimes separated into a new genus under the name *Habranthus pratensis*, is sufficiently hardy to be grown outdoors in very sheltered places and well-drained soils. The foot of a sunny wall or a south border outside a greenhouse will suit it well. Plant the bulbs 6 in. deep in September and cover the ground with dry litter during the winter.

The flowers of this showy plant appear in June. They are trumpet-shaped, brilliant scarlet and carried several together at the top of stiff, foot high stems.

For other hippeastrums see p. 473.

HYACINTHUS (*Hyacinth*). Another of the important families of bulbous rooted plants. Hyacinths need no introduction as they must be familiar to everyone, not only as garden plants but also in bowls and glass jars for the decoration of the home. There are a few species such as *H. amethystinus* and *H. azureus*, but far and away the most important to gardeners are the large flowered hybrids of which there are hundreds of varieties in cultivation. Numbers of these have been raised in Holland in parts of which the light, alluvial soil with water not far beneath the surface is ideal for the cultivation of these bulbs. In many English gardens hyacinths do well for a season or so and then gradually dwindle away usually because the soil is too close in texture or dry in summer. Matters can be improved by working in plenty of peat with sand as well in the case of heavy soils.

A very little well-rotted manure may be used on poor soils but it is better to rely upon fertilisers such as bone meal, 4 oz. per sq. yd. and hoof and horn meal 3 oz. per sq. yd. applied immediately before planting and well raked or forked in. Plant in October or early November and cover the bulbs with about 5 in. of soil. In badly drained places or on very heavy soils it often pays to raise the hyacinth beds a few inches. Space the bulbs at least 8 in. apart.

Little further attention beyond weeding will be necessary until the following July when the bulbs should be carefully lifted as soon as the foliage dies down. Place them in a cool dry place for a few weeks, then shake the soil from them, twist off the withered tops and store them in shallow boxes in a dry shed until planting time. It is only worth keeping good, plump, weighty bulbs.

Hyacinths for indoor culture should be placed in their pots or bowls in early autumn. If the bowls have no drainage holes, special fibre containing charcoal and crushed oyster shell must be used in place of soil. It is very important to moisten this thoroughly before use. Bulbs can be set almost shoulder to shoulder and need barely be covered. For eight to ten weeks after potting the bulbs should be kept in a cool dark place. Thereafter they can be brought into the light and if desired be forced gently.

INCARVILLEA. *See* p. 159.

IRIS. Yet another big family and in this case one which includes many fibrous and rhizomatous rooted members as well as true bulbs. Only the last are included here and for other important sections of the family the reader should see the chapters on herbaceous flowers, rock plants and aquatics.

Bulbous irises are numerous and very varied both in appearance and requirements. The easiest and also the most popular are the so-called Spanish, English and Dutch irises derived from *I. Xiphium* and *I. xiphioides*. These flower during June and early July, average 2 ft. in height, are ideal for cutting and also very attractive for garden display. They will grow in any ordinary garden soil but prefer those that are not liable to dry out quickly in hot weather. They should be planted 3 to 4 in. deep in September in a sunny position. Space them at least 6 in. apart and leave them undisturbed for a year or so. Then, directly they show the least signs of being overcrowded, lift the bulbs in July or early August when the foliage dies down, allow them to dry off for a few weeks in an airy shed, clean, divide into single bulbs and replant in the ordinary way.

Almost as popular is the early flowering *I. reticulata* which has violet coloured, sweetly scented flowers on 8 in. stems in February. *I. Histrio* and *I. histrioides* are rather similar but shorter, stouter and paler blue in colour also a little earlier flowering. All need a warm, sunny position and rather light, well-drained soil. They are excellent for the rock garden and should be planted 2 in. deep in September. Leave them undisturbed for a number of years, but when overcrowded lift, dry off, divide and replant as for Spanish irises

I. tingitana, which is rather like a Spanish iris in appearance but earlier in flower, is less hardy and is usually grown under glass. It will succeed outdoors in some places, particularly if it gets plenty of sun and is in a warm, well-drained soil.

I. susiana, popularly known as the 'Mourning Iris', is a striking plant with very large flowers rather like those of the familiar bearded irises in shape but with white standards heavily veined with black. Its roots are rhizomes, not bulbs, but I include it here rather than amongst herbaceous plants because it needs to be treated more like a bulb with a very marked period of rest after flowering. It should be planted in October in slightly raised beds of light, gritty soil and a very warm, sheltered position. Cover the roots in winter with a little dry litter to protect them from frost. After flowering cover the plants with spare frame lights or panes of glass to keep off rain but leave the sides open so that there is free circulation of air. Leave this covering in position for a couple of months so that the rhizomes get thoroughly ripened and go to rest. This method of cultivation is typical of that required by all the 'oncocyclus' irises, the group to which *I. susiana* belongs, and also by the nearly allied 'regelio-cyclus' irises.

Ixia (*African Corn Lily*). It is a pity that these very graceful bulbous plants are on the borderline of tenderness and cannot therefore be relied upon to succeed outdoors except in very sheltered places and well-drained soils. Ixias flower in June. The starry flowers are borne in slender spikes on wand-like stems about 18 in. in height. They are in a great variety of bright colours usually with a dark contrasting centre which adds to their beauty. They make excellent cut flowers.

The bulbs should be planted 3 in. deep in light, sandy soil. The ideal position is the foot of a wall facing south. Plant in October or November. After flowering cover the plants with panes of glass to keep off rain for a couple of months and so give the bulbs a chance to become fully ripened. Cover the soil with 2 or 3 in. of dry litter from November to March as a protection against frost.

Ixias also do very well in pots in the cool greenhouse for which purpose they should be potted in autumn, five in a 4 in. pot, placed in a cold frame till about February, then brought into the greenhouse with plenty of light and air.

Propagation can be effected by removal of small bulbs at planting or potting time.

Lachenalia. *See* p. 479.

Leucojum (*Snowflake*). This pretty plant is nothing like so well known as the snowdrop, which it resembles in many respects, yet it is not difficult to grow. The conditions which it needs are practically the same as those for snowdrops, i.e. a cool partially shaded place and loamy soil. Sometimes the bulbs do not flower for a year or so after planting and perhaps this puts people off but it is a plant worth waiting for. There are two principal kinds, the spring snowflake, *L. aestivum* which flowers in April and May, and the autumn snowflake, *L. autumnale*, which blooms in October. The first is 18 in. high with nodding, white, green-tipped flowers. The autumn snowflake is a smaller plant, 4 in. high with white and pink blooms. Plant the first in September; the second in July or early August. Cover with 3 in. of soil. Leave undisturbed for a number of years as frequent disturbance checks growth and discourages flowering.

Propagation is most easily effected by dividing the clusters of bulbs when transplanting old plants.

LILIUM (*Lily*). This is the biggest and most important family of hardy bulbs. There are hundreds of species and varieties and whole books have been written about them. It is not possible for me to do more than skim over the surface of so big a subject and readers who seek more information are referred to such standard works as *Lilies of the World* by Woodcock and Stearn and *Lilies for Garden and Greenhouse* by D. T. Macfie.

A few lilies are too tender to be reliable outdoors in this country and there are other species which, though apparently hardy enough have proved very difficult to acclimatise. But in addition to these there are a great many beautiful kinds which will grow well in English gardens without a great deal of trouble.

The first thing to understand about lilies is that some make roots from the base of the flower stem as well as from the bulb whereas others root from the bulb only. In general the stem rooters need to be planted a good deal more deeply than the purely bulb rooting kinds.

Another point that must be grasped is that while a good many lilies will grow in any reasonable kind of soil there are others to which lime is poison and these can only be grown on soils that are at least a little acid. In general these lilies like best a soil containing a fair amount of peat or leaf mould and a little sand.

No lilies like being out of the ground for a long time. Some of the most successful growers treat them like herbaceous perennials rather than bulbs, transplanting them with plenty of soil around the roots in spring just as they are starting into growth. But whatever may be said about this as a method of culture, it is unpractical advice for the beginner who must buy his bulbs from a merchant in the autumn when they are offered for sale. The best thing to do then is to get them as early as possible and plant them at once.

I have prepared a list showing stem rooters and pure bulb rooters. The stem rooters should all be covered with at least 9 in. of soil, but do not cover them to this depth all at once. Only half fill the hole at first. Then the following spring, as growth appears, gradually add a little more soil until the hole is level. Even after this it is advisable to give a few top dressings of peat or leaf mould to a total depth of 2 or 3 in. still further to encourage the production of stem roots.

The bulb rooters should mostly be planted to a depth of about 5 or 6 in. but a few should be even nearer the surface. The most important of these are the Madonna lily, *L. candidum* which only needs to be covered with an inch of soil and will work its way out on to the surface after a time; the Nankeen lily, *L. testaceum*, which should be covered with 3 or 4 in. of soil, and *L. giganteum* which should be planted with the top of its bulb level with the surface, though usually some protection such as with bracken or heather is required in winter. Incidentally the Madonna lily and the Nankeen lily should both be planted very early, in July or August if bulbs can be obtained then, as they start into growth quickly.

A good many lilies will succeed best if they have their 'heads in the sun and feet in the shade'. This is certainly true of the very beautiful Japanese lily, *L. auratum*. The apparent contradiction can be realised by planting the bulbs amongst low growing evergreen shrubs or leafy plants which will shade the ground over the lily roots and so keep it cool and yet permit the flower stems to grow up through the coverage into the sunlight. Dwarf rhododendrons and peonies are two suggestions for this kind of interplanting.

Lilies very definitely do not want to be disturbed every year. If they are growing reasonably well leave them alone and give the beds a good mulch of peat or leaf mould each spring when growth appears.

Animal manure should not be used on the lily beds and most fertilisers are also out of place but bone meal and hoof and horn meal can be used to stimulate plants on poor soils.

Lilies are increased by dividing the clusters of bulbs, by growing single bulb scales into new bulbs, and by seed. The first is the slowest but also the easiest. The gardener has only to wait until one of his lilies has formed a good clump producing several flowers, and then lift it in early autumn, carefully divide the clump into single bulbs and replant with the least possible delay.

Scales for propagation are also obtained in the autumn. Any number may be taken from one bulb, in fact, if desired, the whole bulb may be pulled apart into separate scales. Take care to damage them as little as possible. Press them, right way up, into seed boxes filled with coarse silver sand and peat mixed in equal parts and cover them with half an inch of the same material. Make them moist and stand the boxes in an unheated frame or greenhouse. Bulblets will form at the base of the scales and by the following autumn it will be possible to shake these out of the sand and plant them up in a nursery bed of sandy soil out-doors. Meanwhile the boxes should be watered moderately.

Seed is the quickest method of increasing numbers and is very satisfactory with some lilies. The great popularity of the Regal lily, *L. regale*, is in no small measure due to the fact that it can be raised so freely in this way that the bulbs have been put on the market at a very cheap rate.

As a rule seed is sown, in a mixture containing a lot of sand and peat, in well-drained earthenware pots or pans in early spring. Germination is effected in a frame or unheated greenhouse and the seedlings are not disturbed the first season. The following autumn they are transferred to a nursery bed as in the case of the bulbils grown from scales and in this they are grown on for several years until they reach flowering size.

LIST OF LILIES
STEM-ROOTING LILIES

Auratum, 6 ft., white, gold spotted flowers in July.

Batemanniae, height 3 ft., apricot flowers in August.

Croceum, height 5 ft., orange, maroon-spotted flowers in June.

Davidii, height 4 ft., orange-red flowers in July–August.

Duchartrei, height 2–3 ft., white, purple spotted flowers in July.

Formosanum, height 1 ft., white, trumpet-shaped flowers in July–August.

Hansonii, height 4 ft., yellow, maroon-spotted flowers in June.

Henryi, height 6–7 ft., orange flowers in August–September.

Longiflorum, height 4 ft., white flowers in September (rather tender).

Maxwill, height 6 ft., orange-red flowers in July–August.

Ochraceum, height 4 ft., yellow, maroon-blotched flowers in September.

Princeps, height 6—7 ft., white flowers in July–August (there are several forms of which G. C. Creelman is one of the best).

Regale (*The Regal Lily*), height 4–5 ft., white, gold-flashed flowers in July.

Speciosum, height 4 ft., white, crimson-spotted flowers in September.

Sulphureum, height 6 ft., pale sulphur flowers in September (rather tender).

Tenuifolium, height 1½ ft., orange-yellow flowers in June.

Thunbergianum, height 2 ft., orange flowers in June–July.

Tigrinum (*The Tiger Lily*), height 5–6 ft., orange flowers in August–September.

Wardii, height, 3–4 ft., purplish-pink, maroon spotted flowers in August.

Willmottiae, height 4 ft., orange-red flowers in July–August.

NON STEM-ROOTING LILIES

Canadense, height 3 ft., deep yellow, maroon spotted flowers in July.
Candidum (*The Madonna Lily*), height 4–5 ft., white flowers in June–July.
Chalcedonicum, height 3 ft., scarlet flowers in July.
Giganteum, height 10–12 ft., white flowers in July.
Martagon, height 4 ft., light maroon flowers in June (there are several varieties including a white.)
Monadelphum Szovitzianum, height 3 ft., lemon flowers in July.
Pardalinum, height 5 ft., orange-red, maroon spotted flowers in July.
Pyrenaicum, height 2–3 ft., yellow, maroon spotted flowers in June.
Testaceum (*The Nankeen Lily*), height 4 ft., apricot flowers in June–July.
Umbellatum, height 2–3 ft., yellow to orange-red flowers in June (there are many varieties such as Golden Fleece, Orange King, etc.)

LILY OF THE VALLEY. *See* CONVALLARIA, p. 340.

MONTBRETIA. The montbretia is a garden hybrid between two nearly allied plants, *Crocosmia Pottsii* and *Crocosmia aurea*. It is thus entirely a creation of man and cannot be found growing wild in any part of the world. Its true name is *Crocosmia crocosmaeflora*, not montbretia, but the latter has become too firmly established amongst gardeners to be ignored in a book such as this.

The first montbretias had the merit of growing very freely in almost any soil and making an excellent display in late summer and early autumn though judged individually their flowers were not very wonderful. A great many seedlings have been raised from these early hybrids and numbers of them far excel their parents in size and beauty of flower but few rival the firstcomers in hardiness and ease of culture. Many of the largest flowered kinds need to be lifted each autumn in most gardens and placed in a frame for the winter, and they require more carefully prepared soil than was necessary for the less imposing kinds. Nevertheless they are mostly worth the extra trouble.

Plant in March or April. It is best to obtain growing tufts rather than dry corms but if only the latter are available it is good policy to start them into growth in seed trays filled with a little damp peat and placed in a frame. They can then be transferred to the open ground when they have actually made a few roots and a leaf or so. The dry corms are apt to rot off rather easily if planted directly outdoors without preliminary plumping.

Choose an open, sunny situation and soil that has been prepared as for gladioli. Plant the corms 2 to 3 in. deep and at least 6 in. apart. If the plants are not to be lifted annually but are to be left to form clumps they should be spaced at least 1 ft. apart but this is only wise with the older varieties or in mild districts and places where the winter drainage is exceptionally good.

Little further attention beyond weeding is necessary though a top dressing of peat or leaf mould in early summer will help to prevent checks to growth through drought.

In late October the plants can either be lifted and transferred to an unheated frame in which they may be planted almost shoulder to shoulder, or they may be covered with dry straw or bracken where they stand in their outdoor beds. This latter method is most likely to prove satisfactory on the lighter and better-drained types of soil. If framed the montbretias should be watered very sparingly until February—just sufficient to keep the soil from becoming bone dry—after which water may be given with increasing freedom to prepare them for planting out.

Muscari (*Grape Hyacinth*). Delightful early flowering bulbs for carpeting under trees and shrubs or for the very front of the border. The best known and most generally useful kinds are *M. botryoides* and its improved variety Heavenly Blue. Both have compact spikes of sky blue flowers on 6 in. stems, Heavenly Blue being richer in colour. *M. plumosum* more correctly known as *M. comosum monstrosum* and popularly as the Plume Hyacinth, is a very different plant with much bigger, looser, arching spikes of small blue flowers, the whole spike having quite a feathery appearance. It is a good subject for sunny ledges in the rock garden.

All grape hyacinths should be planted in sunny places and ordinary soil. Plant in September or October, 2 to 3 in. deep and 4 or 5 in. apart (except *M. plumosum* which should be given twice as much room). Leave undisturbed for a number of years till the bulbs get overcrowded when they should be lifted in July as soon as foliage turns yellow. Dry off in an airy shed, separate to single bulbs and replant with as little delay as possible.

Narcissus (*Daffodil*). A good many people still seem to regard the daffodil as in some way different from the narcissus, keeping the first name for the long trumpeted varieties and the second for those with smaller cups or crowns. But the gardener and botanist recognise no distinction between the two and use daffodil merely as the popular

359

English name and narcissus as the Latin botanical one for the same group of plants.

The Royal Horticultural Society's Narcissus Committee has produced a classification of narcissi under eleven main headings which provides a useful survey of the variety to be found in the family. Division I includes all those varieties with true trumpets longer than, or as long as, the backing perianth segments (petals). Division II is known as Incomparabilis and includes those varieties with big, brightly coloured cups which are nevertheless not quite true trumpets. To qualify for this section the length of the cup must be more than one third the length of the perianth segments but not quite their full length and either yellow or red.

Next come the *Barrii* varieties in Division III. These have cups less than one third the length of the perianth segments and always in a bright contrasting colour such as yellow or red. In contrast to the last two are the *Leedsii* varieties in Division IV which may have cups of any size below full trumpet length but always in a pale, non-contrasting colour such as cream, buff or white.

Division V, known as Triandrus, derives its name from the species *N. triandrus* which has small, nodding flowers with very reflexed perianth segments. All varieties and hybrids of this species come into this section. Not unlike it is *N. cyclamineus* so called from the superficial resemblance of its small blooms to those of a cyclamen. This species, together with its forms and hybrids, forms the next Division VI known as Cyclamineus.

Division VII is made up of the well-known and richly fragrant jonquil together with its forms and hybrids. Division VIII takes in the extremely decorative Poetaz hybrids which have several good sized flowers on each stem and are especially useful for cutting. These were obtained by crossing the Poet's narcissi with a species named *N. Tazetta* and the latter gives its name to the division. The early flowering *Polyanthus* varieties, so many of which reach the flower markets from Cornwall and the Scilly Islands early in the year, also belong here. Division IX is made up of the Poet's narcissi themselves and is consequently known as Poeticus. Division X includes all the double flowered daffodils while the sundry remaining species are lumped together in Division XI.

So much, then, for the classification of this great family. Fortunately cultural instructions need not be so varied. With the exception of a few of the species which are most at home in the rock garden in rather light well-drained soil, almost all narcissi will thrive in any ordinary soil. They are perhaps happiest in good loams and fairly rich, alluvial soils but there are few places in which they cannot be made to thrive with a little encouragement. Ground should be dug thoroughly. Well-rotted dung may be used very sparingly on poor soils but as a rule it is better to rely entirely on fertilisers such as bone meal at 4 oz. and hoof and horn meal at 2 oz. per sq. yd. if the quality of the soil is doubtful.

Plant as early in the autumn as possible. If bulbs can be obtained in August so much the better. Planting can be continued till Christmas or after but the later planting is delayed the less satisfactory results are likely to be.

Cover the bulbs with 3 to 6 in. of soil according to size and character of soil (deepest for big bulbs on light soils). Subsequently keep beds free of weeds and pick off flower heads as they fade. Leave the flower stems, however, as sap will pass back from them into the bulbs later in the summer. It is unnecessary to lift narcissi every year. Leave them to grow and multiply until they show signs of becoming overcrowded when they should be dug up carefully in July directly foliage dies down and cleaned in the same manner as hyacinths. Do not leave them lying about for a long time, however, but get them planted again as soon as possible.

If narcissi must be lifted immediately after flowering to make way for other things, replant them at once in a reserve bed and leave them to finish their growth until July when they can be lifted and cleaned as just described. In this reserve bed they can be planted very close.

Many narcissi can also be naturalised very successfully in grass. It is wise to start with good sized bulbs as smaller samples are apt to be starved by the grass before they become well established and able to look after themselves. A special tool for planting in grass can be obtained or, alternatively, the bulbs can be placed beneath lifted turves which should be replaced at once. It is most important that the grass immediately over the bulbs should not be cut until the narcissus foliage has died down as this must not be removed until it has fulfilled its function of feeding the bulbs in preparation for the next year's flowering.

Strong growing trumpet and incomparabilis varieties are specially suitable for naturalising while in fine, short growth many of the species will succeed.

NERINE. *See* p. 484.

ORNITHOGALUM (*Star of Bethlehem*). A few attractive bulbs which are not very well known. The two best are *O. nutans*, with spikes of nodding, silvery flowers marked outside with pale green, and *O. umbellatum* with loose spikes of starry white flowers. Both are about a foot in height and flower in early summer. They will grow in any

The Amateur Gardener

ordinary soil and sunny or lightly shaded place. Plant in autumn 4 in. deep and at least 8 in. apart and leave undisturbed for a number of years.

OSTROWSKIA. One very handsome tuberous rooted species *O. magnifica* is grown but is not very easy to manage. It needs perfect drainage and plenty of sun to ripen its large tubers in late summer. Failing these essentials it is apt to prove impermanent and to disappear after a winter or so. Plant the tubers in October, 3 or 4 in. deep in gritty, rather light soil and a sunny, sheltered position such as the foot of a wall facing south. It will help if some spare frame lights can be supported over the plants in August and September to keep off rain and encourage thorough ripening. The large and very showy white or pale lilac bell-shaped flowers are produced on 3 ft. stems in July.

OXALIS. *See* p. 219 and 486.

PANCRATIUM. *See* p. 486.

POLIANTHES. *See* p. 491.

POLYGONATUM. *See* p. 172.

PUSCHKINIA. One pretty species, *P. scilloides*, is worth a place in the garden. As its name implies it is much like a scilla. The small, loose spikes of blue flowers appear in April and the bulb is a good one to choose for edgings or for planting in the rock garden. Select a sunny position and good, well-drained soil. Plant the bulbs 3 in. deep in September or October and leave them undisturbed until they become overcrowded when they should be treated in exactly the same way as scillas.

RANUNCULUS. All the ranunculi included in this section are very showy, tuberous rooted plants with fully double flowers on 9 in. stems in May and June and not to be confused with the fibrous rooted species some of which are grown as herbaceous perennials or aquatics. They make useful cut flowers and may also be used for a bright display in beds or at the front of borders in the garden.

They need a rather open, loamy soil containing a fair amount of peat or leaf mould. Damp and cold are their enemies. The warmer and more freely drained the position the better so long as it is not the sort of place that becomes arid early in summer. Moisture is needed to complete growth and fatten the small, clawed tubers. As a rule it is best to lift these annually in July when leaves have died down. They are allowed to dry for a while in any airy shed after which they are cleaned off and stored in a cool, dry place until planting time in November or February–March. The former is preferable for the Turban ranunculi and the latter for the French varieties.

362

Plant under 2 in. of soil with the claws of the tubers downwards. Space 4 to 6 in. apart. It is a good plan to surround the tubers with a little sharp silver sand especially if there is any doubt as to the drainage of the land. Ranunculi also make attractive pot plants if potted in autumn about three or four together in a 4 in. pot in ordinary potting soil and placed in an unheated greenhouse or frame.

RICHARDIA. *See* p. 493.

SALVIA. There is one important tuberous rooted species of salvia. This is *S. patens,* notable for the pure blue of its large, sage-like flowers. It is a very handsome, summer flowering perennial for a sunny spot in the herbaceous border in any ordinary soil. Plant the tubers under 4 or 5 in. of soil in mid-April or, better still, start them into growth in large flower pots in the greenhouse or frame in early April and harden them off for planting out at the end of May. Space them at least 15 in. apart. Lift the tubers in autumn before frosts become really severe (usually about the middle of October), allow them to dry off for a week or so in an airy but frost-proof shed and then store them quite dry in a cool airy place in the same manner as dahlia tubers. The roots are reasonably hardy but frost is liable to damage the young growth. The flower stems are 2 ft. or a little more in height.

For other species see pp. 121 and 175.

SCHIZOSTYLIS (*Kaffir Lily*). The only species grown in English gardens, *S. coccinea,* suffers from the drawback of not being quite hardy enough to be reliable in all places outdoors in winter. It is most likely to thrive in a warm, sheltered spot as, for example, in a border at the foot of a wall or building with a southerly aspect, but it must not be allowed to become too dry in summer or growth will be checked and the flower spikes become small in consequence. In well-drained, lightish loams it will often do well right out in the open especially in the south and west. Plant in March or April 3 in. deep and, if possible, start with growing tufts rather than dry corms as in the case of montbretias. In fact the cultivation of schizostylis is very much like that of the choicer forms of montbretia. Once established, however, it is best to leave the plants alone, and cover with a little dry bracken or straw in winter rather than lift and frame annually.

S. coccinea itself has spikes, 18 in. high, of bright scarlet flowers. It has several varieties of which the best is Mrs. Hegarty with very bright, clear rose flowers. Both flower in October and November when there is little colour left in the garden.

SCILLA (*Squill, Bluebell*). In this case the two popular names Squill and Bluebell serve to distinguish two very distinct sections of what is botanically only one genus. The squills are small plants useful in the rock garden, as edgings to beds and borders or for underplanting beneath taller things. *S. sibirica,* the Siberian Squill is very typical of them. It has small, loose spikes of starry, bright blue flowers the whole plant being no more than 3 or 4 in. in height. Planted freely it makes a wonderful carpet of colour in March and April. In contrast to this is our very much bigger native bluebell, *S. nutans,* and the still more robust Spanish bluebell, *S. campanulata* (*S. hispanica*). Both are a foot or more in height with bell-like flowers considerably larger than those of the squills. There are pink and white forms of both Spanish and English bluebells and also of some of the squills. All should be planted in early autumn and left undisturbed for as long as possible. Squills only need to be covered with 2 or 3 in. of soil; bluebells, particularly the English bluebell, should be planted a good deal more deeply—as much as 6 in. on light soils. Squills and Spanish bluebells like sunny places and reasonably well-drained soils. Our native bluebell prefers shadier places and moister soils and is at its best in thin woodlands.

SNOWDROP.—*See* GALANTHUS (p. 349).

SPARAXIS (*African Harlequin Flower*). All that I have said regarding the cultivation of Ixias applies equally to Sparaxis, a related family of South African plants with brightly coloured flowers in loose spikes on slender stems 6 to 12 in. in height. They make excellent pot plants for cool greenhouses but are too tender to be really reliable outdoors except in the mildest regions and even then only in really well-drained, open soils. The smaller kinds, such as the numerous varieties of *S. tricolor,* make delightful rock garden plants in places where they can be grown outdoors with safety. All flower in late spring or early summer.

The lovely plant sometimes known as *S. pulcherrima* I have described under the name Dierama, (see p. 346).

STERNBERGIA (*Lily of the Field*). Despite its name and the legend that it is the authentic 'lily of the field' of the New Testament, *Sternbergia lutea* bears no resemblance to lilies as we know them. It might easily be mistaken for a fine yellow crocus. It flowers in October and has rather wide, strap-shaped leaves. It likes a sunny warm place in reasonably rich but well-drained soil. The bulbs should be covered with 4 in. of soil—rather more if the soil is light—and a pane of glass supported on sticks a few inches over the site will do nothing but good from November to April. Plant in July or August and thereafter leave the plants severely alone for a number of years. When they do get overcrowded, lift and divide at the end of July and replant at once.

Bulbs, Corms and Tubers

TECOPHILAEA (*Chilean Crocus*). One species is sometimes grown in warm, sheltered places and light sandy soils. This is *T. cyanocrocus* a small bulb with widely funnel shaped starry flowers of an astonishingly pure and brilliant shade of blue. It flowers in April and is about 6 in. in height. Plant in September, 4 or 5 in. deep and protect in winter with a good scattering of dry litter.

TIGRIDIA (*Tiger Flower*). These rather tender corms produce brightly coloured and curiously shaped flowers which appear to have only three petals until one looks more closely and realises that there are six, the other three being very small. Colours are bright and varied and the flowers are usually blotched and spotted towards the centre, a feature which accounts for their popular name, Tiger Flower. All should be planted in April or early May in a warm sheltered place and light sandy soil containing just a little well-rotted manure. Cover with 3 in. of soil. Lift all the corms in October and dry them off like gladioli storing them in a similar manner until planting time the following spring.

The flowers are carried on stems 18 in. to 2 ft. in height. Individually they are fleeting but they are produced in succession for a considerable time, the display being at its height in August.

TULIPA (*Tulip*). For centuries tulips have been esteemed by gardeners and hybridised amongst themselves to get new forms and colours. As a result present day garden races bear little or no relationship to the wild species, though this does not mean that none of the species is worth a place in the garden. On the contrary there are some exceptionally beautiful plants among them. Nevertheless they are more the province of the specialist than of the ordinary gardener and to the latter 'tulip' nearly always means the gorgeous hybrids which make so splendid a display during April and May and can be grown so easily in so great a variety of soils and situations.

For like so many other crossbred plants, the garden tulips are hardier and more long suffering than their wild ancestors. There are few gardens in which they cannot be induced to flower for at least a year or so, though, if they are to prove really permanent, it is desirable that the soil should be fairly rich and well drained without being either sour or liable to suffer severely from periods of spring and early summer drought. Later in the summer dryness does not matter, as growth is completed and the bulbs more or less dormant by about the end of June.

In those gardens where, despite efforts to improve the soil, tulips continue to dwindle away after a few years it is still possible to have a magnificent annual display by purchasing new bulbs every second or third autumn from a district, such as that around The Wash, in which tulips are known to thrive. The older varieties can usually be purchased very cheaply and are every bit as attractive as the newcomers in everything but novelty.

Prepare tulip beds by digging them thoroughly and working in a little old stable manure. Failing this hop manure mixed with several times its bulk of peat or leaf mould may be used. Bone meal can also be added with advantage at the rate of 4 oz. per sq. yd. Choose a sunny position where possible or at any rate one not actually overhung by trees. Tulips will not put up with shade to the same extent as daffodils.

Plant in October or early November, 4 in. deep on heavy soils and 5 in. on light. If in the following spring some of the foliage shows signs of browning at the edges as though it had been scorched by fire, spray the plants several times at intervals of about a week with ordinary Bordeaux Mixture.

Unlike daffodils, tulips benefit from annual lifting, drying off and replanting. It is best not to disturb the bulbs until the foliage has died down naturally but if the beds are required for other things they should be lifted immediately after flowering and replanted temporarily elsewhere. They can be laid close together in shallow trenches and bulbs and roots covered with a little soil.

When the leaves have withered, lift the bulbs carefully and lay them in trays in a dry shed for a week or so. Then twist off the tops, shake off any remaining soil, remove the small bulbs, which are seldom worth growing on, and store the rest in a dry place such as a shed or spare room, until the normal planting season in autumn. As a rule it is unwise to plant tulips very early as this may encourage them to make growth too soon and be damaged by winter frost.

Garden varieties of tulips are subdivided into sections in very much the same manner as narcissi. There are the early single tulips which flower in April and are seldom much over a foot in height; the early doubles which are similar in every respect except that the flowers are double; Darwin tulips which flower in May, have stems 2 ft. and more in height and bold, rather squarely built flowers; Cottage tulips, similar in height and flowering time but with variously shaped flowers, in some kinds definitely waisted and in others almost globular; Rembrandt's, resembling the Darwins in all respects except colour which is striped and blotched instead of being mainly plain; Old English tulips which are remarkably regular and refined in form; Parrot tulips with curiously twisted and slashed petals, blotched with green; and Mendel and Triumph tulips which are in many respects intermediate between the early flowering singles and the Darwins in season, height and character of bloom. Varieties within these groups are extremely numerous and detailed descriptions should be sought in trade catalogues.

There are in addition the numerous species to which I have already made reference, and which vary from the 3 in. high, soft pink *T. persica*, to the giant *T. Fosteriana* with its immense glowing scarlet blooms as showy as any garden hybrid. One that should not be overlooked is *T. Kaufmanniana* for this blooms in March and has very gracefully formed short stemmed but large flowers, creamy white within and flushed with carmine outside. It is a gem for the rock garden. Other outstanding species are the scarlet, foot high *T. Eichleri*; similarly coloured but variable *T. Greigii*; scarlet and black *T. Gesneriana*, and graceful, pink and white *T. Clusiana*, often known as the 'Lady Tulip'.

VALLOTA. *See* p. 504.

VELTHEIMIA. *See* p. 504.

WATSONIA. The uninitiated might mistake the watsonias for rather slender, small flowered gladioli. They have, in fact, many points in common but unfortunately they are much more difficult to grow. They are more fastidious as regards soil, more sensitive to variations in water supply and even more in need of sun and warmth. They are most likely to be successful if planted in the same way and at the same time as gladioli in particularly sunny, sheltered places and open but not droughty soils containing plenty of peat or leaf mould. Water very freely in summer. Amongst the best are the many fine forms of *W. Meriana*, 3 to 4 ft. high and with white, salmon or scarlet flowers in early summer. *W. rosea* is 3 ft. high and has soft pink flowers at the end of the summer.

ZEPHYRANTHES (*Flower of the West Wind*). The funnel-shaped flowers of these graceful, bulbous plants are a little like those of a crocus. Unfortunately the plants themselves are far more tender and difficult to manage than crocuses and it is only in warm, sheltered places and sandy soils that they should be risked outdoors in this country. Elsewhere they should be grown in pots or pans in cool greenhouse or frame. Plant in autumn 3 in. deep and protect with dry litter in winter. *Z. candida* with snow white flowers on 6 in. stems in September is one of the most likely to succeed.

CHAPTER XII

Water and Bog Gardens

WATER CAN add greatly to the beauty of most gardens, particularly if it is skilfully employed and used in such a manner as to permit the introduction of aquatic and moisture loving plants. In this connection it should be noted that few plants, least of all water lilies, will thrive in running water. A very slow flowing stream may serve, but a still pool is far better from the gardener's standpoint. Depth of water is important. The larger water lilies and some floating plants, such as the water hawthorn, will thrive in a depth of 18 in. or even 2 ft. of water, but the majority of aquatics prefer the shallow margins of pools and streams where their crowns are covered by, at most, 3 or 4 in. of water.

Some people fear to introduce water to their gardens on the score that this will encourage mosquitoes and gnats in summer. It is perfectly true that a badly stocked water garden can become a breeding ground for these pests but the danger can be overcome by introducing sufficient fish.

In a few cases it may be possible to make use of natural pools and streams, but in most instances the gardener will have to construct his water garden. The first thing to be said here is that clay is seldom satisfactory as a building material. Well prepared concrete is far better and it is wise to include one of the advertised waterproofing preparations, such as Pudlo powder. If this precaution is not taken there will be a slow seepage of water even through quite thick concrete, and this may become a nuisance.

The design of the water garden may range from the completely formal pool, which forms a centre piece of lawn or paved garden, to the natural pool so often used as a charming adjunct to the rock garden. In the former case the lines are likely to be severely rectangular and the sides of the pool vertical, or nearly so, whereas the informal pool will have an irregular shape and the sides will slope like those of a saucer. This saucer shape is very easy to construct and also relieves the gardener of many winter problems, as expanding ice will exert no pressure on the concrete walls as in the case of the vertically sided pool. With the formal pool it is generally advisable to build what is virtually a shelf right round the edge and about a foot below the surface on which soil can be placed or pots stood to accommodate the marginal plants which like to grow in shallow water.

CONSTRUCTING THE POOL. The construction of a small lily pool is well within the scope of any handyman. The real secret of success is to work with really fresh cement and to prepare the concrete with just enough but not too much water. If it is too dry it will not mix and set properly while if it is too wet all the cement will tend to rise to the top and then flake off when it is dry.

The bottom layer of concrete, even in a small pool, should be not less than 4 in. thick. In large pools it is better to have 6 or 8 in. of concrete. The sides should be of the same thickness at the base but may taper a little towards the top, though even at the rim there should be not less than 3 in. of concrete.

Concrete for pool making should be prepared with not less than 1 part of cement to 4 of ballast. A good general mixture is 3 parts by bulk washed gravel, 1 part builder's sand and 1 part cement, but I favour lining a pool made with this mixture with a further 2 in. thickness of concrete prepared with 1 part of cement to 3 parts builder's sand, to which has been added waterproofing powder and liquid used according to manufacturer's instructions.

Mix all the ingredients dry to begin with, turning them four or five times to make certain that they are thoroughly compounded. Then throw the mixture into a cone-shaped heap, make a crater-like hole in the top, pour in water and turn the mixture inwards. This process can be repeated several times, more water being added at each turning until the whole mass assumes the consistency of rather thick porridge or, to use the expressive slang of the navvy, becomes greasy. The concrete is then ready for use and should be thrown into the pool with a shovel and worked to a rough level with a short plank held on edge.

If a second application of finer cement is to be made as described above, no attempt should be made to smooth off the first layer, which should be left with the rough board marks showing on the surface. These will give a 'key' to which the final grout will cling. If, however, only the one application of cement is to be made, it should be smoothed off with the flat of a spade or a builder's trowel. Complete the bottom of the pool first and then build the sides. If these are sloping the concrete can be laid on just as I have described for the bottom, but in the case of vertical sides it will be necessary to make use of shuttering, i.e., planks on edge built one above another to form a temporary wall to hold the concrete in place while it is setting.

The ideal time for doing this kind of constructional work is during mild but rather damp weather. Work should be discontinued if frost threatens, because if concrete freezes before it is set it will be quite useless. In very hot, dry weather it is advisable to cover the concrete with damp sacks and keep these moistened for a day or so to prevent over-rapid drying, which may cause cracking.

If two layers of concrete, one coarse and the other fine, are to be laid, the second should go on just before the first is fully dry, though it must be firm enough to be walked on. If, for some reason or other, there is a delay and the preliminary layer does dry right out, it should be wetted thoroughly before the grout is laid.

The raw edge of the concrete in formal pools can be concealed by setting paving slabs in concrete as a surround to the pool and allowing these slabs to overhang it by a couple of inches. With the informal pool it may be possible to arrange some rocks to overhang the edge, but it is seldom that the whole of the pool can be screened in this manner. Usually it is pleasant to have grass going down to the water edge, at least around part of the circumference of the pool, and then the turves may be laid to overlap the edge of the concrete.

Ordinary concrete made without one of the waterproofing compounds is not fully waterproof. In consequence, unless treated in some way, such pools will gradually empty. The difficulty can be overcome by giving the finished pool two or three coats of one of the elastic bitumen compounds sold for this purpose. Alternatively, they may be given two or three coats of waterglass (sodium silicate) which is sold by most chemists for the purpose of preserving eggs. Thin the waterglass with enough water to give it roughly the consistency of ordinary household paint and then apply it to the surface of the concrete with an ordinary paint brush. Several coats should be given, time being allowed for each to dry before the next is applied.

It is advisable to fill and empty a pool once or twice before trying to stock it with plants or fish, though this precaution is not so necessary if waterglass is used for the final coat. The reason is that there may be certain impurities in the concrete which would be dissolved by the water and would prove harmful to plants or fish. Waterglass, by sealing the pores of the concrete, prevents these chemicals from being dissolved.

If chemical purification of the pool is preferred this can be done by filling it with water and stirring in sufficient syrupy phosphoric acid to turn blue litmus paper pink. It will be found that after a time the water becomes alkaline again, that is pink litmus is turned blue. More acid must be added daily until the water remains acid, that is pink litmus dipped into it remains pink, for at least 24 hours.

370

PLASTIC POOLS. An alternative to lining pools with concrete is to line them with flexible plastic sheets. These can be pre-fabricated to cover pools of almost any size without joins or overlaps so that there is no danger of water seeping out. The plastic also has a certain amount of stretch so that the weight of water in it will carry it down into any small irregularities in the excavation prepared for it. Nevertheless where this method is employed it is desirable to see that such irregularities are kept to a minimum. Flexible plastic sheets can be used to line pools of any shape desired. An alternative is to buy pre-fabricated pools of rigid fibreglass and sink these in holes dug out roughly to the same shape and size, but these are more expensive and do not allow the garden maker to use his own invention in creating shapes to suit the surroundings. Neither plastic sheets nor fibreglass contain any chemicals harmful to plants or fish so both can be stocked immediately.

STOCKING THE POOL. The best time for planting water plants is spring, particularly late April and early May, when many aquatics are just starting into growth. Fish, snails and any other small water creatures which may be fancied should not, as a rule, be introduced at the same time as the plants. It is better to wait a few weeks to give the plants a chance to become established and allow the water to settle after the disturbance and muddying which is almost certain to occur at first.

Soil must, of course, be provided for the plants, though the way in which it is used may be varied quite a lot. Many pond keepers adopt the simple method of spreading good loamy soil all over the bottom of the pool to a depth of at least 6 in., covering this with about an inch of clean gravel or sand and then planting directly in this bed of soil very much as if it were a border on dry land. In this case the water is not introduced until planting is completed. The drawback to this method is that, if the pool is a big one, it takes rather a lot of soil to cover it all over. An alternative is to build up small mounds of soil here and there where plants are required, holding the soil in position with fine mesh wire netting. A variation on this scheme is to plant everything in baskets filled with soil and then sink the baskets in position where required.

The ideal soil for any of these methods is a rather heavy, fairly rich loam. Avoid mud from pond bottoms and stream sides. Do not use dung or artificial manures.

As I have already remarked water plants vary greatly in the depth of water in which they like to grow. There are, for example, some vigorous water lilies which thrive with their roots 2 ft. beneath the surface and many pond weeds, such as the ubiquitous Canadian pond weed and the charming English water violet, also grow well in quite deep water. In contrast there are a great many plants, particularly those found naturally towards the edges of pools and streams, which would be killed outright if submerged more than 6 in. deep. Such are often at their best when no more than just awash with water. The flowering rush, water plantain, marsh marigold and water forget-me-not are familiar examples of this type.

In some cases it will be inevitable that plants must go into their full depth of water straight away, but very often one can arrange to fill the pool gradually at first, and this is certainly the ideal method. After planting run in water to a depth of 2 or 3 in. and then, as plants grow, gradually add more water until, after three or four weeks, the pond is filled.

Do not be surprised if there is considerable muddying at first. This is quite natural and due to the unbalanced condition of life in the water at the outset. It may be some months before the water becomes reasonably clear and, even then, one can never expect a pool that is in really good health to be crystal clear. It is rather like expecting a plot of fertile soil never to produce any weeds. If it did not, one would be pretty certain that there was something wrong with the soil. However, by stocking a pool wisely with a good mixture of plants, including submerged plants which give off oxygen to the water and, in addition, by having sufficient fish in the pool to keep down minute animal life, it is possible to have water which will remain fresh and reasonably clear without being changed at any time. Under these conditions all that is necessary is to bring up the water to its normal level from time to time as it becomes lowered by the normal process of evaporation. Roughly speaking allow one submerged aquatic (oxygenating plant) per square yard of water surface, one water lily to every two or three square yards, one marginal plant every 18 in. around the edge of the pool, and one fish to every six gallons of water. The number of gallons in a pool can be calculated approximately by multiplying the length by the breadth by the depth, all measured in feet, and the result by $6\frac{1}{4}$.

Fish are important not only on account of the interest they add to the pool but also because they devour the larvae of mosquitoes and gnats so preventing the water from becoming a nuisance to the whole neighbourhood. There are many highly ornamental varieties of fish hardy enough to be established in a pool but none better from the standpoint of general utility than the common goldfish and the golden orfe. In winter, if the weather is very cold and the pool is a small one, there may be some danger of it freezing solid. No fish will survive this so either they must be removed in good time to the safety of an inside aquarium or the pool must be well covered with planks and sacks as protection.

WATER PLANTS

Acorus (*Sweet Flag*). The popular name refers to *A. Calamus*, the species commonly grown, which has strong, sword-like leaves similar to those of the common yellow flag iris. The whole plant is scented when bruised. It is grown solely for its foliage and, in addition to the type which is green, there is a form with white, pink and golden variegations. This is a particularly attractive form. Either will grow in very wet bog or in a few inches of water. Both can be propagated by division in May.

Alisma (*Water Plantain*). The common water plantain, *A. Plantago*, is a British wild plant which is worth a place in large water gardens but is not quite choice enough for small ones. It has big, dock-like leaves and loose sprays of pink flowers which are just a little too small and too pale to be really effective. It thrives best in shallow water and, in consequence, is suitable for the margin of a pool or the wettest parts of a bog garden. Propagation is by division or by seed in spring.

Aponogeton (*Water Hawthorn*). There are several species which are occasionally seen in water gardens but the only one that is really common is *A. distachyus*. This is one of the most beautiful of floating aquatics, in fact it almost rivals the water lilies. It has narrow, dark green leaves which lie quite flat on the surface of the water and form a dark carpet to display the small clusters of snow-white flowers which really have a marked perfume of hawthorn. The water hawthorn is hardy and easily grown and will do equally well in quite shallow pools or those of 18 in. depth. There is a form known as 'Aldenhamensis' which has purplish foliage and even larger flowers tinged with pink. Both species and variety can be increased by careful division of the tuberous roots in May.

Arundo. The species usually grown is *A. Donax*, a very strong reed-like plant with broad, grey-green foliage. It will reach a height of 6 or 8 ft. and is really too sturdy for any but the larger pools. Where it can be accommodated, however, there is no more handsome foliage plant for shallow water or the very boggy soil. Division in spring provides the best method of propagation.

Butomus (*Flowering Rush*). Many regard *B. umbellatus* as the most beautiful of all British plants. Colonies of it are to be found in many canals, slow-moving streams and bogs. It makes a sturdy clump of narrow, grass-like leaves from which rise, in July and August, stout, leafless stems terminated by flat clusters of shining pink flowers. This is a really good plant and, despite its height, one which can be accommodated in quite small gardens as it does not spread unduly. Division in May provides a ready means of increase.

CALLA (*Bog Arum*). The species which is usually seen in British gardens, *C. palustris*, is very like the greenhouse arum lily on a reduced scale. It has the same bright green, heart shaped leaves and white 'flowers', but it does not exceed a height of 1 foot. It is reasonably hardy but may require protection from November to April in cold localities or hard winters. Increase by dividing the rhizomes in spring.

CALLITRICHE (*Water Starwort*). Submerged plants grown because they give out oxygen to the water and provide protection for young fish. The species commonly planted is *C. aquatica* which makes a dense curtain of light green shoots.

CALTHA (*Marsh Marigold, King Cup*). This rivals the flowering rush as claimant to be the most beautiful of British wild flowers. Everyone must be familiar with the enormous, buttercup-like flowers of the marsh marigold which fill water meadows and stream sides with colour before most plants have come fully out of their winter rest. These golden blooms belong to *C. palustris*, the commonest but also, in my opinion, the best of its family. It has a number of forms, including a double flowered variety which loses in grace what it gains in solidity. There is also an interesting species known as *C. polypetala* in which the flowers are of even greater size. All thrive in very shallow water or boggy ground. Propagation is most readily effected by division immediately after flowering.

CAREX (*Sedge Grass*). This is a large family of plants all with narrow, grass-like leaves and clusters of small green or brownish flowers similar to those seen on many types of rush. None is of the first merit for the garden, but such kinds as *C. riparia*, Bowles Golden and *C. Pseudocyperus* are worth planting for foliage effect at the margin of the pool in shallow water.

CYPERUS (*Umbrella Grass*). Another example of a well-chosen popular name, for the dainty grass-like flower heads are surrounded by long narrow bracts which really do look like the ribs of an umbrella. There are a great many species, all rather similar in style but mostly too tender for outdoor cultivation. The best for this latter purpose is *C. longus*, which is a British plant, though rare. It grows to a height of 2 or 3 ft. and does best when planted in water 2 to 3 in. deep. Increase it by dividing the roots carefully in May.

Water and Bog Gardens

ELODEA (*Pond Weed*). One species, *E. canadensis*, grows so freely that it soon becomes a dangerous weed in pools and streams. Others are less vigorous and, as they are good oxygenators, are worth planting for this purpose and to provide shelter for fish. All grow completely submerged. Two of the best are *E. crispa* and *E. densa*. Almost any piece detached in spring will grow into a new plant.

ERIOPHORUM (*Cotton Grass*). Before they start to seed there is nothing very striking about any of the cotton grasses which look like rather ordinary rushes 1 to 2 ft. in height. The whole picture changes at seed time when it appears that every blade of 'grass' has become tipped with a snowy tuft of cotton-wool. In parts of Britain cotton grasses can be found literally by the square mile, and in seed they provide a sight not easily forgotten. The best species for the garden are *E. angustifolium* and *E. vaginatum*, but really there is not a great deal of difference in the decorative value of any of the hardy kinds. All thrive in shallow water and can be increased by dividing the roots in spring.

HOTTONIA (*Water Violet*). One of the prettiest of submerged water plants is *H. palustris*, the British water violet. It makes masses of finely divided, light green foliage and in summer thrusts above the surface of the water slender stems bearing pale lilac flowers. It is perfectly hardy, will grow in anything up to about 18 in. of water and can be divided in May.

HYDROCLEIS (*Water Poppy*). The plant which I must deal with under the name *H. Commersonii*, because that is the style which botanists have decided is correct, will be more familiar to gardeners as *Limnocharis Humboldtii*. It is a floating aquatic for water 12–18 in. in depth. The flowers are yellow and undoubtedly poppy-like, though there is no botanical connection between this plant and the poppy. It is beautiful but, unfortunately, none too hardy for which reason it should be given a sunny, sheltered position and, in cold districts, some extra protection in winter, or it may be removed to the greenhouse in October and replanted outdoors in May. Propagation is by division.

IRIS. This great family, in addition to giving us fine plants for the herbaceous border and many choice ones for the rock garden, also includes several moisture loving species of which at least two may be truly regarded as water plants. These are our own native yellow water flag, *I. Pseudacorus*, a rather tall plant with sword-shaped leaves and bright yellow flowers in June, and the Japanese water flag, *I. laevigata*, which is only about 2½ ft. high and has notably showy bluish-purple flowers. Both these will thrive in 2 or 3 in. of water.

I. Kaempferi, often regarded as a water plant, really likes moist soil only and may be killed by water standing over its crowns. It has been very highly developed in gardens and there are many named varieties varying in colour but mostly in shades of blue and purple with white. All these irises can be divided in spring.

JUNCUS (*Rush*). On the whole these rushes are not very interesting or beautiful plants but a few of the best species such as the variegated form of *J. follicularis* in which the green leaves are banded with white, and *J. glaucus* which, as its name implies, has greyish-blue leaves, are worth planting at the margins of pools and streams. They thrive in 2 to 3 in. of water and are easily increased by division.

LIMNANTHEMUM. There is only one species of importance to the owner of an outdoor pool and that is *L. nymphaeoides,* also known as *Villarsia nymphaeoides* or, correctly, as *Nymphoides peltata.* It is a very attractive plant thriving in a foot or more of water and having dark floating leaves surmounted by yellow flowers about as big as florins. When propagation is necessary old roots can be divided carefully in May.

LIMNOCHARIS. *See* HYDROCLEIS (p. 375).

MENTHA (*Mint*). One species of mint thrives either in shallow water or in very wet ground at the edge of the pool. This is *M. aquatica* which has the typical mint aromatic foliage and little, dense clusters of purplish-mauve flowers in early summer. It is a very easy plant to grow but not notably beautiful. Propagation is readily effected by division in spring.

MENYANTHES (*Bog Bean, Buck Bean*). As it is a native of Britain there is no question about the hardiness of the bog bean, *M. trifoliata.* This is a plant for the centre of the pool but not in more than a foot of water. The leaves are bronzy and the white or blush-tinted flowers, though individually small, are produced with great freedom in July. Old plants can be divided in May.

MIMULUS (*Musk, Monkey Flower*). The common "British" water musk, *M. luteus,* will thrive in shallow water or very wet ground. It will succeed very well at the side of a stream and I have found it growing where the current was quite swift, which is unusual for a water plant. It is a very showy plant with brilliant yellow flowers splashed with crimson or maroon in some forms. There is also a variety with semi-double blooms. All can be raised from seed in spring but as a rule division will provide all the plants necessary.

Water and Bog Gardens

MYOSOTIS (*Forget-me-not*). The water forget-me-not, *M. palustris*, is very like the bedding variety but looser in habit and, as a rule, with rather paler flowers. However in this respect there can be considerable variation and very finely coloured forms may be selected. All are plants for very shallow water or wet ground. They can be increased rapidly by seed, sown in spring, or by division at the same time. Flowering time is summer.

MYRIOPHYLLUM (*Water Milfoil*). This genus, which has provided some of the best oxygenating plants for indoor aquariums, has not been lavish with hardy kinds but at least two species are worth planting outdoors. These are *M. verticillatum* and *M. spicatum* both with very finely divided leaves. They grow completely submerged except for the flower spikes which are not conspicuous. Propagate by division in spring.

NUPHAR. In many British pools and slow moving rivers a plant with large yellow flowers in summer is to be seen and is frequently erroneously termed water lily. This is *N. luteum*, which has large, heart-shaped leaves floating on the surface of the water, very much like those of a water lily. It has the merit of thriving even in running water, to which the true water lilies object, but it is very vigorous and quite unsuitable for small pools. It will thrive in water up to 2 ft. deep and does not mind a certain degree of shade. Culture and propagation are the same as for *nymphaea*.

NYMPHAEA (*Water Lily*). This is the biggest and the most important genus of aquatic plants. Probably few amateur gardeners realise just how big it is. There are a number of species to begin with and these have been crossed and inter-crossed to produce hundreds of hybrids, many of the greatest beauty. Water lilies vary very widely in size, vigour, colour and the depth of water in which they thrive. There are miniature types, such as *N. pygmaea*, *N. tetragona* and *N. candida*, which will grow happily in 4 or 5 in. of water and can be established in small tubs or old stone sinks. At the other extreme are very vigorous water lilies, such as *N. alba* and *N. Gladstoniana*, which like to grow in 2 or 3 ft. of water and will soon cover an area of many square yards; in fact they can become a nuisance in any but the largest pools.

It is the intermediate varieties that are of greatest interest to the gardener and these are mostly hybrids of garden origin with 'fancy' names. Amongst the best are Escarboucle, bright crimson; James Brydon, rosy crimson; *Froebelii*, blood red; the numerous forms of *Marliacea*, such as *albida*, white, *chromatella*, yellow, *rosea*, pink, and *ignea*, bright

377

z

carmine; *odorata*, which has fragrant white flowers and several forms with pink, rose or yellow flowers; Lustrous, which is like a pink *Marliacea* but with flowers of extra size, and Albatross, pure white. All these will grow in water 1 to 2 ft. in depth and should be planted at least 4 ft. apart. Where space is more limited the several forms of *Laydekeri* are useful. These include *rosea*, pink; *purpurata*, wine red; and *lilacea*, deep rose.

All these water lilies are best planted in May. They can be grown either in rather rich, loamy soil spread on the bottom of the pool to a depth of at least 6 in. or planted individually in large baskets packed with loamy soil. The kind of basket in which plums are brought to market is excellent for the purpose. It is advisable to overhaul water lilies every year or so and to remove dead leaves annually in the autumn. Old plants can be divided like herbaceous perennials, though it will be found that some varieties are much easier to handle than others. Those with tuberous roots need special care and the occasional use of a sharp knife.

ORONTIUM (*Golden Club*). An interesting plant for the centre of the pool in a depth of 6 to 12 in. of water. The blue-grey leaves appear to project out of the water and the tiny yellow flowers are clustered along a spadix similar to that in the centre of an arum lily, though it should be noted that there is no conspicuous white spathe, however, as in the arum. Propagation is by division in spring. The only species grown is *O. aquaticum*.

PONTEDERIA (*Pickerel Weed*). Good blue pond flowers are not too numerous and *P. cordata* has the twin merits of having light blue flowers borne in dense spikes on 18 in. stems and really handsome broad and shining green leaves. It flowers in July. This is a marginal plant for a few inches of water. It presents no difficulties in culture and can be increased by careful division in May.

SAGITTARIA (*Arrow Head*). The popular name of these plants has reference to the peculiar shape of the leaves which are barbed downwards very much like the head of an arrow. They would be worth growing for their foliage alone but all have the additional attraction of showy white flowers in open spikes. Amongst the best species are *S. sagittifolia*, the common British arrowhead, which flowers in July and August; and *S. japonica* which is even more handsome in leaf and flower. This last has a double flowered form which is extremely beautiful. All are plants for fairly shallow water though they will stand up to 6 or 7 in. of water over their crowns. Division in May provides the best means of increase.

Water and Bog Gardens

SCIRPUS (*Bulrush*). What most people call bulrush is really reed-mace or *typha*. These are the plants with long, cigar-like inflorescences. The true bulrushes (*scirpus*) are far less conspicuous with their small, brownish spikes of 'flowers'. One species, however, is well worth planting for its foliage, in fact it is one of the most popular of foliage plants for the pool. This is *S. Tabernaemontani zebrinus*, more frequently listed as plain *S. zebrinus*. The pointed, rush-like *stems* are pale green widely banded with cream. The whole plant is compact and reaches a height of about 3 ft. It thrives in shallow water and can be divided in spring.

THALIA. The only species grown is *T. dealbata* and undoubtedly this would be much more widely planted were it a little more reliably hardy. It is a handsome plant with broad leaves standing high out of the water and clusters of purple flowers on 6 or 7 ft. stems. It thrives in shallow water and is likely to need winter protection in many parts of the country. For this reason it is best grown in pots so that it can be taken inside without serious root disturbance. Repot in April and divide if desired at the same time.

TYPHA (*Reed Mace, Cat-tail*). These are the plants which are so frequently, but incorrectly, named bulrushes. They all have cigar-like inflorescences and are handsome but as a rule somewhat invasive. One of the best for the small garden is *T. minima* which does not exceed 18 in. in height. *T. japonica*, more frequently seen, grows to about 5 ft. and has a very slender inflorescence. *T. angustifolia* is about the same height with narrow, blue-grey leaves. All are plants for quite shallow water. Division in spring provides the best means of increase though some kinds seed themselves about freely.

VALLISNERIA. Submerged oxygenating plants of which the best for outdoor pools is *V. spiralis*. The leaves are long and narrow like lengths of almost transparent pale green ribbon. Bubbles of oxygen can be seen forming on them freely on any warm day. Nevertheless the vallisneria does not provide such good cover for young fish as some of the more densely growing plants such as *hottonia* and *callitriche*. Increase by division in spring.

VILLARSIA NYMPHAEOIDES.—*See* LIMNANTHEMUM (p. 376).

BOG PLANTS

In the very damp ground surrounding the pool or stream many of the moisture loving plants described in other parts of this book can be used with good effect. Thus from the herbaceous perennials we can borrow *astilbes, aconitums, cimicifugas, funkias, hemerocallis, Iris Kaempferi* and *I. sibirica, lythrum, lysimachia, podophyllum, rodgersia, Saxifraga peltata,* and *trollius.* From the rock garden we can take *dodecatheon* and the moisture-loving *primulas* such as *denticulata, cashmireana, japonica, pulverulenta, Beesiana, Bulleyana, helodoxa, sikkimensis, Florindae, alpicola, rosea* and *Veitchii.* The shrub garden can supply bamboos (*arundinaria* and *bambusa*) in variety, also *Cornus alba, C. sanguinea,* many willows, alders and *taxodium.* Nor must the *gunneras* and *rheums* (ornamental rhubarbs) be overlooked. No plants give a more tropical appearance to the water garden. The leaves of *Gunnera manicata* are often 6 ft. in diameter and the rhubarb-like flower stems may reach 12 ft. in height. The crowns are rather tender and should be protected with bracken or dry leaves in winter. Amongst ferns *Osmunda regalis* is the best for the water garden.

CHAPTER XIII

Lawns and their Maintenance

IT IS customary to say that there are two methods by which lawns may be made, namely from seed and from turf, but this is to overlook a third possibility which, I fancy, is the most usual of all so far as the small garden owner is concerned. I refer to the practice of making a lawn from the turf which already exists on the site.

I have seen some good lawns made in this manner. I remember, for example, an excellent tennis lawn which had been made by the simple process of mowing the meadow in which the owner's house had been built, filling up any small hollows which occurred and levelling out bigger depressions and bumps by cutting the turf in the form of an H with a sharp edging tool, folding back the flaps and then adding to or scraping away some of the soil from underneath.

There is this much to be said in favour of making use of the grasses native to the site. They are certain to be of a kind which thrive reasonably well under the particular conditions of soil and climate, and as much cannot always be said for imported grass. Home-made lawns of this type are often comparatively trouble free in consequence.

On the debit side must be reckoned the fact that the 'natural' lawn seldom has the fine finish and soft, even texture of the carefully 'made' lawn. There are likely to be many small weeds mixed up with the grass, and the grasses themselves will probably contain kinds of a comparatively coarse type, such as annual meadow grass, perennial rye grass and Yorkshire fog. Nevertheless many unsuitable grasses may disappear after a time.

LAWNS FROM TURF

When we come to consider 'made' as distinct from 'natural' lawns, the classification into turf and seed construction holds true. At one time there were more lawns made from turf than from seed, but I scarcely think this is true at the present time. There have been such great improvements during the present century in the selection and supply of suitable grasses for lawn making, and so much has been learned about their cultivation that this has become the most popular and, incidentally, the cheapest method of producing lawns.

Nevertheless, there are many people who, for one reason or another, will prefer to use turf. It has the merit of being extremely quick, a hard wearing sward being obtainable in a matter of weeks instead of months. Added to this it is not so essential to rid the ground so thoroughly of weeds as in the case of sites required for seeding. Good turf will smother quite a number of the weeds, particularly those of an annual character such as chickweed and groundsel, which are often such a nuisance on new building sites. And though it may be argued that there really is no need to worry about these weeds where the lawn is concerned for, being annuals, they will automatically die out at the end of the first year and, provided they are mown regularly, will have no chance to ripen seed and so perpetuate themselves, yet the retort must be made that they can interfere seriously with the seedling grass.

The great drawback of turf is that it almost always contains an unknown combination of grasses together with many weeds; in fact, in this respect it is no improvement on the natural lawn. This is no matter for wonder, because the majority of nurserymen and landscape gardeners obtain their supplies of turf from meadows and fields, often those which have been earmarked for building sites and, in consequence, will have to be stripped of their turf anyway. It is possible to purchase cultivated turf, that is to say turf specially raised for lawn making by sowing suitable mixtures of grass seed on properly prepared ground, but it is inevitable that the price is high and it is seldom that the amateur gardener is prepared to go to so much expense.

CUMBERLAND TURF. There is another special class of turf to which my criticisms regarding weeds and coarse grasses do not apply. This is the sea washed turf, commonly known as Cumberland turf because it is from the Solway estuary that much of it is obtained, though, in point of fact, there are other places around the coast, including Morecambe Bay, Lancashire, from which it can be cut. Sea washed exactly describes it. It is grass which grows on salt marshes near the sea and over which the sea water does occasionally flow at extra high tides or when the wind is blowing inshore. Because of these peculiar conditions and the fine silty nature of the soil, only certain grasses can survive, and these are almost always of a very fine, close-growing character. In consequence sea washed turves are unrivalled for all purposes where an exceptionally fine sward is required, for example on bowling greens, but they are not so suitable for ordinary lawn making where there is to be hard wear and perhaps a minimum of attention. Because of the character of the soil, which may become excessively close with rolling and heavy wear, the turf often dies out and becomes patchy after a few years. Cumberland turf is costly, difficult to maintain and only suitable for special purposes.

PREPARING FOR TURF. I know that it is common practice when a lawn is to be turfed to give it the minimum preparatory treatment consistent with getting a level surface on which to lay the turves. Results can be obtained in this way, but not the best results. The proper method is to treat the lawn like any other permanent feature of the garden and prepare the ground really well, bearing in mind that the first digging will also be the last one.

The soil should be turned right over to a depth of at least 1 ft. and all perennial weed roots picked out. If the site has to be levelled it is essential to keep the fertile top soil on top; that is to say any alteration in levels must be done by juggling with the lower soil, and the top soil (to a depth of at least 9 in. and preferably a foot) must be replaced on top of it. This is because the lower soil is seldom suitable for the cultivation of good grass, lacking the fertility and texture of the top soil. If this preliminary work can be completed in the spring and the soil left fallow all summer it will be an advantage and give an excellent opportunity to get rid of weeds by frequent hoeing.

If the soil is naturally poor it will pay to dig in dung or compost generously. Dressings up to 1 cwt. to 6 sq. yd. may not be out of place. Bone meal, or some other slow acting phosphatic fertiliser could also be added to encourage early root growth, but not too generously as phosphates in excess will stimulate clovers at the expense of fine grasses, and although clovers make a very dark green drought resistant lawn, they also make an extremely slippery one. They are a real menace on all sports lawns.

In any case the soil, after digging, should be allowed to settle for at least a month, and preferably longer. Even then, before the turf is laid, the surface should be trodden, when dry, first in one direction and then at right angles. Finally it must be broken down reasonably fine with fork and rake. This will give a final opportunity to pick out any weed roots which may have been overlooked previously and will also destroy any small weeds which have survived previous cultivations.

LAYING TURF. The best time at which to purchase turves is in autumn, but turf can also be laid in early winter or spring. It is not usually wise to attempt turfing in midwinter unless the weather is particularly mild, nor between May and August, when conditions are usually too dry.

As a rule turf is cut in rectangles 3 ft. long, 1 ft. wide and about 2 in. thick, and these long strips are rolled up for easy transport. The drawback to this method of cutting is that the rolling almost always breaks the soil to some extent and the result is, in consequence, less even than that obtained by cutting turves in foot squares and transporting these flat. The small square turf is, in consequence, frequently favoured by experts, particularly when engaged in the construction of bowling greens or similar swards requiring a very true surface. A drawback is that there are more turves to be handled for any given area, and therefore more labour is involved in laying them.

Before turf is laid it is wise to look it over closely and remove any weeds likely to prove troublesome, such as dandelions and plantains. Next the turves should be trimmed to an even thickness. The simplest method is to make a shallow trough, just big enough to take one turf, and open at one end. The sides of this trough should be 1½ in. high. Then the turves are slid into the box one at a time upside down and are trimmed with a large knife (an old carving knife is ideal) to exactly the depth of the box.

The turves are laid in straight rows starting from one end of the lawn, but the turves in each row are staggered in relation to those in the preceding and succeeding rows. In fact the whole effect is precisely the same as may be observed in any properly made brick wall. The idea is to get a better 'bind' before the turves actually grow into the soil beneath them.

As the turves are laid they may be lightly beaten down on to the surface with a smooth wooden block. A special turf beater can be purchased for this purpose, though it is seldom an investment which the amateur gardener is prepared to make. You can use the back of a spade for beating the turves but it is not as good as a wooden block because it is more likely to bruise the grass and, in any case, a spade back is seldom quite flat. Beating is more likely to be useful on light soil than on heavy and should always be omitted if the turf is very wet. Never use the beater to level out inequalities in the surface. These should be made good by scraping away or adding soil as necessary.

It will probably happen that the lawn site will not be of such a size and shape that every row of turves will finish with whole turves. Half turves, or even smaller pieces, may have to be used to fill up. Never lay these on the extreme end of a row but keep them inside with a whole turf at the end. This is because small pieces have a habit of working loose and are very liable to be kicked out if on the edge.

When all the turves have been laid, sprinkle over them a little fine soil mixed with sand and peat. Old potting soil is excellent for the purpose. Only quite a small quantity should be needed as its purpose is solely to fill up any cracks remaining between the turves. It is brushed down into these with a beech broom and the job is then finished. A week or so later the turf should be knitting nicely to the soil and can be rolled with a light roller and then mown with the cutters set rather high.

LAWNS FROM SEED

Next to making use of the natural grass of the site, seeding provides the cheapest method of making a lawn and, practically without exception, the most satisfactory. This is because the number of grass species capable of making the finest type of lawn is extremely limited and the best results are obtained with either single species or very simple mixtures of two or three species. Natural turf usually contains a greater assortment of grasses, some of them of inferior quality from the standpoint of lawn making, and there is almost always an admixture of weeds into the bargain.

If one starts with seed it is possible to select exactly what one wants in the way of variety and eliminate the second rate as well as the worthless. Rye grass, so often included in cheap mixtures, is undesirable for two reasons: first it is a comparatively coarse grass and produces bents (flower spikes) which are so wiry that the mower often misses them, with the result that they stand up and give the lawn a ragged appearance; and, second, most strains of it do not withstand close mowing well and so gradually die out after the second or third year leaving the ground open to weed infestation.

For high quality lawns the fescues and bent grasses (agrostis) are unsurpassed. For a wide range of purposes an excellent mixture is seven parts by weight Chewing's fescue and three parts by weight *Agrostis tenuis* (a bent grass popularly known as 'Browntop'). Those who prefer a slightly more elaborate mixture, on the principle of not putting all one's eggs in one basket, may use three parts Chewing's fescue, four parts Creeping Red fescue (*Festuca rubra genuina*) and three parts Browntop. If a single grass lawn is preferred, Browntop may be used alone and the result will be a turf of superb evenness provided weeds do not gain the ascendancy in the first year. This they may do if the gardener is not watchful because Browntop establishes itself slowly and is not well adapted to smother an early crop of weeds.

In dry, hot places Crested Dogstail (*Cynosurus cristatus*) may be employed, either by itself or in association with the Smooth-stalked Meadow grass (*Poa pratensis*), another grass which withstands drought. It is even possible to find a grass for those awkward, damp and shady spots which usually remain bare or grow nothing but moss. The Wood Meadow grass (*Poa nemoralis*) is just the thing for them.

The very finest lawns are almost always found on distinctly acid

385

soils. If the soil is already of an acid character (see Chapter I) there is no need to do anything further, but if it is naturally alkaline it may be desirable to work in plenty of dung, compost, leaf mould or peat, and it will certainly be wise to avoid all alkaline dressings such as lime, basic slag and wood ashes.

The initial preparation of the ground is the same for seed as for turf and even more care should be taken to break the soil up thoroughly and eliminate all weeds. Two or three months summer fallow will help immensely to this end.

The best time for sowing grass seed is, as a rule, from mid-August to mid-September though of course it will depend upon the weather. If, for example, early September is excessively dry and hot it may be wise to wait for rain, even if this means sowing as late as the end of the month. After that, however, no further attempt should be made to sow the finer strains until March at earliest and preferably April. Spring sown lawns often do very well though there may be more trouble with weeds than in the autumn. It is not usually possible to germinate grass seeds successfully between May and August.

Before sowing the surface must be broken down to a really fine and crumbly texture and this means waiting for suitable weather. It is impossible to get the right kind of tilth when it is very dry or very wet, and certainly not if the surface is frozen. The final preparation should be with the rake. All lumps and big stones must be removed from the surface, and at the same time a mixture of two parts by weight sulphate of ammonia, four parts superphosphate of lime and one part sulphate of potash should be worked into the surface at the rate of 2 oz. per sq. yd.

SEEDING. Grass seed should be sown at the rate of from $\frac{1}{2}$ to 2 oz. per sq. yd. A heavy rate of seeding will usually give a lawn in shorter time and has the added advantage of smothering weeds more thoroughly. However, if the expense of the 2 oz. seeding is too great, the reader may console himself with the knowledge that a 1 oz. or even a $\frac{1}{2}$ oz. sowing will usually give excellent results provided he is prepared to wait a little longer and take a little more care in the elimination of weeds.

It is important to distribute the seed as evenly as possible, and to facilitate this it is sometimes advised that the whole area to be seeded should be divided into yard squares with garden lines pegged down at right-angles. Personally I think this is carrying things too far and that, unless the area is very big, in which case it may pay to divide it into strips, a more practical scheme is to weigh out the right quantity of seed for the whole lawn and then sow considerably more sparingly than seems necessary and go back over the area a second and, if necessary, a third time. Not only does this give the right rate of seed but also usually results in a very even distribution, particularly if one first sows lengthwise and then crosswise.

The seed is covered first by careful raking and cross raking and then by sprinkling finely sifted soil over it at the rate of 2 lb. per sq. yd. Rolling is only advisable on light soils and then only a very light roller should be used, preferably a wooden one. As a rule this is an operation which the amateur must omit for lack of suitable apparatus.

Protection from birds may be necessary, especially in town gardens. The most effective method is to drive in pegs every yard or so and wind black thread between them in as complicated a pattern as possible. It is also possible to buy special dressings for the seed which will make it distasteful to birds, and some firms offer seed already treated in this manner. The same result can be attained by very slightly damping the seed with paraffin and then dusting it with red lead.

EARLY CARE. If the weather should become very dry after seeding and germination is delayed much beyond a fortnight, it may be necessary to water the lawn, but this should be avoided if possible. If watering does become essential use a lawn sprinkler or a hose fitted with a really fine rose. As a rule, however, germination proceeds quite normally in from five to ten days and a few weeks later the grass will be 2 in. high and ready for its first cutting. This can be done with the ordinary lawn mower provided it is really sharp and set high. A dull mower will drag the seedling grasses out of the ground. Rolling is not likely to be necessary for the first month, but after that, when the grass is beginning to run together and form a real carpet a light roller can be used when the soil is fairly dry. Before rolling or mowing be careful to remove all worm casts.

Little by little, the blades can be set to cut nearer to the ground. Nevertheless very close cutting is not desirable unless the lawn is needed for games demanding a very true surface. It tends to weaken the grass and does not really improve its appearance. For ordinary use mowing to within $\frac{3}{8}$ in. of soil level is sensible and sightly.

ROUTINE MANAGEMENT. Once the lawn has been made, whether from seed, turf or from the native grass of the plot, it is, of course possible to leave it pretty much alone with the exception of mowing, but this kind of treatment will not produce the best results. Good lawns get a lot more looking after than that. They must be fed at regular intervals, watered when the weather is dry, rolled occasionally when conditions are right, opened up with a spiked roller or fork at other times and raked and swept practically all the year round.

Most amateurs tend to put their lawn mowers away from October to March. That is a mistake. Grass does grow, even in late autumn and winter, and occasional cutting is desirable though it may perhaps only be needed twice or three times during the whole of that period. Moreover it is essential to choose a day when the surface is nearly dry. If you cut when the grass is very wet you will probably do more harm than good. For this winter cutting also the blades can be set fairly high to leave the grass say $\frac{3}{4}$ in. long. As the grass starts to grow rapidly in the spring the blades can be lowered and cutting will, of course, become much more frequent. Remember that regular mowing not only keeps the lawn looking nice, but it is also one of the best methods of getting rid of weeds and keeping a good grass sward, though over-close mowing, by killing the grass, may encourage weeds.

Rolling is more necessary for lawns used for games than for purely ornamental lawns. For home use it is seldom necessary to use a roller weighing more than 2 cwt. and it is likely to be most needed in the spring when the grass is growing fastest. Always use it when the surface is moist but not thoroughly wet. Early morning is often the best time for this work.

Towards the end of summer, and sometimes far earlier in the season, lawns which are subject to heavy wear may get too hard in places. This is particularly likely to happen on lawns used for games, the base lines of a tennis court or the creases of a cricket pitch being centre points of damage. This can be overcome by making use of a special light roller made of wood and fitted with spikes. The object is to perforate the turf and slightly lift it. Those who cannot afford a special roller can do the same thing with a fork pushed into the turf about 2 in. and then levered backwards a little, but not enough to break the surface. It is rather a laborious job with a fork because one has to make a fresh set of perforations every 2 or 3 in. In severe cases of hardening due to heavy wear much deeper forking or spiking may be needed. Special machines are made with spikes which will drive 4 or 5 in. into the turf without loosening it, or the same thing can be done with a fork.

The spring toothed grass rake should be much more in evidence in the gardens of amateurs. It is an invaluable tool which will weaken creeping weeds and expose them to the mower, and will also prevent the turf from getting clogged up with dead grass. Use it immediately before rolling or mowing so that the rather rough surface left by the rake is immediately corrected. Rake the lawn in different directions, sometimes working lengthwise, sometimes across. An ordinary steel garden rake is not so good as the special spring toothed rake but may be used, nevertheless.

Brooming is a supplement to raking and, like it, will get rid of a lot of the dead material which otherwise covers the surface of the soil and prevents the grass roots from breathing. It is also necessary to remove worm casts which will otherwise get flattened out by roller and mowing machine and will kill the grass beneath. The best kind of broom is a proper grass besom made from birch branches, but an ordinary yard broom can be used if necessary. Regular brushing is particularly essential in the autumn when worm casts are most abundant.

FEEDING. The grasses in a lawn are so crowded and, for the most part, their roots are so near the surface that they soon exhaust the soil, and unless a regular and considered system of feeding is carried out the quality of the lawn is bound to suffer. Intelligent feeding will not only maintain the strength of the grass but will also have a selective effect, encouraging the finer grasses, and eliminating weeds, clover and coarse grasses. The thing to aim for is a fairly high concentration of nitrogen, preferably in the form of ammonium salts and a definite acidity. Regular small dressings of sulphate of ammonia will help to both ends but, nevertheless, it is not wise to rely on this chemical alone or the feeding will become too unbalanced. Moreover the lawn needs humus just as much as other parts of the garden, so bulky organic dressings must be used as well as chemical fertilisers.

Naturally feeding will have to be adapted to suit the soil, but here is a programme which can be taken as an average and will suit a great many of what one might term ordinary soils. Each spring top dress with a mixture of 3 parts sulphate of ammonia, 5 parts superphosphate of lime, 8 parts fine bone meal, 3 parts dried blood, 1 part sulphate of potash and 2 parts sulphate of iron, all parts to be reckoned by weight. Use this mixture at the rate of 3 ozs. per sq. yd. Then, between May and August, give three or four top dressings of sulphate of ammonia, each at the rate of $\frac{1}{2}$ oz. per sq. yd. but mix it with plenty of sand or fine soil to act as a carrier and so ensure even distribution.

If broad-leaved weeds, such as plantains, daisies, heartsease (*ajuga*), etc. are prevalent, use lawn sand in place of one, or possibly two, of the sulphate of ammonia applications. Lawn sand can be purchased ready for use and then manufacturers' instructions regarding rate should always be followed. If you prefer you can make your own lawn sand. The ingredients are 3 parts sulphate of ammonia, 1 part sulphate of iron, 20 parts fine silver sand all by weight. The mixture must be very well mixed and evenly spread at 4 oz. per sq. yd., no more or it may

The Amateur Gardener

kill the grass as well as the weeds. Lawn sand, it should be remembered, is a fertiliser as well as a weed killer, and properly used can be of considerable benefit. The grass is likely to go black after application but will recover after two or three weeks.

At about the same time as the first dressing of mixed fertiliser is given, and again in early autumn the lawn may receive a dressing of compost made with 1 part of very old dung (the remnants of a mushroom bed are ideal) 2 parts good loamy soil and 1 part sharp sand, all passed through a ⅛ in. mesh sieve. Apply this mixture at 2 lb. per sq. yd.

MOSS AND WEEDS. If a lawn is properly looked after from the first, and the site upon which it is laid has been correctly prepared, there should be no great difficulty with either weeds or moss, but, of course, this is a counsel of perfection which is seldom attained. In actual practice I know only too well how often one has to deal with lawns which have got into shockingly bad condition.

Many weeds can be destroyed with lawn sand, as I have already described, but this treatment is not strong enough to destroy deep-rooting weeds, such as dandelion. No doubt the best method of dealing with the weed problem on lawns today is to treat the grass with one of the selective hormone weed killers such as MCPA or 2 : 4D. These are sold under various trade names and may be in either liquid or powder form, though liquids are the more popular for garden use. It is only necessary to dilute this liquid with the requisite amount of water as specified by the manufacturers, and then water the grass and weeds with it, using an ordinary watering can fitted with a fine rose. It is not necessary to soak the weeds but only to damp them thoroughly for which purpose a gallon of the diluted hormone will cover about 10 square yards. These weed killers are rather slow in action and it may be several days before much effect is seen, but then the weeds will commence to twist and curl and will presently begin to decay and die. Treatment is most effective if carried out during dry weather in spring but these weed killers can be applied at any time of the year. They tend to check the grass a little but do it no permanent injury. Weeds are killed more rapidly and efficiently and the grass recovers more quickly if a light dressing of any good lawn fertilizer, or even of sulphate of ammonia at ½ ounce per square yard, is given a few days before applying the weed killer.

Although these hormone weed killers destroy a wide range of weeds they do not kill everything and there may be a few species left which will have to be dealt with by hand. Yarrow or milfoil belongs to this group and so do the knotweed (*Polygonum aviculare*), pearlwort and the dwarf creeping clovers. Some of these can be weakened.

390

When creeping weeds, such as milfoil or yarrow, clover and mouse-eared chickweed, appear in a lawn they should be cut out at once with a short bladed knife. They can also be weakened, though not eliminated, by frequent raking which exposes them to the blades of the lawn mower. If they are neglected and get a thorough hold of the lawn there is only one remedy, namely to lift the offending turves bodily and either replace with clean turves or with soil and grass seed.

Moss, and the little weed known as pearlwort which is often mistaken for moss, are sometimes indications that the soil is poor but may easily be encouraged by mowing too closely so that the grass is unduly weakened. Moss is particularly likely to occur in damp, shady corners and very often there is no satisfactory method of getting rid of it permanently unless the conditions can be improved by cutting down overhanging trees and removing branches, etc. In other cases a remedy can be effected by laying drains under the lawn, and it is almost always wise to see what the effect will be of a thorough course of compound fertiliser and sulphate of ammonia treatment as described on p. 70.

Some firms offer special preparations for killing moss, one of the best of which is a mercurised lawn sand. A useful mixture to prepare at home is 1 part by weight sulphate of iron and 7 parts fine sand. This is dusted over the lawn at the rate of 4 oz. per sq. yd. The only point to observe is that, while such treatment will kill the moss, it will not eliminate the conditions which caused the growth of moss, nor will it encourage grass, so, unless appropriate steps are taken, the result may simply be a bare patch for a time and then a renewed growth of moss.

REPAIRING WORN PATCHES. Lawns which get a lot of wear are almost certain to become bare in places, particularly towards the end of a dry summer. The quickest way of dealing with this damage is to mark out a rectangle a little larger than the worn place, lift all the turf from this, either with a special turf cutter or with a sharp spade, and then relay with new turves. The drawback of such treatment is that, unless spare turves can be cut from another part of the lawn, which is most unlikely, it will mean that alien grass, and possibly weeds, will be imported, and the patch may become a centre of trouble for the rest of the lawn. In consequence I prefer to reseed with the same grass mixture as that used in the first place. In this case the worn place should be loosened with a fork, the points of which need not be driven in more than 3 or 4 in., and, when a fine crumbly surface has been obtained, the seed is sown and covered in the ordinary way.

WATERING. The finer grasses from which the best lawns are made are not very deep rooting and they tend to suffer quickly during hot dry spells in summer. The only preventive is timely and adequate watering, and the only satisfactory method of watering a lawn is with a sprinkler. Few amateurs realise how long it takes to get the soil under the turf really moist to a depth of 2 or 3 in., and nothing less will serve. To go out for twenty minutes or so with a hose and spray the lawn is worse than useless, while heavy drenchings from an open hose tend to wash the soil away from the grass roots and expose them to scorching. The sprinkler can be left in position for an hour or so without attention and will deliver a fine rain-like spray over a large area. Lawns which have become very hard should be perforated with fork or spiked roller before being watered. It is worth noting that a lawn which is regularly mulched with compost, as I have described on p. 389 will withstand drought for a longer period than one which is not so treated. Pricking or spiking (see p.388) may be necessary before watering if the surface of the lawn has become very hard.

WORMS AND LEATHER JACKETS. These are the two worst pests of the lawn and leather jackets have at times become front page news when, for example, they have threatened Lord's cricket pitch before a series of test matches. The leather jacket is the grub of the familiar daddy-long-legs and it is a sluggish, dark coloured, caterpillar-like creature (though it has no legs like a true caterpillar) which lives in the soil just beneath the surface and devours roots, particularly grass roots. The result is that the grass dies in small patches.

There are several ways of destroying leather jackets. One of the simplest is to soak the lawn very thoroughly with plain water and then cover the surface for a few hours with tarpaulins, boards or anything else that will exclude air. As a result the leather jackets are half suffocated and come up to the surface. If the treatment is carried out towards evening and the covering material is removed the following morning, hundreds of leather jackets may be discovered on the surface from which they can be swept up and destroyed.

A more drastic treatment is to broadcast arsenate of lead over the surface at the rate of 1 oz. per sq. yd. This is a poison and must be used with due caution, but if it is immediately washed into the turf by means of a moderate watering, there is little danger of any harm resulting. The advantage of this treatment is that it remains effective for months and will kill any fresh leather jackets which may find their way into the lawn.

Good results have also been obtained with DDT either dry or in liquid form. A 5 per cent dust applied dry to the surface at the rate of

2 oz. per sq. yd. will kill most leatherjackets beneath the turf and has the advantage of being far less poisonous than arsenate of lead.

Worms do not injure the grass directly; in fact, in some ways, they are beneficial as they drag decaying leaves into the soil, so enriching it, and also tunnel into the turf and aerate it. Unfortunately, worm casts can become a positive menace for, as I have already explained, they get flattened in pasty masses on top of the grass in wet weather and kill it. In consequence the worm population must be strictly limited. This can be done by the arsenate of lead treatment just recommended for leather jackets, though it is advisable to use a stronger concentration, $1\frac{1}{2}$ to 2 oz. per sq. yd. proving most effective.

An alternative for those who do not care to handle poisons is to broadcast mowrah meal over the surface at 4 oz. per sq. yd. and then water in heavily. The mowrah meal treatment is most effective in spring and autumn, February to May and August to December usually being the peak months for results. The worms come to the surface to die and must be swept up after each treatment. Mowrah meal does not remain effective for a long time like arsenate of lead.

A third method is to broadcast derris dust (4 per cent rotenone) over the lawn and water in moderately. The effect of this is fairly lasting.

MOLES. In some districts moles become very troublesome, not only on the lawn but also in other parts of the garden, particularly in seed beds and frames. These creatures are useful in the garden up to a point as they live on soil insects, but they tunnel in all directions just beneath the surface in search of their food and, in consequence, loosen the roots of plants and grass and cause the surface to collapse. Moreover, every few yards they throw up their 'spoil' in a big heap, the familiar mole-hill, and this is not only unsightly but, if left, will kill the grass beneath.

Moles can be trapped in special, steel, spring traps; they can be gassed with cyanide, or they can be poisoned with treated earthworms. Trapping is very effective if one goes about it the right way. Moles are thirsty creatures and will always look for water. If you can find a run which leads to water you can be sure that a number of moles will use it every day. That is the place to set a trap. A square of turf must be removed carefully to expose the run without filling it with soil, the jaws of the trap are opened and set across the run and the turf is then replaced to exclude light. Gloves should be worn when setting the trap because the mole very readily detects the scent of human beings.

To gas moles one introduces a small quantity of calcium cyanide (or one of the proprietary dusts containing this) to each run. A special device for injection can be obtained. Cyanic acid gas is given off by the action of soil moisture on the calcium cyanide. It penetrates the run and kills all living creatures, including the moles. The drawback is that the fumes are also poisonous to human beings, so care must be taken not to inhale them.

To poison moles earthworms well dusted with red squill powder are placed in the runs.

FAIRY RINGS. Sometimes one will see a ring of bright green, strong growing grass on the lawn and immediately inside this an area of dead grass. Country people call these fairy rings because of the old superstition that this is where the fairies dance at night. The trouble is, in fact, due to one or other of several different fungi which live on the grass roots and, gradually penetrating outward from the centre, kill the grass in a circular patch. The bright green appearance immediately beyond this ring is apparently due to the fact that the fungus actually stimulates the grass before it kills it. The remedy is to bore holes every few inches in the ring and fill with a solution of sulphate of iron, 4 oz. per gallon of water.

CHAPTER XIV

Ferns

BOTH FROM the botanical and garden standpoints ferns stand by themselves. Botanically they are separated by being non-flowering plants with a peculiar mode of reproduction by means of spores, which, despite the popular misconception on this point, are in no way analogous to seeds. From the gardener's point of view ferns have numerous peculiarities. In general they appreciate soils considerably looser and more spongy than would be desirable for most other classes of garden plants. Many will thrive in shade, some in dense shade, though it is a mistaken notion to imagine that no ferns like sun. Look along the dry walls which farmers use to divide fields in the Cotswold and Mendip regions and you will see plenty of wild ferns sharing sunny crevices alongside stonecrops and similar rock plants. However, species of this type are definitely in the minority. Most ferns are either woodlanders or hedgerow plants favouring, as a rule, the shady side of the hedge. In general they delight in rather deep, leafy or peaty soils, though it is surprising in what a wide range of soils ferns can be made to grow provided other conditions are favourable.

At this point it is necessary to draw a line between hardy ferns on the one hand and tender or greenhouse varieties on the other. As regards soil and general management, there is no great difference between the two groups, but the first can be grown outdoors throughout the year, whereas the second will require greenhouse protection, at least in winter, and as ferns do not like to be disturbed much at any time this means that greenhouse ferns must usually be grown in pots.

HARDY FERNS

These reached their peak of popularity during the late nineteenth century when many amateur cultivators were engaged in the production or collection of innumerable beautiful varieties. Later the development of the splendid modern races of hardy perennials threw ferns into the background and it is to be feared that some kinds have been lost to cultivation. Nevertheless, specialists have kept the cult going and a great diversity of excellent forms is still available.

It would be impossible in the space available to give descriptions of a representative collection of hardy ferns and for this I must refer

395

readers to fern publications and to catalogues of those nurserymen who specialise in such things. Suffice it to say here that the best hardy ferns for ordinary garden planting are derived from less than a dozen species and yet include innumerable varieties differing from their parents in the formation of fronds, which in some kinds are beautifully crested or waved and in others so subdivided that they suggest fine lace.

These important species are: *Scolopendrium vulgare* (*Phyllitis Scolopendrium*) (Hart's Tongue Fern); *Lastraea* (*Dryopteris*); *Filix-mas* (Male Fern); *L.* (*Athyrium*) *Filix-femina* (Lady Fern); *Polypodium vulgare* (Common Polypody); *Polystichum angulare* (*Setiferum*) (Soft Shield Fern); *P. aculeatum* (Prickly Shield Fern); *Cystopteris fragilis* (Parsley Fern); *Osmunda regalis* (Royal Fern) and *Struthiopteris germanica* (Ostrich Fern).

There are, of course, many others which could be planted in the garden but the best for the beginner will be found amongst those I have listed. The royal fern and its varieties are all very large and, in consequence, not very suitable for small gardens. Most of the others, however, can be planted in borders of ordinary width or in shady rock gardens, on the sides of banks, etc.

CULTURE. No fern really likes to be transplanted at any time of the year but with the hardy species the season when the least damage will be done is in the spring just as the plants are starting into growth. In consequence this is the best time to start a collection and also the period at which old borders of ferns which have become overcrowded may be divided and transplanted with greatest safety.

The soil should be of a more spongy character than that desirable for most other classes of plants. Leaf mould and peat can be used freely in the preparation of the beds and also a little dung, provided it is really old and well rotted; the residue of mushroom or cucumber beds is excellent, but fresh manure is quite unsuitable. Prepare the beds as you would for other plants, thoroughly digging a month or so in advance of the date of planting. Whatever is to be added to the bed should be worked well in and not left lying about in layers.

In planting, follow the ordinary rule of making holes of ample width to take the roots spread out in a natural manner but do not be so heavy with foot or hand in pressing the soil around the roots. The soil should be firm but not hard. Ferns are in the main surface rooting plants and, in consequence, the uppermost roots should only be covered with about an inch of soil.

As a rule very little further attention will be required. The plants should be watered in dry weather and, of course, they must be kept free from weeds. In general it is better to hand weed rather than to hoe as most ferns have so many roots close to the surface that they may be damaged even by careful hoeing.

Dead fronds should be left in the autumn as they serve as a natural protection to the crowns. Cut them off in late March or early April using a pair of sharp secateurs and severing them about an inch from the base.

A collection of hardy ferns may go on in this way in perfect health for ten years or more but there will come a time when some of the plants get too big and occupy more space than can be spared. Then they should be lifted very carefully with a fork in March or early April and divided in the way in which I have already described for hardy plants (p. 136). For large, old plants use two hand forks thrust through the centre of the clump and lever gently apart, but as far as possible divide with the fingers alone and only use a knife very occasionally where it is essential to sever a tough crown. If the plants are examined closely it will be found that there are hard, scale-like fragments clustered round the base of the leaves. These are, in fact, the dead stems of old leaves that have been cut back during the years. They should be removed carefully as they tend to check the free development of the plant.

Ferns require no feeding in the ordinary sense of the word but they will benefit from an annual top dressing in spring of peat or leaf mould with just a little bone meal added. Use a 5 in. potful of bone meal to each bushel of leaf mould or peat and spread this dressing to a depth of about one inch.

GREENHOUSE FERNS

As pot plants for cultivation in the greenhouse ferns are quite as useful as they are for outdoor planting. Many of the hardy varieties which have already been mentioned can also be grown in this way in an unheated greenhouse, but on the whole it is preferable to use the more tender species and varieties, of which there is a very large selection. These exotic ferns range in size from quite small plants, such as the popular *Pteris cretica* and *P. serrulata* so frequently cultivated as room plants, to towering tree ferns which need a tall conservatory to accommodate them. Their requirements, also, are very varied, though the most useful for the amateur are those which succeed in a cool or slightly heated house and partially shaded conditions. Tropical ferns, which require minimum temperatures of 65–70 deg. in winter, are really for the specialist, as are those delicate varieties which have to be grown in dense shade and a very humid atmosphere.

Some Good Kinds to Grow. A useful collection for the amateur would include several species of *adiantum* such as *A. cuneatum* (the common Maidenhair); *A. gracillimum*, a more graceful plant; *A. decorum*, which has larger individual leaflets; and *A. rubellum*, in which the young fronds are tinted with red. In addition to the two species of *pteris* which have already been mentioned, *P. major* is well worth a place. Like the other two it is very tough and will put up with a lot of mismanagement, for which reason it is one of the best ferns to bring into the living room, where the temperature is often variable and much too dry for other more delicate species.

Cyrtomium falcatum is another hard-wearing fern excellent as a room plant, and it is well nigh impossible to kill it. *Asplenium bulbiferum* is a graceful fern very popular with florists. It has the interesting and useful characteristic of forming plantlets all along the old fronds. If these are pegged to the soil and kept moist in spring or early summer the tiny plants will soon form roots of their own, after which they can be detached and potted up, each to grow in time into a new specimen. Incidentally this peculiarity is not confined to *A. bulbiferum*; other ferns show it, including, to a very marked extent, the beautiful hardy form of *Polystichum angulare* known as *proliferum*. Even more beautiful than *A. bulbiferum* is *A. viviparum*, while those who require a big specimen should obtain *A. australasicum*, which differs markedly from the others not only in its greater size but in the fact that the fronds are not divided.

Davallias have in themselves provided the greenhouse owner with a wealth of beautiful material. All species have finely divided fronds and they spread by surface rhizomes which root as they go, so that propagation by division becomes a very simple matter. Two of the best are *D. bullata*, known as the Squirrel's Foot fern because of its very slender rhizomes covered with furry-looking scales, and *D. canariensis*, named the Hare's Foot fern because its rhizomes are stouter and certainly more like a hare's than a squirrel's foot.

An extremely distinctive fern is *Platycerium alcicorne*, appropriately known as the Stag's Horn fern. This will grow quite happily on a block of peat nailed to a board and suspended against a greenhouse wall. It does not require soil, though it can be grown in a pot filled with a compost of equal parts fibrous peat, loam and sphagnum moss. The bluish-grey fronds spread out rather like a stag's horns and the whole plant has a most unusual appearance.

Culture. All the ferns mentioned can be grown with ease in any greenhouse from which frost can be excluded in winter and in which the average temperature in summer is around 60 deg. Very little artificial heat is required, in fact it is likely to do more harm than good. Shading will only be needed from early May until September, and then only on the sunny side of the house. It is not light which must be excluded but merely strong direct sunshine which might scorch the delicate fern fronds.

The atmosphere should be moderately moist, very similar, in fact, to that required by a great many flowering greenhouse plants, including begonias and gloxinias. From April to September the syringe can be used fairly frequently, particularly to damp down between the pots and on the floor and stages. A light overhead dewing in the mornings will also do good during mild weather, provided there is no danger of sunshine playing directly on the fronds while they are still damp.

All these fronds can be grown in the ordinary Innes compost though, if preferred, the proportion of peat or leaf mould can be increased to twice the normal. This will give a more spongy mixture which will make it easier to maintain the necessary moisture and will also help the beginner to avoid the danger of too firm potting.

This is one of the major points in which ferns differ from most other greenhouse plants. Very firm potting is undesirable and the potting stick or rammer will scarcely ever be required. All the firming that is necessary can be done with the fingers and by rapping the pot smartly on a firm wooden bench. Established ferns may be permitted to fill their pots fairly tightly with roots before they are repotted, but they should not be allowed to become badly potbound. Repotting is best done in March just as growth recommences.

These cool house ferns should all be watered freely during their season of rapid growth, which is roughly from April to August, after which the supply should be decreased gradually and only a very moderate quantity of water given in winter.

Despite the fact that ferns are in general moisture lovers, it is most important that they should have good drainage. In consequence, be careful to see that all pots used have adequate drainage holes and that these are covered with a good layer of broken crocks and rough rubble.

If the atmosphere in the fernery becomes too dry and hot, ferns are liable to suffer badly from various pests including red spider, thrips and scale insects. The remedy, apart from correcting faulty treatment, is to fumigate two or three times, at intervals of about a week, with nicotine fumigant.

FERNS AS HOUSE PLANTS. Many greenhouse ferns make good house plants though in almost all cases it is advisable to give them periods of recuperation in a suitable greenhouse as the atmosphere of an ordinary dwelling room can scarcely ever be kept moist enough to suit ferns to perfection. In particular, rooms which are heated by gas are apt to become too dry and hot. Varieties most likely to put up with these conditions for long periods are *Asplenium bulbiferum, Pteris serrulata,* and *Cyrtomium falcatum.*

While spraying indoors is usually impracticable it is possible to damp the fronds down daily with water applied from an ordinary scent spray and in the case of the broader leaved ferns, such as *cyrtomium,* fronds can be sponged occasionally with tepid water which may, with advantage, contain a few drops of milk.

PART III
GARDENING UNDER GLASS

CHAPTER XV

Cloches, Frames and Greenhouses

THERE ARE several things to be gained by adding glass in some form or other to the garden equipment. By its use one can enjoy many plants, including vegetables and fruits, which are not sufficiently hardy to be grown in the open in this country. Then there is the possibility of having crops out of season, either earlier or later than would otherwise be possible. Nor must one overlook the advantage of being able to propagate many plants which otherwise have to be purchased. Seeds can be germinated earlier or more successfully in greenhouse or frame, or even under simple continuous cloches, than in the open, and in some cases seedlings from outdoor sowings can be transferred to the glasshouse during the winter and replanted outdoors in the spring, so gaining a better chance of survival.

As to the precise form in which the glass shall be added, that will depend to a very great extent on the means at the disposal of the gardener. Quite likely he will be content to start with a simple frame or even a few cloches. There is certainly a good deal to be said for such small beginnings, because the principles of glass cultivation are the same whatever the means, and it is good policy to make one's mistakes and gain experience on a small scale before launching out more adventurously.

CLOCHES

The original cloche or handlight was, I believe, devised by French market gardeners, who used it to bring on early lettuces, etc. Often it took the form of a plain bell of glass or a rectangle of glass in a metal frame with a pyramid-shaped 'cap'. The continuous cloche is a comparatively recent development and an immense improvement on the old handlight. There are a number of patents on the market, each with some point of excellence to recommend it. The qualities to look for in a good cloche of this type are rigidity, portability and roominess. The beginner will quite likely start with what is known as the 'A' or tent type of cloche, which simply consists of two pieces of glass held together in the form of a ridge. Later he will probably graduate to the barn type, or something similar, with vertical sides and a sloping top, as this will allow him to grow bigger plants and more of them.

403

These continuous cloches are always open at each end, the idea being that they can be run on one against another to cover any length of row. Generally it is not necessary to block the ends of the rows, but where they are short and there is danger of a cold draught blowing right through, a pane of glass can be stood vertically against each end and held in position with a stick.

Cloches are principally used to bring on early seedlings in the vegetable garden, but they can also be used for the same purpose in the flower garden and can be turned to good account to complete the growth of plants when the weather has become too cold for them to mature without protection; for example, outdoor tomatoes are often ripened in this way during September and October.

If the ground is properly prepared before cloches are to be used, it is often possible to dispense with watering throughout the growth of the crop. This is because the width of soil covered by the cloche is not very great and the rain which is deflected by the glass runs down into the soil on either side of the row and soaks inwards to the roots of the plants. The essential for this to occur freely is that the soil itself should be of a rather spongy texture. This is assured by working in plenty of granulated moss peat and also decayed vegetable refuse or dung prior to planting, and also by cultivating the soil as deeply as possible. Moreover the soil must be thoroughly moistened to a good depth, though not pasty on the surface, before seeds or plants are put in. However, one should not make a fetish of this 'no-watering after planting' policy. If the ground under the cloches does become dry and the plants show signs of suffering in consequence, there should be no hesitation in removing the cloches and watering in the ordinary way.

As there is bound to be a slight crack between each cloche and its neighbours and, moreover, the glasses with which individual cloches are built seldom fit quite tightly together, some air is admitted all the time and this is often enough to give adequate ventilation. Nevertheless it is not possible to lay down hard and fast rules in this case either, and if cloches are to be left in position after the weather gets really warm in spring, it may be necessary to remove one here and there and space the remainder out. I have seen severe leaf scorching occur through leaving unventilated cloches over tomatoes throughout the summer, and far better results obtained by removing altogether one of the side glasses from each cloche so leaving the row completely unprotected on one side.

There is really no end to the ingenuity which can be shown in the use of cloches. Cuttings can be rooted under them, strawberries can be ripened several weeks earlier than in the open air, lettuce seedlings brought through the winter and induced to heart in April or May, and practically every type of vegetable or flower seed germinated at least a month earlier than in the open. A use sometimes overlooked is that of drying off ground sufficiently to enable sowing to proceed.

Those who are interested in food cultivation often practice an extremely intensive rotation of cropping under cloches. Here is a typical programme. Winter lettuces are sown early in October, either alone or with onions. The cloches remain over these until about mid-April when they are transferred to tomatoes previously reared in the greenhouse. By the middle of June the cloches are taken from the tomatoes and placed over the autumn sown onions to ripen them off. From these they go to shallots with the same object, and from them to the spring sown onions, finishing up over the tomatoes again during the last half of September to hasten the ripening of the top trusses. For this purpose the tomatoes are untied from their stakes and laid lengthwise along the rows on clean straw.

FRAMES

A well-made frame will keep out more cold than a cloche and so enable the gardener to grow an even wider range of plants throughout the year. The drawback of the frame by comparison with the cloche is its lack of portability, though this can be overcome to a great extent by using fairly small lights and detachable wooden sides. Frames of this latter character are often known as Dutch frames because they have been highly developed by the Dutch market gardeners. The standard pattern Dutch frame has a light (i.e. the glazed portion of the frame) measuring 62 by 35 ins. and glazed with one pane of glass. The sides are made of 1 in. thick planks, the back being about 10 in. in height and the front 8 in. Various methods are employed for bolting or clipping these sides together so that they can be taken down quickly and moved to other parts of the garden.

The more usual type of frame in private gardens is a much more permanent affair often with brick or concrete sides, though cheaper patterns are made with grooved and tongued boarding. The standard size of light is 6 ft. by 4 ft. but a small size light, 4 ft. by 3 ft., is popular, particularly with amateurs, because it can be handled by one person. As a rule the amount of tilt given from back to front on English frames is greater than with the Dutch type, though this is a feature which varies very greatly with different makes and may be anything from about 4° to 15°. Personally I favour a rather flat type of frame because then it is possible to have a perfectly level bed within the frame and yet keep all the plants within reasonable distance of the glass. Moreover, in the case of small frames if the sides are too high they cut off a considerable amount of light and plants become drawn in consequence.

It is of vital importance that the walls of any frame should be solid and reasonably thick so that they withstand cold and do not admit draughts. Wood frames, if made of more than one plank vertically, should always be tongued and grooved or rebated for plain boards, even if they fit closely at first, are almost certain to gape after a while. Undoubtedly brick or concrete walls give much better protection but there is the drawback that the frame then ceases to be a tenant's fixture, and, in consequence, cannot be shifted with one's household belongings if the property is rented.

A good frame can be of use in a variety of ways. It will do everything that I have outlined for the cloche and is to be preferred for seed germination and striking cuttings because of the greater control it affords over temperature and atmospheric moisture. In addition it can be used to harden off plants raised in the greenhouse and to overwinter many half-hardy plants that would not be safe under cloches.

HARDENING-OFF. This is a process which requires some explanation. Most plants have a wide range of adaptability, a statement which applies as much to temperature as to other things. The process works both ways. For example, if a plant is accustomed, over a long period, to comparatively low temperatures it will become tougher than normal and, in consequence, will quite likely be able to stand even more cold without injury. On the contrary, if a plant is grown in a warm greenhouse for some time it will become more tender and easily injured by temperatures which it would normally endure.

In order to bring seedlings and cuttings along rapidly in the early part of the year it is often necessary to start them in warmth, perhaps a good deal more warmth than that to which they are normally accustomed. If, later on, these same plants are to be transferred to the open air it is essential that they should be accustomed to lower temperatures by gradual stages. It may be possible to go a long way towards achieving this object in the greenhouse, first by cutting out artificial heat and then by giving increased ventilation, but it is never possible to get conditions identical with those outside. In the frame this difficulty can be overcome completely because, when the hardening process has gone sufficiently far, the gardener can remove the frame lights altogether, first of all by day only and then by night as well. Skill in hardening-off is one of the secrets of success with a great many half-hardy or greenhouse raised but outdoor grown plants.

GREENHOUSES

There are many different types of greenhouses and many uses to which they may be put. It would be impossible to deal with them all in the space available, but here are a few of the most important.

First of all greenhouses can be broadly classified as span-roofed, three-quarter span-roofed and lean-to. These main types can be further sub-divided as ordinary greenhouses and forcing houses (or forcing pits) while a further classification can be made into hot houses, temperate or cool houses and cold houses.

Span-roofed Houses. These have an ordinary apex or 'barn' type of roof in which both sloping sides are of equal length. The span-roofed house is the commonest type in private gardens and the one with the widest range of uses. It should, where possible, be built to run north and south so that each side gets an approximately equal amount of sunlight and the door should be at the south end. The span-roofed house can be used for almost any purpose and is as serviceable for growing utility crops, such as tomatoes, winter lettuces or even choice fruit trees, as it is for ornamental plants in pots or planted out in greenhouse borders.

Three-quarter Span. This differs from the full span-roofed house in having one sloping side considerably longer than the other. The shorter side terminates on a wall and, in fact, the three-quarter span-roofed house is most serviceable where a fairly high wall, say 7 to 12 ft., already exists in the garden. It is a type which is rapidly going out of fashion, though it is still to be seen in many old private gardens. Where possible the three-quarter span house should always face south or south-west, unless it is to be used mainly for ferns or shade-loving plants, in which case it may face north. It is a type which at one time was extremely popular for vines and fruit trees permanently planted in borders within the greenhouse.

Lean-to. This type resembles the three-quarter span house but with the short side eliminated, the wall starting from the apex of the house. All the remarks I have made regarding three-quarter spans apply equally to this type, but it is more suitable for the small garden because it is less costly to build. In fact, where a wall 8 ft. or more in height exists a lean-to glasshouse is often the cheapest structure of all. A drawback is that unless the wall faces south the plants within the house inevitably go short of light and may suffer in consequence.

Forcing House. This type of house may be of any of the three preceding types but differs from an ordinary greenhouse in having no vertical glass sides, that is to say the sloping roof comes practically to ground level. In small forcing houses this results in so little head room that it is necessary to excavate a path down the centre and enter the house by descending three or four steps. This is the kind of house often known as a forcing pit. The true pit has a rather limited range of usefulness and is mainly employed by market growers for cucumbers, melons, ferns and other moisture-loving plants as well as for very early forcing of all kinds. The bigger type of forcing house in which there is sufficient head room for a path without excavation also has a limited usefulness in private gardens, though it has the merit of cheapness in construction. It is difficult to install staging economically in this kind of house and this restricts its adaptability for the cultivation of pot plants.

Hot House. The term is synonymous with 'stove' and is used for any class of house in which the temperature averages 70° or over throughout most of the year and certainly never falls below 60°. Naturally a hot house in this climate is an expensive matter for the fuel consumption is considerable. It is necessary for the culture of many tropical plants including some of the most beautiful orchids but is an affair for the specialist rather than for the ordinary amateur.

Temperate House. Any house in which the temperature is maintained around 55 to 65° for the greater part of the year, falling perhaps to 45 or even 40° for short spells in the coldest winter weather is classed as a temperate house. From the amateur's standpoint it is the most useful class of glasshouse, enabling him to grow the widest range of plants. It is seldom that any greenhouse can be maintained at an even temperature throughout, for usually the end nearest the boiler or heating apparatus is hotter than that at the far end. The gardener can turn this to good account by growing the more tender plants in the warm portion and using the other part for the hardier subjects and those which are shortly to be removed to the frame. This feature is further exploited in some houses by having an interior glazed partition which cuts the house into two compartments one warmer than the other. It is possible in most parts of the country to maintain a temperate house at the correct temperature for seven or eight months of the year without artificial heat, and only during the coldest periods is continuous heating likely to be required. In consequence the cost of fuelling can be kept reasonably low.

Cold House. The name may be somewhat misleading for no-one wants to keep a greenhouse intentionally cold. By 'cold house' the gardener simply means one that is not provided with any permanent heating apparatus. An oil lamp or electric radiator may be used occasionally to keep out really severe frost, but most of the time the gardener must maintain the necessary temperature by skilful manipulation of the ventilators and possibly by the use of canvas blinds pulled down at night to retain some of the heat trapped by day. The cold house inevitably has a somewhat limited utility as it will usually be impossible to exclude frost entirely throughout the winter, and this means that really tender plants will succumb. Nevertheless most amateurs start with such a house and gain valuable experience from it before eventually deciding to install heating apparatus.

CHAPTER XVI
Methods of Heating

Directly the gardener considers seriously the question of heating the greenhouse he will find that he is confronted with an embarrassingly large number of possibilities both as regards fuel and apparatus. Coal, coke, electricity, gas and oil can all be used as sources of heat and there are many ways in which each may be employed.

HOT-WATER BOILERS. For the larger type of greenhouse there is much to be said in favour of a coal- or coke-burning boiler heating the greenhouse by way of hot water pipes. Such boilers are economical to run and, if properly managed, they give the right kind of heat, neither too drying nor too concentrated in source. Very small boilers are not so satisfactory as they tend to behave erratically and often go out if left unattended for many hours at a stretch. It certainly takes more skill to manage a tiny boiler heating a house measuring perhaps 8 ft. by 6 ft. than it does to control a big apparatus heating a range of glasshouses. Some improvement can be made by surrounding the boiler with a simple shelter to protect it from direct wind. Another scheme, which I have often seen satisfactorily employed, is to build a potting shed on the end of the greenhouse and install the boiler in this. Alternatives are the oil-fired or gas-heated boiler. Both are, I think, on the whole more costly to operate than a coal- or coke-fired boiler, but they have the immense advantages of being very reliable, easily controlled and readily adaptable to thermostatic control.

Wherever possible 4 in. diameter pipes should be used rather than 2 in. pipes as, within reason, the bigger the surface from which the heat is radiated the better will be the result. For the same reason it is advisable, even in small houses, to have the pipes extending at least their full length and, in bigger houses, running round three sides. There should be at least one flow and one return pipe, while in big installations it is often an advantage to have two returns, so ensuring a steadier flow of water. This flow is almost invariably obtained by the thermo-syphon system, that is to say it is based on the principle that hot water rises and cold water falls. This, incidentally, is the same system that is employed in many car radiators and domestic heating systems. It involves a steady rise in the outflow pipes from the boiler to the farthest point, and an equally steady fall from this point back to the boiler. Ups and downs must be avoided as they will interfere with the flow of water.

The rise and fall respectively need not be more than 1 in. in 10 ft., but it can be greater than this with advantage, the result being a quicker circulation of water.

The boiler itself should be well cased in with bricks or cement to conserve heat and, if the boiler is not alongside the house or built into the wall of the house, any length of pipe connecting the boiler with the house should be heavily lagged or covered with soil with the same object. It is usually most convenient to have the pipes almost against the wall of the house and low down under the staging (if there is any), but occasionally pipes are slung overhead immediately under the roof rafters, this system being most desirable where the purpose of artificial heating is more to dry than to warm the atmosphere, e.g. in carnation houses.

There are a great many different types of coke- or coal-burning boiler designed especially for greenhouse heating, including the very popular horseshoe boiler, which closely resembles the small domestic water heater in design and is most suitable for small and medium sized greenhouses, and the tubular type, which is more efficient but much more expensive to buy and, in consequence, more popular with owners of big glasshouses.

Some boilers can now be obtained with automatic stokers of various designs, some thermostatically controlled so that the temperature of the house is maintained within narrow limits. Unfortunately such stokers are, as a rule, expensive to install and usually involve the use of special fuel or fuel broken very small to overcome the danger of jamming.

HOT WATER HEATING OF GREENHOUSES

Floor area of house in sq. ft.	Approximate length of 4 in. piping required in feet			
	45° F.	50° F.	55° F.	60° F.
60	12	16	20	24
80	15	20	27	30
100	20	28	34	40
120	25	33	42	50
140	30	40	50	60
160	35	47	58	70
180	40	54	66	80
200	45	60	75	90

ELECTRICAL HEATING. Electricity has many advantages but it also suffers from certain serious drawbacks so far as greenhouse heating is concerned. Taking the advantages first the most obvious is the ease with which electricity can be controlled. There is no arduous stoking and, if the house is fitted with a thermostatic control, which is a comparatively easy matter, it is quite possible for the owner to forget the heating altogether for long periods with the assurance that it will not vary more than a few degrees. The heat, if delivered from properly designed radiators, compares favourably with that of hot water pipes.

The principal drawback to electricity is its cost. Even at a penny halfpenny a unit my experience is that electric heating costs about 50 per cent. more to run than a boiler delivering corresponding heat. In many districts electricity costs well over a penny halfpenny a unit and the cost is correspondingly increased. Against this must be reckoned the fact that if the radiators are coupled with a thermostat there is little or no waste heat for the radiator is automatically cut off directly the heat exceeds the required temperature. This results in a considerable saving in current but, even so, it would have to be a badly managed coke or coal boiler which cost as much to run as an electric heating system except on the lowest current rates. A second drawback of electricity frequently overlooked is that any mains failure will cause an immediate (and perhaps unnoticed) cessation of heating.

Broadly speaking there are three ways in which electrical heating may be applied, (1) by low temperature radiators using current on normal mains voltage, usually 220/250; (2) high temperature, fan-assisted heaters operating on mains voltage; (3) low voltage cable or wire often needing no more than 6 volts. The first type is probably still the most popular for ordinary greenhouse heating, though fan-assisted heaters are gaining rapidly in favour because of their portability and the fact that they circulate air without necessity for opening ventilators. Low voltage heating is most favoured for the heating of frames and again there are two alternatives, insulated cable operating on mains voltage or bare wire operating on low voltage, usually either 6 or 12 volts. Cable or wire is simply wound around the sides of the frame or it may be used to warm the soil from beneath by coiling it, serpentine fashion, in the bottom of the frame and covering with soil to a depth of 8 or 9 in. Where low voltage heating or soil warming is employed, a transformer will be necessary. This must be of a type suitable for use outdoors or under wet conditions. In fact all electrical installations in greenhouses, should be of a type able to withstand wet and should be installed by an electrician used to this specialised work.

Soil warming cables can be fitted with a thermostat but an alternative is simply to switch them on for a given number of hours each day. A formula for calculating the heat dosage required is as follows:

Size of frame in square feet × 40 (45 in the North of England) ÷ wattage of heater = hours per day heater should be switched on.

GAS HEATING. Gas fumes can be very damaging to plants and it is possibly the fear of this which has limited the popularity of this form of greenhouse heating. Nevertheless if the gas burners are simply used to heat water in a boiler outside the greenhouse, the heat being conveyed inside by means of hot water pipes in exactly the same manner as from coal or coke boilers, there is not the least reason why any gas fumes should enter the house. Gas combines many of the advantages of both the other sources of heat for it can be readily controlled by thermostatic devices and so left unattended for long periods, while in most districts it compares quite favourably with coal or coke in cost. Any gas company will be able to quote for a suitable installation for almost any type of glasshouse and such apparatus should always be installed by experts.

OIL HEATING. This is the most primitive form of heating for the greenhouse and in many ways the most unsatisfactory. I do not recommend oil heating as a permanent installation in any glasshouse because of the constant danger of fumes, which can be extremely damaging to most plants. Where the paraffin heater does prove itself very useful is for frost protection in otherwise unheated houses. As a rule this means that the heater is only required for short periods at a time, mainly at night, and so the fume danger is greatly reduced, the more so because at the periods when the heaters are required most plants are likely to be dormant or nearly so and, therefore, comparatively resistant to injury.

There are many different types of oil burning apparatus on the market and these can be broadly grouped into two main classes, those with a yellow flame and those with a blue flame. The blue flame heaters are much more efficient, judged from the standpoint of heat produced for fuel consumed, but my experience is that they are more liable to produce fumes and cause damage, especially when burned rather low. The simple yellow flame heater has the merit of being exceptionally reliable provided it is kept spotlessly clean, a precaution, by the way, which applies to all oil heaters. Incidentally the higher the grade of paraffin used the less likelihood there is of harmful fumes being produced.

I have found it possible to exclude frost from a rather exposed lean-to greenhouse with a cubic capacity of 1,500 cubic feet with a single burner white flame heater, but much would depend on the position and structure of the house and it would be wiser to have two heaters at hand so that another could be added if the thermometer fell perilously near freezing point (32° F.).

The Amateur Gardener

There are also more elaborate oil heaters in which the burner or burners warm a small water boiler and the water is carried through pipes. These are perhaps to be preferred in houses of large size.

Incidentally, for the sake of those who have to improvise, I might remark that I have seen frost excluded (or at any rate kept down sufficiently to avoid damage) in big commercial chrysanthemum houses by the simple process of standing hurricane lamps every five or six yards along the paths.

AMOUNT OF HEAT REQUIRED. It is natural that the greenhouse owner should wish to know how much current or fuel will be required to produce a required result but it is far from easy to answer such questions as so very much depends upon factors which will vary from one case to another. The situation of the greenhouse, the soundness of its construction and the thickness of its walls will all obviously have a bearing on the result. Efficiency of apparatus may also make a big difference while in the case of coal or coke stoves the quality of the fuel must also be considered. However bearing in mind that these factors may falsify figures by as much as 25 per cent either way here are some fair averages upon which to base calculations. I am indebted to Col. Alan Monkhouse, of Farm and Garden Electrification Ltd., for the table of electrical heating.

CAPACITY OF ELECTRICAL GREENHOUSE HEATERS

Floor area of Span-roofed Greenhouse sq. ft.	Rating, in watts, of heaters necessary to maintain temperatures of:				
	40° F.	45° F.	50° F.	55° F.	60° F.
	when the outside air temperature is 32° Fahr.				
40	400	620	900	1,120	1,375
60	550	820	1,170	1,500	1,800
80	700	1,000	1,380	1,770	2,100
100	820	1,150	1,580	2,000	2,400
120	920	1,310	1,750	2,200	2,650
140	1,000	1,430	1,900	2,375	2,825
160	1,100	1,560	2,000	2,500	3,000
180	1,180	1,650	2,130	2,630	3,130

In order to ascertain the annual electricity consumption in units (kw.H.)— multiply the appropriate figure in the above table by one of the following coefficients, which vary with the temperature at which it is desired to maintain the greenhouse.

Coefficient	0·8	1·05	1·45	1·95	2·30

414

CHAPTER XVII

General Management

The manner in which a greenhouse is managed will naturally depend to a very great extent on the kind of plants that are grown within it. For this reason it is advisable, when deciding on the occupants of a greenhouse, to select plants which will thrive under similar conditions. It is, for example, a mistake to grow ordinary greenhouse cucumbers and tomatoes in the same house because the first like a very damp atmosphere and the second a comparatively dry one. Admittedly there are one or two varieties of cucumber which will put up with drier conditions and can be used in a tomato house, but that points rather than contradicts the argument. Again tomatoes and grape vines are not a very satisfactory combination as both like plenty of sun and the grape vines, to get it, must be trained quite close under the rafters of the greenhouse, so cutting off much of the light from the tomatoes below.

Nevertheless some general principles of greenhouse management can be enumerated and are most conveniently considered under the headings, temperature control, ventilation (including humidity control), watering, and shading.

TEMPERATURE CONTROL. There is, no doubt, an optimum temperature for every plant at every season of the year but, to begin with, little serious research has been done on this matter and, secondly, practical considerations would make it almost impossible for the ordinary amateur gardener to fulfil such requirements. As a rule his greenhouse contains several different types of plant, sometimes many different kinds, and despite what I have already said regarding the advisability of choosing house mates that do associate reasonably well there is, nevertheless, sure to be some discrepancy between their temperature requirements. Fortunately plants, like human beings, are very adaptable and, provided certain extremes are not exceeded, satisfactory results can be expected.

In the alphabetical section of this chapter, in which I deal with the cultivation of individual greenhouse plants, I have suggested suitable temperatures so far as these are known, but here I would add that it is generally possible to grow all the usual greenhouse, as opposed to hothouse, plants in a structure in which the temperature never falls below 32°, and does not too often fall below 40° in winter and averages 65° in summer with occasional rises to 90° during heat waves. These are the limits within which most amateur gardeners will require to work, and, be it added, the less rapid the fluctuations are the better for the health of the plants.

Temperature control can be obtained in a variety of ways, the most obvious being by the use of a heating apparatus. Nevertheless this should not be employed unnecessarily, for if the necessary temperature can be obtained by natural means without making the atmosphere too stuffy, this is to be preferred. Too much artificial heat will tend to 'draw' plants, that is to say to make them grow tall and spindly with pale leaves and little stamina. This is particularly true in the period October to March, when days are short and light diffused. It is a popular delusion that heat is a substitute for light. In fact, the two are complementary and heat without light is very liable to cause disaster. That is one reason why it is so difficult to get good winter crops of tomatoes or lettuces. In parenthesis I might remark that artificial lighting for greenhouse crops is under investigation but is still in the experimental stage.

Because of this the average temperature of the greenhouse should be much lower in winter than in summer. Big fluctuations, and in particular rapid fluctuations, are to be avoided at all times but are more harmful in winter than in summer.

The amateur who has no heating apparatus can control temperature, often to a remarkable degree, by skilful use of sun heat. In cold weather ventilators, if opened at all by day, should be closed an hour or so before the sun sets, and then at sundown heavy canvas blinds may be pulled over the glass, or felted screens clamped in position, to prevent the escape of heat trapped within the house. Care must be taken not to put such devices in position too early and to remove them betimes in the morning, for their purpose is solely to hold heat and they must not be permitted to rob the plant still more of the scanty winter daylight.

If a heating apparatus is available and it is thermostatically controlled the gardener has little to worry about, for he has merely to set the dial at the desired figure, which should be chosen to suit the most tender plants he is growing, and then leave the rest to the apparatus. Even so it is wise to have a maximum and minimum registering thermometer hung from the rafters of the greenhouse and to set and read it daily as a check on the accuracy of the apparatus.

If the heating apparatus is not under thermostatic control the gardener's task becomes more arduous and a maximum and minimum thermometer is even more essential. It should be read at least morning and evening, preferably midday as well, and the heating apparatus and ventilators regulated accordingly. Bear in mind that too much heat is quite as damaging as too much cold. Incidentally plants which have been scorched in a high temperature look almost exactly like those which have been damaged by frost, a point which the old hand emphasises by referring to frost damaged plants as 'scorched'. In both cases the tissues of the younger leaves and more tender shoots are destroyed, quickly turning brown and withering as a result.

In small houses temperature control in summer is usually a battle against high temperatures and rapid fluctuations. The difficulty with the small house is that it contains such a small volume of air that it very quickly acquires heat and as readily loses it. The result may be a rise of 20 or 30° in the morning when sunshine first shines directly on the glass and, perhaps, before the gardener is about, with a correspondingly rapid fall after dusk. This kind of thing is extremely damaging and must be countered by early and adequate ventilation coupled, if necessary, by shading for a period to slacken the rate at which the temperature rises. At night it may occasionally be necessary to use artificial heat in small houses even in early summer to check the sudden chilling which otherwise occurs.

Ventilation. Ventilation has three objects, (1) to supply plants with an adequate volume of fresh air which they need as a source of both oxygen and carbon dioxide (2) to control temperature and (3) to control atmospheric moisture.

The second of these points I have already mentioned in the preceding section and I need add little here beyond noting that most small greenhouses are inadequately provided with ventilators from the standpoint of temperature control. For example, in a 12 ft. by 10 ft. house with only one ventilator in the roof it is almost impossible to prevent excessively high temperatures on bright summer days even if the door is kept widely open, a policy which, though often essential, is seldom entirely satisfactory as it is apt to cause serious draughts. As regards top ventilators, the minimum which should be regarded as adequate is that the ventilators should total the length of the house, half being on one side and half on the other of the ridge in span-roofed or three-quarter span-roofed houses. Side ventilators in houses with vertical glass should at least total half the area of the top vents while, in addition, there should be a few small ventilators in the brick-work, woodwork or concrete below the level of the staging if any.

As regards point (1), it is only in winter, when many houses have to be kept closed for long periods owing to inadequate heating, that plants are likely to suffer seriously from lack of fresh air. At other seasons this function of ventilation presents no problems at all. If the atmosphere in winter does appear to be getting uncomfortably stuffy the only remedy, apart from making use of every mild spell to give increased ventilation, is to employ a little artificial heat by day and open the ventilators slightly at the same time so that there is, for a while, a steady flow of air without a drop in temperature.

Point (3) is often overlooked completely by the beginner and yet, in some ways, it is the most vital of all. Plants vary greatly in their response to moisture in the atmosphere. Those, such as cacti and succulents, which in nature inhabit desert regions thrive best in dry air and very quickly fall into ill-health if kept in a damp atmosphere, whereas by contrast many foliage plants from tropical forests revel in humidity. Here again is evidence of necessity for choosing house mates with care but, having chosen them, it still remains to maintain something at least approaching the ideal atmospheric conditions. This is done partly by manipulating the ventilators but also by the processes known as damping down and syringing, the first of which refers to the wetting of floor, path and walls and the second to the direct syringing of the plants themselves. In both cases the net result is to increase the amount of moisture in the atmosphere. By frequent damping down and syringing it is quite possible to approach the saturation point of humidity. In some cases shallow trays which can be filled with water are fitted over the hot water pipes or radiators to increase atmospheric moisture. Additional help can be given by covering stages with coarse sifted boiler ashes or small gravel which will hold plenty of moisture when syringed or watered and give it off steadily by evaporation.

It is fairly obvious that by opening ventilators and encouraging the entry of air one will often tend to decrease the dampness of the atmosphere, though this does not hold true during foggy weather, nor during periods of excessive rainfall. It works out in practice like this. If the house is filled with plants which appreciate a more or less normal degree of atmospheric moisture, ventilation is decreased when the weather is very damp or foggy or, alternatively, ventilation is maintained at normal but artificial heat is used to dry the air. In this case it will be the top ventilators that will be kept open and the side ventilators shut. When the weather becomes hot top and side ventilators will be opened to create a through current of air, while if the air within shows signs of becoming too dry, with the result that plants need water with undue frequency and show signs of flagging on every hot day, damping down is carried out at least each morning and possibly more frequently.

To adapt these normal conditions to plants which require above or below the normal amount of humidity is purely a matter of common sense. The dry-air plants will receive even more ventilation during mild weather and will seldom get any damping down, while the wet-air plants will have less ventilation and particularly less side ventilation, which causes a drying current of air, together with more damping down and direct syringing.

A problem which frequently arises in unheated or slightly heated greenhouses growing a normal collection of plants is that there is heavy condensation on the glass inside at night. This collects and drips on to the plants, spotting flowers, and sometimes leaves as well. The remedies are to avoid watering after midday and unnecessary splashing of water at any time and to give a little top ventilation even at night, though this may quite likely necessitate the use of artificial heat to maintain minimum temperature.

WATERING. This is a matter which, I think, gives the beginner more headaches than any other, though in point of fact incorrect heating and incorrect ventilation are quite as likely to bring about his downfall. All the same I know that there is a very general desire to have watering reduced to rule of thumb. Unfortunately this is quite impossible. One cannot say 'Give so much water every so often' about any plant at any time of the year because so much depends on the weather conditions prevailing at the moment, the position and character of the greenhouse and the type of soil in which the plant is growing. All the same there are a few general rules which can be laid down.

Firstly, when a pot plant requires water it should always be given in sufficient quantity to moisten all the soil in the pot. If in doubt lift the pot up and keep on applying water until it begins to trickle out of the drainage hole in the bottom. That will give you a measure of what is needed for this minimum purpose.

There are three ways by which one can gauge the moisture of the soil in a pot. One is to scratch the surface with finger nail or pointed stick. This is seldom practicable because of the root disturbance involved. The second is to lift the pot and judge by its weight, for wet soil weighs more than dry. This requires just a little experience, but if you experiment with a couple of pots of the same size both filled with soil, one thoroughly dry the other wet, you will soon get the idea. The third method is to tap the pot with something hard, such as a small wooden hammer or the leg bone of a chicken. Provided the pot is a sound one, not cracked or faulty in any way, it will give a ringing sound when the soil within it is dry and a dull, heavy note when the soil within it is wet.

My last general remark about watering is never to use a rose on the watering can except when dealing with small seedlings or newly potted plants. A rose tends to give a deceptively wet appearance to the surface while leaving the lower soil inadequately moistened. There is also the danger of wetting the foliage too much or having water collect at the heart of the plant. This is fatal to many things, e.g. winter flowering primulas and greenhouse calceolarias. Even in the case of small seedlings or seed pans before the seed germinates it is often better to give water by holding the pan almost to its rim in a bucket of water so that the moisture soaks up from below through the drainage holes than it is to give it from above through a fine rose. Established plants should always be watered direct from the spout with this held close to the soil to avoid splashing.

Capillary Watering. A new technique of automatic watering relies on the fact that water will rise from below by capillary attraction through particles of fine sand or closely packed soil. The capillary bench is a greenhouse staging covered with some impervious substance such as asbestos cement sheets or strong polythene film. This in turn is covered with a layer of fine sand one or two inches thick. Some device must be arranged for keeping this constantly moist and various equipment is marketed for this purpose. Pot plants are then placed on the damp sand and absorb water from it. If the plants are in clay pots a wick of cotton or glass fibre must be passed through the drainage holes to carry water from the sand to the soil within. Plants in flat bottomed plastic pots do not require wicks. It will be seen that plants on a capillary bench are kept uniformly moist at all times which is contrary to traditional beliefs of what pot plants require but nevertheless seems to suit most plants admirably with the exception of succulents and plants newly potted. The latter should be watered by hand until established when they can be removed to the capillary bench. The capillary action is started by giving each plant a thorough soaking with water. If placed dry on the bench no water is likely to rise.

POTTING

Pots used for greenhouse plants must be clean and also well drained, except for capillary watering. Cleanliness is important because roots will stick to the sides of a dirty pot and it will then be impossible to remove any plant without injuring its roots. Drainage is vital because unless there is a free outlet for surplus moisture the soil in the pot will become waterlogged, air will be driven out and roots will die.

New pots should always be placed to soak for a few hours to get rid of what is known as 'kiln dryness'. Old pots should be scrubbed or at very least rubbed clean with a rag. It often pays to spray them with a sterilising fluid such as formalin (1 pint 40 per cent. purity formalin in 8 gallons water) to kill any disease germs they may contain. If this treatment is adopted leave the pots outdoors for a few days before use.

Drainage is ensured by placing one large piece of broken pot over the drainage hole in the bottom and, if it is a pot bigger than 3 in. in diameter, covering this 'crock' with a few smaller pieces of broken pot and a small wad of sphagnum moss or some of the rough material left in the bottom of the sieve when preparing potting soil. The first crock should be a little curved and placed with its convex side uppermost so that it keeps the drainage hole open.

Many beginners are puzzled by the constant insistence on 'potting plants on', that is to say shifting them from one size pot to the next stage by stage instead of placing them straight away in the biggest pots they are likely to require. Much unnecessary labour, they feel, might be saved by the latter practice. The reason against it is that, even with good drainage, the soil confined in a pot is apt to become stagnant unless it is reasonably filled with roots to draw moisture and air through it. In actual practice it is found that overpotting is one of the commonest causes of failure unless very 'open' composts of the John Innes type are used. In general it is unwise to exceed the following steps in potting on, the figures being for pot diameters in inches measured at the rim: $2\frac{1}{2}$, 4, 7, 12.

COMPOSTS. At one time it was considered necessary to have a different mixture of soil, sand and other ingredients for almost every family of plants and every gardener had his own pet recipes, some of them closely guarded secrets. A series of experiments was carried out at the John Innes Horticultural Institution with the object of finding out whether any simplification of this practice was possible with the rather surprising result that one basic mixture was devised which, with very slight modification, could be used for practically every type of greenhouse plant. This basic mixture is prepared as follows:

7 parts by loose bulk medium loam
3 parts „ „ „ granulated (or moss) peat
2 parts „ „ „ coarse silver sand.

The loam should be top soil cut from a meadow and containing plenty of fibrous roots. It should be stacked for at least a year before use so that it may be well rotted, and it is an advantage if it can be sterilised though this is not essential.

Any good grade peat will do provided it is reasonably free from dust and lumps. Sphagnum moss peat usually has the right 'fluffy' texture. Beech or oak leaf mould may be used instead but should be sterilised first.

The sand should be angular and coarse, many particles only just passing through an $\frac{1}{8}$-in. mesh sieve. Sea sand is not good as it contains too much salt and, in some cases, lime.

The basic potting compost is fortified with fertilisers and again a standard mixture is recommended. This is:

2 parts by weight hoof and horn meal, $\frac{1}{8}$ in. grist. (13% nitrogen)

2 parts „ „ superphosphate of lime (16% phosphoric acid)

1 part „ „ sulphate of potash (48% pure potash).

For most potting up to 4 in. pots, and for all potting in the case of delicate or hothouse plants, 4 oz. of this fertiliser mixture is added to each bushel of the mixed potting compost. For potting on from $4\frac{1}{2}$ to 7 in. size pots for all except delicate and hothouse plants 8 oz. of the fertiliser mixture is added to each bushel of potting compost. For sturdy plants needing 8 in. pots or larger (but still with the exceptions already made) 12 oz. of the fertiliser mixture is used per bushel of potting compost. In my cultural notes I have referred to these as the 'ordinary Innes composts' and where this term is used without qualification it is intended that the various gradations of fertiliser addition should be made as the pot size increases. In other cases I have referred to the three grades as weak, medium and rich respectively.

In addition $\frac{3}{4}$ oz. ground chalk or limestone (not hydrated lime) should be added for each 4 oz. of fertiliser except where the loam used already contains a fair quantity of lime. This addition should not be made in the case of plants commonly described as 'lime hating'.

SIEVING. When dealing with seedlings and small plants it is necessary to sieve loam but it is unwise to overdo this. Very fine soil tends to clog and become waterlogged or hard more readily than coarse soil. In consequence, when dealing with fairly big plants and pots over 5 in. in diameter, it is often best to dispense with the sieve altogether and simply chop the loam up or pull it apart with the fingers into fairly small pieces. Even when dealing with smaller plants it is seldom that a sieve with a mesh below $\frac{1}{2}$ in. will be required.

LOOSENING AND FIRMING ROOTS. When potting plants avoid disturbing their roots overmuch but, if the roots are wound into a tight ball, loosen them gently with the fingers or tease out some of the outer ones with a pointed stick so that the new soil can be worked around them. Always remove the old drainage 'crocks' from the bottom of the ball. Firmness of potting will vary according to the nature of the plant. Not a bad general rule (but it has exceptions) is to firm in proportion to the hardness of growth, plants with hard, woody stems being made firmer than those with soft stems. Also there should be a general tendency to pot more firmly as the bigger pot sizes are reached. Up to 6 in. diameter size adequate firming can almost always be obtained with the fingers pressed into the soil around the edge of the pot, and also by rapping the pot sharply on a wooden bench or table. Above 6 in. pots it is sometimes necessary to use a potting stick i.e. a short length of stick about as thick as a broom handle, rounded at the end and used to force the soil down around the edge of the pot.

Never fill pots with soil right to the brim. Space is necessary so that water can be applied readily. After potting it is usually desirable to water a little more sparingly than usual for a few days and to keep the plants in a slightly warmer and moister atmosphere. This aids quick root growth and prevents unnecessary flagging of foliage.

PROPAGATION UNDER GLASS

Though the methods of increasing plants under glass (broadly seeds, cuttings, layers, grafts or divisions) are the same as outdoors there are certain differences in the technique employed.

SEED. This will be sown in boxes, pans or pots instead of in the open ground and the same caution about providing these with good drainage which I have already made regarding potting applies with at least equal force. Boxes should have at least one good slit in the bottom running their whole length and well covered with pieces of 'crock' and the roughage left in the sieve when preparing composts. In pots and pans it pays to have a good wad of sphagnum moss over the 'crocks'.

The provision of a suitable compost in which to germinate seeds has been investigated at the John Innes Horticultural Institution with similar results to those obtained on potting composts. One standard mixture is found to suit most seeds. The ingredients are: 2 parts (loose bulk) medium loam; 1 part (loose bulk) peat; 1 part (loose bulk) sand. The same provisos regarding the quality and nature of the ingredients apply as in the case of the potting composts. To each bushel of the mixture are added 1½ oz. superphosphate of lime and ¾ oz. ground chalk or limestone. The loam should first be sterilised.

Watering of small seeds needs to be done with great care to avoid disturbance and often the most satisfactory method is to hold the whole receptacle almost but not quite to its rim in a tub of water until the water, soaking up from below, darkens the surface.

It frequently pays to cover seed receptacles with a pane of glass and a sheet of paper to lower the rate of evaporation and so lessen the need for watering but the paper must be removed immediately seedlings appear, the glass itself being tilted a day or so later to admit air and removed altogether a few days after that.

CUTTINGS. Under glass these can often be placed with advantage in a propagating box (really a small frame with glazed light). If this is stood in the greenhouse over the hot water pipes or heating apparatus the soil in which the cuttings are inserted will be warmed from below (bottom heat) and this is found greatly to hasten the rooting of many cuttings. Care must be taken not to overdo this feature nor to keep the frame unventilated for unnecessarily long periods or the cuttings may be weakened dangerously.

The propagating box or close frame, with or without bottom heat, is also found to be a suitable place in which to keep some small grafted or budded plants until they have made a union. Often the frame is partly filled with peat or coconut fibre in which pots or pans containing grafts or cuttings are plunged. This filling serves the dual purpose of conducting heat evenly to the compost and holding moisture.

A standard 'Innes' compost has been devised for cuttings and consists of: 1 part (loose bulk) medium loam; 2 parts (loose bulk) peat; 1 part (loose bulk) sand. No fertilisers are added.

MIST PROPAGATION. Various appliances are now available for keeping cuttings constantly moist by automatically spraying them with water at fairly frequent intervals. Broadly these devices may be divided into two types, those that are controlled by the actual rate of water evaporation and those that work on a simple time basis. Some of these require an electrical mains supply for control but there are a few very simple devices which operate without electricity.

Mist propagation is most satisfactory in spring and summer. The cuttings are not kept close as they are in a normal propagating frame but are usually rooted on the floor or staging of a greenhouse. Coarse sand is the most satisfactory rooting medium and the best results are obtained when this is warmed to about 60°–70° F. from below as, for example, with an electrical soil warming cable. Cuttings should be removed to ordinary compost of soil, sand and peat as soon as they are rooted.

A handy propagating frame to stand on the greenhouse staging

An improvised propagating frame placed over an oil lamp with sacks
hung round to trap the heat

A useful type of span-roofed green-house and garden frame. The frame is fitted with electrical heating while the greenhouse has roller sun blinds

A three-quarter span house with top ventilators on the short side only—not a very commendable practice

A useful lay-out for a greenhouse boiler

An oil heater for the greenhouse

A small garden frame placed on a hot-bed of decaying stable manure

Basal shoots, from which cuttings can be prepared, being removed from old chrysanthemum 'stools'

Inserting prepared chrysanthemum cuttings around the edges of flower pots filled with sandy soil

A 'geranium' (pelargonium) cutting being prepared from a non-flowering
shoot. It is being cut just below a joint

The prepared 'geranium' cuttings are inserted in a small flower pot
in a compost containing plenty of sand

A young chrysanthemum plant ready for re-potting. Note rootlets round the ball of soil

Soil is gently rammed around the chrysanthe-mum roots in the new and slightly larger pot

Repotting selaginella divisions. Only finger pressure is necessary with these small plants

Creating a moist atmosphere in the green-house by wetting the paths

Testing a pot for soil moisture by tapping with a wooden hammer

Another method of creating soil moisture. Ashes on which the pots are standing are syringed with water

Ventilating a frame by tilting the lights on the side away from the wind

When attending to frames a support for the lights will be found very useful

CHAPTER XVIII

Greenhouse Plants and their Cultivation

IN THIS chapter I have arranged alphabetically the more popular or generally useful greenhouse plants and given a short account of the cultivation of each. For information as to the Innes composts to which I make frequent reference the reader should turn to the preceding chapter.

ABUTILON. These are shrubs or climbers and one or two are hardy enough to be grown in the open air all the year round, particularly in the milder parts of the country (see p. 256). All can be put outdoors in summer and the shrubby kinds with leaves variously mottled with silver or gold, such as *A. Selloviunum marmoratum* and *A. Thompsonii*, are quite popular for summer bedding. All these shrubby kinds also make useful greenhouse pot plants, while the climbers, such as *A. insigne*, with deep crimson flowers, and *A. megapotamicum*, with red and yellow flowers, can either be grown in big tubs or be planted out directly in the greenhouse border and trained under the rafters, or against the back wall of a lean-to structure.

Grow them all in the standard 'Innes' potting composts and use 8 to 10 in. pots for the majority, though small plants can be accommodated in 6 in. pots. Re-pot when necessary in February, and during the same month trim the plants to shape. Stems can be shortened by a half or more to prevent plants becoming straggly. Water freely in summer, sparingly in winter. Frost protection only is required and ventilation should be as free as possible consistent with this. The simplest method of propagating is by cuttings of firm young shoots inserted in sandy soil in a propagating frame in summer, preferably with gentle bottom heat.

ACACIA. The hardy tree with rather ferny foliage which one so often sees in front gardens ruthlessly pruned to a mop head is usually called acacia though, in fact, it is really only a false acacia, its true name being robinia. The acacias with which we are concerned now are all more or less tender plants, natives of Australia, and including amongst their number the familiar mimosa (*A. dealbata*). This last is a small tree which can be grown outdoors in specially favoured places, or may be planted in the greenhouse in a big tub or direct in the greenhouse border. It is, however, rather big for the average amateur's greenhouse.

More useful to him are the dwarf shrubby species, such as *A. armata* and *A. Drummondii,* which can be grown in 6 or 8 in. pots in ordinary Innes composts and will produce masses of tiny yellow pompon flowers in late winter and early spring.

Water all fairly freely in summer but very sparingly in winter. Artificial heat is only necessary to exclude frost and the atmosphere at all times should be rather dry. In summer plants may be stood in a dry frame or sunny place outdoors. Cuttings pulled off with a heel of older wood in early summer will usually root readily in sandy soil in a propagating frame within the greenhouse. Acacias do not need frequent re-potting, but when pots become overcrowded with roots they should be shifted to a size larger immediately after flowering. No regular pruning is required.

ACALYPHA. From the gardener's point of view acalyphas may be split into two groups. One, typified by *A. Godseffiana,* is grown principally for its foliage, while the other, of which *A. hispida* is a good example, has, in addition to beauty of leaf, long, catkin-like trails of crimson flowers. All make excellent pot plants and require warm house treatment, i.e. a minimum winter temperature of 55°, rising to 70° or more in summer. They need plenty of water from April to September and a moderate supply the rest of the year. Re-pot, when necessary, in March using the weak Innes compost. Most can be propagated quite easily from early spring cuttings, provided these can be given a fairly high temperature (say 70°) with bottom heat in addition.

ACHIMENES. These are tuberous rooted plants which can be grown as pot plants but are more frequently treated as trailers to be planted in baskets suspended from the rafters. They look very pretty in this way with cascades of thin stems carrying numerous tubular flowers in showy colours, such as red, blue and purple. By potting tubers every few weeks from January to May it is possible to have the plants in bloom from June to September.

Start the tubers in ordinary seed boxes and a rather sandy compost. Place them quite close together and just cover them. Water sparingly at first and place in a temperature of at least 60°. In a week or so the tubers will start to make shoots. When these are 2 in. high transfer to Innes compost with one dose only of fertiliser and grow in the pots or baskets in which they are to flower. The average temperature throughout should be around 66°. The atmosphere should be fairly moist and the plants watered freely until a few weeks after flowering when the water supply should be gradually discontinued and the tubers allowed to dry off. They are stored perfectly dry in the pots or boxes in which they have been growing and in a temperature of about 50° until it is time to start them again, when the tubers are shaken clear of soil and the whole process is renewed. Achimenes can also be raised from seed sown in a temperature of 65° in January–March.

AGAPANTHUS. The so-called blue African lily, *Agapanthus (Africanus) umbellatus*, is most familiar as a pot or tub plant for standing outdoors in sunny places during the summer months. It looks well on a formal terrace or in the angle of a wall. It is, however, too tender to be left outdoors with safety in winter in most parts of the country and it does make a very fine subject for the unheated or slightly heated greenhouse. Grow it in big pots or wooden tubs in medium Innes compost and only re-pot it when it is obviously overcrowded. Then shake it out in March, divide the roots into two or three pieces and re-pot them in the same mixture as before. It likes plenty of water in summer and should have plenty of air. Heat need only be used in winter to exclude frost. From October to March very little water should be given.

AGATHAEA. The only species that is grown to any extent is *A. coelestis*, a bushy, foot-high plant often known as the blue marguerite. This is not a bad descriptive name though it is considerably smaller in bloom than the ordinary white marguerite. It flowers all the summer, will grow in any ordinary soil and only requires winter protection from frost. In fact it will usually withstand a temperature one or two degrees below freezing point without suffering any harm. Grow it in 4 or 5 in. pots and keep it on the staging in as sunny a place as possible. Raise it from seeds sown in spring in a temperature of 60° and treat it like an antirrhinum or stock (see pp. 90, 122). If desired the young shoots can be pinched occasionally to encourage a dwarfer and more bushy habit.

AGAVE. Agaves are natives of desert regions and look like it. They make large stiff rosettes of long, pointed succulent leaves, obviously well fitted to withstand periods of extreme drought. It is for their foliage that they are grown in the garden and many of them are hardy enough to be planted outdoors during the summer. Used in this way they are a popular feature of sub-tropical bedding schemes. Most agaves are rather large plants, the biggest of all being *A. americana*, with leaves up to 6 ft. long and 8 in. wide. There are smaller kinds, such as *A. Taylori* and *A. filifera* which can be grown in 8 or 9 in. pots. All need frost protection only and can be grown without heat for the greater part of the year. Plant them in rather light sandy soil, water moderately in summer and scarcely at all in winter. Re-pot when necessary in March and increase by removing off-shoots at the same time.

ALLAMANDA. All the allamandas are attractive climbing plants, but they require rather higher temperatures than the amateur gardener can usually command. The winter minimum should be 55°, average 60–65°, rising to 80° from May to September. They are fairly vigorous plants which may be grown in large pots or tubs or be planted directly in the greenhouse border in moderately rich soil. Water freely April to August, moderately September to March. If grown in pots, re-pot every third or fourth year in February. Shoots can either be trained on wires or trellis work or over a crinoline frame. The flowers are trumpet-shaped, mainly yellow, and the flowering season is a long one, from April to September with good management. Increase is by cuttings of the previous year's growth taken early in the year and rooted in a propagating frame, temperature 80°.

ALOCASIA. These are very handsome tropical plants grown solely for their foliage. The leaves are like big shields, dark green, variously veined with lighter green, milky white, etc. All are hothouse subjects requiring a minimum temperature of 60° even in winter, and delighting in readings of 80° or more in summer with plenty of moisture; in fact just the conditions one would expect in a tropical jungle. Otherwise they are not difficult to grow. Re-pot when necessary in March. Grow them in Innes compost with one dose only of fertiliser and a little extra peat or leaf mould, and water them freely in summer, moderately in winter. Frequent damping down and syringing will be needed in summer and the glass can be shaded permanently on the sunny side from May to September. Well-grown plants will produce suckers around the main stem and these can be detached at potting time if further stock is required.

ALOE. Far and away the best known of this big family of succulent plants is *A. variegata*, often known as the partridge-breasted aloe, because of the curious buff and white mottling of the leaves. It is an ideal pot plant for the beginner for it is practically impossible to kill it and it will succeed in quite a small pot, say 3 to 5 in. according to the age of the plant. Keep it dry in winter, water moderately in summer. Give it as much sun as possible and frost protection at all times. If necessary it can be stood outdoors all the summer or used as a house plant at any time. Old plants produce offsets which can be detached in March, the proper potting season. Use a rather sandy compost. Other aloes need similar conditions but most take up far more room.

AMARYLLIS.—*See* HIPPEASTRUM (p. 473).

ANTHERICUM. The proper name of the greenhouse anthericum is really chlorophytum, but I have used the familiar name to avoid confusion. *A. variegatum* is the species grown and it is valued for its foliage which is narrow, graceful and shining green striped with cream. It is a very easy plant to grow and I know of one which has thrived for years in a north-facing sitting room quite a long way from the window. It will succeed in any frost-proof greenhouse in sun or shade provided it is watered fairly freely in summer and syringed daily during warm weather. It does not like being baked at any time. These plants throw out long, arching flower stems (the flowers themselves are insignificant) and along these stems little plantlets form which can be detached at practically any time and potted separately to make new plants.

ANTHURIUM. These are precisely the queer, vivid plants which one might imagine would grow in tropical places. They produce very big, handsome, shield-shaped leaves and the flowers (or spathes, to be botanical) look like coloured leaves themselves, being oval and flattish, each with a long yellow 'rat's tail' (the spadix) at the top. The colours of these spathes are very bright including flamingo red, scarlet, rose and orange-red, with white for contrast.

All anthuriums are plants for the hothouse with a minimum winter temperature of 55° rising to 80° or more in summer and with a very moist atmosphere at that season. Water freely, syringe and damp down frequently from April to September, more moderately for the rest of the year. Grow in Innes compost with one dose only of fertiliser and a little extra peat and only re-pot, in March, when absolutely necessary, which may be only every second or third year. Off-shoots can be removed at the same time and potted separately, or root cuttings can be prepared and started in a propagating box with plenty of bottom heat. Anthuriums are not difficult plants provided the necessary temperature and atmospheric moisture can be maintained.

APHELANDRA. This is another family of tropical plants for the hothouse. They are easy to manage provided a winter minimum of 55° can be maintained with an average of around 70° in summer. Water and syringe in the same way as for anthuriums, with which these plants may be associated, but after flowering greatly reduce the water supply and prune back the shoots quite severely. Through the winter be sparing with water, giving only sufficient to keep the soil just moist. The flowers, in compact spikes, are orange-scarlet and can be had from early September throughout the winter until early spring if plants are started in succession. This is done by bringing a few at a time to the warmest part of the house from about March to May. Potting should be done just before the plants are to be started and the weak Innes compost used. Propagation is by cuttings of firm young growths rooted in peat and sand in a propagating box with bottom heat.

ARALIA. The greenhouse aralias are foliage plants with deeply divided leaves. They require rather more warmth than is found in the average greenhouse but can be grown satisfactorily in a minimum of 50° with an average of around 60° in winter, 70° in summer. Apart from this they are easily grown pot plants thriving in ordinary soil and 6 to 10 in. pots according to age of plants. Re-pot annually in ordinary compost in March. Water freely in summer, sparingly in winter, and syringe daily from April to September. Propagation is not very easy and probably best left to the expert, though root cuttings can be grown successfully in a propagating frame within the greenhouse, and plants which have grown tall can have a ring of bark removed around the main stem in spring and a ball of soil and sphagnum moss tied around this and kept moist. When roots are formed from just above the ring the top of the plant is removed and potted on its own.

ARAUCARIA. The monkey puzzle tree with its stiff branches set with hard, shining leaves is a fairly familiar sight, particularly in old gardens. It is quite hardy and in no sense a subject for the greenhouse, but it has a close relative, *A. excelsa*, which makes a useful pot plant for the greenhouse or home. This has the same stiffly branched habit, but the leaves are much smaller and softer, the whole plant looking like a rather formal Christmas tree. It likes cool treatment throughout with no more than frost protection in winter and plenty of light and air at all times. Grow in ordinary Innes composts. Re-pot each March, shifting on to larger sizes as the smaller pots get filled with roots, but avoid over-potting at any time. The best method of increase is by seeds sown in light soil in pots or pans in a warm greenhouse in spring.

ARISTOLOCHIA. This is a big family but not many of its members are of much importance to the amateur gardener. The best is *A. durior*, known as the Dutchman's pipe because of its curious, maroon-coloured flowers shaped like a meerschaum. It is a vigorous climber suitable for a sunny greenhouse, where it can be trained under the rafters, or up the back wall of a lean-to. It likes a rather rich soil, is best planted direct in the greenhouse border and, as it is nearly hardy, only needs artificial heat for the purpose of excluding frost in really cold weather. Ventilate freely when possible and maintain an average atmosphere as regards moisture. Cuttings prepared from young shoots in early summer will generally root readily in sandy soil in a propagating box.

ARUM.—*See* RICHARDIA (p. 493).

ASPARAGUS. The vegetable garden asparagus has two highly decorative relatives both needing the protection of a frost-proof greenhouse. They are *A. plumosus*, familiar to most gardeners as 'asparagus fern', and *A. Sprengeri*, which in gardens is frequently known simply as 'sprengeri'. The first is a climber, though there is a dwarf variety. Both forms have flat, very finely divided leaves and wiry stems and are most useful for cutting and mixing with flowers. *A. Sprengeri* is a trailing plant with small, shining green leaves. It is popular for hanging baskets and also for cutting and various decorative uses such as winding round the handles of ornamental baskets. Both like medium Innes compost, a fair amount of light and not too much heat, though *A. plumosus* can be gently forced (temp. 65°) in spring to get early growth. Re-pot in March when the pots are overcrowded with roots. Old plants can be divided if they get too big, and this is a useful method of propagation, though these ornamental asparaguses can also be increased by seed sown in a greenhouse in spring or early summer. Shoots can be cut in moderation at any time for decorative purposes, but a plant should never be stripped of its foliage.

ASPIDISTRA. This familiar plant can need no introduction. It is unpopular nowadays, probably as a natural reaction from its excessive popularity with our grandparents. Nevertheless it is a useful foliage plant, practically indestructible, thriving in shade too dense for most subjects, and one of the best plants for a living room. Give it the medium Innes compost. Water it moderately at all times of the year, and in summer sponge or syringe the leaves frequently, to keep them free of dirt. Plants can be re-potted in spring when they become overcrowded and big plants can, if desired, be divided at the same time. The aspidistra does not require any artificial heat except to protect it from frost.

ASTILBE. The ordinary astilbes of the herbaceous border (see p. 144) make useful pot plants and, if potted in the autumn, placed in a frame for the winter and brought into a slightly heated greenhouse about February, can be had in bloom in April or May. They should be given plenty of water while making their growth. After flowering the pots should be plunged to their rims outdoors in a cool sheltered position. The roots can then be planted out in the autumn. They should not be forced two years running. It must be understood clearly that these are perfectly hardy plants and that heat is only used to force them into early flower.

AZALEA. Most azaleas are hardy shrubs for the open air (see Chap. IX) but *A. indica*, and the numerous varieties derived from it, are a little tender and, as they make excellent greenhouse pot plants, this is the purpose for which they are commonly employed. They are evergreen shrubs with big, showy, mostly double flowers in various shades of pink, red and crimson and combinations of these, together with white. There are a great many named varieties, particulars of which can be found in any nurseryman's catalogue.

Obtain strong plants in the autumn, pot them up in the smallest pots that will contain their roots in ordinary Innes composts made with lime-free loam. Then place them in a frost-proof greenhouse where they should have plenty of light and as much ventilation as is consistent with a minimum temperature of about 40°. In January or February the temperature can be increased gradually if it is desired to hurry the plants into flower. Temperatures over 70° should be avoided. During this period water freely and syringe daily with tepid water. After flowering harden the plants off and stand them outdoors in a shady place from June to September inclusive. Keep on syringeing with water during hot weather as this prevents attacks by red spider, to which the plants are very subject. Re-pot, if necessary, in April. Return to the greenhouse before frost occurs. Plants can be increased by layering or by cuttings of firm young shoots inserted in sand under a bell glass in June–July but propagation is not easy and is best left to the professional.

BALSAM. Botanically the balsam belongs to the genus impatiens, but I use the popular name here to avoid confusion with the other plants more commonly regarded by the gardener as impatiens. The balsam is *Impatiens Balsamina*, a plant with spikes of large double flowers each not unlike a small camellia. There are various colours including pink, scarlet, violet and white. All should be grown from seed which may be sown successively every fortnight or so from about the middle of March till the middle of May. Germinate the seeds in a temperature of 60° and pot the seedlings singly as soon as they make their first true leaves. Use the John Innes weak potting compost for the first potting and the Innes medium compost for all subsequent pottings, usually two in number, first to 5 in. and then to 8 or 9 in. pots in which the plants will flower. Water freely throughout and syringe frequently in hot weather until the flower buds show signs of opening. The plants should be kept in the greenhouse throughout in a light place and an average temperature of 60°. By successional sowings plants can be had in bloom from July to October.

BEGONIA. This is one of the really important families for the amateur's greenhouse. There are a great many kinds of begonias and a number of them make excellent pot plants, though a few need a little more heat than the amateur can always command. This is particularly true of the winter flowering begonias which can make such a splendid display from about November to February.

From the cultural standpoint the family can conveniently be divided into two groups, one tuberous rooted and the other fibrous rooted. The first is represented principally by the many magnificent hybrids with enormous double flowers in various shades of pink, rose, scarlet, crimson, orange, yellow and white. The catalogues of specialists are filled with named varieties of these.

All these tuberous-rooted begonias are summer flowering. The tubers become completely dormant in the winter and should be kept dry in a cool, frost-proof place. They are started into growth in moist peat or leaf mould towards the end of February in a temperature of 55–60°. The tubers can be arranged quite close together in ordinary seed boxes and should only just be covered. Leaves will appear in a week or so and, when about 2 in. high, the tubers should be potted singly in weak Innes compost and 4 to 6 in. pots. Water moderately at first, more freely as they become established. Damp the staging daily and, as the sun gains power, give shading by day. From June onwards it may be advisable to shade the glass permanently, not too heavily. Throughout maintain a temperature of around 60°. The secret of success with these plants is a mild, slightly damp atmosphere. They will not tolerate excessive heat or drought. Very careful staking is required because of the weight of the flowers. Flower buds may drop off if the plants are kept too dry or the temperature is too cold at night. After flowering gradually withhold water until, by November, the soil is quite dry and the tubers can be shaken out and stored as before.

These begonias can also be raised very readily from seed sown in January or February in a temperature of 65°, though seedlings vary in colour and by no means all will produce double flowers. The seed is extremely small and so should be sown on the surface of a particularly fine compost. Do not cover at all with soil but place a sheet of glass and one of brown paper over each pan. Remove the paper directly germination occurs, tilt the glass a little the next day, remove it two or three days later. The seedlings should be pricked off into ordinary seed boxes filled with seed compost directly they can be handled. Space them 1 in. apart each way. Pot them singly in 2 in. pots as soon as the leaves touch in the boxes. Subsequently grow on like plants raised from tubers.

There is another class of tuberous-rooted begonias, known as *B. pendula,* in which the growths are pendent and the plants are, therefore, ideal for culture in baskets suspended from the greenhouse rafters. All details of culture are the same as for the upright class except that, instead of the tubers being potted after they have been started into growth in boxes, they are placed in baskets lined with moss and filled with the rich Innes compost. Also, as the blooms are comparatively small, no staking is needed.

The fibrous-rooted begonias are even more varied including both species and hybrids. Of the latter, far and away the most important is the winter-flowering group typified by Gloire de Lorraine. This itself has small pink flowers produced in fine sprays. There are other named varieties with deeper pink or white flowers. These are usually raised from cuttings prepared from basal shoots in late winter and early spring. Such cuttings root readily in very sandy soil in a propagating box with gentle bottom heat. They should be potted singly as soon as rooted, first in 2 in. pots, then in 3 in. and finally 5 or 6 in. pots. Use the ordinary Innes composts throughout. During the summer temperature and treatment are the same as for the tuberous-rooted begonias. It is equally important to avoid cold draughts and to maintain a rather moist atmosphere and mild temperature (average 65°). Any flower buds which appear in late summer or early autumn should be removed. Shoots may be pinched once or twice to encourage branching. These begonias are not allowed to dry off in winter, the soil is kept fairly moist throughout and the temperature maintained at the summer level until immediately after flowering, when it may drop 10° for a couple of months to give the plants a partial rest. No shading will be required after September. Plants should be staked neatly and allowed to start flowering in November. After the resting period the plants are re-potted, though not necessarily in a larger pot as over-potting is bad. As soon as new basal shoots appear propagation can be resumed.

Yet another group of begonias is grown principally for their leaves which are handsomely marbled and often very beautifully formed. The best of these are the Rex varieties which, if permitted, will make quite big plants, often several feet in height. They have large, heart-shaped leaves, dark green, variously marked with white. These foliage begonias are all fibrous rooted. They can be raised from seed sown in March or April and treated in the same way as seed from tuberous varieties. Alternatively they can be increased by leaf cuttings, i.e. ordinary mature leaves pegged flat on the surface of sandy soil in a propagating box with bottom heat. A few incisions are made with a sharp knife through the veins of the leaves where they touch the soil. Roots are formed from these cuts and, in time, tiny new plants appear. Apart from this, culture closely resembles that of the winter-flowering begonias as regards temperature, shading and watering, but no resting period need be allowed. Re-potting, when necessary, should be done in March.

Begonia manicata with big, handsome leaves and quite tall spikes of small pink flowers in spring is grown like a Rex variety

The popular summer bedding varieties of *B. semperflorens* (see p. 93) can also be grown as pot plants in the greenhouse with no difference in treatment except that they are potted singly instead of being planted out. Cool moist treatment with shade from hot sun is needed. If desired plants can be retained for several years.

BIGNONIA. These are strong climbers with brilliant, trumpet-shaped flowers. They should, if possible, be planted directly in the greenhouse border or, at the very least, in large tubs. Use fairly rich soil and give a sunny position. Artificial heat is only necessary to maintain a winter minimum of about 40° though one species, *B. venusta*, will produce its orange flowers right on until Christmas time if a temperature of 50–60° can be maintained. The other species commonly grown, *B. Tweediana*, produces its yellow flowers in summer. Remove any weak shoots whenever noted and each January cut back the remaining shoots by about one-third. Water freely in summer, moderately in winter. Propagation is most readily effected by layering stems in the autumn. For the plants sometimes known as *B. radicans* and *B. grandiflora* see Tecoma, p. 501.

BILLBERGIA. At one time it was supposed that these plants required a lot of heat, but experience proves that they can be grown successfully in a minimum winter temperature of 50°, with an average of around 65° in summer. Billbergias have stiff, spiky leaves in rosettes and flowers carried in heads, not in themselves very showy, but surrounded by brilliant bracts. Grow in a moist atmosphere. Water freely in summer, moderately in winter and repot each March in the weak Innes compost. Daily syringeing can be carried out from May to August inclusive. Plants can be increased by removing offsets at potting time.

BLANDFORDIA. Blandfordias are bulbous plants which will thrive in a frost-proof greenhouse without artificial heat for the greater part of the year. Pot the bulbs in weak Innes compost in March. Water very sparingly for the first few weeks and then with increasing freedom as growth increases. Give the plants plenty of sun and air and a fairly dry atmosphere. They will produce their clusters of tubular flowers in various shades of yellow, orange and coppery-red in summer. After flowering the water supply should be gradually decreased and the bulbs kept almost dry from November to March, then re-potted and re-started into growth. Offsets can be removed and potted separately at the same time to increase stock.

BORONIA. These are evergreen shrubs of small size with narrow leaves and an abundance of small scented flowers from late winter to early summer. The best known is *B. megastigma,* in which the flowers are brownish-red and yellow. They make neat pot plants in 5 to 7 in. pots and should be grown in the Innes composts, but with lime-free loam and a little extra peat. Pot very firmly. Boronias need a rather dry atmosphere with plenty of ventilation, minimum temperature of 40° in winter and an average of 60° in summer. Let them have as much sun as possible. Water with care, keeping the soil moist throughout but never sodden. Re-pot annually immediately after flowering but never give a shift into a pot more than one size larger than that already occupied, as over-potting is bad. Propagation is by cuttings of young shoots removed in summer and rooted in sand under a bell glass or in a propagating box. The rooted cuttings should be potted on stage by stage and will need occasional pinching to encourage a bushy habit.

BOUGAINVILLEA. Anyone who has visited the Mediterranean region in early summer will have been struck by the magnificent, magenta flowered climbers which drape so many of the buildings. These are bougainvilleas and they have been developed in gardens so that there are now forms with pink, rose and orange coloured flowers as well as the natural magenta. All are excellent climbers for the greenhouse. They thrive in a minimum winter temperature of 45°, average 55°, rising to an average of 65° in summer. Grow in the ordinary Innes composts. Water fairly freely in spring and summer but gradually reduce in autumn and keep almost dry in winter. In February prune the previous year's growths back to within a few inches of the main vines. Re-pot at the same time if necessary, but it is really better to plant bougainvilleas direct in the greenhouse border. During warm weather syringe daily with tepid water. Cuttings a few inches long prepared from firm young shoots pulled off with a heel of older wood in spring will usually root readily in a propagating box with a fair amount of bottom heat (temperature 70°).

BOUVARDIA. There are few evergreen shrubby plants to surpass the bouvardia for greenhouse display, more particularly as they bloom continuously throughout autumn and early winter. They are not difficult to grow provided a winter temperature of not less than 50° can be maintained. Even in a temperature 10° lower they will not die, but they cannot be expected to open their flowers. In summer they can be stood outdoors in a deep frame with the lights removed most of the time when the weather is mild. There is no need to take them to the greenhouse before the end of September. Water freely in summer,

moderately in autumn and very little during January and February.
Cut back fairly severely at the end of February and place the plants in
a temperature of about 60° to re-start them into growth. Syringe daily
with tepid water at this period and throughout the spring and summer.
Pinch the tips out of the shoots occasionally until late August to encourage a bushy habit. Feed occasionally with liquid manure in summer.
Re-potting, when necessary, should be done at the end of March. Use
weak or medium Innes composts and do not over-pot. Bouvardias can
be increased by ordinary cuttings made from young shoots in spring or
early summer, rooted in sandy soil in a propagating box with bottom
heat. Alternatively root cuttings can be made, each about an inch long
and inserted in March in very sandy soil in a propagating box.

BROWALLIA. The species commonly grown is *B. speciosa major*, a
herbaceous perennial plant which is often treated as an annual. Plants
can be had in flower at almost any time from midsummer to February
by varying the time of seed sowing, but as autumn flowers are valuable
and easily obtained the usual practice is to sow in March in a slightly
heated greenhouse. The seedlings are potted on stage by stage, usually
two or three in a pot until, by July, they occupy the 5 in. pots in which
they will flower. During summer they can be accommodated in a frame
in a sunny position outdoors. Syringe daily during warm weather. At
the end of September take them to a greenhouse, average temperature
55°, minimum 45°. Water moderately and feed weekly with soot water.
It is an advantage to pinch growths occasionally during the early
stages to encourage a branching habit.

BRUNFELSIA. This is a family the naming of which is a little confused
and in some catalogues it may appear as franciscea. The best species is
B. calycina, a really attractive evergreen shrub with big, flattish, deep
blue flowers in summer. It will thrive in a large flower pot or small tub
in the weak Innes compost and, though usually described as a hothouse
plant, will succeed quite well in an average winter temperature of
50–55°, rising to 60–65° in summer. Water freely in spring and summer,
rather sparingly in autumn and winter and syringe in warm weather
only. Re-pot, when necessary, as soon as the flowers fade. At the same
time shoots can be shortened a little to prevent the plants becoming
straggly. Propagate by cuttings of young shoots taken at almost any
time and rooted in a propagating frame with gentle bottom heat.

CALADIUM. Caladiums are amongst the most beautiful of greenhouse
foliage plants. They have very large shield-shaped leaves in an almost
bewildering variety of colours, some mainly green, some almost white,

others mottled with white, pink, purple, etc. All are plants delighting in a warm, moist atmosphere. They can be grown in pots 7–12 in. in diameter, according to the age and variety of the plant, and should have the weak Innes compost with a little extra peat. An average spring temperature of 65° is desirable, minimum 60°, rising in summer to as much as 80° by day. Water freely during the season of growth in spring and summer and, at this period, syringe frequently and damp floors, walls and stages daily. A little shading from strong sun is desirable but should not be overdone. In the autumn gradually reduce the water supply and, when the leaves have died down, keep the tubers quite dry and in a temperature of about 55° until March when they can be restarted in a temperature of 70° and, if necessary, re-potted. Propagation is by careful division of the roots when re-potting.

CALCEOLARIA. Calceolarias are of two main kinds, semi-shrubby varieties, some of which are used for bedding, others for greenhouse display, and true herbaceous plants without woody stems. The latter have been very highly developed by breeders and the best strains produce enormous trusses of big, pouched flowers in a variety of brilliant combinations of yellow and crimson. There are no showier plants in the greenhouse at their season, which is April to June. These herbaceous calceolarias are invariably raised from seed, which may be sown in June or July on the surface of very fine soil in a well-drained pan. Scarcely cover the seed and place a sheet of glass and paper over each pan. Germinate in an unheated, shady frame. Prick off the seedlings into seed boxes in Innes seed compost as soon as they can be handled, and pot them singly in 2½ in. pots in weak Innes potting compost directly they have made four or five leaves each. Throughout this period grow them in an unheated, shady frame with plenty of ventilation on mild days and a fair quantity of water. By October the plants can be moved on into 5 in. pots and should be taken at the same time to the greenhouse. Give them a good light place not too far from the glass. Ventilate fairly freely and maintain a temperature of 45–55°. Water carefully at this period, keeping soil moist but not sodden, and avoid wetting the leaves and crowns unnecessarily. Re-pot into 7 or 8 in. pots in late February or early March using medium Innes compost. Maintain the same temperature avoiding wide fluctuations. The secret of success with calceolarias is a cool, equable atmosphere throughout. Shade lightly in spring if the sun shines strongly.

The most important greenhouse shrubby kinds are John Innes Hybrids with yellow flowers in winter; *C. violacea* with pale violet flowers in summer; *C. Clibranii*, yellow, winter flowering, and *C.*

rugosa hybrida, yellow to crimson, summer flowering. These are usually raised from cuttings of firm young shoots, struck in autumn in the case of the summer flowering kinds and in spring in the case of the winter flowering kinds. Seed can also be used and should be sown in March or April in a cool house. Grow in a frost-proof greenhouse with plenty of light and ventilation and an average quantity of water. If desired plants can be stood in a frame all summer or even outdoors in a sheltered place but they must be kept well watered.

The bedding calceolarias are almost always treated as perennials. They need the protection of a greenhouse, or at least a well-made frame in winter, but are sufficiently hardy to withstand a few degrees of frost without injury. There are two colours, yellow and chestnut red. Both make bushy plants a foot to 18 in. in height with innumerable little pouched flowers in showy clusters throughout the summer. They have the merit of thriving in shady as well as sunny places. Both are commonly increased by cuttings of firm non-flowering shoots struck in sandy soil in a frame in August or September though they can be raised from seed like the greenhouse shrubby kinds. Once rooted cuttings should be ventilated fairly freely, except during cold weather, and hardened off in time for planting outdoors early in May. Bedding calceolarias can also be grown as pot plants for summer flowering in a cool, partly shaded greenhouse.

CALLISTEMON. Bottle brush tree is the popular name of the callistemon, and it is a very good one because the fluffy spikes of red flowers are exactly the shape of the brushes one uses to clean bottles. Callistemons are Australian shrubs with narrow leaves and they need to be grown in a sunny greenhouse with plenty of ventilation and a rather dry atmosphere. Winter temperature need be no more than an average of 50°, rising in summer to 60° or plants may be stood outdoors in a sheltered, sunny spot from June to September. Grow in the ordinary Innes composts. Water fairly freely from April to September, but sparingly for the rest of the year, particularly in cold weather. Re-pot in March, only when the pots become crowded with roots, which may be every second or third year. The best-loved kinds, *C. speciosa* and *C. floribunda,* flower from April to June. After flowering prune lightly to keep plants from becoming straggly. Increase by cuttings of firm young shoots in July or August rooted in sandy soil under a bell glass within the greenhouse. This plant is sometimes known as Metrosideros.

CAMELLIA. Everyone knows and loves the camellia with its large, usually double, perfectly formed flowers and glossy, evergreen leaves. It is a shrub which can be planted outdoors in mild districts and will then grow to considerable size, but in the greenhouse it can be maintained in health for some years in pots no more than 10 or 12 in. in diameter. Camellias are excellent subjects for the slightly heated greenhouse as they require no more than frost protection. For the greater part of the year they can be grown without any heat. The temperature in winter should average 45–50°, in summer 60–65°. Grow in the ordinary Innes composts and re-pot every second or third year, the work being done immediately after flowering. Water freely in spring and summer, rather sparingly in autumn and winter. Flowers will appear from March to May. After flowering the plants should be syringed daily until the end of the summer. There is no reason why they should not stand outdoors from June to September, provided they are in a sheltered place; in fact, this is better than keeping them in the greenhouse, which is apt to get too hot for them in summer. Return to the greenhouse before the first sharp autumn frosts.

Camellias can be increased in a variety of ways, but the simplest for the amateur is to layer young branches in the autumn. A less satisfactory alternative is cuttings of firm young growth removed with a heel of older wood and inserted in sandy soil under a bell glass within the greenhouse in summer.

CAMPANULA. The only campanulas which are of much importance from the greenhouse standpoint are *C. pyramidalis* and *C. isophylla*. It would be hard to imagine two closely related plants more dissimilar in appearance. *C. pyramidalis* makes narrow spires of showy blue or white flowers which may be 5 ft. in height in good soil. *C. isophylla* is a trailing plant with an abundance of thin stems throwing out sprays of starry blue or white flowers. Both flower in summer.

C. pyramidalis is a biennial and so seed must be sown every year. It germinates readily in May in the Innes seed compost and an unheated frame. Prick off seedlings in the ordinary way and, when they are 2 or 3 in. high, pot them singly in weak Innes potting compost. Subsequently grow them in a frame without protection from June to September and with free ventilation during mild weather even in winter. The plants should be potted on by stages in Innes composts, until by March they reach their 8 or 10 in. flowering pots. Throughout they should be treated as almost hardy plants and are, in consequence, ideal for an unheated greenhouse. Give plenty of light at all times and free ventilation whenever the weather permits.

C. isophylla is also practically hardy and requires the same treatment regarding temperature and ventilation. It is easily raised from cuttings of young shoots struck in sandy soil in a propagating box within the greenhouse in spring or early summer. Pot the cuttings in weak Innes potting soil as soon as well rooted and, subsequently, pot on as necessary in the medium Innes compost. The plants are ideal for hanging baskets or may be grown in 4 or 5 in. pots along the edge of the greenhouse staging, which they will festoon with their growth.

CANNA. The familiar canna of summer bedding schemes is also a suitable pot plant for the unheated or slightly heated greenhouse. The fleshy roots rest in winter and can be stored dry in a frost-proof greenhouse from late October until March. It is best to keep them in their pots of soil to prevent shrivelling. In spring they are started into growth in the greenhouse, temperature 55–60°, being watered rather sparingly at first but much more freely as leaves appear. Re-pot as soon as growth commences. Subsequently feed once or twice a week with weak liquid manure. Keep in as sunny a place as possible in a slightly moist atmosphere and average temperature of 60°. After flowering gradually reduce the water supply until the soil is dry by the end of October. Small plants will bloom in 6 in. pots, large ones in 8 or 9 in. pots. Propagation is by division of large roots at potting time or by seeds, which need a temperature of about 70° to ensure germination. It is wise to soak the seeds in water for 24 hours before sowing as they are very hard coated.

CARNATION. The greenhouse carnation is a very different plant from the border carnation. For one thing it is much taller, old specimens often reaching 5 or 6 ft. with quite a hard woody stem at the base, for which reason it is sometimes referred to as the 'tree' carnation. Also, instead of flowering for quite a short while in the summer, it will continue to bloom for months on end; in fact, by careful management, it is possible to cut blooms throughout the year. It is this characteristic which has given it the more popular name of 'perpetual flowering' carnation. Like the border carnation it has been very highly developed and a great number of named varieties exist, to which new ones are added every year. For this reason I make no attempt to suggest varieties, which should be sought in the most recent catalogues of the trade specialists.

Perpetual flowering carnations can be raised from seed but, except for the production of new varieties, this is an unsatisfactory method, as seedlings vary greatly in character and some are certain to be very inferior. The usual method of increase is by cuttings, which can be taken at any time from November to March. The amateur will find that January and February are the most favourable months. Cuttings should be prepared from non-flowering side shoots, the best being those which

2 E   449

form about half-way up the flowering stems. These shoots should be pulled off when 3 in. long. The lower leaves are removed cleanly with a sharp knife and the base of each cutting trimmed just below a joint. The cutting is then ready for insertion in pure silver sand in a propagating frame within the greenhouse. Bottom heat is not necessary and the temperature need be no more than 60°, but the cuttings should be kept close, the frame light only being opened daily for a few minutes to allow condensed moisture to be wiped from it. Under these conditions the cuttings root quickly and, in about a fortnight, will start to grow, when they should be removed immediately and potted singly in 2 or $2\frac{1}{2}$ in. pots and the weak Innes compost. Pot them on as the smaller pots fill with roots, using the progressive Innes composts, until, not later than mid-July, they reach the 6 or 7 in. pots in which they will flower. Alternatively they can, at this stage, be planted in borders of good soil on the floor of the greenhouse. If in pots, they may be stood in a frame outside from June to September and given very free ventilation, in fact the frame lights will only be required at night or to ward off heavy rainstorms.

The plants should be stopped at least twice, the first time when they have made about 7 pairs of leaves, and again when the side growths resulting from the first stopping have themselves made 7 pairs of leaves. Stopping is done by breaking out the topmost joint of each shoot and the effect is to make the plant more bushy. If winter flowers are required, no stopping should be carried out after the middle of July, but for a later supply of flowers stopping can be continued later.

Water moderately throughout the spring and summer but very carefully in autumn and winter, though at no time must the soil be allowed to become dry. Ventilate at all times as freely as is compatible with a summer temperature averaging 60° and a winter temperature averaging 50–55° and never falling below 40°. Be very careful in winter to avoid excessive use of artificial heat which will cause weak growth and will soon put a stop to flowering. Carnations like a rather dry atmosphere but not a hot one, which will encourage attacks by red spider and thrips, their two worst enemies. Top ventilators should be used freely to maintain a constant circulation of air without draughts. The house should be fumigated occasionally with naphthalene to keep down pests, but a special lamp must be used for this purpose.

The flower stems should be disbudded to one bloom each, all the side buds being removed and the terminal bud only retained. Plants that are flowering or about to flower can be fed regularly with one of the advertised carnation fertilisers or a mixture of 3 parts by weight superphosphate of lime, 2 parts sulphate of ammonia, 1 part sulphate of potash, used at half a teaspoonful per plant every week. Excessive or irregular feeding and watering may result in the calyx splitting.

CASSIA. The only species which is likely to interest the amateur is *C. corymbosa*, an evergreen shrub with yellow, pea-type flowers in late summer and autumn. Planted out in a border in the greenhouse it will make a shrub 6 ft. or more high and as much through, but it can be kept to smaller dimensions if its roots are restricted in flower pots 8 to 12 in. in diameter. This cassia only requires frost protection in winter and can be stood outdoors for the summer. Grow in ordinary Innes composts. Water freely from March to October, sparingly in winter. Increase by cuttings of firm young shoots secured in spring or early summer and rooted in a propagating frame within the greenhouse.

CELOSIA. Both the plumed celosias (*C. plumosa*) and the crested types (*C. cristata*) make useful pot plants for the moderately heated greenhouse. They should be raised annually from seed sown in February or March in a temperature of 65°. Pot the seedlings on in ordinary Innes composts from 2½ to 4 in. and then to 5 or 6 in. pots, in which they will bloom. Water moderately and damp staging daily with tepid water. Keep throughout in a lightly shaded greenhouse with an average temperature of 60° or a little more. They will bloom throughout the summer and are extremely decorative. Plants coming into flower can be used for outdoor bedding in July–August but should only be planted out when weather is mild and settled and should then be transferred to the beds with the minimum of root disturbance.

CELSIA. These plants look like neat verbascums and, as they are nearly hardy, they are excellent for the unheated greenhouse. Their spikes of flowers, bright yellow in the case of *C. Arcturus*, pale yellow in *C. cretica*, are 3 to 4 ft. high. The plants will bloom in 6 or 8 in. pots and should be raised annually from seed which can either be sown in February–March for autumn flowering, or in July–August to flower the following summer. The seed will germinate readily in a temperature of 55–60° and seedlings should be potted on in the ordinary manner using the Innes composts. Frost protection only is needed in winter and ventilation should at all times be as free as the weather permits.

CHORIZEMA. These were more popular 50 years ago than they are now. They are trailing plants which can be trained against wires or trellis work on the back wall of a lean-to greenhouse or may be grown over balloon-shaped frames made of wire, a practice which was very popular with the Victorian gardener. They are shrubby Australian plants which should be grown in a cool, airy atmosphere throughout with a minimum temperature of about 40° in winter. Use the ordinary Innes composts with lime-free loam and a little extra peat. Be very careful about watering at all times, keeping the soil moist but never letting it become sodden, particularly in winter. Regular pruning is unnecessary but the shoots of young plants should be pinched occasionally to encourage free branching from the base. Increase by either seeds or cuttings, the former sown in peaty sand in spring, temperature 60°, the cuttings being prepared from firm side shoots removed with a heel in summer and rooted in sand under a bell glass within the greenhouse. There are several species, of which the best are *C. Lowii*, with red and yellow flowers, *C. cordatum splendens*, scarlet, and *C. varium*, red and yellow. All flower in late spring and early summer.

CHRYSANTHEMUMS.—*See* Chapter XIX.

CINERARIA. There are no showier plants for a winter and spring display in a slightly heated greenhouse than the cinerarias. All are treated as annuals and raised every year from seed. At least two sowings should be made, one in April or early May for winter flowers and the other in June or early July for spring flowering. Sow thinly in ordinary Innes seed compost and germinate in a temperature of 55–60°. The summer sowings can be germinated in an unheated frame. Prick off the seedlings when they have three leaves into deep seed boxes and grow on with plenty of light and air throughout. These are almost hardy plants and and they do not like being coddled. Pot singly in 3½ in. pots before they become crowded in the boxes and then move them on to 6 and, in the case of large plants, again into 7 or 8 in. pots directly the smaller receptacles become comfortably filled with roots. The last potting should be made not later than the end of October and the standard Innes composts used throughout. The plants will be happiest in a frame until about the middle of October and should be ventilated freely by day and a little at night, except when the weather is very cold. Even after removal to the greenhouse give as much ventilation as is consistent with a minimum temperature of 40°, average 50°. Stand the plants on the staging as near the glass as possible and in a light place. Watch closely for attacks by the leaf mining maggot which tunnels the leaves causing white, snaky markings. If observed, search for the tiny maggots in these tunnels and kill them with a pin or spray with nicotine insecticide. Water fairly freely in summer, moderately in autumn and winter.

There are a great many varieties, particulars of which will be found in any seedsman's catalogue. These fall into two main groups, the large flowered cinerarias with daisy-like blooms a good 4 in. in diameter, and the star-flowered or 'stellata' types, with smaller but even more numerous flowers. Both are available in a wide range of brilliant colours, including rich shades of blue, purple, pink and crimson, with or without white.

CISSUS. One species, *C. discolor*, is a handsome greenhouse climbing plant with dark green leaves heavily marbled with white and pink. It is an excellent plant to train around a pillar in a large greenhouse, or it can be grown on trellis work against the wall of a lean-to. It is easily grown in ordinary soil but requires a rather higher temperature than that to be found in most small greenhouses, say a minimum of 55° in winter and an average of 65–70° in summer. Water freely from April to September, moderately at other times. Syringe at least once daily in warm weather. *C. discolor* can be grown in large pots but is really happiest planted out in the greenhouse border. It can be increased by cuttings of firm young shoots obtained in early summer and rooted in sandy soil in a propagating box with bottom heat.

CLARKIA. The ordinary annual clarkias, which I have described fully on p. 98 make useful pot plants for the unheated greenhouse. They can be had in bloom in May from a late August sowing, or in June from a March sowing. Cultivation is the same as for outdoors except that the seeds are sown in boxes and the seedlings potted singly in small pots directly they can be handled. Subsequently they are worked on stage by stage to 5 or 6 in. pots in which they will flower.

CLEMATIS. Though most of the clematises are hardy plants unsuited to the greenhouse, there are a few species which are tender and make good greenhouse climbers. The best are *C. indivisa* and its variety *lobata*, both with big clusters of showy white flowers in winter and early spring. They are vigorous climbers and, therefore, only suitable for fairly large greenhouses where they can be trained up pillars, under the rafters or against the back wall of a lean-to. They are happy in ordinary soil and require only frost protection in winter. Give free ventilation in summer and plenty of water at this season, with a moderate supply only in winter. Avoid very high temperatures at any period and syringe at least once daily on warm days from May to September. The average winter temperature need be no higher than 45°, falling to 40° at night. Increase as in the case of hardy clematises, from cuttings or layers.

CLERODENDRUM. From the garden standpoint clerodendrums may conveniently be divided into two groups, the climbing kinds, of which *C. Balfouri* (synonym *C. Thomsoniae*) is the most familiar example, and the bushy kinds, of which *C. fallax* and *C. fragrans* are the ones most commonly seen. All will grow in a moderately heated glasshouse, average winter temperature 55° (minimum 45°) rising in summer to about 65°. *C. Balfouri* can either be grown in a large pot, in which case it is commonly trained over a dome-shaped wire frame 4 ft. or more across to make a bush-like specimen, or it can be planted out in the greenhouse border and trained on trellis work or around a pillar. In either case use the Innes composts and plant or pot in spring. Water very freely from April to September, sparingly at other times. Prune plants immediately after flowering, cutting back the flowering shoots to 2 or 3 in. each. Propagation is by cuttings of firm young non-flowering shoots rooted in spring in sand in a propagating box with bottom heat.

C. fragrans, with flattish heads of white or pink-tinged, scented flowers, is grown in the same manner except that no training is required and far less drastic pruning.

C. fallax is usually grown from seed sown in February or August in a temperature of 70°. The seedlings are potted on in the ordinary way in the standard Innes compost until, by mid-summer (March for August sown seedlings), they reach the 5 or 6 in. pots in which they will flower. Water freely throughout the summer. Maintain in a warm rather moist atmosphere and, in autumn and winter, keep a minimum temperature of 50°, average 60°. Under these conditions the February-sown plants will produce their vivid scarlet heads of tubular flowers most of the autumn, the August-sown ones from June to August. Plants that are about to bloom should be fed with weak liquid manure.

CLIANTHUS. *C. puniceus* is a very beautiful shrub with scarlet flowers shaped like the claws of a lobster. It will grow 6 ft. or more high and is to be seen trained against sunny walls outdoors in the milder parts of the country. It can also be used effectively in an unheated or very slightly heated greenhouse in which it may be grown in large pots, tubs, or planted directly in the greenhouse border. It should have ordinary soil and be watered freely in summer, sparingly in winter. A rather different plant is *C. Dampieri*, with scarlet, purple-spotted flowers and a weak, sprawling habit. It is commonly trained over a balloon-shaped wire frame, or may be planted in a large hanging basket and allowed to trail downwards. It is not an easy plant to grow as it needs perfect drainage, very careful watering at all times and is difficult to propagate, many plants being grafted on *Colutea arborescens*. Give it the standard Innes composts with a little extra peat and lime-free loam. Syringe freely from May to September and give plenty of ventilation.

A hot, dry atmosphere will encourage red spider, a frequent pest of this plant. Both these species of clianthus flower in summer.

CLIVIA. The clivias are fleshy-rooted plants, easy to grow and requiring little heat. From October to January they rest and can be kept in their pots almost dry. At this period a temperature of 45° is ample. In February the bulbs should be given more water and a little more warmth and can be re-potted, if necessary, though over-potting is to be avoided. Use a size which will accommodate the roots comfortably but no more. Pot in the standard Innes composts. Thereafter grow on the staging in a sunny place with an average temperature of 55°. Water with increasing freedom as leaves lengthen, but in late summer gradually reduce the water supply so that, by the end of October, the soil is no more than just not dry. From June to September the plants may stand in a sunny frame. Ventilation should be free throughout. No syringing is necessary. The plants flower in spring, the flowers themselves being trumpet-shaped, in clusters on 2 ft. stems. The original species have largely been replaced by garden hybrids in various shades of red, yellow and orange. All can be increased by division at potting time.

COBAEA. *C. scandens* is most familiar as a climbing plant for outdoor use during the summer months and is then treated as an annual. It is, however, a true perennial, but too tender to survive the winter outdoors. In a frost-proof greenhouse it will make a big plant to cover the back wall of a lean-to or drape under the rafters of a span-roofed greenhouse. It will thrive in any ordinary soil and sunny greenhouse that is frost-proof in winter. Artificial heat will be unnecessary most of the year. Ventilation should be free in spring and summer; watering moderate at this period, sparing in winter. The purplish flowers are a little like Canterbury Bells and appear in summer. Shoots can be cut back fairly severely each February to keep the plants within bounds.

COCOS. *C. Weddelliana* is one of the most graceful of palms, with very slender stems and long narrow leaflets. It is easily grown in a greenhouse with an average winter temperature of 55°, summer 65°, with shade from strong sunshine from May to September. Water freely in spring and summer, rather sparingly the remainder of the year. Syringe at least once daily during summer and also on hot spring days. This palm can be used for short periods as a room plant, but should be returned to the moister and more equable temperature of the greenhouse for recuperation. When indoors sponge the leaves daily with tepid water. Re-pot, when necessary, in March in the ordinary Innes composts. Increase by seeds sown in March in a temperature of 70°.

COLEUS. Most of these plants are grown solely for their foliage though two species, *C. thyrsoideus* and *C. Frederici* are cultivated for their long, narrow sprays of deep blue flowers which appear in the winter. The other coleuses have broad, nettle-shaped leaves which are very handsomely marked in a variety of colours, such as bronze, purple, yellow and various shades of green. They make excellent pot plants and nice specimens may be had in pots no more than 5 in. in diameter. They require a minimum winter temperature of 45°, average 55°, rising in summer to an average of 60–65°. Allow full sunlight except on bright, hot summer days. Water freely from April to September, sparingly October to March. Ventilate as freely as possible consistent with the above temperatures. Plants can be fed with weak liquid manure in place of plain water from May to September. Propagation is very easily effected by cuttings of young shoots which can be rooted at almost any time in sandy soil in a propagating frame with gentle bottom heat. Seeds will also germinate easily in February or March in a temperature of 65°, but seedlings may vary much in the colour of their leaves. Pot on seedlings or rooted cuttings as the smaller pots fill with roots and pinch occasionally to secure a bushy habit. Use Innes composts throughout.

C. thyrsoideus and *C. Frederici* require more heat, particularly in winter when they are forming their flower spikes. At this period the minimum temperature should be 50°, average 60°. Propagation is the same as for the ornamental leaved varieties, but cuttings should be rooted from April to June.

COLUMNEA. The columneas are trailing plants for warm greenhouses. They are seen to best advantage when grown in baskets suspended from the rafters. They will then make cascades of thin stems and bronzy green leaves, with tubular orange-scarlet flowers for half their length in early summer. They should be grown in the weak Innes compost, need an average temperature of 60° in winter, minimum 55°, rising to 65–70° in summer. Water freely from April to September and damp down frequently to maintain a fairly moist atmosphere. Water rather sparingly in autumn and winter and maintain a drier atmosphere. Increase by cuttings made from the ends of shoots in April and rooted in a propagating frame with bottom heat. Re-pot at the end of March.

CONVALLARIA (*Lily of the Valley*). Market growers make much money by forcing this, but it is not a practice which appeals much to amateurs, as the roots are of little use after treatment. For the earliest work, that is to get blooms around Christmas, specially retarded crowns must be obtained and potted eight to ten together in 5 or 6 in. pots in the autumn. Place in a dark place with a temperature of 65–70° and water rather freely. After about a week gradually give light and reduce the temperature a little. Under these conditions blooms will develop in about a month. For a later supply strong roots can be lifted and potted or boxed in October or November. These, after a period of five or six weeks in an unheated frame, may be brought into an ordinary greenhouse, average temperature 55° which a fortnight later may be slowly raised to 65°. In all cases it is desirable to reduce the temperature to 55°, while the plants are actually in bloom to prevent premature fading. After flowering the crowns should be discarded or, if preferred, they can be hardened off and planted in some out of the way corner where some, at least, may establish themselves and make suitable plants for pot culture once again in a few years' time.

CORDYLINE. *Cordyline indivisa* (synonym *Dracaena indivisa*) is a foliage plant frequently erroneously referred to as a palm. It has narrow, sword-like leaves and makes a handsome specimen in pots from 6 to 18 in. in diameter according to the age of the plant. The leaves are green in the type but there are numerous forms, some with wholly red leaves others marked with red. These cordylines can be grown in the ordinary Innes composts and the average temperature of a moderately heated greenhouse, i.e. about 50° winter, never falling below 40°, and rising in summer to an average of 60°. Water very freely in spring and summer, moderately autumn and winter. Good drainage is an important point. Give light shade on the sunny side of the house during bright days in summer. Re-pot when necessary in March. Propagation is by seeds which will germinate in February or March in a temperature of about 60°. Seedlings should be potted on through the various sizes of pot as fast as the smaller ones become filled with roots.

CORONILLA. Only one species is of any importance as a greenhouse plant. This is *C. glauca*, an evergreen shrub with small, grey-green leaves and clusters of small bright yellow, pea flowers in early summer. It is hardy enough to be grown outdoors in some sheltered places but also makes a useful pot plant for the unheated greenhouse. Water freely April to September, moderately October to March. Prune each March sufficiently to keep plants a good shape. Re-pot, if necessary, at the same time using the ordinary Innes composts. Give plenty of light and ventilation at all times. Increase by cuttings of firm young shoots in sandy soil under a bell glass in July–August.

CRASSULA. The crassulas are one of those families about which botanists never seem to be quite decided. In consequence, they are constantly being re-arranged and re-named. For example, the plant which most gardeners know as *C. coccinea* may also turn up as *Kalosanthes coccinea* or *Rochea coccinea*. This is a really showy succulent and well worth growing. It makes an erect plant, freely branched from the base and 18 in. to 24 in. in height. Each stem is closely set with small fleshy leaves and terminated in summer by a head of vivid scarlet, tubular flowers. *C. coccinea* is very easily grown in the ordinary Innes composts and a sunny, well-ventilated greenhouse. Plants can be re-potted in March when necessary; as a rule, 6 in. pots will be found big enough. From then on an average temperature of around 60° should be the aim, falling in autumn and winter to an average of 45°, minimum 40°. Water fairly freely in spring and summer but very sparingly in winter and avoid a damp atmosphere at all times. Cuttings prepared from the tips of non-flowering shoots in late spring or early summer will root readily in sandy soil on the open greenhouse staging.

CRINUM. The crinums are all bulbous plants and some are sufficiently hardy to be grown outdoors in sheltered places, but all make excellent pot plants for the cool or even unheated greenhouse. From October to February the bulbs can be kept almost dry but should not be knocked out of their pots. Re-pot, if overcrowded, in early March using the ordinary Innes composts. Fairly big pots or small wooden tubs will usually be necessary. Water with increasing freedom as leaves lengthen and feed with weak liquid manure while the flower spikes are forming. After flowering in summer gradually reduce the water supply again. Throughout give as sunny a position as possible and as much ventilation as is consistent with a minimum winter temperature of 40°, summer 55°. The simplest method of increase is by removing small bulbs at potting time. The best kinds for greenhouse culture are *C. longifolium*, pink and white, and *C. Moorei*, rosy-red and fragrant (both have white varieties).

CROTON. These are amongst the most popular of all warm greenhouse foliage plants, and justifiably so, for their leaves are of great diversity in shape and colour. The typical croton has long, strap-shaped leaves which, however, may be broader in some kinds, narrower in others and often waved at the edges. All are heavily variegated combining greens, yellows, oranges, bronzes and crimsons.

Crotons are not difficult to grow provided one can maintain the necessary temperatures, namely a winter minimum of 50°, average 60°, rising in summer to an average of 70–75°. From April to September they need plenty of water, both at the roots and in the air. Syringing and damping down should be discontinued when the weather becomes cold. Little shade is necessary, except in very small houses which tend to get overheated. Use the weak Innes compost and re-pot in March, but only when pots are full of roots. Good specimens can be grown in 6–8 in. pots. If desired very big specimens can be grown in large pots or tubs but, as a rule, amateurs will prefer to cut plants back each spring as they get too big to be convenient. Small specimens can be restricted to a single central stem. Cuttings will root at practically any time of the year if inserted in sandy soil in a propagating box with a temperature of about 70° and bottom heat. Water freely while rooting.

CUPHEA. *C. ignea* is the only species much seen in gardens. It is a small plant which can be grown in 5 or 6 in. pots in a cool greenhouse, average winter temperature 50°, summer 60°. The small tubular flowers are a vivid scarlet with a dark ring at the mouth and produced freely throughout the summer. Re-pot as necessary in March and prune to shape at the same time. Use the standard Innes composts. Water fairly freely April to August and feed with liquid manure from May to August. After flowering gradually reduce water supply and keep rather dry from November to March. Increase by cuttings in a propagating box with a little bottom heat in spring or early summer and pinch young plants occasionally to make them branch.

CUPRESSUS (CYPRESS). There is only one cypress of value as a greenhouse plant and this is the so-called mourning cypress, *C. funebris*. It is by no means as mournful as it sounds but is, in fact, a graceful shrub, erect in habit but with pendulous branches and loose, ferny sprays of blue-grey foliage. It will grow readily in an unheated greenhouse and can be stood outdoors from June to September. Good specimens are to be had in 5–7 in. pots. Grow in the standard Innes composts. Re-pot, when necessary, in March and increase by seeds germinated in spring in a temperature of 60–65°.

CYCAS (*Sago Palm*). To the gardener the cycas is just another palm, though the botanist will not allow that it is a palm at all. It is the leaves of this plant which are so commonly used by florists to make wreaths. In growth the plant is rather too big for the average greenhouse and needs too high a temperature, a winter minimum of 50°, average 60°, rising in summer to 75° and with plenty of moisture in the air as well as at the roots. The plants are undeniably handsome, shaped like a shuttlecock with big, spreading, fan-like leaves often 5 or 6 ft. long. Grow in big pots or plant directly in the greenhouse border in rather rich soil. Plant or pot in March. Water freely in spring and summer, moderately autumn and winter. Increase by suckers removed from the base of the plant at potting time or by seeds germinated in spring in a temperature of 70°.

CYCLAMEN. Here by contrast is one of the very best plants for the amateur gardener. The greenhouse cyclamen is nearly hardy, can be grown successfully with a minimum amount of heat, and fine specimens can be had in 5 or 6 in. pots. Moreover cyclamens flower in winter when colour is most welcome.

There are two ways of starting. Seed may be sown in August in an unheated greenhouse and the seedlings grown on to flower 15 months later, or, alternatively, developed corms can be purchased in August and potted to flower the same winter. Assuming seed is used, it should be sown thinly in ordinary Innes seed compost and only just covered. Prick the seedlings off into boxes of the same soil when they have two leaves, spacing them 2 in. apart each way. Directly their leaves touch in the boxes pot singly in 3 in. pots. Keep in a cool sunny greenhouse, average temperature 50° (minimum 40°), all the winter and pot on in spring and early summer until, by the end of June, they reach the 5 or 6 in. pots in which they will bloom. For these successive pottings use the ordinary Innes composts. As the corm forms take care to keep it on top of the soil. Throughout maintain an equable temperature, average 60° in summer, with shade during hot weather, plenty of moisture at the roots and a moderate quantity in the air. Stages can be damped daily in summer, but this should be discontinued in autumn and winter.

For flowering arrange the plants on the staging in a light, sunny greenhouse, average temperature 55°. Plants will bloom successionally from about November to March. After this remove faded flowers and gradually reduce the water supply. At the end of May the pots may be stood in a shady frame outdoors and kept almost dry until August, when the corms should be shaken out and re-potted. Return to the frame and give a gradually increasing quantity of water as leaves appear. Bring into the greenhouse about the middle of October and grow on as before.

If a start is made with corms instead of seeds, the process simply begins as from the second August after seed sowing, i.e. the corms are purchased dormant, or nearly so, and are re-potted and grown on as just described. Alternatively plants may be purchased in winter already in bloom and grown on from that stage.

The principal point to avoid is too hot and dry an atmosphere, which will encourage attacks by red spider and mite. Ventilation should be as free as possible, consistent with the average temperatures given. All the greenhouse varieties are obtained from one species, *C. persicum*. There are a great many shades of pink and scarlet together with pure white, and in the best strains the butterfly-like flowers are of great size.

CYPERUS. *C. alternifolius* is often known as the 'umbrella grass' because its narrow leaves radiate from the top of a foot-high stem very much like the spokes of an umbrella. It is an attractive foliage plant readily grown in a slightly heated greenhouse, minimum winter temperature 45°, though it will stand much higher temperatures. Good plants can be had in 4 or 5 in. pots in the medium Innes compost. Re-pot in February or March and increase by division at the same time, or by seed germinated in a temperature of 60° in spring. Shade in summer from strong sunshine. Water freely at this period and syringe frequently. Keep just moist in winter.

CYTISUS.—*See* GENISTA (p. 469).

DAPHNE. In addition to the hardy daphnes (see p. 275) there is a splendid greenhouse variety named *D. indica*. This is a dwarf, spreading shrub with evergreen leaves and heavily perfumed pink flowers in February and March. It can be grown in 5 to 7 in. pots and should be re-potted in March or April immediately after flowering. Use the standard Innes composts and pots that are just big enough to accommodate the roots. Plants may be stood in a frame or sheltered position outdoors from June to September, but the remainder of the year should be in a frost-proof greenhouse, average temperature 50°. Water freely from March to September, rather sparingly October to February. No pruning is required. Propagation is a little difficult, the usual method being to graft on to seedlings of *D. Laureola*, but cuttings can be rooted in August–September in sand under a bell glass within the greenhouse, or branches can be layered in autumn.

DATURA. An alternative name for this plant is Brugmansia. Several species are grown but all are big, showy plants with large leaves and equally large trumpet-shaped flowers, white in *D. suaveolens*, orange-red in *D. sanguinea*. They are often seen in sub-tropical summer bedding schemes but are also useful greenhouse plants where there is room for them. Grow them in big pots or plant them out in the greenhouse border. Give plenty of water from April to September and syringe and damp down frequently when the weather is warm. In winter water moderately and keep a fairly dry atmosphere. Winter temperature should not fall below 45°. In summer no artificial heat is needed, in fact plants can stand outdoors in a sunny sheltered place. Re-pot annually in March using the standard Innes composts. Increase by cuttings

461

prepared in spring from the ends of shoots and rooted in sandy soil in a propagating box with bottom heat, temperature 70°.

DESFONTAINEA. The only species grown, *D. spinosa*, looks rather like a small holly bush until, in August, it suddenly bursts out into the most astonishing scarlet, tubular flowers. It is an easy plant to grow as long as it is realised that it is nearly hardy. It may be stood outdoors in a sheltered position, but shaded from the midday sun, from the end of May until the end of September. Pot it firmly in the ordinary Innes composts. Grow with plenty of air throughout and an average winter temperature of 50°, which may fall to 40° for short periods without harm. Water carefully at all times, keeping the soil moist but never sodden. Pots should be very well drained. The plant can be increased from cuttings of firm young shoots in August under a bell glass within the greenhouse. Cuttings should be potted on as necessary until they reach 5 or 6 in. pots, after which annual re-potting in March will be required.

DEUTZIA. The deutzias are deciduous shrubs, many of them hardy, but *D. gracilis* is just a little tender and is such a good pot plant that it is usually grown in this way in the cool greenhouse. Pot in autumn in the ordinary Innes composts. Keep in an unheated frame until January and then bring into a light airy greenhouse, average temperature 55°. Water moderately at first, more freely as growth lengthens. The sprays of small white flowers will commence to open in early March if the above temperature can be maintained. After flowering cut back fairly severely to points at which new shoots are commencing to grow. Keep in the greenhouse or a frame till mid-May, then stand outdoors in a sunny place. Water freely and feed occasionally with weak liquid manure. In this way plenty of new growth will be made to flower again the following year. Propagation is by cuttings of young shoots obtained in late spring or early summer and rooted in a propagating box within the greenhouse.

DICENTRA. The familiar bleeding heart of the herbaceous border (see p. 152) makes a good pot plant for the cool or unheated greenhouse. Roots can be lifted from the open ground in October, potted in ordinary soil in the smallest pots that will contain them (usually 5 to 6 in.), placed in a frame for a few weeks to get established and then brought into the greenhouse. Treatment should be quite cool the first year but plants firmly established in pots can be forced in a temperature of 60 to 65° to give bloom by January or February. After flowering harden off and stand outdoors in a sheltered place from May to October, when the process can be repeated as before.

DIDISCUS. *D. caerulea* is a dainty annual, sometimes known as the blue lace flower, with heads of tiny blue flowers on 18 in. stems in July. It makes a good pot plant for the practically unheated greenhouse and can be raised from seed sown in a temperature of 55° in February. Pot on singly in the ordinary Innes composts until 4 to 5 in. pots are reached by June. Water moderately. The correct name is *Trachymene caerulea*.

DIEFFENBACHIA. These once popular plants have passed out of favour, probably because they need too much artificial heat. There are several good species all grown for their foliage. The leaves are usually broad, deep green, variously marked with yellow or white. These are tropical plants requiring a minimum temperature of 55° in winter, rising to 65° or more from April to September. Water freely from March to September, rather sparingly in autumn and winter. Shade from direct sunshine in summer and syringe daily. Grow in 6 or 7 in. pots in weak Innes compost. Increase by cuttings of short pieces of stem in spring, rooting these in a propagating frame with a temperature of 70° and bottom heat. It is advisable to keep up an annual supply of young plants as the old ones lose much of their beauty.

DIPLACUS. These plants are closely related to mimulus and are sometimes merged into that family. The most important species is *D. glutinosus*, an evergreen shrubby plant which needs some support and can be trained around a cane or up a small pillar. It has pouched, orange-yellow flowers most of the summer. It will grow in a cool greenhouse, average winter temperature 50°, summer 60°. Water moderately in winter, freely from April to September. Prune sufficiently to keep in shape each February and re-pot, if necessary, the following month using the ordinary Innes composts. Increase by cuttings of firm young shoots which will root readily in sandy soil in a propagating box at almost any time in spring or summer.

DIPLADENIA. The dipladenias are beautiful flowering climbers which were once very popular but slipped out of cultivation as warm greenhouses became too expensive to run. They need comparatively high temperatures, certainly a minimum of 55° in winter with a rise of 10 or 15° during the summer months. They are of moderate vigour, with trumpet-shaped flowers throughout the summer and autumn. There are numerous varieties, two of the best being *D. boliviensis*, which is blush-pink, and *D. Brearleyana*, reddish-crimson and of exceptional vigour. Grow in the weak Innes compost in large pots or tubs with very good drainage. Re-pot, when necessary, in early March and prune each autumn, but only those shoots which have by then finished flowering. These may be cut right out. Water sparingly from October to February, moderately during the spring months and very freely from May to September. Syringe daily during hot weather to keep down red spider. Increase by short cuttings of young shoots taken in spring and rooted in a propagating frame, temperature 70°, with bottom heat.

DRACAENA. Foliage plants closely allied to the cordylines, in fact *C. indivisa* is sometimes called *Dracaena indivisa*. There are many garden-raised varieties which differ in the colour, markings and shape of their leaves some being narrow, others quite broad. All will make shapely plants in pots 6 to 12 in. in diameter. Grow in a moderately heated greenhouse, average winter temperature 55°, rising in summer to 65°. Use the standard Innes composts. Water freely from April to September and syringe daily in warm weather, also damp between pots to maintain moisture in the air. Keep a much drier atmosphere in winter and water moderately. Re-pot in March. Increase by seeds germinated in a temperature of 60–65° in spring, or by cuttings or pieces of root in sandy peat in spring in a propagating box, temperature 70°, with bottom heat.

ECHEVERIA. The best-known species is *E. secunda*, a very popular summer bedding plant. It makes a neat rosette of fleshy, grey-green leaves from which spring, in late summer, elegant little sprays of reddish flowers 9 in. to a foot in height. It is half hardy, that is to say it requires the protection of a cool greenhouse or well-made frame from October to April inclusive but the rest of the year can be planted out in any sunny place and well-drained soil. Propagation is by division in the spring or by seeds sown in a temperature of 60–65° in March.

Of more interest for the greenhouse owner are the larger species, such as *E. metallica*. This is very much like the bedding type but with rosettes at least twice as big and a series of branches terminated by further rosettes. It makes a handsome pot plant for the cool greenhouse, i.e. no heat from April to October and just enough heat to keep out frost the rest of the year. It is propagated like *E. secunda* and should be re-potted in March. Keep all echeverias almost dry in winter but water moderately in summer.

EPACRIS. The beginner might easily mistake these small shrubby plants for heathers, though in point of fact they are quite unrelated. Some flower in winter or early spring, some in summer, but the former are the more valuable for the greenhouse owner. Of these the best are *E. hyacinthiflora* and *E. purpurascens* which, with their numerous varieties and hybrids, give a colour range from white to heather-red.

They grow about 2 ft. in height, and thrive in an airy greenhouse with average winter temperature 55°. In summer they can be stood out in a sunny frame. Prune rather hard immediately after flowering and then, about three weeks later, re-pot using the ordinary Innes composts without lime, according to pot size. Pot firmly. Water rather sparingly at first, then more freely, but do no more than keep soil moist from October to March. After pruning, daily syringeing is advisable for a few weeks, but the rest of the year the atmosphere should be moderately dry. Increase by cuttings of firm shoots in sand under a bell glass in June, but cuttings root very irregularly.

ERICA. The greenhouse heathers, or heaths, are quite as important as the hardy outdoor varieties, particularly as many of the best flower in winter. They have the neat habit and free-flowering characteristic of the hardy heathers and will grow with a minimum of artificial heat, but are a little difficult to manage because they are very sensitive to watering. The aim should be to keep the soil just moist throughout but never dry or sodden. This involves a soil of really good texture and thoroughly drained pots. Use the ordinary Innes composts, but see that loam and peat are of superlatively good texture, the loam lime-free. Pot very firmly. Re-pot as necessary in spring immediately after flowering. *E. hyemalis* can be pruned fairly severely immediately after flowering, but other varieties are best with little or no pruning, though occasional pinching of badly placed shoots will help to keep the plants shapely. During the summer months the plants are best stood outdoors in a sunny, sheltered position, the pots plunged to their rims in ashes to reduce the necessity for frequent watering. No syringing or damping is necessary at any time. Propagation is by cuttings of short side growths in June–July, rooted in sand under a bell glass or in a propagating box. The best kinds are *E. hyemalis*, pink and white, and *E. gracilis*, heather-red.

ERYTHRINA. Only one species is much grown, *E. Crista-galli*, popularly known as the coral tree, though, as we know it in greenhouses, it is more of a herbaceous plant than a tree. It makes a bushy specimen 5 or 6 ft. high, with clusters of scarlet pea-type flowers in summer. It needs a cool, airy greenhouse in summer, but in winter should have a minimum temperature of 45°, rising to 60° in March to start it into growth. Water freely from April to August, then gradually reduce the supply and keep almost dry from late October to early March. Re-pot, if necessary, in Innes composts and gradually increase water supply. Propagation is by cuttings removed with a heel in spring and rooted in a propagating box with some bottom heat.

EUCALYPTUS. Despite the fact that the various species of eucalyptus are all large trees, several can be grown as pot plants in the cool greenhouse. The best for this purpose is *E. globulus*, known in Australia as the blue gum tree with attractive, aromatic, blue-grey leaves. It can be grown in the ordinary Innes composts and in a light airy greenhouse with an average winter temperature around 50° and frost protection at all times. In summer the plants can be stood outdoors in a sheltered place. Water freely from April to September, moderately at other times. Re-pot as necessary in March. Increase by seeds sown in a temperature of 65° in spring, or by cuttings of side shoots rooted in May–June in a propagating box with gentle bottom heat.

EUCHARIS. *Eucharis grandiflora* (synonym *amazonica*) is one of the most beautiful of warm greenhouse plants. It has broad shining leaves and numerous erect stems, terminated in spring (and sometimes again in summer) by large, nodding, pure white and intensely fragrant flowers. The plant is bulbous rooted and increased by careful removal of small bulbs immediately after flowering. Pot in the weak Innes compost. Water sparingly at first, very freely as growth commences. Keep in a temperature of 65–75° during spring and summer with some shade during hot weather, abundant water and syringing at least twice daily. Give no shade in the autumn and winter. Keep in an average temperature of 55° for a month or so in winter and water sparingly, but raise the temperature to 65–70° in February when the flowers will soon be produced.

EUPATORIUM. This is a big family containing several useful flowering plants for the greenhouse, with compact, fluffy heads of tiny flowers, the most valuable species blooming in mid-winter. One of the best is *E. vernale*, which has white flowers in January–February and is 2–3 ft. high. All will grow in the ordinary Innes composts and can be re-potted immediately after flowering. Water freely in summer and feed with liquid manure while the plants are growing. From October to March water rather sparingly. No heat is needed from April to October. In winter an average temperature of 55° should be maintained. Increase by cuttings prepared from basal shoots in spring and rooted in sand in a propagating box within the greenhouse.

EUPHORBIA. This is one of the very large families of plants and one well provided with weeds, though it also includes a few members of outstanding importance to the gardener. Of these one of the best for the greenhouse owner is *E. fulgens* (synonym *jacquinaeflora*), a herbaceous plant with slender, arching stems carrying for half their length in mid-winter, small clusters of the brightest orange-scarlet flowers imaginable. It needs warm greenhouse treatment, i.e. a minimum winter temperature of 55°, rising to 60–65° by day, with a fair amount of moisture in the atmosphere. In summer the temperature can average as much as 75° with frequent damping down. Water freely in spring and summer, moderately in autumn and winter. Grow in the weak Innes compost throughout. After flowering keep rather dry for a few weeks then, when growth re-starts, re-pot and give more water. Propagation can be effected at about the same time by removing young side growths and rooting in a propagating box, temperature 70° with bottom heat. *E. splendens*, a spiny plant with scarlet flowers in summer requires similar treatment. For *E. pulcherrima* see poinsettia (p. 490).

EXACUM. There is no neater pot plant than *E. affine*. In a 5 or 6 in. pot it will make a perfect rounded bush a foot high, covered all over with flattish, pale blue flowers each with a centre of bright yellow stamens and with the additional attraction of fragrance. This fine plant is at its best in late summer, but a succession can be had by making several sowings. Seed provides the best method of propagation and should be germinated in a temperature of 60–65°. Sow from February to April. Pot on through the ordinary Innes composts and keep in a cool, sunny greenhouse throughout, watering fairly freely. Syringe daily during warm weather. If desired, plants may be wintered in a frost-proof greenhouse, but it is really better to raise a new stock every year from seed.

FATSIA. *Fatsia japonica* is also known as *Aralia japonica* and *A. Sieboldii*, so do not be surprised to find three plants with different names looking exactly alike. It is a fairly hardy shrub, often grown in the open air in the milder parts of the country, but making an excellent foliage plant for the unheated greenhouse or living room. It has big, fig-like leaves, requires no artificial heat at any season and should be grown in the ordinary Innes composts. Water it freely in spring and summer, moderately in autumn and winter. It may stand outdoors from May to October in any sheltered place. Good specimens are to be grown in 8 or 9 in. pots and should only be re-potted when absolutely necessary; then do the work in March. Propagate by seeds germinated in a warm greenhouse in spring or by cuttings of firm young growth in a propagating box at the same season.

FICUS. This is another foliage plant, but for the warm rather than the unheated greenhouse. The best-known kind is *F. elastica*, the india-rubber plant, with big leathery leaves, much longer than they are broad. There is also a useful climbing species known as *F. repens* which will cling to the wall of a greenhouse. Both need a minimum winter temperature of 50°, with an average around 60°, rising to 70° in summer. Water freely in spring and summer and syringe frequently in warm weather. Damp down to maintain moisture in the air and shade from strong sunshine. Grow in the weak Innes compost and re-pot, when necessary, in March. *F. elastica* is increased by removing, in early summer, single eyes or buds with a leaf attached and rooting these in sandy soil in a propagating box, temperature 70° with bottom heat. *F. repens* is increased by ordinary cuttings in spring rooted under similar conditions. Several other species are available now.

FRANCOA (*Bridal Wreath*). The bridal wreath commonly grown is *Francoa ramosa*, a beautiful and easily managed plant with slender 2 ft. spikes of white flowers in summer. It is a favourite window plant with cottagers. The ideal place for it is a greenhouse with frost protection in winter but otherwise no artificial heat and plenty of light and ventilation. During summer the plants can, if desired, be placed in a frame. Good specimens are to be had in 5 to 7 in. pots in the ordinary Innes composts. They should be watered freely in summer and fed occasionally with weak liquid manure. At other times water moderately. Re-pot annually in March and increase by seed sown in an unheated greenhouse in June.

FREESIA. There are no more delightful bulbous-rooted plants for the cool greenhouse than these. They may be had in bloom from December to April by starting batches in succession, and are quite easy to grow provided no attempt is made to force unduly fast. Obtain bulbs in July or early August and pot, a few at a time, from then until early October. Place six or seven bulbs in a 5 in. pot in weak Innes compost and just cover with soil. Stand in a cold frame for at least eight weeks, keeping the soil moist, but no more, and ventilating freely except during cold weather. When plenty of roots have been made bring the pots into a well-lighted greenhouse, average temperature 50°, which may rise to 60° when the flower stems have formed. If a few pots are brought in every week or so from October to December there will be a continuity of bloom. After flowering grow on under similar conditions for a few weeks and then gradually reduce the water supply until, by June, the soil is quite dry. Keep in this condition in a frame or airy greenhouse until July, when the cycle recommences. The species are not now so important as the many named hybrids in a great variety of shades of cream, orange, lilac, blue, pink, rose and salmon. All have the heavy freesia perfume. Increase by seeds sown as soon as ripe in an unheated greenhouse or frame, or by removing small bulbs at potting time.

FUCHSIA. The fuchsia is almost hardy, and no more than frost protection is required. Magnificent specimens can be obtained by growing on from year to year and carefully pinching young growth to build up enormous pyramids, covered throughout the summer with graceful, drooping flowers. There is no difficulty whatsoever about culture. The fuchsia will grow in any ordinary soil, the Innes composts being ideal. Ventilation should be as free as possible at all times, subject to exclusion of frost. Shade is not essential but will be found an advantage on hot summer days, as high temperatures are at all times undesirable. Water fairly freely throughout the season of growth, from about April to September, but keep rather dry in winter, especially when the temperatures are low. After the leaves have fallen the plants can be pruned fairly severely, if desired, to economise space and the pots may then be stood close together in any out of the way corner, but should be brought back on to the staging directly growth appears in spring. Re-potting should be done in March. Propagation is easily effected by cuttings of young, non-flowering growth, which will root quickly in sandy soil in a propagating box or under a bell glass in spring or late summer. There are single and double-flowered varieties in shades and combinations of red, mauve, purple, pink and white.

GARDENIA. The fragrant, rather stiff and usually very double flowers of the gardenia are chiefly valued for floral decorations and button-holes, but the plants (to be exact they are evergreen shrubs) also make excellent specimens for a nicely-heated glasshouse. Winter temperature should average 55°, and certainly not fall below 45°. In summer it can rise to 70 and even 80° with advantage, with shade from strong sunshine and daily syringing. At this period the plants can also be fed generously with weak liquid manure. In autumn and winter keep considerably drier and discontinue syringing. Plants can be had in bloom successively from about March to June by starting some in January, some in February and some in March. For this purpose the temperature should be raised to 65° and more water given. Re-pot in the weak Innes compost just before the plants are started. At the same time they can be moderately pruned to maintain a neat shape. Propagation is by cuttings of firm young wood obtained a few weeks after starting and rooted in sandy soil in a propagating box, temperature 70°. The best kinds are *G. citriodora*, *G. florida* and *G. Fortunei*, all white.

GENISTA. The shrub which every gardener knows as *Genista fragrans* botanists tell us should be *Cytisus fragrans*, but I have retained the familiar name to avoid confusion. It is everybody's plant, easily grown with little or no heat, and also readily forced in a temperature around 60–65° to get early flowers at Christmas time or soon after. Without heat it will bloom in April. It makes a neat bush in a 4 to 7 in. pot, according to age, smothered for several weeks on end in bright golden-yellow, pea-type flowers. Grow it from cuttings, which will root quickly in sandy soil in a propagating box in either spring or late summer. Pot on through the various sizes of pot and stages of Innes compost and pinch occasionally to secure a very bushy habit. The first year keep in a light, slightly heated greenhouse with no more than frost protection. Stand outdoors from June to September in a sunny place. The following year some plants can be brought into the greenhouse in September and the temperature gradually raised to 65° to get early flowers, while others can be kept in a practically unheated greenhouse until a couple of months later, when forcing may commence. Yet a third batch can be grown cool (minimum temp. 40°) throughout. In all cases water freely while the plants are making their growth and flowering, but more sparingly towards the end of the summer and early autumn before they are started into growth.

GERANIUM.—*See* PELARGONIUM (p. 488).

GESNERIA. Tuberous-rooted plants for the warm greenhouse which, for some reason, have not been grown so much in recent years as formerly. All are handsome plants with ornamental foliage and spikes of drooping, tubular flowers, usually in bright colours, such as orange, scarlet and yellow. Many are autumn or winter flowering. They probably need a little more heat and care than the amateur can, as a rule, manage. Treatment is very similar to that of gloxinias, tubers being kept quite dry after flowering until about February or March, when they are shaken out of their soil, re-potted in the weak Innes compost with a little extra peat, watered moderately and started in a temperature of 60–70°. Watering is gradually increased. Plants are frequently syringed and damped down and are shaded in summer from strong sunshine. After flowering the water supply is gradually decreased and the temperature allowed to drop back to an average of 60°. Finally the soil is allowed to dry off completely and the pots stored on their sides in a dry place, temperature 50–55°. It is possible to propagate by dividing the tubers at potting time, but a more satisfactory method is to prepare cuttings of young shoots in spring and root in sandy peat in a propagating box, temperature 70° with bottom heat and plenty of water.

GLORIOSA. The gloriosas are very handsome, climbing, tuberous-rooted plants with reflexed lily-like flowers which, in the best-known species, *G. superba*, are orange-red and yellow. They do not require very high temperatures and can be stored dry from October to March in a temperature of 45–50°. Then re-pot in weak Innes compost and start in a temperature of about 60°. Water sparingly at first, freely later, and tie the rather slender growths to bamboo canes or trellis work. Feed frequently with weak liquid manure. After flowering in summer gradually reduce the water supply until the foliage dies down and the bulbs can be stored dry once more. The simplest method of increase is to remove small bulbs at potting time.

GLOXINIA. Even the tuberous-rooted begonias cannot surpass gloxinias for display during the summer months. The modern garden forms all have large bell-shaped flowers, mostly in very rich colours, including velvety crimsons and purples, together with many kinds which are heavily spotted or netted with crimson, purple or pink on a white base. The deep green, velvety leaves are also very handsome and the whole habit of the plant, dwarf and compact, is ideal for the small greenhouse. The one drawback is that gloxinias require a little more warmth and moisture than the amateur can always manage conveniently. The roots are tuberous and can be stored dry from October to February. Do not shake them out of their soil but keep them in the pots on their sides in a dry atmosphere and a temperature of 50°. In February shake the soil from the tubers and arrange them practically shoulder to shoulder in seed boxes filled with moist leaf mould or granulated peat, but do not cover the tubers. Then place them in a temperature of 60–65° to start them. Directly they have two or three leaves each pot them singly in weak Innes compost with a little extra peat, first in 3 in. and later in 5 to 6 in. pots. Keep them growing in the same temperature and a fairly moist atmosphere. Water freely once established and syringe between the pots (but not over the leaves) daily. From May to September give shade on the sunny side of the house. Feed with weak liquid manure as soon as flower buds appear. After flowering gradually reduce the water supply until the soil is quite dry by the end of October. The best method of propagation is by seed which should be sown, and the seedlings handled, in the same way as described for tuberous-rooted begonias, but with slightly higher temperatures.

GREVILLEA. The grevilleas are shrubs, a few of which are hardy enough to be grown outdoors in sheltered places. *Grevillea robusta* is, however, invariably treated as a greenhouse foliage plant. It has handsome, deeply divided, ferny leaves and, in a 7–8 in. pot, will make a good specimen 3 or 4 ft. high. It can be grown in any frost-proof greenhouse without artificial heat for the greater part of the year. Water freely from April to September, moderately the rest of the year. Grow in the ordinary Innes composts. Re-pot when necessary in March. Increase by cuttings prepared from the tops of plants in early summer and rooted in a propagating box or, the more usual method, by seeds sown in March in a temperature of 65°.

HAEMANTHUS. These bulbous-rooted plants are sometimes known by the popular name Blood Flower. The showiest species is *H. coccineus*. It has close heads of small scarlet flowers in August–September, and requires a fair amount of heat, say an average of 60° in winter, minimum 50°, rising to 70–75° in summer. Water very sparingly from October to March, then with increasing freedom as growth commences. Give full sun throughout, but maintain a fairly moist atmosphere by damping down. Re-pot when necessary in early April. Increase by removing small bulbs at this period. There are also some hardier species, such as *H. Katherinae*, deep red, and *H. puniceus*, orange-red, which can be grown in temperatures 10° lower than those recommended for *H. coccineus*. *H. Katherinae* flowers in spring, should be re-potted in August or September and rested in late summer. *H. puniceus* flowers in summer, should be re-potted in October and rested from August to October.

HEDYCHIUM. Here again is a family containing some members requiring a good deal of heat, though others can be grown in a minimum winter temperature of 45°, average 55°, rising in summer to 65–70°. Of these hardier kinds the best is *H. Gardnerianum*, with fragrant yellow flowers in summer. It should be grown in 8 to 10 in. pots in weak Innes compost. Re-pot early March and water rather freely from April until after flowering, then reduce the water supply and keep almost dry from November to February inclusive. Increase by division at potting time. The best of the more tender kinds is *H. coronarium*, with fragrant while flowers in summer. Culture is exactly as above, except that temperatures should be increased to an average of 60° in winter, 70–75° in summer.

HELIOTROPIUM (*Heliotrope*). The common heliotrope, or cherry pie, can be grown either as a greenhouse pot plant or used for summer bedding outdoors from June to September. There are various improved garden forms, such as Lord Roberts, with flowers of extra size or deeper colour. All have the typical heliotrope fragrance. These selected forms should be raised from cuttings which can be prepared from young shoots in spring or summer and rooted in sandy soil in a propagating box, preferably with a little bottom heat. The common heliotrope can be increased from seed sown in a temperature of 60–65° in February or March. Pot on the seedlings or rooted cuttings in the ordinary Innes composts until they reach the 5 or 6 in. pots in which they will flower. Alternatively harden them off carefully for planting out early in June in a sunny position. Water rather freely while in growth. After flowering reduce the water supply and keep on the dry side from October to February in an average temperature of 50°, minimum 40°. Bedded out plants can be lifted at the end of September, pruned fairly hard and potted in the smallest pots that will take their roots, after which they should be returned to the greenhouse and given the same treatment as those grown in pots throughout. Very large specimens, or even standards on 2 or 3 ft. stems, can be grown by careful training and pinching carried out over several years.

HIBISCUS. There are species of hibiscus which are perfectly hardy, and these I have dealt with elsewhere (see pp. 106, 284). Here I am concerned with tropical or sub-tropical species which need greenhouse protection and, in some cases, fairly high temperatures. The grandest of these are undoubtedly the numerous varieties of *H. Rosa-sinensis*, a tropical tree of considerable size in its native habitat, but capable of being grown in a large pot or tub in a greenhouse with an average winter temperature of 60°, rising to 70–75° in summer. An alternative is to plant directly in the greenhouse border, so allowing more freedom. The type has very large scarlet flowers, but there are many varieties, some double-flowered, others pink, yellow or buff, or with various combinations of these colours. All should be grown in the weak Innes compost and re-potted as necessary in March. Water very freely from March to October, moderately November to February. Syringe frequently in summer. Give full sun throughout. Prune sufficiently to keep plants in bounds at potting time. Increase by cuttings of firm young shoots taken at almost any time and rooted in a propagating box, temperature 65–70° with bottom heat.

HIPPEASTRUM. These bulbous plants have been much confused with amaryllis, to which they are closely related, in fact it is now stated that amaryllis is the correct name for the plants commonly known in gardens as hippeastrums. They are very showy bulbs for the warm greenhouse, flowering from March to June and resting in winter. The bulbs are rather big but should not be over-potted. Pots 6 to 7 in. in diameter are adequate for a single bulb. Keep almost dry from October to February in a temperature of 45 to 50°. Re-pot, if necessary, directly the bulbs show signs of growing, using the weak Innes compost, but usually bulbs can go three years with top dressing only. Water with increasing freedom from March onwards and raise the temperature to 65° (55° for newly potted bulbs), syringeing at least once daily. Under these conditions the strap-shaped leaves will lengthen rapidly and the stiff flower spikes, terminated by clusters of large trumpet-shaped flowers in brilliant shades of scarlet and crimson, will appear. After blooming place the pots on a sunny shelf in the greenhouse in an average temperature of 55–60°. As the foliage shows signs of dying down, gradually reduce the water supply until, by the autumn, the soil is no more than just not dry. Increase by seeds sown in a temperature of 65–70° in spring, or by removing offsets at potting time.

Hoya. The hoyas are climbing plants with very regular star-shaped clusters of flowers which look as if made of wax, hence the popular name 'wax flower'. The species usually grown is *H. carnosa*, in which the flowers are very pale pink and at their best in July–August. It is quite an easy plant for a cool greenhouse, average winter temperature 45°, summer 60°. The plants may be grown in large pots in the medium Innes compost, but a better plan is to plant directly in the greenhouse border in good loamy soil with plenty of peat and sand and a little crushed charcoal. The stems twine so should have suitable support, such as a pillar or trellis. Water freely in spring and summer, moderately autumn and winter. Thin out overcrowded shoots and shorten weak stems every February. Plants in pots or tubs should be re-potted every second or third year in March. This hoya can be propagated by cuttings of firm young shoots taken in spring and rooted in a propagating box with bottom heat. Alternatively year-old shoots can be layered in autumn.

Humea. The only species grown in gardens is *H. elegans*. It is not often seen in amateur collections but invariably figures in groups of greenhouse plants at flower shows and always attracts notice because of its tall, feathery plumes of tiny pinkish-brown flowers. These are often 6 ft. in height. *H. elegans* is a biennial and, in consequence, must be raised from seed every year. Sow any time in spring or early summer in a greenhouse in Innes seed compost covering very lightly and germinating in a temperature of 60–65°. Prick off in the same compost as early as possible and then, when the seedlings are 2 or 3 in. high, pot singly in 3 in. pots. From these move to 5 in. pots and then to 8 or 10 in. pots, using the graded Innes composts throughout and being specially careful about drainage. Give plenty of water. Damp down around the pots daily in hot weather and grow throughout the summer in an unheated and unshaded greenhouse. In autumn and winter water very carefully and maintain an average temperature of 50°.

April sown plants will flower early the following summer, July sown plants late the following summer. Plants should be discarded immediately after flowering.

HYDRANGEA. The common hydrangea with its great trusses of blue, pink, reddish or white flowers is hardy enough to be grown outdoors in many sheltered places, but is primarily a greenhouse shrub in this country. Small specimens, in pots 6 in. in diameter and each carrying one truss of bloom, can be obtained by striking cuttings every August. They should be inserted singly in small pots filled with sandy soil and rooted in an unheated and shaded frame. Directly these pots are nicely filled with roots move on to 4 in. pots and then, the following March, to 6 in. pots, using the ordinary Innes composts. Keep all winter in a frost-proof greenhouse, average temperature 45°. Water moderately till April, then with increasing freedom. It is almost impossible to overwater hydrangeas in summer provided soil is porous and drainage good. To get early flowers the temperature can be raised to an average of 60° in April, or the plants can be grown on without heat to flower in June. Bigger specimens can be obtained by growing on these young plants for two, three or more years. Stand outdoors in a sunny place after flowering plunging the pots to their rims in peat or ashes. Return to a frost-proof greenhouse early in October. Re-pot early in March. The only pruning necessary is to cut back flowering stems to side growths or good growth buds immediately the blooms fade.

Blue flowers are only produced in soils that are rather acid, and then only from plants that normally have coloured flowers. White kinds cannot be made to bear blue flowers. One way of ensuring an acid soil is to prepare a mixture of 3 parts by bulk old cucumber loam, 1 part oak leaf mould and add to each cwt. of this mixture $2\frac{1}{2}$ lb. of aluminium sulphate. This mixture can be used for all pottings after the plants leave the propagating frame.

IMANTOPHYLLUM.—*See* CLIVIA (p. 455).

IMPATIENS. I have dealt with the balsam which, strictly speaking is an impatiens, on p. 440. Here I am concerned only with those species which commonly pass under the name 'impatiens' in gardens. The two most important are *I. Holstii* and *I. Sultani*. Both are bushy plants a couple of feet in height, with vivid scarlet flowers produced throughout the summer. They are sometimes used for summer bedding schemes, for which purpose they should not be put outdoors until all danger of frost is passed, usually the second week in June in the London area. They should then have a sunny, warm position. As greenhouse plants they are excellent for the moderately heated structure, average winter temperature 50–55°, summer 60–65°. They are readily raised from cuttings of young non-flowering growths, which will root at almost any time in spring or summer in sandy soil in a propagating box with gentle bottom heat, or from seed sown in February–March in a temperature of 60–65°. Grow the plants on in the ordinary Innes composts, potting them on as necessary. Good specimens can be had in 6 or 7 in. pots. Water very freely in summer, more sparingly in winter, especially during cold weather. Give full sun throughout. Ventilate as freely as possible consistent with the temperatures indicated.

IPOMAEA. These plants are very closely allied to convolvulus and a good deal of confusion in naming exists (see p. 99). Here I am concerned with two fine climbing plants for the slightly heated greenhouse, *I. Leari* and *I. rubro-caerulea*. Both are vigorous twiners which can be trained up a pillar or under the rafters. They flower in summer and the blooms are large and funnel-shaped, Oxford blue in the first named Cambridge blue in the second. There is an even better form of *I. caerulea* known as Heavenly Blue, in which the colour is paler and purer. All can be grown in large pots or tubs, but it is better to plant them directly in the greenhouse border in ordinary well-drained soil. Maintain an average winter temperature of 50°, rising to 60–65° in summer. Water freely in spring and summer, moderately in autumn and winter. No pruning is necessary, though overgrown plants can be cut back in March. Propagation is easily effected by seeds sown singly in small pots in March and germinated in a temperature of about 60°. The seedlings should be potted on in the ordinary Innes composts as necessary and will flower the first summer. As they do not make very big plants the first year they then make useful pot specimens for the greenhouse staging, with the shoots trained around three or four thin bamboo canes stuck into a 6 or 8 in. pot.

ISOLEPIS. *I. gracilis* is a very graceful ornamental rush with grass-like leaves and slender stems terminated in summer by tiny green flowers, from which it gets its popular name of Job's Tears. It is an easily grown pot plant for the cool or warm greenhouse, and good specimens are to be had in 4 in. pots. Grow with plenty of water from April to September and in a fairly damp atmosphere. In winter water more sparingly and keep a drier atmosphere. Frost protection only is essential though the plant will stand quite high temperatures. The plant can also be grown in hanging baskets. Re-pot in March, using the ordinary Innes composts, and propagate, if desired, by division at the same time.

Greenhouse Plants and their Cultivation

Alternatively plants can be raised from seed sown in March in a temperature of 65°, seedlings being potted on as necessary throughout the first summer.

Ixia.—*See* p. 354.

Ixora. These are brilliant evergreen shrubs for the warm greenhouse. They produce their large clusters of vividly coloured flowers in summer. The best for the amateur is *I. coccinea*, in which the flowers are orange-scarlet. Good compact specimens are to be had in 6 or 7 in. pots. Grow them in the weak Innes compost. Re-pot old plants in March but young plants, which can be raised from cuttings of firm growth rooted in a propagating box with bottom heat at almost any time of year, should be potted on from stage to stage directly the smaller pots become filled with roots. Grow in a spring and summer temperature of around 70°, with plenty of water at the roots and in the atmosphere. Plants can be syringed twice daily in warm weather. Keep a much drier atmosphere in autumn and winter and reduce the temperature to an average of 60°. Plants can be pruned to shape in February just before potting.

Jacaranda. The only species cultivated is *J. mimosifolia* and, despite the fact that it is a flowering plant, it is grown mainly for its finely cut foliage. It makes a good specimen in a large pot or can be planted direct in the greenhouse border and allowed to form a big shrub or small tree. The weak Innes compost will suit it and it needs a moderate temperature, winter minimum 55°, summer 65–70°. Pot plants can be re-potted as necessary in March. All may be pruned to shape each February. Shade is, as a rule, unnecessary. Water should be given freely in spring and summer, moderately in autumn and winter. Increase is most readily effected by seeds sown in a warm greenhouse in spring. Young plants need a rather higher temperature than those which are older.

Jasminum (*Jasmine*). The hardy jasmines will be found in another chapter (see p. 287) but it is often overlooked that there are also some equally delightful species for the greenhouse. These can conveniently be considered under two headings, cool house kinds which will thrive in an average winter temperature of 50°, which may fall as low as 40° at times without harm, and warm house species requiring an average winter temperature of 60°, minimum 50°. There should be a corresponding difference in summer temperatures, 60° being the average for the cool house species, 70° for the warm kinds. The best species in these two groups are: Cool house—*Jasminum grandiflorum*, with white

477

fragrant flowers in summer, and *J. primulinum*, with yellow flowers in winter: Warm house—*Jasminum Sambac* and *J. gracillimum*, both with white fragrant flowers in winter. All are climbers of moderate vigour which may be trained up pillars or under the rafters. Grow directly in the greenhouse border in good loamy soil, or in large pots or tubs in medium Innes compost. Plant or pot in March. Water freely in spring and summer, moderately in autumn and winter. No shading should be needed, except possibly from very strong sunshine in small houses. Prune sufficiently to keep in bounds, immediately after flowering in the case of winter flowering kinds, or in February in the case of summer flowering kinds. Propagate by cuttings of firm young shoots in spring, pulled off with a heel and rooted in sandy soil in a propagating frame, with bottom heat in the case of the warm house kinds only.

JUSTICIA. *Justicia carnea* is a very showy plant for the greenhouse which may also turn up under the name *Jacobinea carnea*. It has compact heads of hooded pink flowers which are at their best in September and October. Good specimens can be had in pots 7 to 8 in. in diameter. Grow from cuttings, which will root readily in spring in a propagating frame, temperature 60°. Pot these singly in 3 in. pots directly they are rooted and then work on stage by stage to the 7 to 8 in. pots in which they will flower, using the ordinary Innes composts. Old plants can be re-potted each March. Grow in a sunny greenhouse, temperature 55–65° April to September, 45–55° October to March. Water freely in spring and summer and feed with weak liquid manure. Keep soil only just moist in autumn and winter. Prune fairly severely immediately after flowering.

KALANCHOË. These are succulent-leaved plants closely allied to crassula and requiring identical treatment (see p. 457). The best are *K. carnea*, with pink flowers, *K. flammea*, orange-scarlet, and *K. kewensis*, bright rose. All bloom in summer.

KALOSANTHES.—*See* CRASSULA (p. 457).

KENTIA. The two most useful of all palms for pot culture are *Kentia Belmoreana* and *K. Forsteriana*. They are both easily grown in a slightly heated greenhouse, average winter temperature 50°, rising in summer to 60°. Give shade from May to September and water freely from April to September, moderately the rest of the year. Syringe plants at least twice daily in spring and summer. Re-pot when necessary in March, using the ordinary Innes composts. Increase by seeds which may be sown singly in small pots in March and germinated in a temperature of 70–75°.

LACHENALIA. The lachenalias deserve to be better known, for they flower in winter or very early spring with very little artificial heat and are extremely easy to manage. They are bulbous-rooted plants, and the bulbs should be potted five or six together in a 5 in. pot in August or early September in weak Innes compost. Cover with ½ in. of soil and place the pots for at least two months in an unheated frame. Then, when plenty of roots have been formed, bring the pots into a sunny greenhouse, average temperature 50°, which may rise to 60° for the last few weeks while flowers are developing. After blooming reduce the temperature again to 55° and grow on in the same manner as freesias (see p. 468) slowly reducing the water supply so that, by the end of June, the soil is quite dry. The flowers are orange-red or yellow, tubular, drooping and arranged in slender spikes remotely like those of the cowslip, hence the popular name Cape cowslip. Lachenalias may also be grown in hanging baskets with very good effect. Propagation is by seeds sown in a temperature of 60° in March, or by removal or small bulbs at potting time.

LANTANA. There was a time when the lantana was almost as popular a plant, both for summer bedding and for greenhouse display, as the verbena, to which it is related and which it resembles in flower. It has slipped out of favour but is, nevertheless, a useful and showy plant, bushy and branching in habit, usually 2 to 3 ft. high with bright clusters of flowers throughout the summer. The flowers themselves are in various shades of violet and red, together with white. Lantanas should be raised from seed sown in a temperature of 65° in February-March or from cuttings struck in spring or autumn in a propagating frame and should be grown on in a moderately heated, airy, sunny greenhouse with plenty of water while they are making their growth and in a temperature of 45° with very little water from October to February. Use the ordinary Innes composts. Give good drainage and prune rather hard in February to keep plants compact. If preferred, lantanas can be planted outdoors early in June and lifted, re-potted and brought back into the greenhouse at the end of September.

LAPAGERIA. There are no climbers more beautiful than the lapagerias, and they will grow in any slightly heated glasshouse, minimum winter temperature 40°, average 45–50°. Plants can be grown in large pots or tubs, but it is better to place them directly in the greenhouse border and train them around pillars or on wires beneath the rafters, from which their handsome, long bell-shaped flowers will hang throughout the summer. Plant or pot in March and water very freely from April to September, in fact it is almost impossible to give them too much, provided the soil is open and well drained. In autumn and winter far less water is needed. Give some shade throughout the summer and syringe daily to maintain a moist atmosphere. In a dry greenhouse plants are likely to be severely attacked by thrips and red spider. The best species is *L. rosea*, with rosy-red flowers. There is also a good pure white form. Both can be increased by layering in autumn or spring.

LIBONIA. *Libonia floribunda* is a small evergreen shrub with numerous tubular scarlet and yellow flowers in the autumn. It is suitable for growing in pots 5 to 7 in. in diameter and can be cultivated in any greenhouse with an average winter temperature of 55°, in fact it will survive considerably lower temperatures, though these may check flowering. Grow in the ordinary Innes composts, re-potting in March or early April. From early June till September plants may be stood in a frame. Water fairly freely at this period, moderately in autumn and sparingly after flowering until re-potted. Prune lightly immediately after flowering. Propagation is by cuttings rooted in spring in a propagating frame, preferably with some bottom heat.

LILIUM (*Lily*). A great many lilies can be grown in the greenhouse and, as most of them are hardy, or almost so, they are good subjects for the unheated structure. Few will tolerate much artificial heat, but the various forms of *L. longiflorum*, of which the best are *eximium* and *Harrisii*, can be flowered early in a temperature of 65° once they are well established in their pots. All lilies for the greenhouse should be potted in the autumn. In most cases a 6 in. pot will accommodate one bulb, or two or three bulbs may be placed in pots 8 to 10 in. in diameter. Use the weak Innes compost and make certain that pot drainage is good. Place the bulbs fairly low in the pots, especially in the case of stem rooting kinds, and do not completely fill the pots at first but leave room for top dressing with similar soil as shoots lengthen. After potting place in an unheated frame for at least two months so that roots may be formed freely before top growth starts. Completely hardy lilies can be left in the frame with advantage until their flower stems are already well formed, and only brought into the greenhouse for the last few weeks. Lilies should have free ventilation throughout and plenty of light. Water freely while in growth, but after flowering gradually reduce the water supply until, by the time growth dies down, the soil is no more than just moist. Then allow to rest for a month or so before re-potting. Those lilies which are hurried along in heat to get early flowers should not be forced two years running.

The best lilies for pot cultivation are *L. longiflorum*, with long, trumpet-shaped, white flowers (this is the popular white lily of the florists' shops); its variety *Harrisii*, which is both earlier in bloom and finer; *L. speciosum*, with reflexed pink and white flowers in late summer; its numerous varieties, such as *Melpomene* and *rubrum*, in which there is more and deeper colouring; *L. auratum*, the immense golden ray lily of Japan; *L. formosanum*, which is a little like *longiflorum* but with longer and more slender trumpets, and *L. regale*, with widely opened trumpet-shaped flowers, white a little suffused with gold. This last is one of the easiest of all lilies to grow and can be flowered in eighteen months from seed. *L. longiflorum* and its varieties are the best kinds for gentle forcing and by this means can be had in bloom from about February to June.

LILY OF THE VALLEY.—*See* CONVALLARIA (p. 456).

LIPPIA. The well-known lemon-scented verbena, *L. citriodora*, which is hardy enough to be grown outdoors in a sheltered place, is described on p. 292. It can also be grown in unheated greenhouses and conservatories, but should then be watered and ventilated freely in summer to prevent attacks by red spider and thrips. Syringe daily during warm weather. Winter temperature should average 50°, rising to 60° in summer, and ventilation must be as free as possible consistent with these readings. After flowering cut the young shoots back rather severely and keep rather dry and cool for a couple of months to give the plants a rest. The best method of increase is by cuttings of young shoots, which will root readily in a propagating frame in early summer.

LUCULIA. *Luculia gratissima* is a greenhouse shrub which deserves to be better known as it has clusters of very charming and exceptionally fragrant pink flowers in the autumn. It is rather too big for pot culture, but may be grown in a tub or planted out in the greenhouse border in any good loam with a little extra peat and sand. Water freely in spring and summer, rather sparingly autumn and winter.

MANETTIA. Though one frequently sees *Manettia inflata* at shows, it seldom figures in amateurs' greenhouses, despite the fact that it is a pretty and easily grown plant. It is a small, evergreen climber which can be grown in pots 6 to 10 in. in diameter and either trained beneath the rafters or wound around a few bamboo canes to form a bush-like specimen. The small, tubular, scarlet and yellow flowers are produced freely the greater part of the year. Winter temperature need be no higher than 55°, rising in summer to 60–65°. It will thrive in the ordinary Innes composts, can be raised readily from cuttings of young shoots which root quickly in a propagating box in spring, and should be worked on through the smaller size pots as quickly as these become filled with roots. Water fairly freely from April to September, rather sparingly October to March. Light shade will be needed on hot days only.

MARANTA. These are handsome foliage plants for the well-heated greenhouse. They are not in the least difficult to grow in pots in the weak Innes compost, provided an average winter temperature of 60° can be maintained, rising in summer to 70°. Like most other hothouse plants they need abundant moisture in both soil and atmosphere throughout the spring and summer, but should be watered more moderately from September to December and be kept rather dry for the first two months of the year. Re-pot, as necessary, in March and increase by division at this time. The leaves are large and handsomely variegated with white, grey, purple or pale green on a dark green base.

MARGUERITE. Botanically the common marguerite is a species of chrysanthemum, but its full name, *Chrysanthemum frutescens*, is seldom used in the garden. Though it makes quite a good pot plant to flower in the unheated greenhouse in summer, it is far more commonly grown for summer bedding and window boxes. For all purposes it is best to propagate by means of cuttings of young, non-flowering shoots, which root readily in a propagating frame in March and April and also in August and September. When rooted, pot the cuttings singly in 3 in. pots and work them on as necessary using the ordinary Innes composts until, by late May, they are planted out or reach the 5 or 6 in. pots in which they will bloom. In autumn and winter water very sparingly and keep in a sunny greenhouse with frost protection only. In spring and summer ventilate as freely as possible consistent with an average temperature of 55–60°. Old plants can be kept from year to year and will eventually make quite big bushes though, alternatively, they can be pruned severely each autumn to keep them smaller. If desired, some plants can also be lifted in late September from the summer beds and potted for return to the greenhouse. The common marguerite is white but there is also a good golden form not seen as often as it deserves.

MAURANDIA. *M. Barclayana* is a pretty trailing or climbing plant which can be grown in baskets suspended from the rafters or in pots placed at the edge of the greenhouse staging. It has purple flowers freely produced during the summer and early autumn. Cuttings can be rooted in the spring, but the usual method of increase is by seeds sown in March in a temperature of 60°. Pot on as necessary in the ordinary Innes composts until the plants reach the 4 to 5 in. pots in which they will bloom. Alternatively several plants can be accommodated in a hanging basket of ordinary size. Water freely while in growth, but very sparingly from November to March inclusive. Re-pot each March. In February the previous year's shoots can be cut hard back.

METROSIDEROS.—*See* CALLISTEMON (p. 447).

MIMOSA (*Sensitive Plant*). The plant commonly known in gardens as mimosa is, in fact, an acacia (see p. 433), but there is a genuine mimosa occasionally grown as a pot plant. This is *M. pudica*, a small branching plant with finely cut leaves which have the curious habit of folding up when touched, hence the popular name Sensitive Plant. It is grown mainly as a curiosity and will thrive in any light, sunny greenhouse with an average winter temperature of 60°, rising in summer to about 70°. Water and syringe freely in spring and summer and shade from direct sunshine. Use the ordinary Innes composts. Re-pot in March and increase by seeds germinated in February or March in a temperature of 70°. The plant is usually treated as an annual though it can be grown on from year to year.

MIMULUS (*Musk*). The true musk, *Mimulus moschatus*, was once a very popular greenhouse pot plant on account of its distinctive fragrance, but when it lost this in the early part of the century it fell out of favour. Nevertheless it is still worth growing for its yellow flowers, particularly the form of it known as Harrison's Musk, which is rather stronger growing and more showy. It can be raised from seeds sown in March in a temperature of 60°, or by cuttings of young growth rooted in a propagating frame in spring. Grow on in the ordinary Innes composts, potting as necessary until the plants reach 5 or 6 in. pots in which they will bloom. Water very freely but make certain that the pots are well drained. Grow in a cool, airy, lightly shaded greenhouse, minimum temperature 40°. No artificial heat is needed for the greater part of the year.

MYRTUS (*Myrtle*). This evergreen flowering shrub is hardy enough to be grown outdoors in a sheltered position in many parts of the country, but it also makes an excellent pot specimen for the unheated greenhouse. *M. communis* is the only species grown. In an open border it will make a compact bush 8 or 10 ft. high, but pot culture restricts it and good specimens, 3 or 4 ft. high, are to be had in 8 or 9 in. pots. These will produce their small but abundant, fragrant white flowers in summer. Grow in ordinary Innes composts and re-pot when necessary in March. If desired plants can be pruned to shape at the same time, though pruning is not essential. Water fairly freely in spring and summer, rather sparingly autumn and winter. If desired the plants can be stood outdoors from June to September inclusive, preferably in a sheltered but not too sunny position. Increase by cuttings of young shoots pulled off with a heel in August–September and rooted in a propagating frame with a little bottom heat.

NEPENTHES (*Pitcher plant*). The pitcher plants are so called because some of their leaves have been modified into large, pitcher-like structures which serve as insect traps. They are not only curious and interesting on this account but also distinctly beautiful, as the pitchers are often handsomely marked with crimson, purple and brown. The plants can be grown in either pots or teak baskets, and the best position for them is suspended from the greenhouse rafters. They need a damp, warm atmosphere with abundant moisture during the growing season both in the air and at the roots. Grow them in a compost of about 2 parts by bulk fibrous peat and 1 part sphagnum moss with no soil at all. Place in the pots or baskets in March and water rather carefully at first until the roots are established. Subsequently water very freely from April to September inclusive, but no more than moderately from October to March. Syringing should be continued throughout the year once daily even in winter, and maybe two or three times daily in summer. Temperatures should average 65° from October to March, 75° April to September. Shade rather heavily from direct sunshine. Propagation is not a very easy matter for the amateur but can be effected by means of stem cuttings obtained in spring or early summer and rooted singly in small pots filled with peat and sphagnum moss and placed in a propagating box, temperature 80° with bottom heat. Seeds may also be germinated under similar conditions.

NERINE. The nerines are amongst the best bulbous-rooted plants for the amateur's greenhouse. They flower in autumn, are very easy to grow and do not require high temperatures. Obtain bulbs in July or early August and pot them singly in 4 in. pots, or three or four together in 6 in. pots using the weak Innes compost. Place straight away in a sunny, unheated greenhouse. Water very sparingly at first, but with increasing freedom as growth appears. Then, in a month or so, the heads of showy scarlet or pink blooms will develop on stiff 18 in. stems before the leaves appear. After they fade, continue to water fairly freely and grow on in the greenhouse in an average temperature of 45°, minimum 40°. Give plenty of ventilation and full sunshine throughout. In May the foliage will show signs of dying down. Pots may then be stood on a shelf near the glass and the water supply cut down until, for some weeks, the soil is absolutely dry. Then, in August, at the first sign of growth, soak well and continue to water moderately. Nerines flower most freely when rather pot bound and should only be re-potted every third or fourth year. They can then be split up or merely potted on into larger sizes. Most of the kinds now cultivated are hybrids with fancy names, such as Scarlet Beauty, Lucifer, etc. and will be found fully described in the catalogues of bulb merchants.

NERIUM (*Oleander*). The oleander, like the myrtle, is a native of Southern Europe and almost hardy. It can be grown in a greenhouse with frost protection only and is a really beautiful shrub which, if planted out in the greenhouse border, will grow in time 6 or 8 ft. high and rather more through. Smaller plants are to be had in 8 or 10 in. pots or tubs. The common species, *N. Oleander*, produces its large clusters of bright pink flowers in late spring or early summer. Pot or plant in medium Innes compost in March and only re-pot when absolutely necessary due to overcrowding. Water freely from March to September, rather sparingly the remainder of the year. In summer, after flowering, plants can be stood outdoors for a month or so, but must be brought inside before there is danger of frost. Throughout the warm weather syringe frequently. In too hot and dry an atmosphere red spider may be very troublesome. Immediately after blooming prune all young growth rather hard and, subsequently, keep a little dry for a few weeks until growth recommences. In winter it is only necessary to maintain a minimum temperature of 40°. Earlier blooms can be obtained by raising the temperature in March to about 60°, but nothing in the nature of hard forcing should be attempted. Propagation is by cuttings of firm shoots rooted in a propagating frame in late summer.

NICOTIANA. All the nicotianas make good pot plants for the unheated greenhouse and can be had in flower throughout the summer. Treat them as already described on p. 115 except that, instead of being planted out, the seedlings should be potted on singly in the ordinary Innes composts into 4 or 5 in. pots in which they will bloom. Give shade from strong direct sunshine.

NIDULARIUM. For a well-heated greenhouse the nidulariums make excellent pot plants, for they are neat in habit, have handsome foliage and showy flower spikes. The long, strap-shaped leaves are produced in rosettes and the central leaves are usually scarlet in contrast to the violet or purple flowers. Nidulariums should be grown in the weak Innes compost in a temperature of 70° or more from April to September, 60–65° October to March. Give them light shade during hot weather only. Syringe and damp down frequently in spring and summer. Water freely April to September, moderately the rest of the year. Re-pot as necessary in March. Increase by removing offshoots.

OPHIOPOGON. These are plants grown mainly for their narrow, graceful foliage, which in some varieties, such as *O. Jaburan variegatus*, is handsomely variegated with yellow or white. They also produce slender spikes of blue or lilac flowers in summer, but these are of lesser importance. Grow in the ordinary Innes composts in the smallest pots that will contain the roots and re-pot every second or third year in March. Water very freely in spring and summer, moderately autumn and winter. The plants will thrive equally well in full sun or partial shade and can be brought into the dwelling house for periods, for they make good room plants. All that is required is frost protection in winter. Most of the year no artificial heat is essential though warmth is not detrimental. Increase by dividing the plants at potting time.

ORCHIDS.—*See* Chapter XX.

ORNITHOGALUM (*Star of Bethlehem*). Both the ornithogalums which are described on p. 361 may also be grown as pot plants in the cool greenhouse. Pot them in weak Innes compost in early autumn. Stand them in a frame for a month or so and then bring them into a light, airy greenhouse. No heat is needed though, if early flowers are required, a temperature of 60° can be maintained. There are some other species which are tender and, therefore, only suitable for the greenhouse, notably *O. arabicum* and *O. lacteum*, the latter being the South African Chincherinchee, both with white flowers in summer. Culture is the same as for the hardy kinds, except that frost protection should be given.

OXALIS. In addition to the hardy species, described on p. 219, there are some slightly tender kinds which make splendid pot or basket plants for the frost-proof, but otherwise unheated, greenhouse. The best of these are *O. Bowiei*, summer flowering, and *O. rosea* and *O. floribunda*, both spring flowering. All are rose pink. Pot in the autumn in 4 or 5 in. pots, or place several together in baskets, using the weak Innes compost, and grow in a sunny greenhouse with ventilation as free as possible, subject to a minimum temperature of 35°. Water rather sparingly in autumn and winter, but moderately from March to about the end of August, or until foliage dies down. Then keep quite dry for about six weeks until re-potting time. Increase by removal of offsets when potting.

PANCRATIUM. These are bulbous-rooted plants with white, fragrant flowers in summer. They are very showy and make good specimens for large pots in the slightly heated greenhouse. Re-pot in March, but annual re-potting is seldom required. Keep in a light, airy greenhouse, average temperature 50°, watering rather sparingly at first but freely later. After flowering gradually reduce the water supply and keep almost dry from about November to February inclusive. At this period only frost protection is required. Use the weak Innes compost. Increase by removing small bulbs at potting time. These instructions apply to the best species for the amateur, *P. maritimum*. There are other kinds, such as *P. canariense*, which require much higher temperatures, especially in spring and early summer.

PANICUM. *P. variegatum* is the garden name of a useful trailing grass with white-striped, and sometimes pink-tinged, foliage. It makes a very pretty edging to the greenhouse staging. It will grow in the weak Innes compost and needs a winter temperature of around 50°. In summer it will thrive in an unheated greenhouse. Water freely in spring and summer, moderately autumn and winter. Re-pot in March and increase by cuttings rooted in spring or summer in very sandy soil in a propagating frame, preferably with a little bottom heat.

PANDANUS. Very useful foliage plants of which the best is *P. Veitchii*. This has strap-shaped leaves striped with cream and forming a large, palm-like rosette. In decorative value it may be compared with the best of the dracaenas. Unfortunately it needs a fairly warm temperature most of the time, though it may be used as a house plant for short periods. Grow in the weak Innes compost, re-potting when necessary in March. Good specimens can be had in 8 or 9 in. pots. Cultural details are the same as for dracaena (see p. 464) except that the best method of propagation is by removal of offsets at potting time.

PASSIFLORA (*Passion Flower*). The blue passion flower, *Passiflora caerulea*, can be grown in an unheated greenhouse and is usually more successful there than outdoors. There are also some excellent varieties of it, including Constance Elliot which has white flowers. *P. edulis*, the species which produces the passion fruit, requires more warmth. All can be grown in large pots or tubs, but are better planted directly in the greenhouse border in good soil with free drainage. Give them plenty of room and place them where they can climb up a pillar or trellis. The sunnier the position the better. Plant or pot in March and water very freely from April to September. Growth can also be syringed daily during hot weather. In autumn and winter keep the soil just moist and the atmosphere dry. A winter temperature of 45° will be sufficient. In February overgrown plants can be reduced a little and weak shoots removed. Propagation is by cuttings of firm young growth rooted in spring or early summer in a propagating frame in the greenhouse.

PELARGONIUM (*Geranium*). It is a pity that geranium should have been chosen for the popular name of pelargonium for it is also the correct botanical name of a separate genus of plants, some of which are good, hardy herbaceous perennials (see p. 207). The novice should note well that the familiar scarlet flowered geraniums of the summer border are, in fact, pelargoniums and dealt with here. In addition to these popular plants, which are known as zonal-leaved pelargoniums, there are several other types, including ivy-leaved pelargoniums, which are climbing or trailing plants flowering, like the zonal-leaved kinds, all the summer and well on into the autumn, too, if in a mild climate; the show and regal pelargoniums which are purely greenhouse plants, similar to the zonal-leaved type in habit, but flowering from April to June and with bigger blooms, usually strikingly blotched with maroon or crimson on a red, pink, salmon or mauve base; and the scented-leaved pelargoniums, most of which have insignificant flowers but leaves which are not only fragrant but often much divided, so that some have an almost fern-like appearance.

All pelargoniums are easily grown pot plants, thriving in the ordinary Innes composts and capable of being raised from cuttings struck in either spring or late summer in a temperature of 55–60°. Cuttings will, as a rule, strike quite readily on the open greenhouse staging or, in August, even in a frame outdoors. Too much heat and moisture are not desirable as it may cause decay. Pot the spring struck cuttings singly in 3½ in. pots directly they are rooted, the autumn struck cuttings in early March, and thereafter move them on to larger pots as quickly as the smaller ones become filled with roots. Good flowering plants are to be had in 5 or 6 in. pots though, if desired, old plants can be retained and will eventually make big specimens in pots 8 to 10 in. in diameter.

Zonal and ivy-leaved geraniums required for bedding should be hardened off in a frame during late April and early May and planted out towards the end of May or early June in well-drained soil and a sunny position. The ivy-leaved kinds can either be trained up sticks about 3 ft. in height, or allowed to trail over the soil.

The regal and show pelargoniums should be kept in the greenhouse, average temperature 55°, until they have finished flowering and may then be stood in a frame or even outdoors in a sheltered, sunny position. At this period they must be kept rather dry for a few weeks, but early in August the plants should be cut back quite severely and watered with gradually increasing freedom to encourage new growth. They can be re-potted directly new shoots appear. A few plants may be pruned and watered in June to give a supply of early cuttings which can be rooted in July and potted singly in 3 in. pots by September. These cuttings give better results than those taken later.

All pelargoniums require frost protection in winter and should be housed about the end of September. Keep in a sunny, airy greenhouse, average temperature 45–50°, and water rather sparingly until growth starts again in March.

It is also possible to treat zonal-leaved pelargoniums as winter flowering greenhouse plants, the method being to grow the plants in pots throughout and prevent them from flowering in the summer by pinching off the flower buds as fast as they appear. The plants can stand in a sunny frame from June till late September and then be brought into a greenhouse, temperature 55°. From this time onwards blooms can be allowed to develop naturally.

Varieties of all types are very numerous and particulars will be found in the catalogues of specialists.

PETUNIA. The ordinary petunias as used for summer bedding (see p. 117) also make excellent pot plants for flowering in the unheated greenhouse in summer. The best kinds for the purpose are the large-flowered hybrids and the double-flowered varieties, but as the latter sometimes produce little seed they must often be increased by cuttings of young growth rooted in a propagating frame at any time during the spring or summer. Pot on the cuttings, in the ordinary Innes composts till they reach 4 or 5 in. pots. Seedlings should be treated as already described (see p. 118), except that they are placed in 4 or 5 in. pots instead of being planted out.

PHOENIX. A family of large and handsome palms of which the best for the amateur is *P. Roebelenii.* This is as useful for decorative purposes as the two kentias described on p. 478 and requires identical treatment. *P. Roebelenii* can be used for short periods for indoor decoration but should be returned to the greenhouse to recuperate as it does not thrive for long in the dry atmosphere of a dwelling house.

PILEA. The best known species, *P. muscosa,* is popularly known as the Artillery Plant because, when it is about to flower, the buds will suddenly burst open and throw out a smoke-like puff of pollen. It is worth growing for its foliage as well as this oddity of habit. Another useful species is *P. Cadierei.* This has dark green leaves striped and margined with silver and the whole plant grows about 9 in. high. Both species are easily managed in a moderately heated greenhouse, winter temperature

55°, summer 65° or over. Water freely while in growth, moderately afterwards. Grow in pots in the weak Innes compost, re-potting each March. Increase by cuttings prepared from the ends of young shoots and rooted in spring or early summer in a propagating frame with gentle bottom heat.

PLUMBAGO. The only greenhouse species of importance is *Plumbago capensis*, a vigorous climber with big clusters of light blue phlox-like flowers throughout the summer. It is one of the best climbing plants for the greenhouse and it requires no more than frost protection in winter. It can be grown in large pots or tubs, but is better planted direct in the greenhouse border in rather rich, well-drained soil. Plant it where it can be trained around a pillar, up a wall or beneath the rafters, and be sure to give it plenty of headroom. Plant or pot in March. Water freely from April to September, moderately October to March. Give as much ventilation throughout as is consistent with frost protection in winter and an average of 55–60° in summer. Foliage can be syringed daily in warm weather. Prune each March, shortening most of the previous year's growths to 8 or 9 in. Propagation is most readily effected by cuttings of young shoots pulled off with a heel in April and rooted in sandy soil in a propagating frame.

POINSETTIA. The handsome shrubby plant which all gardeners know as poinsettia is, in fact, a euphorbia, its full name being *E. pulcherrima*. It is a plant for the well-heated greenhouse and its great merit is that it produces its large scarlet bracts in mid-winter. The flowers, which are at the base of the bracts, are themselves insignificant.Good plants may be had in 7 or 8 in. pots in the weak Innes compost, but with fairly generous feeding for the last two or three months. Any re-potting necessary should be done in March. From then on water with steadily increasing freedom and maintain an average temperature of 65°. Syringe once daily, but give a fair amount of ventilation by day and only light shade on the sunny side of the house from May to September. From September to December the average temperature can drop to 60° to harden the wood. After flowering prune the year's growth to within a few inches of the base and reduce the temperature to an average of 55° until it is time for re-potting in March. During this period of comparative rest the soil should be kept relatively dry.

Propagation is by cuttings, 6 or 7 in. long, removed in spring with a heel of older wood to prevent bleeding. Insert these in sandy soil in a propagating frame, temperature 65°, with some bottom heat. Pot the cuttings on by stages until, by about mid-July, they reach the 7 or 8 in. pots in which they will bloom.

POLIANTHES (*Tuberose*). *P. tuberosa*, popularly known as the Tuberose, is a bulbous-rooted plant of which one hears a lot, though it is seldom to be seen. The explanation is that, though beautiful and fragrant, it is not a very satisfactory plant in this country, even under greenhouse conditions, and bulbs usually have to be re-imported every year. The single or double creamy-white flowers are produced in short spikes sometimes on rather overlong stems, though this fault can be avoided by giving the plants plenty of light throughout. Pot the bulbs in autumn or spring two or three together in 5 or 6 in. pots in weak Innes compost. Water very sparingly at first, but with increasing freedom as growth lengthens. A temperature of 65° will help to start the bulbs into growth, but once this end is achieved the plants will do better in a temperature 55–65°. While in bloom in summer or early autumn keep the house cool and equable. Syringe frequently while in growth.

PRIMULA. Without the numerous tender primulas the amateur's greenhouse would be a far less interesting place in winter and early spring than it is. Of the four important species which are grown, namely *P. obconica*, *P. sinensis*, *P. malacoides* and *P. kewensis*, the first three have given rise to a great number of varieties, and together are the most important group of flowering plants in the slightly heated greenhouse from November to April. *P. malacoides* and *P. kewensis* are almost hardy and can be grown practically without heat, except during the coldest weather.

These greenhouse primulas are all treated as annuals and raised from seed each year. The first sowing should be of *P. kewensis* in February or March followed by *P. obconica* and *P. sinensis* varieties, together with the stellata forms of *P. sinensis*, in April, all in the greenhouse in a temperature of 60°. A further sowing for succession can be made a month or six weeks after the first. *P. malacoides* may be sown in April, May and June. In all cases sow thinly in Innes seed compost and cover very lightly. Directly they can be handled, prick off the seedlings 1½ in. apart each way into well-drained trays or pans filled with the same compost. Keep them in a light airy greenhouse, shaded on the sunny side and with an average temperature of 60°, or in a frame with similar conditions. Pot singly in 2½ in. pots directly the seedlings touch in the trays. For this use the weak Innes compost. Pot again into 5 in. pots, using the medium Innes compost, directly the smaller pots become filled with roots. Big plants can receive one more shift into 6 or 7 in. pots in October, but as a rule 5 in. pots will serve for flowering. By mid-October frame plants should be removed to the greenhouse with plenty of ventilation, full light and an average temperature of 50 to

55°. Make no attempt to force the plants. Water moderately throughout, taking care to avoid wetting the leaves unduly, and above all not allowing water to lodge in the crown of the plants. Pick off any decaying or mildewed leaves. After flowering discard the plants. *P. kewensis* is bright yellow, *P. sinensis* is to be had in various shades of pink, carmine, crimson, salmon, orange and slate, together with white, *P. obconica* includes many beautiful shades of pink, rose, mauve, pale blue and white while *P. malacoides* has a range from white and palest pink to carmine. *P. obconica* and, to a lesser degree, *P. malacoides*, cause a skin rash in some persons.

The Show Auricula is also a primula and though a perfectly hardy plant must be grown under glass to preserve its flowers and the bloom of its leaves from weather damage. Plants can be raised from seed sown in spring or from divisions in June or July when repotting. Plants may be kept in a cool place outdoors all through the summer and will only need greenhouse protection from October to May. Little or no heat should be necessary but shade from strong sunshine is essential.

REHMANNIA. *R. angulata* is a tender herbaceous plant suitable for the slightly heated greenhouse. It has long spikes of rose-pink, trumpet-shaped flowers in spring and early summer and makes a good specimen in 6 or 7 in. pots. Grow in the ordinary Innes composts. Re-pot in March. Frost protection only is required. Grow in as light a place as possible. Water freely from April to October, sparingly November to March. Give shade from direct sunshine in warm weather. Propagation is usually effected by seeds germinated in May in a temperature of 60–65°, the plants being treated as biennials and discarded after flowering, though, in fact, they are true perennials and can be kept for many years. Division at potting time provides an alternative method of increase.

RHODODENDRON. The hardy rhododendrons have little place in the greenhouse though small bushes are sometimes potted in autumn and allowed to flower in a cold or slightly heated house in spring. But there are, in addition, a number of slightly tender species and hybrids, often known collectively as Himalayan rhododendrons, which are brilliant early-flowering evergreen shrubs for a cool greenhouse in which there is plenty of room. They need the same type of peaty soil which suits the outdoor types, are better grown directly in a border than in pots or tubs and need no more than a winter temperature of 40–45°. They bloom very early in the spring and have showy flower trusses similar to those of the hardy kinds in various shades of pink, salmon, orange and red, together with white. The so-called Javanese rhododendrons require similar soil but a higher temperature, 50° being the minimum in winter. If either type is grown in pots, re-pot when necessary immediately after flowering. This is also the best time for planting. Water freely from March to September, moderately the rest of the year. No pruning is needed, but faded flower heads should be removed. Daily syringing is advisable in hot weather. When grown in pots, the Himalayan kinds can be stood outdoors in a sheltered place from June to September. Increase is as for the hardy kinds (see p. 306).

RHYNCHOSPERMUM. *Rhynchospermum jasminoides* is a very beautiful climbing plant which also passes under the name *Trachelospermum jasminoides*. It is evergreen and has clusters of fragrant white flowers, not unlike those of the summer jasmine, at their best in July and August. It requires no more than frost protection, will grow in any cool greenhouse and may be trained on wires under the rafters, up pillars or against a wall. It can be grown in large pots, but is better planted directly in the greenhouse border in fairly rich but light and well-drained soil. Plant or pot in March. Water very freely in spring and summer, rather sparingly in autumn and winter, and syringe daily while the weather is warm. Give shade from direct sunshine May to September and avoid high temperatures. Shoots can be thinned out and shortened moderately immediately after flowering. Increase is by cuttings of firm young growth taken in summer and rooted in sandy soil in a propagating frame.

RICHARDIA. *R. aethiopica* is the familiar white arum lily often called 'calla' in gardens and should be correctly known as *Zantedeschia aethiopica*. There are also other species, some with coloured spathes, notably *R. Pentlandii*, which is deep yellow, and *R. Elliottiana*, a slightly paler yellow. All have fleshy roots. *R. aethiopica* should be re-potted in August or early September in the weak Innes compost and pots 6 or 7 in. in diameter. Alternatively two or three roots (each with one strong shoot) can be placed in a 10 or 12 in. pot. Stand the pots in a frame until late September with free ventilation, in fact, lights are only likely to be needed on cold nights. Water moderately at first, rather more freely as growth lengthens. Directly there is danger of frost bring the plants into a greenhouse, average temperature 45–50°. Later the temperature can be increased gradually to as much as 60° if early flowers are required, but over-hasty forcing is undesirable. Plants will flower from January to May according to the amount of heat employed. After flowering gradually harden the plants off, allowing the temperature to drop to 50–55° and giving increasing ventilation. By the end of May or early June the plants can be tapped out of their pots and planted outdoors in any sheltered place. Continue to water freely during dry weather.

R. Elliottiana and *R. Pentlandii* require a little more warmth in winter, and an average of 55° should be maintained throughout. Re-potting in the case of these species is best done in February as the flowers are produced in summer. They are kept in a greenhouse throughout.

Propagation in all cases is by careful division at potting time.

Rosa. Though roses are grown in greenhouses in vast numbers by commercial growers particularly to provide cut blooms for market, they are not ideal plants for the amateur. Only the polyantha pompon roses make really showy pot plants, and all need rather careful management or they are apt to become badly infested by red spider and thrips. Just a few climbing varieties thrive well under cool greenhouse conditions, notable amongst these being Marechal Niel, with yellow flowers, and Niphetos, which is pure white. These, however, should not be grown in pots if it is at all possible to plant them directly in the greenhouse border in deep, rich soil. Roses to be grown in pots should be young (maidens are best) and must be potted in autumn, one root in every 8 or 9 in. pot, using medium Innes compost. Make no attempt to force them the first year. They should stand in an unheated frame for at least two months after potting to form roots and, even then, should only be brought into an unheated greenhouse. Prune them in the ordinary way (see p. 327) during January and then water, moderately at first, more freely later as growth proceeds. Give full light and plenty of ventilation. When weather is hot syringe at least once daily. After flowering plunge the pots outdoors in a sunny position and continue to water freely. The following year plants well established in pots can be brought into flower early by placing them in a cool greenhouse in December or early January and gradually raising the temperature to an average of 60° by March.

Permanent climbers planted in greenhouses should be pruned when they lose their leaves in the autumn. In most cases it is enough to remove some of the older wood altogether, also weak shoots, and shorten other growths by a foot or so. Pests are most likely to be troublesome when the atmosphere in the house becomes too hot and dry in summer. Propagation is as for outdoor roses.

Saintpaulia (*African Violet*). The only species grown is *Saintpaulia ionantha*. This is a small but exceptionally beautiful plant with soft, dark green leaves and abundant violet-coloured flowers produced throughout the autumn and winter. There is no better pot plant for a moderately heated glasshouse. Good specimens can be had in pots as small as 3 in., or several plants can be grown together in a 6 in. pot or pan. Saintpaulia will thrive in sun or shade, and good specimens may often be seen under the staging, provided it is not too dark. Pot in March or April in the weak Innes compost with a little extra peat and grow in a temperature of 60–65° from April to September, when the temperature may be lowered to 55°. Give abundant water in summer, a very moderate supply in autumn and winter. Weak liquid manure can be used occasionally while plants are in flower. Propagation can be effected by division at potting time, by seeds sown in February in a temperature of 65° (the seeds are very small and should be handled in the same way as those of the begonia) or by well-developed leaves which will root readily and soon form new plants if pegged on to the surface of sandy peat in a propagating frame, temperature 70–75°, and kept moist.

SALVIA. The common scarlet salvia, *S. splendens*, is a very popular summer bedding plant which can also be used as a greenhouse pot plant for either summer or autumn flowering. In addition there are several other species, such as the blue-flowered *S. patens*, and shrubby, scarlet-flowered *S. Grahamii*, which can be grown in the greenhouse or be planted outdoors in summer. Culture varies according to species.

S. splendens and its varieties are frequently raised from seed sown in a temperature of 65° in January or February, but they can also be increased by cuttings of young shoots taken in spring and rooted in a propagating frame with gentle bottom heat. The seedlings or rooted cuttings are potted on in the ordinary Innes composts and either gradually hardened off for planting outdoors in a sunny place in early June, or worked on into 6 or 7 in. pots and kept in the greenhouse or a sunny frame from June to September. All plants should be back in the greenhouse by the end of September if required for a second year. Maintain an average temperature of 50–55° throughout autumn and winter and water rather sparingly. Water freely throughout the spring and summer. If plants are needed for autumn flowering, pick off all flowering stems until the end of September.

S. patens has tuberous roots rather like those of a dahlia and, like a dahlia, can be stored quite dry and out of soil from October to March. The roots should be in a frost-proof place. In March or early April pot in weak Innes compost using the smallest pots that will accommodate the roots. Water sparingly at first, more freely later, keeping in a temperature of 50–55°. The plants will make growth quickly and can either be planted out at the end of May or allowed to flower in pots in the greenhouse. In the case of outdoor planted roots, lift in October directly the foliage is blackened by frost and remove to a frost-proof store as before. Potted plants should be dried off gradually during September and October, and thereafter stored dry. Propagation is readily effected by cuttings of young growth in spring treated like dahlias, or by careful division of the roots at this season.

S. Grahamii is a shrub several feet in height and with a spreading habit. It can be grown in large pots in medium Innes compost and requires no more than frost protection in winter. Water sparingly October–March, freely April–September and keep in a sunny place throughout. The plant blooms throughout the summer. Propagation is by cuttings of firm young shoots in summer in a propagating frame.

SAXIFRAGA. The only saxifrage which is treated as a greenhouse plant is *S. sarmentosa*, often known as Mother of Thousands. It is a plant with slender, trailing shoots and roundish leaves which, in some varieties, are handsomely variegated with white and red. Along the length of these shoots appear tiny plantlets complete with roots, hence the popular name Mother of Thousands. The flowers are white, spidery and produced in summer, but it is grown mainly for its leaves and graceful habit. It is a first class plant for a hanging basket and, as it is almost hardy, can be grown in a greenhouse without heat. It also succeeds well as a window plant. Water freely in spring and summer, rather sparingly the rest of the year, and re-pot when necessary in March or April using the weak Innes compost. There is no difficulty about propagation as the plantlets can be removed and potted separately at almost any time of the year.

SCHIZANTHUS (*Butterfly Flower*). This most graceful flowering plant is an annual and so must be renewed from seed every year. If seeds are sown in March or April in a greenhouse with a temperature of 55° to 60° plants will be obtained to flower in August and September. A second sowing made late in August or during the first week in September will give plants to flower the following April or May. Sow thinly in ordinary John Innes compost. Prick off the seedlings into a similar mixture as soon as they can be handled and pot singly in 3-inch pots about three weeks later using the weak Innes potting compost. Pot on into 5-inch and later into 6-inch or 7-inch pots as required, using the same compost throughout. Some of the best plants may even go into 8-inch or 9-inch pots for flowering. Do not pot between November or February inclusive. All plants should have their growing tips pinched out when they are three or four inches high. As their stems lengthen they should be carefully staked and several thin stakes will be necessary for each of the larger specimens. These should be arranged to spread growth out a little like a shuttlecock.

Schizanthus appreciate cool, airy treatment throughout. In winter the temperature may average 50° and fall to 40° at times without harm. As much air as possible should be given consistent with the maintenance of these temperatures. Water fairly freely in spring and summer but rather sparingly in autumn and winter.

The flowers are usually attractively marked and the colour range includes pink, mauve, purple, carmine, crimson and white with marking of a deeper shade than the ground colour or of yellow or bronze. The large varieties will reach a height of 3 to 4 feet but there are dwarf forms which will not exceed 18 inches.

SELAGINELLA. To most amateurs the selaginellas are either 'ferns' or 'mosses' though, in fact, they have no connection, belonging to a different natural order than either of these. They are grown for their trailing (or in some species erect) moss-like foliage, which in many kinds is bronze, gold or emerald green. Selaginellas can be grown in quite small pots, or several plants together in a 6 or 7 in. pan. Use the weak Innes compost with a little extra peat and re-pot, when necessary, in March. Grow in a temperature of 45–50° in winter, 60–65° in summer, and give shade from direct sunshine from May to September inclusive. Keep the soil fairly moist throughout but make certain that drainage is good. Propagation is effected by division when potting. The trailing kinds are excellent for the front of the staging or for hanging baskets.

SMILAX. Here is another instance of the botanist and the gardener between them making a grand muddle of naming. There are genuine species of smilax grown in the garden, but they are hot house plants and comparatively rare. The cool house plant which every gardener knows as 'smilax' is a usurper of the name, being genuinely an asparagus or, according to some authorities, a myrsiphyllum. I have used the name smilax here as it is the one to which gardeners would turn automatically. *Smilax* (or *Asparagus*) *medeoloides* is a trailing, evergreen plant much used, cut, in floral decorations and also, growing, in hanging baskets. It is cultivated solely for its long trails of bright green 'leaves' and is an easily managed plant in any frost-proof greenhouse. It will thrive in sun or partial shade, can be raised easily from seed sown in February or March in a temperature of 65° and should be grown in the weak Innes compost throughout. Water freely in spring and summer.

rather sparingly autumn and winter. During warm weather the plants can be syringed daily. Re-potting of young plants should be done as frequently as necessary to prevent pots becoming overfilled with roots. Old plants can be re-potted in March or April.

SOLANUM. There are two totally distinct types of solanum popular as greenhouse plants. The better known is the bushy *S. Capsicastrum*, often known as the Winter Cherry, because of the bright orange-scarlet fruits about the shape and size of cherries which are produced in mid-winter. It is a very popular plant for Christmas decorations and will make a neat, evergreen bush in 5 or 6 in. pots. It is usually grown from seed sown in the greenhouse, temperature 65°, in February or early March. The seedlings are potted on in the ordinary Innes composts until, by the end of May, they reach the 5 or 6 in. pots in which they will flower. Keep well watered during the summer and stand outdoors or in a sunny frame from June to September, as plenty of air will help the flowers to set. From late September onwards keep in a light, airy greenhouse, average temperature 50°, and water moderately.

If desired, plants can be kept from one year to another, but better results are obtained with young plants. An alternative method of propagation is to take cuttings of young shoots, plenty of which can be obtained in March or April from old cut back plants placed in a temperature of 60–65°. These will root freely in sandy soil in a propagating frame with gentle bottom heat.

The other type of greenhouse solanum consists of vigorous climbing plants, of which the best is *S. jasminoides*. This bears clusters of white flowers, rather like those of summer jasmine, and is in bloom throughout the summer. It can be grown in large pots, but is better planted out in the greenhouse border in rich, well-drained soil. It should have plenty of head room and may be trained to wires under the rafters, up a pillar or against a wall. It needs frost protection in winter, but can be grown without heat for most of the year. Water freely from April to September, sparingly from October to March. Regular pruning is unnecessary, but weak or old stems can be removed and overgrown vines shortened each February. Increase by cuttings of young shoots rooted in spring in sandy soil in a propagating frame with gentle bottom heat. Another even more vigorous kind with lilac-blue flowers is *S. Wendlandii*. It requires similar treatment.

SPARRMANIA. *S. africana* is the only species grown and it is a useful, if rather large, flowering shrub for the cool greenhouse. In habit it looks a little like a large pelargonium with semi-woody growth and clusters of white flowers, which can be had most of the year. Left to its own devices it will grow 10 ft. or more high, but fairly small specimens can be maintained in pots by hard pruning each February. Re-pot in March in the weak Innes compost. Water freely from the time growth commences until October, but sparingly in autumn and winter. Plants can be stood outdoors in a sunny place from June to September inclusive, in fact the conditions required are very much the same as for zonal-leaved pelargoniums. Increase is by cuttings in a propagating frame in spring or early summer.

STATICE. In addition to the well-known annual statices (see p. 122) and the hardy perennial kinds (see p. 178) there are several beautiful species grown mainly as pot plants in the greenhouse. The best of these are *S. profusa*, which is a perennial, rather like the hardy *S. latifolia* in habit, with densely branched heads of small purple flowers in late summer, and *S. Suworowii*, an annual with pink flowers carried in long, narrow, erect spikes which are branched like a candelabrum. It is an extremely distinctive plant and well worth growing. *S. profusa* is increased by cuttings prepared in spring from side shoots and rooted in a propagating frame with a little bottom heat. The cuttings are potted on in the ordinary Innes composts until they reach 5 or 6 in. pots in which the plants will bloom. Throughout the spring and summer they should have an average temperature of 55–60°, falling in autumn and winter to 45–50°. Water freely in spring and summer, but very sparingly the rest of the year. Old plants can be re-potted in March. *S. puberula*, which is rather similar in appearance, can be raised readily from seed sown in January–February.

S. Suworowii is also raised from seed sown in a temperature of 60° in February or early March. The seedlings are potted on through the usual Innes composts until they reach 4 or 5 in. pots in which they will flower during the summer. After flowering the plants should be discarded. Full sun should be given throughout. Artificial heat is unlikely to be necessary after April.

STEPHANOTIS. Only one species is grown, *S. floribunda*. This is an exceptionally beautiful climber with clusters of intensely fragrant, tubular, waxy-white flowers in late spring. It is a vigorous twiner and should be planted, for preference, directly in the greenhouse border in a position where it has plenty of headroom and wires or a trellis up which to climb. Maintain a temperature of 65° or more from April to September, and 55–60° October to March for it is a warmth loving plant; indeed if a little more heat can be given, so much the better. Water very freely April to September and syringe at least once daily,

except when flowering, when the atmosphere should be a little drier.
Immediately after flowering all shoots can be shortened considerably
to encourage vigorous new growth to bloom the following year.
Increase by cuttings of firm young growth removed with a heel of
older wood in spring and rooted in a propagating frame, temperature
65–70° with some bottom heat as well. Grow throughout in the weak
Innes compost.

STRELITZIA (*Bird of Paradise Flower*). *Strelitzia Reginae* is one of the
most exotic looking of all greenhouse plants. It grows 5 or 6 ft. high with
a corresponding spread and needs very large pots or small tubs so is not
a suitable subject for small greenhouses. The leaves are several feet in
length, evergreen and very handsome, while the flowers, which are
carried on stout, stiffly erect stems 4 or 5 ft. in height, are shaped
rather like the crest of a bird of paradise and are orange and violet. The
plant always attracts much comment when in bloom and is at its best
in May and June.

Grow in the weak Innes compost and re-pot, when necessary, in
March. During the autumn and winter keep in an average temperature of
55°, though a little more warmth is advantageous. If possible the average should be raised to 65° from April onwards. Water very freely
while the plant is making growth from about April to September and
maintain a moist atmosphere during this period, but be rather sparing
with water the rest of the year, especially during cold weather. No
shade is needed at any time. Increase can be effected by seeds, but a
simpler method for the amateur is to divide old plants at potting time.
The divisions should be given a little extra warmth and syringed
frequently until well established.

STREPTOCARPUS. This is one of the most important of flowering plants
for the moderately heated greenhouse to give colour in summer and
early autumn. Most of the kinds now cultivated are hybrids. They have
very showy, trumpet-shaped flowers produced freely in loose clusters
on erect 12–18 in. stems. They may be raised from seeds which are
sown in a temperature of 65° either in January or February for autumn
flowering or July for flowering the following summer. Being very
small the seeds should be treated exactly like those of begonia (see p.
440). Plants can also be propagated from mature leaves, which will root
readily and form new plants if pegged to the surface of sandy peat in a
propagating frame with bottom heat in spring or summer. Seed is the
better method for the amateur. Grow on in the weak Innes compost
throughout, potting seedlings first into 3 in., then into 4 in., and finally
into 5 or 6 in. pots in which they will flower. Water freely throughout

this period and give weak liquid manure occasionally when in the final pots. Syringe between the pots frequently in summer to maintain moisture in the atmosphere. Shade from direct sunshine from May to September. If plants are to be kept from year to year they should be wintered rather dry, though not bone dry, in a light greenhouse, average temperature 50°, but are seldom worth keeping beyond their second year.

STREPTOSOLEN. *S. Jamesonii* is the only species cultivated and this is a greenhouse climber with brilliant orange flowers in early summer. Good specimens can be had in large pots or grown direct in the greenhouse border under the ordinary cool house conditions, i.e. winter temperature of 50–55°, summer 60–65°. Grow in the medium Innes compost, giving plenty of water from April to September and keeping the soil just moist the rest of the year. A little shade is required from strong direct sunshine. Flowering shoots should be pruned hard immediately the flowers fade to prevent the plant from becoming straggly. Increase by cuttings of young growth rooted in spring or summer in a propagating frame, preferably with a little bottom heat.

TACSONIA. These are very brightly coloured climbers closely allied to the passion flower (see p. 487) but too vigorous for the ordinary greenhouse, requiring big, moderately heated conservatories to be really satisfactory. Plant in rich, loamy soil direct in the greenhouse border in March and train to wires, beneath the rafters or up walls. Grow in a rather moist atmosphere with daily syringing in spring and summer and water very freely at this period. In winter the air should be much drier, the water supply moderate and the temperature around 45°. Plants can be thinned out and pruned back moderately each February. One of the best kinds is *Van Volxemii*, with scarlet flowers. All bloom in summer. Propagation is the same as for passiflora (see p. 488).

TECOMA. Another family of vigorous and brilliant greenhouse climbers, and this time closely related to the bignonias, some of which are hardy enough to be grown outdoors in sheltered places (see p. 443). Tecomas have big, tubular, orange, red or pink flowers in summer. They can be grown in large pots or tubs, but are better planted direct in the border in a sunny greenhouse with plenty of headroom, so that they can be trained to wires or trellis work. Water freely in spring and summer, very sparingly autumn and winter. Syringeing is only required in hot weather to keep down red spider, and heat only needed in winter in exclude frost. Prune back the previous year's growth by about one-third to one-half each February and remove some of the oldest vines altogether. The tecomas can be increased readily by cuttings prepared from the ends of shoots in spring and rooted in sandy soil in a propagating frame with bottom heat.

THUNBERGIA. Many species of thunbergia require too much heat for the average privately owned greenhouse, but *T. alata* and its hybrids are easily managed without artificial heat for the greater part of the year, though a moderate degree of warmth is necessary to germinate the seeds by which it is most readily propagated. It is an attractive trailing or twining plant with cream and dark purple flowers throughout the summer and it is usually treated as an annual, plants being discarded in autumn after flowering. Germinate the seeds in a temperature of 65° in March. Pot on the seedlings through the ordinary Innes composts until, by early June, they reach the 5 in. pots or hanging baskets in which they will flower. Water freely throughout the growing season. Give all the sunlight possible and ventilate as freely as possible consistent with an average temperature of 55–60°.

TILLANDSIA. These plants have dropped out of favour, but one or two kinds are still worth growing, either for their handsome foliage or for their curiously flattened spikes of flowers with showy coloured bracts. Two of the best are *T. Lindeniana*, with deep olive green leaves and blue flowers surrounded by pink bracts, and *T. splendens*, which has leaves banded with deep brown on a green base and white flowers with pink bracts. All make excellent pot plants for the moderately heated greenhouse in sun or shade. Good specimens are to be had in 5 or 6 in. pots. A temperature of 55–60° should be maintained in winter, rising to 70° or more in summer. Water very freely and syringe frequently from April to September, but give only a moderate water supply and no syringing in autumn and winter. Grow in the weak Innes compost and re-pot, when necessary, in March. Plants can be increased at the same time by breaking off rooted offsets.

TRACHELIUM. *T. caeruleum* is a dainty plant with dome-shaped heads of feathery blue flowers on 18 in. stems throughout the summer. It is almost always grown as an annual, seed being sown in February or March in a temperature of 60° and the seedlings potted on in the ordinary Innes composts until, by late May or early June, they reach 4 or 5 in. pots. Stake carefully with a few thin twigs or split bamboo canes. Keep in a sunny greenhouse throughout with free ventilation and an average temperature of 55°. Water fairly freely throughout the season. After flowering it is best to discard the plants. There is a pure white variety.

TRADESCANTIA. This is one of those plants which has so many synonyms that it is almost impossible to sort things out correctly.

Rhoeo or zebrina is probably the correct name for the plant which every gardener knows as *Tradescantia zebrina*. It is one of the most useful small trailing foliage plants with which to drape the front of the staging in greenhouses or to use in hanging baskets. It has oval, glossy leaves of bright green striped with white. There is also another kind, known as *T. discolor*, in which the leaves are green above and pale purple beneath. Both will grow in the ordinary greenhouse temperature, minimum 45° in winter rising to 60° or 65° in summer. They can be grown in small pots or hanging baskets or may be planted direct in a border of soil. Water freely in spring and summer, moderately autumn and winter. Give a little shade from strong sunshine in summer and syringe occasionally to keep the air reasonably moist. Pot in spring in the weak Innes compost and increased by cuttings of young shoots dibbled in sandy soil in a propagating frame at almost any time of the year.

TRITONIA. This genus is closely allied to the familiar hardy plants known as montbretias, but *T. crocata*, the only species likely to be found in British gardens, is an attractive but rather tender corm grown as a pot plant in slightly heated greenhouses. The flowers are bright orange or, in some forms, orange-red on slender foot high stems and are at their best in early summer. Pot four or five corms together during November in weak Innes compost in a 4 in. pot, place in an unheated greenhouse or frame for a couple of months and then, when plenty of roots have been formed, bring into a slightly heated house to hurry the plants into bloom. Water very sparingly at first, but with increasing freedom as growth lengthens. After flowering gradually reduce the water supply so that, by about August, the foliage dies down and the corms can be stored dry until re-potting time. Propagation is by removal of small corms when potting.

TROPAEOLUM. Here again matters have been confused for the beginner as the tropaeolum family includes the plant with which he is familiar as nasturtium (see p. 113). However, there are a few species commonly grown under glass or only used for summer bedding outdoors and kept in a glasshouse for the rest of the year which retain the name tropaeolum in most gardens. The best of these are varieties of *T. Lobbianum*, of which there are a great number, many with double scarlet or yellow flowers, though there are also single-flowered forms. All are trailing or climbing plants of moderate vigour which make excellent pot plants if trained around two or three bamboo canes or over a crinoline framework of wire. They can be increased very readily by cuttings of young shoots in spring or late summer. These cuttings should be inserted in very sandy soil and rooted in a propagating frame, preferably with gentle bottom heat. Single-flowered kinds can be raised from seed sown in February or July. Pot on the seedlings or rooted cuttings through the ordinary Innes composts until they reach 5–7 in. pots, which will be large enough for good sized flowering plants. A temperature of 45–50° should be maintained from October to March and can rise to 55° or more from the latter date on. Plants can either be flowered in a sunny greenhouse, or may be planted out in well-drained soil and a sunny place in early June. In either place they will bloom most of the summer.

TUBEROSE.—*See* POLIANTHES (p. 491).

VALLOTA (*Scarborough Lily*). *V. purpurea* is a bulbous plant with trumpet-shaped flowers in a cluster on stiff stems in late summer and early autumn. The flowers are scarlet rather than purple, as the name would suggest, and very showy. The leaves are strap-shaped, similar to those of an amaryllis. There are several forms, one known as *major*, of extra size, and another *minor*, which is comparatively small. All have the merit of being very easily grown, requiring little or no artificial heat and making, for short periods, excellent room plants. Pot the bulbs in March in weak Innes compost, one bulb in a 4 or 5 in. pot. Water very sparingly at first and then more freely as growth appears. From this period on keep in a sunny greenhouse with a temperature of 50° or more, though it will not hurt if it occasionally drops to 45°. After flowering reduce the quantity of water fairly rapidly and keep the soil no more than barely moist from November to March. Re-potting is not essential every year as vallotas flower most freely when slightly pot bound. They can be increased easily by division at potting time.

VELTHEIMIA. This is another family of bulbous-rooted plants requiring much the same conditions regarding temperature as the Vallotas. They should, however, be potted in August or September as they flower in winter. Water moderately during the succeeding months and then, after the flowers fade, gradually reduce the water supply until the soil is almost dry by June, when the plants may rest in an unheated greenhouse. Winter temperature need not exceed 55°, but frost must be excluded at all times. The flowers are orange, tubular and clustered in a small spike at the top of a bare stem, the whole having somewhat the appearance of a small red hot poker.

VERBENA, LEMON-SCENTED.—*See* LIPPIA (p. 481).

ZANTEDESCHIA.—*See* RICHARDIA (p. 493).

CHAPTER XIX

Chrysanthemums Indoors and Out

NO COMPLETELY exotic flower has obtained so great a hold on British gardeners as the chrysanthemum. There are chrysanthemum societies in all parts of the British Isles, a great many of these hold shows devoted exclusively to the chrysanthemum and in addition there are chrysanthemum classes in most of the general autumn flower shows. The literature of the chrysanthemum is extensive and the number of amateur and professional specialists immense. The chrysanthemum has often been termed the autumn queen of flowers, a description which would place it second to the rose alone and this is no exaggeration.

TYPES. In formulating any classification of this great family the first division to make is between outdoor (or border) and greenhouse varieties. The distinction is less one of hardiness than of season. All chrysanthemum flowers are damaged by frost. In consequence any variety which blooms after the end of September is unreliable for outdoor cultivation without protection. On the other hand August and early September blooming varieties can be flowered outdoors even in the north, though they may need some protection to bring them safely through severe winters.

In addition to this seasonal division there are many subdivisions principally based upon the shape and size of the flowers. There are, for example, single, anemone centred (semi-double) and fully double flowered forms in both outdoor and indoor sections. The doubles may be further grouped into large flowered exhibition types and smaller flowered decorative types. Then there are forms with the outer petals curving outwards (recurving) and, in contrast, others with all the petals curving inwards (incurving). What may be described as a super-development of the last named is the exhibition incurve in which the petals are placed with such accuracy that each bloom makes a perfect globe. The production of the faultless incurve is, perhaps, the height of the chrysanthemum grower's art.

Even so the list of chrysanthemum types is not complete. To it must be added the pompon, with masses of small rounded blooms; the thread petalled type and rather similar though more substantial Rayonante, both out of favour at present; and the comparatively new

Korean, a race of very hardy chrysanthemums which were at first mainly single flowered but are being rapidly developed to include other types of bloom.

The cascade chrysanthemum is yet another interesting class. It is the habit of this that is distinctive, the stems being particularly wiry and freely branched. Left to its own devices it makes a big bush but with a little skilful training it can be made to hang down in a perfect cascade of growth and flower.

PROPAGATION. All chrysanthemums can be increased by division of the roots but in practice this method is not used except, occasionally, for the Koreans and the commoner outdoor types. Increase by cuttings is the general rule and results in a healthier and more satisfactory plant.

Seed, which provides the only other means of increase, germinates readily in a warm greenhouse in spring but seedlings vary greatly in colour and sometimes in type so this is not a satisfactory means of increasing selected varieties except in the case of the 'Charm' varieties. It is, however, the method by which most new varieties are produced.

Cuttings can be taken at any time of the year, December to March being the main propagating season with extension to April for small plants to be flowered in 4 or 5 in. pots.

The best cuttings are those prepared from shoots which come through the soil direct from the roots. Shoots from the old woody stems can be used but seldom make such satisfactory plants or produce such good blooms. They often have a tendency to flower prematurely, or to produce blind buds.

Plenty of suitable basal shoots are usually produced by the plant after it has finished flowering. As far as possible work should commence on the greenhouse varieties, particularly those that are to be flowered on second crown buds (see p. 510) the outdoor varieties being left until February and March.

All the cuttings are taken in exactly the same way. The shoots are severed when about 2 to 2½ in. long. They are cut off below soil level and prepared by being trimmed cleanly just below a joint. The lower leaves, if any, are removed and the cutting is dibbled, about three quarters of an inch deep, into sandy soil. This may be in a pot, box or bed but should, for preference, be in a slightly heated greenhouse. Cuttings can be struck without heat but it is more difficult and there are likely to be more failures than when a temperature of 45–50° can be maintained irrespective of weather.

The cuttings need not be kept in a very close, damp atmosphere, but they should be watered fairly freely and be shaded from strong sunshine. They usually flag a little at first but pick up after a week or so and are beginning to root in from two to three weeks.

POTTING. As soon as the cuttings commence to grow they should be lifted carefully and potted singly in small flower pots and a rather fine compost. The John Innes formula for first potting (see p. 421) will do excellently. Thereafter the plants should be grown on steadily in a temperature of about 50° with as much ventilation as the weather allows and all the daylight possible.

They will need to be potted on as the pots become filled with roots. First they will go into 4 in. pots and then, in the case of indoor varieties into the 8½ or 9 in. pots in which they will flower. For each successive potting the soil mixture is made rather coarser than before and more fertiliser is added (see p. 422). Some growers prefer to add a little well-rotted dung to the compost for the final potting and this certainly does help to counteract any mineral deficiencies in the soil.

The final potting for indoor varieties should not be later than mid-June; usually it is nearly a month earlier than this. Outdoor chrysanthemums often do not get beyond their first pots as they can generally be planted outdoors early in May and, as they are rooted late, they have not outgrown their first pots by that date.

All potting, and especially the later pottings of indoor varieties, should be very firm.

PLANTING OUTDOOR CHRYSANTHEMUMS. The ground in which outdoor chrysanthemums are to be planted out must be well dug and moderately manured. Well rotted stable manure is best for this purpose but any form of bulky organic manure may be used at the rate of about 1 cwt. to 12 sq. yd. Get this preparatory work finished at least a month in advance of planting time so that the ground may have time to settle. Finish off with a dusting of bone meal, 4 oz. per sq. yd., well raked in.

Plant out when the soil is in good working condition, neither too wet nor too dry, and choose a period when the weather seems fairly settled and mild. For two or three weeks prior to this the plants should be in an unheated frame with gradually increasing ventilation to harden them off and it is unwise to plant out until they have had at least a week without any protection other than that given by the surrounding walls of the frame.

Plant firmly and space the plants at least eighteen inches apart each way. A more usual method for cutting or exhibition is to have them eighteen inches apart in double rows with 2½ foot alleyways between.

SUMMER TREATMENT. Apart from stopping and disbudding which I have described separately (see p. 509), summer treatment resolves itself into staking and tying, necessary for both outdoor and indoor types; watering, usually only necessary with plants in pots; feeding, and the maintenance of a close watch for pests or disease.

Pot plants can usually be stood outdoors by the first week in June. A sunny position should be chosen, open but free from cutting draughts. It is an advantage if the pots can stand on a good ash base or on slates or planks. This will prevent worms entering through the drainage holes, blocking the latter up and disturbing the roots.

Water may be needed daily during hot weather. Sufficient must be given at each application to soak right through the soil and run out at the drainage hole in the bottom of the pot. No more should be given till the soil begins to look dry or the pot rings when struck with a small wooden hammer.

Support is best given by 4 ft. bamboo canes—at least one per plant and preferably more in the case of big specimens. In the case of pot plants it is a wise precaution to have stout stakes driven firmly into the standing ground every few feet, with a horizontal wire strained between these $3\frac{1}{2}$ ft. above ground level. Then each cane can be tied to this wire, which will prevent many breakages during windy weather.

FEEDING. This may commence as soon as the plants are well settled in their summer quarters and continue until the flower buds commence to show colour. Little and often is the rule and feeding should be varied a little. There are many good proprietary chrysanthemum fertilisers which should be used according to manufacturers' instructions. These may be varied with natural liquid manure made by steeping well decayed dung in water and diluting the liquid to the colour of straw. This can then be used freely as for plain water.

A good chemical fertiliser can be made at home with four parts by weight superphosphate of lime, two parts sulphate of ammonia and one part sulphate of potash. Use this mixture at the rate of a teaspoonful per plant or per gallon of water every five to ten days.

AUTUMN PROTECTION. By the end of September most indoor varieties should be removed from their summer standing ground and be brought into a greenhouse. Outdoor varieties that have not finished blooming should be protected in some way, as with hessian pulled each night over a framework of laths. A few degrees of frost may be enough to damage the flowers or flower buds though the plants themselves will suffer no harm from much colder weather.

Give the plants as much room as possible in the greenhouse. The more light and air they get the better. Overcrowding will encourage such diseases as mildew and may spoil the quality of the flowers.

Nevertheless too much heat is equally bad and will weaken the plants. Never forget that they are nearly hardy, that little more than frost protection is required and that the more sturdy the plants are the better it will be for them.

TREATMENT AFTER FLOWERING. When the blooms fade or have been cut the plants, whether indoors or out, should be cut back to within a few inches of soil level. This will encourage the production of the basal shoots already described as providing the best material for propagation. At this stage it is an advantage to lift outdoor varieties and transfer them to a frame or greenhouse. The roots can be packed quite close together providing there is a good dividing mark between one variety and another. This measure of protection will encourage the production of cuttings and provide an insurance against losses in the open border, which are likely to occur particularly in wet cold winters.

STOPPING. In linked operations of stopping and disbudding lies much of the art of chrysanthemum culture. To understand either a knowledge of the natural habit of the chrysanthemum is necessary.

Left to its own devices a rooted cutting, after growing a single stem for a while, will produce a small flower bud. This is known as a 'break bud' because it prevents further extension of that particular shoot and causes it to branch or 'break'. This flower bud rarely develops into a bloom and is important mainly because of its function in causing branching.

The shoots which appear as a result of this 'breaking' will grow on again without further branching until they too are terminated by flower buds. These are known as 'first crown buds' and are usually quite capable of developing into good flowers.

Whether they do so or not the plant, if left alone, will produce a fresh lot of shoots just below the flower buds and these will again grow on upwards. In time more buds will terminate the new shoots and these are generally exactly like the earlier buds in every respect except the time at which they appear. They are known as 'second crown' buds.

Again the process of branching and extension will continue but this is the last time that the plant will grow on upwards. The next lot of buds to appear will be different in character from those that have gone before. Not only will they terminate each shoot but there will be other flower buds clustering in the leaf axils below the central buds. These take the place of the growth buds which formerly appeared in this position and so effectively put a stop to growth for the season. This last group of buds are known as 'terminal buds'.

It will be seen that the gardener usually has a choice of three distinct sets of flower buds. All differ in the time at which they appear and the last also differs in kind.

By deciding arbitrarily which of these buds shall flower and which shall not, the gardener can influence to a considerable degree the time at which the flowers are produced. This is known as timing and may be of first rate importance to him. By means of it he may so manipulate things that a chrysanthemum which would normally be too late or too early for his particular show is, in fact, just right on the day. He can also use it to hasten the outdoor flowering of varieties which might otherwise be so late that they would be damaged by frost.

There is yet another consideration. Experience has proved that, despite the similarity in appearance of the first two of this bud series, the quality of bloom produced by each is not always identical. There are some varieties which give a more perfect flower from the first crown bud than from the second crown bud and vice versa. The clever exhibitor will naturally cash in on knowledge of this sort.

Nor is it necessary for the gardener to wait until the plant branches naturally through the production of one or other of these buds. He can hasten nature's process by nipping out the growing tip of the plant at any stage. For example if he knows that a certain variety will take ten weeks from the production of its break bud to the production of its first crown bud and that this will be a week too late for his purpose, he may pinch the tip out of the young plant a week before the break bud is due to appear. Later buds may be 'timed' in the same way.

Finally there is the peculiarity of the terminal bud to be considered. This seldom produces as good an individual bloom as either of the crown buds but, unlike them, it is surrounded by a lot of other flower buds at practically the same stage of development. Consequently if all are left they will together form a spray of small flowers which for certain decorative purposes is more effective than a solitary large bloom.

DISBUDDING. So much then, for stopping and timing. Now how does the gardener pin the plant down to flower on the particular bud or buds he has selected? Simply by removing all other growths which might interfere with this. In practice this, as a rule, means the removal of the shoots which appear in the axils of the leaves below the first or second crown buds—whichever the grower decides to use.

This kind of disbudding is really very little different from that applied to many other kinds of flower but the chrysanthemum grower, perhaps liking to be different, seldom calls it disbudding, but refers to it as 'taking the bud'. This is apt to be misleading for the beginner as the bud is not taken in the sense of being removed but just the reverse. One might, in fact, refer to it as 'taking for keeps', the point being that the bud is very carefully preserved for flowering and all growth which might interfere with this is removed.

Stopping and bud-taking suggestions will be found in most catalogues issued by chrysanthemum specialists. They use a peculiar jargon of their own which needs a little understanding. Here are a few of the usual phrases with their meaning:

'Natural break, first crown'—meaning that the plant is to be allowed to grow on and branch once naturally after which the first bud that appears will be preserved for flowering.

'Stop April 20th, for first crown'—which is similar to the last except that the tip of the rooted cutting is to be pinched out on April 20th instead of being allowed to grow on until a break bud appears and stops it.

'Natural break, second crown'—which means that the cutting is to be allowed to branch naturally and then, when the first crown bud appears this is to be rubbed off and the plant left to branch again and produce second crown buds which will then be preserved for flowering.

'Stop May 1st and June 1st for second crown buds'—the object in this case being to anticipate the normal branching of the plant twice over and so get a second crown but considerably earlier than by natural means.

One last point. It may appear from all this talk about branching that the later the bud retained the more flowers the plant will carry. Left alone in other respects this would be exactly the result obtained. But this by no means always suits the chrysanthemum grower's ideas. Too many flowers means that all will be small. So, if the plant is being grown for exhibition, there is usually a drastic thinning out of shoots after each stopping or natural branching. It may be that at the finish, when a plant has branched twice and is forming second crown buds, it has no more than two or three shoots and consequently two or three buds. Occasionally, for very keen competition in large-flowered exhibition classes, no more than one bloom per plant is permitted. For decorative purposes more flowers may be retained but even with these, if solitary, rather than spray blooms are required, the plant is usually restricted to about eight final stems.

CHAPTER XX

Orchids

THERE IS widespread belief that orchids are difficult to grow and very expensive. Both ideas are true of certain kinds of orchid but it is quite possible for many beautiful species and varieties to be grown in an ordinary greenhouse with no more skill than would be required to produce good plants of, say, begonias or cyclamen, and at a very similar cost. Orchid growing on a small scale has been developed very widely in the Midlands and North of England. It is no uncommon thing in those parts of the country to meet miners, cotton spinners and other industrial workers who cultivate orchids as a hobby in houses no more than 8 ft. wide by 12 ft. long. There is not the least reason why orchids should not enjoy the same general popularity in other parts of the country.

As regards culture, orchids can conveniently be considered under three headings; cool house kinds; those requiring the conditions known as 'intermediate', and genuine hot house varieties. It is only the last that must remain in the province of the specialist and the well-to-do. Temperatures averaging 70 deg. or more in winter can only be maintained at considerable cost in fuel and it is not surprising that nurserymen have to ask fairly high prices for orchids which are so expensive to maintain.

WHAT TO GROW. The cool house orchids are undoubtedly the easiest for the beginner. Included in this group are most of the *odontoglossums*, which are unrivalled as cut flowers; *odontiodas*, handsome hybrids from the last; the *cymbidiums*, which will possibly withstand more ill treatment than any other genus of orchids; the very numerous *cypripediums* obtained from that grand plant, *Cypripedium insigne*, and *oncidiums*, in my opinion the most graceful of all orchids. All these can be grown in any greenhouse in which a minimum winter temperature of 45 deg. can be maintained. In fact it will not hurt if the temperature occasionally falls to 40 deg. I have even heard of *cymbidiums* which survived two or three years in an unheated greenhouse in which some of the panes had been broken by bombing. Moreover these plants had had very little attention. True they were in bad condition, but they were alive and quickly responded to better treatment. In the cool house the average summer temperature should be around 60 deg. with 50–55 deg. as the average during the winter months.

If a little more warmth is available, say a minimum of 55 deg. in winter with an average of 60 deg. rising to 70 or 75 deg. in summer, the orchid grower can include *miltonias*, many *cattleyas*, including the hybrid *brasso-* and *laelio-cattleyas*, the *laelias* and *brassavolas* themselves and those *cypripediums* which have mottled leaves as distinct from the plain green leaves of *Cypripedium insigne*. Some *dendrobiums* can also be grown, though there are species which require higher temperatures to be really satisfactory.

In the hot house with a minimum winter temperature of 65 deg. and a summer average something over 80 deg. one can grow *angraecums*, *vandas*, *calanthes*, *phaius*, *phalaenopsis* and many other genera.

MANAGEMENT OF THE ORCHID HOUSE. So much then for temperatures which, it will be seen, very closely resemble those required by other classes of greenhouse plants. Much the same also applies to ventilation and atmospheric moisture. Most cultivated orchids are, or have originated from, tropical or semi-tropical plants thriving in humid forests and similar places. It follows that they require a fair amount of moisture in the greenhouse atmosphere. For this reason it is seldom wise to cultivate orchids on open lath staging. They can be managed in this way, but it is easier to grow them successfully on a solid staging with the pots stood on an ash or gravel base. It is then possible to damp down between the pots daily or, in hot weather, two or three times daily using an ordinary garden syringe or a watering can with a fine rose. An alternative, and one which has much to recommend it, is to erect a lath staging 6 or 8 in. above one of the solid type, stand the plants on the upper staging and apply the moisture to the lower one. This simplifies the work of daily damping down and ensures a good circulation of air around the plants and a free outlet for surplus water from the pots in which they are grown.

Ventilation follows the same general lines as for other greenhouse plants, though it is particularly important that the orchid house should be fitted with side as well as top ventilators so that some air can be admitted even in cold weather. Cold draughts must be avoided at all times, also any sudden and rapid fluctuation of the temperature. In general ventilation will be fairly free from April to September and then more and more sparing as the winter approaches. In mid-winter it will only be possible to open the side ventilators a little for a few hours on fine days.

POTTING AND COMPOSTS. It is in the compost in which the plants are grown that orchids vary most widely from other greenhouse plants. Here, for once, we have to forsake the standard potting composts which are so useful elsewhere and employ special mixtures for the various genera. New materials also make their appearance, notably sphagnum moss and osmunda fibre, the latter being obtained from the decayed foliage and roots of the royal fern. Loam does not enter very largely into orchid composts except in the case of *cypripediums, cymbidiums* and *calanthes*. Old time growers usually employ finely crushed crocks to keep the compost open, but there is no real objection to the use of coarse silver sand as for other greenhouse plants. When osmunda fibre is not obtainable good grade orchid peat should be used instead, but it is not quite as satisfactory as the fibre.

Typical potting composts are as follows. For *cypripediums* of the *insigne* type and also for *cymbidiums* and *calanthes* 1 part by loose bulk of osmunda fibre or fibrous peat, 1 part sphagnum moss and 3 parts good fibrous loam, which must be lime free. The sphagnum moss should be well chopped up and the osmunda fibre and loam pulled to pieces but, except for small plants, not put through a sieve.

For cool house orchids, such as *odontoglossums, oncidiums* and *odontiodas*, equal parts of osmunda fibre or fibrous peat and sphagnum moss. For *cattleyas, laelias, dendrobiums, aerides* and *vandas* 2 to 3 parts of osmunda fibre to 1 part of peat.

In all cases sufficient sand or broken crocks must be added to keep the compost open.

The actual operation of potting differs in some important respects from that of other greenhouse plants. First considerably more drainage material is used, the pots usually being filled at least one-third with broken crocks, on top of which may be placed a good wad of sphagnum moss. On this porous base the plant is set in position and the compost placed around it in the ordinary way, being worked between the roots with the fingers and, where necessary, a small potting stick. Finally a few live pieces of sphagnum moss are dibbled into the surface so that they quickly grow and form a living carpet right over the top of the pot.

Many orchids make pseudo-bulbs, that is to say bulb-like parts which stick up above the soil and from which the leaves and flower stems grow. Each year fresh pseudo-bulbs are added in front of the old ones and, when orchids of this type are re-potted, the older pseudo-bulbs with attached rhizome and roots should always be cut off and discarded unless required to provide extra plants. They tend to harbour pests and disease germs and are a hindrance rather than a help to the plant. The best time for potting orchids is when they commence to make new roots. This will vary according to the species under consideration but it is quite easy to ascertain as some of the roots are produced on the surface and can be seen quite clearly. It is seldom that annual repotting is necessary. Most kinds can remain in their pots for two or even three years without disturbance, though it is wise to over-haul all plants annually and, if necessary, remove a little of the top compost and replace with fresh compost and live sphagnum moss. For a week or so after re-potting orchids should always be kept a little warmer and in a slightly moister atmosphere than normally but water should be rather reduced.

WATERING. This task, with both newly potted plants and those well established, is perhaps the most difficult part of culture for the novice to learn. There is no easy guide as in the case of other greenhouse plants. Tapping the pots will not help, nor can their degree of moisture be gauged easily by testing their weight. It is really a matter which must be learnt by experience, the ideal being to keep the compost moist right through during the growing season, but never sodden. In the case of those kinds which make pseudo-bulbs, very little water will be needed during the resting period, lasting usually two or three months and start-ing some time after the plants have flowered. Orchids which have no pseudo-bulbs need water throughout the year though, of course, less when they are resting than when they are growing rapidly.

PROPAGATION. The only really satisfactory method of propagation for the amateur grower is by division, which can be carried out at potting time. Those varieties which have no pseudo-bulbs are divided just like any other fibrous rooted plants. It will be found that orchids with pseudo-bulbs also make rhizomes, that is creeping stems lying flat on the surface of the compost. It is from these rhizomes that the pseudo-bulbs grow. Division in this case consists in cutting through the rhizome so that each portion contains at least two pseudo-bulbs. Care must be taken to avoid unnecessary injury to the roots.

New orchids are, of course, produced by hybridisation and sub-sequent seed raising, but this is entirely a job for the specialist.

CHAPTER XXI
Cacti and Succulents

ALTHOUGH IT is customary to talk of cacti and succulents as though they were distinct groups of plants the actual fact is that the term succulents, embracing as it does all fleshy-leaved plants, includes cacti which merely form a section in the group. Cacti all belong to one family of plants, the *Cactaceae,* whereas succulents belong to many different families often quite unrelated. The thick, fleshy-leaves or stems common to all these plants are constructed to hold moisture and so enable them to withstand long periods of drought. This really gives the key to the cultivation of all cacti and succulents. They all come from regions where drought is common and many are desert plants accustomed to a maximum of sunshine and, at any rate for long periods, a minimum of water.

In their native habitats these plants mostly go to rest during the dry season and then grow very actively when rain does fall. Almost all are used to stony or sandy soils and for successful cultivation must have a more open and gritty compost than is common for other classes of greenhouse plants.

Not that all cacti and succulents are tender and need greenhouse protection. A few are hardy enough to stand outdoors throughout the year, at any rate in the milder parts of the country and near the coast. Nevertheless it is as pot plants that cacti and succulents are most familiar and most useful to the amateur gardener.

There is great variety in form and character amongst these plants and though some seldom produce flowers and are grown principally for their strange shape, patterned spines or dense covering of filaments others bloom quite freely and are often of exceptional beauty. It is possible, in a greenhouse from which frost can be excluded at all times and in which average temperatures of around 45 deg. winter and 60 deg. summer can be maintained, to grow a wide selection of these plants. It is even possible to cultivate many cacti and succulents successfully on a sunny window ledge. In summer, if desired, they can be stood outside, but in winter they must be brought within the room lest they be damaged by frost.

In general cacti and succulents are very tough plants in the sense that they will put up with a lot of ill-treatment, and it is perhaps for this reason that they so often appeal to people who have to garden under very unfavourable conditions, as, for example, in the heart of a big city. Nevertheless, if the best results are to be obtained, it is desirable to give the plants what they need, which is plenty of sun and moisture during the growing period, sharp drainage at all times and a rather dry, buoyant atmosphere even in winter. This will involve the use of a little artificial heat at times, not so much to raise the temperature as to keep air on the move and rid it of surplus moisture.

Many cacti and succulents are naturally small plants, while others grow so slowly that they can be kept in small pots for a good many years. Such kinds are most useful to the town and window gardener, who can accommodate a considerable variety of plants in a small area.

The things to be avoided are drip, damp and shade, all of which, if permitted for long, will encourage soft growth and eventual decay.

It must not be assumed from what has already been said that when the plants are growing, which is usually between April and August, water should be given in dribs and drabs. In desert regions long periods of drought are often interspersed with periods of heavy rainfall. In consequence the cactus grower must water his plants quite as freely while they are growing as he would ordinary greenhouse plants. It is only at the end of this period that the water can should be put away or used very sparingly. Roughly speaking from April to August inclusive cacti and succulents will need watering two or three times a week, whereas from September to March water may only be required on an average every four to six weeks. If the weather is damp or cold the plants may be left for much longer periods without water. Even if they shrivel slightly during this resting season they will suffer no serious harm and will plump up and start to grow freely again when the spring arrives.

A good compost for the majority of cacti and succulents can be prepared with 6 parts by bulk of medium loam or good garden soil, 2 parts of coarse silver sand, such as that recommended for the John Innes mixtures, 2 parts of brick crushed into fragments ranging from dust to $\frac{1}{4}$ in. diameter and 1 part of old mortar rubble crushed in the same way. More drainage crocks should be used in the bottom of each pot than is normal for greenhouse plants. March is the best season for potting and the roots should be made reasonably firm.

If it is desired to put cacti out of doors for the summer months care must be taken not to do this until all danger of frost is passed, which usually means not until the end of the first week in June. For the same reason the plants should be safely housed again at least by the end of September. In most cases it is best to place the plants outside in their flower pots, plunging these to their rims in a bed of ashes or sand, but a few succulents can with advantage be actually planted out on rockeries or on sunny borders. Many of the mesembryanthemums will grow freely in this way and make a splendid display with their brilliant flowers during July and August.

Propagation can in many cases be effected by careful division or removal of offsets at potting time. Some kinds however, and the mesembryanthemums are notable examples, have a more shrubby habit with a single woody stem at the base which cannot be divided. With these cuttings often provide a ready means of increase. The cuttings should be prepared from young, non-flowering growths, either side-shoots or the tips of stems, and July and August are usually the most favourable months for taking these, though propagation can be continued at almost any time of the year. The cuttings should be prepared in the ordinary way and inserted in pure sand or very sandy soil in a close frame or under a bell glass, preferably within the greenhouse.

In a few instances propagation can be carried out by leaves alone. *Sedum Stahlii* is a notable example of this. Its little, globular leaves fall off of their own accord in the autumn and will often root in the ashes on the greenhouse staging without any further attention. Many hundreds of plants can be raised in a short time by this method.

Seed is a universal method of propagation for practically all cacti and succulents though, as the seed is often extremely small, it must be handled with care. Sow it on the surface of a very fine, sandy compost and cover either very lightly or not at all. In either case each pan or pot of seed should be protected with a pane of glass. When water is required give it by holding the pot or pan almost to its rim in water and not by applying water from above, even from a fine rose.

It is not possible in the scope of this book to give complete lists of desirable cacti and succulents as these run into many thousands. They will be found in the catalogues of trade specialists and also in books devoted exclusively to this subject. However, here are a few suggestions for the beginner.

Amongst succulents some of the *aloes* should certainly be included, particularly *A. variegata*, popularly known as the partridge-breasted aloe because of the partridge-like marking on its leaves; *crassulas*, some of which have very brilliant flowers; the nearly allied *rocheas*; *echeverias*, of which one, *E. secunda*, used to be a popular summer bedding plant and is still in the front rank as a formal edging; *mesembryanthemums* in enormous variety; *sedums* and *sempervivums*, both of which include a number of completely hardy kinds, *haworthias* and *gasterias*.

Cacti suitable for the beginner include *cereus*, of which the Old

Man cactus, *C. senilis*, is interesting on account of its long, white filaments like a grey beard; *echinocactus*; *echinocereus*; *echinopsis*; *epiphyllum* (trailing plants, these, to be grown in a hanging basket or a pot on the edge of the staging); *mammillaria*; *nyctocereus*, the so-called night flowering cacti; *opuntia*; *pachycereus*; *pereskia*, which roots very readily from cuttings and is sometimes used as a stock on which other cacti are grafted, though I do not recommend this method; *phyllocactus*, a genus in which some of the most gorgeous flowers are to be found; *pilocereus*; *rhipsalis* and *zygocactus*.

CHAPTER XXII

House Plants

I N RECENT years there has been a great revival of interest in plants grown in living rooms. The Scandinavians, with their centrally heated homes with double windows to keep out draughts, have pioneered the return of many an almost forgotten plant and, while we in this country may not enjoy the same advantages, it has been shown that there is a wide range of plants which are suitable for growing in the house.

Many of these would have been familiar to our Victorian grand-parents, others have only been seen until recently in botanic gardens and in hot houses. It would be fair to say that most of them are very unlikely to flower indoors but that is not the point for they are grown mainly for their decorative foliage to provide something of interest the year round.

Decorative they are, indeed, as many a window display designer has found, and it is now no uncommon sight in London and other big towns to see large plants of monstera, ficus, hedera, philodendron etc., adding to the interest of a shop window display.

Apart from the decorative value of their foliage the great attractions which these plants have for many people are their toughness under adverse conditions, their willingness to grow in poor light and the minimum of attention they require. Many of them can be grown in the same pots for several years provided some attention is given to feeding; some can be propagated quite easily by the amateur with a greenhouse or frame; many can be trained to fit in with schemes of interior decor-ation.

Almost without exception the plants described in this chapter have decorative foliage; valuable either for its colour, its variegation or its almost sculptural effect. There is an undeniable attraction in the leaves of many of these plants and, while a single plant can be used with great effect, many plants can be used together in baskets or wire or wicker plant-stands.

GENERAL CULTIVATION

Most of the plants described are good-tempered and will survive, if not exactly thrive, in poor conditions. As with most plants, however, the better the conditions are the better they will grow and even when in the list of plants it is said that a plant can be grown in a shady room, away from the window, it will benefit from being brought nearer the light on occasions.

It is unfortunately true that the leaves of house plants will gather dust but an occasional sponging with clean luke-warm water will remove this and benefit the plant as well. An occasional spraying with clean tepid water (except those plants with hairy leaves), also helps, and for this, where the number of plants concerned is small, there is nothing better than a cheap scent atomizer.

WATERING. Experience will be a great help here but some indication of the needs of the various species will be found in the alphabetical list. Generally speaking, no plant likes to be in a perpetually sodden state although some require much more water than others, particularly in the growing season—usually from March to October. Plants in small pots require watering more frequently than those in larger pots.

During the winter months when growth is almost at a standstill watering will be required less frequently and some plants will be better if left almost dry during that period, certainly being allowed to dry out completely between waterings. As a general rule water should not be allowed to remain in the containers in which the plants are standing and it is beneficial if the pots are supported on small blocks of wood so that air can circulate freely round them.

Those plants which require more water than others should be watered once, then again, and even a third time, as soon as the water has run through the pot. If possible, however, it is best to immerse the pots up to their rims in water for a while to allow them to soak up water from below. It is usually best to use tepid water and most plants benefit from being stood outside in the garden for a while during a light summer shower, but not in heavy rain lest the leaves become broken.

FEEDING. During the growing season the plants will benefit from an occasional feeding, especially if they are to remain in the same pot for several years. For this a proprietary fertiliser can be used, the manufacturer's instruction being followed. Care should be taken, however, not to over-feed as this is one of the chief causes of decline in the health of the plant.

REPOTTING. As I have already mentioned some plants can remain for several years in the same pot provided they are fed properly. However, there will come a time when most plants will benefit from repotting and, generally speaking, this will be when the growth of the plant has practically or completely stopped (when this happens in the growing period, not in the dormant period), and the plant looks generally unhealthy with yellowing leaves. As a general indication, if the plant when knocked out of its pot is found to be root-bound then it is time to repot. This is best done in April or May so that the plants can settle down to make new roots during the summer, before the dormant period. For most plants a good open soil, light in texture, can be used; better still if it is peaty. To this add the same amount of fibrous leaf mould and half the amount of sharp sand. Alternatively plants may be grown in vermiculite and fed with nutrient solution, following the manufacturer's instructions. The advantages of using vermiculite are its lightness in weight and that no drainage holes need be provided in the container.

CONTAINERS. Most florists' shops now stock a variety of containers in metal, wire, wicker etc., many of them very attractive, and among these it will be possible to find some to harmonize with the decorations of almost any kind of room.

Wicker or wire baskets, like birdcages, containing a climbing or trailing plant such as hedera or philodendron can look very pleasant hung in a window. Plant stands in metal or wood are now available in several different designs or sizes and in these a variety of plants can be arranged to give pleasing effects. For plants hung on walls some form of drip container is essential and wall brackets or pot-holders incorporating these can be obtained.

ARRANGEMENT. The arrangement of plants in a living room is, of course, very much a matter of personal taste and a great deal of pleasure can be obtained from using a number of different plants in different arrangements. It is not necessary for all plants to be near the light; many will tolerate conditions of shade and many in fact, dislike direct sunlight.

The stark, almost geometric beauty of some leaves, such as those of *Ficus elastica decora,* can be very effective against a plain wall if single specimen plants are used or equally as effective to add height and point in a display of lower growing plants, while plants such as *Fatshedera Lizei* and *Philodendron scandens* trained as climbers or trailers have a quality of line which can be used to great advantage in a window.

PESTS AND DISEASES. Few troubles will be encountered and a weekly spray with clean water will keep at bay attacks of mealy bug, scale insects, aphis and red spider. Individual picking off will also be possible as only small numbers of plants are concerned. Fungus diseases seldom occur but when they do the treatment is to pick off and burn affected leaves and to correct the condition which encouraged the disease—this usually means keeping the plant in a slightly warmer atmosphere and watering less, since it is cold, moist conditions which allow the disease to gain a foothold. While it is not a disease or a pest, it will be found that escaping gas will affect most plants, causing their leaves to yellow and drop off. Certain plants such as monsteras, philodendrons, hederas and ficus are not affected.

PROPAGATION. In the list of plants I have given at the end of this chapter the method of propagation has been given but a general note on propagation by cuttings will be found in chapter XVII, while in chapter XVIII under the various greenhouse plants I have described other methods such as removing offsets. It is worth noting that cuttings of certain house plants such as hederas and tradescantias can be rooted in jars of plain water. When rooted they should be potted up in small pots, taking care not to break off the tiny roots.

SOME RECOMMENDED PLANTS

Many of the plants described in Chapter XIV on Ferns, Chapter XVIII on Greenhouse Plants and in Chapter XXI, Cacti and Succulents, can be used as house plants and I have referred the reader to these in the appropriate place. Certain nurserymen specialize in these plants and their catalogues should be consulted for lists of up-to-date varieties.

ALOE.—*See* p. 436.

ANTHURIUM.—*See* p. 437.

ARALIA.—*See* p. 438.

ASPIDISTRA.—*See* p. 439.

BEGONIA.—*See* p. 440.

BELOPERONE. The Shrimp Plant, *Beloperone guttata* a native of tropical America, is a bushy plant growing about 18 in. high and bearing, in good conditions, masses of purple spotted white flowers with orange-brown bracts. Keep the plant warm and moist for the best effect, but avoid wetting the leaves. Propagate by cuttings taken after flowering.

BILLBERGIA.—*See* p. 443.

CHLOROPHYTUM.—*See* ANTHERICUM (p. 437).

CISSUS.—*See* p. 453.

COCOS.—*See* p. 455.

CODIAEUM.—*See* CROTON (p. 458).

COLUMNEA.—*See* p. 456.

CRASSULA.—*See* p. 457.

CROSSANDRA. *C. infundibuliformis* is a free-flowering plant with orange-red flower spikes with many bracts. Rather a difficult plant but worth attempting to grow well because of its long flowering period and its olive-green leaves with their wavy margins. Avoid draughts and try to keep a minimum temperature of 55°. Do not over-water, especially in winter. Propagation is by cuttings taken almost at any time or by seed.

CROTON.—*See* p. 458,

CYPERUS.—*See* p. 461.

DIEFFENBACHIA.—*See* p. 463.

DIZYGOTHECA.—*See* ARALIA (p. 438).

EUPHORBIA.—*See* p. 466.

FATSHEDERA. This is a bigeneric hybrid between *Fatsia japonica Moseri* and *Hedera japonica*. It is an excellent plant for a cool room and will do well in the shade. Its attractively lobed deep green leaves are reminiscent of the ivy which is one of its parents. In a sunny position it can attain a height of 8 or 10 feet on a single stem, less in the shade, while if the growing tip is pinched out in March the plant will send out branching sideshoots. It requires ample water in the summer months but less from October to March. The usual variety is *F. Li̇ei* but there is a form *F. Li̇ei variegata* which has cream edges to the leaves.

FATSIA.—*See* p. 467.

FICUS.—*See* p. 467.

FITTONIA. *Fittonia Verschaffeltii argyroneura* is a difficult plant as it dislikes draughts and its leaves must not touch the soil but well grown it is a lovely sight as it has silver or white markings along the veins. It requires moist warm conditions away from direct sunlight. Propagation is by cuttings of firm shoots in a propagating frame in the greenhouse, in spring or by division of the plants in February or March.

FUCHSIA.—*See* p. 469.

GERANIUM.—*See* PELARGONIUM (p. 488).

HEDERA. There are many species and varieties of ivy, a number of which can be grown to advantage in pots in the house. Many have variegated or mottled leaves, in others the leaves are crisped and curled. All grow well in a compost of two parts of loam, one part of leaf mould or decayed manure and one part of sand. Propagation is by cuttings in well-drained pots in a cold frame.

While nurserymen's catalogues list a large number of kinds, most of them are varieties of *H. canariensis*, the Canary Island Ivy or *H. Helix*, the Common Ivy .While many require strong light and a cool atmosphere others can be found which will tolerate positions in centrally-heated rooms and all look effective trained up a window frame or against a wall.

HOYA.—*See* p. 474.

IXORA.—*See* p. 477.

KALANCHOË.—*See* p. 478.

MARANTA.—*See* p. 482.

MISCANTHUS. This tall, hardy perennial grass is often used in bedding out schemes where its zebra-striped leaves, 3 to 4 feet long are very decorative. Easy to grow, it likes a cool position in a north or east window, with plenty of water in the growing period. There are a number of species, the most popular being *M. sinensis* (often known as *Eulalia japonica* or just *Eulalia*), green leaves with a white mid-rib, and its varieties, *gracillimus*, dwarf, narrow-leaved; *variegatus*, leaves striped yellow or white; and *zebrinus*, leaves cross-banded yellow.

MONSTERA. The varieties of *Monstera deliciosa* are among the most handsome and trouble-free plants for the house. Their deep green, perforated or deeply cut leaves are strikingly attractive while their habit of growth is both curious and interesting. New leaves break from a long sheath at the back of the previous leaf stem and are often more cut or divided on one side than another. Thus plants may be grown in which some leaves are unperforated or cut, others perforated or cut down one side and not the other, some with one cut on one side and two or three on the other and so on, so that as each new leaf appears it is a gamble as to its form.

A further curious attraction lies in the way in which fleshy aerial roots emerge from the stems and in moist conditions grow down into the soil in the pot to draw up further moisture and sustenance for the leaves. Propagation is by leaf or stem cuttings, taken at any time and inserted in sandy soil in a propagating frame in the greenhouse.

NIDULARIUM.—*See* p. 485.

OPHIOPOGON.—*See* p. 486.

PANDANUS.—*See* p. 487.

PEPEROMIA. There are over 400 peppers but the best for growing in the home are *P. glabella* with dark green leaves and *P. Sandersii* and its variety *argyreia* with dark green and silver stripes. All have fleshy leaves, growing close together. They require warmth and should be kept out of stray sunlight. Always use tepid water for watering and never over-water. If the pots can be sunk in moist peat so much the better. Propagation is by cuttings of shoots or single joints with a leaf attached, in a warm propagating frame, in spring.

PHILODENDRON. There are many philodendrons but only a few are available commercially in this country although the range is widening. They vary a good deal, some being of erect habit with large, perforated or indented leaves, sometimes cut into narrow segments as far as the mid-rib, as in *P. pinnatifidum*, while others are climbers or trailers. Of the latter *P. scandens* is the best known and with its heart-shaped, alternate, grey green leaves it makes an attractive plant and can either be trained against a wall or a window or can be grown as a trailer from a hanging basket. Like the monsteras mentioned earlier, to which it is closely related, it has aerial roots. All the philodendrons will do well in a north window and do not need much heat. Plenty of water is required in the growing season but do not over-water. The foliage should be sponged occasionally or wiped over. Propagation is by stem cuttings at any time, placed in a propagating frame in the greenhouse.

PHOENIX.—*See* p. 489.

PILEA.—*See* p. 489.

PLECTRANTHUS. These pretty little plants are allied to the coleus and are useful trailing plants to grow in a window or a hanging basket. They require plenty of water in the summer and should be shielded from direct sunlight. The small heart-shaped, serrated leaves are aromatic and pale blue or lavender flowers grow at the end of the stems in autumn and early winter. The most popular species is *P. Oertendahlii*. Propagation is by cuttings of side shoots inserted in sandy soil in a propagating frame during March or April.

RHOEO.—*See* TRADESCANTIA (p. 502).

RHOICISSUS. Closely related to cissus (p. 453) there is one species *R. rhomboidea*, the Grape Ivy, introduced a few years ago. It is a rapidly growing climber with glossy, toothed leaves. It should be grown in a light window in a warm room and should be sprayed regularly with tepid water but should not be over-watered. Propagation is by 2 in. cuttings of young growth, taken with a heel of old wood and inserted in sandy soil under a bell glass.

SAINTPAULIA.—*See* p. 494.

SANSEVERIA. These strangely attractive plants are commonly known as 'Mother-in-Law's Tongue' or 'Bow-string Hemp', the former because the leaves are long and pointed and the latter because the natives of

Tropical West Africa use the coarse, strong fibres as bow strings. The leaves are thick and fleshy, attaining a length of 2-3 feet and tapering to a point. They are banded and striped golden yellow and dark green, and grow upright out of the soil from the rootstock. The plant is very hardy, does not mind shady corners of the room or variations in temperature and is very long-lived. The only thing it will not stand is overwatering and it should be kept practically bone dry during the winter months and only watered occasionally at other times of the year. Propagation is by leaf or root cuttings in a propagation frame at any time or by division in spring.

SCINDAPSUS. This is another plant closely allied to the monstera and philodendron and the two species *S. aureus,* with heart-shaped leaves blotched with pale yellow and *S. pictus,* dark green leaves, and its variety *argyraeus* with silver spotted leaves, make attractive trailers or climbers. They should be kept away from direct bright sunlight and given plenty of water in summer and autumn and sprayed frequently. It has aerial roots and these will grow into a piece of dead tree stump if it can be provided. Propagation is by division of the roots in spring.

SPARRMANIA.—*See* p. 498.

SYNGONIUM. Both *S. podophyllum* and *S. Vellozianum* make attractive trailing plants with aerial roots. The leaves in older plants have three fingers and are dark green and leathery while in their younger state they lack the indentations. They should be given a warm, moist, shaded position and the pots should be stood in wet peat. Propagation is by stem cuttings in a warm propagating frame in spring.

TETRASTIGMA. This a rapid climber of the Vine family closely related to the Cissus (*see* p. 453). It is a somewhat difficult plant as overwatering will result in the loss of leaves and buds, but when grown well it is very attractive as the leaves are large and glossy green. It should be grown against a light trellis in a shady window and given very little water. The species grown are *T. obtectum, T. serrulatum* and *T. Vionieriana.* Propagation is by cuttings in a propagating frame.

TRADESCANTIA.—*See* p. 502.

ZEBRINA.—*See* TRADESCANTIA (p. 502).

PART IV

VEGETABLES

CHAPTER XXIII

Planning the Vegetable Garden

Iℕ devising a plan for the vegetable garden a great deal must depend on the shape and size of the plot available. Nevertheless certain general principles can be laid down. It is, for example, always advisable to make some provision for rotational cropping even though it may not be possible to adhere to this rigidly. The position of 'permanent' crops, such as rhubarb, herbs, etc. must also receive careful attention and, if frames are to be included, these must be given a specially suitable spot.

Rotational Cropping. This is a scheme which is very familiar to the farmer and should be more widely adopted by the gardener. It is based on two principal facts; first that crops make different demands upon the soil, some requiring more of one food, others of another, and second that they suffer from different pests and diseases. If the same crop is grown in the same place every year it is more likely to exhaust the soil or to be attacked by some foe than if it is grown in a different place as often as possible.

Obvious difficulties arise from the mere haphazard re-arrangement of crops every year and a far better policy is to practise a logical system of rotation. This may be a two year, three year or four year rotation, according to the time that will elapse before any particular crop comes back to the same ground.

For garden work the three year rotation is the one most commonly adopted. There are quite a number of variations of this but all conform roughly to the same basic plan.

The plot is divided into three approximately equal sections which for the sake of clarity we will designate A, B and C. One of these is devoted mainly to brassicas (i.e. cabbages, savoys, Brussels sprouts, broccoli etc.), another to root crops and the third to peas, beans and miscellaneous small crops. Let us suppose that the first year these are planted in the sequence brassicas on plot A, root crops on plot B, peas and beans, etc. on plot C. The following year all these crops will move on one place, the brassicas going to plot B, the root crops to C, and the peas and beans to A. Next year they will move on again so that the root crops will be on plot A, the peas and beans on plot B and the brassicas on plot C. The fourth year they will be back where they started.

531

As I have already remarked, there are all kinds of variations of this basic scheme to meet the needs of particular gardens. For example if it is the intention to grow enough potatoes, besides other root crops, to supply the whole family throughout the year, it is highly probable that the root crop section will have to be increased in size out of proportion to the others. In this case the root crop plot may be reserved for potatoes alone and carrots, parsnips, turnips and beetroots, may go along with the peas and beans.

Then there is the question of intercropping to be considered, a matter which I have discussed more fully below, and the necessity for allowing reasonable time for cultivation between one crop and another. The chief points to observe are that identical or closely related crops should not follow one another closely, nor those which suffer from the same pests and diseases, and that the scheme followed should be orderly and pre-arranged rather than improvised.

INTERCROPPING. This is a device whereby the gardener seeks to increase the cropping capacity of his ground by letting two or more vegetables occupy the same plot of ground at the same time. In theory it is possible to do this without allowing either of them to take up more room than they would if planted alone, but in practice this seldom works out satisfactorily. As a matter of fact a good deal of experience is necessary to make intercropping a real success and I think it tends to be more often a snare than a help to the beginner. The trouble is that one or other of the crops almost always grows away too quickly to the detriment of the slow starter which gets starved and stunted in consequence. Nevertheless, provided the ground is in thoroughly good condition and the gardener knows what he is about, good results can be obtained by intercropping.

Here are a few suggestions: peas must normally be planted in rows at least as far apart as the height of the pea when fully grown, i.e. 3-ft. peas should be planted a minimum of 3 ft. apart row to row; 4-ft. peas, 4 ft., and so on. This allows room for single or even double rows of lettuces, radishes, summer spinach or some other small crop which does not mind a certain amount of shade. Summer turnips and shorthorn carrots may be grown in the same way or between rows of runner beans, which must also be planted widely because of the shade they throw.

The trouble arises when the gardener tries to intercrop two vegetables either of which might reasonably be expected to cover the whole area with its foliage. I have, for example, often seen an attempt made to plant winter greens between the rows of potatoes. This is only successful if the potatoes are really widely spaced and are almost ready for lifting at the time when the greens are put out. Under other circumstances the greens are almost invariably smothered by the potato haulm.

CATCH CROPPING. This is another scheme for getting two crops from one plot of ground but in this case instead of the crops being grown at the same time, they follow one another in quick succession. Catch cropping is most useful when ground has been prepared a considerable time in advance for some particular crop.

Celery provides a good example. The trenches in which this is to be grown are generally dug and manured quite early in the spring, sometimes even in late winter, though the plants are seldom put out before early June. This means that for two months or more the ground is lying idle and there is time to harvest a quick-growing crop such as radishes or early lettuces. Here again, however, considerable forethought is necessary for it is the easiest thing in the world to practise catch cropping and then find that the first crop is still not ready for gathering when the following crop is already spoiling for want of being put out.

SUCCESSIONAL CROPPING. The difference between successional cropping and catch cropping is that the following crop is of the same kind as that which preceded it, the idea being to lengthen the period at which the crop is available rather than to make double use of the ground. Indeed it by no means follows that the successional crop will be planted on the same ground, this being the exception rather than the rule.

Many vegetables have a comparatively short season when only one sowing or planting is made; peas and lettuces are both good examples of this. Two or three weeks and the crop is over. Unless the gardener practises successional cropping he will be in danger of having a glut at the peak season followed almost immediately by a complete lack of supplies.

The art of successional cropping is to know just how much to sow or plant each time and what time lag to allow between the successive sowings. A study of the table of average yields which appears on p. 526 may help to solve the first problem while as regards the second, it is a fairly safe general rule to space the sowings of summer crops at approximately fortnightly intervals from beginning to end of the possible sowing season.

It should be noted that in many cases succession can also be improved by choosing several varieties which mature at different times, e.g. early, mid-season and late potatoes, broccolis, peas, etc.

REGULATING SUPPLY. This is perhaps the most difficult task of all for the new-comer to vegetable growing; indeed it has tripped up many experienced gardeners. The only thing to do is to set about the whole

AVERAGE YIELD OF VEGETABLES

Vegetable	Yield			
	Per Acre	Per Rod	Per Square Yard	Per Foot of Row
Beans, Broad - -	4 tons	56 lb.	2 lb.	8 oz.
„ French - -	3 „	42 „	1½ „	4 „
„ Runner - -	10 „	140 „	5 „	4 lb.
„ Haricot* - -	15 cwt.	10-12 lb.	5-6 oz.	—
Beetroot - - -	12 tons	168 lb.	5½ „	14 oz.
Broccoli - - -	8 „	112 „	3¾ „	19 „
Brussels Sprouts - -	4 „	56 „	2 „	9 „
Cabbage (Spring) -	9 „	126 „	4 „	11 „
„ (Autumn and Winter) -	15 „	210 „	7 „	1½ lb.
Cauliflowers - -	6 „	84 „	3 „	1 „
Carrots (Main Crop) -	14 „	196 „	6½ „	12 oz.
„ (Early) - -	8 „	112 „	3¾ „	5 „
Endive - - -	—	300 heads	10 heads	¾ head
Kale - - - -	10 tons	140 lb.	5 lb.	1½ lb.
Leek - - - -	10 „	140 „	5 „	13 oz.
Lettuce - - -	—	300-400 heads	10-13 heads	1½-2 heads
Mushrooms - -	—	—	10 lb.	—
Onions - - -	12 tons	168 lb.	5½ „	10 oz.
Parsnip - - -	10 „	140 „	5 „	13 „
Peas - - - -	3 „	42 „	1½ „	6 „
Potatoes (Main Crop) -	10 „	140 „	5 „	1¼ lb.
Savoys - - -	15 „	210 „	7 „	1½ „
Shallots - - -	—	240 „	8 „	10 oz.
Spinach (Summer) -	8 tons	112 „	3¾ „	5 „
Swedes - - -	13 „	182 „	6 „	14 „
Turnips (Main Crop) -	13 „	182 „	6 „	14 „
Tomatoes (Under Glass)	30 „	420 „	15 „	6 lb. per plant
„ (Outdoors) -	20 „	280 „	10 „	4 lb. per plant

* Seeds only.

The above figures can only give a rough guide to average production. Yield varies greatly according to soil, weather, and degree of cultural skill. Figures 50 per cent. in excess of those given may often be obtained under favourable conditions.

In almost all cases the weights quoted are for maincrop varieties allowed to mature. Earlies may be harvested at practically any stage of growth, so no reliable weights can be given. Exception is made in the case of early carrots, as figures are taken from the average market yield of shorthorn varieties allowed to develop.

CONTINUITY CHART FOR PRINCIPAL VEGETABLES

Jan. Feb. Mar. Apr. May June July Aug. Sept. Oct. Nov. Dec.

Artichokes		
Beet		
Beans (Broad)		
„ (French)		
„ (Runner)		
Broccoli		
„ (Sprouting)		
Brussels Sprouts		
Cabbages		
Carrots		
Cauliflowers		
Celery		
Coleworts		
Endive		
Kale		
Kohl Rabi		
Leeks		
Lettuces		
Onions		
Parsnips		
Peas		
Potatoes		
Savoys		
Shallots		
Spinach		
„ Beet		
Turnips		
Turnip Tops		
Vegetable Marrows		

The times at which vegetables are available from the open ground are indicated by continuous lines, while the dotted lines show the additional period during which they may be stored or preserved. With careful management it may be possible to extend the season of some of the crops even further.

planning of the vegetable garden in a methodical way. First of all try to make a rough estimate of the quantity of each vegetable that will be required to supply the household throughout the period when that vegetable is in season. The table on p. 535 is designed to help to this end.

Pay particular heed to two periods, one from about the middle of May to the middle of June and the other during August and September. During the first there is liable to be a severe shortage of supplies, or at any rate an almost complete lack of variety. Winter vegetables such as cabbages, savoys and Brussels sprouts are over, spring crops such as broccoli and kale are also over or very scarce and the true summer crops are not yet ready. Very often there is practically nothing but spring cabbage and potatoes left at this season. The difficulty can be overcome by making early sowings of peas and broad beans under cloches and also by carrying over a batch of spinach or seakale beet from the preceding year. Summer cabbages raised in warmth and planted out in early April will also help and, if frames are available, shorthorn carrots can be pulled in June without artificial heat. Again a glance at the tables on pp. 534-5 will suggest many ways in which the gap can be breached.

As regards the August–September period, the trouble is not a shortage but a glut. Almost everything is turning in at once then and only a few of the crops are of a type which can be kept at all readily. There will be peas, beans of every kind, cabbages, cauliflowers, spinach, carrots, beetroots, lettuces, tomatoes, to say nothing of potatoes, turnips, swedes and possibly an early batch of celery. The way to get over this difficulty is by successional cropping and also by making provision for bottling or drying those crops which lend themselves to such methods of preservation.

Another difficulty which arises in the regulation of supply is the lack of variety likely to occur in winter. Of course, if the gardener has planned wisely there will be plenty of root crops in store but once Christmas is past and the main flush of Brussels sprouts and winter cabbage is over, there is often little beyond savoys to provide fresh green vegetables until the spring supplies turn in.

In favoured localities it is possible to grow winter heading broccoli but there are many places in which these are not successful. Turnips sown in August and allowed to stand unthinned in the rows will provide useful supplies of greens from about March onwards. There are numerous kinds of kale, notably the Curled Scotch kale and the Thousand Headed kale, which can be picked throughout winter and early spring. Further variety can be provided by forcing seakale, chicory and salsify in a warm, dark place. If frames are available they may be filled with winter lettuce and endive. Even after the celery is finished the flavour of celery can be maintained in the salad bowl with grated celeriac, a relation to celery which is well worth growing.

MANURING THE VEGETABLE GARDEN. Dung or well-rotted compost should form the basis of all feeding in the vegetable garden, but it does not follow that dung or compost should therefore be applied indiscriminately all over the garden every autumn or winter. For one thing that would be wasteful and for another it might prove positively harmful for there are some vegetables which do best on ground that was dunged for a previous crop rather than immediately prior to sowing or planting. Carrots and beetroots both come into this class and it is also true of August and September planted brassicas, which are apt to make too much soft growth if planted on newly manured ground.

SUGGESTED THREE-YEAR ROTATION

A	Cabbages, cauliflowers, Brussels sprouts, kale, savoys, and other brassicas. Preceded by, or intercropped with, lettuces, radishes, and other small salads. Plot dressed with animal manure or compost and limed (not together). Crops fed while in growth with nitrate of soda or sulphate of ammonia.
B	Potatoes. Followed by broccoli, spring cabbage, coleworts, leeks, and late sown turnip (for tops). Plot dressed with animal manure or compost, but *not* lime. *Complete* artificial fertiliser applied, just prior to planting potatoes.
C	Carrots, parsnips, turnips and beetroots. Peas and beans with summer spinach and lettuces between. No animal manure or compost except for pea and bean trenches. Wood ashes forked in. *Complete* fertiliser (low nitrogen ratio) applied just prior to sowing.
D	Onions. Plot dressed with animal manure or compost and wood ashes. Nitrate of soda after thinning.

The scheme is applicable to plots of any size or shape, so no dimensions are necessary. The only essential is that sections A, B, and C should be of approximately the same area. They need not be of the same shape. The second year the order of the crops from top to bottom is C, A, B, D; the third year B, C, A, D; the fourth year the same as first year. Onions are not included in the rotation because they appear to derive greater benefit from being grown on the same plot for a number of years. If however it is preferred to include them, they should go to plot C.

The rotational cropping scheme will help the gardener to solve such problems in the simplest possible manner as some sections of the garden can be manured right through and others simply treated with appropriate chemicals (see diagram, p. 537). Note, however, that even for those vegetables which like freshly dunged soil and get it there is generally advantage to be gained by using some chemical fertilisers as well. These as a rule can be applied most conveniently and economically as top dressings just before the crop is sown or planted. Those who like to do things the most scientific way will use separate chemicals, varying these to suit the individual crop and the known deficiencies of the soil. Those who cannot be bothered with such refinements should use a well-blended fertiliser, with an analysis showing approximately equal quantities of nitrogen, phosphates and potash, for all their crops —and they will probably get just as good results this way as the other.

THE UTILITY FRAME

I do not propose here to give detailed instructions for the management of each crop in the frame. This will be found under the headings of the vegetables themselves. My purpose rather is to indicate the various uses to which a frame may be put.

A frame is a great asset to the vegetable garden. It may be either heated or unheated but it will have wider uses if the latter. In any case the frame should be given a sunny, but reasonably sheltered, position; for example, it may stand at the foot of a wall facing south or on the south side of a greenhouse or potting shed.

There are many different types of frame and almost any of them can be turned to account in the vegetable garden but perhaps the most useful is the standard type of nursery frame with either 6 ft. by 4 ft. or 4 ft. by 3 ft. lights. This kind of frame may have wooden, brick or concrete walls and should be only a little higher at the back than in front. A 6 in. fall from back to front will be sufficient for a 6 ft. light and this can be reduced to 4 in. for a 4 ft. light. This will run off water satisfactorily and the advantage of having a rather flat 'roof' to the frame is that all the plants in it may be reasonably close to the glass. If some plants are far from the glass they will tend to get drawn and weakly.

There are two distinct purposes for which the frame may be used in the vegetable garden; one to rear seedlings and harden off young plants and the other to bring crops to maturity at an earlier or later date than would be possible outdoors. Of the two the first is usually of greater importance to the amateur but there is no reason why both objects should not be combined to some extent.

SEED IN FRAMES. Outdoor seed sowing can seldom start before the extreme end of February and in many cases must be delayed until late in March. In a frame it is possible to get a good seed bed and satisfactory germination at least a month earlier even without artificial heat in the case of hardy plants such as Brussels sprouts, cauliflowers, broccolis, leeks, onions, peas and lettuces. Tender vegetables such as tomatoes, cucumbers, vegetable marrows and French and runner beans can also be raised in a frame but as they need protection from frost and a higher temperature to effect germination it will either be necessary to delay sowing until about April or to provide the frame with some method of heating, even if this is no more than a hot bed of ample size (see p. 542).

Seedlings can either be raised in boxes stood on a floor of ashes or sand in the frame or, if preferred, a bed of soil can be prepared in the frame and the seeds sown direct into this. The former method has the advantage that successive batches of seedlings can be passed through the frame more rapidly and easily but it has the drawback that the seeds and seedlings will require more attention, particularly as regards watering. In sunny weather the soil in shallow seed trays dries out rapidly, whereas a good bed of soil will retain its moisture for a much longer period.

Taking the crops in chronological order according to sowing date, those which might most advantageously be reared in a frame are onions, leeks, broad beans, lettuces, Brussels sprouts, cauliflowers, early broccolis, summer cabbages, tomatoes, celery, vegetable marrows, cucumbers, French beans and runner beans.

FRAME CROPS. Crops to be brought to maturity in a frame can be divided into two groups, 'summer' crops and 'winter' crops. The former will be of greater importance to the amateur as he can combine them readily with the seed raising to which reference has just been made. Winter crops will in general occupy the frame from about September or October until at least March and that really rules out the possibility of any seed raising.

The three best summer crops for the frame are cucumbers, tomatoes and melons in that order of merit. The idea of growing tomatoes in frames may appear novel to many readers but it can be managed quite successfully especially if the frame can be made a little deeper than previously advocated. This extra depth can easily be added to a normal frame by having detachable wooden sides which can be lifted on or off as required.

Cucumbers are a familiar summer frame crop and usually do very well. Either the ordinary frame cucumber may be grown or the hardier ridge cucumber, which has the merit of being more prolific and easily managed.

Melons are a distinctly tricky crop and I do not recommend them to the beginner. All the same I have seen some very satisfactory and profitable yields obtained by skilful management.

The two most successful winter crops for the frame are lettuces and endive. The description 'winter' is perhaps a slight exaggeration in the case of lettuce for it is unlikely that any crop will be fit for cutting between November and mid-March, but October and April supplies can be obtained quite easily and are both very welcome. Endive, being hardier, can actually be cut in winter. Alternative crops are radishes, which can be sown very early in the year for pulling from late February onwards, early carrots and mustard and cress.

CLOCHES

Cloches of many kinds and ingenious patterns can be used with great advantage in the vegetable garden to enable early sowings to be made and to help young plants through the treacherous spring months. Even in summer cloches can be used like miniature greenhouses to hasten the growth of tomatoes, cucumbers, aubergines and other rather 'tender' vegetables, while in autumn they are serviceable as protection against frost and to ripen off tomatoes and onions. Very elaborate cropping schemes are sometimes used so that the cloches are in almost constant use, being passed from one crop to another with the minimum delay. Such schemes require considerable knowledge and very careful timing if the whole programme is not to get into a muddle. I have referred more fully to these matters on p. 403.

THE UTILITY GREENHOUSE

At the commencement it is more important to have a frame than a greenhouse, but if funds and space permit both to be included in the vegetable garden, so much the better. A greenhouse will do many but not all the things that can be done with a frame and it has a few additional functions as well.

It is not possible satisfactorily to harden off plants in a greenhouse and that is where the frame scores. Perhaps this needs a little explanation. Any plant, however naturally hardy, will tend to be made more tender than usual if it is raised under glass. If such a plant is suddenly placed outdoors without any preliminary preparation, it is likely to receive a severe check to growth which may even be sufficient to kill it outright. To overcome this difficulty the gardener uses the process known as hardening off. During this the plant is gradually accustomed to greater degrees of exposure. This begins with increased ventilation during all favourable periods. With the frame there comes a time when the light is dispensed with altogether unless the weather becomes unseasonably cold or rough. Now there is no way of dispensing with the glass in a greenhouse; the most that can be done is to throw the ventilators wide open and open the door and this does not harden the inmates so thoroughly as exposure in a lightless frame.

With these reservations, however, it may be said that all the seedlings suggested for frame rearing may also be germinated in a greenhouse and many of them several weeks earlier if heating is available. In addition, all the crops suggested for the frame may be brought to maturity in a greenhouse with equal or greater success and, in the case of tomatoes, cucumbers and melons there is great advantage in the extra head room available.

A greater variety of winter crops can be included with the aid of artificial heat. The skilled grower can even ripen tomatoes and obtain moderate yields of cucumbers at this season. But one word of warning is necessary. No amount of artificial heat can make up for lack of daylight. In fact too much heat without balancing light can result in drawn, weakly plants and eventual disaster. Much of the skill of producing winter crops lies in knowing just how much heat can be used to keep plants growing without causing this weakness and that is knowledge which must be gained by experience rather than from books.

As regards the type of house most suitable for the vegetable garden, I favour a span roof house with walls not exceeding 2½ ft. in height. If the glass comes right to ground level that is an advantage from many points of view but it does mean that a little more heat will be necessary when dealing with tender or very early crops. A house of this type should run as nearly as possible north and south so that each side gets an approximately equal amount of sunshine.

An alternative is the lean-to house which is quite good provided it is built against a wall or building with a southerly aspect.

In all cases ample provision must be made for ventilation. Many small, cheap houses offered to the amateur are inadequately equipped in this respect. In the case of the span roofed type there should be top ventilators on both sides of the ridge and the total length of these should certainly not be less than half the length of the house. There should also be deep ventilators in the side in these houses which have vertical glass above the walls, while the 'forcing' type of house with roof rafters resting directly on the side walls should have small wooden ventilators in these walls. A visit to a nursery or the nursery quarters of a public park will show the type of ventilation which the professional deems necessary.

HOTBEDS

The hotbed is a very ancient method of generating heat. It is based on the observation that a rapidly fermenting heap of dung becomes very warm. Fresh stable manure containing a fair proportion of straw produces the greatest degree of heat over the longest period and is therefore best for hotbed construction but plain straw or chaff treated with one of the proprietory substances sold for preparing mushroom compost will make quite a good substitute.

The idea is to build a flat topped heap of well-trodden dung 2 to 3 feet in height and a little larger than a portable garden frame. The frame is then stood on top of this fermenting heap and a 6 or 8 in. layer of good soil placed in it. The heat from the rotting manure warms the soil and is trapped by the frame light so converting the frame into a miniature hothouse. Seeds, cuttings or young plants can be placed in the soil.

Sometimes the manure is placed in a pit instead of being built into a heap with the idea that this will conserve the heat better. Care must be taken that the pit does not become waterlogged with the result that the dung is chilled.

Always it is wise to wait a few days before putting lights in position so that ammonia fumes may escape.

CHAPTER XXIV

Vegetables and their Cultivation

IN THIS chapter the principal vegetables likely to be grown in the amateur's garden are arranged alphabetically for easy reference and brief cultural directions are given for each, together with some suggestions regarding varieties. Regarding this last point, however, it should be noted that new varieties of merit are constantly being introduced and that many large seed firms list their own specialities. Trade catalogues should be consulted for information regarding these. Moreover in some cases 'strain' is more important than variety, that is to say it is more vital to obtain seed from firms of repute who maintain the highest standard in their stocks than to purchase a 'name' without regard to the source from which it comes.

ARTICHOKE–GLOBE

This is a vegetable for the epicure rather than for the general gardener. Judged on weight of crop per rod it is not profitable as the only parts of the plant which are edible are the tips of the scales protecting the inflorescence. The plants are extremely ornamental particularly in foliage and worth growing from this standpoint alone.

There are two methods of raising globe artichokes, one from seed and the other by means of off-sets or divisions. The former has the merit of being cheap but best results are obtained with off-sets taken from plants selected for the quality of their produce. These off-sets should be detached early in April and planted at once in deeply-dug, well-manured ground and well-drained, sunny position. Space them at least 3 ft. apart each way.

Seed may be sown in a frame or unheated greenhouse in March or in shallow drills outdoors in April. The seedlings are transplanted a few inches apart each way to well broken, reasonably rich soil, directly they can be handled conveniently, and are transferred to their final quarters the following spring, when planting is exactly the same as for off-sets.

Subsequent treatment is the same in each case. The ground should be well mulched with decayed manure each May and thoroughly watered in summer during dry weather. Weak liquid manure can be substituted for plain water if available. Dead leaves are cut off towards the end of October and the crowns covered lightly with bracken or straw as a protection against frost. This should be left in position until March or early April.

No crop should be cut the first summer after planting. Subsequently the flower heads are cut as soon as they are of good size and the outer scales feel fleshy. The plants will go on cropping for several years but it is most profitable to replace them after the third year.

There are no varieties of globe artichoke in the ordinary sense of the word but it is important to obtain a good strain, that is to say seed or off-shoots from plants that are known to have given good results.

ARTICHOKE—JERUSALEM

There could hardly be a greater contrast between this and the globe artichoke. Though the latter is a vegetable for the epicure, the Jerusalem artichoke is one for everyone—or at any rate, everyone who likes its rather peculiar flavour and somewhat slushy texture. It is a very profitable crop judged on the basis of weight lifted per rod and it can be grown anywhere. It is cultivated for the tubers which are formed in big clumps underground, rather like an immense root of potatoes. Growth above ground is tall, stiffly erect and very similar to that of a sunflower, to which the plant is related.

The Jerusalem artichoke is grown from tubers which can be separated from the parent clump when it is lifted. It is advisable to choose well shaped tubers of medium to large size for planting. They are put in during January or February, as soon as the ground is in workable condition. Almost any plot will serve but best results are obtained when it is deeply dug and dressed with dung or compost at 2 to 3 cwt. per rod. Plant 15 ins. apart in rows 2½ to 3 ft. apart and cover the tubers with 4 or 5 ins. of soil. No earthing up is needed as in the case of potatoes. It is sufficient after planting to keep the plot clear of weeds.

The plants and tubers are perfectly hardy and may be left in the ground all winter if desired, being lifted for kitchen use as required, though it is usually convenient to lift at least part of the crop in November and store in a shed or outhouse under a little dry soil. Do not leave the tubers exposed or they will shrivel fairly quickly.

'Named' varieties in the ordinary sense are seldom offered but there is considerable difference in stocks and it is advisable to exercise care in choosing a good one. There are pink-skinned and white-skinned forms of which I prefer the latter, and the most desirable types have large, roundish, shallow-eyed tubers.

Planting Brussels sprouts. Note the well-rooted plants and holes of ample size

Cutting Brussels sprouts, considered by many experts a better method than picking them

Brussels sprouts correctly spaced. The ground has been well limed as a precaution against club root

Breaking down soil with the back of a fork used with swinging blows

Raking the soil still further to break down the surface to a fine tilth

A shallow trench for pea seeds is scooped out with a spade held flat

Sowing seeds in drills which are a model of straightness and evenness

Drawing a deep seed drill with a swan necked draw hoe

A shallow drill is drawn with the corner of a Dutch hoe

Pea seeds are spaced out evenly in the shallow trench-type drill

Seeds sown in a drill are covered by gently raking soil over them

Planting potatoes by using the soil from one trench to cover the tubers in the next

Earthing up potatoes by drawing soil from between the rows towards the potato haulms

Spraying potatoes against blight. A stick is used to turn the haulms back

Digging potatoes. If there has been disease the haulm should be removed

Making a potato clamp. The ridge-shaped heap of potatoes stands on straw and is covered with a thick layer of straw

The clamp completed. The straw has been covered with beaten earth and a couple of drain pipes inserted to act as ventilation shafts

Staking runner beans. One stake is provided for each plant

Using brushy hazel twigs to provide support for dwarf peas

Well-staked rows of tall peas which have been sown successionally to give a continuous supply for several weeks

A well-stocked allotment of the regulation 10 perch size

A walled vegetable garden neatly laid out in rectangular plots for easy cropping

Pulling carrots. First the roots are loosened by an upward heave with a fork

Removing carrots from a small outdoor clamp

A good crop of globe beetroots showing the beneficial effect of early and adequate thinning

Bending down onion tops to hasten the ripening of the bulbs

Onions stored in 'ropes' formed by plaiting the withered onion tops to three strands of string or raffia

Tomatoes growing on in four-inch pots and well spaced out on the
greenhouse staging so that each plant has ample space

A grand crop of tomatoes in an amateur's greenhouse. The plants are
growing in twelve-inch pots

Tomatoes planted in a bed made on the greenhouse staging, a method
which involves less labour than tomatoes grown in pots

A utility greenhouse planted with dwarf and climbing French beans

Planting outdoor tomatoes. Pots have been sunk alongside the plants to facilitate watering

Removing a side shoot from a tomato plant. The earlier this is done the better

Outdoor tomatoes growing under special tall cloches from which one side can be removed during warm weather

Ridge cucumbers growing on a slightly raised but flat topped bed of rich soil

A promising batch of greenhouse cucumbers just commencing to crop

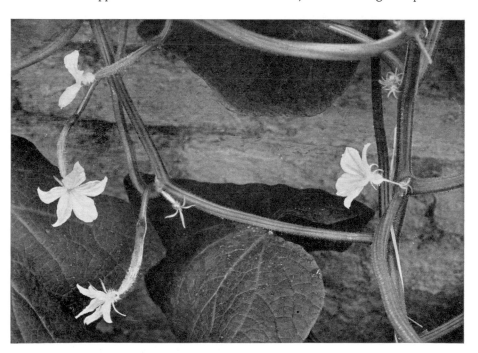

Cucumbers in flower. Female flowers with embryo fruits attached are seen on the left while a thin stalked male bloom is seen on the right

Celery newly planted in a well-prepared trench

Completing the earthing up of celery for blanching

Lettuce seedlings which have been raised under cloches

Autumn sown broad beans under barn cloches

Well-blanched seakale. The root has been covered with a flower pot and straw

Forcing rhubarb by covering a strong root with a flower pot and soil

Earthenware forcing pots in use over outdoor roots of rhubarb

Pulling outdoor forced rhubarb. Strawy manure has been used to generate warmth

Preparing a bed of stable manure for a green-house crop of mushrooms

Spawning a mushroom bed by placing small pieces of spawn in the prepared bed

A good crop, or 'flush', of mushrooms obtained in a darkened shed

ASPARAGUS

Another vegetable for the epicure but, unlike the globe artichoke, one which will give quite a considerable return of food in relation to the ground occupied. The drawbacks with asparagus are that it takes rather a long time to come into bearing and then continues to occupy the same ground for a number of years, which means that, unless the plot is well manured and cleaned to begin with, it will soon become worked out or covered with weeds. When dealing with new gardens it is generally wise to wait a year or so before making the asparagus bed so that the ground can be got into thoroughly good condition first.

Asparagus can easily be raised from seed sown in a frame or sheltered bed outdoors early in April. Sow thinly in drills $\frac{1}{2}$ in. deep and 9–12 ins. apart. Best roots are obtained by thinning the small seedlings to 9 ins. but if space cannot be spared for this, leave them standing 3 or 4 ins. apart. Transplant to permanent beds the following April. An alternative is to sow the seed directly in the bed in which the asparagus is to grow and then thin the seedlings to 12 in. apart. The rows themselves should be 15 in. apart. The method has the merit of permitting the seedlings to grow unchecked so that they more rapidly attain cropping size. Usually, however, the amateur will prefer to start by purchasing two year old roots, which can be obtained from most nurserymen. Such roots should be planted in early April 1 ft. apart in rows at least 15 in. apart.

Some plants produce in summer berries containing the seeds whereas other plants never carry any berries but only anther-bearing flowers. The former are known as females the latter as males. Experiment has shown that the males produce the heavier crop of edible shoots so it is an advantage if a bed can be formed entirely of them. Unfortunately it will not be until the second season at earliest that the two sexes can be distinguished among seedlings so if this scheme is to be followed either there must be a further delay of a year before the bed is planted or the females must be picked out after planting and the spaces made good later.

As a rule asparagus is grown in long, narrow beds raised a little above the surrounding ground to ensure good drainage round the crowns. A convenient width for the beds is 4 ft., which will allow for three rows lengthwise with 9 ins. separating the outer rows from the edge of the bed.

Excavate the soil to a depth of at least 2 ft., break up the bottom with a fork, replace the top soil and at the same time mix in well-rotted stable or farmyard manure at the rate of 1 cwt. to 5 sq. yds. Build the bed up at least 6 ins. above the surrounding level.

Allow the bed to settle for at least a month and then plant the crowns with their roots well spread out and cover with 3 ins. of soil.

Take no crop the first year. In subsequent years commence to cut the young shoots in May and continue until the middle of June. The shoots are cut when they are 3 to 4 ins. high and are severed well below soil level.

After June the plants are allowed to grow unchecked and make plenty of top growth which is not removed until it turns yellow at the end of October. It is then cut off just above soil level.

The asparagus bed should be fed each spring with a good thick mulch of well-broken and thoroughly rotted manure or, failing this, hop manure as advised by the manufacturers. Some growers also give salt, 1 oz. per sq. yd., each March.

There are not a great many varieties, two of the best in size and quality being Connover's Colossal and Giant French.

AUBERGINE (EGG PLANT)

This is a vegetable very little cultivated in this country though it is popular on the Continent. The plant is grown for its thick sausage shaped fruits which can be cooked in a variety of ways and are esteemed a delicacy by gourmets.

Seed should be sown during January, February or March, in well-drained pans or boxes filled with an ordinary seed mixture (see p. 423). Germination is effected in a warm greenhouse, temperature about 60 to 65°. The seedlings are potted singly in 2½ in. pots as soon as they can be handled and are moved from these into 6 or 7 in. pots when the first are nicely filled with roots. For all this potting the John Innes compost recommended on p. 421 should be used.

Grow the plants throughout in a sunny greenhouse (or from May in a frame) with an average temperature of 60°, which might rise to 80° on sunny days but should never fall below 50°. Water rather freely. Pinch out the tip of each plant at about 6 in. high and subsequently train growths to stakes or wires. When fruits form restrict them to about five or six per plant and thereafter feed liberally with weak liquid manure or a good compound fertiliser.

The fruits are ready for use when they become fully coloured and a little soft, in fact about the condition in which tomatoes would be picked.

Not many varieties are listed as a rule in this country. The Long Purple is the kind most frequently planted. An improvement is New York Purple and there is also a white fruited kind.

BEANS—BROAD

Broad beans are hardier than any of the other popular types and, unlike runner and French beans, are grown solely for their seeds. They are a profitable crop for they give a heavy yield and will thrive with a minimum of attention.

There are few soils in which broad beans will not succeed, though they do best on the richer types of loam. Digging should be as thorough as possible and well-rotted manure or compost used sparingly in the preparation of the ground as it is seldom wise to give more than 1 cwt. to 15 sq. yds. An alternative is to follow this crop after brassicas, potatoes or some other crop for which the ground has already been well manured. In this case the dressing can be omitted. In any case it is wise to give extra phosphates and potash as, for example, superphosphate of lime, 3 ozs. per sq. yd. and sulphate of potash, 1 oz. per sq. yd., raked in immediately before sowing. Broad beans do best in soils that are neutral or at most only slightly acid, so if there is any doubt on this point, a dressing of lime or chalk should be given at the appropriate rate, see p. 27.

Seed can be sown in three ways. Outdoors in late October or early November; in deep boxes in a warm greenhouse or frame during January or February; or outdoors in spring any time from about the end of March until early June. Autumn sowing became unpopular as so often the seedlings suffered badly during the winter months. It revived thanks to the introduction of the continuous type of cloche which can be used to protect the seedlings, as much from excessive rain and wind as from cold.

Box sowing is very satisfactory provided the seedlings are not subjected to too much heat (a temperature of 60° is ample) and are well hardened off before being planted out. This can usually be done with safety during the first half of April. By either autumn sowing or box sowing a crop of beans can be picked in early June.

The main crop for use from mid-summer to August is obtained from early April sowing outdoors. Some gardeners make a successional sowing in May to crop in September and this can be most useful.

For all outdoor sowings the beans should be placed 6 in. apart in drills 1½ in. deep and 2 ft. apart, or alternatively two rows can be spaced at 18 in. and then a wide alley-way of 2 ft. 6 in. left between this pair of rows and the next. On heavy soils it is sometimes best to sow the seeds on the surface, not in drills, and cover by drawing the soil over the seeds in a low ridge.

No thinning is required and little after care beyond weeding and hoeing until the plants have set their first clusters of beans. Then the growing tip of each should be broken off to prevent further extension and hasten the maturing of the crop.

Seeds raised in boxes are spaced a couple of inches apart each way and covered with ¾ in. of soil. They are not pricked off but are left to grow undisturbed until they can be planted outdoors. Planting should be with a trowel; the roots must be dropped into good, deep holes and the plants spaced as for beans sown outdoors.

Picking should commence directly the beans inside the pods are of good size. Start from the bottom clusters and work upwards. If a few pods are removed at a time from each plant the rest will be encouraged to develop more quickly.

There are a good many varieties, many of which do not differ greatly. Good standard kinds are Green Windsor and Seville Longpod. The latter is the heavier cropper and makes the hardier plant but Green Windsor has the merit that the beans keep their colour better when bottled. There are, in addition, numerous selections and sub-varieties of these two types such as Early Longpod, Masterpiece, Green Longpod, Bunyards Exhibition (a particularly big longpod bean), Giant or Four-Seeded Windsor and Harkington White (Windsor type but extra broad pods).

BEANS—FRENCH

For some reason the French bean is not nearly so popular in this country as the runner bean. On the Continent the opposite is true and it is my conviction that the French bean makes far and away the better eating of the two. However, that is for the individual gardener to decide for himself. Some less controversial advantages which the French bean has over the runner are that it grows more quickly, starts to crop earlier, is a little hardier and takes up less room. There are two principal types, dwarf and climbing, but the latter are not frequently seen in this country and I doubt that they have any real advantage though they may give a slightly heavier crop per sq. yd. of ground.

Though French beans will grow in most ordinary garden soils they do best in those that are light and rich. Well-rotted dung can be used freely in the preparation of the ground at rates up to 1 cwt. to 8 sq. yds. The deeper the digging the better, for the plants appreciate an open root run and plenty of moisture. Before sowing, dust the ground with superphosphate of lime 3 ozs., and sulphate of potash 1½ ozs. per sq. yd.

Outdoor sowing should not be attempted until the last week in April except in very sheltered places or under cloches. Earlier crops can be obtained by sowing seeds in deep boxes in a greenhouse or frame during early April and hardening the seedlings off for planting out towards the end of May. In boxes the seeds should be spaced 3 in. apart each way. Outdoors they should be spaced 6 in. apart in drills 1 in. deep and 18 in. apart. These distances are also the right ones for planting out greenhouse-raised seedlings.

The secret of producing good French beans is to keep them growing fast throughout. Water them freely if the weather is dry and then mulch with grass clippings or very strawy manure. Start to pick beans when they are 3 or 4 in. long and never let any beans get big and coarse on the plants as this checks further production. I think a good many people leave French beans to grow too big and consequently do not appreciate their delicate texture and flavour.

If it turns out that more beans have been grown than are required for use green, leave some of the plants unpicked altogether and let them ripen their whole crop. The dried seeds can then be shelled out and used as haricots. They will keep in a cool, dry place for years.

The best variety I have grown is The Prince. Other good kinds are Canadian Wonder Improved, Masterpiece and Black Prince.

FORCING. French beans can be grown under glass in pots or direct in a bed of soil. From a January sowing in a greenhouse with a temperature of 60° beans may be had by May while February or early March sowings in frame or cloche will yield June pickings. Use a soil mixture similar to that recommended for tomatoes and grow under as even conditions of temperature and moisture as possible throughout. At no time need the temperature exceed 65° and some ventilation can be given directly the house reaches 55°. The minimum should be 45° and it is wise to keep well above this while the plants are in flower. If grown in pots three seeds may be sown in each 8 in. pot.

BEANS—HARICOT

From the botanical stand-point there is really no difference between the haricot bean and the French bean and it is grown in exactly the same way in the garden with the sole difference that instead of the beans being picked green they are all left to ripen, after which the seeds are shelled out and stored in a cool, dry place for winter use. All the details I have given regarding the cultivation of French beans apply equally to haricot beans. The crop is not a very heavy one, seldom more than 6 ozs. of ripened beans per sq. yd., and I doubt whether it is a profitable one for the gardener in ordinary times. It is probably better for him to leave the cultivation of haricot beans to farmers in warmer climates than our own.

There are both dwarf and climbing haricots, just as there are dwarf and climbing French beans. Two of the best varieties I have tried, both dwarfs, are Brown Dutch, with brown seeds, and Comtesse de Chambord with white seeds, but the ordinary dwarf French bean Masterpiece also makes an excellent haricot.

BEANS—RUNNER

There are few crops which will give a greater return for less trouble than the runner bean. It will grow practically anywhere, on heavy or light soils and sunny or partially shaded positions. I have seen quite good crops taken from town gardens with the plants grown in boxes and trained against most unpromising looking fences and walls.

The preparation of the ground is the same as for French beans. Some people grow runner beans in trenches prepared in much the same manner as for celery and this is not at all a bad plan as it saves labour and materials, but in heavy soils the trenches are apt to serve as drains for surface water with disastrous results for the plants growing in them.

Runner beans are very tender and the least frost will kill them so it is not safe to sow seed out of doors until the first week in May except in the most favoured localities or where the plants are to be covered by cloches. An alternative is to raise seedlings in boxes in the same way as described for French beans and plant them out when properly hardened off. Do not sow until the end of April nor plant out before the first week in June.

The spacing for seeds outdoors or for plants is 8 in. apart in double rows 10 to 12 in. apart. Between each pair of double rows at least 5 ft. should be left. These spacings are for plants to be grown on stakes. An alternative method of cultivation is to turn the plants into big, loose bushes by constantly pinching out the points of the runners. This is the method used by most commercial growers and excellent crops can be obtained, though individually the beans are seldom of the length and straightness of those obtained from staked plants. If the bush method is to be used the plants must be spaced at least 2 ft. from plant to plant and 3 ft. from row to row.

Where beans are to be grown on stakes these should be put in position directly the seedlings appear. Poles 8 ft. long are best and should be lashed securely at the top to a horizontal spar running the length of the row. A row of fully-grown runner beans presents a tremendous resistance to wind.

It pays to mulch the ground between bean rows with strawy manure early in June. This not only feeds them but also keeps the soil cool and moist, encourages root growth and helps the setting of the bean flowers. Some growers syringe their beans every evening with clear water while they are in flower as an additional aid to setting, but I think the main cause of flower dropping is cold at night and it is in consequence very much a seasonal trouble about which nothing can be done.

The beans should be picked young and none allowed to remain to ripen on the plants unless a few plants are set aside especially to supply seed which should be shelled out when the pods become dry and commence to split open.

There are a good many varieties but a well-selected strain of Scarlet Emperor still takes a lot of beating for ordinary kitchen use. For exhibition one of the very long podded kinds is preferable, such as Prizewinner or Streamline, while for early work Princeps should be grown.

BEETROOT

There are three principal types of beetroot, the globe, in which the roots are shaped more or less like a cricket ball, the long-rooted, which may be as much as a foot in length, gradually tapering to a point, and the tankard or intermediate type, obtained by crossing the other two. This deserves to be better known as it gives a heavy weight of crop without needing very deep soil. The roots are roughly canister-shaped, shorter and less tapering than those of the long beetroot.

The beetroot needs a well-tilled and reasonably rich soil but too much dung is liable to cause forking of the roots. The best policy is to choose a plot that was thoroughly manured for a previous crop and then prepare it for beetroot by digging or half trenching and finishing off with a top dressing of artificial fertilisers well raked in. For this purpose sulphate of ammonia may be used at 1 oz. per sq. yd., with a similar weight of sulphate of potash and 4 ozs. of superphosphate of lime. Use these fertilisers a week or so prior to sowing and rake in very thoroughly.

A first sowing outdoors, preferably of a globe-rooted kind, should be made from the middle to the end of April. It should be followed by a main sowing of a tankard or long-rooted beetroot during the first half of May. In all cases sow in drills 1 in. deep and 12 in. apart, drop in the seeds in twos or threes, 4 in. apart in the case of globe varieties and 6 in. with the other types. When the seedlings are 1 in. high, reduce them to one at each point. At this stage seedlings transplant quite well and surplus can be used to fill any gaps in the rows. If growth is slow give a top dressing of nitrate of soda, 1 oz. to 12 ft. of row and hoe in. No other treatment is necessary beyond an occasional hoeing to keep down weeds.

Many people leave beetroot in the ground too long with the result that the roots get coarse and woody and some commence to crack. Globe kinds should be lifted, a few at a time as required, from the period at which they are a couple of inches in diameter. None should be left to grow beyond the size of cricket balls. If they cannot be used at this stage, lift them and store them in a shed or outhouse, covering them with dry soil or sand. Long and tankard-rooted beetroots should be lifted during late September and be stored in the same way. They will keep till April or May.

There are numerous varieties, particularly of the globe- and long-rooted types and many seedsmen list their own specialities. Good standard varieties are Crimson Globe, Veitch's Intermediate, Cheltenham Greentop, Nutting's Red and Red Globe.

FORCING. An extra early crop for June–July use can be obtained by sowing a globe-rooted variety in a frame or under cloches. Preparation of the soil is exactly as for outdoor culture. Seed can be sown in February in drills 8 in. apart, seedlings being thinned to 4 in. Ventilate freely on fine days from April onwards.

BORECOLE—SEE KALE

BROCCOLI

There is a good deal of confusion as to the difference between broccoli and cauliflower and in fact thanks to hybridisation there is really no hard and fast distinction between them. Roughly speaking broccoli may be described as biennials, that is to say plants which are sown from seed one year to mature the next, whereas cauliflowers are annuals, i.e. they are sown and harvested in the same year. Another distinction might be made on the score of flavour and texture as the cauliflower is generally considered superior to broccoli in both these respects. But there are a good many exceptions to both these distinction, some early broccoli heading the same year as sown and some so resembling cauliflowers in texture that they are termed 'cauliflower headed'.

The sprouting broccoli is a very different plant in appearance from the ordinary heading type. Instead of making a close, white curd it produces a number of separate shoots each terminating in a cluster of flowers. These are cut just before the flowers open and it is these flower shoots and buds which form the edible part of the plant. When cooked they have rather the appearance and flavour of asparagus.

Both heading and sprouting broccoli are raised from seed sown in spring. A first sowing of early varieties of the heading type can be made in early March in a frame but the main sowing of heading and sprouting varieties will not come until April and can be outdoors, with a further small sowing of late sprouting broccoli in mid-May.

In all cases sprinkle the seed thinly in drills $\frac{1}{4}$ in. deep and 6 in. apart. If the seed is sown very thinly the seedlings can be left to grow until they are big enough for removal to their final quarters, but should the seedlings appear crowded they must be pricked off 2 or 3 in. apart in rows 6 to 8 in. apart as soon as they can be handled. The object is to get sturdy, well-rooted plants for putting out in May, June and July.

Meanwhile the final bed should be prepared by deep digging or trenching. Dung or compost may be worked in at about 2 cwt. per rod. In addition give extra phosphates and potash as, for example, basic slag, 4 to 6 oz. per sq. yd. and sulphate of potash 1 to $1\frac{1}{2}$ oz. per sq. yd. These fertilisers should be applied as a top dressing after completion of digging and worked in as the ground is broken down for planting.

Do not pull the seedlings out of the seed bed but lift them with a fork. Plant very firmly with a trowel or spade, not a dibber, and space the plants at least 2 ft. apart in rows $2\frac{1}{2}$ ft. apart. Water in well if the weather is dry and water the seedlings before they are lifted from the seed bed.

When the plants are well established and a foot or more in height, spread a little well-rotted manure or compost down the rows and draw soil over this and up around the stems from between the rows. Fresh roots will be formed from the stems into the soil and manure and these will give better anchorage and growth.

Heading broccoli are ready for gathering when the curds are well developed but before they commence to open. It is rather a tricky business as they develop very rapidly in mild weather and the plants need to be examined daily. It is a good plan to protect the forming curds from frost and sun by breaking down a few inside leaves over them but do not forget to examine the curds under these leaves.

Sprouting broccoli is cut directly the flower shoots are well developed but before any flower buds commence to open into yellow bloom. Here again almost daily cutting is necessary.

Because of their habit of turning in all at once it is necessary to plant quite small patches of heading broccoli for private consumption and to make use of early, main crop and late varieties of which a great selection will be found in every seed catalogue. A few outstanding kinds are

Michaelmas White, usually fit to cut in October; Veitch's Self-Protecting, ready in October–November; Roscoff 1 to 5, which are cut from about December to early May in the order of their numerals, but are all rather tender; Lenten Monarch, March–April; Knight's Self-Protecting and St. George for April cutting; May Queen and Late Queen, to cut in May, and either Methven's June or Clucas's June which are generally ready a little earlier than their name suggests.

BRUSSELS SPROUTS

One of the most useful brassicas for the amateur as, unlike so many others of its family, picking can be continued for a considerable time from one batch of plants. For this reason there is seldom any waste as so often occurs with broccoli, cauliflowers, cabbages, or savoys.

Brussels sprouts need a rich, firm soil. It should be dug or trenched as long as possible in advance of planting so that the soil may have ample time to settle. Dung or compost can be used with advantage at rates up to 1 cwt. to 10 sq. yd. and it is almost always desirable to add some extra phosphates and potash immediately prior to planting. These can be in the form of superphosphate of lime, 3 oz. per sq. yd., and sulphate of potash, 1 oz. per sq. yd.

Seed should be sown in a separate seed bed at least two months before the plants are required for putting out. It is usually desirable to make two separate sowings, one about mid-March in a frame or sheltered position outdoors and another in the open during the first half of April. For a very early supply seeds may be sown in an unheated greenhouse or frame in early February or outdoors in early September. In the latter case the seedlings will be transferred to a frame in late October and kept there until the following spring.

Sow in drills half an inch deep or alternatively sow broadcast and cover with half an inch of fine soil. Scatter the seed as thinly as possible and so avoid the necessity of pricking off. When the plants have five or six leaves each, transplant them to their final quarters at least 2 ft. apart in rows 2½ ft. apart. Plant very firmly and water freely if the weather is dry. About two months later top dress down the rows with well-rotted dung and draw soil over this towards the stem. If the plants grow very large and are in an exposed place, it may be necessary to stake them and it is certainly better to do this than to risk their being blown over.

Commence to pick when the bottom sprouts are of useful size and continue up the stem, leaving the head until last. Treated in this way one batch of sprouts should continue to yield for two or three months and by growing two batches, one of an early and the other of a late variety, sprouts can be had from late August until February.

The principal difficulty met with is that many of the sprouts come loose instead of being nice tight 'buttons'. There are three possible causes, a poor strain of seed, loose soil or insufficient potash and too much nitrogen in the soil.

Varieties are numerous, most seedsmen offering their own specialities. Amongst the best are those raised at the Cambridge Experimental Station and known as Cambridge No. 1 (early), Cambridge No. 3 (mid-season) and Cambridge No. 5 (late). Fillbasket is specially good for exhibition; Harrison's XXX, is heavy cropping and early, and The Wroxton is a good old variety of medium height.

CABBAGE

It is possible to cut cabbage throughout the year but it takes a little skill and forethought to do it. The method is to make use of varieties from three separate groups of cabbage; very quick-growing varieties that will mature in early summer from a spring sowing, slower growing kinds that will be ready in autumn and winter from a spring sowing, and those varieties which can be sown in August to heart the following spring.

The first sowing can be made under glass, preferably with a little artificial heat in January or early February. Seed should be sown thinly in boxes and the seedlings pricked off 2 or 3 in. apart each way into a bed of reasonably rich soil in a frame the following month. Here they are hardened off until, four or five weeks later, they are sturdy enough to go outdoors in rich soil and a fairly sheltered position. If a suitable variety, such as Primo, is chosen heads should be ready for cutting from June onwards.

A second sowing of a similar variety should be made in March in a frame or sheltered place outdoors. Two more sowings, one of an autumn and one of a winter cabbage, should be made in April, the seeds being sown very thinly in $\frac{1}{2}$-in. deep drills and left undisturbed until they can be planted in late May or early June. It is sometimes wise to make yet another sowing of a winter kind about mid-May treating it in the same way but not planting out the seedlings until July.

The last sowing of a spring cabbage is made some time between the middle of July and the middle of August. The precise date will vary according to district and soil and if you cannot get any local advice on this point it is probably best to make two separate sowings the first season, one early and the other late and in subsequent years adjust matters according to results. Seedlings from this summer sowing will be treated just like the spring seedlings and planted in their final quarters in September or early October. Some seedlings can be left in the seed bed throughout the winter and used to fill up gaps the following March.

In all cases the bed for the final planting should be in an open position and the soil reasonably rich. For summer supplies more dung can be used than for winter and spring cabbage, say 4 cwt. per rod for the former and 2 cwt. for the latter. An alternative is to follow the spring cabbage—i.e. those raised from a July–August sowing—after potatoes or some other crop for which dung has already been used, in which case no further manure need be added but only potash and phosphates in the form of artificial fertilisers. It is, in any case, always wise to give some extra potash and phosphate besides dung as, for example, super-phosphate of lime 3 oz. and sulphate of potash $1\frac{1}{2}$ oz. per sq. yd.

Plant spring and early summer maturing cabbages 1 ft. apart in rows 18 in. apart. Autumn and winter maturing kinds make bigger plants and need more room, usually 18 in. in the rows and $2-2\frac{1}{2}$ ft. between the rows.

Lift the seedlings from the seed bed with a fork, injuring the roots as little as possible, plant firmly with a trowel and water in well. About six weeks after planting summer, autumn and winter maturing cabbages will benefit from a top dressing of nitrate of soda, 1 oz. to every 6 ft. of row well hoed or watered in. In the case of spring cabbages this dressing should be delayed until March or early April.

Varieties are extremely numerous and I can only mention a few of the best known. They are grouped according to the classes already described. For early summer cutting, Primo, Greyhound and Velocity; for summer and autumn cutting, Winnigstadt, Enfield Market and Wheeler's Imperial; for winter cutting, Long Standing, January King and Christmas Drumhead; for spring cutting, Early Offenham, Harbinger, Flower of Spring, First and Best and Ellam's Early.

CARDOON

One of the less well-known vegetables but much appreciated by epicures. It is a plant very like the globe artichoke in appearance but instead of being grown for the flower heads it is prized for the stems, which are blanched and served either cooked or raw.

Cardoons are raised from seed sown in a moderately heated green-house in February, in a frame in March or outdoors towards the end of April. Seed should be sown thinly and the seedlings pricked off a few inches apart into deep boxes or a frame bed and hardened off for planting out between the end of May and the beginning of July. Cardoons make big plants and should be given plenty of room, at least 18 in. in the rows and 3 ft. between the rows. Plant them in an open, sunny position and moderately rich, well-drained soil. Well-rotted dung can be used in the preparation of this site at the rate of 1 cwt. to 12 sq. yd.

Little subsequent attention is required, beyond weeding and hoeing, until early September when the leaves should be tied together at the top and the stems wrapped in brown paper. Soil is then drawn up around this exactly as when earthing celery and the plants left for at least two months, by which time they should be thoroughly blanched. The whole plant is then lifted and the roots trimmed off, again in a similar manner to the preparation for table of celery. Dig a few plants at a time as needed and, if hard weather threatens, protect the remaining plants with straw where they grow.

CARROTS

There are several very distinct types of carrot and selection should be made from amongst them according to the purpose for which the crop is required. For very early supplies in frames the stump rooted, forcing varieties are best. Shorthorn carrots can also be grown out of doors for an early crop while to follow on the stump-rooted type is most serviceable. In this the roots are longer than those of the stump-rooted varieties and they do not taper so much; in fact they are rather the shape and size of a candle. For the main crop, to be stored for winter use, either an intermediate or a long-rooted carrot should be chosen, according to the nature of the soil. The long-rooted varieties give the heaviest crops but they do need deep, well-cultivated soils.

All carrots do best on rather open, easily-worked, reasonably rich soils. Dung, if used at all, should be applied sparingly and several months before sowing, but it is better to provide a site which was manured for a previous crop and to prepare this with artificials alone. A suitable dressing is sulphate of ammonia, 1 oz. per sq. yd., superphosphate of lime, 3 oz. per sq. yd. and sulphate of potash, $1\frac{1}{2}$ oz. per sq. yd. Rake this in thoroughly just before sowing.

The earliest crops are obtained in frames or greenhouses and sowing can commence in January if a temperature of $55°$ can be maintained. For these early crops, sow very thinly in drills $\frac{1}{4}$ in. deep and 8 in. apart and do not thin out the seedlings. Let them stand until they are big enough to use and then pull out the most forward first, leaving the rest to gain size.

Outdoor sowing can, as a rule, commence early in March though it is no use sowing if the ground is wet and cold. Better wait three or four weeks than risk bad germination. Drills should be ½ in. deep and 9 in. apart for stump-rooted and shorthorn varieties, 1 ft. to 15 in. apart for intermediate and long-rooted kinds. Successional sowings of early and second early varieties can be made every fortnight or so until midsummer. As a rule it is not wise to sow the main crop for storing until the latter half of April and in some districts it pays to wait until early June for by this means the carrot fly is avoided. This fly lays its eggs in the soil near the seedlings, small white maggots hatch out in a week or so and eat their way into the young carrot roots. The pest is very damaging in some places and certain seasons.

Early carrots need not be thinned but main crop carrots should be singled out to at least 4 in. apart in the rows. For exhibition this may be increased to 8 in. Do this while the seedlings are still quite small and be careful to press the soil firmly around the roots after thinning. If left loose the carrot fly is encouraged. It often pays to top dress along the rows with sulphate of ammonia or nitrate of soda, 1 oz. to 6 ft. of row, immediately after thinning.

Early carrots should be pulled as required for use while the main crop should be dug about mid-September or at latest by mid-October. If left too long the roots get coarse and some will crack. Such roots do not store well.

Main crop carrots lifted in good condition will keep until the spring if placed in a dry, airy shed and covered with dry sand or fine soil. Alternatively they can be stored in small clamps outdoors. First cut off the tops, then pack the roots in a low ridge with their tops outwards, as shown in the photograph on p. 552. Finally cover them with about 3 in. of sand or sifted boiler ashes. The clamp should be made in a sheltered place.

There are a great many varieties of carrot though a good many of these don't differ markedly from one another. Reliable standard kinds are as follows: *Early Sowing in Frames*: Early French Forcing Horn; *Early Sowing Outdoors*: Red Cored Early Market, Early Gem; *Summer Use*: Early Nantes; *Autumn and Winter Use*: James' Scarlet Intermediate and St. Valery.

CAULIFLOWER

Because of their comparatively short season of growth it is essential that cauliflower shall receive no check from start to finish. The soil chosen for them should be rich and well watered and care must be taken that seedlings raised under glass are properly hardened off before they are planted out, otherwise they may be chilled and set back for several weeks.

Cauliflowers can be cut outdoors in June from a sowing made in February in a warm greenhouse, provided an early variety is chosen. An alternative method is to sow the seed outdoors in September, transfer the seedlings to an unheated frame the following month and allow the seedlings to remain there throughout the winter. In either case the seedlings should be hardened off for planting out as early in spring as the weather allows. Later crops are obtained by sowing seed in a frame or sheltered position outdoors in March and planting out in late April or May.

In all cases the position chosen for planting should be open, sunny, but not too exposed. The ground must be dug as deeply as possible, in fact if it can be trenched so much the better, and manure should be used liberally; 1 cwt. to 6 sq. yd. will not be too much in most cases. In addition dust with superphosphate of lime, 2 oz. per sq. yd. a week or so prior to planting.

Plant firmly with a trowel, 18 in. apart each way for the early varieties and 2 ft. apart in rows 2½ ft. apart for the late summer and autumn kinds. Top dress with Nitro-chalk, 2 oz. to 6 ft. of row when the plants are well established and draw a little soil from between the rows over the fertiliser and around the stems of the plants at the same time. Water freely if the weather is dry. Very weak liquid manure can be used instead of water.

When curds begin to form break some of the inner leaves down over them as a protection from sunlight which will spoil their whiteness. In autumn the broken leaves also serve to protect the curds from frost.

Cauliflowers should be cut directly the curds are of good size and before they commence to open. Like broccoli they tend to turn in all at once and so it is important in small gardens to make successional sowings or plantings every few weeks and not have one big batch.

Good crops of early cauliflowers can also be produced under glass. The seedlings are raised in the ordinary way and are planted out in a bed of rich soil on the floor of the greenhouse as soon as they have five or six leaves each. Space them 18 in. apart each way. Grow them on in an average temperature of 55°. Keep well watered and ventilate freely whenever the weather is favourable. The more light and air the plants get the better. This is quite a good utility crop to precede tomatoes. It will probably be necessary to plant the tomatoes in the greenhouse before the cauliflowers are cut and room should be left for this but the tomatoes will not be very big by the time the cauliflowers are removed.

Varieties are fairly numerous, amongst the most reliable being First Crop and Early Snowball, which can be cut in June or July; Early Erfurt, and Early London, both of which can be cut in August; Veitch's Autumn Giant and Majestic, which are ready in September–October, and Veitch's Self-Protecting for November and December cutting in sheltered places. All the Year Round as its name implies, can be sown at various times to mature fairly early or quite late in the cauliflower season.

CELERIAC

This is a useful alternative to celery and one which can be grown more easily in many gardens. It is cultivated for its thick root which, when fully grown, is about the size of a good turnip and has the flavour of celery. The roots can be grated in salads or can be sliced and cooked in stews, soups, etc. It is sometimes stated that celeriac will grow in ground not rich enough for celery. This may be so but it is a comparative distinction only and does not mean that celeriac should be planted in poor, dry places. On the contrary, the ground should be dug thoroughly and well manured, for preference with farmyard or stable manure at about 1 cwt. to 8 sq. yd. The position should be open, not too dry.

Seed is sown in an unheated greenhouse or frame early in April, the usual method being to sow thinly in earthenware pans or shallow wooden boxes. The seedlings are pricked off 2 in. apart each way into deeper boxes directly they can be handled and while still very small. It is a task requiring some skill and patience. Water well, keep in a greenhouse or frame for a further week or so and then stand in a sheltered position outdoors to harden off.

Plant out towards the end of May or during June. The plants should be 1 ft. apart in rows 18 in. apart. Subsequently keep well watered if the weather is dry but do not attempt to earth up in any way. A top dressing of Nitro-chalk, 1 oz. per sq. yd. can be given a few weeks after planting out. No further attention should be necessary until October, by which time the roots should be well formed and ready for lifting. In sheltered districts celeriac can be left outdoors all winter and lifted as required, but in exposed places it is better to dig the whole crop in October and place the roots in a shed, covering them with sand or dry soil.

There are no important varieties but it is very vital to get a good strain of seed. Some poor strains make big plants but no swollen roots.

CELERY

This most useful of autumn and winter salad vegetables is not too easy to grow. It needs very good soil, plenty of moisture while in growth and yet good drainage. To reconcile these needs it is necessary to use plenty of well-rotted dung or, failing this, good compost, together with leaf mould and peat to make the soil rather open and spongy.

Celery is reasonably hardy but the seed is so small and germinates so slowly unless in a warm place that it is better to raise it under glass in boxes or pans of fine soil than to chance sowing it in the open air. The earliest crops are obtained from early March sowings made in a greenhouse with a temperature of 55 to 60° while the main crop seed can be sown in an unheated greenhouse or frame about mid-April.

Sow on the surface of an ordinary seed compost, see p. 423 and cover with the merest sprinkling of fine soil. In addition cover each box or pan with a pane of glass and a sheet of brown paper but remove this directly germination takes place.

Directly they can be handled the seedlings should be pricked off into deeper seed boxes filled with a similar compost. The earlier this can be done the better and the seedlings must be separated out singly at this stage. They are so small and often the roots are so tangled together that it is easy to put them in in small clumps by mistake. Space them 2 in. apart each way. Water them in well and return them to the greenhouse or frame for a further fortnight after which they can be gradually hardened off for planting out.

A common mistake is to sow too early, with the result that the seedlings get over-crowded and checked before they have been properly hardened off and are ready for putting outdoors. Final planting out should be done some time between mid-May and the end of June and the ground must be prepared for the plants as long as possible in advance.

It is customary, though not absolutely essential, to grow celery in trenches which may be either 15 in. wide to take a single row of plants or 18 to 20 in. wide to take a double row. Soil from the trench is dug out to a depth of at least 2 and preferably 3 ft.; the subsoil, if poor, is replaced with good soil from another part of the garden, and then the trench is nearly but not quite refilled with the top soil mixed liberally with well-rotted dung. 1 cwt. of dung to every 24 ft. of trench is not too much. Leave a depression about 4 in. deep in which the plants will be placed. This will give them a little protection from cold winds and will make it easy to flood them with water in dry weather. Plant with a trowel, 1 ft. apart down the middle of the trench in the case of single rows, or at each side if two rows are to be planted.

A few weeks after planting a top dressing of nitrate of soda or sulphate of ammonia should be given down the trenches at the rate of 1 oz. to 12 ft. and this can be repeated a fortnight later. Water liberally in dry weather and occasionally substitute weak liquid manure for plain water.

Earthing up to blanch the stems should not be started until the plants are fully grown as it checks further progress. As a rule the earliest crop planted in mid-May is ready for earthing during the first half of August, while the main crop is earthed during September and early October. First of all remove any off-shoots that have formed round the base of each plant. Then tie the stems together with a piece of raffia and draw the soil from each side of the trench towards the plants and up around them. Some growers tie a brown paper collar round the plants first before earthing up to prevent soil falling into their hearts.

It takes about six weeks to blanch celery properly and subsequently it can be left just as it is to be dug as required. From November onwards it is advisable to place a couple of planks on edge along the summit of each ridge to shoot off water and prevent it soaking down into the hearts of the plants. After the ridge has been opened at one end to dig a few sticks the soil should be returned as a protection against frost.

There are numerous excellent varieties but the main distinction is to be made between white- and pink-skinned types. Of these Solid White, Wright's Giant White, Standard Bearer Pink, Clayworth Prize Pink are good examples.

There is also a variety known as Golden Self Blanching. This has naturally pale-coloured stems and if it is planted 9 in. apart each way in a squarish bed the leaves cast sufficient shade to complete the blanching to a very pale, golden colour. This variety is not of the highest quality nor does it make sticks of very great size but it is extremely economical to grow and is certainly excellent for cooking. Because of the close planting it is essential to grow it in very rich soil and to water freely. It is most suitable for summer and early autumn use.

CHICORY

This is not a popular vegetable in this country though it is extensively grown on the Continent as a salad for winter use. For this purpose the leaves and stems are forced and blanched in heat. Suitable roots for forcing are obtained by sowing seed outdoors in

April or May in drills ½ in. deep and 1 ft. apart. Sow the seed very thinly. Previously the ground should have been well dug and given a dressing of dung or compost at the rate of 1 cwt. to 12 sq. yd. followed by a top dressing of superphosphate of lime, 2 oz. per sq. yd. The seedlings are thinned to 9 in. apart as soon as they have their first true leaves. Subsequently they need little care beyond hoeing and weeding until November, by which time they should have formed good roots, 1 ft. or more in length and not unlike thin parsnips. These are lifted a few at a time, any remaining leaves are cut off just above the crowns and they are packed 2 or 3 in. apart in boxes or fairly large flower pots filled with any old potting soil. They are then brought into a warm greenhouse or shed and kept completely dark either by inverting an empty flower pot over each pot of roots or by placing them in a specially darkened forcing pit which can often most conveniently be made under the greenhouse staging. It is very important to exclude all light, otherwise the leaves will not be fully blanched and will be very bitter. The temperature should be 60° or more and the soil must be watered moderately. The blanched shoots are cut off at soil level when 6 or 7 in. high. They are served in salads in the same way as lettuces or endives or can be cooked and served hot. The forced roots are of no further use and should be thrown away.

The Witloof chicory is generally regarded as the best variety.

CHIVES

This member of the onion family is very easily grown and is remarkable for its mild flavour. Many people prefer it on this account to spring onions as an ingredient of salads and it can also be used instead of onions as flavouring in soups, stews, etc.

Chives are exceptionally easy to grow. All that is necessary is to obtain a good clump as early in March as possible, split it up into small tufts, each with two or three shoots and some roots attached, and plant these firmly 6 in. apart in rows about 9 in. apart in any ordinary garden soil and reasonably open position. No further attention is required except for occasional hoeing and weeding, until the plants get overcrowded, when they can be lifted, divided and replanted in March as at the commencement.

When chives are required for kitchen use, the shoots are simply cut off at soil level. Take a few from each plant and growth will continue unchecked.

There are no varieties.

COLEWORTS (COLLARDS)

A small, hardy type of cabbage which is sometimes grown for autumn and early winter cutting. The utility of the colewort has been considerably diminished by the introduction of better-hearted types which can be had at the same time but it has the merits of taking up very little room, being sufficiently quick growing to be planted as a catch crop after early potatoes or peas, and sufficiently hardy to withstand very cold weather. Those who like a 'green' cabbage in contradistinction to one with a big white heart will like the colewort.

Sow seed in June and July and plant out from July to September in ground prepared as for cabbage. Space 9 in. apart in rows 15 in. apart. After cutting the main heads leave the stumps to shoot again. They will give a good crop of spring greens.

CORN SALAD

A vegetable which is more frequently written about than grown in this country. One is constantly coming across references to it in books and articles, but I have seldom seen a crop in growth. This is not because of any difficulty in cultivation for corn salad is one of the easiest of vegetables to grow. Probably the real explanation of its unpopularity is that it is an unfamiliar ingredient of salads and a good many people who have tried it do not much care for its rather undistinguished and earthy flavour.

Corn salad is a low-growing annual plant which is cultivated for its leaves. These are cut when the plants are a few inches high, before they commence to flower, and are served in salad with lettuce and the other more familiar ingredients.

Seed should be sown sparingly, either broadcast or in $\frac{1}{2}$-in. deep drills, 4 in. apart. Thin the seedlings to 4-in. apart. Frequent small sowings should be made at fortnightly intervals from about mid-March until the end of September. Late sowings for autumn and winter use are best made in a frame or may be covered later with cloches. The ground chosen should be open, or slightly shaded and the soil well dug and fairly rich. Water freely in dry weather.

There are no varieties of importance.

COUVE TRONCHUDA

Another vegetable that is very little known in this country, though it is much esteemed on the Continent. It is a member of the cabbage family and has cabbagy-looking leaves with enormous white mid-ribs.

The green part of the leaf is cooked and used exactly like cabbage while the mid-rib is separated and cooked and served like seakale.

To be good, couve tronchuda must be planted in very rich soil with plenty of moisture to keep it growing fast. In poor soil or a dry year it tends to be coarse and tough. Sow seed in March or early April in an ordinary seed bed as for cabbage and transplant the seedlings in May or early June. They should be planted at least 2 ft. apart each way, preferably more, and will benefit from a top dressing of dung or several feeds with liquid manure when well established.

Start to cut the leaves, a few at a time, as soon as they are big enough to be serviceable.

There are no varieties.

CRESS

Cress is usually grown as a salad vegetable, to accompany mustard, see p. 588, but those who find the flavour of mustard too strong can, if they prefer, have cress alone.

Outdoor crops can be grown from April to September, while under glass in a temperature of 50–60° cress can be grown for the remaining months of the year; but many will prefer to have it in frames even in summer if only for the sake of keeping it clean. No special soil is required as long as it is fine and sandy. In fact it is possible to grow cress in sand alone. Cress should be grown in shallow trays or in pots and in either case the seed should be broadcast thinly and evenly all over the surface. No soil covering is needed but boards or slates should be laid over the boxes or pots for the first 5 or 6 days until germination occurs. Then remove this covering and let the cress have full light until it is ready for cutting somewhere between the 12th and 18th day from sowing.

Cut with scissors just above soil level when the seedlings are 2–3 in. high.

Note that cress takes about half again as long as mustard to grow, a point which must be allowed for when making sowings to cut at the same time. For a constant supply it is advisable to make a small sowing every 7 to 10 days.

CUCUMBER

The 'frame' or 'house' cucumber needs a good deal of warmth to succeed and is a crop only to be grown under glass. In contrast the 'ridge' cucumber is much hardier and good crops can be obtained in the open during the summer months. The fruits are inferior in size and appearance but not in flavour to those of the glasshouse type.

UNDER GLASS. Frame cucumbers need a very rich, open-textured soil containing abundant humus. They must have good drainage and yet the compost must be sufficiently spongy to hold ample moisture even when the atmosphere is very warm. The usual practice is to make up a special bed with a mixture of good, turfy loam, fresh or decayed stable manure containing plenty of straw bedding, bone meal and lime. Add 1 lb. of fine bone meal and a similar weight of hydrated lime to each barrowload of loam some weeks before it is required. Then, when it is time to make the bed, use two barrowloads of this prepared loam to one barrowload of stable manure and mix well. Build into a flat-topped bed, a foot deep, as much through at the top and about 18 in. wide at the base. This bed can run the whole length of the house if desired. One cucumber will be planted every 3 ft. along its length. The bed should be built on some kind of firm base such as slates, galvanised iron sheets or even clean straw to check wandering roots and provide a getaway for surplus water. In an ordinary greenhouse with side walls 2 ft. or more high it may be on the staging but if low-walled 'forcing houses' are used, the bed is best made on the floor.

An alternative method of bed making, popular in many private gardens though not with commercial growers is to spread a 6-in. deep layer of the compost to a width of about 3 ft. and any desired length and make a low mound with ½ bushel of compost every 3 ft. along this shallow bed. One cucumber is planted on the summit of each mound. The advantage gained by this is that of really sharp drainage round the 'collar' of the plant where stem joins root. Decay is liable to occur here if it is kept too wet. The drawback of the mounded bed is that not only the collar but the roots themselves may get dry at times and that will mean a check to growth. I have seen excellent cucumbers produced from both types of bed but I think the flat-topped kind is the better for the amateur who is likely to be away from home all day.

As regard the choice of fresh or rotted stable manure, the former gives a bed of better texture but care must be taken to see that the manure is really well-mixed with the soil and that there is no considerable escape of ammonia gas after the bed is planted. If there is, severe leaf scorching may result. Note well that the manure must contain plenty of straw either rotted or fresh. This is essential to give the necessary open, rather flaky texture so liked by cucumbers.

Beds can be made and seed sown at almost any time of the year, according to the period at which the crop is required, but usual practice with amateurs is to make one sowing in January or early February for an early crop, another in mid-March for the main crop, with possibly a May sowing for a late supply.

The seeds are sown singly in small earthenware pots filled with the usual seed compost,(see p. 423). They are watered moderately and placed in a greenhouse with a temperature of 65 to 70°. Stand in a box covered with glass or cover the pots themselves with glass and brown paper. Germination is usually very rapid and may take no more than two days. Directly the seedlings can be seen the covering must be removed. Most gardeners plant direct from these small pots but some prefer to grow on for a while in 6 in. pots to which the seedlings should be transferred when they have four or five leaves each. In this case each plant is tied to a short stake and all tendrils and flowers are removed.

The bed should have a temperature of at least 65° before the plants are put into it. That is the advantage of using fresh stable manure because as it ferments it generates heat. Otherwise one must wait for the heat of the house to penetrate into the compost. Plant with the top of the ball of soil just level with the surface of the bed. Water in freely. Be careful always to use water heated at least to the temperature of the greenhouse which should certainly not fall below 60° throughout and may rise to 80° with sun heat.

A good deal depends upon the correct training and pinching of the plants. The main shoot is trained over wires directly towards the apex of the house and about 13 in. below the glass. As side growths form they are tied horizontally along the wires and each is pinched at the second leaf beyond the first fruit formed. The main growth is pinched when it reaches the top of the house or a length of 7 or 8 ft. Secondary shoots forming from the first side growths will also carry fruits and must be stopped two leaves beyond these. Later in the season, after the plants have been cropping for some time, some of the older growths that have already carried a lot of cucumbers are cut right out and young shoots are trained in their place.

Cucumbers produce flowers of two sexes, male and female. They can be distinguished quite easily by the fact that immediately behind the female flower is a tiny embryo cucumber, whereas the male flower is simply carried on a thin stalk. These male flowers should be picked off as soon as they can be distinguished as it is not desirable that the female flowers should be fertilised. If they are the cucumbers will produce seeds and will not be nearly so palatable. There is no need to reduce the number of female flowers unless the plants are weak. No fruits are allowed to form on the main stem, only on side shoots.

Throughout the season the atmosphere should be pleasantly warm and very moist. If it is allowed to become dry the foliage is likely to be scorched and to be attacked by red spider, a minute pest which breeds in thousands on the under sides of the leaves, sucks the juice from them and turns them a curiously mottled, greyish-yellow colour. The best preventive for red spider is moisture and this is maintained by damping the floors, walls and stages of the house and syringing the leaves two or three times a day with tepid water. The frequency of syringing will depend on the temperature and time of year, being most frequent on bright warm summer days and least frequent in dull, cold weather.

The cucumber is a surface-rooting plant and after a short time a good many white roots will probably appear on top of the soil. This is the signal for top dressing with a mixture of equal parts well-rotted stable manure and good loam, which should be spread 1 in. thick all over the bed, mounds included, but not around the stems where they enter the soil. Two or three such top dressings can be given during the course of a season, being repeated each time fresh roots appear on the surface.

In winter, spring and autumn cucumbers can usually do with all the light they can get, but in summer unrestricted sunshine is usually too much for them under glass and some shading should be given. This may take the form of a thin stipple of whitewash or one of the advertised shading compounds applied to the glass from a spraying machine fitted with a fine nozzle. Do not err on the side of shading too heavily or the plants will be weakened.

Cucumbers should be cut regularly, when of good size but before they commence to yellow. It is a mistake to let them hang too long as this checks cropping; on the other hand immature fruits are bitter.

Sometimes, particularly towards the end of the cropping season, a good many of the fruits will wither from the end backwards. This is always a sign that the plants are weak and may be due to over-cropping, under-feeding or a decaying root system, due to over or under watering and general deterioration of the bed. Sometimes such plants can be encouraged to bear a few more good fruits by being heavily top dressed and thoroughly pruned to get rid of old growth.

FRAMES. Culture in frames differs in no marked respect from that of cucumbers under glass except in the method of training. Each plant is pinched when it has made about six leaves. Subsequently four new shoots are allowed to form and these are trained towards the four corners of the frame, being pegged to the soil with pieces of wire bent like large hairpins. These runners are in turn pinched when they reach the confines of the frame and most of the fruits are produced on the secondary side growths. As a rule one plant is sufficient for each 6 ft. by 4 ft. frame light and is planted in the centre of the frame.

It is a great advantage if the frame can stand on a good hotbed. Mid-April is a suitable time for planting.

There are many varieties of frame cucumber but one of the best for general purposes is Butcher's Disease Resisting. Improved Telegraph has fine quality fruits but a somewhat shorter season. A variety named Conqueror is remarkable for the fact that it will thrive in a much drier and cooler atmosphere than any other frame cucumber and is in consequence a good kind for those who wish to grow cucumbers along with other plants, such as tomatoes.

OUTDOORS. Ridge cucumbers require a rather different system of culture. The seed is sown and germinated in a similar manner but not before the last fortnight in April, as the seedlings must not be planted out until the first week in June. The plants are given as sunny and sheltered a position as possible in well-dug soil that has been thoroughly dressed with decayed manure. One may use as much as 1 cwt. of manure for 4 or 5 sq. yd. of bed. Contrary to popular belief, it is not good policy to plant ridge cucumbers on a ridge, as they tend to dry out too quickly, but the bed must be well drained. The plants are pinched as for cucumbers grown in frames, the runners being stopped again when about 3 ft. long.

Male flowers are not picked off as with the frame cucumber for it is desirable that the female flowers should be fertilised. In fact, if fruits fail to set properly, it is good policy to fertilise them by hand. This is done by picking off some of the male blooms when fully open and shaking them over the female flowers.

Ridge cucumbers will be killed by the first touch of autumn frost, but are quite capable of giving a heavy crop during August and September. They should be watered freely during dry weather.

Earlier crops can be obtained by growing ridge cucumbers under barn type cloches. In this case plants can often be put out safely early in May. Two shoots per plant instead of four should be retained after the first pinching and these trained in opposite directions along the line of cloches. After about mid-June the cloches may be removed and the plants allowed to spread more widely. Yet another alternative is to grow ridge cucumbers in frames in which case they are stopped like ordinary frame cucumbers. If the frame is well made and in a sheltered place it is possible to plant about the middle of April.

Varieties are not very numerous and the one with which I have been most successful is Stockwood Ridge. The frame cucumber, Conqueror, can also be grown as a ridge variety and is particularly good under cloches.

ENDIVE

This vegetable looks rather like a lettuce and is used in salads in exactly the same way as lettuces. It is rather more bitter in flavour and on this account some people do not like it, but the bitterness is less marked if the endive is grown quickly throughout and is thoroughly blanched. The great merit of this salad vegetable is its hardiness and the fact that it can be grown in winter without artificial heat.

The soil should be reasonably rich and well dug. Well-rotted dung can be used at the rate of up to 1 cwt. to 8 sq. yd. In addition super-phosphate of lime should be raked into the bed immediately before sowing, at the rate of 2 oz. per sq. yd. Sow thinly in drills ½ in. deep and 1 ft. apart. A first sowing can be made in April, with further sowings at intervals of about three weeks until mid-August, but because of its value as a winter salad it is the later sowings which are most important.

Seedlings should be thinned to 9 in. apart and can be transplanted elsewhere if desired. From the last sowing it is a good plan to transplant some of the thinnings to a frame or unheated greenhouse and then to cover the remaining plants in the seed rows with cloches towards the end of October.

A week or so after thinning Nitro-chalk or nitrate of soda can be dusted down the rows at the rate of 1 oz. to 12 ft. and a similar dressing given three weeks later.

No other attention, beyond regular hoeing and weeding, is necessary until the plants are well grown, when they should be blanched either by covering each with an inverted plate or piece of wood or, in the case of frame- or cloche-grown plants, by darkening the glass or throwing sacks over it. The more light that can be excluded the better, for the aim should be to blanch all green colouring out of the leaves. It will take about six weeks to do this and the endives are then ready for use.

Good kinds are Moss Curled and Batavian, the former with very curly and deeply-cut leaves which have a most attractive appearance, and the latter with almost plain leaves. The Batavian has the merit, however, of being even hardier than the Moss Curled.

GARLIC

The flavour of garlic is too strong for most English people though it is extremely popular in some parts of the Continent. Most people will find it sufficient to have half a dozen plants to be used as flavouring.

The cultivation of garlic is very similar to that of shallots. At the end of each season of growth the plant forms a cluster of small bulbs, the whole cluster being known as a 'clove'. This should be split up into separate bulbs some of which can be replanted in February or early March, 6 in. apart in rows 1 ft. apart. The bulbs should be given a sunny position in well-drained, fairly rich ground and should be barely covered with soil. Thereafter leave them alone with the exception of weeding and hoeing, until the foliage turns yellow in July, when the whole plant is lifted and hung up in a cool, airy shed for a week or so to dry off. Some of the cloves can then be kept for kitchen use and others set aside for replanting the following year. All should be stored in a cool, dry, airy, but frost-proof place.

There are no varieties.

GOOD KING HENRY

This little-known vegetable is sometimes grown as a substitute for spinach, its merit being that it is perennial and will grow in almost any soil and situation. Consequently a few plants can be put in and left to grow on year after year to be cut from as occasion arises.

Good King Henry can be grown quite easily from seed sown outdoors in April in drills ½ in. deep and 18 in. apart. Thin the seedlings to about 9 in. apart and then, the following year, take out every alternate plant so that the remainder are left standing 18 in. square. It is in the spring that the leaves are most welcome and they are pulled off a few from each plant as needed. Do not strip any one plant of foliage or it will be checked too severely.

GOURDS

Botanically these have the same origin as vegetable marrows and from the garden standpoint they are treated in exactly the same manner with the one difference that the fruits (gourds) are not cut until they are fully ripe, when the skins turn from green to yellow or orange and become very hard. The gourd can then be stored for several months in any cool, dry, airy place.

The fruits are used in the same way as pumpkins but it should be noted that some of the very ornamental varieties have little flesh and are grown more for decoration than utility.

HAMBURG PARSLEY

This vegetable, so well known on the Continent, is very little grown in English gardens, yet it is perfectly hardy, easy to grow and serviceable. The foliage is used for seasoning in the same way as ordinary parsley, while the long, thin tap roots are cooked like parsnips and have a delicate flavour. They can be served alone or used in soups and stews.

Hamburg parsley is grown from seed which should be sown in March or April in drills $\frac{1}{4}$ in. deep and at least 1 ft. apart. Choose reasonably rich but not freshly manured ground and an open, sunny position. Thin the seedlings to 1 ft. apart and subsequently keep the bed well hoed throughout the summer. A few leaves can be picked from each plant at any time during the summer for use in place of ordinary parsley, but no plant should be stripped of leaves at any time as this would weaken the roots. These are full grown by the end of October and may be lifted for use at any time from that date onwards during the winter.

There is no need to store the roots as they are perfectly hardy and can be left in the ground all winter to be dug as required, though in very cold districts it may be convenient to dig up a few roots and place them in sand or dry soil in a shed so that a supply is available even when the ground is so hard frozen that digging becomes impossible.

There are no varieties.

HORSE RADISH

This is one of the easiest of all vegetables to grow badly, though it is not so simple to grow it well. By this I mean that roots of a sort can be produced merely by planting small roots or even pieces cut from roots in any soil and situation and leaving them alone, but that such samples are likely to be thin, much branched and not of the type which the cook likes. Her ideal is a thick, straight root, which certainly is most profitable in the kitchen.

Such roots are produced by choosing an open situation, digging the soil deeply and breaking up all large lumps, working in a little well-rotted manure and then, in March, making holes with a thick dibber (an old spade handle is ideal) and dropping into each of these one small horse radish root right way up. The top of each root should be just below soil level. It is not essential that the root should have a crown attached though it is better if it has. No further attention is necessary beyond weeding and hoeing until November, when the whole bed should be lifted, the best roots sorted out for kitchen use and the remainder divided or cut up into suitable lengths for replanting. All should then be laid in sand or ashes in a sheltered place, the planting roots to be put in the following March and the others to be used as needed.

KALE (BORECOLE)

These are members of the brassica family and thus very closely allied to the cabbage and broccoli. In appearance and habit they are a most varied lot. There are, for example, the Scotch kales with densely curled leaves; in contrast there are varieties with almost plain leaves, such as Cottager's kale and Thousand Headed and others which are grown more for the young shoots than for the leaves, such as the Asparagus kale. Almost all are very profitable and hardy vegetables, particularly serviceable between the New Year and the end of May, when green crops tend to become scarce and variety is lacking.

Seed should be sown outdoors in April or early May in any open position and well-broken ground. Sow thinly in drills $\frac{1}{2}$ in. deep and 6 in. apart. When the seedlings have made four or five leaves each, transplant them to their permanent positions, where they should be spaced 18 in. apart in rows at least $2\frac{1}{2}$ ft. apart for the larger growing kinds, though these distances can be reduced to 1 ft. and 2 ft. respectively for smaller sorts such as the Dwarf Scotch Curled.

The ground should be prepared exactly as for winter cabbage and planting should be carried out in the same way. It is good policy, though not essential, to top dress along the rows with well-rotted dung about mid-July and draw soil from between the rows over the dung and up around the stems in a low ridge. This helps to steady the plants and encourages them to make further roots and more vigorous growth.

There is a popular idea that no kale should be cut until there has been fairly sharp frost. It is perfectly true that the flavour of the kale is improved after cold weather but it is quite possible to start using the leaves early in the autumn even before there has been any frost at all. The right method is to cut the leaves from the plants, starting from the bottom and working up and allowing a small stump of stalk to remain. The tops should be removed last of all, though even after they have been cut off there may still be some secondary growth from the lower part of the stem. In this way it is possible to gather useful food from a single plantation of kale for several months.

Varieties are numerous and varied including Cottager's, with slightly waved leaves and tender sprouts; Dwarf Green Curled and Tall Green Curled, well described by their names; Hungry Gap, hardy and late, and Thousand Headed, which certainly takes a lot of beating for crop.

KOHL RABI

Many attempts have been made to popularise this vegetable but it has never been really widely grown. Its merits are that it has the flavour of a mild turnip but can be grown successfully in soils and during seasons which are too dry for turnips. Actually the part of the plant which is eaten is not a root at all, though it looks like one, but a swollen stem. The Kohl Rabi, like the turnip, is a member of the brassica family.

Prepare the ground in exactly the same way as for summer cabbages, being fairly generous with dung. The seed can either be sown very thinly where the plants are to grow or, alternatively, can be raised in a seed bed as for cabbages, the seedlings being transplanted to final quarters at an early stage. In either case the plants should be spaced 1 ft. apart in rows 18 in. apart. Keep them growing as quickly as possible during the summer by frequent hoeing and an occasional light top dressing of nitrate of soda, 1 oz. per sq. yd. Pull the roots for table use when they are about the size of tennis balls. A common mistake is to let them get too big, when they are strong in flavour and tough.

Kohl Rabi cannot be stored for any length of time like turnips and in order to ensure a supply from August to about Christmas, small successional sowings should be made every four weeks or so, starting in mid-April and finishing in early August.

There are no varieties worth speaking about but there are two colour forms, the green and the purple, of which I think the former is to be preferred as it has the more delicate flavour.

LEEKS

These can be extremely profitable if well grown but they need a deep and rather rich soil and must have a long season of growth. For exhibition, seed is usually sown in a warm greenhouse in January or February, the seedlings being pricked off $1\frac{1}{2}$ in. each way into fairly deep trays as soon as they can be handled and then gradually hardened off for planting outdoors in April. An alternative is to raise the seedlings in a frame from a late February sowing. For ordinary kitchen use it is satisfactory to sow seed outdoors at the end of March or early in April in an open position and well-broken soil, into which superphosphate of lime has been raked, at 2 oz. per sq. yd., immediately prior to sowing. The resultant seedlings will be lifted and planted in June or July, the earlier the better.

For ordinary purposes plant in rows 18 in. apart spacing the plants 9 in. apart. Make the holes with a stout dibber—one made out of an old spade handle is excellent. The holes should be about 10 in. deep and one plant be dropped well down into each hole so that only the tops of the leaves project above ground level. The soil is not replaced immediately in the hole but instead the plants are well watered in direct from the spout of a watering can so that some soil is washed down round the roots. Later on the holes will automatically fill up, both from the action of rain and when the bed is hoed. This will blanch the stems for several inches and further blanching can be secured by drawing soil from between the rows towards and around the plants.

For exhibition purposes an even greater length of blanched stem is required and this is obtained by planting the leeks in trenches prepared as for single rows of celery (see p. 577) and spaced at least 3 ft. apart. The leeks are planted 1 ft. apart in these trenches. As the leeks grow, soil is gradually drawn into the trenches and, later, from between the trenches towards the plants to form a steep-sided ridge. In fact in some cases planks on edge are used to hold the soil up. In this way the leeks are encouraged to grow a very long stem which is blanched from top to bottom. Pure white stems 3 ft. in length may often be seen at shows. Note particularly that the blanching is done gradually throughout the season of growth, not all at once at the end of the season as in the case of celery and endive. Exhibition leeks are usually fed generously during the growing season with weak liquid manure and small top dressings of nitrate of soda or soot well hoed in.

Leeks are in season from about August until the following April or May. They are quite hardy, so it is unnecessary to lift and store the crop; they can be dug from the open ground at any time during the winter as required for use.

Most firms list their own specialities, but good standard varieties are Musselburgh and The Lion. In the North of England a type known as the pot leek is extremely popular and there are special competitions for it. This has a very thick but quite short stem and it is grown in the same manner as leeks for kitchen use, though with special attention to the richness of the soil when extra weighty exhibition specimens are needed.

LETTUCE

It is possible, but not easy, to get lettuce throughout the year. Outdoor supplies can be obtained from late April to the end of October without protection, while in greenhouses, frames and cloches, winter and early spring supplies can be grown. The chief difficulty with the mid-winter lettuce, however, is that there are few varieties which will heart during the short days. Any attempt to force ordinary lettuces to do so by increasing the amount of artificial heat, results either in disease or in the production of a few big leaves without any hearts. This difficulty can only be overcome by using special winter hearting kinds such as Cheshunt Early Giant, though a fair amount of skill is needed to grow even these successfully. There are, in addition, so-called hardy lettuces which can be left outdoors all the winter in sheltered positions, but these are seldom fit to cut before the end of April.

Apart from this difference between summer and winter hearting varieties, there are two principal types of lettuce, the cabbage and the cos. The former is the familiar, round hearted lettuce of the greengrocers' shops and far and away the more popular type in this country. The cos lettuce has long, boat-shaped leaves of a much crisper texture. Some people prefer it to the cabbage lettuce but that is not the general verdict. Both require the same culture.

The secret of success with all lettuces is to grow them swiftly and without check in rather rich, well-watered but open-textured soil. Though lettuces can be grown in a certain amount of shade a sunny position is better, especially for early and late supplies. In mid-summer a little shade is sometimes an advantage as it minimises the necessity for watering.

In all cases the ground should be dug as deeply as practicable. Well-rotted manure may be used freely up to 1 cwt. to 6 sq. yds. In addition, immediately prior to sowing, rake in at the rate of 3-4 oz. per sq. yd. a mixture of six parts by weight superphosphate of lime, two parts sulphate of ammonia and three parts sulphate of potash.

Individual sowings should be fairly small but should be repeated at frequent intervals as lettuces will not stand long and must be cut as soon as ready for use. The first sowings are made under glass in a temperature of 55 to 60° during January and February. Seed can be sown thinly in boxes or pans and must be very lightly covered. The seedlings are pricked off 2 in. apart each way into deep seed trays as soon as possible and are then hardened off in a frame for planting out during a mild, damp spell from mid-March to early April. Take them from the boxes with plenty of soil round the roots and plant firmly but not too deeply with a trowel, spacing the plants 1 ft. apart each way.

Outdoor sowing can commence as early in March as the ground becomes workable and thereafter a small sowing can be made every fortnight or three weeks until mid-August. Sow very thinly in drills $\frac{1}{4}$ in. deep and 12 to 15 in. apart, and thin out the seedlings to 12 in. when they have three or four leaves each. The thinnings can be transplanted elsewhere if required and will usually heart up about a week or ten days later than those plants left undisturbed, though they seldom make such big hearts. In September a sowing can be made in a frame or greenhouse or, alternatively, in a very sheltered place outdoors, with the object of transplanting the seedlings to a frame or greenhouse later on.

Once they have been thinned, lettuces require very little attention, though, if growth is slow, a dusting of nitrate of soda or Nitro-chalk, 1 oz. per 10 ft. of row, well hoed in, will often help. The trouble is most likely to occur if the weather is very hot and the soil becomes thoroughly dry. In this case watering may be essential but once started must be continued as long as the drought continues.

If growth is too slow, the soil poor, or the weather very hot, lettuces are liable to run to seed before they form a heart. The remedy for this is better cultivation, more liberal use of dung and freer supplies of water.

There are a great many varieties of both cabbage and cos lettuce and every seedsman lists his own specialities. Synonyms abound and it is said of one popular variety that it has appeared under no less than a hundred and ten different names. Amongst the most reliable of the cabbage type are All the Year Round, Continuity (this stands drought better than most but in some people's eyes a drawback is that the leaves are tinged with bronze), Trocadero, Tom Thumb (a small variety which can be spaced at 6 in.) Webb's Wonderful (New York), with crinkled leaves almost as crisp as those of the cos lettuce, and Iceberg, another crisp-leaved lettuce. To stand the winter outdoors, Stanstead Park is one of the most reliable, but Arctic King gives a better heart. For winter cultivation in greenhouses, Cheshunt Early Giant, Loos Tennis Ball and May Queen are best, while for spring cutting from frames and cloches, Cheshunt Early Ball, Blackpool Improved, Winter Crop and May Queen are good. Reliable cos varieties for summer cutting are Paris White and Jumbo. To stand the winter outdoors and heart in the spring, Brown Cos and Hardy Winter White are the two best.

FORCING. In winter under glass, the chief difficulty is to get enough light to counterbalance the artificial heat and keep the plants growing steadily. The frame or greenhouse should be in the sunniest place available and the glass must be kept spotlessly clean. The bed in which the plants are grown must be near the glass and the temperature should never rise much above 60° with 50° as the mean. Ventilation must be given freely whenever outside conditions are favourable and there is no fog. In frames ventilation may be even more liberal and temperatures lower though this will mean slower growth and a later crop.

Sowings for these winter and early spring lettuces should be made from early September to mid-October in a temperature of about 55°.

Seedlings should be transplanted when they have three or four leaves and roots must be kept quite close to the surface. Deep planting will encourage disease; so will overcrowding, so adopt same spacings as for outdoor plants.

For special varieties see above.

MINT

This is one of those odd plants which will grow like a weed in one place and absolutely refuse to take in another. It does best in an open, sunny position and reasonably rich soil which is neither very heavy nor very light. Roots should be obtained in March and spread out thinly all over the bed. Then cover them with about 1 in. of fine soil; old potting soil is admirable for the purpose though ordinary garden soil can be used. After this, leave the bed severely alone, simply pulling out by hand any weeds that appear. You cannot use a hoe or other tool on the mint bed with safety.

There may not be a great deal of growth the first year, but as long as the roots do make some shoots and leaves, it is satisfactory. By the second year they should be growing strongly and the bed will soon be a mat of roots covered with dense mint growth, from which shoots can be picked as required.

When the bed becomes so crowded that growth falls off in consequence, the roots should be lifted in March, carefully divided and replanted in freshly dug, moderately manured ground.

FORCING. To get a winter supply of mint lift a few good roots in October, break them up into single pieces and strew these thinly in ordinary seed boxes filled with old potting soil. Cover them with half an inch of the same material, place them in a frame for a month or so and then bring them into a warm greenhouse with a temperature of about 60-70°. Water moderately and growth should start very quickly. These forced roots are not of much use afterwards and should be thrown away.

There are no important garden varieties of mint but there are several different species cultivated, of which far and away the best is the familiar Spearmint, with smooth, dark green, notched leaves.

MUSHROOMS

This is probably the most difficult crop for the beginner to manage. Even experts find mushrooms 'chancy'. Sometimes they crop excellently and at others, though apparently given identical treatment, are a failure.

Mushrooms can be grown both indoors and out but the crop in the open is even more risky than that under cover and can only be obtained with any degree of certainty from about mid-August to the end of October. Under cover it is possible to have mushrooms the whole year round provided a temperature of around 55° can be maintained. It is not at all essential to have a greenhouse, in fact it is rather a drawback than otherwise as the mushrooms must be grown in complete darkness, so if a greenhouse is used it will be necessary either to cover the glass completely or to build inside the house some kind of large box or frame in which the mushrooms can be grown.

At one time it was supposed that mushrooms could only be cultivated in horse manure. It has now been proved possible to get excellent results from clean straw or chaff rotted down by means of special chemical preparations. When one of these preparations is used, manufacturers' instructions must be followed to the letter.

If horse manure is employed there are two essentials, first of all to get really fresh manure containing a fair amount of straw and secondly to make certain that it comes from healthy, stable-fed animals. There must be no shavings or sawdust in the manure. Take out any pieces of twig or other refuse and then build the manure into a stack 3 ft. high, 3 ft. through and of any convenient length. Cover this all over with 1 in. of soil.

A week later turn the stack completely, bringing the inside parts out and vice versa. At the same time water thoroughly any parts which appear dry. Continue to turn the stack in the same way every fourth or fifth day for three weeks, by which time the manure should have decayed to such an extent that the straw can be easily broken and the whole mass appears brown and rotten. If there is any smell of ammonia when the heap is turned, it is not sufficiently rotted.

The decayed manure is either made into beds or placed in boxes of any convenient size and 9 to 12 in. depth. Indoor beds are usually flat, 2 to 3 ft. wide, 8 to 10 in. deep and of any convenient length. Outdoors ridge beds are preferred as they shoot off rain more readily. The ridge is about 3 ft. wide at the base, $2\frac{1}{2}$ ft. high, a little rounded on top and of any desired length. In all cases the manure should be trodden down firmly layer by layer as the box is filled or the bed made. Plunge a thermometer well down into the manure and take a reading daily. When the temperature falls to between 70° and 75° the bed is ready for spawning.

It is possible to obtain either brick spawn or 'pure culture' spawn in bottles or cartons. The latter is much to be preferred as the brick spawn is often too dry and old to be any good. In either case the spawn should be broken up by hand into small lumps each about as big as a walnut, and these should be buried 1 in. deep and 9 in. apart all over the bed. Then cover the whole bed with a 6-in. layer of clean, dry straw or, if the bed is outdoors, use 1 ft. of straw for additional protection. About ten days later, remove a little of the straw and examine the bed. Dig into the manure with a pointed stick. If there are fine, white filaments running this way and that, the spawn is growing and the bed is ready for casing. This should be done with rather heavy, loamy soil spread 1 in. thick over flat beds or 1½ in. over ridge beds and beaten down quite smooth with the back of a spade. This casing is put directly on the manure and the straw covering must be removed while the work is being done but should be replaced directly the whole bed is cased.

In the case of inside beds, if any heating apparatus is available maintain a temperature of about 60° until mushrooms appear through the casing and then let the temperature fall to about 50–55°. Keep the atmosphere damp by syringing paths and walls daily with tepid water. Water the beds also when they become dry but be very careful to avoid over-watering.

It usually takes about six weeks from the time a bed is spawned to the time at which the first mushrooms can be gathered and with good management the bed will continue to crop for a further month or six weeks. The mushrooms should be gathered regularly directly they are large enough for use and they may either be broken off carefully at bed level or cut with a sharp knife, but cutting is preferable.

Inside beds can be made at any time of the year provided the necessary temperatures can be maintained. The best time for making an outside bed is in the middle of July.

It is sometimes possible to introduce mushroom spawn to fields and so obtain what is virtually a naturalised crop. This is, however, even more risky than cultivation in outdoor beds. The method is to raise a turf every yard or so with a sharp spade and insert two or three pieces of brick spawn beneath, replacing the turf at once. It will help if a little rotted horse manure can be scattered under the turf with the spawn. The best time for this experiment is in mid-July and the most favourable place a meadow which has been grazed by horses.

MUSTARD

The plant grown in the vegetable garden as 'mustard' is not true mustard but a close ally named rape. It is grown as a salad to be cut while still in the seed-leaf stage of development and should be grown as quickly as possible so that the leaves may be tender and have a mild flavour. It is possible to have supplies the whole year round by sowing in a warm greenhouse from November to February, in an unheated greenhouse or frame in March and September and either outdoors or in a frame for the remaining months.

Under glass the seed is usually sown in shallow seed trays filled with any fine soil—old potting soil mixed with a little extra sand is admirable. Outdoors a sheltered, slightly shaded position should be chosen for preference and the soil raked as finely as possible. In either case the seed is sprinkled thinly all over the surface and pressed lightly into the soil with a smooth, wooden block. No further covering of soil is required but a slate or board should be placed over each box to exclude light. Water moderately with tepid water. Directly germination occurs, remove the covering slates or boards. The seedlings are cut off close to soil level with a pair of scissors when they are 2-3 in. high.

As a rule mustard germinates about four to five days after sowing and is ready for cutting in eight to twelve days. Successional sowings should be made about once a week.

ONIONS

Onions of ordinary size and quality can quite easily be grown in most soils but the big bulbs which one sees at exhibitions require a considerable degree of skill on the part of the gardener.

Bulbs can be produced in two different ways; either seed can be sown in a special seed bed or in boxes, the seedlings being transferred to their final quarters at a later stage, or it can be sown directly in the ground in which the bulbs are to mature. Good results can be obtained by either method but, if the second system is to be followed, it is essential to have a finely broken seed bed with a surface texture not liable to become caked after heavy rain. On heavy soils this means working in a good deal of opening material such as strawy manure, leaf mould, peat, wood ashes and sand. Many gardeners place such importance on the texture of the onion bed that they do not allow it to form part of the usual rotational cropping system, but instead keep it in one position for a number of years. I have seen beds of this type which had become so fine and open with constant cultivation that a walking stick could be pushed down to its full length. This idea of using the same bed for many years is satisfactory as long as the onions do not suffer from any soil-borne disease or pest but undoubtedly it is safer to give the onions a fresh plot each year as with other crops.

Rotted manure can be used in the preparation of the onion bed at rates up to 1 cwt. to 6 sq. yd. In addition, rake in superphosphate of lime, 2-3 oz. per sq. yd. and sulphate of potash, 1 oz. per sq. yd. prior to sowing or planting.

Outdoor sowing can commence as early in March as the ground is in workable condition. Sow in drills ½ in. deep and 1 ft. apart. Thin the seedlings when they are about 4 in. high to 4 in. apart if small bulbs are required, 6 in. apart for medium sized bulbs or 12 in. for the very large, exhibition bulbs. The thinnings can be used as salading or may be transplanted elsewhere. Top dress with nitrate of soda, 1 oz. to 12 ft. of row, a week or so after thinning and give a second, similar dressing in June.

Towards the end of August, bend over the leaves just above bulb level and a fortnight or three weeks later, loosen the bulbs in the soil with a fork to check growth and encourage ripening. Towards the end of September, lift the bulbs completely and spread them out to dry either on the surface of the ground or in a frame or greenhouse. After a further day or so, store in a cool, dry, airy place either on open slat shelves or strung up in ropes. This roping is done by plaiting the withered onion leaves together with two or three strands of raffia or string.

Onions to be transplanted can either be sown under glass in January or February or outdoors in mid-August. The glasshouse sowing should be made in boxes filled with ordinary seed compost (see page 423) and germination should be effected in a temperature of 50° to 60°. The boxes can be shaded at first but the seedlings must have all light possible once they have germinated. Either sow the seeds singly 1 in. apart each way or prick off the seedlings 1½ in. apart each way when they are 2 in. high. Transfer to a frame in March and harden off for planting out in mid-April. Plant with a trowel and, contrary to general advice, make rather deep holes so that the roots can be dropped vertically into the soil and the base of the stems covered to a depth of about ½ in. Shallow planting with the stem right on top of the soil usually causes quite a severe check. Space 6 in. apart in rows for medium bulbs, 1 ft. for big bulbs. Water in well if the ground is at all dry. Subsequently treat exactly as for outdoor sown plants but bend down the tops, loosen the bulbs and lift and dry off a week to a fortnight earlier.

Mid-August sowings are made in a sheltered but sunny position and finely broken, well-drained soil. The seedlings are left unthinned throughout the winter, are lifted carefully with a small fork during the latter half of March and planted exactly like the greenhouse raised seedlings. If desired, some of the seedlings can be left undisturbed in the seed bed, the thinnings being used for planting out. Bulbs from these late summer sowings will be ready for use from June onwards but should not be stored until the foliage dies down, which will probably be towards the end of July or early in August.

Salad onions are produced by sowing thinly in drills 9 in. apart at fortnightly intervals from March to June and again in mid-August. No thinning is carried out and the onions are pulled as soon as they are big enough for salading. A mild flavoured variety is generally preferred.

There are a great many varieties of onion and almost every seedsman offers his own specialities. For exhibition Ailsa Craig or selections from it are generally preferred. For kitchen use a smaller and more solid fleshed onion is better, for example Up-to-Date, James's Long Keeping, Bedfordshire Champion, Rousham Park Hero or Solidity. Most of these varieties can also be sown in August, though Giant Rocca and Tripoli are often recommended because they stand the winter so well. They are not good varieties for storing. If some onions are required for salad use only, White Lisbon is good because of its mild flavour. Up-to-Date, Rousham Park Hero, Improved Reading and White Spanish appear to be highly resistant to the onion white rot disease so should be used in all gardens in which this disease has proved troublesome.

PARSLEY

This is one of the few vegetables that are required in most gardens throughout the year. For this purpose at least three separate sowings should be made; the first as early in March as soil and weather conditions will allow, the second towards the end of May or early June, and the third early in August. In each case seed should be sown directly in the ground in which the plants are to grow. The soil need not be particularly rich but should be well dug and the position should be open and sunny. Quite a common practice is to use parsley as an edging for beds in the kitchen garden. Sow in drills $\frac{1}{4}$ in. deep, or broadcast, in which case the seed should be covered with $\frac{1}{4}$ in. of fine soil.

Germination is, as a rule, rather slow so there is no need to worry if no seedlings appear for four or five weeks. When the seedlings are 1 in. or so high, thin them out to 6 in. apart and subsequently leave them to grow with occasional weeding or hoeing. Cutting can begin as soon as the plants are nicely grown and if only a few leaves are taken from each plant at a time cropping will continue for many weeks. Some of the seedlings from the last sowing in August can be transferred at thinning time to a frame or to a very sheltered border in which they can be covered with cloches. The remaining plants can be left where they are, either to take their chance with the winter weather or to be covered later on with cloches or spare frame lights supported on bricks. As a rule no protection is needed before the end of October and even then only light covering is required to keep off the most severe cold.

Varieties are not numerous. Any good strain of Moss Curled will give satisfactory results.

For Hamburg parsley, see page 587.

PARSNIPS

These have the merit of extreme hardiness, which makes it possible to produce winter crops in districts too cold for turnips or carrots. A drawback is that parsnips grow rather slowly and therefore require a long season if really big roots are to be formed. For this reason the earlier in March that seed can be sown the better, provided the soil is in good working condition, but the seed bed must be reasonably dry and crumbly. It is better to wait until April or even early May than to sow in a sticky seed bed.

For exhibition purposes ground must be trenched at least two and preferably three feet deep, but for ordinary kitchen purposes deep digging is usually sufficient. The seeds are comparatively big and the best method of sowing is to drop them in twos or threes 4 in. apart in drills 1 in. deep and 18 in. apart. Then if all the seeds germinate they can be singled out to 8 in. apart. It is no use trying to transplant the thinnings as they will not produce good roots.

Do not use any animal manure on the parsnip bed but try if possible to choose a position that was manured thoroughly for a preceding crop such as brassicas or potatoes. Prior to sowing dust the surface with superphosphate or lime, 3 oz. per sq. yd., sulphate of ammonia, 1 oz. per sq. yd. and either sulphate or muriate of potash, $1\frac{1}{2}$ oz. per sq. yd. It is usually an advantage to give a top dressing of nitrate of soda or Nitro chalk at the rate of 1 oz. to 10 ft. of row immediately after thinning. Dust this in a double band a couple of inches wide along each side of the rows and hoe in at once. Subsequently hoeing will be the only attention required until the end of October, when lifting may commence.

Most of the roots can be left in the ground all winter to be dug as needed, but it is convenient to lift a few and store in sand, ashes or dry soil in a shed so that roots are available even when the weather is too unpleasant or the ground too hard frozen to work outdoors.

An alternative method of cultivation sometimes practised by exhibitors is, after trenching the ground, to bore holes with a crowbar, 1 ft. apart in rows at least 18 in. apart. These holes should be about 2 ft. deep and 2 in. in diameter at the top. They are almost filled with any old sifted potting soil. Two or three seeds are then sown in each hole and covered with 1 in. of the same fine soil. Later the seedlings are singled out. The idea is that the root follows the direction of the bored hole and is, in consequence, exceptionally straight and well formed.

It should also be noted that when lifting parsnips for exhibition it is very important to get as great a length of root as possible, even including the long, thin 'tail' of the root. This may necessitate opening a trench 3 ft. or more deep at one end of the parsnip bed and working towards the plants with a fork so as to get them out intact and without any injury.

There are not a great many varieties though some seedsmen offer specialities and re-selections of well-known standard kinds such as Tender and True, Hollow Crown and Offenham.

PEAS

One of the most important of all the kitchen garden crops and certainly one that pays for good cultivation. Some gardeners grow peas in trenches prepared in much the same way as celery trenches (see p. 577), but a better method is to dig the ground as deeply as possible throughout, working in dung or compost at the rate of about 1 cwt. to 8 sq. yds. The position should always be as open and sunny as possible. Prior to sowing dust the surface with superphosphate of lime, 3 oz. per sq. yd. and either sulphate or muriate of potash, 1½ oz. per sq. yd. Peas do best in ground that is reasonably well supplied with lime but as lime cannot be given economically at the same time as dung it is advisable to choose a plot that was limed previously.

There are two methods of sowing, one in the ordinary V-shaped drills drawn with the corner of a hoe, in which case it is usual to draw two such drills about 9 in. apart to form a double row and then leave an alleyway at least as wide as the eventual height of the peas. The alternative is to sow in shallow, flat-bottomed trenches scooped out with a spade held almost horizontal. Such trenches should be about 2 in. deep. Two lines of peas are sown in each trench, one on either side, and the trench is then half filled with fine soil, thus leaving a small depression which serves to hold water should the peas require watering in hot weather. In either case the seeds themselves should be sown singly at least 2 in. apart. If mice or birds are troublesome place the peas before sowing in a tin can with a very little paraffin, shake them well, so that they all get moistened, and then dust them with red lead.

Peas are split up into early, second early, mid-season and late varieties and also into dwarf and tall kinds. It so happens that a good many of the earlies are also dwarf, whereas most of the lates are tall, but this by no means holds true for all varieties. The difference between early and late peas, by the way, is simply in the time they take to reach maturity from the sowing date. Roughly speaking the very earliest varieties will commence to fill their pods about ten weeks from the date of sowing; second early varieties will take twelve to thirteen weeks to reach the same stage of development; mid-season, thirteen to fourteen weeks; late kinds, about fifteen weeks. It is quite possible and indeed desirable to sow early varieties late in the season to get a catch crop before the weather gets too cold. Some gardeners use early varieties for all their sowings but a drawback to this is that the earlies seldom give quite such a heavy crop plant for plant as the slower growing varieties.

Whatever kinds are used successional sowing should be practised with the object of spreading the picking season from early June to at least the end of September and possibly mid-October in a favourable year. This will mean a first sowing of an early in late February or early March, followed by a similar sowing a fortnight later with perhaps a main-crop sown end of March, mid-April and mid-May and a return to a first early to be sown the first week in June.

Varieties below 2 ft. in height need not be staked though I think it best to give some support, even if it is only a string down each side of the row, to even the dwarfest kinds. Those over 2 ft. in height must be staked and brushy hazel branches are best for this purpose. They should be put in as soon as the seedlings appear, a row of sticks down each side of the line and they must be pushed well into the soil as the wind resistance of a well-grown row of peas is considerable.

Peas thrive on plenty of moisture, particularly when the pods begin to fill and it pays then to water freely either with plain water or, better still, with weak liquid manure from the time the pods can be seen unless, of course, the weather should be wet. Pick early and regularly as this encourages the plants to go on bearing. Do not allow any of the pods to ripen or turn yellow on the plants. If possible spread a mulch of strawy manure or grass clippings a couple of inches thick between the rows in May.

There are a great many varieties of peas and almost every nurseryman lists specialities almost all of which are excellent. It is impossible to name more than a few standard kinds, of which these are representative: *First early*: Little Marvel (18 in.); Early Superb (2 ft.); Foremost (3½ ft.); Meteor (1 ft. to 18 in.); Gradus (4 ft.) and Kelvedon Wonder (18 in.). *Second Early*: Senator (4 ft.); The Lincoln (2 ft.); and Duplex (2½ ft.). *Maincrop*: Onward (2½ ft.); Admiral Beatty (4 ft.); Giant

Stride (2 ft.); Kelvedon Triumph (3 ft.); Stratagem (2 ft.). *Late:* Autocrat (5 ft.); V.C. (5 to 6 ft.) and Ne Plus Ultra (6 ft.).

POTATOES

There are few soils in which potatoes will not grow tolerably well though the ideal is undoubtedly a light, easily worked loam and the nearer one can get to this the better. The position for the potato bed should always be as open as possible. In shade the haulm tends to get excessively long and crops are likely to be light.

Dung can be used freely in the preparation of practically all soils. An average dressing is 1 cwt. to 12 sq. yd. and this can be increased to as much as 1 cwt. to 6 sq. yd. on the poorer and lighter types of soil. However, it is seldom wise to rely on dung only. Potatoes need plenty of phosphates and potash, in both of which dung is likely to be deficient. Immediately prior to planting dust the ground at the rate of 5 oz. per sq. yd. with a mixture of five parts by weight superphosphate of lime, three parts sulphate of ammonia and two parts sulphate of potash.

Potatoes are grown from tubers which are often known as seed potatoes though in fact they have nothing to do with real seed. Any healthy tubers can be used for the purpose but commercial growers usually try to supply tubers averaging about 2 oz. in weight, as these give a satisfactory result and are economical. Larger tubers are extravagant unless they are divided, which takes time and is not satisfactory with all varieties while smaller tubers do not give a sufficiently strong plant.

It is a great advantage, though not absolutely essential if tubers can be purchased early in November. Failing this they should be obtained in January or February. Place them in shallow trays in a fairly light but frost-proof place to sprout. Stand the tubers on end in the trays with their eyes uppermost. The temperature of the sprouting shed should be round about 45°. If it is too hot or too dark sprouts will be long and weakly; if it is too cold the tubers will be chilled or perhaps even frozen and killed. The ideals to aim for are short, sturdy green or purplish looking sprouts by the time the potatoes are required for planting.

Planting should commence in March for the earliest varieties and continue throughout April for the later kinds. The very first planting should be made in as sheltered a position as possible as the young growth is tender and likely to be killed by even a few degrees of frost. April plantings are usually quite safe right out in the open.

There are a number of methods of planting, the essential thing being to space the tubers 1 ft. to 15 in. apart in rows $2\frac{1}{2}$ to 3 ft. apart and to cover them with 2 to 3 in. of good soil. Perhaps the quickest method is to dig out a shallow V-shaped trench with a spade, place the tubers in this and then use the soil from the next trench to fill up the preceding one. An alternative is to draw the same soil back into the trench again with a rake or hoe, while some gardeners use a draw hoe to make the trenches. I have seen potatoes planted with a big dibber but do not like this method as the hole tends to be too pointed and so leaves the potato suspended with a space beneath it.

Earthing up should commence as soon as the shoots appear through the soil. At first only a little soil is drawn from between the rows right over the young potato shoots. A few days later the process is repeated, with a third earthing up ten days or so later so that finally all the soil is drawn up into broad, rounded ridges with the potato shoots growing through their summits. The idea is to give plenty of loose soil into which the potato can grow and form its tubers. On poor soil it is an excellent plan to give a further dusting of the mixed fertiliser already recommended prior to the first earthing up. It should be used at the rate of 3 oz. to every 12 ft. of row.

No further attention should be needed until the earliest varieties are ready to dig, which may be any time in June according to season, variety and time of planting. The only way to make sure is to scrape a little soil away from one of the ridges and examine some of the tubers. Start to dig as soon as they are the size of hens' eggs and only lift a few roots at a time, just as many, in fact, as are required for immediate use. These early potatoes soon spoil when out of the ground.

Mid-season and late potatoes must be left much longer and will need to be sprayed with Bordeaux or Burgundy mixture or one of the advertised copper fungicides about the first week in July as a precautionary measure against Potato Blight, the commonest and most destructive of all potato diseases. Cover both the upper and under sides of the leaves with the spray and give a second application at the end of the month and a third about three weeks later. Near industrial centres, where the air is much polluted by factory smoke, this spraying may have to be omitted as under these conditions it can cause severe leaf scorching.

Second early potatoes are usually ready for digging in August as soon as the first earlies are finished, but if they are to be kept for winter they should be left in the ground until the skins are firm and cannot be removed by pressure with the thumb. The same test should be applied to maincrop and late potatoes which are usually ready towards the end of September and early October respectively.

Dig with a broad tined fork and be as careful as possible not to bruise or spear any of the tubers. Remove those that are under sized, damaged or diseased in any way. The remainder can be stored for winter use either in a frost-proof shed or in a clamp made outdoors.

A clamp is made by spreading clean straw on the ground to a depth of about 1 ft., piling the tubers on this, covering them with more straw to the depth of 1 ft. and then with soil at least 9 in. thick beaten down smoothly with the back of a spade. Usually clamps are made in the shape of a ridge 4 to 5 ft. through at the base, 3 to 4 ft. high and of any desired length, but conical clamps are sometimes more suitable for the small garden. Essentials are a good layer of drainage material underneath and a good thick covering of straw and soil to keep out frost and rain. In the summit of the clamp some provision should be made for ventilation, the usual method being to draw some of the straw through the covering soil or place drainpipes to form 'chimneys' as shown in the illustration on p. 533. In a well-made clamp potatoes will withstand the coldest weather without injury. Clamps with thin walls are a menace. When a clamp is opened so that potatoes may be removed for use the end must be sealed up again with sacks and soil to keep out frost.

When potatoes are stored in sheds they must be kept in the dark. If they are in thin sacks and the shed has windows it will be necessary to cover the sacks in some way, otherwise the outside potatoes will become green and bitter.

Varieties are numerous and tend to change fairly rapidly. This is because many kinds deteriorate with the passage of years. The trouble can be checked to a considerable extent by cultivating seed potatoes exclusively in those areas which are relatively free from virus disease. All the same it is rather important to keep up-to-date on information regarding potato varieties and in particular to find out what kinds are known to give good crops in the particular locality in which they are to be grown.

There are four main groups or subdivisions, first earlies, second earlies, maincrops and lates. These differ in the time they take to reach maturity, the first earlies needing something like three months from planting to digging, second earlies four months, main-crops five months and lates six. There is usually a considerable difference between the weights of crop lifted from earlies and main-crops but not so much between the intermediate groups nor between main-crops and lates. In fact I am disposed to think that the cultivation of very late potatoes might be discontinued in most private gardens with advantage as they occupy the ground so long and are often difficult to lift before the soil gets very wet and cold.

Here are a few of the best kinds at the time of writing. *First Earlies*: Arran Crest, Arran Pilot, Epicure, Sharpe's Express, Duke of York (syn. Midlothian Early), Eclipse (syn. Sir John Llewellyn), Dunbar Cavalier. *Second Earlies*: Arran Comrade, British Queen, Great Scot, Ulster Monarch. *Main Crop*: Arran Banner, Arran Peak, Doon Star (rather subject to dry rot), Gladstone, King Edward, Dunbar Standard, Majestic, Red King, Redskin. *Late*: Arran Chief, Arran Victory, Kerr's Pink, Arran Cairn.

RADISHES

These are very quick-growing plants and make an excellent catch crop to be taken off a plot of ground prepared well in advance for another crop. For example, radishes can be sown in the celery trenches and on plots prepared for late peas or autumn and winter brassicas. It is hardly possible to have too rich a soil for the purpose for the more quickly radishes can be grown the more tender and crisp they are to eat.

Sowings should be made every fortnight or three weeks outdoors, starting as early in March as soil conditions allow and continuing until mid-August. Earlier supplies can be obtained by sowing in a frame in February, while winter radishes can be had either by growing a hardy variety such as Black Spanish from a September sowing or by growing ordinary radishes in a slightly heated frame or greenhouse, from September, October and January sowings.

Seed can either be sown broadcast or in $\frac{1}{2}$ in. deep drills 4 to 5 in. apart. In either case sow very thinly and so avoid the necessity for thinning out. Broadcast seed should be covered with $\frac{1}{4}$ in. of fine soil. Water freely in dry weather.

Radishes should be ready for pulling within six or seven weeks of sowing except in winter and early spring when they will take rather longer. Use the most forward roots first.

Varieties are not numerous but there are two distinct types, the round or olive-rooted radish, of which French Breakfast is typical, and the long, tap-rooted radish. The former is easily the more popular and better for general cultivation. There is also the black skinned variety known as Black Spanish which is very hardy and so suitable for winter cultivation.

RHUBARB

One of the small number of perennials grown in the vegetable garden. Rhubarb roots may occupy the same soil for a number of years and, in consequence, initial preparation should be very thorough. Dig the ground deeply, working in dung or compost at 1 cwt. to 8 to 10 sq. yd.

March is the best planting season and good roots can be purchased from the nurseryman. They should be spaced 3 ft. apart each way. As they are generally rather big it is most convenient to plant them with a spade. The roots must be planted just so deep that the whole of the woody part of the crown is covered but the shoots on it just appear through the soil. Plant very firmly and water in freely should the ground be dry.

Do not pull any sticks the first year and be rather moderate in pulling the second year. If any flowering spikes appear, cut them off at once.

It is also possible to raise rhubarb from seed and some varieties mature surprisingly quickly, e.g. Glaskin's Perpetual. Seed should be sown very thinly in a frame in March or outdoors in April in drills ½ in. deep and 1 ft. apart. Thin the seedlings to 6 in. apart and transplant them to their permanent quarters the following March. Subsequently the same details of cultivation apply as for purchased roots.

FORCING. Early rhubarb is usually greatly appreciated from January to March. The first supplies are obtained in heated greenhouses or sheds and later ones by covering roots outdoors.

For indoor forcing strong roots (at least two years from planting) should be lifted, as required, from November to January. Allow them to lie outdoors for a day or so exposed to frost, then bring them into the greenhouse or shed, place them in boxes or large pots or even pack them very close together on the floor and surround them with any old potting soil. Water moderately and then make the place quite dark. If the roots are in pots they can be covered with other inverted pots; if they are packed on the floor a framework may be built over them and covered with sacks or linoleum, while another excellent method is to plant under the greenhouse staging and hang thick sacks in front to keep out all light.

In a temperature of 60 to 75 degrees growth will be rapid and sticks will be ready for pulling within four or five weeks.

For outdoor forcing, roots should be covered with special forcing pots, boxes or barrels where they are growing in their permanent beds. If possible surround and almost cover these pots or boxes with dead tree leaves and strawy stable manure, mixed in about equal parts. This will generate some heat and so increase the rate of growth, but it is not absolutely essential. Again it is essential to exclude all light so that the tops of the forcing pots should be covered with lids, while barrels, etc. from which the bottom has been knocked, should also be suitably covered. As a rule outdoor roots do not require any watering while they are being forced.

There are not many varieties of rhubarb, three of the best being Champagne, Victoria and Glaskin's Perpetual. The first two excel in colour but Glaskin's Perpetual gives a yield for a very long time and, as already remarked, grows readily and rapidly from seed.

SAGE

This useful herb is a perennial of shrubby habit. It will eventually make a bush 3 ft. high and as much through.

Sage can be grown from cuttings of firm, young growth taken in August or September and inserted in a frame or under a bell glass in rather sandy soil or, alternatively, seed can be sown in a frame in March or outdoors in April. Seedlings should be pricked off 2 or 3 in. apart in lightish soil and a sunny place as soon as they can be handled and the following autumn or spring be transplanted to their permanent quarters. Cuttings taken in late summer will be rooted and ready for permanent beds the following spring. In all cases the final planting should be in full sun and well drained, though not necessarily particularly rich, soil. Space the plants at least 18 in. apart.

Young shoots can be cut or leaves removed from established plants at any time as required for use provided no plant is heavily stripped at any one time. For drying, sage is cut in late June, just before the plants come into flower. The young shoots are tied up in small bundles and hung head downwards in a cool, airy place until quite dry.

There are no named varieties of sage but there is an ornamental form with reddish leaves which has the same aromatic properties as the ordinary green leaved sage.

SALSIFY

This not very common vegetable is grown for its roots, which are rather like thin parsnips in appearance and have, in the opinion of many persons, a very good flavour. In fact the plant is sometimes known as the Vegetable Oyster.

Salsify is grown from seed, which should be sown outdoors in April in drills $\frac{1}{2}$ in. deep and at least 1 ft. apart. The position should be open and sunny, the soil deeply dug and prepared as for parsnips (see p. 600). Thin the seedlings to 8 in. apart while still quite small and subsequently keep the soil well hoed and free of weeds.

Early in November the whole crop should be lifted, the tops cut off and the roots stored in sand, ashes or fine, dry soil in a shed or outhouse.

There are no varieties.

SAVOY

This is really no more than a variety of cabbage with very crinkled leaves. The twin merits of the savoy are that it is exceptionally hardy and has produced some fine late varieties which can be cut from January to April after most winter cabbages are over. There are also early varieties of savoy for use in autumn for those who prefer them to ordinary cabbage.

Cultivation is identical with that of autumn or winter cabbage and seed should be sown in April or, for a very late supply, about mid-May. It is common practice to follow the later varieties of savoy after early potatoes and peas.

Amongst the best varieties are Best of All, Drumhead Early, Drumhead Late, the four forms of Ormskirk known as Early, Medium Late and Extra Late, and Omega, another very late and hardy savoy.

SCORZONERA

Another of the less known root vegetables but one which is worth growing for variety. It makes long, tapering roots not unlike those of salsify, but with black skins.

Scorzonera is grown from seed sown in late April or early May outdoors in deeply dug, reasonably rich soil but for preference in soil that has not been freshly manured. Sow thinly in drills ½ in. deep and 1 ft. apart. Thin the seedlings to 8 in. and lift the roots at the end of September or early in October for storing in sand, ashes or dry soil in the same way as salsify.

There are no varieties.

SEAKALE

This is a vegetable for connoisseurs and it is grown for its young shoots which must be blanched in order to be palatable. If grown in the light they are green and excessively bitter.

Seakale can be raised from seed sown in shallow drills outdoors in April but it usually takes two years to get plants large enough for forcing in this way. Given very favourable conditions some of the most forward roots may be ready for forcing the first autumn. The more usual method of culture is from root cuttings. These are obtained in autumn from the plants that are to be forced. Any side roots from about the thickness of a lead pencil to that of a man's thumb may be used. Cuttings can be from 4 to 10 in. long but there is no need for them to contain any obvious crown or shoot. When preparing them it is advisable to cut the bottom of each piece on the slant and the top squarely across, the reason being that the cuttings must be put in the right way up and unless there is some distinguishing mark it is very difficult to tell which end is which after they have been made

Tie the cuttings in small bundles and lay them in sand or ashes in any sheltered place outdoors until early March. Then plant them out in deeply dug, rather rich soil. Dung can be used in the preparation of this bed at the rate of 1 cwt. to 10 to 12 sq. yd. Drop the roots, right way up, into dibber holes 1 ft. apart in rows 18 in. apart. The holes must be just so deep that the top of each cutting is about ½ in. below the surface. Keep the bed clean and well hoed all summer.

In November lift all the roots, cut off thongy side growths to provide a new lot of cuttings and reserve the strong main roots and crowns for forcing. Alternatively part of the bed may be left intact for forcing outdoors.

Forcing. For the earliest crop this should be done in a greenhouse or shed with a temperature of 60°–75°. Pot the crowns three or four together in 6 or 7 in. pots in any old potting soil, water moderately and place in complete darkness (see notes on forcing rhubarb). It is advisable to force only a few potfuls at a time and to bring a succession of pots into the forcing house every week or ten days from November to January or February.

Later supplies can be had by covering strong outdoor plants with inverted flower pots or by heaping fine sand, ashes, or even sandy soil over them to a depth of 8 or 9 in. If flower pots are used the hole in the bottom of each must be blocked up in some way to keep out light.

In all cases the shoots should be cut at soil level when they are 6 to 9 in. long.

Roots which have been forced are of little further use.

There are no varieties of any importance but it is desirable to get a good strain from a reliable source.

SEAKALE BEET

This is a variety of beetroot which is cultivated for its foliage and not for its roots. The central rib of each leaf is very large and can be separated from the remainder of the leaf and served as a substitute for seakale, while the green part is cooked separately and served as spinach. It is a useful vegetable, capable of giving a big crop for a long period and it has the additional merit of being hardy.

Seed should be sown in late March or early April and again during the first half of August. Sow in a sunny place (fairly sheltered for the August sowing) in drills 1 in. deep and 18 in. apart, dropping the seeds in pairs 8 or 9 in. apart. Single out the seedlings to one at each station. No further attention is required beyond hoeing and weeding.

Leaves can be cut a few at a time as required directly the plants are growing freely. Provided no plant is stripped at any one time, the bed will continue to yield for several months. From the spring sowing it should be possible to gather leaves and mid-ribs from June to October, while the August sowing will give a few leaves in autumn and a lot more in the spring.

There are no varieties of any importance.

SHALLOTS

Some people prefer shallots to onions because of their milder flavour. They also have the merit of being much easier to grow and in consequence will often give a good crop in places where onions fail. Small shallots are excellent for pickling, while the larger bulbs can be used for flavouring and some of the best kept for replanting.

It is always better to grow shallots in this way, from carefully selected bulbs, than to raise them from seed, as seedlings have a tendency to run to flower, in which case they seldom produce a satisfactory crop. Bulbs can be planted in either autumn or spring, late October and late February being the most favourable times. I favour autumn planting on well-drained soil in the South and West but in cold places or heavy soils spring planting is better.

In either case it is only necessary to press the bulbs firmly into the soil until they are about half covered. Space them 8 in. apart in rows 12 to 15 in. apart, giving them an open position and well dug soil which has been moderately manured. Dung can be used at the rate of about 1 cwt. to 12 sq. yd. and superphosphate of lime 3 oz. per sq. yd. and sulphate of potash 1 oz. per sq. yd. may be raked in with advantage prior to planting. A few weeks later go over the bed carefully and firm any bulbs which appear loose. Frost may push them out or sometimes mice and birds will disturb them before they are rooted. Keep the bed well hoed.

Early in June draw the soil a little away from the clusters of bulbs which by this time will be forming around the parent bulb. Directly the foliage turns yellow, which is usually during the latter half of July, lift the plants with a fork and spread them out to dry in an airy shed. A few days later the clusters can be split up into separate bulbs, sorted according to size and the best selected for replanting. Then all can be stored until required in any cool, dry, airy place.

SPINACH

I have spoken repeatedly of the importance of sowing some vegetables at short intervals for succession but this applies to none more vitally than spinach, which has a very short season, especially when the weather is hot. If a big batch is sown at one time it is almost certain that most of it will go to seed before it can be used. The ideal for an ordinary family of three or four persons is to sow a 30 ft. row of summer spinach every ten days or fortnight from mid-March until mid-July and then, a month later make one sowing, in a sheltered position, of a winter spinach to be used in autumn and again from March to May.

All spinach requires rich, deeply dug ground and summer supplies need, in addition, plenty of moisture. If possible, make the spinach bed in a place where it will be easy to turn the hose on the plants during droughty spells. It is not a bad plan to make the May, June and July sowings in a partially shady place as this reduces the need for such frequent watering.

Dung or compost can be used freely in the preparation of the bed; 1 cwt. to 6 sq. yd. will not be too much on dry or sandy soils. While the plants are in growth feed them once or twice with small doses of nitrate of soda, 1 oz. to 10 ft. of row. Winter spinach must not be fed too freely or it may grow too soft and be killed by frost. Cut down the application of dung to 1 cwt. to 15 sq. yd., rake in sulphate of potash at $\frac{1}{2}$ oz. per sq. yd. prior to sowing and give no nitrate of soda until early April.

All spinach should be sown thinly in drills 1 in. deep and 9 in. to 1 ft. apart. Thin the seedlings to 3 in. apart as early as possible. Start to cut as soon as the outer leaves are of a usable size.

Good varieties of the summer type are Round Seeded, Long Standing, King of Denmark and Monarch Long Standing. Good varieties of winter spinach are Prickly Seeded Long Standing and Hollandia.

SPINACH BEET

Practically all that has been said regarding seakale beet applies equally to spinach beet with the one difference that the leaves have not the thick, white mid-ribs which distinguish seakale beet. Consequently spinach beet is purely a spinach substitute, not a seakale substitute as well. It is grown in precisely the same way as seakale beet and has the same capacity for cropping for a very long time.

There are no varieties of any importance.

SWEDES

The garden swede is very closely allied to the turnip and is grown in the same way. It has the merit of great hardiness and swedes will often winter outdoors without any protection. It also gives a very heavy crop, though roots of the largest size are not really desirable as they are inferior in texture and flavour to smaller specimens.

The position chosen for swedes should be open and sunny, well dug and, for preference, well manured for a preceding crop. If this is impossible, dung can be used sparingly provided it is dug in at least three months before the swedes are to be sown. In any case, dust the ground with superphosphate of lime 3 oz. to the sq. yd., sulphate of ammonia or Nitro-chalk, 2 oz. per sq. yd. and sulphate or muriate of potash, 1 oz. per sq. yd. immediately prior to sowing.

Sow in May or early June in drills ½ in. deep and 15 in. apart. Thin the seedlings to 6 in. apart. If the plants appear to grow slowly during the summer give them one top dressing of nitrate of soda, 1 oz. to 10 ft. of row and hoe it in.

At least part of the crop should be lifted at the end of October or early in November and stored in dry sand or fine soil in an outhouse in case the weather should be so severe that outdoor roots are damaged or it is impossible to lift them.

The most important varieties are Purple Top, Bronze Top and Green Top.

SWEET CORN

This vegetable, so immensely popular with Americans and colonials, is easily grown from seed sown outdoors early in May. Choose a sunny, rather sheltered position and prepare the soil by digging it deeply and manuring it generously. Well rotted dung can be used at rates up to 1 cwt. to 8 sq. yd. and additional superphosphate of lime and sulphate of potash given, the former at 3 oz. and the latter at 1 oz. per sq. yd. Drop the seeds into small dibber holes ½ in. deep, 15 in. apart in rows 3 ft. apart. It is better to have several short rows than one long one because the plants are wind pollinated and in a compact block there is more chance of the pollen being blown from one plant to another.

Keep well watered in dry weather. Feed with weak liquid manure. When the plants come into flower, frequently shake the male tassels which top the stems and so assist in the distribution of the pollen.

The cobs for which the plants are grown are formed low down on the main stems. Sometimes strong plants will produce a number of cobs but as a rule it is wise to restrict them to no more than three.

It is very important to gather the cobs at exactly the right stage of development, which is when the seeds are milky. The test is to open the covering sheath very carefully (it can be slit with a knife if necessary) and push the point of a penknife into one of the seeds. If transparent juice comes out, the cob is too young. If the interior of the seed has the consistency and appearance of a hard boiled egg, the crop is too old. If a white, milky liquid comes out, it is just ripe.

There are a great many varieties of sweet corn and it is important to choose one which matures fairly quickly, otherwise many of the cobs will be spoiled by frost before they are ready for use. Golden Bantam is one of the best in flavour but a little slow in growth and small in size. The John Innes Hybrids 1 and 2 are both first class while other satisfactory kinds are Golden Cross Bantam, Sen Cross and Early White Columbia.

Note particularly that, though sweet corn and maize are both varieties of the same plant, they are distinct from the garden standpoint, bearing much the same relationship to one another as garden marrow-fat peas and blue field peas. The sweet corns, as their name implies, are sweet and succulent, whereas maize has relatively little flavour and is grown to be ripened and used as poultry food, etc. There are also ' dent ' corns which are intermediate between the two and some varieties of which are good enough for human consumption. Gold Standard is one of these.

THYME

This most important of garden herbs is a dwarf shrubby perennial which makes an attractive edging for vegetable beds or can be grown in the herb border.

Thyme can either be raised from seed sown thinly in April in a frame or sheltered place outdoors or from cuttings of firm young growth struck under a hand-light or in an unheated frame in July and August. Both methods are equally satisfactory but seed is probably the simpler for the amateur. Transfer the tiny seedlings to a bed of fine soil outdoors in May or early June, planting them 2 or 3 in. apart in rows 9 in. apart. From this nursery bed remove them to their final quarters the following autumn or spring, spacing them at least 9 in. apart each way. The ground need not be particularly good but it should be well drained and the position as sunny as possible.

For immediate use thyme can be gathered at any period of the year but for drying it should be cut in June, just before it comes into flower. Tie the shoots up in small bundles and suspend these in a cool, airy place but not in full sun. When the leaves are quite dry they can be crumbled and stored in stoppered bottles.

TOMATOES

The tomato is a half hardy plant which can only be grown in the open in this country from about the commencement of June until the end of September. This is too short a season for anything like a full crop to be obtained and in consequence the tomato is primarily regarded as a glasshouse plant, though in some warm, sheltered places fairly extensive plantations are also made in the open. Under glass it is quite possible to gather ripe tomatoes from January to December but a good deal of skill is required for winter and early spring crops. The reason for this is that artificial heat does not entirely take the place of sunlight and in winter it is the lack of light which often brings about disaster. For these reasons I would advise the beginner to concentrate upon producing ripe tomatoes from about mid-summer until early autumn and then, as he feels his skill and understanding increasing, lengthen the season by earlier and later sowings.

For this main crop under glass seed should be sown towards the end of February in a temperature of 60–65°. Seed can be broadcast thinly in ordinary seed trays but a better method is to space the seeds singly 1 in. apart each way. I use a piece of glass to carry the seeds and the point of a pen-knife to flick them off on to the soil. Use the John Innes seed compost (p. 423) and cover the seeds with the same compost to a depth of $\frac{1}{8}$ in. Moisten with tepid water from a can fitted with a fine rose and cover each box with a pane of glass and a sheet of brown paper.

In the right temperature germination should be rapid and within ten days or so seedlings should be spearing through the soil. Remove the brown paper at once and tilt the glass with a small stone. A couple of days later remove the glass as well. Keep the trays on the greenhouse staging in as light a position as possible.

Directly the seed leaves are well formed, prick the seedlings off into other seed trays, spacing them 3 in. apart each way or, better still, pot them up singly in $2\frac{1}{2}$-in. pots. Keep them on the staging in a temperature averaging 60° and not falling below 50° at any time. Water fairly freely, always using water warmed to the temperature of the house. As soon as the small pots begin to fill with roots, which will probably be about three weeks after potting, move the plants on into 4-in. pots. For both these pottings or for trays into which the seedlings are pricked off, the composts described on p. 421 should be used.

Meanwhile the soil in which the tomatoes are to fruit should be prepared. This may be in a border on the floor of the greenhouse; in troughs about 1 ft. deep and wide and of any convenient length; in boxes of the orange box type, or in flower pots not less than 8 in. in diameter. Growth is very much under the gardener's control in pots, boxes and troughs and the earliest crops are usually obtained in this way, but a drawback is that the plants require more frequent attention. For the amateur who is likely to be away from home most of the day, bed culture on the floor of the house is most satisfactory.

For pots, boxes and troughs the rich John Innes compost (p. 422) is as satisfactory as any. If desired this can also be used to make up beds on the floor of the house but usually this is impracticable because of the quantity of soil required. The method is then to use existing soil well dug and enriched with rotted stable manure, 1 cwt. to 10 to 12 sq. yd. After digging the surface is dusted with bone meal, hoof and horn meal and sulphate of potash all at 4 oz. per sq. yd. Get the bed prepared at least a fortnight in advance of planting time.

The tomatoes should be ready for planting from the 4-in. pots or for removal to large pots, boxes or troughs by about the first week in April. Plant or pot them very firmly and let the top of the old pot ball be a little below the surface of the ground. In beds space the plants at least 15 in. and preferably 18 in. apart in rows at least 2 and preferably 3 ft. apart. If it is a big greenhouse and there are many rows of plants, it is advisable to have a still wider alleyway between every third or fourth row.

After planting the tomatoes should be well watered in and subsequently they should receive gradually increasing quantities of water. For the first week or so this will average about one pint per plant per day but by the time the tomatoes are carrying three or four trusses of fruit this quantity should have been increased to an average of something like a gallon per plant per day. But do not try to work entirely by rule of thumb. The ideal is to keep the soil moist right through the pot or box or, in the case of beds, for the full area and depth occupied by the roots, an area which is, of course, steadily increasing. Always water direct from the spout of the watering can, not through a rose, and never water if the surface of the soil is still wet.

As a rule each tomato plant is restricted to a single stem. Side shoots, one of which will form in the angle between each leaf and the main stem, should be rubbed out as soon as seen. The plant itself is generally stopped, that is to say the top is pinched out, when it has formed six trusses of flowers but in that case the uppermost side shoot is retained and allowed to grow on again, so forming a new top. The idea is temporarily to throw the whole strength of the plant into the production of the first six trusses and so hasten the date on which ripe fruits can be gathered.

Of course in the meantime the plants must be supported in some way. There are a great many methods of doing this. The simplest is to use a 6 or 7-ft. bamboo cane for each plant. A cheaper and quite satisfactory scheme is to use 4 or 5-ply tomato fillis. Loop this round the base of the plant and tie in a non-running knot. Then twist the fillis round the plant two or three times in a clock-wise direction and fasten at its upper end to wires strained horizontally just beneath the rafters of the greenhouse. As the plant continues to grow it will be wound round the fillis still in a clock-wise direction.

Correct feeding is almost as important as watering. Even though the soil was well prepared and properly enriched to begin with, more food is likely to be needed directly the fruits begin to swell. Both artificial fertilisers and animal manure should be used for this purpose. Good compound tomato fertilisers can be purchased ready mixed or you can prepare your own with three parts by weight superphosphate of lime, two parts sulphate of ammonia and two parts sulphate of potash. Use this mixture at a teaspoonful per plant approximately once every week or ten days from the time the fruits commence to swell until the last trusses are commencing to ripen. In addition give two or three light top dressings of old stable manure or farmyard manure at intervals of a few weeks, each to be spread all over the bed or surface of pots, boxes, etc. to a depth of about $\frac{1}{2}$ in.

When the flowers are fully developed, syringe the plants daily with clear water to assist in pollination.

The temperature in the greenhouse from May to September should average 60°, rising to as much as 85° or even 90° on hot, sunny days but never falling below 50°. Ventilate freely as soon as the thermometer rises above 60°. In small houses it is sometimes necessary to throw open the door as well as all ventilators on really hot, summer days and some temporary shading such as thin tiffany may be required in addition. Too much heat will cause leaf scorching and will make the fruits ripen unevenly. In particular avoid rapid temperature rises on bright mornings following chilly nights.

It is often said that tomatoes require a dry atmosphere. If this means dry by comparison with that needed for cucumbers it is true, but it is quite easy to have too little moisture in the air even for the tomato. This will cause bad setting and particularly the condition known as dry set, in which the tiny fruitlets refuse to swell and remain for weeks like pinheads. The remedy is to splash water about on the paths and walls on sunny days or even to syringe the plants themselves.

Commence to pick fruits directly they are half coloured. They can be finished indoors in a sunny window or in a box or drawer and their removal will help the other fruits to ripen quickly. Always pick complete with calyx and stem, breaking the latter off at the knuckle. At the end of the season if there are any green fruits remaining on the plants they can be picked and used for chutney.

RING CULTURE. Some plants, notably tomatoes, chrysanthemums and carnations grow well in bottomless 'pots' standing on a bed of gravel or ashes. Real pots with the bottoms knocked out can be used but most ring culture is carried out in special rings made of bitumenised cardboard or 'whalehide'. Rings 9 in. in diameter and 9 in. deep are suitable for strong growing plants. They are filled with ordinary potting soil and are stood on a bed of clean washed gravel or well weathered boiler ashes at least 6 in. deep. The plants are raised in the normal way from seed or cuttings and are planted in the rings while still quite small. At first water is supplied to the rings just as it would be to plants in normal pots but as soon as the plants have rooted through the soil in the rings into the gravel or ashes below water is supplied direct to this aggregate, and to this alone. Any solid or liquid food required is applied to the soil in the rings from which the plants derive all the chemicals they require but they get their major water supply from the aggregate.

OUTDOOR CULTURE. The cultivation of tomatoes in the open follows the same general principles as under glass but differs in some important details. Seed should not be sown before March 10th, in fact I have often had excellent results from seed sown as late as April 12th. If the seed is put in too early the plants get too big before they can be transplanted to their fruiting quarters. The only exception is in the case of plants that are to be protected with special cloches after planting out and for this purpose the seed should be sown the first week in March. Otherwise details of germination and early potting of the seedlings is the same as for greenhouse plants.

The tomato plants should be worked on into 4-in. pots a fortnight or three weeks before planting out. They must be carefully hardened off by being placed in a frame and given steadily increasing ventilation on all favourable days, but even with the best treatment they will remain susceptible to a few degrees of frost. This means that in many places it is not safe to plant tomatoes outdoors without protection before the end of the first week in June. Near the coast and in the South of England it is often possible to plant towards the end of May, while in some very favoured places early May planting can be considered but generally this involves temporary protection with cloches.

Prepare the ground by deep digging and a moderate use of well-rotted dung but not more than 1 cwt. to 10 sq. yd. If not available, use well-rotted compost at the same rate or plenty of peat or leaf mould to supply the necessary humus. In any case use fertilisers as advised for indoor crops.

Plant 15 to 18 in. apart in rows 2½ ft. apart, or alternatively have two rows spaced at 20 in. and then an alleyway of 3 ft. Let the rows run as nearly as possible north and south or, if there is to be one row only, it can run east and west in front of a south-facing wall or fence. The sunnier the position the better but if it can be sheltered from the north and east it is all to the good. Water the plants in but subsequently only give water if the soil appears dry.

Remove side shoots exactly as advised for indoor plants but stop the plants by pinching out the growing point when three, or at most four, flower trusses have been formed. This is as many as can reasonably be expected to ripen outdoors.

Either stake the plants individually, each with a 4-ft. bamboo cane or similar stick, or alternatively drive strong 4-ft. stakes at 10-ft. intervals along the rows, strain one wire along the tops of these posts and then string the plants individually from beds to wire.

Commence to pick at a rather earlier stage than with greenhouse plants as it is difficult enough to get a whole crop to ripen outdoors under the most favourable circumstances.

Top dressings with dung are usually unnecessary outdoors but the plants can be fed with artificials as already described.

Keep a sharp look out for sharp frosts from the end of September onwards and gather the whole crop, however green the fruits may be, before such a frost occurs. Many of the fruits can be ripened subsequently indoors packed in boxes in a dark place while the very green ones can be used for chutney.

An alternative is to pull the plants up roots and all before a sharp frost occurs and hang them in a greenhouse as already described (see p. 618), while yet another method is to untie them, remove the stakes and just lay the plants down lengthwise along the row when they can be covered quite easily with barn type cloches. If this is done it is advisable to spread some clean straw on the ground first.

It is possible to grow tomatoes outdoors under special type cloches throughout the summer. These cloches are much taller than the ordinary type and they are made in such a way that one side can be removed completely. The complete cloche should be employed from the time the plants are put out in the first half of May until about mid June, after which the west side if the rows run north and south or the south side if the rows run east and west, should be removed. This side is returned towards the end of September and subsequently left in position as long as the plants continue to ripen their fruits.

When tomatoes are grown under these cloches the stakes are driven in at an angle of 45° along the length of the row, leaning from the south towards the north if in north-south rows. If the plants are in east-west rows the stakes can lean to either east or west, whichever is more convenient.

There are a great many varieties of tomatoes and though some of the old kinds remain good, others lose their vitality after a time and must be replaced, so that it is advisable to keep up-to-date on these. Here are a few which I have personally found good.

For greenhouse culture: Potentate, Plumpton King, E.S.1., Best of All, Ailsa Craig, Kondine Red, Clibran's Victory, Stoner's M.P., Stoner's Exhibition and Carter's Fruit.

For outdoor cultivation: Early Market, Carter's Sunrise, Outdoor Girl, Earliest of All, Harbinger, Market King and Essex Wonder.

BUSH TOMATO. A distinct type of tomato which finds favour with some gardeners is known as the bush. This does not make one central stem but branches almost at once into several stems and these in turn branch again. The bush is, in fact, aptly described by its name and a good type will not exceed a height of 2 ft. and will perhaps by the end of the season measure 2 ft. through.

Methods of stopping and training differ quite a lot but I have found it best as a rule to restrict each plant to about four stems and stop each of these not later than the first week in August. Each plant should be provided with four stakes placed around it in a small circle and the various stems should be tied individually to these stakes.

The chief merits of the bush are for cultivation in pots in small greenhouses where there is little head room, for cultivation in deep frames or for planting outdoors under big barn type cloches.

Typical bush varieties are Amateur and First in the Field.

TURNIPS

Summer turnips are not an easy crop in all gardens as unless they can be grown quickly and without check the roots tend to be tough and strong flavoured. To counteract this the ground should be as rich as possible and very deeply dug but it is not desirable to use dung immediately prior to sowing as this tends to cause forking. Either choose a plot that was manured for a preceding crop or give a moderate dressing of well-rotted dung (1 cwt. to 15 sq. yd.) at least three months prior to sowing. Fertilisers should be used as for swedes and it is advisable to give this whether or not dung is applied.

Do not rely on one sowing only as in the case of swedes, but make small successional sowings every three or four weeks starting as early in March as the condition of the ground will allow and continuing until the end of July. This will make it possible to use the roots while they are still fairly small and tender.

The final sowing for winter storing need not be made until the end of July provided the ground is in really good order and water can be supplied should the weather become dry. Failing these necessities it is advisable to sow three or four weeks earlier as growth may be delayed.

All seed should be sown in $\frac{1}{2}$ in. deep drills 10 in. apart except for the final sowing which may be in rows 15 in. apart because for storing the roots will be allowed to attain greater size. If the seed is sown very thinly no thinning may be needed in the case of summer turnips but the seedlings should be spaced at least 4 in. apart at this season and for the last sowing 6 in. apart. Small top dressings of nitrate of soda can be given along the rows as for swedes.

Turnips should not be left in the ground all winter like swedes but the whole crop should be lifted at the end of October or early in November and stored in a shed or outhouse. Cover the roots with a little dry soil, sand or ashes.

Turnip tops make a welcome change in spring from kale and broccoli. They are produced by sowing seed rather more thickly than usual early in September and leaving the seedlings unthinned throughout the winter. Space the rows 9 in. apart and cut the tops at ground level as required from March onwards.

There are a good many varieties of turnip and most seedsmen offer specialities of their own. For summer use Orange Jelly and Golden Ball, with orange flesh, and Milan Early White and Snowball, both with white flesh, are excellent. For winter use and providing turnip tops in spring Greentop Stone and Manchester Market are hardy and reliable.

VEGETABLE MARROW

This is an extremely tender vegetable and one which will be killed by even a few degrees of frost so it is practically essential to start it under glass. The usual method is to sow seeds singly or in pairs in small flower pots towards the end of April or the first week in May. Almost any light soil can be used for the purpose and the John Innes seed compost (see p. 423) is excellent.

Germinate in an unheated greenhouse or frame, and if frost threatens at night see that the plants are well protected with brown paper or sacks. Germination is, as a rule, very rapid and within three or four weeks of sowing the pots should be well filled with roots and the plants already 4 or 5 in. high with several strong leaves each.

Unless protection can be given do not on any account plant outdoors before the first week in June except in specially favoured regions such as Cornwall and Devon.

The old method of growing marrows was on raised beds composed chiefly of decaying turves with any other vegetable refuse that might be available and a little dung. Excellent crops can be produced in this way but a drawback is that the plants are liable to need a lot of watering in dry weather. For this reason it is really better to plant marrows on the flat in ordinary beds well dug and liberally dressed with dung. It can be used at rates up to 1 cwt. to 5 sq. yd.

There are two types of marrow—bush and trailing. The former should be planted 2 ft. apart each way and the latter at least 3 ft. Water in well after planting and keep on watering every day or so for the first ten days or fortnight until the plants are growing freely.

Bush marrows will need no further attention beyond fertilising the female flowers. This is done by picking well-developed male blooms and inverting them over the females, which can be distinguished by the fact that each is attached to an embryo marrow. Do this fairly frequently and, for preference, when the sun is shining and the pollen is dry.

Trailing marrows should be fertilised in the same way and in addition the points of the runners should be pinched out occasionally to encourage the formation of side growths. These are usually more productive of female flowers than the main runners, which often carry nothing but male blooms.

Cut the marrows while they are still quite young and feel a little soft if pressed with the thumbs at the blossom end. In September one or two fruits per plant may be allowed to remain to attain full size and ripen. If they are cut when the skins show a yellow tinge and feel really hard, they will keep for many months in any cool and perfectly dry place, such as on a shelf in a spare room.

To produce very large marrows for exhibition the number of fruits should be considerably restricted and the plants should be fed freely with weak, liquid manure from the time the fruits commence to form.

There are numerous varieties, the most useful being Long White Trailing, Long Green Trailing, Bush White and Bush Green. Rotherside Orange is a trailing variety of exceptional quality while Table Dainty gives a number of rather small marrows. Custard Marrows and Squashes, some of which are highly ornamental, are grown in the same way.

WATERCRESS

The best watercress is produced in specially made beds flooded with slowly running water, but it is possible to grow it in the garden without any water at all except that which is applied from a can or hose.

To deal with the former method first, the beds may be of any convenient size but are not generally more than 4 ft. wide and should certainly not be more than 10 in. deep. They are lined with concrete and provided with valves or sluices to enable the flow of water to be controlled at all seasons. The bottom of each bed is covered with 3 in. of good loamy soil and a little clean gravel or sand is spread on top of this to keep the soil down. Cuttings from young shoots taken from any good watercress plants during spring, summer or early autumn are dibbled into the bed 6 in. apart each way. Water is then admitted, but only to a depth of $1\frac{1}{2}$ in. at first. Later, as the plants grow, a greater depth of water is maintained, but never more than 4 in.

Commence to cut as soon as the bed is covered with growth. Do not cut the whole of any one plant but leave a couple of inches at the base to throw up fresh shoots. A bed treated in this way will continue to crop for many months.

To grow watercress without running water, dig a trench 1 ft. deep and about 2 ft. wide and break up the subsoil with a fork. Then put 6 in. of rotted manure in the bottom, cover with 3 in. of soil and either sow watercress seed in this thinly in April and August or plant cuttings as for the water beds. Water the trenches freely whenever the soil appears dry.

There are no varieties of importance but get seed or cuttings from a reliable source as strains vary widely.

PART V
FRUITS

CHAPTER XXV

Making a Fruit Garden

THERE ARE few gardens in the British Isles in which fruit cannot be grown, though it would be misleading to pretend that it can be grown with equal success everywhere. Contrary to popular belief, soil is not as important as situation. Highly successful orchards are to be seen on land varying from stiff clays to quite light sands or gravels, and though it is probably true to say that the ideal soil for an orchard is a medium well-drained loam, this is by no means essential. Perhaps the most useful thing that can be said on this subject is that any ground that is capable of producing good crops of potatoes, cabbages and similar common vegetables, is also suitable for the cultivation of fruit of all kinds.

SITUATION. This is, as I have already remarked, far more critical and it is not, as so frequently supposed, the very sheltered position that is always most suitable. The real danger with fruit is frost at blossom time, that is to say in spring. Now frost behaves in a peculiar way. Still cold air tends to flow downwards like water and in consequence spring frosts are often most severe in valleys and hollows, in fact in just the very places which seem so delightfully sheltered and suitable for planting fruit trees. Hillsides, which are exposed to all the winds that blow, are generally relatively free from spring frosts and, provided the altitude is not too great, are often ideal for orchard planting.

I have mentioned altitude and this must be taken into consideration for even in the south of England fruit trees are unlikely to crop reliably above certain heights. As a rule it is considered that 700 ft. is about the maximum for successful fruit growing though in exceptional cases this may be increased.

I do not want to give the impression that fruit should not be planted in low lying places. As a matter of fact far more depends upon the relative height of the ground to that immediately around it than upon its actual height above sea level. A hollow on a high plateau may be more of a frost trap than a small knoll not much above sea level. Moreover, however frosty the situation, it is still probable that fruit crops will be obtained as frequently as two years out of three on the average, which may be quite enough to satisfy the amateur gardener though it would be fatal to the success of a commercial grower.

Many people get the idea that they cannot include fruit in their gardens because of the amount of room it will take up. With modern stocks and forms of training this is not true. It is possible to include some fruit even in the smallest gardens by making use of what are known as dwarfing stocks and such forms as the single stem cordon. This, no doubt, necessitates a little further explanation.

FORMS OF TREE. Any fruit tree left entirely to its own devices would in time form a big branching bush or tree many feet in height and circumference. The gardener sets out to adapt the shape of the tree to his own requirements. So far as the bigger fruits, apples, pears, plums, etc., are concerned there are seven forms of tree in fairly common use. I will take them in the order of the space they occupy from the biggest downwards. First, then, there is the standard, which has a main trunk 5–6 ft. high on top of which are a number of branches radiating in all directions, forming a roughly globular head, in fact what we commonly call a tree. Next to this is the half standard, similar in all respects except that the main trunk is only about 4 ft. in height. Third comes the bush, in which the main stem is still further reduced, usually in present day trees to about 2 ft. though some old specimens may have main trunks as short as 1 ft. or less. Again branches radiate in all directions, forming a big, goblet-shaped specimen without undue formality.

The pyramid appears rather similar at first sight but on closer inspection proves to be much more regular in shape. It has a main stem continued vertically right through the centre of the tree and from this, from bottom to top, branches radiate roughly at right angles, the bottom branches being longer than those at the top, giving to the whole tree the shape not so much of a pyramid as of a cone. This form was very popular a generation or so ago but then fell into disuse, mainly because of the amount of pruning necessary to keep it in trim. Latterly there has been renewed interest in this form particularly when the trees are worked on dwarfing stocks (see p. 629) and so can be kept quite small.

Coming down the scale another stage, we find the horizontal trained or espalier tree and the fan trained tree. The former has an unbroken central stem like the pyramid with branches or 'arms' at right angles to it but in one plane only, not all round the trunk as in the pyramid. The object of the espalier trained tree, as its name implies, is to occupy a position on an espalier fence, that is to say a series of wires stretched horizontally between uprights embedded firmly in the soil.

The fan trained tree bears about the same relationship to the horizontally trained tree as the bush does to the pyramid, that is to say it is less formal though it occupies approximately the same amount of space. The name gives a satisfactory description for the branches are roughly arranged like the ribs of a fan, radiating from a short main stem but in one plane so that the tree can be planted against a fence or wall.

Finally there is the cordon trained tree which has several variations such as single, double, triple, oblique and horizontal. All are based on the same general idea, namely to have a main stem (or two or three stems in the case of the multiple cordons) to which all side growth is pruned comparatively closely. The great advantage of the cordon is that it occupies very little space and so gives the owner of a small garden the opportunity to grow a considerable variety of fruit.

DISTANCE OF PLANTING. Roughly speaking the standard tree needs a circle 25–30 ft. in diameter, that is to say no other tree of similar type can be planted closer to it than that. The half standard occupies about the same amount of ground, perhaps a little less, much depending upon the type of stock on which it is worked (see p. 630). A bush or pyramid needs from 10–15 ft.; dwarf pyramid 3 ft. by 6 ft.; horizontal and fan trained trees 12–15 ft.; and single stemmed cordons 2 ft. in one direction and 6 ft. in the other, i.e. if several rows of cordons are to be planted they should be at least 6 ft. apart though the trees in the rows are spaced only 2 ft. apart.

THE INFLUENCE OF STOCK. I have already referred several times to the stock and implied that it has an influence on the ultimate size of the tree. This is a very important matter and one which the amateur fruit grower should consider carefully.

First of all it must be understood clearly that only the tree fruits (apples, pears, plums, cherries, peaches, etc.) are worked on stocks, that is to say grafted or budded to a root system other than their own. Soft fruits, such as currants and gooseberries, and cane fruits such as raspberries and loganberries are grown from cuttings, layers or off-shoots and their roots are of their own providing.

The original reason for grafting or budding tree fruits was simply that they cannot readily be grown from cuttings or layers and that seedlings varied too much in character to be of any real value. In consequence the only satisfactory method of propagating a good variety was by grafting it either on to a seedling or on to some type of allied tree which could be raised from either cuttings or layers. It was quickly observed that this method of increase actually has definite advantages because root systems vary greatly and have a marked influence upon the growth and fruiting characteristics of the tree.

Standardised stocks have now been produced for several types of fruit, including apples, pears and plums and each of these has a known and predictable influence.

To take Paradise apples as an example, there are now eighteen such stocks classified and known under numbers which often bear the prefix 'Malling' after the East Malling Research Station where much of this work of collection and identification was carried out. Only a few are of importance to the gardener. No. IX is notably dwarfing in character. Even a naturally vigorous apple such as Bramley Seedling, when grafted on it, makes quite a small tree and I have seen ten year old bushes of this variety no more than 6 ft. across though on an old fashioned crab stock they would have been three or four times that diameter at the same age. Moreover No. IX stock brings apples into bearing exceptionally early. It is no uncommon occurrence for some fruit to be produced the year after grafting, whereas on crab stock it might be eight to ten years before any fruit was produced by the same variety.

No. II stock is more vigorous and less precocious than No. IX but still moderately dwarfing and has been found the ideal root system for a great many apples both in commercial orchards and private gardens when trees are to be grown as bushes or are to be espalier trained. No. I stock is a little more vigorous still at any rate in the early years, though later it may lag behind No. II. Nos. XII and XVI stocks carry this tale of vigour a stage further and are sufficiently sturdy to make good half standards or even, with vigorous varieties and good soil, a full standard. Of the two No. XVI is to be preferred.

It will be seen that by choosing his stock wisely to suit the main peculiarities of the variety and the purposes for which it is required, the fruit grower can solve a lot of his problems and in particular avoid a great deal of unnecessary pruning later on.

PLANNING AN ORCHARD

In the case of very small fruit gardens the question of planning will scarcely arise as fruit trees will probably have to go wherever room can be found for them and, most likely, share the ground with other crops. There is nothing against this except that it should be borne in mind that most fruit trees and particularly currants, raspberries, cherries and brambles, make a great many roots near the surface which rules out the possibility of much digging or forking close to them. These roots will generally extend at least as far as the branches. Another point is that some of the sprays used to keep down pests and diseases on fruit trees are damaging to other plants. This is notably the case with winter washes used to kill insect eggs. The difficulty can be overcome to some extent by covering under crops with sacking while spraying is in progress.

With bigger orchards the first thing to observe is that whatever system of planting is adopted it should be symmetrical throughout. This is not merely a matter of appearance but also one of utility for if the trees are evenly spaced and in straight lines cultivation will be easier and the trees themselves will be encouraged to make well-balanced growth. Quite a number of different systems of planting have been used but the two most important are those known as square and triangular, shown in the diagrams on p. 634.

In small orchards it is probable that only one or two specimens of each variety will be included and the most that can be advised in this case is to keep fruits of a kind together, that is to say all apples in one part of the orchard, pears in another and so on. With bigger plantations this grouping should be extended to varieties though not without some qualification. The point is that even within a given kind of fruit, such as apples or pears, there is considerable varietal difference in growth and also in reaction to spray fluids, fertilisers, etc. For example apple Cox's Orange Pippin is often damaged by fluids containing copper once it is in full leaf, whereas apple Stirling Castle is equally intolerant of lime sulphur at this stage. If one variety is planted alongside the other spraying can become a somewhat complicated business but if Cox's Orange Pippins are all in one row and Stirling Castles in another, the problem is greatly simplified.

FERTILITY. The reason I stated that qualification was necessary to this general rule of grouping varieties together is that most fruit trees are to a greater or lesser degree self sterile. This simply means that they do not set a good crop, or in some cases any crop at all, unless the blossom is fertilised with pollen from another variety of the same kind of fruit. This point must be understood clearly. Apple blossom can only be fertilised with pollen from an apple, pear blossom from a pear, and so on. But the blossom of such a variety of apple as, say, Cox's Orange Pippin needs to be fertilised with pollen from another variety of apple such as Laxton's Superb or Worcester Pearmain. It is important that 'mates' chosen for this purpose shall flower at the same time.

When planting a big orchard it is necessary to intermingle these good mating varieties. There is no need for them to be actually side by side so long as they are within 40–50 ft. of one another. Quite a usual plan in commercial establishments is to have two or three rows of one variety followed by a single row of the pollinating kind.

UNDER PLANTING. The next question to consider is that of under planting, either with vegetables or with soft fruits. This can be a bit of a snare because although there is plenty of room for the under crops at the outset the fruit trees soon fill up all the space. In addition there are the problems of spraying and fertilising already remarked upon to be considered. All the same, interplanting is usually good policy in small gardens for the first five or six years and for this purpose black currants or gooseberries are generally employed.

WALLS AND FENCES. In private gardens there are almost always fences and walls which can be turned to good account for fruit. There are suitable varieties for every conceivable aspect from full sun to full shade and I have indicated these in a list at the end of this section. Cleverly used, walls and fences can greatly extend the fresh fruit season, the sunny walls giving a crop earlier than can be obtained in the open and the shady ones extending it after the normal crop has been gathered.

Beware of one point, however. The soil at the foot of a wall or fence is almost always relatively dry and until fruit trees have had time to root out for some feet they may need considerable supplies of water.

SOIL PREPARATION

There is really nothing very special to be said about the preparation of soil for fruit trees. Provided the ground is broken up as deeply as practicable and is in reasonably good condition fruit trees should succeed in it. Contrary to what is often stated it is an excellent plan to add some well-rotted dung prior to planting. It must be thoroughly decayed; fresh manure is undoubtedly harmful at this stage. Moreover the dressing should not be too heavy; 2 cwt. per rod is ample. Nor should it be left lying about in layers between one spit and another; get it thoroughly mixed into the soil to a depth of 18 in. or so. At the same time give bone meal, 6 oz. per sq. yd. and any potash fertiliser at the appropriate rate. Muriate of potash is quite suitable and usually cheap and can be used at 1 oz. per sq. yd.

Finally, get the digging done as long as possible in advance of the time of planting. An ideal plan is to use the site of the fruit garden for a crop of early potatoes, get these cleared as soon after mid-summer as possible and then dig or half trench the ground in August or September for planting early in November.

PLANTING

The chief point to observe about planting is to do it when the soil is in the right condition. It is fatal to plant fruit trees when the ground is waterlogged or frostbound. In some seasons there are only a few weeks during which this work can be carried out with real success so it is important to make the best possible use of the time when conditions are favourable. Other things being equal, the best period for planting is usually from the fourth week in October to the end of November. By December the ground is almost always too wet and cold and this state of things is likely to continue at least until the end of February, by which date sap is rising and there is little time left to complete planting.

A good test for the condition of the soil is to try digging a few holes. If the soil clings to spade and boots and, still more, if the holes tend to fill with water, planting should not be attempted. The ideal is that the soil should be crumbly; sufficiently moist to bind together when squeezed in the palm of the hand but dry enough for the ball so formed to break up again when tossed on to the surface.

If trees or bushes arrive from the nursery when soil conditions are unfavourable for planting, they should be heeled in temporarily. This simply means that a trench is dug large enough to accommodate the roots, the trees are lined out in this as close together as possible, the soil returned over the roots and made firm. Treated in this way they will take no harm for several weeks.

As regards the actual planting, the vital points are to spread the roots out fully and not cover them too deeply. A common fault is to make holes too deep and narrow. Remember that the normal habit of fruit tree roots is to grow out more or less horizontally. Not many roots plunge steeply into the soil and this is, in any case, an undesirable characteristic.

Speaking generally, holes for apples, pears, plums, etc. should be about 3 ft. wide and 1 ft. deep but these dimensions may need to be varied a little to suit individual peculiarities of growth. In any case the hole should be wide enough to accommodate the longest root fully extended in a natural manner and deep enough to permit the uppermost roots to be covered with 4 in. of soil.

It is wise to drive stakes into position in the centre of each hole before the trees are planted. Even bush trees need staking for a year or so though quite short stakes will do in this case. For standards they should be long enough to reach to the top of the main stem where it forks, and go down a couple of feet into the soil. It often pays to have a second stake driven in at an angle to the main stake and bound to it as a stay.

Before actually planting the trees examine the roots carefully and cut off any portions that are badly broken or bruised. These are in any case not likely to be of much use to the tree and if left they may decay and cause trouble.

It is a great help to have an assistant when planting. He can hold the tree and jerk it gently up and down while the planter returns the soil a little at a time, the finer and more crumbly portions first. When all the roots are just covered with soil this should be trodden down firmly. Then the rest of the soil is returned but left loose.

Get the newly planted trees tied securely to their stakes directly planting is finished but first bind some old sacking or fragments of inner tubing around the bark where the tie will come. This is to prevent any possibility of the cord cutting into the bark or chafing it. Ties should be renewed fairly frequently during the first few years as the trunks will expand rapidly and the ties will soon become too tight.

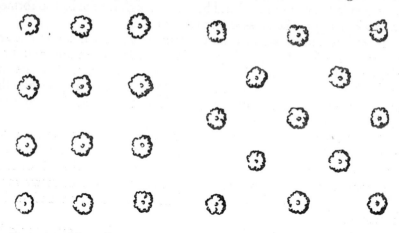

TWO SYSTEMS OF PLANTING FRUIT TREES
The 'square' system is shown on the left and the 'triangular' on the right

CHAPTER XXVI

Fruit Propagation

The nurseryman produces fruit trees by five different means, seeds, cuttings, grafts, buds and layers. Seeds are only used to raise new varieties or stocks upon which accepted kinds are grafted or budded. The reason is that there can be no guarantee that a seedling will resemble its parent in any respect except, of course, that an apple will always produce an apple, a pear a pear and so on. But in all the important details of size, colour, flavour, etc. it is almost certain that the seedling will differ widely from the fruit from which it was obtained. Moreover the change is very seldom one for the better, the chances being in favour of deterioration rather than improvement. This remains true even when careful crosses have been made between parents selected for special points of excellence. Nurserymen who specialise in raising new varieties of fruit have to rear many hundreds of seedlings in order to get one fit to put on the market.

There is, of course, nothing to prevent the amateur from sowing pips and seeds on the off-chance of getting something good as long as he realises just what the chances are. He should also know that seedlings are, as a rule, slow in giving any fruit. In the case of apples and pears, for example, it may be ten years before a seedling produces a single fruit by which its quality may be judged and even then further years must elapse before its cropping capabilities can be fully proved. This tardiness can often be overcome by grafting shoots from the seedling on to one of the dwarfing stocks to which I have already referred. Seedling apples can be worked in this way on No. IX stock and brought into bearing in two or three years and this is the usual method adopted by commercial raisers.

The actual handling of fruit seeds is the same as that for the seeds of other hardy trees and shrubs. The fruits are gathered when they part readily from the tree, and are then stood in a dry and fairly warm place until they become quite ripe. The seeds are then removed from them and stored in a cool, dry spot until the following March, when they are sown either outdoors in shallow drills or, a better policy, separately in small pots in a frame. If in pots the seedlings should be planted out in good soil the following autumn and subsequently left to grow with a minimum of thinning or pruning which only delays fruit production.

CUTTINGS. Soft fruits, such as gooseberries and currants, are always raised from cuttings taken in the autumn as soon as or just before the leaves fall. Wood of the current year's growth is used for this purpose, that is to say the young stems which have grown during the preceding summer. They must be firm and well ripened at the base but it does not matter if they are still fairly soft at the tips as these can be discarded. Stems about 12 in. in length are ideal but shorter pieces will serve. Each potential cutting is either severed from the parent plant just below a joint, i.e. the point at which a leaf stalk joins the stem, or alternatively, if it is a side growth and not a terminal shoot, it is pulled away from the main branch with a strip of old bark, a method usually referred to as taking a 'slip'. The technical term for this is 'heel cutting' as opposed to a 'plain cutting' and many gardeners assert that a heel cutting has a better chance of rooting. The drawback of this method is that it leaves an ugly instead of a clean wound on the parent plant and so affords greater chance for infection by disease germs.

If the heel type of cutting is taken the thin strip of bark left at the foot of the cutting must be trimmed neatly back. With the plain cutting no further preparation is necessary providing the cut has been made quite cleanly just beneath a joint. If the cut is ragged or removed from a joint these faults should be rectified.

There is only one other point to note, namely that with gooseberry and red and white currant cuttings it is advisable to nick out all buds on the lower half of each shoot with the point of a penknife. The object of this is to prevent any shoots forming below soil level as these are a nuisance, tending to block up the centre of the bush and hindering picking. This precaution is not necessary in the case of black currants because with these all old wood is cut out annually and therefore the sucker growths, which incidentally always produce the best fruit, do not overcrowd the bush.

All these cuttings are inserted in the same way. They are lined out about 1 ft. apart in straight-backed trenches about 4–5 in. deep in well-broken soil and an open but not too exposed position. These trenches are best chopped out with a sharp spade and the back of each should be kept as nearly vertical as possible so that the cuttings stand upright. The soil is returned around the cuttings and made thoroughly firm with the foot. No further treatment is necessary beyond the usual summer watering and hoeing until the following autumn, by which time the cuttings should be sufficiently well rooted to be lifted and planted in fruiting quarters.

A few failures will usually occur and need cause no concern but if there are many blanks in the cutting bed it is probable that the shoots selected were either too soft or too hard. With a few varieties, particularly of gooseberry, it is difficult to get the right kind of shoot to make a good cutting. The gooseberry Leveller is a notable offender in this respect. The difficulty can be overcome by setting apart a few bushes for propagation early in the year, cutting them back to within a few inches of the soil level and then, when shoots appear in spring, gradually drawing the soil around them to a height of 7 or 8 in., much as when earthing potatoes. This will keep the bases of the shoots sufficiently soft to make satisfactory cuttings when they are severed for this purpose the following autumn.

GRAFTING. If the larger fruits, apples, pears, cherries, etc. could be easily raised from cuttings no doubt this method would be largely used despite certain objections. Unfortunately most varieties either entirely refuse to root or can only be induced to root with the greatest difficulty. In consequence for hundreds of years it has been a practice, as I have already explained, to graft or bud them on suitable root stocks, and the advantages accruing from this have already been outlined.

First let it be understood that budding is not really a distinct operation from grafting but only a form of it.

Grafting is done in early spring usually between the third week in March and the middle of April, just as the sap is beginning to rise freely. The shoots of the fruit tree which is to be propagated are known as scions and the roots to which these scions are to be joined are known as stocks.

Scions can be prepared from any firm, well-ripened young growths, shoots, in fact, identical with those used as cuttings in the case of soft fruits. Very often sufficient of these can be obtained in the ordinary course of winter pruning. Fairly strong shoots terminating branches are ideal for the purpose and should be obtained in winter preferably before the end of January. They can be cut off quite roughly, labelled clearly and heeled-in in a shallow trench made in a cool, shady position such as under a north wall. The object of this is to hold them back so that by grafting time they are more backward than the stocks to which they are to be joined.

These stocks should be planted in autumn in well-prepared soil and allowed to grow for at least a year before being grafted. Stocks which are to form young trees should at the time of grafting have one main stem about as thick as a man's thumb and this is cut cleanly through about 15 in. above soil level a month before the time of grafting.

There are many different kinds of grafting but as far as the formation of young trees is concerned only one need interest us. This is the whip graft.

To make a successful whip graft one needs a very sharp knife, a supply of soft raffia or twine and some grafting wax which can be obtained from any dealer in horticultural sundries. Select one of the shoots reserved as a scion and, starting immediately behind a bud, make a long, straight, downward cut coming out on the opposite side of the shoot about 2 in. from the point of entry. The effect of this is to shape the bottom of the shoot into a long, thin wedge. Turn the shoot over and, starting about a quarter of the way down the first cut draw the knife upwards in the opposite direction so forming a thin slip or tongue as shown in the illustration. Now make two exactly similar cuts in the reverse direction at the top of the beheaded stock. These cuts should be identical in length and width with those made on the scion so that scion and stock can be fitted together perfectly like a well-made piece of cabinet making. Do this and bind them together with raffia or twine. Then cover the whole wounded area with grafting wax which will need to be warmed to make it work freely.

If the scion is a long one the top can be cut off a couple of inches above the top of the stock. Some very strong shoots may be cut into two or three separate scions. There is nothing against this provided all the wood is properly ripened, but beware of using soft, downy looking wood for this purpose. The tips of even the best shoots have to be thrown away on this account.

Two other methods of grafting are used but not for raising young trees. Both are serviceable for converting older trees to newer or more suitable kinds of fruit. One is known as rind grafting and the other as frame or stub grafting. In both cases a start must be made by gathering scions in winter just as for whip grafting but the method of preparing the trees which are to be grafted is different. For rind grafting each main bough or branch is cut off 1 ft. or so above the trunk of the tree, thus leaving a number of short thick stumps. For frame grafting there are two alternatives. Either every side growth along the length of each main branch is removed, leaving the branches bare but unshortened, or no preparation at all is done at this stage.

A rind graft is particularly simple to make. The scion is cut with one long, sloping incision like that made for the whip graft but without the reverse cut. The stock is prepared by slitting the bark vertically from the top downwards for a length equal to that of the cut made on the scion. The flaps of bark on each side of this incision are gently raised from the hard wood beneath and the tapering wedge of the scion is pressed down beneath them so that its cut surface lies snugly inwards against the moist wood of the stock. Two or three scions can be inserted in this way round the top of each stump if it is a big one.

All are then bound in together with a raffia tie and covered with grafting wax.

FRAME WORKING. For frame grafting, if all side growths were removed in autumn, L-shaped incisions are made in the bark every few inches along each main branch. Again the flap of branch so formed is raised and the scions, prepared in the same way as for rind grafting, are slipped beneath, bound in and waxed.

If the side growths were not removed in winter a different method is employed. A short, downward incision is made on the upper side of each side growth half an inch above its base. The scion is prepared with a double cut forming a rather blunt wedge. The side growth is then bent downwards so opening the cut, the scion is slipped into position and the shoot is immediately released so that it springs back and grips the scion. Finally the shoot is cut off just beyond the point at which the scion was inserted. By this method no tying is necessary and it only remains to wax the wound in the ordinary way.

The advantage of frame grafting is that the whole main framework of the tree, however old, is retained and the conversion is made with the minimum of delay. The tree that has been headed back for rind grafting may take a number of years to regain its former productiveness.

BUDDING. This is a simpler and more certain method of making a union between stock and scion. It is the form of grafting invariably used first by nurserymen when working up young stock for sale, their practice being to bud all their stocks in July or August following the autumn of planting, and then, the next spring, to graft any which may have failed when budded. Budding is far more satisfactory than grafting for stone fruits as it does not necessitate severe heading back of the stock and consequently does not render it so liable to attack by diseases such as Silver Leaf. The limitation of budding is that it can only be applied to quite young wood and does not provide a satisfactory method of re-working old trees.

All the work is done in summer, usually from about the middle of July to the end of August. The limiting factors as regards time are, at the commencement, the earliest date at which ripe buds can be obtained, and at the end of the period, the latest date at which the bark of the stock will part cleanly from the wood.

The 'buds' referred to are, in fact, dormant growth buds, one of which will be found in the angle between the leaf stalk and stem on practically every young shoot in summer. Suitable wood for budding can be obtained when doing summer pruning for well developed side growths (laterals) are just what is needed. The tips of these are usually still soft and downy and should be discarded but the lower half of each should be firm, woody and suitable. The leaves are removed from the selected shoots but the leaf stalks are retained.

The stock should be anything from two to four years old and should for preference be about as thick as a man's thumb. It is prepared by making a T-shaped incision in the bark about a foot above soil level. The down cut of the T should be a little over an inch long and the cross cut $\frac{1}{2}$ in. wide. The flaps of bark on each side of this down cut are raised with the thin end of a budding knife. Now a bud is cut by inserting the blade of the knife $\frac{1}{2}$ in. below one of the leaf stalks on the selected shoot and drawing it in and up beneath the bud and out again on the same side well above the leaf stalk. This gives a shield-shaped portion of bark and wood with a leaf stalk and bud. Holding this by the leaf stalk turn it over, grip between thumb nail and knife point the slip of wood contained within the bark and whip it out. Now square off the top of the shield-shaped portion of bark $\frac{1}{3}$ in. above the bud. Still holding it by the leaf stalk slip it beneath the flaps of bark on the stock, keeping the bud uppermost and outwards. Push it down until the squared top of the bud lies snugly against the top of the T. Finally bind it in position with soft raffia, being careful to carry the tie well above and well below the cut portion.

Six or seven weeks later examine ties as some may be cutting into the bark of the stock due to its growth. If this is the case, remove the old tie and replace with a fresh one.

Nothing further is done until the following February when the whole of the top growth of the stock is cut off just above the point of budding. This concentrates all the sap from the roots on to the inserted bud which by this time should have made a good union and will therefore be ready to grow away strongly.

LAYERING. As a method of propagation layering is not very frequently applied to fruit trees themselves, though a special form known as tip layering is used for bramble fruits, but it is the best method of increasing many fruit stocks, notably paradise and quince stocks. The method in this case is very simple. The stocks are planted in the ordinary way in straight rows. Then in February they are cut back to within a few inches of ground level. The following spring strong basal growth will appear from each beheaded stock. The best shoots are selected and pegged down horizontally to the soil the following winter. The remaining weaker shoots are cut out. Side shoots will soon form freely along the lengths of the pegged stems. Soil is drawn up around these a little at a time, just as when earthing potatoes, until eventually there is a

Planting a tree against a fence. The roots are spread out well

Planting cordon-trained apples in a wide, shallow trench

A close up of fruit tree planting showing the necessity for a wide hole

A well-planted row of cordon trained apples in a small garden

On the left is a grafted apple stock. Right a scion is prepared for whip grafting

The prepared scion fitted to a stock which has been cut in the reverse manner

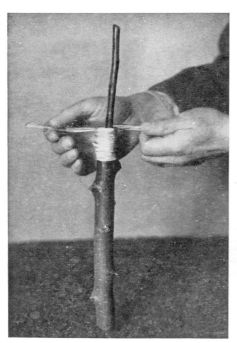

Stock and scion are bound together with raffia

When completed the whole wounded area is sealed with warm grafting wax

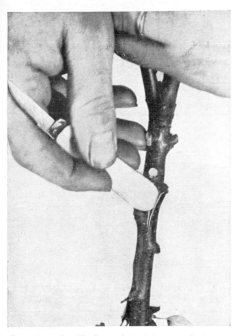

Opening the T-shaped incision made in an apple stock which is to be budded

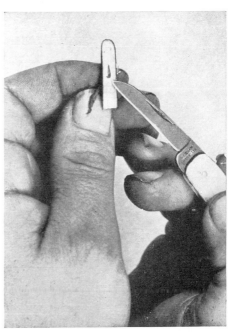

The bud ready for insertion. The knife point indicates the interior surface of the bud itself

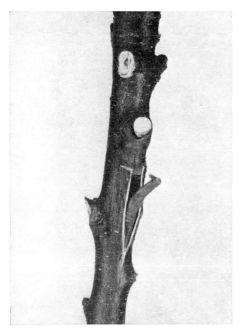

The prepared bud slipped beneath the flaps of bark left by the T-cut

The bud is bound firmly in position with raffia. No wax is required

Pegging down a strawberry runner. A small flower-pot has been sunk in the ground to receive the runner

Firming in a newly planted strawberry. Note the crown of the plant just level with the surface of the soil

Picking strawberries which have been protected from birds by covering them with fish net supported on a framework of canes

Strawing strawberries to protect the berries from mud splashes

Planting a raspberry cane

The newly planted cane is pruned severely

Correct pruning of established canes

Tipping raspberry canes in February

Summer pruning a gooseberry. A lateral is being shortened to about five leaves

Winter pruning a gooseberry to counteract a natural tendency to 'weep'

A cherry before April pruning   The same tree after correct pruning

June pruning of a standard plum tree using long-handled pruners   The plum after pruning to keep branches properly spaced

Leader pruning of a bush apple. The cross lines show where the leaders should be cut

Lateral pruning of a bush apple to a fruit bud. The shoot had been summer pruned

Bud development on a typical two year old apple branch. Just above the knife are two summer pruned laterals. The knife points at a dart. Lower down the shoot are several fruit buds

Spraying a young half-standard plum with a garden syringe

A pneumatic sprayer in use on a bush apple tree

Winter spraying a standard plum with a barrow **spraying machine**

A special high pressure foot spraying apparatus in use

Root pruning an over vigorous fig tree. This is usually done in October

Notching above a dormant apple bud to start it into growth

Spreading a mulch of dung to encourage growth in bush apples

Ringing an apple to check growth and encourage fruitfulness

651

Well-trained and correctly pruned espalier (horizontal) trained apple trees

Single-stemmed cordon apple trees obliquely trained to bring the whole stems within arms reach

A typical garden specimen of bush apple showing the open formation

A well-trained fan peach against a greenhouse wall

A fan-trained peach in flower. This specimen has been trained to wires stretched horizontally beneath the roof glass of the greenhouse

Thinning grapes. Note the stick to steady and turn the bunch

A correctly thinned bunch of grapes. All surplus berries have been removed

Tying in summer growth on a wall-trained peach tree

Winter pruning a vine. The arrow indicates lateral which may be removed or pruned to one bud; the line, the correct pruning point for another lateral which stands alone

Tying down vine laterals in spring. This must be done a little at a time as the young shoots are very brittle

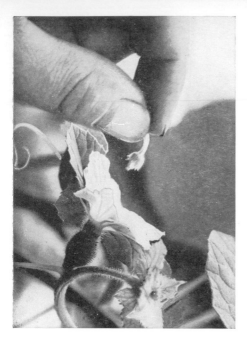

Fertilising a female melon flower with pollen from a male bloom

Melons grown outdoors with the aid of barn-type cloches

Melons ripening in the greenhouse. Note the mounds of soil on which the plants are growing, also the nets to take the weight of the fruits

ridge right down the row a couple of feet wide and six inches in height. Most of the shoots will make roots into this soil. The following autumn they can be pulled away from the parent plant with roots attached and be planted up on their own.

Tip layering as applied to blackberries and loganberries is done in July and August. Any strong, young canes can be used. These are bent down so that the tip of each touches the soil and then weighted in this position with a stone or held down with a peg. In a very short time roots will grow from the tip which will also continue to grow on, producing a further shoot. By the autumn the new plant should be sufficiently well rooted to be severed from its parent just behind the point of layering.

CHAPTER XXVII

Pruning Fruit Trees

BEFORE ENTERING upon a discussion of the principles underlying all pruning and a general outline of the methods employed I think it is as well to get quite clear upon the reasons for pruning at all. Many people imagine that it is to get fruit, whereas this is far from being the case. It is almost always the unpruned fruit tree which will bear most rapidly and heavily. So much is this the case that one of the big problems which faces the fruit grower is to devise a system of pruning which will achieve the desired ends without unduly delaying or reducing the production of fruit.

What, then, are these ends? In the main they are four in number, as follows:

1. To form each tree to a specified shape and, in particular, to get branches where they are most needed to suit the convenience of the gardener.

2. To allow sufficient light to reach leaves and fruits and prevent rubbing of one branch against another.

3. To get rid of dead, diseased and pest infested wood.

4. To prevent over-cropping and so improve the standard of quality of the crop and regulate yield from one year to another.

The regulation of yield from year to year referred to under 4 above requires some explanation. Many fruit growers complain that their trees only carry a crop every second year. So marked in certain instances in this habit of biennial bearing that it was at one time thought to be unavoidable. Further experience has shown this to be wrong. The habit is due to the exhaustion of the tree in the year during which it is carrying a crop. So much strength goes into the actual production of that one crop that the tree is unable at the same time to produce fruit buds to crop again the following year. The next year, having no fruit to ripen, it can make more buds and so the cycle continues. If the strain on the tree in the 'on' year is suitably reduced the tree will make sufficient fruit buds not to have an 'off' year.

Pruning falls into two main stages. First there is the initial pruning, during which the main framework of the tree is formed. During this period object 1 (see above) predominates. Following this comes the permanent pruning of the tree, after the main framework has been formed. It is then that objects 2, 3 and 4 come into greatest prominence. But there is no clean-cut division between the two periods. Roughly speaking for the first six or seven years of the life of an apple, pear, plum or cherry initial pruning will be carried out, after which there will be a more or less gradual transition to permanent pruning. But common sense must always be used and the actual growth of the trees considered.

TERMS. Before passing on to a consideration of the actual methods of pruning employed, it is necessary to explain certain technical terms which will constantly crop up. Chief amongst these are 'leader', 'lateral', 'fruit bud', 'growth bud' and 'spur'. 'Dark' is occasionally used for a short growth terminated by a fruit bud.

A leader is any young shoot that is required to extend a main branch or start a new branch.

A lateral is any other young shoot and not necessarily one growing out sideways from a branch. Usually, of course, laterals are of this type but occasionally a terminal shoot may have to be treated as a lateral if it is not required as a leader under the terms explained above.

A fruit bud contains a cluster of flower buds and will only produce fruit if some of these flowers are fertilised with pollen. It is necessary to be able to distinguish a fruit bud from a growth bud (see below) and this is really a matter of experience and observation. Fruit buds are in general larger, fatter and rounder than growth buds and definitely more noticeable in autumn when most pruning is done.

A growth bud is one which will in the normal course of things produce a shoot and not a flower. As a rule a growth bud will be found in the angle formed by every leaf stalk where it joins the stem.

A spur is a group of fruit buds and is a characteristic development on many mature fruit trees. Sometimes spurs become extremely complicated, branching freely and covering an area of many square inches. As a rule such complex spur systems are undesirable, much simpler systems being more satisfactory.

INITIAL PRUNING. If any young shoot is shortened in autumn or winter it will tend, the following year, to produce a number of new shoots from just below the point of cutting. The gardener makes use of this tendency to get branches where he requires them. Let us for a moment consider the early formation into a bush of a maiden apple, i.e. one which has just completed its first year of growth after budding or grafting and has only one main stem with perhaps a few small side shoots (feathers, the professional calls them) near the base. A bush is shaped like a goblet standing on a short leg or main trunk. This trunk needs to be about 2–2½ ft. in length, so, sometime between late October and early March, the maiden is beheaded 2–2½ ft. above soil level and any feathers (i.e. small shoots) below this point are removed.

The following spring the tree produces several shoots from just below the point of pruning and the gardener retains about three of these to make the first main branches. Others are rubbed out quite early. Those retained are situated as nearly as possible at equal points all round the stem.

From now on the object will be to get main branches roughly 15 in. apart sideways and 3–4 ft. apart vertically. Note particularly that a greater distance is necessary between branches that overtop one another than between branches which are beside one another.

By the end of the second year the three shoots retained after the first pruning will probably have grown 2 to 3 ft. each and be well spaced out at the tips. There is, in consequence, room for more branches, so the pruner cuts back to approximately the points at which the branches are 15 in. apart.

The following year still more shoots will come from each of the pruned stems and the gardener will retain sufficient of these, perhaps two per stem, to fill the available space, still bearing in mind that the branches are to be roughly 15 in. apart laterally. But by this time it may be possible to add some more branches vertically as well as outwards so adding an inner ring to the tree. If so do not forget that the vertical spacing must be greater because the branches will tend to sag with the weight of their crop. This process goes on until the bush covers a circle 8–10 ft. in diameter and has, perhaps, twenty-four branches.

A standard or half standard is formed in much the same way except that the main stem of the maiden is allowed to grow on unchecked until it has attained the required height for the trunk of the finished tree, 4–4½ ft. in the case of half standards, 6 ft. in the case of full standards. The top is then removed and the head branches allowed to form, as in the case of the bush tree.

The formation of a fan-trained tree follows the same general lines as that of the bush but that instead of selecting shoots situated all round the main trunk they are retained in one plane only. Otherwise the same method of encouraging branches at about 15 in. intervals is adopted.

A little more care is called for in forming the horizontally trained tree for in this the branches must be placed with considerable accuracy (see illustration on p. 652). The usual scheme is to have one pair of horizontal arms every 15 in. up the main central stem. The method is as follows: The maiden tree, in autumn or winter, is pruned back to within 18 in. of ground level. In the spring three shoots are retained as near the pruning cut as possible. The two most conveniently placed are bent down to left and right respectively and fixed to canes or wires. The third is trained vertically, usually to a stout cane. The next autumn the vertical growth is cut back to within 18 in. of the horizontally trained shoots. In the spring three shoots are again retained, two to form a second pair of arms and the third to continue the central stem. The process can go on indefinitely until the desired number of arms have been formed.

There is some difference of opinion as to whether the horizontal arms themselves should or should not be pruned. They are not required to branch and therefore it would seem most logical to leave them unpruned but usually they fail to make sufficient new growth when treated in this way. This fault can only be overcome by light cutting back each autumn.

There remains the cordon tree to consider. This, the reader will remember, has a single (or sometimes double or triple) main stem to which all other growth is kept fairly closely pruned. As branching is not required it follows logically that no pruning of the leader should be carried out. It is allowed to extend vertically until it reaches the desired height for the completed cordon, when further development is prevented by cutting out all further leader growth when pruning in autumn or winter. If a multiple stemmed cordon is to be formed the maiden is cut back to within about a foot of the ground and two or three stems are trained vertically. Subsequently each stem is treated like a single stemmed cordon.

In all this talk about the formation of young trees I have said nothing about the treatment of side shoots. What is to become of these while the main framework is being formed? The answer will depend a lot on the variety and form of tree, the kind of stock upon which it is worked and on the character of the soil in which it is grown. If laterals are left unpruned many of them will start to carry fruit along most of their length in their second year. That may seem very nice and a good many amateurs are only too pleased to allow their trees to bear as quickly and heavily as possible. But bearing places a great strain on the tree and may result in a cessation of growth. That must not be allowed while the framework of the tree is being formed. In consequence it is almost certain that some of the laterals will have to be removed or shortened to lessen the number of fruit buds. In the case of the trained trees, especially the horizontally trained and cordon trained types, it will be essential to shorten the laterals to maintain the characteristic shape of the specimen.

This shortening is best done in two operations, one carried out in summer and the other in winter. Summer pruning is done as soon as the laterals become woody near the base. Young growth has a soft, downy appearance which passes slowly with age. With apples and pears the right condition of growth is generally reached late in July or early in August according to variety in the South and Midlands. Plums and cherries may be a week or so earlier, while gooseberries and currants will probably be ready for summer pruning by early July.

The method is to cut every half woody shoot to within about five well-developed leaves of its base. Generally there are a few poorly developed leaves near the bottom of the shoot. Take no account of these when reckoning the approximate point of pruning. In the autumn these summer pruned shoots are either left as they are or, if the tree is a cordon or horizontally trained one, are further cut back to a length of two or three buds.

The following year these side shoots are likely to produce some new growth which can be summer pruned to one leaf. On the older part, below the point of the first summer pruning, they will generally form some fruit buds and when these are observed the shoot can be pruned back to one of them; precisely which one will depend upon whether it is wished to keep a strictly formal specimen with very short fruiting spurs or to build up a looser but more prolific tree.

PERMANENT PRUNING. As the tree takes its permanent shape the gardener becomes progressively less concerned with the production of new branches and more with the regulation of fruitfulness. Another point which he must watch is the spacing of the branches, for trees, as they age, tend to spread out and droop. In consequence branches which were originally well spaced may become too close with age and some must be removed.

The precise amount of pruning which has to be carried out on the adult tree will vary according to its character. Often bushes, half standards and standards can go practically unpruned for a number of years with no more than an occasional thinning out of stems or branches which rub together and, of course, removal of dead or diseased wood. But as a rule there will be something to do each autumn. Some branches may be damaged by overcropping or be showing signs of waning vitality. Either such branches should themselves be cut back quite severely, even if this means going into wood that is several years old, or a neighbouring branch should be cut back. The object is to get strong new shoots from which one or more may be selected to replace the old one and the principle upon which the gardener works is the old one that 'growth follows the knife'.

Elsewhere it may be seen that a tree is making long, thin growths which could not carry the weight of fruit even if they produced it. Such should be shortened sufficiently to give them necessary stiffness and in this case each cut should be made, if possible, just above a good, plump fruit bud.

Some varieties of fruit, such as apples Worcester Pearmain and Irish Peach and pear Jargonelle, make a great many fruit buds right at the tips of side growths. These should have very little pruning unless they are grown as trained trees, in which case their natural habit will have to be modified by summer pruning. Similar remarks apply to naturally vigorous varieties such as apples Bramley's Seedling, Newton Wonder and Blenheim Orange which tend to make wood at the expense of fruit if heavily pruned, especially in autumn or winter. But it is really wise to avoid such varieties when choosing trees for training and to select instead varieties of moderate vigour which tend to form fruit spurs easily. Apples Cox's Orange Pippin, Charles Ross, Rival, Beauty of Bath and Laxton's Superb and most choice dessert pears are examples of this type.

Formal specimens such as pyramids and fan, horizontal or cordon trained trees must always have a considerable amount of pruning, especially of side growths, or they quickly get out of shape. Summer pruning on the lines already indicated will be needed throughout their life whereas it can be largely omitted in the case of bushes and standards after the initial years. It will be followed by winter pruning to keep spurs and fruiting side shoots as compact as possible. Prune to fruit buds wherever these exist but, failing them, to the first, second or third growth bud reckoned from the base of each shoot.

RENOVATION OF OLD TREES. Still later in the life of the tree it may happen that laterals which, in the early days carried no more than two or three fruit buds each, become densely crowded with spurs and fruit buds. Blossom production in spring may be immense but the high hopes of the gardener when he sees this grand display may not come to fruition.

The trouble is that the tree is now producing too many fruit buds and not enough new growth. It is in need of renovation. There are several ways in which this may be done. First of all the spurs themselves can be thinned out or reduced. Some can be removed entirely and others left with only two or three fruit buds. Secondly many main branches (not just one here and there as already described) may be headed back quite severely (dehorning is the technical term for this) with the object of making them produce new wood and so giving the gardener fresh material upon which to work. Feeding also has a bearing on this problem for by increasing the rate of application, particularly of nitrogenous foods, further growth can be encouraged.

ROOT PRUNING. It is not always the branches alone which need pruning. Sometimes the roots also grow too vigorously with the result that the tree makes too much growth and does not fruit as it should. This is particularly liable to happen with young trees that are grafted on vigorous stocks or are planted on very rich land.

One remedy is to cut back some of the roots. This is best done in October or early November. The method is to dig a trench around the tree three or four feet away from it and work towards it with a fork, uncovering the roots and severing any thick ones, particularly those which tend to dive down steeply into the subsoil. Finer roots are preserved and, when the pruning is judged to have gone sufficiently far, are spread out again, covered with soil and made thoroughly firm.

Some gardeners believe that only one half of a fruit tree should be root pruned at a time, the other half being left until the following year. Personally I think that this encourages unbalanced growth and prefer to go right round the tree at one operation. If there is fear that this may prove too drastic, stop while still several feet from the base of the tree.

Young fruit trees are often most efficaciously root pruned by lifting and re-planting them. This should be done in autumn directly they have lost most of their leaves.

It should be noted that excessive vigour may be caused by incorrect feeding, particularly by giving too much dung or nitrogenous fertiliser. Obviously the best way to counter this is to stop the practice that has caused it. Potash fertilisers only, for a few years, and no pruning at all may bring an over vigorous tree into bearing.

SPECIALISED METHODS OF PRUNING. In addition to the methods I have described there are several specialised methods of pruning which have their keen advocates. Notable among these are the Lorette system devised by M. Lorette in France, and the renewal system largely developed in Kent for commercial apple orchards.

The Lorette system is an extremely severe method of pruning most suitable for small, trained trees. Under it the fruiting spurs are produced very close to the main branches and a particularly neat specimen results. It is said to be applicable to all apple and pear varieties but in England very mixed results have been obtained with it, possibly due to the fact that our climate is, in general, cooler and moister than that of France.

Briefly the Lorette system depends upon forcing into growth and turning into fruit buds certain very tiny buds, known as stipulary buds, which normally remain dormant. These buds are situated at the extreme base of each shoot. In order to force these buds to grow the shoots must be cut back very severely—to within $\frac{1}{4}$ inch of the base. The precise condition of growth where this is done is important as it must be fairly ripe but not really hard and woody. Three summer prunings are usually advised. In mid-June all side shoots that have attained pencil thickness are cut back to $\frac{1}{4}$ inch. In mid-July the process is repeated on shoots that have attained the required thickness since June. In mid-August any further shoots that have reached pencil thickness are also cut back in a similar manner. Shoots which are not thick enough to be pruned in mid-August are tied downwards to check the flow of sap. Leaders of main branches are shortened by about one third in mid-April. There is no winter pruning at all.

But there are so many qualifications to this general outline of treatment that anyone who really intends to apply the method seriously should study a book on the subject.

Renewal pruning is almost dramatically opposed to Lorette pruning in that it is directed towards encouraging the formation of fruit buds throughout the length of young branches. All close summer pruning is eliminated and the work is entirely done in winter.

About two out of every three year-old shoots are then cut back to a length of about 1 inch and the next one left unpruned. These unpruned shoots should form fruit buds freely the following summer and carry a crop the summer after that. They can be shortened a little and left to bear for a second year after which they are cut right out. Meanwhile the shoots which were severely shortened will have made more strong growths some of which will have been retained to provide new fruiting wood.

Great judgement is required when using this method an d feeding must be carefully supervised to ensure that the trees make the required amount of strong new growth each year. Moreover, as trees treated in this manner tend to acquire an increasingly weeping habit each year, strong young stems growing upwards from the topmost part of each bent branch must be retained to act as replacement leaders. Each year a few of the very weeping branches are cut back to these replacement leaders.

Once again this is a system for experienced fruit growers rather than for novices and I would advise any amateurs who are interested to study a book on the subject or see a practical demonstration of the method before trying to put it into effect.

RINGING. This is a device for checking excessive vigour and encouraging fruitfulness without going to the labour of root pruning. It works well with apples and pears but is less satisfactory with stone fruits. The work is done early in May. A ring of bark, $\frac{1}{4}$ in. wide, is removed around the main trunk 2 to 3 ft. above soil level. In the case of bushes with short trunks it is usually better to cut one ring near the base of each main bough.

The object is to check the free flow of sap for a limited period, i.e. until the ring has healed over again. If the ring is too wide the healing process may take too long and the tree die of starvation. Some growers prefer to make two half rings one a few inches above the other, while another scheme is to cut a ring which nearly but not quite encircles the trunk. I have not found these precautions necessary providing the width of $\frac{1}{4}$ in. is not exceeded.

It is not essential to protect the ring in any way but there is no harm in coating it with warm grafting wax or binding a piece of adhesive tape around it.

KNIFE-EDGE RINGING. This is a special form of ringing used mainly on individual branches with the object of encouraging growth where it has not previously occurred. For example a young branch fails to develop any fruit buds or laterals over a portion of its length. In early May the edge of a sharp knife is drawn around the branch at the top of the bare portion in such a way as to cut through the bark and soft tissues without actually removing anything. The sap flow is checked but for a much shorter period than would result from ordinary ringing. It is long enough, however, to start into growth buds below the ring which had previously remained dormant.

NOTCHING. This is a variation on the foregoing practice applied to individual buds. If a triangular notch of bark is removed in early May just above a dormant bud it will be encouraged to start into growth, whereas a similar notch made just below the bud will check its growth. Such methods are often of service when forming trained trees to get shoots and fruit buds just where they are needed.

FRUITS WHICH BEAR ON YOUNG WOOD. So far I have written as though all fruit trees and bushes with which we are concerned produce their fruit on spurs and upon the older wood. There are a few kinds which bear either exclusively or mainly upon the young wood, usually that produced the previous year. The raspberry is the most obvious example.

It throws up fresh canes from the roots every summer and these carry fruit the following summer and then die out. Blackberries and loganberries have exactly the same characteristic and black currants carry it to a lesser degree. Peaches, nectarines and Morello cherries are other common fruits in which year-old wood is more important for fruit production than older wood.

With all these the gardener's endeavour must be to maintain a sufficient production of young growth each year to carry the next year's crop. This is partly done by adequate manuring and soil cultivation and partly by thinning out young growth as it appears, leaving only sufficient for next year's requirements and so concentrating all the available strength of the plant upon it. Quite a complicated process of disbudding is used in the case of peaches, nectarines and Morello cherries and I have described this in some detail under the heading 'Pruning' on p. 713.

In all this class of pruning the object is to get rid of as much as possible of the old fruiting wood soon after the crop has been gathered and to retain the best young growth to crop the following year.

CHAPTER XXVIII

A Spraying Programme

PESTS AND diseases are discussed in detail in a separate chapter (see p. 747) but the spraying of fruit trees is such a special matter and so much of it is carried out purely for prevention, even though no pest or disease is actually seen, that separate description is necessary here.

WINTER WASHING. If we follow the calendar year work commences in January with the application of tar oil wash. This can be given to all fruit trees and bushes. Its purpose is to clean the trees as thoroughly as possible both from obvious growths such as those of moss, lichen and green 'scum' and also from the less obvious but more dangerous eggs of pests, chiefly those of green flies and allied species of aphis. Tar oil is damaging to trees once the buds have commenced to swell, but the later it can be applied up to this stage the better because insect eggs are more vulnerable as the spring draws near. Generally it is unwise to continue tar oil spraying after the end of January on apples and pears or after the middle of the month on cherries and plums.

Two pests which have been very much on the increase in some orchards are capsid bug and red spider. Neither of these is seriously damaged by tar oil wash, in fact there is good evidence that tar oil actually encourages red spider by killing some of its natural enemies. These pests can be controlled by spraying with petroleum oil winter wash, often known as white oil emulsion, a month to six weeks after the tar oil application. Lime sulphur, used to control scab disease, will also kill red spider, and if attacks occur despite these precautions derris may be used as a spray early in June. Derris used as a spring or summer spray is also useful but probably the best control can be obtained with chlorbenside applied in spring or, if necessary, in summer.

A considerable amount of thought has been given to the problem of devising one spray which will combine the functions of tar oil and petroleum oil. The most effective is that known as DNC Petroleum Oil. It is used at the same time as the ordinary petroleum oil, that is to say in a normal season up to about mid-March on apples and pears, and it does give a reasonably good control of aphides, capsids and red spider. Nevertheless it appears probable that where infestations are very severe it is still better to give two separate applications, tar oil in January, petroleum oil in early March.

ANTI-SCAB TREATMENT. The next step, as far as apples and pears are concerned, is to keep scab under control. This is a disease which spots and cracks the skins of these fruits. Though it does not penetrate to the flesh it often checks development and is, in any case, very unsightly.

Scab is controlled with either a sulphur or copper wash. Lime sulphur is generally employed for apples and pears though colloidal sulphur is now running it close.

The first application is given when the blossom buds are sufficiently open to show the tiny clusters of green flower buds within. This is known as green bud stage. Lime sulphur is then used at full winter strength, colloidal sulphur at normal strength. A second application at the same strength is given ten days to a fortnight later when the buds are showing colour, pink in the case of apples, white with pears. A third dose is applied immediately the blossom falls or, more precisely, when about three quarters of the blossom is actually on the ground. At this stage lime sulphur must be reduced to summer strength but colloidal sulphur can still be applied at normal strength. In bad cases where scab has been persistent further applications are given in mid-June and mid-July, still at summer strength for lime sulphur, normal strength for colloidal sulphur.

CATERPILLARS AND GRUBS. Meanwhile other foes may have been launching an attack. First of all there will be winter moth caterpillars which are small, green or brownish and move by looping themselves. Sometimes they appear almost as soon as the blossom buds open and strip the trees of their first leaves. They can be killed by prompt spraying with arsenate of lead. This is highly poisonous and those gardeners who do not like to handle powerful poisons can use either derris or pyrethrum instead.

After the winter moths come the sawflies and codlin moths. Apple sawfly is often terribly destructive. It lays its eggs in the fully open blossom and the tiny maggots eat into the fruits, producing the familiar maggoty apple. The codlin moth caterpillar behaves in just the same way but appears later. There are not often any sawfly maggots left after mid-July whereas apples may still contain codlin moth caterpillars in August.

To counter apple sawfly the apple grower mixes nicotine or BHC with the lime sulphur applied after blossom fall. Codlin moth is controlled by spraying with arsenate of lead or DDT when the eggs begin to hatch out, usually the second week in June. Unfortunately DDT applied at this late date may greatly encourage red spider.

In early June the fruit grower will have to turn his attention to the raspberries. They, too, may become maggoty with the grubs of the raspberry beetle unless he dusts the open flowers with derris and repeats the treatment, this time on the fruits, towards the end of June.

GREASE BANDS. There is only one other routine measure which should be taken whether foes are seen or not. This is the application of grease bands to all fruit trees about mid-September. The grease band is simply a piece of grease proof paper about 6 in. wide wrapped tightly round the main trunk of the tree about 3 ft. above ground level or, in the case of bushes, one band around each main bough at the same height from the ground. The band is then thoroughly smeared with special sticky 'grease'. The purpose of the paper is simply to prevent the grease from injuring the bark. There are some proprietary brands which can be applied direct to the bark of mature trees.

The purpose of the grease is to trap any insects which may try to crawl up the trunk from the soil to the branches. Principal among these are the female winter moths, which are wingless. As they pupate in the soil and lay their eggs on the branches the grease band is quite an effective method of catching them. Incidentally codlin moth caterpillars often crawl from fallen apples back to the branches of an apple tree to pupate, so if this pest has been troublesome it is worth while getting grease bands in position two months earlier than usual, that is to say in mid-July instead of mid-September. In any case the grease bands should be kept in position, the grease being renewed from time to time, throughout the winter.

This brief account of routine pest control in a fruit garden does not rule out the possibility of a great deal of extra spraying having to be done. This will depend upon just what foes materialise and full particulars regarding these will be found in the chapter already referred to.

CHAPTER XXIX

Cropping Problems

ONE OF the perennial complaints of the amateur fruit grower is that some of his trees do not bear. I have already referred to some of the possible causes of this earlier in this section, but as there is so much confusion of thought on the subject of bad fertility it seems wise to assemble all the relative facts in one section.

Many trees about which the gardener feels uneasy are simply not sufficiently mature to produce fruits. The actual age at which any tree should commence to fruit will depend upon several things, such as the variety of tree, the type of stock on which it is grafted and, to a lesser degree, the form in which it is trained. Some stocks, such as Paradise Apple No. IX or Quince C. induce comparatively early fruitfulness; others, such as crab stock and free pear stock delay fruitfulness. A naturally slow fruiting variety, such as the apples Bramley's Seedling or Blenheim Orange, worked on crab stock cannot reasonably be expected to produce much fruit until it is fifteen years old. A naturally precocious variety such as Stirling Castle, worked on No. IX stock may quite likely produce a fairly heavy crop at three years. That gives an idea of the kind of difference which may occur from this cause.

Over severe pruning may prevent fruiting by destroying most or all the flower buds.

A tree that is growing very vigorously, making, perhaps, shoots a yard long each year, is unlikely to fruit well. Here again before taking drastic action one must decide whether this vigour is the normal exuberance of youth or due to faulty feeding. A young tree on a sturdy stock should make a good deal of growth and it would be a mistake to check it too soon. However, if the growth really is abnormal and possibly due to too rich soil, it can be checked by correcting the manurial programme, by root pruning in October by bark ringing in May (see p. 666) or by allowing grass to grow under the trees.

Then there is the question of pollination to be considered. In order that fruit may be formed the blossom must be fertilised with ripe pollen, and in most cases it is far better, if not actually essential, that this pollen should come from another tree of the same kind but different variety (see p. 631). In some cases there is even incompatibility between certain varieties. This is most marked in cherries and is fully described under that heading.

Even when there is plenty of pollen of the right kind it may be that the weather prevents bees from carrying it from flower to flower and tree to tree. Bees are practically the only natural agents of pollen distribution in fruit trees. They will not fly far if the weather is bad and in any case in some districts there are insufficient bees to give satisfactory pollination even when the weather is good. The remedy is to pollinate by hand; not such a lengthy business as it sounds if the orchard is not too big. The pollen is collected on a camel-hair brush or rabbit's tail tied to a stick and dusted lightly over the blossoms to be pollinated.

Again there is the possibility that the essential organs of the blossom may be killed by frosts. It is not necessary that the blossom should be killed outright. The most sensitive part of the flower is the stigma or central organ and frost may destroy this even before the blossom opens. Such flowers can be detected by very careful examination as they have a tiny black eye.

Novices are often misled by the fact that fruits form and even, perhaps, get as big as marbles only to fall off. They think that this could not occur unless the blossom had been pollinated. On the contrary, these fruits are often the result of imperfect pollination, as can be proved by cutting them open. Instead of having plump seeds within they either have empty husks or no seeds at all.

Another cause of failure to fruit may be an early attack by sawfly grubs or other pests which eat into the fruits and cause them to fall prematurely. This can be ascertained by cutting open some of the defective fruits.

Lastly there is the often overlooked point that big supplies of readily available food, particularly nitrogen, are required during the first few weeks after pollination. If the soil is rather poor or dry this food may not be available. It not infrequently happens that a previously barren tree can be brought into bearing by giving in April a top dressing of a quick-acting nitrogenous fertiliser such as Nitro-chalk or sulphate of ammonia.

MANURING

A great deal depends upon the correct feeding of fruit trees. Failure to grasp the importance of this accounts for many disappointments. Vigour control is partly a matter of right feeding though it is also influenced by stock (see p. 629) and pruning (see pp. 658-67).

Nitrogen and potash are the two foods which have the most marked effect, the former mainly on growth and the latter on fruitfulness though to some extent the two are linked. Phosphates play a comparatively small part except in the case of strawberries. Lime does not have anything like so marked an effect as was at one time thought and lack of lime is seldom if ever the main cause of poor stone formation in plums, cherries, etc. In some districts magnesium deficiency is the cause of poor growth and early defoliation.

Here are a few danger signs. Very vigorous growth with dark green leaves and poorly coloured fruits indicates an excess of nitrogen. Poor growth, with small, pale leaves is an indication of too little nitrogen. Potash shortage will cause severe scorching of the leaf edges, a condition which is often erroneously ascribed to disease. Excess of potash is not likely to occur and in any case will probably only cause excessive colouring of fruit with some diminution of growth.

An excessive amount of lime will cause yellowing of the foliage and poor growth. Lack of magnesium will result in an early leaf fall affecting most markedly the young shoots which may only retain a few leaves at base and tip, the middle portions being bare. This deficiency may also be diagnosed by the regular, brown smudging of the leaves between the veins.

Routine feeding must be adjusted to meet the growth of the trees and the known or observed deficiencies of the soil, but an average programme from which deviations can be made as seems necessary is as follows:

In winter or early spring a top dressing of well-rotted farmyard or stable manure at the rate of 2 cwt. per rod for apples, pears and gooseberries, $2\frac{1}{2}$ cwt. for plums, cherries and currants. At the same time, or in autumn, sulphate of potash 2 lb. per rod. Every second autumn basic slag or bone meal 7 lb. per rod. For strawberries superphosphate of lime each spring 4 lb. per rod.

If no dung is available Nitro-chalk or sulphate of ammonia could be substituted at 4 lb. per rod for any of these fruits.

If leaf edge scorching appears, two applications of potash fertiliser could be given per year till the trouble clears up. Should the scorching be of the smudgy, intervenal type associated with magnesium deficiency, sulphate of magnesium could be added to the spring dressings at the rate of 2 lb. per rod, or alternatively magnesium limestone could be used at 14 lb. per rod. This latter is lasting and safe but rather slow in action.

In the case of trees which show a marked tendency to bear one year and miss the next it will often pay to give an extra dressing of

Nitro-chalk or sulphate of ammonia at 2 lb. per rod in April. This is particularly likely to prove beneficial if the trees have not been making much new growth for this is an almost certain indication that the biennial bearing is due to weakness and, in particular, to lack of readily available nitrogen at the critical time when the fruit should be commencing to swell.

CHAPTER XXX
Fruits and their Cultivation

IN THIS chapter I have done exactly as I did for vegetables in Chapter XXIV, namely arranged the principal fruits alphabetically with concise cultural instructions for each and brief lists of varieties. New varieties of fruit do appear from time to time but they are by no means as numerous as in the case of vegetables, nor do they 'catch on' so readily. In consequence the list I have given can be taken as including in general the best for planting.

APPLES

The apple is the most popular hard fruit grown in this country and undoubtedly the most widely planted. It suits the climate well and succeeds in most parts of the British Isles subject to the reservations regarding altitude and frost susceptibility made on p. 627. Nevertheless even in places too subject to spring frosts to be suitable for the majority of hardy fruits it is sometimes possible to grow apples successfully by choosing late flowering kinds. The season of apple blossom is in any case later than that of any other tree fruit, extending over the whole of May in a normal season and there are a few varieties such as Crawley Beauty, Edward VII, Royal Jubilee and Court Pendu Plat which often carry on into early June, by which date there is seldom much danger of damaging frost.

SOILS. Apples succeed best on medium loamy soils that are reasonably well drained. They can also be grown on quite light soils but in such places stronger growing stocks should be used and a rather higher rate of manuring practised. Trouble is most likely to occur on very heavy soils, particularly if badly drained. Under such conditions apples are apt to suffer from canker and to die back badly after the first few years.

The two most vital foods are nitrogen and potash. So far in extensive experiments phosphatic fertilisers have not shown much effect but in view of the importance of maintaining the general fertility of soil it is advisable to give some phosphatic fertiliser even in apple orchards.

When ground is being prepared for planting it should be dug as deeply as appears reasonable taking into account the character of the subsoil. A moderate quantity (about 2 cwt. per rod) of well-rotted dung should be worked in at the same time. It is also advisable to give some extra potash which can be in the form of wood ashes, 6 oz. per sq. yd., or any of the potassic fertilisers recommended in Chapter V. Lime is not essential in any great quantity and provided the pH of the soil (see p. 27) is not below 6 there should be no necessity to add lime.

TYPES OF TREE. Apples can be trained in a number of different ways. Where there is ample space and the labour of picking is not a great consideration, full standards may be planted. These are particularly suitable for orchards which are to be grassed down eventually. Half standards are being increasingly planted, while bushes are the most popular type of all. Bushes on a Paradise stock of medium vigour, such as Malling No. II are suitable for even quite small gardens and may be planted 15 ft. apart. On Malling No. IX this distance can be decreased to 10 ft.

Apples are not as suitable as other fruits for growing against walls, though they will succeed in such a position, particularly if the wall faces west. For this mode of training and also when grown against wire fences in the open the horizontal tree rather than the fan trained is almost invariably used.

For trees on dwarfing root stocks the dwarf pyramid method of training is rapidly gaining favour. The cultivation of cordon trained apple trees has recently become very popular, particularly with the owners of small gardens. The single stem cordon on Malling No. II or No. IX stock can be planted as close as 2 ft. in the rows and so offers great scope for variety in a small garden.

STOCKS AND PROPAGATION. I have already had a good deal to say about apple stocks on p. 629. It only remains for me to re-emphasise here the importance of getting trees worked on the right kind of stock for the purpose for which they are intended. As a rule it is advisable to rely on the nurseryman's advice on this point. The natural vigour and habit of the trees must be taken into account and also the richness of the soil on which they are to be planted. For example Malling No. IX stock would be very suitable for a small bush of Bramley's Seedling on good soil but would unduly dwarf a weak growing apple such as Stirling Castle especially if on poor soil. Crab stock is still the only fully satisfactory variety for big standards that are to be grassed under.

Propagation is either by grafting in March–April or by budding in July–August.

FERTILITY. There are practically no apples that are fully self-fertile, certainly none in general cultivation. A few are fully self-sterile, that is to say they will set no fruit unless their blossom is fertilised with pollen from another variety of apple. But the great majority of varieties are partially self-fertile, that is to say they will set a moderate crop with their own pollen but a much better crop with pollen from another variety. There is no inter-incompatibility amongst apples. This rather formidable term simply means that any variety of apple will serve to pollinate any other, providing of course, its pollen is ripe at the correct time.

The blossom season extends over about a month but for any one tree it only lasts about ten days to a fortnight and it is probable that out of that the effective period for pollination is only five or six days. Varieties which are to act as 'mates' must overlap in their full blossom period during those five or six days.

There are, in addition, a few kinds of apple which produce little or no fertile pollen. Bramley's Seedling is a notable example. These do not make good pollinators for any variety and are specially indicated in the list on pp. 681-5.

SEASON. Early apples, such as Gladstone, Beauty of Bath and James Grieve, are ready to eat when picked, or perhaps it would be better to say should not be picked until they are ready to eat. This is not true of the later kinds which must be picked before they are blown off the tree but may not be ready for use until many months later. In other words the ripening process for these kinds goes on after the apples have parted from the tree. An extreme example of this kind is Sturmer Pippin, which is usually ready for gathering by the second or third week in October but is hard, woody and tasteless at that time though it develops into a magnificent dessert apple by the following May. In the table of varieties at the end of this section and also in most nurserymen's catalogues, the season of use of each variety is indicated after the name. It should be understood clearly that this is not necessarily the time at which the fruit should be picked. In the case of varieties in season during August and September the dates of picking and using are likely to coincide. October apples are usually picked two or three weeks in advance of their season of use, while all later apples are gathered by the middle of October.

AGE OF TREE. For planting young trees are preferable to old ones. Because of this the expert may be well advised to start with maiden trees, i.e. apples at the end of their first season of growth after budding or grafting. Less experienced gardeners will probably prefer a tree which has been formed for a year or so by an expert but four years should be regarded as the maximum age for any tree other than a standard or half standard. These, because of their greater size, have not begun to take proper shape until about the fifth or sixth year. Because of this greater age there is increased risk in transplanting them and they are more likely to suffer a check.

PLANTING. Apples can be planted at any time between mid-October and mid-March in a normal season, or, to put it another way, between the times when the leaves begin to fall off fairly freely to the date at which the buds show signs of bursting in the spring. The middle part of this period is seldom favourable owing to poor weather and bad soil condition. Late planting can be very successful if the following spring is damp but may be disastrous if the spring is dry. On the whole the best time for planting is from about the last week in October to the end of November.

There is nothing special to be said about the actual methods of planting beyond emphasizing that the union between stock and scion (see p. 637), which can usually be identified quite distinctly in a young tree as a marked swelling well above the uppermost roots, must not be buried beneath the soil. If it is buried the apple is likely in time to make roots of its own above those of the stock and these may entirely upset the influence of the stock.

TREATMENT OF YOUNG TREES. The first year after planting trees should never be allowed to bear fruit. If they do produce blossom, which is unlikely, it should be picked at once. The trees must be pruned fairly severely either immediately after planting or, if planted in the autumn, the February following. In general, leaders (see p. 659) should be cut back by half their length or more and side growths either eliminated or shortened to no more than 1 inch. The object is to reduce the strain on the roots for the first few months of growth and so give the tree a chance to make satisfactory shoots during the first summer. Very often newly planted trees, especially if they have been badly handled and the roots have been allowed to dry out unduly, make very little progress the first year and then it becomes essential to cut right back into two year old or even three year old wood, which wastes time and useful material.

Every other encouragement should also be given to the trees to make good growth. If the weather in spring is dry, heavy watering will help and may be followed by a mulch of straw or grass clippings to keep the moisture in. If the soil was properly prepared no manure should be necessary this first year or at any rate not before the autumn when a top dressing of sulphate or muriate of potash, 2 oz. per sq. yd., may be given. In the case of trained trees, particularly cordons and horizontally trained trees, summer pruning should be carried out in late July or early August and the general rules given on p. 662 must be followed.

PRUNING. Once a tree is established, pruning should proceed on absolutely normal lines (see pp. 662–3). For the first five or six years the framework of the tree is built up and then there is a gradual transition to adult pruning with the object of maintaining regular production of fruit.

There are, in apples, certain marked differences of growth between one variety and another which must be taken into account when pruning, especially in the later stages when the trees are coming into full bearing. Broadly speaking varieties can be classified under two headings from this point of view. These are (1) varieties which form fruit buds and spurs readily and do not make a great deal of wood; (2) varieties which do not form fruit buds freely and tend to produce a lot of wood. In addition one might add a third group of tip bearing varieties but I think too much has been made of this characteristic with the result that novices have become confused. From the point of view of pruning tip bearers may be amalgamated with Group 2 above, the principal difference being that they do not usually make a lot of wood and so are likely to need harder leader pruning and more frequent dehorning (see pp. 664). The point about the tip bearer is that it tends to produce quite a lot of fruit at the ends of both side growths and, sometimes, leaders as well. In consequence too much lateral pruning may diminish the crop very seriously.

Examples of the two groups are:—Group 1. Arthur Turner, Beauty of Bath, Charles Ross, Cox's Orange Pippin, Crawley Beauty, Early Victoria, Edward VII, Ellison's Orange, Exquisite, Golden Noble, Grenadier, Herring's Pippin, James Grieve, King of the Pippins, Lane's Prince Albert, Laxton's Superb, Rival and Stirling Castle; Group 2. Allington Pippin, Bismark, Blenheim Orange, Bramley's Seedling, Encore, Newton Wonder and Warner's King. To these may be added the tip bearers: Irish Peach, Lord Lambourne, Worcester Pearmain.

When pruning for fruit the side growths of all varieties in Group 1 can, if necessary, be pruned a good deal more severely than those of varieties in Group 2. I say if necessary advisedly because it is not essential to prune any apple severely unless it has to be stimulated into fresh growth for some reason or other or there is a necessity to shorten weak stems or eliminate diseased wood. Obviously it is varieties of Group 1 which will make the best trained trees, especially horizontal trained specimens, as they will submit more readily to the hard pruning necessary to maintain the characteristic shape of such specimens.

In the case of the more vigorous apples coming under Group 2 it is essential to be as sparing as possible with the secateurs. If side growths are cut back too often and too hard the result will be a thicket of new growth and very little fruit. When such varieties are trained, as much as possible of the pruning should be done in summer as this will tend to check, rather than increase, their natural vigour.

FEEDING. Routine feeding for apples resolves itself, as a rule, into the application of dung, or a nitrogenous fertiliser such as sulphate of ammonia or Nitro-chalk in the spring, and potash in the form of wood ashes or any potassic fertiliser in the autumn. The average dressing for adult trees of normal vigour would be dung at the rate of 1 cwt. to 15 sq. yd., or Nitro-chalk at 2 oz. per sq. yd., followed by wood ashes at 6 oz. or sulphate of potash at 1 oz. per sq. yd. Every third year there should be, in addition, an autumn dressing of basic slag, 6–8 oz. per sq. yd.

THINNING. If the spring is favourable for fertilisation and the trees are in good condition they will very likely set more fruit than they can bring to perfection. Some natural thinning will occur and there is often quite a heavy drop of fruit towards the end of June for which the gardener must make due allowance. Nevertheless it is often necessary to reduce the fruits still further by hand. This should be done a little at a time during June and July. Dessert varieties can be allowed to carry more fruit than cookers because the individual fruits are not required to be so large. As a rough guide dessert apples should not exceed two per cluster and should be at least 3 inches apart along the branch, whereas cookers should hang singly and be spaced 6 to 8 inches apart though often the final thinning can be left until the fruits removed are large enough to be serviceable.

When thinning give preference to the most perfect fruitlets and, other things being equal, remove the central fruit in each cluster as this is often mis-shapen.

PICKING. Apples are ready to pick directly they part readily from the tree. The test is to lift the fruit gently without twisting or tearing it. If it comes away easily, well and good; if not, let it hang a little longer.

It does not follow that all the fruits on any one tree will be ready for gathering at the same time. It often pays to go over a tree several times at intervals of a few days. The picking season extends from the end of July for early varieties such as Mr. Gladstone, to the third or fourth week in October for late kinds, such as Sturmer Pippin. Care should be taken not to bruise or damage the fruit in any way, especially if it is to be kept.

GOOD VARIETIES OF APPLE

Abbreviations: C, cooking; D, dessert; CD, cooking or dessert; SS, self-sterile; P.S.F., partially self-fertile. (Note that Self-sterile varieties should not be planted alone nor should they be used as pollinators for other varieties. Even partially self-fertile varieties will give better crops if associated with other varieties of apple flowering at approximately the same time.)

Name	Use	Season	Pick	Type	Colour	Flavour	Pruning	Flowering	Fertility	Cropping
ALLINGTON PIPPIN	D	Oct.-Dec.	early Sept.	medium, round, conical	lemon, faintly flushed red	good	moderate, to upward pointing buds	mid-season	PSF	very good
ANNIE ELIZABETH	D	Dec.-June	mid Oct.	large, oblong, conical, un-even	yellow, flushed and striped deep red	good, acid	light to out-ward pointing buds	late	PSF	good when established
ARTHUR TURNER	C	July-Oct.	Sept.	very large, even	yellow, flushed brownish red	good, acid	light	mid-season	PSF	very good
BARNACK BEAUTY	CD	Dec.-Mar.	mid Oct.	medium, oval, regular	golden, flushed & striped red	good, crisp	light	mid-season	PSF	fair
BEAUTY OF BATH	D	August	when ripe	medium, flattened	yellow, very flushed and striped with red	good	light	early	PSF	irregular
BEAUTY OF KENT	C	Nov.-Mar.	mid Oct.	large, conical, ovate	deep yellow striped deep red	good, juicy	light	mid-season	PSF	very good
BELLE DE BOSKOOP	D	Dec.-April	mid Oct.	medium, flattened	dull yellow-red russeted	good, sweet	moderate	early	SS	good
BISMARCK	C	Nov.-Jan.	mid Oct.	large, tapering, angular	yellow, flushed deep crimson	good	light	early	PSF	good
BLENHEIM ORANGE	DC	Nov.-Jan.	mid Oct.	fairly large, flattened, round	yellow, flushed & russeted	sub-acid excellent, crisp & good cooker	light to up-ward point-ing buds	mid-season	SS	good when established
BRAMLEY's SEEDLING	C	Nov.-April	mid Oct.	large, round, flat	yellow, flushed red	excellent, acid	very light	mid-season	SS	very good
BROWNLEE's RUSSET	D	Jan.-April	mid Oct.	medium, flat, irregular	brownish green russet	good	moderate to outward pointing buds	early	PSF	irregular
CHARLES ROSS	DC	Oct.-Nov.	mid Oct.	large, round, even	yellowish green, flushed & striped red	moderate	moderate	mid-season	PSF	good

681

GOOD VARIETIES OF APPLE—(Continued)

Name	Use	Season	Pick	Type	Colour	Flavour	Pruning	Flowering	Fertility	Cropping
CLAYGATE PEARMAIN	D	Dec.-Feb.	mid Oct.	medium, round, flattened	dull, green flushed and russeted	excellent	moderate to upward pointing buds	mid-season	PSF	good
COURT PENDU PLAT	D	Dec.-Mar.	mid Oct.	small, round flattened	yellow, flushed dull red and russeted	good	fairly hard to outward pointing buds	late	PSF	very good
COX'S ORANGE PIPPIN	D	Nov.-Feb.	mid Oct.	medium, round,regular	yellow, faintly russeted and striped brownish red	excellent	hard	mid-season	PSF	usually good
CRAWLEY BEAUTY	C	Dec.-April	mid Oct.	medium, round, regular	greenish yellow, flushed red	good	moderate to upward point-ing buds	very late	PSF	very good
CRIMSON BRAMLEY	C	Nov.-April	mid Oct.	large, round, flat	deep crimson	very good	very light	mid-season	SS	good
CRIMSON COX	D	Nov.-Feb.	mid Oct.	medium, round, regular	deep crimson	excellent	hard	mid-season	PSF	very good
CUTLER GRIEVE	D	Nov.-Jan.	mid Oct.	medium, flattened, conical	yellow, covered red flush&stripes	moderate	moderate to outward pointing buds	mid-season	PSF	good
DEVONSHIRE QUARRENDEN	D	Aug.-Sept.	when ripe	small to medium, flat	deep crimson	good	moderate to upward pointing buds	mid-season	PSF	irregular
EARLY VICTORIA (EMNETH EARLY)	C	July-Aug.	as needed	large, conical, irregular	yellowish green	good	moderate	mid-season	PSF	very heavy needs thinning
EDWARD VII	C	Jan.-April	mid Oct.	large, oblong, regular	pale yellow, flushed brownish red	very good cooks red	moderate	late	PSF	very good
EGREMONT RUSSET	D	Oct.-Dec.	late Sept.	medium, round, regular	yellow, heavily russeted	good	moderate	early	PSF	very good

Variety	Use	In use	Picking time	Size & shape	Colour	Quality	Vigour	Flowering season	Pollination	Fertility
ELLISON'S ORANGE	D	Sept.–Oct.	late Sept.	medium, slightly conical	golden yellow striped crimson	good	moderate	mid-season	PSF	very good
EMPEROR ALEXANDER	C	Sept.–Nov.	mid Sept.	large, conical	yellow, red striped	good	moderate	mid-season	PSF	fair
ENCORE	C	Jan.–June	mid Oct.	large, flattened	grass green, yellow, flushed brown	good, acid	light	mid-season	PSF	good
EPICURE	D	Sept.	when ripe	round, regular	yellow, red streaks	very good	moderate	early	PSF	very good
EXQUISITE	D	Sept.–Oct.	late Aug.	tall, angular	yellow, red streaks	very good, soft	moderate to upward pointing buds	mid-season	PSF	fair
FORTUNE	D	Sept.	early Sept.	conical, irregular	yellow, striped red	good	moderate	mid-season	PSF	good
GASCOYNE'S SCARLET	D	Sept.–Jan.	by mid Oct.	large, slightly flattened, oval	brilliant scarlet, heavy bloom	good	light to upward pointing buds	late	PSF	uncertain
GLADSTONE	D	July–Aug.	when ripe	medium	red with yellow streaks	good	moderate	mid-season	PSF	good
GOLDEN NOBLE	C	Sept.–Jan.	by early Oct.	round, regular	clear yellow	excellent cooks yellow	light	mid-season	PSF	good
GOLDEN SPIRE	C	Sept.–Oct.	by mid Oct.	tall, conical oblong, medium	clear yellow, red flush and streaks	good	moderate	early	PSF	good
GRAVENSTEIN	D	Oct.–Dec.	late Sept.			good, soft	moderate	early	SS	good
GRENADIER	C	Aug.–Sept.	mid Aug.	large, round	pale yellow	good, acid	moderate to upward pointing buds	mid-season	PSF	very good
HERRING'S PIPPIN	CD	Oct.–Nov.	early Oct.	large, conical medium, flattened	bright red yellowish, streaked dull red	good, soft very good eaten immediately	light	mid-season	PSF	very good
IRISH PEACH	D	Aug.	when ripe				moderate	very early	PSF	irregular
JAMES GRIEVE	D	Sept.–Oct.	mid Sept.	medium, conical	lemon yellow, striped red	v. good, soft	moderate	mid-season	PSF	very good
KING'S ACRE PIPPIN	D	Dec.–Jan.	mid Oct.	medium, irregular	greenish, streaked dull red	v. good	moderate	mid-season	PSF	good

Name	Use	Season	Pick	Type	Colour	Flavour	Pruning	Flowering	Fertility	Cropping
KING OF THE PIPPINS	D	Oct.-Nov.	by mid Oct.	medium, conical	orange, red flush	medium, crisp	moderate to outward pointing buds	mid-season	PSF	good
LADY SUDELEY	D	Aug.-Oct.	when ripe	large, conical	yellow, scarlet striped	good, eaten immediately	moderate	mid-season	PSF	good
LANE'S PRINCE ALBERT	C	Nov.-Mar.	early Oct.	large, regular	grass green, red flush	v. good, acid	hard, to upward pointing buds	mid-season	PSF	very good
LORD DERBY	C	Oct.-Dec.	late Sept.	large, conical	green	excellent cooks red	light, to outward pointing buds	mid-season	PSF	good
LORD LAMBOURNE	D	Oct.	late Sept.	medium, conical	yellow, deep red flush and stripes	excellent soft flesh	light	early	PSF	very good
MILLER'S SEEDLING	D	Aug.-Sept.	late Aug.	medium, conical	pale yellow, few stripes	good, crisp, soft	light, to outside bud	early	PSF	heavy
MOTHER (AMERICAN)	D	Oct.-Nov.	late Sept.	tall, conical	yellow, heavy scarlet flush	v. good	moderate	late	PSF	irregular
MONARCH	C	Dec.-April	mid Oct.	medium, conical	pale yellow, flushed and striped red	good	light	mid-season	PSF	very good
NEWTON WONDER	C	Dec.-May	mid Oct.	large, broad	yellowish, green, red flush and few stripes	v. good	very light	mid-season	PSF	irregular
ORLEANS REINETTE	D	Jan.-Feb.	mid Oct.	flat, regular	orange yellow, red stripes	excellent	light	late	PSF	fair
PEASGOOD'S NONSUCH	CD	Sept.-Nov.	by mid Sept.	large, regular	yellow, crimson flush and stripes	good, soft	light, to upward pointing buds	mid-season	PSF	irregular
REV. W. WILKS	C	Oct.-Nov.	by mid Oct.	enormous, flat, conical	cream with scarlet dots	good	moderate, to upward pointing buds	mid-season	PSF	good

684

Variety	Type	Season of use	Picking time	Size / shape	Colour	Flavour / quality	Vigour	Flowering	SS	Cropping
RIBSTON PIPPIN	D	Nov.-Jan.	mid Oct.	medium-large, conical, irregular	russet, flushed and streaked scarlet	excellent	light, to upward pointing buds	early	SS	moderate
RIVAL	CD	Oct.-Dec.	by mid Oct	medium, flattened regular	yellow, carmine flush and stripes	moderate cooks well	light	mid-season	PSF	fair
ST. CECELIA	D	Dec.-Mar.	early Oct	medium, oval	yellow, russeted red striped	excellent	light	mid-season	PSF	good
ST. EDMUND'S RUSSET	D	Sept.-Oct.	when ripe late Aug	small, flattish round, regular	orange russet	excellent	moderate	mid-season	PSF	good
ST. EVERARD	D	Sept.			yellow, red stripes and russet	v. good	moderate	mid-season	PSF	irregular
SALTCOTE P-PPIN	C	Dec.-Jan.	mid Oct	large, conical	brownish red	good	moderate	mid-season	PSF	good
STIRLING CASTLE	D	Sept.-Oct.	early Sept	large, round	pea green to pale yellow	good, acid	hard	mid-season	PSF	very good
STURMER PIPPIN	D	Mar.-June	late Oct	medium, large	yellowish, brown flush and russet	v. good	light	mid-season	PSF	good
S. T. WRIGHT	C	Sept.-Oct.	mid Sept	large, flat	pale yellow striped pink	good	moderate	mid-season	PSF	good
SUPERB (LAXTON'S)	D	Dec.-Mar.	mid Oct	medium, round	yellow flushed dull red	v. good	moderate, to upward pointing buds	mid-season	PSF	good, sometimes biennial
WARNER'S KING	C	Nov.-Jan.	late Sept	enormous, flat, conical	bright green to yellow, russety spots	good, acid	light, to upward pointing buds	mid-season	SS	moderate
WELLINGTON (syn. DUMELOW'S SEEDLING)	C	Nov.-Mar.	mid Oct	medium, flattened	pale yellow, flushed red	v. good, acid	light	mid-season	PSF	moderate
WORCESTER PEARMAIN	D	Sept.-Oct.	when ripe	medium, conical	yellow, heavily flushed scarlet	v. good if left on tree till ripe	light	mid-season	PSF	very good very regular

STORING. Early apples should be used as soon as possible after gathering but mid-season and late varieties may be kept for periods varying from a month to eight or nine months according to variety and condition.

There are several methods of storing apples, the best for the amateur being to wrap each fruit separately in waxed paper and pack fairly tightly in the type of box in which apples are imported from abroad. These measure about 1 ft. by 1 ft. by 18 in. and will hold three to five layers of apples. The boxes should then be placed in a cool, dark place. It is an advantage if the atmosphere is a little moist. A shed with a good roof but an earthen floor is ideal as the floor will hold a little moisture and give just the right degree of humidity to the atmosphere. Failing this an outhouse or spare room may be used. Before the apples are wrapped, however, they should be spread out thinly for a week or so to sweat which they will always do after picking. No attempt should be made to pack them away until all this surplus moisture has evaporated from their skins.

An alternative method of storing apples is to spread them out in a single layer on an open slatted shelf but this is not so satisfactory as the fruits tend to wither prematurely. It has one advantage, however, most noticeable in a bad season, namely that decaying fruits can be detected at once and removed.

APRICOTS

Apricots do not grow well in the open in most parts of the country unless planted against sunny walls or in similar sheltered and warm positions. They succeed admirably under glass, however, either in unheated houses or with a small amount of artificial heat to start them into growth.

SOILS. Their requirements are similar to those of plums, that is to say they grow best in a soil rather richer than desirable for apples. It must be really well drained. They do particularly well on fertile loams overlying chalk though, despite the popular belief to the contrary, lime is not essential to them.

TYPES OF TREE. Apricots are almost always trained in fan formation. These should be planted at least 15 ft. apart. It is possible to grow them against walls as horizontal trained trees but this is not nearly so satisfactory. In the open they may take the form of small bushes or half standards, but as I have already remarked are only likely to succeed in the warmest counties Planting distances are 12–15 ft. for bushes, 15–20 ft. for half standards.

STOCKS AND PROPAGATION. Apricots are increased by budding on to suitable root stocks and for this purpose practically any of the ordinary plum stocks may be used. The best are Black Damas, Mussel and St. Julien. Budding is carried out from July to August.

FERTILITY. Unlike many other hardy fruits apricots do not appear to suffer from self- or inter-sterility. In consequence single trees may be planted with every prospect of success. Nevertheless as the blossom is produced very early in the year there are seldom sufficient bees flying at the time to ensure satisfactory pollination and this should be carried out by hand with a camel-hair brush or rabbit's tail. Do the work as far as possible on fine, dry days towards noon when the blossom is fully open. Hand pollination is always essential under glass.

SEASON. Apricots cannot be stored for any length of time. They must be used practically as they are picked from the trees, unless of course they are bottled or preserved in some similar way. Roughly speaking the season of apricots grown under glass can be extended from about mid-July until the end of September, by choosing early, mid-season and late varieties.

AGE OF TREE. As with apples it is best to start with young trees and those who feel themselves competent to do so should purchase maidens and train them according to their requirements. Less experienced gardeners will no doubt prefer to have a slightly older tree, but in no case should the age exceed four years.

PLANTING. This can be done at any time during the dormant period from approximately the end of October until about mid-March. In greenhouses apricots are best planted early in November but outdoors it may happen that soil conditions are not ideal then and the work must be delayed in consequence. The general rules for planting should be observed and the uppermost roots kept fairly close to the surface. Be careful not to injure the roots unnecessarily when planting as this may cause a troublesome production of suckers.

TREATMENT OF YOUNG TREES. After planting trees should be pruned rather severely, leaders being cut back by as much as two-thirds their length and weak shoots removed or shortened to a few inches. Trees planted under glass should be watered freely in February and receive further moderate applications of water every few weeks from the time they start into growth. No trees should be allowed to produce fruit the first year after planting. New growth should be restricted to that required to fill the available space.

PRUNING. Apricots bear on wood of all ages in the same way as plums. Pruning should be as light as possible compatible with keeping the trees to the desired form. Quite a lot of the work can be done in summer by shortening side growths to the sixth good leaf reckoned from the base. In the case of trained trees, badly placed shoots which cannot easily be tied back to the training wires can be rubbed out as soon as noticed. In winter it will only be necessary to shorten leaders to points at which branches are required (see p. 659) and, where side growths are over-crowded, to cut some of these still further back.

In the case of old trees it often pays to retain an occasional strong, young shoot at practically full length and tie it in to take the place of an older branch which can be removed the following year. As in the case of plums, hard pruning may encourage Silver Leaf or Gumming.

FEEDING. Here again the requirements are very similar to those of plums, nitrogen and potash being the particular requirements but with the emphasis on the former. Good treatment is to give an annual spring mulch of well-rotted dung at the rate of 1 cwt. to 10 sq. yd. followed by a potash fertiliser such as sulphate of potash at 1 oz. per sq. yd. in autumn. Basic slag may be given every third year as in the case of apples.

THINNING. As a rule apricots can carry all the fruit they set but occasionally when the branches are very heavily laden a little thinning out is repaid. It should not be commenced until the stones are formed, a point which can be ascertained by cutting through any typical fruit. There is often quite a heavy natural fall just before this period and earlier thinning may leave the gardener with an unsatisfactory crop.

PICKING. This should be done as soon as the fruits are well coloured and part readily from the tree. As with other fruits it is advisable to go over any one tree several times rather than strip it at one operation.

CULTIVATION UNDER GLASS. In the main the treatment of apricots under glass is the same as for outdoor trees but a few special points require emphasis. It is vital to give the border a thorough soaking of water each winter. This is the only time at which sub-soil reserves can be replenished without injury to the roots. Trees can either be allowed to start naturally into growth, which they will do in a normal season about March, or a little artificial heat can be applied in February and the ventilators closed at the same time. The temperature at this stage should not exceed an average of 55 degrees.

During the summer it is important to maintain sufficient moisture in the atmosphere which can be done by syringing the trees with house warmed water morning and evening and thoroughly damping the paths and walls at the same time. Failure to observe this precaution may result in a bad attack of red spiders or of frog flies.

Ventilation throughout should be as free as possible, subject to maintaining an average temperature of 55°, rising to 65° in summer. When the leaves fall in autumn the house should be thrown wide open so that the wood becomes quite dormant in winter.

VARIETIES. Good apricots are Hemskirk, August; Moorpark, August–September; and New Large Early, July. Of these the last named is the most satisfactory outdoors.

BLACKBERRIES AND OTHER BRAMBLE FRUITS

These are very useful for filling odd corners in the garden, and for clothing screens, pillars or even arches, though if the last method of training is contemplated, fairly drastic pruning and frequent tying will be necessary with most varieties. A drawback to blackberries in the small garden is that they take up rather a lot of room and that their extremely spiny and vigorous growth can be a nuisance. There is now at least one thornless variety which may be preferred on this account.

SOILS. Blackberries and allied bramble fruits are not fussy regarding soil. They will thrive in light sands and stiff clays but they do respond well to generous feeding. In consequence the ground should be dug thoroughly prior to planting, and well-rotted manure or compost should be incorporated at the rate of 1 cwt. to 8–12 sq. yd. It will usually also pay to give additional potash either as wood ashes or as one of the chemical salts such as sulphate or muriate of potash.

TYPES OF PLANT. Blackberries and the allied bramble fruits are always grown naturally, that is to say they are allowed to make new sucker-like growths from the base every year, though these can be trained in a variety of ways to cover walls or fences, to be grown around pillars or tied to horizontally-trained wires. One good method of training is to drive in stout posts 10–12 ft. apart and strain three horizontal wires between these, 1 ft. 6 in., 3 ft. and 5 ft. above ground level. One plant is grown between each pair of posts and is restricted to six main stems which are trained to left and right along wires.

PROPAGATION. The best method of propagation is that known as tip layering. Strong, young canes are bent downwards in June or July and their tips are held to the soil either by the weight of a stone or with a forked peg driven into the ground. In a few weeks, roots will be formed and new shoots will start to grow. The parent stem can then be severed and the following spring the young plant may be transferred to a nursery bed to grow on until, by the autumn, it is strong enough to go into its permanent positions.

AGE TO PLANT. It is highly desirable to start with young plants. Nurseries usually offer year-old plants from tip layers and these are entirely successful, though they should not be allowed to fruit until their second year from planting.

PLANTING. Bramble fruits are notably surface-rooting. In consequence wide, rather shallow holes, should be prepared for them. The best period for planting, is from mid-October to mid-November, but work can be continued during any open weather until the end of March. Plants should be at least 6 ft. apart; very vigorous kinds such as Himalaya need double this amount of room, apart. If more than one row is contemplated these should be at least 8 ft. apart.

TREATMENT OF YOUNG PLANTS. This is much the same as for raspberries, that is to say, the February following planting, or immediately in the case of late planted canes, all growth should be cut back to within about 9 in. of soil level. As a result, fairly strong, young canes should be formed the first summer and these will require no pruning until they have carried fruit the following summer, after which they should be cut out.

PRUNING. The last sentence of the preceding paragraph really describes the very simple pruning of bramble fruits; that is to say, once they have started to crop it is necessary to cut out each year all the old fruiting canes to make way for the young shoots from the base. This pruning should be done as soon as possible after the crop has been gathered. During the early summer it is an advantage to tie young growth to one side out of the way of the older fruiting stems. In this way it will be possible to gather the fruits easily without risk of damaging the rather brittle young shoots.

FEEDING. This should follow the same general lines as for raspberries, a mulch with dung or compost applied each spring being the most important feed. In addition some extra nitrogen and potash should be given annually in the form of concentrated fertilisers such as dried blood (3 oz. per sq. yd.) and sulphate of potash ($1\frac{1}{2}$ oz. per sq. yd.).

VARIETIES. Good varieties of the common blackberry with their seasons of ripening are Bedford Giant, August; Himalaya (syn. Black Diamond), August; John Innes, September; Merton Early, August;

Merton Thornless, August–September, and Parsley-leaved, August–September. Useful hybrid berries are Boysenberry, very vigorous and often not very heavy cropping but with large, red fruits; Loganberry, too well known to need description and still the best bramble fruit for the private garden; Phenomenal Berry, very like a Loganberry in appearance and habit; Veitchberry, a hybrid between blackberry and raspberry, and Wineberry (often known as Japanese Wineberry) which is perhaps more valuable for ornament than for utility.

CHERRIES

There are two distinct types of cherry, sweet and sour. The latter are easier to grow for they will succeed in every situation, even trained against walls facing due north.

Soils. All cherries succeed best on medium to light soils, particularly good light loams overlying chalk. The sour cherries will also grow on poorer types of soil but no type of cherry likes a heavy, badly drained clay. Very shallow soils are unsuitable for cherries not only because they dry out too rapidly in summer but because they encourage gumming, a troublesome disease (see p. 780).

Preparation should be thorough and dung can be used fairly freely, say 1 cwt. to 12 sq. yd. In spite of the fact that cherries do so well on ground overlying chalk this seems to be due less to a liking for lime than for a need of summer moisture which the chalk holds. It is, in any case, a fact that cherries will grow quite well in lime-free soils provided they are suitable in other respects.

Types of Tree. Cherries dislike hard pruning and therefore succeed best in the freer forms of training such as standard, half standard or large bush. They can also be trained against walls, fences, etc., in which case the fan system is best. Occasionally one sees cherries trained as cordons but these are seldom satisfactory. Minimum planting distances are: standards, 30 ft.; half standards, 25 ft.; bushes, 15 ft.; fan trained, 15 ft.

Stocks and Propagation. Cherries, like other tree fruits, are propagated by grafting or budding, usually the latter, on to suitable root stocks. That most commonly used is the Gean or Wild cherry also known as Mazzard. It is a vigorous stock but has to serve for all purposes as no thoroughly satisfactory dwarfing stock has been found. Forms of Morello cherry are being tried.

FERTILITY. The question of fertility assumes particular importance in the case of cherries. Most varieties are fully self-sterile, that is to say they will not set any fruit if pollinated with their own pollen. In addition there is a great deal of inter-sterility, that is to say there are many varieties which will not pollinate one another. A great deal of work has been done on this problem but much still remains to be found out. I have set out below, in table form, the principal facts as at present known. It will be seen that the varieties are arranged in groups. All varieties in one group are inter-sterile. Varieties from different groups can be planted together as pollinators but even then it is wise to choose kinds that bloom at the same time. However, this is not quite as important as with other fruits as the cherry blossom season is a short one and many kinds overlap sufficiently for pollination to take place even though they do not bloom at exactly the same time.

POLLINATION TABLE FOR CHERRIES

1	2	3	4

Bedford Prolific (*e*)
Black Eagle (*m*)
Black Tartarian A (*e*)
Black Tartarian B (*e*)
Early Rivers (*m*)
Knight's Early
  Black (*m*)
	Bigarreau
	  Schrecken (*m*)
	Black Heart (*e*)
	Frogmore Bigar-
	  reau (*l*)
	Waterloo (*m*)
		Bigarreau
		  Napoleon (*l*)
		Emperor Francis (*e*)
			Kentish Bigar-
			  reau (*l*)
			Ludwig Bigar-
			  reau (*m*)

5	**6**	**7**	**8**

Late Black Bigar-
  reau (*m*)
Turkey
  Heart (*e*)
	Elton (*l*)
	Governor Wood (*l*)
		Géante d'Hedel-
		  fingen (*l*)
		Monstreuse de
		  Mezel (*m*)
			Noir de
			  Schmidt (*m*)
			Peggy Rivers (*e*)

9	**10**	**11**	**12**

Ursula Rivers (*m*)	Bigarreau
	  Jaboulay (*e*)
	Black Tartarian
	  D (*e*)
		Guigne
		  d'Annonay (*e*)
			Morello (*l*)
			Noir de
			  Guben (*e*)
			Florence (*l*)
			Noble (*l*)

With the exception of varieties in Square 12, all of which are inter-fertile, varieties within any one square are not fertile, either individually or collectively. All can be successfully cross-pollinated by varieties from any of the other squares. Letters in brackets mean: (*e*) early flowering, (*m*) mid-season flowering, (*l*) late flowering.

There are just a few varieties of cherry which are self-fertile, that is to say will produce fruit when fertilised with their own pollen. In addition these varieties are also universal donors, in other words they will serve to fertilise any other variety of cherry in bloom at the same time.

The only other point to observe about cherry fertility is that the flowering season is exceptionally early and therefore the blossom is particularly liable to be cut by frost or to suffer from lack of attention by bees.

SEASON. Cherries are in season from mid-June to mid-August and cannot be kept once they are ripe except by bottling or some such artificial means.

AGE OF TREE. Within reason the younger the tree to be planted the better but as most amateurs will prefer to start with a specimen that has been formed by an expert it is usually necessary to plant three to five year old trees, the greater age for standards or half standards. Those who feel competent to do their own initial pruning will be well advised to start with one or two year old trees whatever the form of training.

PLANTING. This should be done between mid-October and mid-March, preference being given to the early part of this period providing the soil is in good order. Cherries generally make many spreading roots and should in consequence be planted in wide, rather shallow holes, the uppermost roots to be covered with about 4–5 in. of good soil.

TREATMENT OF YOUNG TREES. Though established cherries dislike hard pruning it is as a rule necessary to cut them back fairly severely after planting to ensure good growth the first season. Most branches may be shortened by about half the length of growth they made the previous summer. Weakly shoots should be pruned to 2 or 3 in. or cut out altogether.

The spring following planting it is well to give a generous mulch of dung or grass clippings. The soil for several feet around each tree should be kept clear of weeds and grass even though it is intended eventually to grass the orchard down.

Summer pruning the first year is usually unnecessary except in the case of trained trees in which badly placed shoots may be rubbed out early.

GOOD VARIETIES OF CHERRY

Name	Use	Season	Colour	Flavour	Flowering	Fertility	Group	Cropping
ARCHDUKE	DC	July	dark red	sweet	late	PSF	0	good
BIGARREAU NAPOLEON	D	August	yellow and red	excellent	late	SS	3	good
BIGARREAU SCHRECKEN	D	June	black	good	mid-season	SS	2	good
BLACK HEART	D	July	black	fair	early	SS	2	good
BLACK TARTARIAN	D	July	black	excellent	early	SS	1	good
EARLY RIVERS	D	June	black	excellent	mid-season	SS	1	good
ELTON	D	July	red	excellent	late	SS	6	fair
FLEMISH RED	C	July	red	acid	late	SF	0	very good
FLORENCE	D	August	yellow and red	good	late	SS	0	good
FROGMORE BIGARREAU	D	July	red	good	late	SS	2	good
GÉANTE D'HEDELFINGEN	D	August	deep red	excellent	late	SS	7	good
GOVERNOR WOOD	D	July	yellow and red	good	late	SS	6	good
KENTISH BIGARREAU	D	July	yellow and red	good	late	SS	4	good
KENTISH RED	C	July	red	acid	late	SF	0	good
KNIGHT'S EARLY BLACK	D	June	black	good	mid-season	SS	1	fair
LATE DUKE	DC	August	deep red	fair	late	PSF	0	good
MAY DUKE	DC	June	black	fair	late	PSF	0	good
MORELLO	C	August	black or dark red	acid	late	SF	0	very good
NOBLE (TRADESCANT'S HEART)	D	August	black	excellent	late	SS	0	fair
NOIR DU GUBEN	D	June	dark red	fair	early	SS	0	good
PEGGY RIVERS	D	July	red	good	early	SS	8	good
ROYAL DUKE	DC	July	deep red	good	late	PSF	0	fair
TURKEY HEART	D	August	black	fair	early	SS	5	good
WATERLOO	D	June	black	excellent	mid-season	SS	2	fair

Abbreviations: SS, self-sterile but also inter-sterile; SF, self-fertile; PSF, partially self-fertile.

Some cherries are not only self-sterile but also inter-sterile with certain other varieties. This makes it essential to select cross-pollinating varieties with some care. In the column above headed 'Group' the figures indicate the respective pollination groups of the cherries listed. Those marked o may be planted with each other or with any other variety, provided flowering times overlap. With the remainder varieties bearing the same number should not be planted to pollinate one another but may be planted with any varieties bearing different figures.

PRUNING. The sweet cherry, like the plum, bears on both year old and older wood and forms spurs freely. The main problems in pruning are to keep an open shapely tree and avoid silver leaf and gumming. Infection by silver leaf fungus is very likely to occur during autumn and winter through wounds made in pruning, while gumming always tends to appear on trees that have been pruned too severely. In consequence pruning should be confined to the spring and summer and be as light as possible.

My own plan is to do most of the work in April just as the trees are starting into growth. They are then thinned moderately, no more in fact than is necessary to get rid of crossing or rubbing branches and to maintain the desired shape of tree.

Side growths can frequently be retained unpruned as they will then form fruit buds throughout their length. If they tend to get overcrowded some can be shortened to five leaves in July or early August.

Leaders can be left unpruned unless they are tending to become weak, in which case they may be shortened by one third in April.

Trained Trees will of necessity need rather more pruning. Leaders must be cut back to a point at which they are about 15 in. apart. As much as possible of the side growth should be laid in between the main branches but badly placed shoots should be cut out in April or shortened to five leaves in July–August.

A different system of pruning is necessary in the case of sour cherries, including Morello, because these bear mainly on year old wood. Pruning is very similar to that of peaches and nectarines. In the early stages while the tree is being formed leaders must be cut back as described above to get branches where they are needed. But side growths must, as far as possible, be replaced annually. This is done mainly by a process of disbudding carried out gradually from May to August. Each year old side growth will, during this period, produce a number of new shoots. Two only are retained, one as near as possible to the base of the old growth and one at its tip. All the rest are rubbed out as early as possible. The terminal shoot is pinched when it is 3 or 4 in. long, its purpose being solely to draw sap through the stem and so help any fruits it may be carrying to swell. The basal shoot is allowed to grow unhampered. As soon as possible after the crop has been gathered all the old side growths are cut out and the new basal shoots are tied back in their places.

FEEDING. Nitrogen is the most important food for cherries but must be balanced with a moderate quantity of potash. The usual practice for cultivated orchards is to give a mulch of dung in spring, about 1 cwt.

to 10 sq. yd., followed by a potash fertiliser, such as sulphate of potash in autumn at 1–2 oz. per sq. yd. In the case of grass orchards, Nitro-chalk, 2–3 oz. per sq. yd. may supplement the dung.

PICKING. This should commence as soon as the fruits are well coloured and part readily from the spurs. Commercial orchards are usually stripped at one operation but it will pay the amateur to go over his trees several times, so extending the season for a fortnight or more and getting a much higher average quality of fruit.

The wood of cherry trees is rather brittle and, in consequence, easily broken, so care should be taken when moving ladders around large standard trees not to injure branches and twigs more than is inevitable.

COB NUTS

Cob nuts, and filberts which are simply a variety of cob with long awns, are not frequently grown in private gardens probably because they are not very profitable on a small scale. Nevertheless they have a limited usefulness, especially for forming wind breaks or making hedges with a utility as well as an ornamental value.

SOILS. All will succeed in a great variety of soils. The only places where they cannot be grown successfully are very thin soils and heavy, water-logged clays. They are native to the country and therefore well adapted to our peculiar climate. In spite of the fact that they flower in February they are not damaged by frost and can be planted in hollows which would be unsuitable for most other fruits.

In preparing the ground digging should be thorough and a little well-rotted dung can be used with advantage, say about 1 cwt. to 20 sq. yd.

TYPES OF TREE. Nuts are almost invariably grown as open centred bushes, with either a very short leg or no leg at all. They have a habit of throwing up strong growths direct from the roots and occasionally it pays to retain one of these to replace an older, worn out growth but it is not wise to encourage the production of suckers too much or the bushes will soon become shapeless and overcrowded.

Bushes should be spaced at least 12 ft. apart.

PROPAGATION. Unlike most other fruit trees, nuts are grown on their own roots, not budded or grafted on stocks. Another method of increase is by the suckers referred to in the preceding paragraph. These can be detached in autumn or winter with some roots and, if planted on their own, will soon grow into sturdy bushes.

Another method of propagation is by layering in autumn. This is done by bending whippy shoots down to soil level, notching them at a joint where they touch the soil and then pegging them down at this point or weighting them with a heavy stone. The layers form roots from the point of notching the following year and can be severed after a twelvemonth.

Nuts can also be raised from seeds sown in March outdoors but as seedlings vary greatly in character and are often inferior to their parents, this is not a good method.

FERTILITY. Despite their hardiness and the fact that they are self-fertile, nuts often fail to crop properly. This is due to the fact that some varieties produce little or no good pollen or few pollen bearing catkins. Other kinds, such as Cosford and Pearson's Prolific, produce plenty of pollen even when quite young and it is therefore a good policy either to form plantations exclusively of these kinds or to mix them with other kinds in the proportion of at least one good pollinator to four others.

AGE OF TREE. The best method is to start with year old suckers or layers, which means, of course, that the gardener must form his own tree from the outset. If he fears to do so and prefers to start with a partly formed bush he may purchase three year old plants but should not exceed this age.

PLANTING. There is nothing special to be said about this. The work is done from mid-October until mid-March as for most other fruits and the general instructions given on pages 633–4 should be followed.

TREATMENT OF YOUNG TREES. Immediately after planting it is wise to prune severely, in fact very much as for black currants (see p. 700). All strong branches are cut back to within about 1 ft. of ground level or the main trunk and weak shoots are removed. No special precautions are necessary the first summer but the soil around the bushes should be kept clear of weeds and may be mulched with dung or grass clippings in spring.

PRUNING. The pruning of established nut bushes is little understood by amateurs and failure to treat the bushes properly often accounts for bad crops. First it must be understood that two distinct types of flower are produced; the catkins which are the male flowers and produce pollen only and the female flowers which are very small and bright red. In spite of the colour of these females it is quite difficult to see them and they are often overlooked. Nevertheless they are very important as it is from them, and them alone, that nuts will be produced. Both types of flower appear in February and March but usually on any particular bush the catkins open a little before the female flowers.

Apart from shaping the bushes, which can be done in November, the important pruning is carried out during the blossom period. Side growths are cut back to the first catkin reckoning from the tip or, if the shoot carries no catkins, to the first female flower. Shoots that are carrying catkins only may be left unpruned until the catkins fade, when they are best shortened to two buds.

During the operation of shaping the bushes in November suckers should be removed unless required to replace old branches as already described.

FEEDING. As a rule nuts get on quite well without a great deal of feeding but if dung can be spared a light top dressing can be given each spring. Bushes that are not making sufficient growth can be stimulated with Nitro-chalk or sulphate of ammonia applied in April, 2 oz. per sq. yd. Each autumn give basic slag, 6 oz. per sq. yd., and sulphate of potash 1 oz. per sq. yd.

PICKING. This should be done towards the end of September or early in October when the nuts part readily from the bushes and the husks are yellowing.

STORING. Nuts will keep quite a long time in any cool, dry place but a better method of storing is to pack them into glass jars or earthenware crocks with plenty of salt sprinkled between and over them.

VARIETIES. Good cobnuts and filberts are Cosford, Pearson's Prolific, Duke of Edinburgh, Kentish Cob, Merveille de Bolwyllen, Red Filbert, and White Filbert. The first two are good pollinators for themselves and for other varieties.

CURRANTS, BLACK

This is amongst the most satisfactory of small fruits for the amateur gardener. It succeeds well in most districts and usually crops heavily from about the third year onwards. The profitable life of a black currant bush is rather short compared with that of some other fruits, seldom extending much beyond the twelfth year, but new stock can be produced easily at home by means of cuttings taken from the old plants.

SOILS. Black currants succeed best in rather rich soils and can stand more nitrogen than most other fruits. They need plenty of moisture during the growing season but dislike stagnation in winter and there-fore require good drainage. The ideal is a deep, well cultivated, rather light loam and the worst types of soil are those which are very thin and overlie stone or chalk. Cultivation should be thorough prior to planting and well-rotted dung may be worked in at the rate of 1 cwt. to 10 or 12 sq. yds.

It does not very much matter whether the position is sunny or in partial shade as long as it is open overhead. In fact one method of extending the season is to plant some bushes, preferably of a late variety, in a place with a cool, northerly aspect and so encourage the berries to hang a long time.

TYPES OF PLANT. Black currants are always grown as bushes, usually without any main stem or 'leg' but with a number of strong shoots coming direct from the roots. Plant at least 5 ft. apart each way.

PROPAGATION. This is by cuttings prepared in autumn from well ripened shoots formed the previous summer. Each cutting should be about 1 ft. long, trimmed at the base just below a joint and inserted firmly some 4 in. deep in good soil outdoors. The cuttings root readily and can be transferred either to a nursery bed or fruiting quarters the following autumn.

FERTILITY. All varieties are self-fertile, that is to say any particular plant will set fruit when pollinated with its own pollen. They are, as a matter of fact, usually self-pollinated, either by insects or by the pollen falling from the anthers direct on to the stigmas. Bad fertility is fre-quently due to cold, damp weather when the flowers are open and lack of insects to carry the pollen.

Frequently the basal flowers in each truss set berries whereas the tip flowers fail, a fault referred to as 'running off'. This is due to the fact that the flowers at the top of the truss generally have such short pistils that the stigmas are within the anthers. In consequence it is easy for the pollen to fall on to them without the help of insects. In contrast the pistils of the lower flowers are long, the stigmas sticking out beyond the anthers and so missing the pollen. This fault can be overcome by hand pollination with a rabbit's tail or camel hair brush on fine, dry days when the flowers are fully open.

SEASON. The only way in which black currants can be kept is by bottling them and the quicker they are used after picking the better. The season for fresh fruit extends from July to early September.

AGE TO PLANT. It is advisable to start with quite young plants, certainly no more than two years old.

PLANTING. This should be done while the bushes are dormant from about the middle of October until mid-March. Late planting is not so desirable unless the bushes can be well watered for the first few months. Late October and early November is usually the most favourable period.

The plants are extremely surface rooting and in consequence the uppermost roots should only be covered with 2 in. of soil. The bushes generally lift with a mass of fibrous roots which dry out and shrivel rapidly if exposed to the air so the quicker they can be planted the better.

Black currants make big bushes and should not be planted closer than 5 ft. each way.

TREATMENT OF YOUNG BUSHES. The February following planting or, in the case of late planted bushes, immediately after planting, all strong stems should be cut back to within 4–6 in. of ground level and weak stems removed. No fruit will be produced the first season but the bushes will be encouraged to make strong growth to fruit the following year. No further pruning is necessary until a crop has been gathered.

They will benefit from a moderate mulch of strawy manure or grass clippings applied in April and renewed about June.

PRUNING. Established black currants should be pruned as soon as possible after the crop has been gathered in late summer or early autumn. The crop is borne on year-old wood. In consequence if bushes are growing well all old wood that has just carried fruit can be cut right out together with any weak young growth, the strong young growth being retained at full length to crop the following year. The more strong stems there are coming direct from the roots the better. Suckers are not harmful.

Bushes that are not making a great deal of new wood may either be cut back to within 8 to 9 in. of soil level, in which case they will bear no fruit the next year but should make strong growth, or alternatively a little of the old wood can be removed and the rest retained with whatever new growth it may be carrying. In either case the bushes should be fed more liberally than usual.

FEEDING. Nitrogen is the most important item and can be given in spring in the form of any quick-acting nitrogenous fertiliser such as Nitro-chalk or sulphate of ammonia either of which may be used at 2 oz. per sq. yd. In addition there should be an annual mulch in spring of well-rotted dung, 1 cwt. to 10 sq. yd. It is wise to give some extra potash in autumn as, for example, sulphate of potash, 1 oz. per sq. yd. Phosphates may be required on some soils and can be given in autumn as basic slag or bonemeal, or in spring as superphosphate of lime.

PICKING. For exhibition the fruits are almost invariably picked on the truss but for home use it pays to pick individual berries and go over the bushes several times at intervals of a few days. The fruits at the top of the truss invariably ripen before those lower down and by this means can be removed first. The difference is more marked with some varieties than others.

VARIETIES. Good black currants are Baldwin, late; Boskoop Giant, early; Daniel's September, late; Davison's Eight, mid-season; Sea-brook's Black, mid-season, and Wellington XXX, second early. The variety Edina, also known as Victoria and Goliath, is not recommended owing to its susceptibility to lime-sulphur, a spray which must frequently be used to keep the currant big-bud mite under control.

CURRANTS, RED AND WHITE

These differ from black currants both in their habit of growth and method of bearing. They crop heavily and succeed in most places but are less useful than black currants and so should generally be planted on a smaller scale.

SOILS. Requirements are very similar to those of black currants but they will withstand drought a little better and do not need quite such liberal supplies of nitrogen. In preparing the ground dung can be used at 1 cwt. to 15 sq. yd. and sulphate of potash should usually be added at 1 oz. per sq. yd.

TYPES OF PLANT. Unlike the black currant, red and white currants are grown as bushes with a distinct main stem or 'leg' about 4-5 in. high. Occasionally one sees bushes with a good deal of sucker growth direct from the roots. This is not definitely harmful but it is not as satisfactory for garden purposes as the more orthodox type of bush. All bushes should be planted at least 5 ft. apart. Red and white currants can also be trained in various ways. Single, double or triple stemmed cordons are quite popular and very high class fruits can be produced in this way. Planting distance is 1 ft. in the rows for single cordons, 18 in. for twin stems and 2 ft. for triple cordons. Rows should be at least 4 ft. apart.

PROPAGATION. This is done by cuttings prepared and rooted in the same way as those of the black currant, except that all buds are nicked out of the lower half of each cutting to prevent the formation of suckers.

FERTILITY. All varieties are fully self-fertile and in consequence single bushes may be grown with satisfactory results. Red and white currants flower early and are therefore apt to suffer from frost if planted in hollows and similar frost pockets. For the same reason hand pollination is often well repaid as few bees may be flying when the plants are in bloom.

SEASON. This is a little earlier than for black currants, being mainly in July though some fruits may be ready in June. There is no method of storing other than by bottling.

AGE TO PLANT. As for black currants.

PLANTING. The same instructions as those given for black currants apply.

TREATMENT OF YOUNG BUSHES. It generally pays to cut back rather severely after planting in order to ensure good growth the first year. However, it is possible to get some fruit the first year by leaving the best branches at half their original length and cutting others back by about two-thirds. In other respects treatment is the same as for black currants.

PRUNING. Established bushes should be both summer and winter pruned, the main work being done in July. Unlike black currants, red and white currants fruit on old as well as on one-year wood and form spurs freely like an apple or plum. In July all strong side-growths should be shortened to about six leaves. This will encourage the formation of fruit buds. In winter there will be little further to do beyond shortening the leading shoots by a few inches each and, where fruit buds are showing prominently on the summer pruned side growths, cutting back to these. An attempt should be made to keep the centre of each bush reasonably open, in fact rather like an apple bush on a smaller scale.

Cordons are treated very much like apple cordons, that is to say the leading shoot of each plant is left unpruned, side growths are shortened to six leaves in July and are further cut back to two or three buds in October–November.

FEEDING. The same general routine may be followed as advised for black currants but with rather less emphasis on nitrogen and more on potash. If dung is available for spring use it will not as a rule be necessary to give a nitrogenous fertiliser as well. Potash should be used fairly freely every autumn as red and white currants both show the effects of potash deficiency very quickly. Sulphate of potash is the most suitable form and can be used at 2 oz. per sq. yd.

PICKING. As for black currants.

VARIETIES. The best red currants for garden planting are Earliest of Fourlands, very early; Fay's Prolific, early; Laxton's No. 1, early; Perfection, mid-season; Raby Castle, mid-season; Rivers Late Red (syn. Prince Albert), late; Victoria (syn. Wilson's Long Bunch), very late.

Good white currants are White Dutch, mid-season, and White Versailles, early.

FIGS

These exotic fruits are not very widely grown in this country except under glass, but in warm, sheltered places, particularly near the coast, good crops can be ripened outdoors most summers.

SOIL. The really important points about soil are that it must not be too rich and must be well drained. Dung should be used very sparingly in the initial preparation of the ground as it may cause rank growth which will prove unfruitful. If there is any doubt about the drainage it is good policy to remove the soil to a depth of 2 or 3 ft. and place a good layer of brickbats or clinkers in the bottom. This is almost always a wise precaution when figs are to be grown under glass and often the border is further restricted with bricks or concrete to a width of about 3 ft. It is also wise policy to sprinkle a little ground chalk or limestone right through the soil while preparing it.

TYPE OF TREE. Figs are usually grown either as bushes with quite a short central trunk or as fan trained specimens against walls. Occasionally one sees half standards in the open but these are seldom satisfactory except in the warmest localities. Allow at least 15 ft. between fan trained trees; 25 ft. between half-standards.

PROPAGATION. Figs are raised on their own roots, the usual method being by cuttings prepared from firm, young growths detached in autumn and rooted singly in 4 or 5 in. pots. These should be filled with rather sandy potting compost and be plunged in ashes in a frame or cool greenhouse. The cuttings themselves should be prepared in the ordinary way, that is each should be severed just below a joint, but lower buds must be nicked out as advised for red currants and gooseberries.

FERTILITY. The fig has a curious system of flowering. The flowers, of two separate sexes, are carried inside the young fig and can only be seen if this is cut in half. In the warm, Mediterranean countries to which the fig is native these flowers are fertilised by a special kind of wasp which crawls into the fruit through a hole in the end and carries the pollen from male to female flowers. But fertilisation is not essential with most cultivated varieties. Perfectly good crops of fully developed figs are produced without any outside agency. When failure occurs and the figs drop off instead of swelling, it is usually due to some fault in management, not to bad fertilisation.

SEASON. Outdoor figs are in season at the end of summer and in early autumn but under glass it is usually possible to get two separate crops from the same trees, one quite early in the summer and the other at approximately the same time as outdoor figs.

AGE OF TREE. It is best to start with two or three year old trees which should, for preference, be purchased in pots.

PLANTING. In the case of figs lifted from the open ground the usual instructions for planting (see pp. 633–4) should be followed. With figs purchased in pots the only difference is that the roots, which are likely to be bound fairly tightly in a ball, should be carefully loosened and spread out before they are planted. In both cases the work should be done between mid-October and mid-March, preferably early in that period, especially in the case of figs to be grown under glass.

TREATMENT OF YOUNG TREES. After planting the trees must be pruned fairly severely. The following spring a moderate mulch of dung should be applied. Trees under glass will need frequent and generous watering from April to September. Apart from this no special attention is required for the first season and no crop should be allowed to form.

MODE OF BEARING. Before describing the pruning of figs it is necessary to understand the way in which the fruits are produced. It is possible for a fig to produce three separate crops in one year and it is usual for it to try to produce at least two crops. Under glass two crops can usually be matured but in the open it is never possible in this country to ripen more than one crop. Pruning must be adjusted accordingly.

The first crop is produced on wood of the previous year's growth, in fact the young fruit are already well formed on the wood in the autumn. They remain there practically without alteration in size until the spring when, if the temperature can be raised to about 60–65° they commence to swell fairly rapidly and will ripen in about three months. By this method a crop can be obtained quite easily by the end of June or early July, the trees being started into growth at the end of March or early in April.

The second crop is carried on the tips of the previous year's growth or from beside the scars left by the removal, while still small, of the first fruits described in the preceding paragraph. The tip fruits will also be present in the autumn but will be no bigger than peas whereas the first crop figs will be much more forward at that time. This second crop is the only one which can be secured outdoors and all other fruits should be removed.

The third crop is produced on short side growths from the current year's wood. Under glass it may ripen in the autumn but in practice it is seldom obtained, two crops being sufficient for the strength of the tree.

PRUNING. This is generally directed towards maintaining a suitable supply of strong, young wood and restricting the tree to those fruits which it is able to ripen. The main pruning is done as soon as the leaves fall in the autumn. Some of the oldest wood is cut right out and any thin or weak shoots removed but the best young branches are trained in at full length. In summer, side growths not required to extend the main branches, are shortened to five or six leaves in much the same manner as with apples.

Trees that are making too much new wood and bearing badly should be root pruned in October.

FEEDING. Avoid too much dung as this tends to produce rank growth at the expense of fruit. Weak trees can have a light mulch each spring, otherwise artificials will prove sufficient; Nitro-chalk or sulphate of ammonia at $1\frac{1}{2}$ oz. per sq. yd. in March and bone meal 4 oz. and sulphate of potash 1 oz. per sq. yd. in October.

THINNING. With all trees, outdoors or under glass, only the best of the swelling fruits should be retained. Smaller fruits should be removed in spring or early summer. This thinning is additional to the removal of all fruits of unwanted crops.

PICKING. Figs are ready for picking when they commence to get soft and part readily from the tree.

VARIETIES. The best all round variety is Brown Turkey as it crops freely and is hardy. The skin is nearly brown when ripe. White Marseilles has a pale green skin and ripens early but is not as reliable as Brown Turkey.

GOOSEBERRIES

Together with black currants these are the most useful bush fruits for the small garden. There are few places in which they will not succeed and they probably have a wider soil range than any other fruit. The flowering season is early and in consequence spring frosts may do much damage in low lying places.

SOILS. The ideal is a medium, well-drained loam and extremes towards sand or clay should as far as possible be avoided. Both heavy and light land can be improved by liberal additions of well-rotted dung to which gooseberries respond well. In all cases it is wise to give some additional potash when preparing the ground as gooseberries are especially sensitive to potash deficiency. The results of the latter will be shown in poor growth and leaf scorching, often followed by premature defoliation.

Gooseberries may be planted under fruit trees or be interplanted with vegetables. They associate well with plums as, like them, they like a generous rate of manuring.

TYPES OF PLANT. The bush form is generally adopted and gooseberries are grown with a distinct main stem or 'leg' like red and white currants. It is impossible to form an open, goblet-shaped bush in quite the same manner as with currants but the main stems should be well spaced to allow easy gathering of the crop. Such bushes should be planted at least 4 ft. apart.

Gooseberries are also grown as cordons with one, two or three main stems. Very big fruits of exhibition quality are produced in this way. Spacing is as for red and white currant cordons.

PROPAGATION. This is carried out by cuttings taken in exactly the same way as those of the red and white currant. Note particularly that the lower buds on each cutting should be nicked out with the point of a sharp penknife to prevent the cutting forming sucker shoots from below ground level. Such suckers are not harmful in the way in which they would be with a fruit cultivated on a stock but they are a great nuisance and make it very difficult to carry out cultural operations.

FERTILITY. All gooseberries appear to be self- and inter-fertile and so no problems on this score arise. Nevertheless because of the earliness of their flowering it is sometimes necessary to take special precautions to ensure pollination. Individual bushes can be protected during the flowering period with old curtains or muslin spread across them and, if few bees are flying, the flowers can be fertilised by hand with a camel-hair brush or rabbit's tail.

SEASON. By planting early, mid-season and late varieties and commencing to pick as soon as the most forward fruits are large enough for cooking, it is possible to have gooseberries from about Whitsuntide until the end of August. Many varieties which are listed as dessert gooseberries can also be used for cooking in the green state. When the set is heavy it is a distinct advantage to thin fruits towards the end of May or early in June by which time the thinnings are usually serviceable. The remaining fruits can be left to grow bigger or to ripen for dessert.

The only methods of storing are by bottling or canning.

AGE TO PLANT. Once again I would stress the importance of starting with young stock; year-old rooted cuttings for preference but certainly nothing older than three years.

PLANTING. This follows precisely the same lines as for red, white and black currants. The uppermost roots should be covered with about 3 in. of soil. Space bushes at least 4 ft. apart, and single stem cordons 1 ft. in rows and 4 ft. between rows. Double and triple stem cordons are spaced a minimum of 18 in. and 27 in. in the rows.

TREATMENT OF YOUNG PLANTS. Again there is little to add to what has already been said regarding red and white currants except that it is particularly important to get good growth the first year after planting and therefore more than ever necessary to be rather severe in pruning and liberal with mulches and water.

PRUNING. In the case of bush trees pruning, after the first year, may resolve itself into thinning out all over crowded branchlets and shortening all leaders sufficiently to correct any peculiarities in habit. Some gooseberries are satisfactory in this respect but many have a semi-weeping habit while others grow too erect. In the case of the weepers, each leading growth should be cut back to the top of the arch and to a bud pointing upwards. With those varieties which are too erect in habit leaders should be shortened by about one third and cut to an outward pointing bud.

Cordons require more pruning to maintain their distinctive shape. Leading shoots are left untouched until the maximum desired height is obtained after which they are removed. Side shoots are pruned in July to six leaves each and are further cut back to two or three buds in October–November, or to a fruit bud if any have formed.

Feeding. Again it is necessary to emphasise that potash is of particular importance and has an almost controlling effect on growth. Give a generous mulch of well-rotted dung each spring if possible or, failing this, some other bulky, organic manure such as shoddy or well-made compost and every autumn a potassic fertiliser such as sulphate of potash, about $1\frac{1}{2}$ oz. per sq. yd. If bushes fail to make satisfactory growth or show indications of dying back, the rate of feeding can be increased to as much as 1 cwt. to 6 sq. yd. of dung and 3 oz. per sq. yd. sulphate of potash.

Thinning. This should be done when the fruits are of usable size. See 'Season', p. 707.

Picking. For dessert use gooseberries should not be picked until they cease to be hard and acquire their full colour. For cooking they can be picked as soon as of sufficient size.

Varieties. Good gooseberries are Careless, white, mid-season; Crown Bob, red, mid-season; Cousen's Seedling, yellow, very late; Dan's Mistake, red, mid-season; Early Sulphur, yellow, early; Golden Drop, yellow, mid-season; Gunner, yellow, late; Keepsake, green, late; Lancashire Lad, red, mid-season; Lancer, green, mid-season; Langley Gage, white, mid-season; Leveller, yellow, mid-season; May Duke, red, early; Whinham's Industry, red, mid-season; Whitesmith, white, mid-season; and White Lion, white, late. Of these my pick of three would be Careless, Lancashire Lad and Leveller.

GRAPES

Grapes cannot as a rule be cultivated very satisfactorily in the open air in this country. A few of the hardiest varieties will succeed in certain sheltered places but in general outdoor cultivation is a risky business and good crops are only obtained occasionally. Those who require a regular supply of grapes should undoubtedly plant under glass and it is with the indoor cultivation of grapes that the following notes are chiefly concerned.

Type of House. Vines can be grown satisfactorily in almost any kind of greenhouse but the ideal vinery should not be less than 12 ft. wide and 20 ft. long and should have glass extending to within 2 ft. of soil level. For early crops a lean-to house against a wall facing south, or a little west of south, is best. For the main crop a span-roofed house running north and south is very suitable.

The vine border may be inside the vinery, outside, or partly in and partly out. The inside border encourages early growth as the soil warms up quickly in the spring. It is, however, entirely dependent upon the gardener for its water supply and therefore taxes his skill and time to a greater extent than the outside border. The latter has the merit of being easy to manage and requiring little attention for the greater part of the year but growth tends to be late and, if rainfall should be excessive, there is no easy means of protecting the roots from it. The border partly inside and partly out has much to recommend it as it combines the advantages of both methods.

Whatever type of house is used it must be provided with suitable training wires. These must be strained horizontally at least 9 in. below the glass and should extend the full length of the vinery. There should be one wire every 15 in., i.e. a wire for each lateral.

SOIL. A medium loamy soil is best for grapes. Drainage is of paramount importance, so much so that if there is any doubt about its adequacy a special border should be prepared with drainage trenches in the bottom leading to a properly constructed soak-away (see p. 41), or main drain.

If the ordinary soil of the garden is reasonably good it can be used as the basis of the compost. A fairly liberal addition of very well decayed dung, preferably horse manure, should be made, the precise quantity depending on the known quality of the soil. The average will be one barrow load of dung to every eight barrow loads of soil. In addition mix in about half a barrow load of well broken old mortar rubble or chalk broken up as small as possible, 1 lb. of bone meal and ½ lb. of sulphate of potash.

If the natural soil of the garden is not good or its suitability for vines is in doubt, remove it altogether from the vine border and replace with loam or, better still, chopped turves obtained from a meadow in a good condition. The same additions should be made as recommended for garden soil. The border must be at least 4 ft. wide, preferably more, and should extend the full length of the vinery. The depth must not be less than 3 ft. The border should be completed at least two months before planting so that the soil may have ample time to settle.

TYPES OF TRAINING. Two methods are commonly used, one the single rod system and the other the extension or multiple stem system. In the former a number of vines are planted side by side about 4 ft. apart. Each is restricted to a single main stem which is trained directly from soil level to the apex of the house, following the line of the roof rafters. Under the extension system one vine may fill quite a large house, a notable example being the Great Vine at Hampton Court. The first growth from the roots is trained horizontally beneath the eaves and from it subsidiary rods are trained parallel with the roof rafters to the apex of the house at approximately 4 ft. intervals.

The single rod system is now most in favour with experienced growers and is certainly the best for the amateur.

PROPAGATION. Vines can be increased by cuttings or single eyes. Cuttings are taken in autumn directly the foliage has fallen. They are prepared from well-ripened growth formed during the previous summer, suitable wood for the purpose being that which has just finished carrying a crop of grapes, in fact the very kind of growth which would in any case be removed at the winter pruning (see p. 714). Each cutting should be about 1 ft. in length. severed at the base just below a joint or leaf. The cuttings are potted singly in rather sandy compost in well-drained 4 or 5 in. pots. Stand these in the greenhouse or vinery and keep moderately watered. The cuttings should be well rooted by the following autumn when they may be planted in their permanent quarters or, if preferred, can be transferred to larger pots and grown on for another year.

Many growers think that single eyes make sturdier plants than cuttings. This method is certainly economical of material. The best time to obtain these eyes is about the end of August. The 'eye' in question is in fact a dormant growth bud, one of which will be found at the base of practically every leaf at that time of the year. The eye can either be scooped out with a portion of bark, as when preparing a rose bud (see p. 332) or can be cut with a section of stem about $\frac{1}{2}$ in. long. In either case the eyes should be inserted in sandy soil in 3 in. pots in such a manner that they are just level with the surface. Pack the pots in coconut fibre or fine peat in a box or frame placed over the hot water pipes. Do not cover the box or frame but water fairly freely.

The eyes usually start into growth quite quickly and after a few weeks may have filled the small pot with roots, in which case they should be potted on into 5 or 6 in. pots, filled with ordinary potting compost (see p. 421). Subsequent treatment is as for vines raised from cuttings.

FERTILITY. Most vines are self-fertile, that is to say it is quite possible to grow one variety only in a greenhouse and yet get good crops.

SEASON. By growing early and late varieties and starting the former into growth with artificial heat, it is possible to have ripe grapes from June to Christmas or even later but considerable skill is necessary in producing both very early and very late crops. The beginner will be well advised to be satisfied with an autumn crop for the first few years.

AGE OF VINE. As with other fruits it is undoubtedly best to start with young plants. Year old cuttings or rooted eyes transplant without any difficulty and will grow on into fine fruiting vines in time but it will be several years before a crop is gathered. Most amateurs prefer to start with something more advanced and the nurseryman meets this requirement by offering so-called 'fruiting vines' in pots. These are usually three or four years old and must be planted with considerable care if they are not to receive a severe check. Such vines should always be purchased in pots.

PLANTING. Home grown vines, whether year-old cuttings or well-rooted eyes, can with advantage be planted in September or early October, before growth ceases for the year. Fruiting vines (see above) should be purchased in November but not planted until the following March. Meanwhile they should simply stand in the vinery in their pots and become acclimatised.

The young vines can be planted with little or no root disturbance but in the case of the older plant, which will probably have its roots bound round in a tight ball, it is essential to disentangle these before planting. This must be done carefully and a pointed stick can be used to tease out the tangled roots which should then be spread out in a wide hole, sufficiently deep to allow the uppermost to be covered with 3 in. of soil. Work fine soil around and between them and make thoroughly firm.

TREATMENT OF YOUNG VINES. Home grown vines that have been planted in September or October will require no pruning the first winter. Fruiting vines should be pruned about a month before they are planted. They are cut back to 3 ft. from soil level.

The first spring one strong growth is trained under the rafters towards the apex of the house. Any side shoots are pinched when they have made one or two leaves. When the main shoot has grown 6 ft. it is also pinched. Following this further side growths will appear. One of these, as near the end as possible, is trained on towards the apex and the rest of the shoots are allowed to grow unstopped until mid-September when they should all be pinched.

By this means the grower will obtain by the end of the first year anything from 7 to 10 ft. of growth, the lower part of which will be beginning to get stout and woody. When all the leaves have fallen he will cut this back to a length of 5 ft. Any side growths remaining should be cut right back to the main rod.

Meanwhile the vine border should be well watered throughout the summer. No artificial heat should be needed but in hot weather the vine should be syringed daily with tepid water and the path and walls damped down.

Ventilation should be free throughout subject to avoidance of draughts and rapid falls in temperature.

TREATMENT OF ESTABLISHED VINES. After the first year fruiting vines should be able to carry a small crop which will, of course, increase every succeeding year. Home grown cuttings will take a further year or so of foundation pruning on the lines of first year treatment before they are sturdy enough to crop.

STARTING INTO GROWTH. Vines required for an early crop are started into growth in January or February by closing the ventilators and raising the temperature to about 55°. Prior to this the border, if an inside one, should have been very thoroughly soaked with house warmed water. It is also wise to give a good mulch of well-rotted dung at the time the vines are to be started.

TEMPERATURE. Subsequently an average temperature of 55 to 60° rising to 70 or 75° with sun heat should be maintained except during the flowering period when an increase of about 5° is to be preferred. As the summer advances and the grapes become well formed, the maximum temperature may rise to 90° with sun heat but every effort should be used to prevent higher temperatures than this as they may cause scorching of leaves and berries. For the final week or so, while the grapes are getting their full colour, it is better to have a lower temperature again with a night average of 60°.

VENTILATION. Throughout ventilation should be as free as possible compatible with the maintenance of these temperatures. More ventilation must be given while the flowers are setting even though this means increased fire heat. There should be another increase in ventilation while the pips are being formed.

WATERING. At no time must the vine border be allowed to become dry. If the winter watering has been properly done the soil will be moist throughout to begin with. Subsequently water is likely to be needed every three or four weeks throughout the season, depending on the weather. Not less than 5 gal. per sq. yd. should be given at each application. However, avoid watering by rule of thumb. Watch the soil carefully and give water when it appears to be getting dry. In all cases water warmed to the temperature of the house should be used.

HUMIDITY. A fairly damp atmosphere must be maintained throughout the season of growth except for a week or ten days when the vines are in flower and again when the grapes are colouring. For the first few weeks, until the shoots are 4 or 5 in. long, the vines should be syringed daily with tepid water. Subsequently shallow trays placed over the hot water pipes should be kept full of water and the floor of the house be damped once or twice daily.

In addition to the mulch of dung applied before starting the vine into growth a further mulch should be applied when the berries are set and commencing to swell. In addition it is advisable to give a potash fertiliser such as sulphate of potash each autumn, 3 oz. per sq. yd., and a compound vine manure may be used in winter or spring according to manufacturers' instructions.

STOPPING AND DISBUDDING. A great deal of the pruning of the vine is done by a process of disbudding and pinching carried out throughout the spring and summer. The ideal is to have one side growth approximately every 15 in. on each side of the main rod. Any surplus side growths over and above this number are rubbed out as soon as possible. Each selected side growth is pinched either two leaves beyond the point at which it produces a bunch of flowers or, if it fails to produce flowers, when it has reached a length of 2 to 3 ft. Any subsidiary side growths which come from it are stopped at the first leaf. The main rod is stopped when it reaches the apex of the house.

TYING. All young growth must be tied down to the training wires a little at a time. The shoots are very brittle to begin with and if pulled down too quickly will snap off. The method is to loop a piece of soft raffia around the tip of the growth, attach the other end of the tie to the wire and then shorten the tie daily until the growth lies parallel with the wire.

FERTILISATION. This can be ensured partly by correct temperature and ventilation and partly by jarring the vines daily while in bloom or dusting the flowers with a camel hair brush.

THINNING. About a fortnight after the berries are set, thinning should be carried out. This is a skilled job and it is not easy to tell the novice exactly what to remove and what to retain. Speaking generally a vine bunch contains about twice as many berries as it can develop fully. The surplus must be cut out with a special pair of pointed, vine scissors. All berries at the tips of the branchlets should be retained and the thinning confined mainly to the interior of the bunch. It should be most drastic towards the point and least severe around the shoulders, which will in any case extend and so give the berries more room to develop.

Great care must be taken not to bruise the very tender fruits. The bunches should not be touched by hand but may be held and turned as necessary with a small, forked stick.

Thinning should so far as possible be completed at one operation but the novice will usually find it necessary to go back to the bunches two or three times during the following weeks.

PRUNING. Winter pruning is not done until all the leaves have fallen from the vine. It can in most cases be left with advantage until the early part of December, later in the case of late vines. Do not, however, delay after the beginning of January or sap may be rising in which case the cut surfaces may bleed. When bleeding does occur it must be checked at once. This can be done either by treating the cut surface with a styptic or by charring them with a red hot iron.

If the summer stopping and disbudding has been properly done winter pruning is really very simple. All laterals, whether they have carried fruit or not, are shortened to two buds and that is all there is to it. Some growers prefer to cut back to one bud, arguing that as only one new lateral will be required at each spur the following spring, one bud is sufficient. Personally I prefer to have two as an insurance. If both start into growth the weaker can be rubbed out. If one fails there is a second string to one's bow.

CLEANING. Directly pruning has been completed any loose bark on the main rod should be removed. This loose bark is only likely to be found on the older vines. Contrary to oft-repeated advice it is not wise to scrape vines with either an old kitchen knife or any other implement. Simply rub the loose bark off with the palm of the hand. Then paint the whole rod thoroughly with Gishurst Compound, using an old, stiff paint brush for the purpose. Work this compound well into any rough places. Its purpose is to kill mealy bugs and other insects.

WINTER TREATMENT. During the winter from the time the grapes are cut until it is desired to start the vine into growth, the freest possible ventilation should be given and no artificial heat should be used. The vine rods themselves are perfectly hardy and should be encouraged to become thoroughly dormant during the winter.

During this dormant period it is an advantage to untie the main rods from the training wires and let them hang down on long strings. Incidentally it is convenient to do this before pruning as it saves the use of steps for this operation. The vines should be allowed to continue hanging until the new shoots are 2 or 3 in. long in the spring, after which the rod should be tied back in the normal position. The purpose of this is to encourage complete dormancy in winter and even out the flow of sap when it starts to rise. With the vines in their normal position the sap will tend to flow to the top first with the result that the lower eyes may not start into growth.

VARIETIES. There are many varieties of grape but for greenhouse cultivation the amateur need only be concerned with the following seven. Black Hamburgh is the best all round variety for heated or unheated houses, an easliy grown grape of good quality. Muscat of Alexandria is a pale yellow grape which sets the standard for quality but it is more difficult to grow and needs warmth. Gros Colmar is remarkable for the size of the black berries and is very late ripening but is of inferior quality. Foster's Seedling is a good white grape for an unheated or slightly heated greenhouse. Madresfield Court is an early ripening black grapes of good quality and Mrs. Pince and Alicante are black grapes which keep well and were once much grown but are not so reliable as some of the others named.

MEDLARS

Medlars are seldom planted in great quantity in this country but one or two trees make an acceptable feature in the garden and are valuable for ornament as well as for the crop which they will give.

SOIL. Unlike most fruit trees the medlar succeeds best in rather moist types of soil though they must not be so damp that they become seriously waterlogged in winter. A fairly stiff loam is ideal. Lighter soils can be made suitable by a liberal use of dung and well-rotted compost. The situation should be open and as sunny as possible.

TYPES OF TREE. Usually medlars are grown as standards or half standards. Occasionally bushes are grown but these are not on the whole so satisfactory and certainly not so ornamental. At least 25 ft. should be left between standards, 15 ft. between bushes.

PROPAGATION. Medlars are increased by grafting or budding on to suitable stocks. Any of the ordinary pear stocks (see p. 724) may be used for this purpose and the work is done in exactly the same way as for pears.

AGE OF TREE. Start with trees not more than four years old whenever possible.

PLANTING. This should be done at any time between late October and mid-March when the soil is in good working order. Details are as for apples.

TREATMENT OF YOUNG TREES. The same as for apples (see p. 678).

PRUNING. In the early stages of growth pruning is carried out in the same way as for apples. Established trees that have come into bearing are seldom pruned at all. The most they are likely to need is an occasional thinning of overcrowded branches and the removal of any wood that has become damaged or diseased. This should be done in autumn, as soon as possible after leaf fall.

FEEDING. As a rule very little feeding is required after the first few years but if the trees fail to make satisfactory growth they may be mulched with well-rotted dung each spring and treated with a potassic fertiliser such as sulphate of potash, 1 oz. per sq. yd., each autumn.

THINNING. No thinning is necessary.

PICKING AND STORING. Medlars should be allowed to hang on the trees as late as possible in the autumn but not after they commence to fall. Usually they must be gathered towards the end of October or in the early part of November. They are not at that time quite ready for use and should be laid in single layers, with the eye of each fruit downwards, on a shelf in any cool, dry but airy place, such as a store shed or spare room. After a few weeks the fruits will become much darker and develop the soft condition known as bletted. At this stage the flesh looks rather like that of a banana which is over ripe. It is at this stage that medlars are ready for table.

VARIETIES. Dutch, Nottingham and Royal are all reliable.

MELONS

From the cultural standpoint melons more closely resemble vegetables than fruits and some may argue that if tomatoes and cucumbers are to be included amongst vegetables, melons should find their right place there likewise. Nevertheless custom decrees that the melon should be classified with fruits rather than with vegetables. Hence its inclusion here.

SOILS. As melons are almost always grown either in a greenhouse or frame, the soil can be specially prepared for them in a way that is impossible with more permanent fruits. The compost must be rich and open in texture, in fact very similar to that employed for cucumbers.

A satisfactory mixture can be prepared with 3 parts by bulk of turfy medium loam, 1 part well-rotted stable manure and a liberal sprinkling of bone meal and wood ashes. This should be spread to a depth of about 6 in. over a porous base such as a good layer of clinkers or clean straw. The bed should be about 3 ft. wide and of any convenient length. Every 3 ft. a low, rounded mound should be made with about two bucketfuls of the same compost. One plant will be placed on the summit of each mound. The object of this is to ensure perfect drainage at the collar of the plant, i.e. where the stem enters the soil.

RAISING SEEDLINGS. Melons are propagated from seed, which is germinated in a warm greenhouse for an early crop or an unheated greenhouse or frame for a late summer crop. A minimum temperature of about 65° is necessary for germination, so in the unheated greenhouse it is seldom wise to sow before the beginning of May. In a heated house the first sowing can be made in January, provided the necessary temperature can be maintained throughout.

The seeds are sown singly in small, well-drained flower pots, filled with the usual seed compost (see p. 423). The seed pots should be plunged to their rims in coconut fibre or peat in a box or propagating frame stood over the heating apparatus or hot water pipes, and covered with glass or a light, the object being to maintain as damp an atmosphere as possible.

Germination is, as a rule, rapid. As soon as the seedlings appear ventilation should be given and a few days later the pots may be removed to the ordinary staging of the greenhouse.

PLANTING. By the time the young plants have their fourth true leaf they may be planted on the previously prepared mounds. Be careful not to plant too deeply, in fact only just to cover the soil in the pot ball. Water in well and decrease ventilation for a few days until growth resumes freely.

TRAINING. The principal shoot of each plant is trained to wires fixed as for vines (see p. 709). It should be led directly towards the apex of the house following the lines of the roof rafters. Side growths are tied out along the training wires and are stopped when they have made about 1 ft. of growth each. The main shoot is itself stopped when it has grown about 6 ft.

FERTILISING FLOWERS. Flowers and fruits will be produced on the side growths only. There are two sorts of flower, male and female, and they can be distinguished easily by the fact that immediately beneath each female flower is an embryo fruit rather like a large pea, whereas the male flower has nothing but a thin stalk.

It is essential that the female flowers which are to produce fruits should be fertilised by pollen from the males. Moreover no fruit must be allowed to get ahead of any other on one particular plant. In consequence as far as possible all the flowers required on one plant must be set on the same day. This is assured by picking off all female flowers until the plant is well developed and four flowers open approximately together on different side growths. This will usually be about one month after planting out. These four selected female blooms must be fertilised by securing a male flower, not necessarily from the same plant, that has ripe pollen on it, and dusting this over the centre of each female bloom. A good test for the pollen is to stroke the flower across the palm of the hand. If the pollen is ripe, yellow dust-like grains will be seen quite clearly on the skin.

It is advisable to fertilise the same flowers two or three times on successive days. As far as possible the work should be done when the sun is shining and towards midday. The atmosphere of the house should be allowed to dry a little and the temperature to rise a few degrees. If fertilisation is successful the fruits will commence to swell rapidly in a few days. If instead they turn yellow, it will be necessary to look for a fresh set of female flowers and treat them in the same way.

FEEDING AND GENERAL MANAGEMENT. Ventilation throughout should be as free as possible consistent with a minimum temperature of 65°, rising to 80° or 85° on sunny days.

Throughout the plants should be watered freely but care should be taken to keep the collar of each plant dry. Failure to observe this point may result in canker of the main stem at or just above soil level. Some growers place a zinc collar round the bottom of each plant to protect it from accidental splashes of water. It is also good policy to sprinkle the base of the plant with sulphur from time to time.

After a few weeks, white rootlets will appear on the surface of the compost. At this stage give a top dressing, 1 in. thick, of well-rotted stable manure mixed with an equal bulk of good soil. Repeat this dressing as often as roots re-appear on the surface. No other feeding is required.

As the fruits gain in size they must be supported. This is done with special melon nets, one to each fruit, the net itself being slung to the training wires beneath the rafters.

CULTIVATION IN FRAMES. The only difference in the treatment of melons in frames from that of melons in greenhouses, is in the training.

Two plants are sufficient for an ordinary 6 ft. by 4 ft. frame. They should be set as nearly as possible equidistant on the centre line of the frame, that is to say about 2 ft. from each end and 2 ft. from each side.

The point is pinched out of each plant when it is about 6 in. in height. Subsequently four shoots only are retained per plant and these are trained towards the four corners of the frame. They can be pegged in position with pieces of galvanised wire bent to the shape of hair pins. These primary runners are stopped when they reach the confines of the frame. Fruits can either be produced on them or on secondary side growths from them, whichever is more convenient.

The same instructions apply regarding fertilisation of all flowers on one day. Sometimes it is possible to obtain four fruits per plant in frames but as a rule two or three fruits are sufficient.

Unless the frames are heated it is unwise to plant in them before the first week in June.

VARIETIES. Good melons for frame and greenhouse culture are Cantaloupe, Hero of Lockinge, King George, Superlative and Tiger.

MULBERRY

Like the medlar, the mulberry is usually a lone tree in the garden, grown as much for ornament as for utility. Nevertheless it can be extremely profitable, old mulberries in particular bearing very heavy crops.

SOILS. This should be rather rich and well supplied with moisture though not waterlogged, in fact very much the kind of soil which would grow culinary plums well. The situation must be open and sunny and plenty of room should be allowed, for though mulberries grow slowly at first, they make big trees in the long run. Preparation should be thorough and a moderate amount of well-rotted dung can be mixed with the soil before planting. Lime is not essential. It is a good plan to add coarse bone meal at 4 oz. per sq. yd. and kainit at 3 oz. per sq. yd.

TYPES OF TREE. Mulberries are almost always grown as standards. Occasionally one may see bushes but these are not so satisfactory because of the spreading habit of the branches.

PROPAGATION. The simplest method of increasing mulberries is by layering. For this purpose fairly young branches should be used and pegged down to the soil in autumn.

Seed is sometimes employed as a means of propagation but is not very satisfactory. It is germinated outdoors in March.

Cuttings will root if prepared partly from current and partly from two year old wood. These cuttings should be about 15 in. long and must be taken in autumn. They are inserted firmly 4 or 5 in. deep in rather sandy soil in a sheltered position outdoors.

A fourth method of propagation is by grafting good forms of mulberry on to seedling mulberries. This is done in March in the same manner as for apples.

FERTILITY. It must be fairly obvious to all that mulberries are self fertile from the fact that as already stated the trees are usually isolated and there is seldom another mulberry in the immediate neighbourhood.

AGE OF TREE. Because mulberries are usually slow in coming into bearing there is a temptation to start with well-developed trees already five or six years old. This is a mistake as such trees invariably suffer a severe check when transplanted and take some years to recover. It is far better to begin with two or three year old specimens even though this may mean waiting ten or twelve years for fruit.

PLANTING. The period of semi-dormancy from about mid-October to mid-March is the correct time for planting mulberries with the emphasis more than ever on the early part of that time. If planting can be completed by the end of October so much the better. If more than one tree is to be planted fully 30 ft. must be left between them.

The roots tend to spread laterally to a considerable extent and must be accommodated in wide, rather shallow holes. The uppermost roots should be covered with 5 in. of soil and staking should be secure from the outset.

TREATMENT OF YOUNG TREES. This is exactly the same as for young apples.

PRUNING. Young trees are formed and branches obtained where required by the methods detailed on pp. 658-9. Bear in mind the ultimate spreading habit of the mulberry and allow ample space between branches that are one above the other. Once the main framework of branches is formed, little further pruning is required. All the work should be done in autumn immediately after leaf-fall.

FEEDING. Young trees can be fed in the same way as plums but old trees seldom require any attention except possibly an occasional top dressing of dung in spring.

THINNING. Unnecessary.

PICKING AND STORING. Mulberries are ready to pick when they become a dark crimson in late August or early September. They cannot be kept by any other means than bottling.

PEACHES AND NECTARINES

Like the apricot these are fruits for sunny regions and they can only be grown outdoors with success in warm parts of the country. They do well under glass if given plenty of light and ventilation and not permitted to become over heated in the summer. The nectarine is simply a smooth skinned form of the peach and is identical in every other aspect.

SOILS. A medium loamy soil gives the best results and good drainage is absolutely essential. In greenhouses it generally pays to make up a special border for the trees, excavating the existing soil to a depth of 2 ft. or more, a width of at least 4 ft. and a length of at least 6 ft. per tree and replacing with chopped turf mixed with about one twelfth its own bulk of well-rotted dung, a similar quantity of old mortar rubble and a good sprinkling of coarsely crushed bones and wood ashes. In any case a good layer of clinkers or land drain pipes should be placed in the bottom of the bed connecting with a main drain or soak-away outside to take away surplus moisture.

Outdoors peaches and nectarines succeed best against walls facing south or south-west. In a few very mild places they can also be grown in the open without any form of protection but this is rare.

TYPES OF TREE. The fan system of training is almost invariably followed both with glasshouse trees and with those planted against walls outdoors. Such trees should be planted a minimum of 15 ft. apart. Occasionally small bushes are formed in pots, and bushes are also being trained out of doors in the southern half of England with some success.

STOCKS AND PROPAGATION. Peaches and nectarines can be raised easily from stones. This is rather a pity as amateurs frequently do it and are then bitterly disappointed with the quality of the resultant fruit. Seedlings seldom come up to their parents in any respect, least of all quality, and are generally serviceable only as stocks for well tried varieties.

Budding is the best method of increase and should be done in July or early August in the same manner as for apples or plums. Plum stocks or seedling almonds are most commonly used to provide the necessary roots. Of the former Brompton appears to be most satisfactory.

FERTILITY. All varieties of both peach and nectarine appear to be fully self-fertile but as they are dependent on bees for fertilisation and in this country flower too early to be reliably pollinated by such means, it is advisable to go over the fully open blossom with a rabbit's tail or camel hair brush. As far as possible this should be done on fine, sunny days when the pollen is dry and parting readily from the anthers.

SEASON. By planting early, mid-season and late varieties, starting some into growth with artifical heat and leaving others to start naturally in unheated houses, it is possible to pick ripe peaches and nectarines from June to October. The fruits cannot be stored by any means and the only method of extending the season beyond these dates is by bottling or canning.

AGE OF TREE. Once again it is necessary to impress the importance of starting with quite young trees, certainly no more than three years old. Maidens or two year old specimens transplant even better but, of course, take a little longer to come into bearing. However, peaches and nectarines properly managed are not slow in cropping and will usually give some fruit by their fifth or sixth year.

PLANTING. This can be done at any time from mid-October to mid-March but early planting is desirable, particularly under glass, and is then usually possible as soil conditions are under the gardener's control. In other respects planting follows the general lines already detailed on pp. 633–4, the only point to add being that, when planting against walls outdoors, it is desirable to keep the base of the tree at least 9 in. away from the wall rather than plant hard up against it.

TREATMENT OF YOUNG TREES. Pruning after planting should be very severe to ensure strong growth the first season. For the same reason two mulches of strawy manure may be given, the first in March and the second in May or early June. Watering should be generous even with outside trees as against walls they seldom get sufficient moisture from natural rainfall.

PRUNING. In the early stages the framework of the tree is built up as described on pp. 659–60. The main branches of fan trained specimens should be approximately 1 ft. apart and side growths may be laid in between these as close as 6 in. to one another.

By about the third year it will be possible to modify this initial pruning and encourage the production of some flowers and fruit. The system employed is the same as that used for Morello and other sour cherries. Peaches and nectarines bear on year-old side growths and a sufficient but not excessive number of these must be obtained annually.

The method is to remove all unwanted shoots, a few at a time, quite early in the season, usually in May and June. Roughly speaking two new side growths are retained for each fruiting side growth, one as near as possible to its base and the other at its tip. The former will replace it in the autumn whilst the latter is retained solely to draw sap through the fruiting lateral and so assist in the swelling and ripening of the crop.

In the autumn, as soon as the fruit has been gathered, it simply remains to cut out the old laterals entirely and train the young growths in their place. Note particularly that frame work pruning to extend the tree further and obtain more branches, may be going on concurrently with the pruning for fruit which I have just described.

WATERING. The first essential with peaches and nectarines, particularly those under glass, is to give the soil a very thorough soaking of water before they start into growth in late winter. As much as 50 gals. per sq. yd. may be necessary at this stage as it is the only period at which subsoil reserves can be replenished.

In addition to the winter watering, more water will be required whenever the border shows signs of dryness and sufficient must be given to soak well down. Under glass the trees should be syringed daily with house warmed water throughout the growing season except during the time when they are in bloom and while the peaches are colouring.

FEEDING. Just as the trees start into growth a mulch of well-rotted dung, 1 cwt. to 6 sq. yd., should be given. This may be supplemented in the case of old trees that are making insufficient new growth by a nitrogenous fertiliser such as Nitro-chalk, 1 to 2 oz. per sq. yd. In autumn give sulphate of potash, 2 oz. per sq. yd., and in alternate years basic slag, 6 oz. per sq. yd. and hydrated lime 8 oz. per sq. yd.

TEMPERATURE. Ventilation should be as free as possible throughout while avoiding draughts and sudden drops in temperature. Overheating and too dry an atmosphere will almost certainly result in an attack by red spiders or frog flies.

Great heat is undesirable at any time. Early peaches and nectarines can be started into growth in February by closing the house and raising the temperature to 50°. In the summer every effort should be made to keep the temperature below 80°. After the crop has been gathered the peach and nectarine house should be thrown wide open, for, as with grape vines, it is essential that peaches and nectarines should become completely dormant during the winter months.

VARIETIES. Good peaches are Duke of York, July; Dymond, September; Hale's Early, July; Peregrine, August; Royal George, September, and Sea Eagle, September. Of these Hale's Early is one of the most reliable for outdoor planting.

Good nectarines are Early Rivers, July; Elruge, August; Humboldt, August–September; Lord Napier, August; Pine Apple, September and River's Orange, September. Of these Early Rivers is the best for outdoor planting.

PEARS

Pears are not quite as satisfactory in this country as either apples or plums but they do well in some districts, particularly those with plenty of sunshine. They are quite suitable for small gardens as they respond to pruning well and can be trained in restricted forms.

SOILS. A medium to light, well-drained loam is the best type of soil. In other respects it needs similar conditions to the apple. As the flowering season is early, it is advisable to choose a sheltered position otherwise there is danger of the blossom either being killed outright by frost or at any rate being damaged so badly that fertilisation is impeded.

The ground should be prepared in exactly the same way as for apples with a moderate dressing of manure and extra potash, particularly if this is believed to be deficient in the soil. Heavy soils which are liable to become waterlogged in winter must be drained adequately.

The choicest varieties of dessert pear crop most satisfactorily when planted against a wall facing south or south-west.

TYPES OF TREE. All the forms commonly employed for apples may also be used for pears but only the less choice varieties should be planted as standards or half standards. The best dessert pears should always be grown as small bushes, pyramids, espalier trained trees or cordons. Pears make particularly good cordons as most varieties form fruit buds freely and submit to severe pruning readily.

Planting distances are as for apples.

STOCKS AND PROPAGATION. This is always done by budding or grafting in the same way as for apples. Budding is carried out between mid-July and early September and grafting towards the end of March or early in April.

There are two main groups of stock, the one seedlings, which may be obtained from garden pears, perry pears or wildings, and the other quince. The seedling stocks are in general more vigorous than the quince stocks and are therefore more suitable for large trees such as standards and half standards. However the quince is itself variable and an effort has been made to classify the different types in a similar manner to the Paradise stocks for apples. Three of these types are of importance to the fruit grower and they are known respectively as Malling A., Malling B. and Malling C. The first two are moderately vigorous and suitable for bushes on soils of average fertility. Malling C. is more dwarfing and should be used for cordons and other trained trees. There is a fourth variety of quince, Malling D., which should be avoided as trees worked on it frequently break or blow out. All can be raised by layers in the same way as Paradise apple stocks and by this means can be kept absolutely true to type.

Not all varieties of pear make a good union direct with the quince stock in any of these forms. Examples are Jargonelle, Joséphine de Malines, Marguerite Marrilat, Marie Louise, Souvenir de Congrès and to a lesser extent Dr. Jules Guyot and Williams. When these varieties are to be grown on quince stocks they are double worked, that is to say first of all another variety that is known to make a good union with quince is grafted to it and then, when it is growing nicely, it is cut back and the incompatible variety is grafted on to it. Pitmaston Duchess and Fertility are often used as intermediate stocks in this way.

FERTILITY. Most varieties are partially self-fertile, that is to say they will set some fruit with their own pollen but give a better crop if pollinated from another pear tree of different variety. There is little or no incompatibility between one variety and another but a few are unsatisfactory pollinators because they produce little pollen. Provided several varieties of pear are planted fairly near together and they all bloom at approximately the same time, there is unlikely to be much difficulty in securing proper fertilisation as long as the weather is favourable at blossom time and the position is a suitable one. In this respect, however, it should be noted that the pear, like the apple, is dependent on bees to carry pollen and if the weather is cold, damp or windy, or the position very exposed, these insects may not venture far from the hive. Under such conditions it is wise to pollinate by hand with a rabbit's tail or camel hair brush, bringing the pollen from one tree to another.

SEASON. By planting early, mid-season and late varieties and storing the two last correctly ripe pears can be enjoyed from the end of July until Christmas or later.

GOOD VARIETIES OF PEAR

Name	Use	Season	Pick	Type	Colour	Flavour	Pruning	Flowering	Fertility	Cropping
Beurré d'Amanlis	D	September	As ripe	medium, pear-shaped	yellow, flushed brown	good	moderate to upward pointing buds	early	SS	good
Beurré Bedford	D	October	September	large, tapering	yellow, flushed red	good	moderate	mid-season	PSF	good
Beurré Clairgeau	C	Nov.-Dec.	October	large, pear-shaped	yellow, flushed crimson	fair	moderate to outward pointing buds	early	PSF	very good
Beurré Diel	D	Oct.-Dec.	September	large, oval	yellow, flushed brown	good	hard	mid-season	SS	fair
Beurré Hardy	D	October	September	medium, conical	brown, russet	very good	light	early	PSF	irregular
Beurré Superfin	D	October	September	medium, pear-shaped	yellow	very good	fairly hard	mid-season	PSF	good
Calebasse Bosc Catillac	D C	Sept.-Oct. Dec.-Apr.	September October	very long large, round	brown russet green	fair good cooked	hard light	early mid-season	PSF SS	unreliable irregular
Clap's Favourite	D	Aug.-Sept.	as ripe	medium, pear-shaped	yellow, striped red	good	moderate to outward pointing buds	mid-season	PSF	good
Conference Dr. Jules Guyot	D D	Oct.-Nov. September	late Sept. as ripe	medium, long large, oval	green, russet yellow, slight flush	very good good	moderate fairly hard to outward pointing buds	early late	PSF PSF	very good good
Doyenné du Comice	D	November	October	medium, broad pear-shaped	golden russet	very good	moderate fairly hard	late	PSF	unreliable
Doyenné d'Ete	D	July-Aug.	as ripe	small, round	yellow, flushed brown	fair	hard	early	SS	good
Durondeau	D	Oct.-Nov.	late Sept.	large, pear-shaped	brown, flushed red	very good	light	early	PSF	good
Emile d'Heyst Fertility	D CD	Oct.-Nov. October	late Sept. September	long, oval medium, conical	yellow yellow, russet	good poor	hard fairly hard	early late	PSF PSF	good very good

GLOU MORCEAU	D	Dec.-Jan.	October	large, round	green	very good	fairly hard to upward pointing buds	late	PSF	good
HESSLE (HAZEL)	D	October	September	small, round	brown	fair	light	late	PSF	very good
JARGONELLE	D	August	as ripe	medium, long	greenish yellow	good	light	early	SS	very good
JOSÉPHINE DE MALINES	D	Dec.-Feb.	October	small, conical	greenish yellow	very good	light	mid-season	SS	good
LAXTON'S SUPERB	D	Aug.-Sept.	as ripe	medium, pear-shaped	yellow	good	fairly hard	mid-season	PFS	very good
LOUISE BONNE OF JERSEY	D	October	late Sept.	medium, conical	yellow, flushed red	very good	fairly hard	early	PSF	very good
MARGUERITE MARILLAT	D	Sept.-Oct.	September	large, pear-shaped	yellow, flushed red	fair	moderate to outward pointing buds	mid-season	SS	good
MARIE LOUISE	D	Oct.-Nov.	late Sept.	medium, oval	greenish yellow	good	fairly hard	late	PSF	good
PITMASTON DUCHESS	CD	Oct.-Nov.	late Sept.	large, pear-shaped	yellow	fair	moderate	late	SS	unreliable
SECKLE	D	Oct.-Nov.	late Sept.	small, round	brown	very good	hard to outward pointing buds	mid-season	PSF	good
SOUVENIR DE CONGRÈS	D	September	as ripe	large, pear-shaped	yellow, flushed red	good	fairly hard	early	PSF	good
TRIOMPHE DE VIENNE	D	September	as ripe	medium, conical	yellow, flushed red	good	moderate	late	PSF	good
VICAR OF WINKFIELD	C	Nov.-Jan.	October	large, long	green	good cooked	light	early	SS	very good
WILLIAMS EON CHRÉTIEN	D	September	as ripe	large, pear-shaped	yellow, slight flush	good	fairly hard	mid-season	PSF	very good
WINTER NELIS	D	Nov.-Jan.	October	small, round	green to yellowish	very good	hard	late	PSF	good

Abbreviations: C, cooking; D, dessert; CD, cooking or dessert; SS, self-sterile; P.S.F., partially self-fertile. Note that CONFERENCE is not a suitable pollinator for BEURRÉ D'AMANLIS, nor is SECKLE for LOUISE BONNE. Varieties marked sterile should not be planted alone nor used as pollinators for other pears. Even partially self-fertile varieties will give better crops if associated with other varieties of pear flowering at approximately the same time.

AGE OF TREE. All the remarks I have made under this heading regarding apples apply equally here.

PLANTING. This follows exactly the same lines as with apples, with perhaps a little more emphasis on planting only when the soil is in tip top condition. It is on the whole better to work in the late October–early November period or in February–March rather than in midwinter when conditions are seldom favourable.

TREATMENT OF YOUNG TREES. Precisely the same as for apples.

PRUNING. The general principles of pruning described in Chapter XXVI apply to pears but as most varieties make fruit buds and spurs more readily than apples it is possible to be a little more severe without upsetting the balance of growth. It is for this reason that most pears make such good trained trees. If side growths are shortened to about five leaves in late July or early August, many of them will have commenced to form fruit buds by the autumn and can be cut back to 2 or 3 in. then. However, this severe treatment is not essential and when pears are grown as standards, half standards or bushes and the main framework of branches has been formed, they can, if desired, be left pretty much alone.

A few varieties have the habit of forming fruit buds at the tips of shoots. With these kinds light pruning is particularly desirable. The most familiar examples are Jargonelle and Josephine de Malines.

Because of the freedom with which spurs are produced it may be necessary to carry out drastic spur thinning or reduction in the case of old trees. De-horning (see p. 664) is also beneficial if insufficient new growth is being made.

FEEDING. Here again the general instructions given for apples apply also to pears, the two most vital foods being nitrogen and potash. There is, however, if anything a little greater necessity for nitrogen with pears than with apples and in consequence spring dressings of manure can be a little heavier, say up to the rate of 1 cwt. to 10 sq. yd.

THINNING. This follows the general lines described for apples (p. 680) but should be a little more severe, especially for big dessert pears such as Pitmaston Duchess or Durondeau which may be left as much as 9 in. apart.

PICKING. Early pears are ready for picking at the end of July. Like early apples they will not keep and should be used up as gathered. The picking season continues until about mid-October and some of the later varieties will store for a period though few will last as long as the latest apples.

Storing. Pears must be stored in a warmer and drier atmosphere than that necessary for apples. A spare room or airy cupboard is a very good place in which to keep them and they should be spread out in single layers, not packed into boxes like apples. Once ripe they commence to decay from the centre very rapidly, a condition known as sleepiness, and quickly become unfit to eat. Pears in store should therefore be examined frequently and used directly they are in suitable condition.

PLUMS

Plums are easily grown in most parts of the country but on account of their very early flowering season are apt to crop unreliably in very cold or exposed places. Also they do not, as a rule, take kindly to very hard pruning and, as they frequently make a good deal of growth, they are not quite as suitable for small gardens as are apples or pears. Damsons on account of their hardiness, are sometimes planted as windbreaks.

Soil. The better grades of loam are most suitable. Plums require more nitrogen than apples or pears and more moisture during the growing season. For this reason plum orchards should never be grassed down in the way so common with apple orchards after the first few years. Good drainage is essential. The position should be reasonably open without being too exposed, for the reasons already explained.

The soil can be prepared by thorough digging and the addition of well-rotted dung or compost at the rate of 1 cwt. to 10–12 sq. yd. At the same time it is desirable to give extra potash either as wood ashes, 6–8 oz. per sq. yd., or sulphate of potash, $1\frac{1}{2}$ oz. per sq. yd.

Types of Tree. Plums succeed particularly well as standards or half standards as they can then be allowed to grow freely with a minimum of pruning once the head of branches has been formed. The drawback is that the trees soon get very large and all cultural operations become difficult, ladders being required for picking, etc. Both standards and half standards must be planted a minimum of 30 ft. apart. Plums can also be grown as bushes planted 15–20 ft. apart and choice dessert varieties are often trained against sunny walls, in which case the fan system is usually employed. Such specimens should be at least 15 ft. apart. Even when trained the more freedom the trees can be allowed the better, i.e. a high wall is better than a low one for plums.

Propagation. This is almost invariably by budding in summer though grafting in spring is also employed.

A number of stocks are used, the two most popular being Myrobalan and Brompton. Both can be increased by layering and in this way can be kept true to type in a manner impossible with seedling stocks. Several types of Myrobalan stock have been classified in the same way as the classified Paradise stocks of apples. Of these the most satisfactory so far is Myrobalan B., a vigorous stock which makes excellent standards or half standards.

Other stocks are Common Plum, Mussel, Pershore, St. Julian, Black Damas, Mariana and Brussels. Some incompatibility exists between certain of these stocks and some varieties of plum. For example Czar, Pond's Seedling, President and most of the Damsons do not make a satisfactory union with Common Plum though this is a very good, semi-dwarfing stock for many other varieties. Mariana is vigorous and increasing in favour. Suckers from the Pershore or Yellow Egg Plum make good stocks for plums that are to be trained or grown as small bushes.

There are just a few varieties of plum which are occasionally grown on their own roots and can in that case be increased by suckers. Notable amongst these are Blaisdon Red, Pershore and Warwickshire Drooper. The suckers are removed with roots in late October or early November and planted in the ordinary way. Note particularly, however, that this method of propagation is only possible if the plum is on its own roots. If it has been grafted or budded, the suckers will resemble the stock.

FERTILITY. Some plums are fully self-fertile but more are either self-sterile or partially self-sterile and need the presence of a mate flowering at approximately the same time.

It should be noted that poor fertility in plums is quite as often due to bad weather at blossom time as to lack of suitable pollen. Hand pollination and the provision of some shelter will often solve the fertility problem.

SEASON. The earliest plums are ripe towards the end of July and the season continues until early October. There is no method of keeping plums once they have been picked other than by bottling or canning.

AGE OF TREE. The remarks I have already made with regard to most tree fruits (see apples, pears, etc.), apply equally to plums. Other things being equal the younger the tree at the time of planting the more likely is it to make a good start. The drawback to planting young trees is that plums are sometimes slow in coming into bearing. If one starts with a maiden it may be six or seven years before one gathers any crop.

PLANTING. This should be done at the usual season for tree fruits, namely during any open weather from about the middle of October until the middle of March. Plums are surface rooting and in consequence must not be planted too deeply. Spread the roots out in wide, rather shallow holes and cover the uppermost with about 5 in. of soil. Be sure to plant very firmly and, in the case of large trees, make certain that these are properly staked; in fact two stakes per tree, one vertical and the other inclined towards direction of the prevailing wind are often desirable.

TREATMENT OF YOUNG TREES. Though established plums do not like hard pruning, it is advisable to be fairly severe after planting. In any case the main shoots must be cut back to the points at which branches are required as explained in the chapter on pruning (p. 658).

A good mulch of strawy manure or grass clippings applied in the spring following planting will help to keep the trees growing strongly. This is particularly important with plums in the early stages for if the trees hang fire at the outset it is sometimes difficult to get them going again. Apart from this no special treatment is called for during the first year.

PRUNING. Young trees are shaped by the ordinary methods applied to apples and pears but a change over should be made to lighter pruning at an earlier stage. This is not difficult because as a rule plums branch quite freely on their own account; in fact by the fourth or fifth year it may be necessary to carry out some thinning of branches to prevent overcrowding, rather than keep on pruning for fresh branch formation.

Once the trees are well formed very little pruning is required except in the case of trained specimens. Watch must be kept for dead or diseased wood so that this may be removed promptly. For the rest it is generally sufficient to cut out a crossing branch here and there and keep the centre of the tree reasonably open. It is an advantage to do as much as possible of this pruning in June or, if this is impossible because it would interfere too much with the crop, in early autumn directly the plums have been gathered. The reason for this departure from normal pruning practice is that there is less danger of infection by Silver Leaf, the worst disease of plums, if pruning is done in summer than if it is done in winter.

Trained trees can also be pruned to a very large extent during the summer months, the system followed being almost identical with that

GOOD VARIETIES OF PLUM

Name	Use	Season	Type	Colour	Flavour	Flowering	Fertility	Cropping
Belle de Louvain	C	August	large, egg-shaped	red	fair	late	SF	good
Bryanston Gage	D	September	medium, round	yellowish	very good	mid-season	SS	good
Blaisdon Red	C	September	medium, oval	red	poor	mid-season	SF	very good
Cambridge Gage	D	September	medium, round	green	very good	late	PSF	good
Coe's Golden Crop	D	September	medium, oval	yellow	very good	early	SS	fair
Czar	C	August	medium, round	black	poor	late	SF	very good
Denniston's Superb Gage	D	August	medium, round	yellow	very good	early	SF	good
Delicious	D	September	large, oval	red	very good			good
Early Transparent Gage	D	August	small, round	yellow	very good	early	SF	fair
Giant Prune	C	September	large, oval	purple	fair	mid-season	SF	good
Gisborne's Prolific	C	August	medium, oval	yellow	poor	late	SF	very good
Golden Transparent Gage	D	October	large, round	yellow	very good	late	SF	fair
Green Gage	D	August	medium, round	green	very good	mid-season	SF	fair
Jefferson's Gage	D	September	large, oval	yellow	very good	early	PSF	fair
Kirke's Blue	D	September	medium, round	purple	very good	late	SS	fair
Late Transparent Gage	D	September	large, round	yellow	very good	late	SS	fair
Magnum Bonum (Warwickshire Drooper)	D	September	medium, round	yellowish	good	early	PSF	good
Merryweather Damson	C	September	small, round	blue-black	good	mid-season	SF	very good
Monarch	C	September	large, round	purple	fair	early	SF	good
Oullin's Golden Gage	D	August	large, round	yellow	very good	late	SF	fair
Pershore	C	August	medium, egg-shaped	yellow	fair	late	SF	very good
Pond's Seedling	C	September	large, oval	red	fair	late	SS	good
President	C	October	large, oval	purple	good	early	SS	poor
Purple Pershore	C	August	medium, oval	red	fair	late	SF	very good
Rivers Early Prolific	C	July	small, round	black	good	early	PSF	good
Victoria	CD	August	large, oval	red	good	mid-season	SF	good
Warwickshire Drooper	C	September	large, oval	yellow	good	mid-season	SF	very good

Abbreviations: C, cooking; D, dessert; CD, cooking or dessert; SS, self-sterile; S.F., self-fertile; P.S.F., partially self-fertile. Self-sterile varieties should not be planted alone while even partially self-fertile varieties will give better crops if associated with other varieties of plums flowering at approximately the same time.

for apples, that is to say side growths which cannot be trained in at full length are shortened to about five leaves when they commence to get hard and woody at the base, which in practice usually means in the last half of July. These summer pruned side growths can be further cut back when they form fruit buds which may be either the same season or the following season.

FEEDING. This is similar to that carried out for apples but with greater emphasis on nitrogen and less on potash. The plum orchard must never be cultivated deeply because of the number of surface roots formed but a good mulch of dung or compost applied each spring will feed these roots and protect them at the same time. As much as 1 cwt. to 8 sq. yd. can be given to trees that are not making too much new growth. Failing dung or compost use a nitrogenous fertiliser such as Nitro-chalk 2 oz. per sq. yd. In any case give extra potash each autumn such as sulphate of potash, 1 oz. per sq. yd. Every alternate autumn give in addition basic slag at 6 oz. per sq. yd.

QUINCES

Surprisingly few quinces are grown in English gardens apparently because most English people do not know what use to make of the fruits. Perhaps if it were more generally realised what excellent jam and jelly they make and how freely the trees crop we might see more quinces.

SOIL. Quinces require precisely the same conditions as pears with perhaps a little more emphasis on moisture during the season of growth. This does not mean, however, that they will thrive in stagnant, water-logged soils. A good, rich loam with plenty of humus is ideal.

TYPES OF TREE. Quinces could be grown in practically any of the forms used for pears but are almost invariably grown as bushes.

PROPAGATION. The quince can be increased by layering (p. 640), and bushes which are known to be on their own roots can also be propagated by suckers detached with roots in autumn. Occasionally selected quinces are grafted or budded on to common forms, in which case, of course, the suckers will not be of the stock type and cannot be used to increase the improved variety worked on it.

FERTILITY. Quinces are fully self-fertile and incidentally will also serve to pollinate pears or can be pollinated by pears.

AGE OF TREE. As for pears.

PLANTING. As for pears.

TREATMENT OF YOUNG TREES. As for pears.

PRUNING. After the initial stages of formation, which is the same as for pears, very little pruning is required; just a little thinning out to prevent overcrowding and to preserve the chosen shape of the bush. This can be done in autumn or winter.

FEEDING. As a rule very little feeding is required but if the bushes do not make sufficient growth or fail to crop satisfactorily, they can be fed in the same manner as pears.

VARIETIES. The best variety is Meech's Prolific, with pear-shaped fruits. Apple or English is round fruited.

RASPBERRIES

There is no difficulty about the cultivation of raspberries and as they flower comparatively late it is possible to get crops in many places where other fruits fail. The principal point to observe is to purchase healthy stock at the outset. Raspberries are rather subject to disease and far too much of this has been distributed by nurseries. Government certified stock is now available and is generally to be preferred to uncertified canes.

SOIL. The conditions which suit raspberries best very closely resemble those required for black currants; that is to say the soil should be reasonably rich, well supplied with moisture during the spring and summer but not waterlogged in winter. The last point is of vital importance. There is probably no fruit which reacts more quickly to bad drainage and it is one of the commonest causes of failure.

The soil should be particularly well cultivated at the outset as raspberries make masses of fine roots just beneath the surface, in consequence of which very little cultivation can be carried out once the plantation has been made. The plot should be dug deeply, dressed with well-rotted dung at the rate of 1 cwt. to 8–10 sq. yd. and given additional potash such as sulphate of potash 2 oz. per sq. yd.

The situation may be open or in partial shade but should not be under overhanging trees.

PROPAGATION. The raspberry is increased by means of off-shoots or suckers which are freely produced without any special encouragement. These suckers should be removed with roots at any time during the normal planting season. The only important point to note is that suckers must not only be perfectly healthy themselves but must be produced from plants which are also healthy. Failure to observe this point results in the spread of disease and accounts for the weakness of so many raspberry plantations.

FERTILITY. No problems of self- or inter-fertility occur with raspberries. All varieties will set fruit with their own pollen and as a rule no difficulties occur. Occasionally one meets plantations in which the set is very bad or many of the fruits are malformed. More often than not this is due to a faulty strain, that is to say it is a hereditary characteristic. The only remedy is to scrap the entire stock and replant with good canes. Bad setting may also be due to attacks by the Raspberry Beetle (see p. 785).

SEASON. The normal raspberry season is July but there are also kinds which fruit in the autumn and at least one variety, Lloyd George, will often bear a double crop, one in summer and another in autumn. The difficulty with the autumn fruits, however, is that frequently they form so late that they fail to ripen properly.

AGE OF PLANTS. Only year old canes can be used for planting as, after fruiting, the canes die down and only the young growth remains. Indeed the raspberry plantation itself should not be retained too long. My own policy is to re-make a quarter of the plantation every year.

PLANTING. This can be done at any time from October to March inclusive but the best results are seldom obtained from mid-winter planting. If the work cannot be completed by the middle of November it is generally best to leave it until March. Late planting often gives very good results providing the plants are well cared for and not allowed to suffer from drought.

Plant the canes singly 2 ft. apart in rows 6 ft. apart. Spread the roots out widely and only cover the uppermost with 2 in. of soil. Make the soil very firm.

TREATMENT OF YOUNG PLANTS. After planting the canes must be cut back to within about 9 in. of soil level. In the case of autumn planted stock this can be done the following February. If planting is left to the spring pruning should be done immediately. No crop will be produced the first year except in the case of autumn fruiting varieties but the hard pruning should result in plenty of young growth to fruit the following year. These new canes are generally tied to wires strained between posts, 8–10 ft. apart. As a rule two training wires are sufficient, one 2 ft. and the other 5 ft. above ground level. However I have found it possible to grow some varieties without any support.

A generous mulch of strawy manure or grass clippings should be spread all over the plantation in April or early May. Weeds should be removed by hand or by very light hoeing. At no time must a fork or spade be used near raspberry canes because of the surface roots to which I have already made reference.

No pruning of summer fruiting varieties will be required the first year, after the initial hard cutting back described above.

PRUNING. In subsequent years summer fruiting raspberries are pruned as soon as possible after the crop has been gathered. All the canes that have just borne fruit are cut out at ground level. Some growers reduce the young canes to six or seven per root at the same time, choosing those that are strongest and nearest to the training wires. My own policy is to allow the plants rather more freedom. The young canes are thinned to about 9 in. apart and any which are growing right out in the alley-ways between the rows are removed but otherwise each plant is allowed to spread to a considerable extent. In this way after a year or so a row of raspberries presents rather the appearance of a thin hedge, perhaps 2 ft. or more wide and with canes evenly spaced throughout. I find that very good crops are obtainable in this way and that a minimum of support is required. After the first year I often dispense with training wires altogether in the case of compact varieties such as Lloyd George. It also appears that the fruits benefit from the shade provided by the surrounding canes, but more feeding and mulching is required because of the heavy demands made on the soil.

Some varieties grow very strongly and with these it is desirable to shorten the young canes a little in February. They may be cut back to a level height of about 6 ft. With shorter kinds this supplementary pruning is not necessary.

A different system of pruning is needed for autumn fruiting raspberries. These are left until February when all the canes are cut back to within 9 in. of soil level.

In the case of Lloyd George and other varieties which are mainly summer fruiting but may also produce a small autumn crop, the best policy is to prune as for summer raspberries and then, in February, to shorten by a foot or so any canes which, in autumn, bore fruit at their tips only and to remove any canes which, in autumn, fruited throughout their length.

FEEDING. The most important item in the routine feeding of raspberries is a good annual mulch of strawy dung applied in March or April at the rate of 1 cwt. to 6 or 8 sq. yd. This serves the dual purpose of feeding the roots and protecting them from drought. The dung can be used at the rate of 1 cwt. to 8 sq. yd. but it must be well decayed. Failing dung, decayed vegetable refuse such as grass clippings can be used in the same way.

Additional potash should be given either at the same time or in autumn. Sulphate of potash is the most suitable form and can be used at $1\frac{1}{2}$–2 oz. per sq. yd.

VIRUS DISEASE. Raspberries are liable to be attacked by incurable virus diseases which may sap them of strength and greatly reduce cropping. That known as mosaic is particularly common. It produces a yellow mottling or variegation of the leaves and reduced growth. Some varieties are more susceptible than others or suffer more severely. Lloyd George is one of the worst in these respects. The Ministry of Agriculture certifies some stocks as free from virus and these are to be preferred to uncertified stocks unless it is known that these are free of infection.

VARIETIES. Good raspberries are Hailsham, autumn fruiting; Lloyd George, summer and autumn; Norfolk Giant, July; Newburgh, July; Pyne's Royal, July, and Red Cross, June–July. A good yellow-fruited variety is Yellow Antwerp.

STRAWBERRIES

Strawberries are not at all difficult to grow. The only trouble is that so many plants are required in order to get good pickings throughout the season. Most amateurs make the mistake of having too small a strawberry bed with the result that they can only fill a dish with fruit for a few days at the height of the season. Really a bed of a hundred plants is about the smallest that is serviceable for a family of two adults and two children.

SOIL. Most strawberries do well on rich, medium to heavy loams provided they are properly drained in winter. A few varieties, such as Royal Sovereign, do well on sandy loams. If drainage is bad the plants are apt to rot but this difficulty can be overcome by planting along the summits of broad, low ridges. On light soils it is essential to manure heavily, as much to maintain moisture in summer as for the sake of the food which the dung contains. In any case the soil must be dug deeply and it is wise to add dung or compost at the rate of not less than 5 cwt. per rod. Phosphates are of more importance with strawberries than with other fruits and in consequence bone meal can be used in the initial preparation at 4 oz. per sq. yd. Additional potash should be given as for raspberries.

PROPAGATION. Alpine strawberries, which are varieties with very small fruits and a prolonged fruiting season, are usually increased by seed which can be raised in a warm greenhouse in February or in a frame in March–April. The seedlings, after hardening off, are planted out in June. They fruit a little the first summer and give a full crop the second year.

All the familiar large-fruited strawberries are propagated by runners which are freely produced throughout the summer.

It is good policy, though not essential, to set aside a few plants specially for propagation, removing the flowers from these and so encouraging the production of runners. If propagation is carried out on the ordinary fruiting bed it is apt to become rather a mess by the end of the summer. In any case it is advisable to restrict plants to about four to six runners each.

Plantlets are formed every few inches along each runner but only one should be retained and that the nearest to the parent plant. The tip of the runner must be pinched off immediately beyond this.

The plantlets will often root themselves where they touch the soil but a more satisfactory method is to peg them down to the soil with a piece of wire bent like a hairpin. Some growers peg them into small pots filled with ordinary potting soil and sunk to their rims in the strawberry bed. This certainly makes it possible to transplant the rooted runners when weather conditions are unfavourable but in my experience it checks the growth of the plantlets and in consequence I seldom use it, preferring the open ground runner.

If all goes well the plantlets will be rooted nicely in about five to six weeks, when the runners can be severed from the parent plants. Wait a further week, then lift the rooted plantlets with good balls of soil and transfer them immediately to the new strawberry bed.

A point of very great importance is to propagate only from thoroughly healthy and vigorous plants which come from a stock of proved cropping capacity. Failure to observe these precautions will result in rapid deterioration of stock.

FERTILITY. A few varieties of strawberry are partially or fully self-sterile, due to the fact that they produce little or no good pollen of their own. Notable examples of this are Tardive de Leopold and Oberschlesien. In consequence these varieties must not be planted by themselves. They should be inter-planted with another variety known to produce a good supply of pollen, though it is quite sufficient to have one row of the pollen-bearing strawberry to every three rows of the self-sterile kind. Useful pollinators are Royal Sovereign and Huxley Giant.

SEASON. The main strawberry season is in late June and early July but there are both early and late varieties which will extend it by as much as six or eight weeks. Full advantage should be taken of this fact when selecting varieties.

AGE OF PLANTS. It is always essential to start with young plants, i.e. seedlings in the case of alpines and freshly rooted runners with the large fruited strawberries. The strawberry bed soon wears out and becomes unprofitable. In consequence it is wise to renew it frequently, the usual practice being to replace a third of the bed every year so that no plant remains in the bed more than three years.

PLANTING. This can be done in late summer, early autumn or spring but undoubtedly the best results are obtained from August-September planting. If runners are to be ready by this time they must be pegged down early, which is one of the advantages of having a separate bed for propagation.

The vital point about planting is to keep the crown of each plant level with the surface of the soil. If the crown is buried it is almost certain to rot during winter. This means that the uppermost part of the roots is only just covered with soil. Make the plants thoroughly firm, otherwise the soil will settle away from them and leave some of the roots exposed, which is quite as bad as having the crowns covered.

If the planting is to be left until March, it is a considerable advantage to use pot rooted runners (see p. 738). In any case spring planted strawberries should not be allowed to fruit the first summer. Any flowers which they produce should be cut off at once.

Space large fruited strawberries 15 in. apart in rows $2\frac{1}{2}$ ft. apart. These distances may be reduced a little for alpine kinds.

CARE OF THE PLANTS. Clean straw or the special straw mats sold for the purpose should be placed around the plants in May, just before they come into flower. The straw serves a double purpose: it keeps the berries clear of the soil and so preserves them from mud splashes and it makes a useful mulch, which encourages root growth. The straw and mats should be removed in August as they may harbour pests or the spores of disease.

Apart from this the principal cultural operation is to remove any runners not required for propagation. This should be done frequently throughout the summer as the runners, if left, make an unnecessary drain on the strength of the plants, reducing their capacity to fruit the following year.

Protection from birds is another essential when the berries commence to colour. For this purpose the strawberry bed may be made in a permanent fruit cage covered with wire netting or small mesh fish netting can be spread over a suitable framework when the need arises. In any case care must be taken to see that there are no holes nor any spaces at soil level for if there are the birds will very quickly find them.

Some growers make a practice of burning the straw on the beds instead of removing it. They do this on a dry and rather windy day so that the straw is kept burning briskly and does not smoulder too long around any particular plant. All the strawberry foliage is destroyed but they claim that the plants very quickly recover and that the treatment does get rid of all pests. There is no doubt a good deal in this but it requires a lot of confidence to do it and I do not recommend the treatment to the beginner.

FEEDING. An annual mulch of dung given in April in the same way as for raspberries should be the staple item in routine feeding. It may be supplemented by an application made at the same time of superphosphate of lime, 3 oz. per sq. yd. and sulphate of potash, 2 oz. per sq. yd.

STRAWBERRIES UNDER GLASS. Strawberries can be forced quite easily if early rooted runners are transferred in July to 6 in. pots filled with ordinary potting compost (see p. 421). The pots should be placed in a frame but no protection need be given until October. From then onwards lights will be required during very cold weather though ventilation should be given freely during favourable periods.

From January to March the plants can be removed, in suitable batches, to a greenhouse with an average temperature of about 50°. Arrange them as near the glass as possible and in a light place. Water sparingly at first but more freely as the plants grow and flowers are produced. These flowers must be fertilised by hand with a camel hair brush. From this stage onwards the temperature can be raised little by little to a maximum of 70° as the fruits swell and colour but it is advisable to drop again to about 60° for the last few days.

Another method of enjoying early strawberries is to cover some of the plants in the ordinary outdoor bed with barn type cloches. These should be placed in position about mid-February. Little or no ventilation will be required but if the weather is bright and sunny it may be necessary to shade lightly with whitewash for the last week or so while the fruits are colouring.

DETERIORATION OF STOCK. I have already referred to the fact that strawberries often deteriorate rather rapidly. This is largely due to the fact that they are very subject to a series of virus diseases most of which weaken the plants without killing them. Certain varieties of strawberry carry some of these viruses without showing any outward symptoms (Huxley Giant is rather a bad offender in this respect). The trouble has become so widespread that it is unwise to purchase any strawberries unless the plants are known to be healthy or, better still, carry a Ministry of Agriculture certificate for freedom from virus. Much work is being done in breeding virus free varieties and also in selecting from existing varieties particular plants which are free from disease. From these selected plants others are propagated by runners and, by careful isolation and rogueing, are kept free from infection. In this way a splendid stock of Strawberry Royal Sovereign has been produced and distributed under the name Royal Sovereign (E.M. 40).

VARIETIES. Good strawberries are Huxley (syn. Brenda Gautrey) mid-season; Oberschlesien, mid-season; Royal Sovereign, early; Sir Joseph Paxton, mid-season; Tardive de Leopold, late; Waterloo, late; Western Queen, mid-season. Perle de Prague, early; Climax, rather late, and Cambridge Early, very early. Of these my choice would be Royal Sovereign (E.M. 40), Climax and Cambridge Early.

WALNUT

Walnuts are planted more for ornament than for utility and they have the reputation of taking an exceptionally long time to come into bearing. This is true of certain varieties but there are walnuts which will commence to crop within ten or twelve years of planting and these should be obtained whenever possible. Unfortunately selected varieties are very difficult to purchase in this country, most of the trees offered being seedlings of unknown worth.

SOIL. Walnuts are not particular as regards soil and may be grown successfully practically anywhere except in waterlogged places or on very poor land. They should be planted in open, sunny places. The ground should be well dug some time in advance and at the same time be enriched with a little well-rotted manure and a sprinkling of bone meal and potash, e.g. sulphate of potash, 2 oz. per sq. yd.

TYPES OF TREE. The standard form is almost invariably employed for walnuts. The trees make a good deal of growth and do not submit to severe pruning so should be given plenty of room. A minimum of 35 ft. should be allowed between trees.

PROPAGATION. Seeds are frequently used as the means of increase but the results are not satisfactory as varieties selected for early fruiting will not breed true to type by this means and in fact seedlings may vary in many ways from their parents. However, if seeds are to be used they should be sown outdoors in March, 1 in. apart in an open, sunny situation.

A better method of increase is to graft shoots from selected walnuts on to seedlings which have previously been potted and placed in a greenhouse in a temperature of 60–65°. This is usually done in early spring. The grafts are treated in the ordinary way (see p. 637), and are then placed, pots and all, in a propagating frame in which the atmosphere is kept rather warm and moist. They should remain here until a good union has been made and the grafts are growing freely when they are removed to the ordinary greenhouse staging and gradually hardened off for transfer outdoors in early summer.

Outdoor budding has also been tried but is not very effective except in hot summers. A special method known as patch budding is employed. The bud is cut with a rectangular piece of bark and an exactly similar rectangle of bark is removed from the stock. The bud is then used to patch this rectangle and is bound in position. This work is done between late May and late July.

FERTILITY. Walnuts produce two kinds of flower, male and female, on the same tree. They are self-fertile but the trouble with many varieties is that they either produce few male catkins or only start to bear male catkins at an advanced age. Other kinds bear catkins early and these are the ones to plant for early fruiting or alternatively they may be mixed with slower varieties as advised in the case of cob nuts (see p. 696).

AGE OF TREE. It is an advantage to start with quite young trees, say two or three years old, but as a rule these are rather difficult to obtain. Nurserymen seem to prefer to sell older specimens up to seven or eight years in spite of the fact that they do not transplant so easily.

PLANTING. This can be done at any time from mid-October to mid-March and the general instructions already given on pp. 633-4 need no addition.

TREATMENT OF YOUNG TREES. Prune rather severely after planting with the object of getting a well branched head. Subsequently the trees should be treated in the same way as standard apples (see p. 659).

PRUNING. The first few years pruning is the same as for the formation of young standard apples (see p. 659). Once the head of branches is well formed little further pruning is necessary. Badly placed, over-crowded, damaged or diseased branches can be removed each November.

FEEDING. Usually unnecessary.

PICKING AND STORING. The nuts should be left on the tree until they fall naturally or can easily be shaken down. Then remove the outer husks, wipe the shells as clean as possible with a damp cloth and store them in earthenware crocks or large glass jars with plenty of salt sprinkled between and over them. If desired an equal quantity of dry coconut fibre may be mixed with the salt. Stored in this way walnuts should keep quite satisfactorily until January or later.

PART VI

DEALING WITH FOES

CHAPTER XXXI

Diagnosis and Treatment

I DO NOT regard it as part of the amateur gardener's job to be able to identify any great number of the multitudinous pests and diseases which may afflict his plants nor do I consider it part of my task in this volume to supply detailed information on these matters. But I do think that every keen amateur should be able to do two things; first to make a rough diagnosis of most symptoms which will at least identify them as characteristic of a certain group of allied troubles, and second to recognise at sight a few extremely common foes. The purpose of this chapter is to satisfy these two needs.

GROUP DIAGNOSIS

The value of the general classification is that it will often suggest a line of treatment which can at least be pursued while the advice of an expert is being sought—and I certainly advise that in all cases of doubt advantage should be taken of one of the many services which exist. The reason for knowing the everyday pests and diseases is so obvious that I need not enlarge upon it—after all we none of us run to a doctor to be told that we have a cold.

When faced with any unusual condition in plants I suggest that one should first ask oneself the question 'Is this likely to be the work of some animal (including, under this heading, insects), is it a disease caused by an infection of some kind, or could it be put down to faulty cultivation?' As a rule a little investigation will enable the right answer to be found.

PESTS. This is a convenient term under which to group all the troubles caused by animals. Quite a lot of this kind of damage is too obvious to need any explanation. A tree that has been badly barked tells its own tale though one may not, at first sight, be quite certain whether the bark has been removed by the gnawing of rabbits or rats, the chewing of cattle or goats, the clawing of cats or the penknife of a mischievous child.

When whole pieces are removed from leaves, stems or fruits one can be fairly certain that an animal is responsible, though it may be a very small one—for do not forget that throughout I am using 'animal' in its widest sense and including slugs, woodlice, caterpillars, beetles, weevils etc. Often a close search of the plant or its surroundings will reveal the culprit and if it can be found actually at work all doubt will be set at rest. A good many pests feed at night and hide by day, so when other methods have failed it is always wise to visit the plants after dark and examine them carefully with a torch.

However there are many insects which live on plants without ever taking a bite out of them. These are suckers of sap and they usually work with such a fine proboscis or probe that they leave no visible wound. All the innumerable greenflies, blackflies and other aphides belong to this group as do the allied capsid bugs which do so much damage to fruit trees and garden plants, also red spiders, mites, thrips, whitefly and scale insects. Fortunately many of these 'stay put' on their chosen host for quite long periods, so are easy enough to identify, though in some cases a small hand lens may be needed to make them plainly visible. Always have a good look at the tender tips of young shoots and the undersides of the younger leaves if you have any cause to suspect that foes of this type are at work. Sucking insects will usually check growth and cause some yellowing or silvering, often accompanied by distortion and severe cockling. These will quite likely be the first symptoms to attract the gardener's eye, and it will only be after closer inspection that the insects themselves will be detected.

DISEASES. A great many of the diseases which affect plants are caused by fungi. Often the symptoms are easy even for the novice to recognise. Mildew, for example, causes the same type of powdery white outgrowth on the leaves and stems of plants as it will on a piece of cloth in a damp cupboard. The fungi concerned are quite distinct, by-the-way, and a plant cannot catch mildew from the cloth despite the similarity in outward appearance. The same is true of most other fungi and it is a remarkable (and for the gardener a fortunate) fact that their range is, as a rule, so very limited that, for example, the mildew which grows on a pea will not live on an apple tree nor even the apple tree mildew on a plum tree.

Then there are moulds which produce fluffy white outgrowths similar to those one finds on mouldy jam or bread: rusts, so called because they produce rusty-looking spots on the leaves or stems attacked; and a whole host of 'spot' diseases in which brown or blackish spots of varying size develop, usually on leaves or fruits. Spotting can be caused by other agencies than fungi, such as spraying with a caustic fluid, but a tell-tale characteristic of the fungus spot is that it spreads outwards, gradually getting bigger and bigger. If it is examined closely it will be seen that the central part, usually the darkest, is completely dead whereas the marginal area is in process of destruction and may actually have a slight outgrowth of mould upon it.

There are also a number of fungi which attack plants at soil level. 'Damping off' is a disease of this type and one which every gardener with a greenhouse or frame will meet before long. The stem rots right through and the plant topples over just as if it had been bitten off at soil level. There are, in fact, soil caterpillars and other creatures which will eat through stems at just this point and at first the beginner may be puzzled to distinguish damage of this character caused by a pest from that due to a disease, but a little experience will teach him that the insect always makes a clean job of it whereas the stem that has been destroyed by fungi is more or less blackened in the process.

There are a few plant diseases which are caused by bacteria and I do not regard these as being very easy for the amateur to diagnose in a general way though he may learn to distinguish a few specific and common kinds such as the soft rot of cabbages and celery. But as a rule it would be wise to regard these as diseases requiring the advice of an expert.

The last group of diseases is due to virus infection. There are a great many of these and some of them are difficult for the amateur to diagnose as the symptoms are very much like those caused by bad cultivation, in fact it is quite certain that a great many of the failures which once were ascribed, even by experts, to overwatering, over-feeding and the like were, in fact, caused by unrecognised viruses. But this much can be said with safety; if a plant is very much deformed or dwarfed, or if its leaves are curiously variegated or streaked it is wise to suspect virus infection and get a sample to an expert as quickly as possible. Viruses are carried from plant to plant mainly by the agency of sucking insects such as aphides and thrips so the presence of these actually increases the probability that the symptoms I have just outlined are caused by virus infection.

PHYSIOLOGICAL DISORDERS. Under this heading are grouped all those ailments which are caused, not by any attack by an outside organism be it pest or disease, but by some fault in the actual living conditions of the plant. These troubles are sometimes the most difficult of all to diagnose and it is certainly hard to think of any general rules which will enable the novice to distinguish them from the effects of certain fungi and viruses. Nevertheless there are some points which may help to put him on the right track.

Draughts and drought will both cause leaf scorching and so will exposure to excessive heat (especially under glass) or to some kinds of fumes, notably those from creosote or a badly adjusted paraffin lamp. Scorching can also be due to lack of potash or magnesium in the soil and to an overdose of certain fertilisers, or to the direct effect upon the leaves of some chemicals. However in all these cases the damage can be distinguished from the browning caused by fungus disease by the fact that it ends quite cleanly and sharply and does not tail off to a zone in which the tissue is in process of destruction as the fungus grows through it. The damaged part of the leaf is, as a rule, quite dry and papery and may even appear transparent when held up to the light. Admittedly dry spotting is a feature of some virus diseases but generally such spots are quite small and accompanied by other symptoms such as distortion or variegation which give them away.

Bad drainage will often produce a progressive yellowing of the foliage until, if the condition is not rectified, the plant dies. This occurs commonly with pot plants grown in badly-drained pots and the cause may often be traced to earthworms which have entered the pots through the drainage holes and blocked them with their casts. The remedy, in this case, is to stand the pots on slates, boards or sharp boiler ashes through which worms will not pass.

A rather special case of drainage trouble is often found in low-lying orchards. Here the trouble occurs in winter and is not noticed at first because the trees are dormant. Growth apparently starts normally in the spring but is, in fact, sustained only by the sap remaining in the branches. Directly this is exhausted the leaves collapse and within a few weeks the trees are quite dead.

Some queer symptoms can be caused by deficiency of certain essential foods in the soil. I have already referred to the scorching which may be caused by lack of potash or magnesium. In the first instance it is the leaf margin that is most damaged whereas with magnesium scorching there is a smudgy discoloration between the veins of the leaves which may look extremely like a fungal disease to an inexperienced eye. A central decay of the roots of beetroots and swedes may be caused by boron deficiency while severe yellowing of many plants may result from a shortage of iron. In all cases where this kind of trouble is suspected it is wise to consult an expert as much harm may result from wrong treatment.

As the autumn approaches it is inevitable that the leaves of most outdoor plants suffer an increasing amount of weather damage, which may vary in intensity from a slight spotting to extensive discoloration. In spring late frosts will often play havoc with tender young leaves and shoots, while some plants may be killed outright especially if they have been raised in a warm greenhouse and put out with insufficient hardening off. Chilling at this season may result in a complete cessation of growth and a change in the colour of leaves from normal green to a bluish or purplish shade.

GROUP TREATMENT

While the number of different pests and diseases which may attack garden plants is very great the number of remedial or preventive measures is comparatively small. In practice the amateur will find that just as he is using the same half dozen or so fertilisers in different combinations for practically all his plants so a very few stock remedies will see him through most of his troubles if applied at the right time and in the right way. Therein lies the value of the group classification which I have outlined, for once the trouble can be placed in its right class it is highly probable that a suitable treatment can be determined.

BITING INSECTS. Suppose, for example, we decide that the damage is due to an animal which bites holes in the stems or leaves. It may be a caterpillar, a beetle or a weevil but in any case it is highly probable that the quickest way to get rid of it will be to poison it much as one would poison rats or mice. Several suitable poisons are available.

Derris and pyrethrum are mainly insect poisons which can be used with complete safety. DDT and Gamma BHC (lindane) have greater killing power and are harmless to human beings in the quantities in which they are used for plant dusting or spraying.

The essential in all cases is to get the appropriate spray or dust on the plants at the first sign of attack and to cover all the leaves as evenly as possible so that the insect, whatever it may be, cannot take a bite anywhere without taking a fatal dose of poison at the same time.

SUCKING INSECTS. But perhaps our diagnosis is in favour of the sucking rather than the biting type of pest. If so the line of attack will have to be slightly different because the insect lives on the sap direct without taking pieces out of the surface of the leaf. Either it will be necessary to poison the sap itself with what is known as systemic insecticide such as schradan or the gardener can make use of what are known as contact poisons, that is chemicals which kill merely by coming in direct contact with the body of the insect. It so happens that both DDT and derris will operate in this way, but the former is not effective against aphides. Nicotine, however, is an extremely effective contact poison and can be used against a great variety of sucking insects, including all aphides, with devastating results. Moreover it can be applied as a vapour as well as in dust or spray form and this is often the best method for dealing with greenhouse pests. There are, however, two drawbacks, one that nicotine is poisonous to warm-blooded creatures and the other (which to some extent cancels out the first drawback) that it soon loses its poisonous properties on exposure to the air. For the first reason it is unwise to use nicotine within ten days or so of gathering crops and for the second it is often necessary to make several applications at fairly short intervals to catch successive broods of insects. BHC in its various forms is also an effective contact spray and for many purposes is the best and safest for use in the private garden.

FUNGAL DISEASES. If our rough diagnosis favours a disease caused by a fungus, our choice of a remedy will be equally restricted. Some compound of copper or sulphur is almost certain to give results and the four in most general use are Bordeaux mixture (copper), lime-sulphur and the so-called colloidal copper and colloidal sulphur sprays. The sulphur sprays are particularly effective against mildews of all kinds and for fruit trees, whereas the copper sprays are more suitable for spots and rusts in the vegetable and flower garden. If only people would make a habit of spraying their potatoes and outdoor tomatoes as a matter of course with Bordeaux mixture in July and August they would have little or no trouble with the late blight disease which now destroys so many promising crops. Two newer fungicides that are not based on either sulphur or copper are captan which is useful for certain diseases (but not mildews) that appear resistant to other remedies and dinocap, effective against mildews.

Though these fungicides (the correct name for any chemicals which kill fungi) can be used to check the further spread of diseases which have already made their appearance they are still more effective as preventives and it is for this reason that many gardeners carry out regular routine spraying year by year whatever does, or does not, turn up. In all cases the fungicide should cover the leaves completely, above and below, so that wherever the spore of a fungus starts to grow it will come in contact with a film of chemical poisonous to it.

It is possible to purchase both copper and sulphur dusts for use where a dry powder is more convenient than a wet spray.

VIRUS DISEASES. So far no satisfactory method has been found of combating virus diseases once plants are infected by them, but as they are spread mainly by sucking insects, principally aphides and thrips, any measures taken to reduce the number of these by suitable sprayings or fumigations will also limit the virus. In addition infected plants should be destroyed so that they cease to act as carriers.

BACTERIAL DISEASES. These also defy treatment and leave the gardener

A greaseband on the trunk of a standard fruit tree. Many insects have been caught

An earwig trap made by stuffing hay into a flower pot and inverting this on a plant stake

Sliced carrots impaled on sticks make effective traps for wireworms. They can be lifted daily and examined

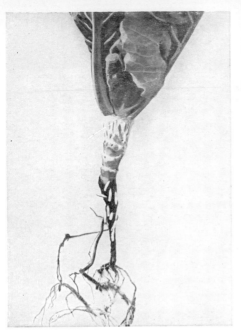

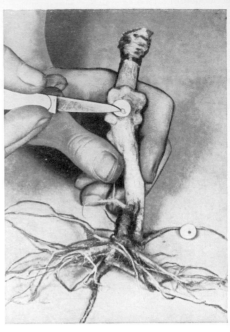

Maggots of the cabbage root fly at work on the stem and roots of a broccoli plant

The galls caused by the cabbage gall weevil. If cut open the maggot will usually be found

The very distinctive and stinking swellings caused by club root

Caterpillars of the cabbage white butterfly at work on Brussels sprouts

A daffodil badly affected by the bulb eelworm

The distinctive damage caused by the chrysanthemum leaf miner

Red spider damage to a vine leaf. The colour is a mottled grey

These bean leaves have been scalloped by pea and bean weevils

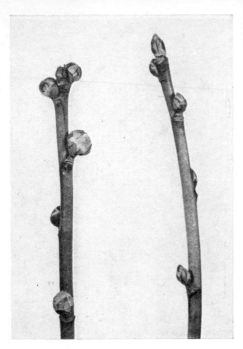

On the left is a black currant shoot attacked by big bud, with a healthy shoot on the right

Canker wounds on apple branches. These will eventually cause the branches to die

Aphides (greenflies) at work on apple leaves showing the distortion they cause

Plum leaves showing symptoms of silver leaf (bottom) with healthy leaves above

An apple badly attacked by scab

Capsid bug damage to an apple

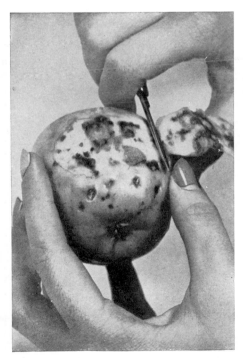

Peeling an apple suffering from bitter pit

Apples suffering from brown rot

Potato leaves showing symptoms of late blight disease

A potato tuber suffering from the fungus disease known as common scab

Blossom end rot of a tomato fruit

An onion attacked by neck rot

Wire stem of cabbage (right) with healthy plant on left

Tomato leaf mould disease in an advanced state

A box of stock seedlings suffering from damping off disease

A dahlia plant stunted by virus disease. Affected plants should be burnt

Mosaic mottling of raspberry due to virus infection

A potato suffering from virus leaf roll with healthy plants surrounding it

with the rather thankless task of promptly destroying every infected plant as the best possible means of preventing further trouble. However something can also be achieved by keeping down slugs and snails and in other ways protecting plants from wounds through which infection may enter.

PHYSIOLOGICAL DISORDERS. With these the remedy is almost always the obvious one of removing as quickly as possible the faulty condition which has caused the trouble. One word of warning may not be out of place. Do not rush from one extreme to another. Because a plant has been in too cold a place it will not help to transfer it to one which is too hot; nor, if the soil has been short of some essential food, is it wise to apply the appropriate fertiliser at rates in excess of those ordinarily recommended. What is needed is to get matters back to normal and keep them there.

SOIL PESTS AND DISEASES. So far the treatments I have suggested have been applicable mainly to those foes which attack the aerial parts of plants. But there are also a number of pests and diseases which are to be found in the soil and in the main attack the roots or lower parts of their victims. Ordinary sprays and dusts are seldom effective against these and special measures must be employed.

Many soil insects can either be driven out or killed with naphthalene. The more finely this is powdered the better and it should be raked or lightly forked into the soil rather than dug in deeply for most such pests will be found quite close to the surface. This treatment is most suitable for vacant ground but small quantities of naphthalene (say up to 2 oz. per square yard) can usually be applied around plants without injuring them seriously.

Some pests can be trapped, and such baits as sliced potatoes or carrots are frequently used for the purpose. These are impaled on sharpened sticks and buried just beneath the surface. Then they can be lifted every other day and any insects feeding on them collected and destroyed.

Slugs, snails, woodlice and leatherjackets can be poisoned in various ways. A very little powdered metaldehyde mixed with bran makes a good slug and snail poison. Alternatively Paris green and bran can be used and this will also kill some of the other pests named, though for woodlice dried blood and Paris green is still most effective.

Onion and carrot fly eggs, which are laid in the soil in May and June near the seedlings to be attacked, can be killed by sprinkling 4 per cent. calomel dust around the plants at this season. Calomel dust is also fairly effective against club root, a smelly disease which attacks the cabbage family causing them to swell and lose all their fibre. For this purpose calomel is sprinkled in the holes when the young plants are put out. Nevertheless the best method of ridding land altogether of the club root organism is to keep it well limed.

A more recent treatment for fly larvae in the soil is to apply a soil insecticide containing BHC but this must be used with caution where root crops are to be grown as it may impart an unpleasant taste to them. Apart from this disadvantage (greatly reduced in the form of BHC known as lindane) this is a most efficient treatment. Carrot seed can be treated with a BHC seed dressing prior to sowing and this gives a measure of protection against fly larvae with a minimum risk of tainting.

A fungicide which can be used with safety even around young seedlings is Cheshunt Compound. A solution is watered freely on the ground and is very effective in stopping the spread of damping off disease and some other soil borne fungi. It is not sufficiently powerful, however, to clear the soil of all diseases any more than the insecticides just mentioned will rid it of all insects.

CHAPTER XXXII

Sterilisation and Fumigation

WHERE soil is heavily infected with disease causing organisms or pests some form of sterilisation is usually the only method by which it can be cleared completely. Unfortunately this is too costly to be carried out on a large scale and must usually be confined to seed and potting composts (see p. 421) and greenhouse borders.

Either heat or chemicals may be used to sterilise soil, or more accurately, partially sterilise it for that is all that is desirable. Complete sterilisation would render it unfit for cultivation for a considerable period.

Heat may be applied dry or wet but extremes either way are to be avoided because either may have a bad effect upon the texture of the soil. For this reason steam is one of the best sources of heat as it will neither char the soil nor make it sodden. Special apparatus can be obtained for steaming large or small quantities of soil, but quite satisfactory results can be obtained in a copper of the ordinary domestic type if the soil is placed in a small sack and suspended over, but not actually in, a few inches of fast boiling water. Let the soil be rather dry to begin with and do not try to handle too much at a time—half a bushel will be ample. Get the water boiling fast before the sack is placed in position and then clap a lid over all and cover with further sacks to trap the heat. The ideal is to raise the temperature of the soil as quickly as possible to about 200° Fahr. and keep it at that for twenty minutes or so. Very slow heating or over-long sterilisation are equally undesirable.

Small electrical sterilisers are also available and are very effective. The method commonly used is to pass the current from the mains (210–240 volts) directly through the soil from large metal plates spaced not more than 7 in. apart. The resistance set up by the soil is sufficient to cause considerable heating but when the soil against the plates reaches boiling point it rapidly dries and then acts as an effective insulator preventing further passage of electricity.

Various chemicals are used for soil sterilisation but formaldehyde is as satisfactory as any. It is usually purchased as formalin (40 per cent. formaldehyde) and to prepare this for use it is diluted with 49 times its own bulk of water, i.e. approximately 1 pint of formalin to 6 gallons of water. The soil is thoroughly watered with this (if it can be spread out on a hard floor for the purpose so much the better) and then it is heaped up and covered with sacks for 48 hours to trap the fumes. Subsequently it is uncovered and spread out again and left until it has lost all smell of formaldehyde, which may take a month or so. Two gallons of diluted formalin is sufficient to treat a bushel of soil.

GREENHOUSE FUMIGATION

In a closed space a vapour has many advantages over either a liquid or a dust as an insect killer because every nook and cranny is penetrated and there can be no question of some part of the plant being missed. Nicotine is much used for the purpose and is very effective against aphides and thrips. Liquid nicotine specially manufactured for the purpose can be vaporised over a small spirit lamp, or special 'shreds' or cones impregnated with nicotine can be ignited and left to smoulder in the house.

Several of the best synthetic insecticides such as DDT, BHC and azobenzene, can be obtained in the form of smoke generators. These are rather like small fireworks which have only to be ignited and left to distribute their fumes.

In all cases the house must be kept as tightly closed as possible for about twelve hours after fumigation to trap the fumes and give them a chance to do their work. Cracks in ventilators and doors should be covered with damp sacks or be plugged in some way. Operators should leave the house directly the chemical has been applied or they may be poisoned too. This is particularly vital in the case of calcium cyanide as hydrocyanic acid gas is a deadly poison to human beings. Houses that are being fumigated should be locked and the key kept in safe custody so that no one may enter the house unawares.

It is usually most convenient to fumigate in the evening. The following morning ventilators should be thrown open to allow remaining fumes to escape and no one should remain in the house for more than a few moments until it has been thoroughly ventilated. As a rule damage to plants is least likely to occur if the atmosphere of the house is a little drier and warmer than usual while fumigation is being carried out.

CHAPTER XXXIII

Common Pests and Diseases

FOR SIMPLICITY of reference I have arranged many of the commoner pests and diseases in alphabetical sequence in this chapter with short descriptions and an account of the best method of dealing with each.

AMERICAN BLIGHT.—*See* WOOLLY APHIS p. 796.

ANTS. These can cause a lot of damage by loosening soil especially in pots, seed boxes, seed beds and around small plants. On lawns they may throw up ant hills. They will sometimes attack and damage blossoms and ripening fruits and also do indirect damage by transporting aphides from one plant to another.

There are several proprietary ant killers which can be purchased from dealers in sundries and should be used strictly in accordance with manufacturer's instructions. Alternatively, if nests can be found, a hole can be bored into each with a dibber, a tablespoonful of carbon bisulphide poured in and the hole blocked immediately with soil to trap the fumes. In greenhouses and frames pyrethrum, derris, BHC or DDT powder can be sprinkled around pots and boxes. Greasebands placed around the trunks or main branches of trees will catch many ants ascending and descending.

APHIDES. This is the general name used to cover the numerous insects known to the gardener as greenflies, blackflies and plant lice. They are all small, soft-bodied creatures some winged but mostly wingless and slow moving. They tend to cluster around the tips of young shoots or on the undersides of leaves, from which they suck the sap. They check growth, often cause severe distortion and frequently carry virus diseases from one plant to another.

Spraying with malathion, nicotine, BHC, derris or pyrethrum provides the best remedy but must be commenced directly infestation is noted because it is essential to get the spray into direct contact with the insects and this is almost impossible once leaves have become severely distorted. Soft soap, at the rate of 1 oz. per gallon, or one of the proprietary 'spreaders' added to the spray will make it more effective. Menazon is an excellent new remedy (see p. 802). In all cases the spray should be mixed at the strength recommended by the manufacturers as different brands differ in concentration.

On fruit trees the eggs of aphides, which are mostly laid on the ends of the young shoots, can be killed in winter with tar oil, DNC or thiocyanate winter washes. Tar oil is used at the rate of 5 pints to 10 gallons while the trees are quite dormant in December or January. DNC and thiocyanate can be used on apples as late as the first fortnight in March when the buds of the trees are already loosening and showing a green tip. Manufacturer's instructions regarding strength should be followed.

A special kind of aphis attacks the roots of some plants, notably auriculas and lettuces. Valuable plants may be lifted and dipped in a solution of derris or pyrethrum some of which may also be poured into the holes from which they have been removed.

For woolly aphis see p. 796.

BACTERIAL CANKER.—*See* GUMMING (p. 780.)

BASAL ROT. There are several different fungi which attack the bulbs of narcissi and tulips causing them to rot at the bottom and these are all known by the name 'basal rot'. As the treatment is the same it is not necessary to be able to distinguish between one kind of basal rot and another. All bulbs should be very carefully examined before they are planted so that any which show signs of decay may be destroyed. Bulbs should always be stored in a cool, dry place as this minimises risk of infection. If bulbs are being sterilised against eelworm by being immersed in water for 3 hours at 110° F., it is wise to add 4 fluid ounces of formalin to every 5 gallons of water in the bath.

BEES, LEAF-CUTTING. Certain species of bee cut pieces out of leaves to form their nests. These pieces are always clearly removed from the edges of the leaves in the form of semi-circles and so it is usually possible to recognize the culprit from the kind of damage done. Though leaf-cutting bees are seldom sufficiently numerous to constitute a serious danger to the garden they can be most annoying. Unfortunately there is very little that can be done effectively to get rid of them except to catch the bees with a fine mesh butterfly net and destroy them.

BEETLES. In general beetles, in contrast to weevils, tend to be friends rather than foes of the gardener as they are mainly carnivorous. There are, however, one or two notable exceptions such as the Raspberry Beetle, described on page 785, the Flea Beetle, described on page 778, the Asparagus Beetle, a small but rather striking fellow in black with orange markings, and the pea and bean beetle who is more a worry to seedsmen than to gardeners. The grubs of the Asparagus Beetle feed on the leaves of asparagus and may leave the stems quite bare. An occasional dusting with DDT will account for it. The pea and bean weevil drills tiny holes into pea and bean seeds. There is nothing that can be done about it in the garden, but seedsmen have ingenious machines which pick out the holed seeds and discard them. One other group of beetles that may occasionally prove troublesome are the Bark Beetles and Shot Borers, all of which are very small, brown or blackish beetles which bore tunnels into the wood of various trees. Usually only old trees or those that are in poor health are attacked, so good general cultivation is the first line of defence. All wounds should be protected with Stockholm Tar or an approved wound dressing.

Big Bud. This condition is all too common in black currants and is occasionally found in red and white currants and even gooseberries. The dormant buds become swollen and globular instead of being comparatively small and a little pointed. The condition can be detected very easily towards the end of the winter. It is due to the infestation of the buds by great numbers of tiny mites, which later migrate to other buds. Besides destroying many of the buds these mites often carry virus disease, particularly the destructive virus which causes 'reversion'.

The mite is checked by picking off the swollen buds in winter and spraying in spring, when the most forward leaves are as big as shillings, with lime sulphur wash used at 1 pint to 6 galls. of water. For a serious attack a stronger solution should be used, 1 pint in 2 galls. of water. This will cause scorch and one year's crop will be lost.

Birds. Many species of birds can be a considerable nuisance in the garden though there are few birds which do not also do some good to compensate for any harm they may do. Probably one may place completely on the black list jays, wood-pigeons and bullfinches and in some districts rooks and crows can be very troublesome. There is no simple or single remedy. Netting or similar protective measures are the only ones likely to give complete immunity. Sprays such as alum and quassia may give a little protection by rendering berries etc., too bitter to be palatable but their true value seems very doubtful. The same is true of most birds scarers, for after a while birds become used to even the most terrifying of these.

Bitter Pit. This is a very common physiological disease of apples and pears in which the surface becomes marked with small, darkish depressions. If the skin is peeled it will be found that beneath each 'pit' there is a small area of brown flesh. Closely allied to this is the condition known as 'cork' in which there are small brown areas of flesh throughout the fruit and not merely near the surface. Both troubles are connected with dry spells of weather during the growing season and are likely to be most marked on soils that dry out rapidly. Some varieties are more subject to bitter pit than others.

Anything that can be done to improve the moisture-holding qualities of the soil, as for example by working in dung or compost, will help to prevent this disease.

BLACK FLY. The name is given to one of the many kinds of aphis. Black fly is particularly troublesome on broad beans. On this crop, apart from spraying with derris or pyrethrum considerable benefit is to be gained by early sowing and by pinching out the tips of the plants when the first clusters of pods commence to form. On other plants and trees remedies are the same as for other aphides (see p. 765).

BLACKLEG. A disease which attacks the stems of potatoes at and just above soil level, causing them to go black and die, with the result that the foliage withers and the whole plant collapses. As a rule only an odd plant is affected here and there in the potato bed and the disease is seldom very serious. No cure is known, but as the disease is carried in the seed tubers care should be taken to destroy all affected plants and to examine the planting sets with care. Destroy any which are soft or rotten at the end removed from the eyes.

BLACK SPOT. Though a great many diseases cause black spots to appear on leaves or fruits the name 'Black Spot' is reserved for a specific and extremely serious disease of roses. The foliage is attacked and the disease progresses rapidly in summer, the circular blackish spots increasing in size until eventually the leaf is destroyed and falls prematurely. Badly attacked leaves should be removed and burned. Plants should be sprayed fortnightly from July to September with captan, thiram or copper white oil emulsion, according to maker's instructions. In winter, when all leaves have fallen, the bare branches and the surface soil can be sprayed with copper sulphate, 1 oz. per gallon of water. In severe cases it will pay to remove the surface inch of soil from beneath all affected roses in winter, burn it and replace with fresh soil from another part of the garden where no roses have been grown. In less serious cases it will help to mulch the rose beds with dry grass clippings in April and maintain this mulch throughout the summer, so checking the rise of disease spores from the soil to the leaves.

BLIGHT (POTATO). I have referred to this very widespread disease under the general heading Potatoes on page 604. The disease is caused by a fungus which first attacks the leaves of potatoes and tomatoes, causing them to develop black spots and patches which rapidly spread until all the leaves and even the stems are killed. On potatoes the disease usually passes quickly to the tubers causing them to develop brown, decayed patches which may extend deep down into the flesh. On tomatoes the fruits are usually attacked and these develop black streaks and blotches which soon cause the whole fruit to go rotten. The disease cannot be cured but it can be prevented by spraying potatoes and tomatoes in good time with Bordeaux mixture and repeating at intervals of three or four weeks until the autumn. As the disease usually starts in the west of England about mid-June and then quickly spreads eastward to reach the London area about the first week in July the first preventive spraying should be timed to precede these dates by a few days.

BLOSSOM-END ROT. A physiological disease of tomatoes which sometimes causes heavy loss of crop. The fruits only are attacked and always at the end farthest removed from the stalk. First a dark spot appears. This rapidly gains in size, becomes black and hard and finally the end of the fruit is flattened.

Despite appearances to the contrary the disease is not primarily due to a fungus but is caused by shortage of water. It may be a week or so after the period of dryness before the spots make their appearance. There is no cure for affected fruits but the disease can be prevented or checked once it has started by regular and adequate watering. Affected fruits should be removed and burned before secondary infections start in them.

BLOTCHY RIPENING. A condition of tomato fruits which prevents them from turning red evenly. Instead the fruits have greenish or yellowish blotches or areas irregularly disposed. This condition is sometimes a symptom of virus disease but more commonly it is due to unbalanced feeding and can be corrected by giving the plants a fertiliser containing plenty of potash as well as nitrogen and phosphates. A good proprietary tomato fertiliser may be used or the mixture I recommend on page 617 under the general heading Tomatoes.

BOTRYTIS. This disease is commonly known as 'grey mould' because, as it develops, a fluffy, greyish mould appears all over the affected area. In the early stages the attacked tissue decays, becoming soft and black in the process.

This is an extremely common trouble and one which attacks an unusually wide range of plants. Strawberries are often severely affected, the fruits suffering most and becoming very bitter as they rot. Lettuces are frequent victims, the main stem suffering most severely just above soil level, so that the whole plant collapses. In roses it causes serious die back of the year-old wood most of which may die during the winter. The seed heads of giant sunflowers are often completely rotted. Cucumber, melon and marrow fruits may become infected. Tomato stems and fruits are also attacked and infection is most likely to start at points where leaves or shoots have been cut off. In fact it is a characteristic of this fungus to seek entry through some small wound though it is also capable of breaking its own way into perfectly sound tissue.

Botrytis is an almost impossible disease to control once it has secured a firm hold but it needs a damp, cool atmosphere to stimulate it to its worst attacks and is always most troublesome in autumn outdoors, and in winter or early spring under glass. Careful watering and ventilation combined with a little artificial heat will go far to prevent it in glass houses. Outdoor crops should be harvested so far as possible before the weather becomes cold and wet and should be stored in dry, well-ventilated places. Spraying with Bordeaux mixture or captan and frequent dusting with flowers of sulphur will help to check the spread of botrytis. In the case of winter lettuces, which often suffer severely, great care should be taken not to plant too deeply and to choose varieties which are suitable for winter cropping.

BROWN ROT. A widespread disease of fruits which causes serious losses in many years. Apples, pears, plums, cherries, peaches and nectarines are frequently attacked. First there is a soft brown rot of the flesh which later develops a series of small, whitish pustules often arranged in a series of concentric rings. Eventually the whole fruit withers and may hang for months on the tree in a mummified condition. The spurs or twigs on which the fruit hangs often become infected, with the result that the bark withers and the shoot eventually dies.

Spraying has not proved effective against this disease. Trouble almost invariably starts through some small wound, so the first line of defence is to eliminate pests and protect the fruits from accidental damage and bruising. In apples brown rot often follows the damage caused by caterpillars of the codlin moth. All affected fruits must be removed and burned or buried as soon as noted. Spurs and twigs which show signs of the disease should also be cut off and burned.

BUD-DROPPING. The flower buds of various plants are apt to drop without apparent cause just before they open. This trouble is particularly common with sweet peas, lupins (especially the white varieties), begonias, runner beans and tomatoes. It is usually due to sudden changes in temperature, especially to cold nights, and may be encouraged by draughts and under or over watering.

Under glass care should be taken to maintain reasonably even temperatures and to water correctly according to the nature of the plant. Outdoors it is more difficult to control the trouble as the gardener is often at the mercy of the weather, but if the soil is dry, a good watering followed by syringing overhead with tepid water may help.

CANE BLIGHT. A damaging disease of raspberries caused by a fungus which attacks the fruiting canes at or near ground level causing the canes to wither and die. Infection usually occurs through wounds and these are often caused by the Raspberry Cane Midge. In consequence anything that is done to kill this pest will also reduce Cane Blight. In addition all infected canes should be cut right out, not just broken off at the point of infection.

CANE MIDGE. A tiny pest which seems to be on the increase. The tiny red maggots bore into the tender parts of young raspberry canes near ground level. The direct damage is not usually very serious but the wounds caused by these maggots give entry to the fungus which causes Cane Blight. The young canes should be sprayed in late May with either DDT or BHC and this treatment should be repeated in early July and again in August to catch successive broods.

CANE SPOT. A common, though often not a very serious disease, of raspberries and loganberries. It is caused by a fungus which attacks the canes causing them to develop numerous small, greyish, purple-rimmed spots. The canes are weakened and may, in very severe cases, be killed. Occasionally fruits are also infected and become lop-sided. The remedy is to spray with lime sulphur at 1 pint to 2 gallons in mid-March and again when the fruit flower buds are just open enough to show some petal colour at $\frac{1}{2}$ pint to 2 gallons.

CANKER. The most troublesome canker is that which attacks apples and, to a much lesser degree, pears, but there is also a distinct form of canker which causes similar trouble on roses. In all cases it is the wood that is attacked, often the wood of the older branches or main trunk. The fungus eats into this causing deep, gaping wounds with gnarled edges. Eventually the flow of sap is so checked that the branch, or even the whole tree dies.

Small branches, twigs and spurs that are cankered should be removed and burned. Wounds on larger branches may be painted with 'Medo', a proprietary dressing which checks the fungus and helps the wood to heal, and lead paint or Stockholm Tar used to protect pruning cuts. Some varieties are much more subject to canker than others and should be avoided in places where the disease has caused much trouble. Canker is also encouraged by bad drainage and cold, heavy sub-soils.

CAPSID BUGS. These are insects allied to aphides and much like them in appearance but mostly more active and less numerous. They often cause an amount of damage quite disproportionate to their numbers. Leaves, stems and fruits are all liable to be attacked and a great variety of plants are affected, fruit trees suffering particularly badly. Leaves and shoots become distorted, flower buds fail to develop or have deformed or missing petals, while fruits show rough, brown uneven scabs and may be greatly stunted.

Spring and summer spraying with nicotine insecticide, malathion, BHC or DDT are useful methods of control but with very choice plants such as exhibition chrysanthemums and dahlias it is also wise to search for the bugs and destroy them by hand. With fruit trees additional control can be obtained by spraying with winter petroleum emulsion when the buds are on the point of bursting in late February or early March.

CATERPILLARS. It is not necessary for the amateur to be able to recognise and name the great variety of caterpillars which may invade gardens as all are pests and all may be destroyed by spraying with derris, pyrethrum, DDT or BHC. Hand picking is often the quickest and surest method of stopping an attack, especially in the early stages. On fruit trees caterpillar damage can be much reduced by spraying with tar oil winter wash while the trees are dormant in December or January, or with DNC or thiocyanate winter wash in late February or early March. Greasebanding in September will catch the female winter moths which produce many of the spring caterpillars on fruit trees but the bands must be fixed tightly round the trunks or main branches at least 2 ft. above soil level and they must be kept sticky all the winter.

CHAFERS. These are beetles one of which, the cockchafer, is very common and may often be encountered just after dusk on a summer evening flying rapidly with a droning noise. It lives on the leaves of many trees and can be most troublesome. Even more destructive, however, are the larvae which are found half coiled in the soil. They are big with brown, horny heads and swollen, white bodies which have a darker hue towards the tail. They attack the roots of a great variety of plants.

Dusts containing BHC will kill the beetles, while the grubs can be attacked by boring holes in the soil and pouring in carbon disulphide which is an effective soil fumigant. As a rule, however, handpicking while digging in winter is sufficient to keep this pest down.

CHLOROSIS. One of the commonest of the 'deficiency' diseases, i.e. disorders caused by the lack of something in the soil. Chlorosis is often due to lack of iron, resulting in insufficient green colouring matter in the leaves, which consequently become pale yellow in patches or all over. Excess of lime will often bring about deficiency of iron resulting in chlorosis and in such cases a remedy may be effected by giving heavy dressings of peat, oak leaf mould, dung or other humus-forming substances which will tend to make the soil less alkaline and restore a more normal balance of available plant foods. Sequestrenes have proved very beneficial (see p. 69). It is, however, usually wise to consult an expert as the causes of chlorosis are numerous and difficult to diagnose.

CHOCOLATE SPOT. One of the numerous spot diseases and extremely common on broad beans. The name aptly describes the condition except that 'blotch' might be a better word than spot. There is no satisfactory remedy, but as the disease is only likely to be serious after severe weather it can be prevented by giving early beans as much shelter as possible. Be generous with phosphatic and potassic fertilisers in the preparation of the soil as this will tend to harden growth.

CLUB ROOT. Quite the worst disease the grower of cabbages and allied crops has to face. Club root is caused by a soil-borne organism which attacks the roots of all kinds of brassicas, and some allied plants into the bargain. At first there is a notable lack of fibrous roots. Soon the main roots swell, often to an astonishing size, and then they gradually decay with a most obnoxious smell. The small round swellings on the extreme base of the stem caused by the cabbage gall weevil (see p. 779) are often mistaken for club root but are easily distinguished, first by the fact that they are on the base of the stem and not on the root itself, and secondly because, if they are broken open, they will be found to be hollow, probably with one or two of the white larvae feeding within.

Club root thrives on acid soils and one of the most effective remedies for it is to apply so much lime that the soil becomes markedly alkaline (*p*H 7.5 or thereabouts, see p. 27). This and a thorough rest from cabbage crops for three or four years is the only complete cure, but the severity of attacks can be greatly diminished by sprinkling a little 4 per cent. calomel dust into each hole at planting time or by pouring in about half a pint of a solution made by dissolving 1 oz. mercuric chloride in 10 gallons of water (this solution is very poisonous). The seed bed can also be soaked with the mercuric chloride solution before sowing. All affected plants should be lifted and burned.

CODLIN MOTH. This is one of the two insects responsible for most maggoty apples, the other being the apple sawfly (see p. 787). It is the small white caterpillar of the codlin moth which does the damage. It enters the fruit, often by way of the eye, about midsummer or a little later and feeds in the core and surrounding flesh, leaving the fruit a few weeks later by another tunnel and then forming a cocoon in some sheltered place.

Features by which this pest can be distinguished from the sawfly are that the attack starts some weeks later when the fruit is already well formed and that there is no unpleasant smell from the damaged flesh.

DDT may be used but in the spring and summer it is very likely to kill useful insects and therefore cause an increase in red spider infestation. If bands of sacking are tied round the trunks of the apple trees in July many of the caterpillars will pupate beneath them and can either be collected by hand in the autumn or be killed where they are by soaking the bands with tar oil wash at the normal winter spraying.

CROWN GALL. A very curious disease which attacks a great variety of plants including fruit trees, ornamental trees and shrubs, including roses and occasionally beetroot, causing them to develop large, roughened tumour-like swellings. The disease is caused by a bacterium and though often extremely unsightly it does not seem greatly to affect the vigour or condition of the plants attacked. No satisfactory remedy has been devised but when roots are attacked it is best to remove and burn them.

CUCKOO SPIT. This insect has acquired its popular name because it usually appears first of all at cuckoo time and it covers itself with a spittle-like mass of sap for protection. In some localities it is simply known as the spittle bug. The creature itself, when it can be cleared of its covering, is found to be small and yellowish white. It lives by sucking sap but is seldom in sufficient numbers to do great damage.

Any of the remedies recommended for aphides may be used but it is wise first of all to hose the plants or syringe heavily with clear water to remove as much as possible of the spittle covering and expose the insect to the insecticide. In gardens hand picking is usually the simplest and most satisfactory method of getting rid of this pest.

CUTWORMS. This is a useful general name which we have copied from the Americans who use it to describe all those caterpillars which live in the soil and attack plants at the base so that they topple over with the appearance of having been cut off at or about soil level. There are several different kinds of cutworm, each the caterpillar of a different moth, but treatment for all is the same, namely to hoe frequently so as to expose the cutworms for handpicking or to their natural enemies birds, and to hoe or fork into the soil an insecticide containing lindane. Whenever plants are attacked, search in the surface soil immediately around them as it is highly probable the cutworms will be found.

DAMPING OFF. Another general term applied to several distinct fungi which attack seedling plants at or just above soil level causing them to rot and topple over much as they would if they had been attacked by cutworms but with the difference that the stem is always blackened to some extent by the fungal decay. Damping off can spread very rapidly in the damp, stuffy conditions which favour it. Thin sowing and early picking off or potting are two of the best preventives as are careful watering and adequate ventilation. The disease is unlikely to prove troublesome in sterilised soil (see p. 763). The spread of attacks can be checked or much limited by soaking the soil around the seedlings with Cheshunt Compound. This can be purchased ready for dissolving in water at the strength stated on the container. Alternatively soil can be watered or sprayed with captan.

DIE-BACK. A name given to two quite distinct diseases one of which attacks plums and apricots while the other attacks roses and gooseberries. The effect of both is rather similar, whole branches dying quite rapidly but whereas with the fungus which causes the disease in plums and apricots it is difficult to find any centre of infection, in roses and gooseberries a careful examination will usually reveal patches of dark-coloured, decayed bark at the base of the affected branch or branches. All infected branches should be removed and burned, while with plums and apricots improved drainage and adequate feeding with a fertiliser containing nitrogen and potash will usually effect an improvement. Similar treatment will also help roses and gooseberries and, in addition, an application of Bordeaux mixture in April or early May will help. Gooseberries may also be sprayed with copper sulphate, 1 ounce per gallon of water, in winter while still dormant but just before the buds burst.

DRY SET. Sometimes the fruits of tomatoes, though apparently set, fail to swell but remain the size of a large pin head. This is known as dry set and is caused by too hot and dry an atmosphere. Freer ventilation and daily syringing of the plants with water will soon improve matters.

EARTHWORMS. In the ordinary way earthworms are not pests at all but on the contrary are highly beneficial to the garden because they drag decaying leaves into it, pass their bodies through the soil, breaking it up and moving it in the process, and, by making tunnels in it, admitting air. But all these activities, excellent as they are in the right place, can be damaging in the wrong one. Earthworms are a menace in pots and seed boxes, for they block up drainage holes with their casts and disturb roots by their constant tunnelling. On lawns they can be equally troublesome as their casts flatten out over the grass and smother it. Chlordane is a useful worm killer (see p. 799).

I have discussed other means of control on lawns on p. 392. Worms in pots and boxes can be driven out by watering with a deep pink solution of permanganate of potash or with lime water made by pouring 1 gallon of water on half a pound of quick lime, leaving for 24 hours and then decanting the clear liquor.

EARWIGS. These are too familiar to need description but the damage they do in the garden is often wrongly ascribed to other causes. Earwigs have a special partiality to petals, which they devour greedily so giving the blooms a very ragged appearance. They also attack leaves, which get to look rusty and distorted in consequence in much the same manner as when attacked by capsid bugs. As the earwigs work by night and hide by day it is not surprising that they so often go undetected.

There are several lines of attack, one to trap the earwigs, which can be done readily enough by making use of their love of dark hiding places, and others by poisoning them either with dusts or with poison baits. Traps can be made by inverting small, hay-stuffed flower pots on canes, by placing old, hollow broad bean stalks in the branches of the plant attacked or by suspending slightly opened match boxes from them. DDT or BHC dusts can be scattered where earwigs are seen.

The best poison bait is made by dissolving 4 oz. sodium fluoride in a little water, thinning half pint black treacle with a little more water, mixing treacle and sodium fluoride together and then adding the lot to 2 lb. of bran with just sufficient extra water to make a damp, crumbly mash.

EELWORMS. Beginners often say they have seen eelworms attacking the roots of their plants. In fact this is quite impossible both because the true eelworm is microscopic in size and also because it lives inside the plant in either the root or stem. What the novice has actually observed are almost invariably larger kinds of nematode worm which are eel-shaped and transparent like the genuine eelworm but amply large enough to be seen with the naked eye—in fact they are often a third of an inch in length. These big nematode worms are comparatively harmless as they feed mainly on decaying matter in the soil. When found on roots they are usually attacking tissue that is already rotting from some other cause, though occasionally they may do some direct damage to living tissue.

It is quite otherwise with eelworms which are invariably destructive. Within the plant they breed in immense numbers feeding on the sap and hampering normal development so that growth is checked, stems become stunted, thickened and spongy while in some cases leaves are distorted or made thread like.

A great many plants suffer from eelworms but fortunately most have their particular species so that, for example, the eelworm which damages potatoes will not also attack phloxes, nor will the phlox eelworm infest narcissi, onions or chrysanthemums.

As at some stage in their existence eelworms pass into the soil to attack other plants some soil treatment is necessary in addition to measures applied to the plant itself. Where the quantity of soil is small sterilisation (see p. 763) provides the complete answer but on a large scale outdoors this is impracticable and starvation is the only possible means of destroying the pests. This may mean growing no crop similar to that attacked for three or four years.

As regards the plants themselves burning is often the only course but some bulbs, notably narcissi, and also the 'stools' of some plants, notably chrysanthemums, can be cleared of eelworms without injury to themselves by immersing them in water at a steady temperature of 115° Fahr., for a period of five minutes. If the water gets any hotter, the plants or 'stools' may be destroyed while a lower temperature will not kill the eelworms. Special apparatus is available but this is mostly of a type more suitable for large nurseries than for private gardens.

Frequent syringing with nicotine in spring and early summer will greatly check the spread of chrysanthemum eelworm.

One special method of control, applicable to phloxes, is to work up a new stock of plants from root cuttings. This depends upon the fact that the phlox eelworm lives in the stems and, in consequence, the roots are clear. Of course the new stock of plants will soon become reinfested if grown in the same soil as the parents.

FIRE. A highly descriptive name given to a fairly common disease of tulips which withers leaves and buds or open flowers as if they had been sprayed with a caustic chemical. It is caused by a fungus and can be controlled by spraying with thiram.

FLEA BEETLE. This is a very small, blackish beetle which jumps when disturbed. It attacks all kinds of brassica seedlings including cabbages and turnips, eating small round holes in the leaves so that they look as if they had been perforated. One remedy is to keep the seedlings growing fast by watering them freely and giving them a small dose of nitrate of soda so that they quickly pass out of the stage at which they are tempting to the flea beetles. A more positive line of attack is to sprinkle the seedlings with 2 per cent. DDT dust.

FLY (CARROT, ONION, CABBAGE ROOT). There are a great many flies which are pests of one plant or another, but I am using the term here in its common garden application which is to three distinct pests the cabbage root fly, the onion fly and the carrot fly. Though in fact quite unrelated all three have points of great similarity, at least for the gardener. In each it is the maggot of the fly that does the damage, and in each the maggot is small, white and attacks the roots, or, in the case of the onion, the bulb. In all three cases the fly responsible lays her eggs in the soil near the base of the plant so that when the maggots hatch out they have food close at hand. Plants that are attacked stop growing, and in onions and cabbages the leaves take on a leaden hue. Sometimes they recover, but often small plants are killed outright.

Carrot, onion and cabbage root fly can be controlled with BHC dust and the last two also with 4 per cent. calomel dust sprinkled on the surface soil in a narrow band round the plants during May and early June when the flies are about. Care is needed in using BHC on carrots because of the risk of tainting the crop. It is safer to use a BHC seed dressing on the seed before sowing. Incidentally late sowings often escape attack as they come through after the fly has finished its egg-laying season.

Common Pests and Diseases

For celery fly see Leaf Miners (p. 781).

One other group of flies which can be very troublesome are the narcissus flies, the dirty-coloured larvae of which feed within the bulbs of daffodils and narcissi. With the large narcissus fly only one larva will be found in each attacked bulb, but when the small narcissus fly is involved numerous small larvae will be found. The remedy is the same for each, namely to lift all suspected bulbs, burn those seriously damaged and immerse the remainder for one hour in water kept at a steady temperature of 110° F. Frequent hoeing and raking of narcissus beds during the spring will help by filling up cracks in which the flies might otherwise lay their eggs.

FOOT ROT. A term applied to almost any rot which attacks plants at the base of the stem causing the upper part to collapse. Strictly speaking most of these diseases should be referred to as damping off and 'foot rot' as a name should be confined to a bacterial disease of cucumbers and melons which is also sometimes known as canker. The stems become soft and rotten just above ground level and this effectively strangles the rest of the plant. Anything which helps to keep the base of the stem rather dry will check the disease. Some gardeners plant on mounds of soil, others plant in the small pots in which the seedlings were raised merely breaking the bottom of the pot and standing it on the bed so that the roots may penetrate to the soil beneath. The rest of the pot remains as a collar to keep the neck of the plant dry. Occasional dusting with flowers of sulphur or a mixture of 10 parts of hydrated lime and 3 parts of finely powdered copper sulphate will also help.

GALL WEEVIL. The small white grub of this weevil enters the base of the stem of all plants of the cabbage tribe including turnips and swedes, causing small rounded galls to form. These swellings are frequently mistaken for those caused by club root (see p. 773). Gall weevil does little damage and it is usually sufficient to break open any galls noted when planting brassicas and kill the grubs within. A light dusting of finely powdered naphthalene raked into the seed bed prior to planting will help to keep the weevil away.

GREENBACK. A very common physiological trouble of tomatoes caused by lack of potash in the soil or sometimes by too much exposure of the fruit to strong sunshine. The chief symptom is the refusal of the fruit to ripen properly around the stalk where there is a band of hard

779

green of yellowish flesh. The remedy is to give more potash to the soil, and to leave sufficient foliage to shade the fruits.

GUMMING. All stone fruits and particularly plums and cherries are liable to exude large masses of resinous gum from time to time. Frequently little or no harm results but sometimes the gum is the symptom of a disease probably of bacterial origin. In such cases whole branches may die back quite suddenly sometimes in the middle of the summer and eventually whole trees may be destroyed. Cut off and burn withering branches and paint wounds with Stockholm tar or one of the advertised tree dressings. Apart from this necessary removal of diseased wood avoid hard pruning. Improve the drainage of the soil where this appears to be poor. Give regular dressings of potassic fertilisers. This disease is known as Bacterial Canker.

HOLLOW HEART. A condition common in some varieties of potato on certain soils and particularly in wet seasons. The centre of the potato is hollow though not actually decayed. Varieties which naturally produce very large tubers are most likely to suffer and the trouble may be aggravated by an excess of nitrogenous fertiliser with lack of balancing phosphates and potash. Extremes of soil moisture, however, are mainly to blame and improvements in the texture and drainage of the soil will help more than anything else to eliminate hollow heart.

LEAF CURL. One of the commonest diseases of peaches and nectarines particularly outdoors. Almonds are also affected. The trouble starts in spring when young leaves develop curled patches. These patches redden and become thickened until the leaf may be destroyed. Twigs may also be attacked and die back in consequence. The disease is always most troublesome when the weather is cold. Affected leaves and twigs should be removed and burned. If the disease has proved troublesome in former years spray with Bordeaux mixture, lime sulphur or captan at the end of February or early in March just before the buds commence to open.

LEAF HOPPERS (*Frog Flies*). Though very common these toublesome little insects are often overlooked. They are about the size of greenflies, the adults yellowish and winged, the young similar but wingless. They will be found on the undersides of the younger leaves, from which they suck the sap, and they are often mistaken for aphides. Two distinctive features are the white mottling of the attacked leaves, with little or no distortion, and the white, papery, cast-off skins of the growing frog flies which will usually be found attached to the undersides of the leaves even many weeks after an attack has finished. However accurate distinction between frog flies and aphides is not very vital for the gardener as the treatment is the same for both—namely spraying with malathion, BHC, nicotine, derris or pyrethrum.

LEAF MINERS. The grubs of several different kinds of flies attack the leaves of plants by tunnelling within them, eating out the soft, fleshy part without disturbing the skin, which remains as a protection to them. The chrysanthemum leaf miner is a well-known example of this type of pest and it can be extremely troublesome. Badly attacked leaves appear to be covered with snaky white lines which, on closer inspection, prove to be the tunnels left by the grubs in their passage through the leaves. Exactly similar damage is done by the cineraria leaf miner. The celery leaf miner burrows out a blister-like patch rather than a tunnel and the lilac and holly leaf miners produce a rather similar effect.

If the attacked leaves are run between the fingers the grubs can usually be felt as small lumps. In mild cases the quickest way to check the damage is to go over the leaves in this way one by one and kill the grubs with a pin or the point of a penknife. More extensive damage can be dealt with by spraying fairly frequently with nicotine, DDT, BHC, or malathion.

LEAF MOULD. This is one of the commonest diseases of tomatoes grown under glass. It is the foliage that is attacked and the damage is usually at its worst towards the end of the season. Damp, cold air and lack of ventilation encourage it. The first indication that something is wrong is the appearance of khaki-coloured spots on the undersides of the leaves. These spread rapidly and the leaf eventually withers.

If plants are adequately spaced and properly ventilated leaf mould is likely to be at a minimum. Some varieties show considerable resistance. When attacks do occur all badly affected leaves should be removed and burned and the plants sprayed at once with Bordeaux mixture or colloidal sulphur.

LEAF SCORCH. Leaf scorching of various kinds may occur from a great variety of causes including excessive temperatures, lack of water, an overdose of certain fertilisers such as sulphate of ammonia or calcium cyanamide and exposure to draughts. The term is also commonly used for a specific disease very common in fruit trees and also occurring in ornamental trees and shrubs and herbaceous plants of many kinds. This kind of leaf scorch is due to lack of potash and the typical symptom is a yellowing of the leaf margin early in summer followed by browning and withering from the outer edge inwards. The remedy is to apply a quick-acting potash fertiliser, such as sulphate of potash to the soil.

LEAF SPOT. An omnibus name given to a number of quite unrelated diseases all of which cause small spots to appear on the leaves. The most important are Carnation Leaf Spot which atacks both carnations and pinks, causing them to develop bleached spots; Celery Leaf Spot which is confined to celery and produces spots which are pale at first but which may eventually cause the whole leaf to wither, and Strawberry Leaf Spot which produces small reddish spots on the leaves of strawberries Carnations should be dusted with flowers of sulphur, and celery seed should be soaked for 3 hours before sowing in 1 part by volume of commercial formalin in 300 parts of water. In addition celery seedlings may be sprayed, also plants in summer, with Bordeaux mixture; strawberry may also be sprayed with Bordeaux mixture fortnightly during April and May. Burn all badly affected leaves.

LEATHERJACKETS. These may be mistaken for cutworms (see p. 775) as they look rather like caterpillars, live in the soil and attack the roots of plants or bite them off at soil level. Closer examination will show that they are not caterpillars as they have no legs. The colour is dark grey or almost black, the leatherjackets are extremely slow in their movements and they have soft but very tough skins. They are the larvae of the flies known as daddy-long-legs or crane flies.

Remedies are mostly the same as those recommended for cutworms but when leatherjackets become troublesome on lawns (which they may do by eating the grass roots and causing the grass to die in patches) an effective cure is to broadcast DDT dust at 2 oz. per sq. yd. over the surface. BHC is also very effective.

LILY DISEASE. There are many diseases of lilies but that commonly known as 'lily disease' is a form of botrytis (see p. 769) which is particularly liable to attack the white Madonna lily, causing the leaves to wither from the bottom of the plant upwards. If the disease has proved troublesome plants should be sprayed every week or so with Bordeaux mixture from April until they are about to come into flower.

MEALY BUG. This is a serious pest in many greenhouses. It attacks vines and a great variety of tender shrubs and ornamental plants, sucking sap from their stems or leaves. It is small, bug-like and covered with a whitish, waxy substance which gives it its popular name. As a rule individual treatment is necessary, each affected plant being sponged with derris or one of the proprietary summer petroleum emulsion insecticides or with malathion. Mass treatment by fumigation with nicotine (see p. 803) is sometimes possible.

MICE. There is no need to introduce these universal pests which will eat seeds and small bulbs so cleanly that the novice is often left wondering where they have disappeared. Any of the advertised poisons and viruses can be used and also the usual household mousetraps baited with fat, nuts or cheese. Of non-proprietary poisons I have found none more effective than phosphorous paste which can be spread on pieces of bread or any of the baits mentioned above. If seeds are damped with paraffin and then dusted with red lead prior to sowing they are unlikely to be attacked.

MIDGE (PEAR). The small yellowish-white maggots of this pest feed within the young fruits of pears causing them to be become deformed, turn black and fall. All such fruitlets should be collected and burnt. In addition the trees may be sprayed with nicotine when the blossom is fully open. If poultry are allowed to feed beneath the trees from April to June they will peck up many of the maggots.

MILDEW (POWDERY). There are a great many different mildews each attacking one particular family of plants. They are mostly alike in causing a white, powdery outgrowth on the part affected usually the leaves or younger stems though occasionally the fruits. American gooseberry mildew is peculiar in producing a thick, greyish felt on the gooseberries.

All powdery mildews can be attacked with sulphur. Flowers of sulphur may be dusted over the leaves or colloidal sulphur sprayed on them. Dinocap and thiram are also effective against powdery mildews.

For gooseberry mildew it is necessary to spray with lime sulphur at summer strength when the fruit is set and again three or four weeks later.

MILLEPEDES. These are soil pests varying a good deal in size and appearance but all thin in proportion to their length with a great number of small legs. They are often confused with centipedes but may be distinguished by the fact that they are relatively inactive and usually comparatively dull in colour, greyish or blackish in contrast to the yellow or orange of centipedes. The centipede is always dashing about and is, in fact, doing the gardener a good turn for he is looking out for other insects to eat. Millepedes eat roots though they often follow in the wake of other pests rather than initiate the trouble themselves. They can be trapped in sliced carrots or potatoes buried just beneath the surface of the soil. A lindane soil insecticide hoed or forked in will kill these pests.

MOLES. These are both friends and foes of the gardener—friends because they live on many soil insects, foes because in tunnelling to find their food they loosen the soil around roots and under seedlings, causing beds to collapse and plants to lose their roothold. Moreover on lawns they throw up unsightly molehills which, if not immediately removed, will smother and kill the grass.

There are two ways of dealing with moles apart from burying wire netting vertically in the soil around seed beds or special plots to prevent moles entering them. One is to trap the moles with special steel mole-traps which can be purchased for the purpose; the other to gas them in their burrows. Traps should be set across main runs, especially those leading to water as these will be used frequently and probably by many different moles. Soil or turf must be removed to allow the trap to be placed in position but should be returned immediately so that the run remains covered and dark. It is wise to wear gloves when setting the traps to avoid leaving any scent on them. Gassing is generally done with special smoke generators or 'fuses' which are ignited and then inserted in the runs. These runs should be sealed with a turf or peice of wood to trap the fumes.

MOSAIC. This is a name given to a sympton rather than to a disease, the condition being one of irregular pale green or yellowish mottling of the leaves. It generally indicates virus infection of some kind and a great many plants are capable of showing mosaic symptoms though it would be a mistake to assume on that account that the same virus was at work in all cases. However far and away the most important mosaic from the gardener's standpoint is that which attacks raspberries causing, in addition to the typical mottling, a slow deterioration in the vigour and cropping capacity of the canes. Some varieties are especially susceptible, the popular Lloyd George being one of the worst in this respect.

There is no cure and no preventive. Affected canes should always be removed and burned as noted. The disease is not carried in the soil so, provided the infected canes are removed roots and all, others may be planted in their place without danger. Note particularly that yellowing or bronzing of raspberry leaves is common in late summer especially if the weather is hot and is, as a rule, due to failure of surface roots for lack of moisture. True mosaic shows as a distinctive and immediately recognisable yellow variegation on the normal green background and is most easily detected about midsummer.

NECK ROT. Next to mildew this is the commonest disease of onions. To a lesser extent it also attacks shallots and garlic. The name is a good one because the principal symptom is a soft rot starting at the neck of the bulb. The trouble often does not commence until after the onions are lifted and placed in store. Bulbs with thick, soft stems are more liable to be attacked than those with thin, dry well-ripened necks and the principal method of control is to carry out good culture throughout so that the bulbs are properly ripened. Lift in fine, dry weather and do not store while still damp. See that the store is cool, airy and dry.

RABBITS. A vast amount of damage may be done by rabbits especially to young trees and shrubs of all kinds and also in the vegetable garden to young green crops. Trees and shrubs are barked near soil level and die as a result of the interruption to the flow of sap.

There is really only one way of dealing with rabbits on a large scale and that is to enclose the whole garden in wire netting which should have a mesh of not more than 1¼ in. and must be a minimum of four feet in height of which 6 in. should be buried in the soil. Individual trees can be protected with circles of wire netting or bundles of brushwood tied around the trunks. There are also various rabbit deterrents on the market to be painted on the trunks or main stems of trees and shrubs. Foetid animal oil, obtainable from most country chemists, can be used in this way.

RASPBERRY BEETLE. The adult beetle, small and greyish, damages the flowers of raspberry canes but it is its tiny white maggot which is the gardener's worst enemy as this enters the raspberry fruits and feeds within them. The remedy is to dust or spray with derris just after the blossom period and again when the earliest fruits commence to colour.

RATS. These are seldom as troublesome as mice to the gardener but they will sometimes cause serious damage to roots, bulbs or seeds in store and occasionally may bark young trees and shrubs in a similar manner to rabbits. Remedies are as for mice, the various proprietary viruses being convenient and, as a rule, effective.

RED SPIDER. There are a number of different kinds of red spider, each with its favourite host plant, but the gardener has no need to distinguish between them as all are harmful and all are to be tackled in much the same manner. Red spiders love a hot, dry atmosphere and are repelled by coolness and moisture. Hence one of the best methods of keeping them under control is to make frequent use of the syringe with nothing more potent than clear water. If this does not prove enough, a malathion, derris, or sulphur spray may be used — lime sulphur on fruit trees gives a partial control and derris in early June a better check. In the case of fruit trees that have been badly attacked, it is wise to spray with petroleum oil winter wash or thiocyanate winter wash in early March to kill eggs or to use one of the summer ovicides.

It should be noted that indiscriminate use of DDT insecticide may increase the severity of red spider attacks by destroying insects which prey on red spider. For this reason it is undesirable to use DDT on fruit trees after mid-April.

Under glass azobenzene may be used in the form of proprietary aerosols or smokes applied according to manufacturer's instructions, or plants can be sprayed with malathion or derris.

The red spider often escapes identification because it is so very small and so little like what its name would suggest. To the naked eye it looks no bigger than a grain of rust, though a pocket lens will reveal it to be a living creature with a roundish body and eight legs. It lives on the undersides of leaves, especially in the angles of the veins. It sucks sap like an aphis and the effect is to check growth and give the leaf a curiously grey, mottled appearance which is immediately detectable by the experienced gardener.

REVERSION. This very common disease of blackcurrants has a most misleading name. It was given because the affected bush gradually changes in character, developing a simpler, less lobed type of foliage, a bunched habit at the top and a progressive loss of fertility all of which features were supposed to be typical of a reversion to some primitive type. In fact this is a perfectly straightforward disease caused by a virus infection and spread by the big bud mite (see p. 767). The disease can be identified most readily in June or July. If at that time bushes are producing a great deal of small growth giving them a bunched or 'nettleheaded' appearance and if it is found that most of the leaves have less than five pairs of subsidiary veins on the main lobe, it is probable that reversion is the cause. Such bushes should be grubbed and burned at once as they are a source of infection. Steps should also be taken to eliminate big bud from the plantation.

RHODODENDRON BUG. One of the commonest pests of rhododendrons. The bug is a small black insect which may not be easy to detect but the damage it causes is distinctive enough, the leaves appearing rusty beneath and mottled above. When only a few plants are attacked a careful search of the foliage should be made for the bugs, but larger outbreaks are best dealt with by spraying in mid-June and again in early July with nicotine or DDT. In very bad cases it may be necessary to remove and burn all terminal growth in March even though this will mean sacrificing all bloom for a year.

ROOT ROT. There are a number of different fungi which attack the roots of plants, causing them to decay. Peas are particularly subject to a form known as black root rot because roots and stem base turn black. Privet is subject to attack by the honey fungus which will also damage the roots of many other ornamental shrubs and trees and fruit trees also. Toadstools appear above ground and are honey coloured— hence the popular name.

In most cases there is little that can be done except remove and burn the affected plants. Ground in which the honey fungus is believed to be at work may be soaked with sulphate of iron solution 4 oz. per gallon of water. Under glass soil may be sterilised but this is usually impracticable in the open garden.

ROSY RUSTIC MOTH. The green caterpillars of this moth feed within the stems of potatoes (and occasionally, some other plants) hollowing them out and causing them to flag. As the caterpillars are completely protected within the stems sprays and dusts are useless and the only remedy is to cut off and burn wilting stems.

RUST. A great number of diseases pass under the name 'rust' though some are quite unrelated and most are confined to one family of plants only. The three most troublesome are hollyhock rust, antirrhinum rust and chrysanthemum rust, each confined to the plant named. They are alike in producing rust-coloured spots or pustules on the under sides of the leaves, which are eventually killed. In the case of the orange rose rust these spots are a bright orange in colour.

All rusts are rather difficult to cure and if only a few plants are attacked it is usually best to destroy them. On a larger scale remove and burn the worst leaves and spray the plants fairly frequently with Bordeaux mixture or one of the advertised colloidal copper fungicides.

SAWFLY, APPLE. A pest which, with the codlin moth, is responsible for the majority of maggoty apples. The points of difference between it and the codlin moth I have explained on p. 774. The best remedy for sawfly is to spray with nicotine, DDT, or BHC when nearly all the blossom has fallen from the trees.

SCAB (APPLE AND PEAR). This is far and away the most troublesome disease of apples and pears. It is not a killer, but fruits are much disfigured by the roundish, black, shrunken spots some of which may run together or develop into deep, dry cracks. These spots are only skin deep, but they check the development of the fruit and may make it undersized or lopsided. Moreover the spurs and twigs are also attacked, the bark developing small blisters and eventually dying. These wounds often form a starting place for canker.

Scab must be kept down by routine spraying as it is much too common and widespread to be left for treatment if and when it turns up. Lime sulphur is a good remedy and should be used three or four times in a season—at full, or 'winter', strength in March or April when the buds are at the state known as 'green cluster', again at the same strength at the 'pink bud' or 'white bud' stage, and at the reduced summer strength as soon as the blossom falls. In severe cases a further summer strength application may be given a month later. Some varieties are liable to be damaged by lime sulphur after blossom fall and these should only have the first two applications. Alternatively captan can be used with safety on all varieties but as it is soon washed off it is necessary to spray at about fortnightly intervals from early April to August with the exception of the blossom period.

SCAB (POTATO). One of the commonest diseases of the potato. It attacks the skin, causing it to develop rusty looking scabs slightly raised above the surface. The flesh beneath these scabs remains unaffected but the appearance of the tubers is seriously impaired.

The fungus which causes potato scab is carried in the soil and flourishes in alkaline conditions, such as may exist in naturally chalky soils or those that have been heavily limed. It is seldom a serious problem in moderately acid soils. One remedy, therefore, is to avoid the use of lime on ground that is shortly to receive potatoes. Another is to use liberal quantities of peat or leaf mould in the preparation of the ground as these will tend to make it more acid. Incidentally gritty soil particles which wound the skin of the potato appear to make it more liable to infection and for this reason, also it is wise to surround planting sets with soft, yielding material such as peat, leaf mould or grass clippings. Rotational cropping will also help to keep the disease down by starving the fungus.

SCALDING. Under glass rapid fluctuations of temperature accompanied by bright sunshine will often cause direct scalding or scorching of young leaves and fruits. Tomatoes and grapes are particularly likely to suffer, the leaves withering from the margin as if they had been burned. The bunches of grapes themselves may also be affected and develop brown, sunken patches on the side exposed to the sun. The remedy in all cases is to give more ventilation while the sun is shining and, if necessary, to give some shade.

SCALE INSECTS. A number of insects attach themselves to the leaves, stems or bark of various plants and trees, looking rather like tiny limpets or mussels, and feeding by sucking sap from their hosts. Fruit trees can be cleared of scale insects by spraying in winter with tar-oil or DNC winter washes. These are too strong to use on plants in leaf which must be cleared by spraying or sponging with malathion, a summer petroleum emulsion or a mixture of this and nicotine. Under glass fumigation with nicotine may be carried out.

SHANKING. This common disease of old or overcropped vines may easily be mistaken for scalding. The grapes turn brown and collapse just before they ripen, and on close examination it will be found that the stalk which attaches the berry to the bunch has withered. This is a feature which may be used to identify shanking at once, coupled with the fact that the whole berry collapses, not merely a patch on the sunny or exposed side. Shanking is always an indication that the roots are giving out and this in turn may mean that the vine border has become waterlogged through bad drainage, or that the soil is exhausted. The remedy is then to remake the border the following autumn.

SILVER LEAF. This most destructive disease of plums is also found to a lesser extent on other stone fruits, hawthorns and even Portugal laurels. Silver leaf is not an easy disease for the beginner to diagnose until he has been shown it, and then he will never mistake it for anything else. The leaves of an affected branch gradually assume a metallic, silvery sheen which is most obvious about midsummer. Later the branch dies but this may take a year or so. On the dead wood a plentiful growth of purplish-mauve fungus appears and it is from this that spores are distributed to infect new trees. It is a legal offence to allow wood killed by silver leaf to remain on the trees after July 15 of any year. It is wise policy to cut all silvered boughs out before the autumn, even though they are not yet dead. All this wood should be burnt at once. Pruning should, as far as possible, be confined to the summer months when danger of infection is least, and all pruning cuts should be painted with warm grafting wax, Stockholm tar or one of the advertised wound dressings.

SLUGS AND SNAILS. These need no introduction to the gardener. Even the novice can hardly fail to know and hate them within a few months for they are the universal pests of every garden. Curiously enough slugs seem to be destructive in inverse proportion to their size, it being the small grey and black species which do far and away the most damage. Slugs and snails are for the most part night workers, and by day they hide in dark crannies or in the soil. In consequence their depredations are often wrongly blamed upon some other creature. A search after dark with the aid of a torch will usually set doubts at rest. The appearance of ragged holes in the leaves of plants, sometimes with tell-tale slime trails leading to them, will warn the more experienced gardener what he is up against. Fortunately there are a number of excellent slug poisons on the market. Two first-class recipes which can be made at home are powdered metaldehyde mixed with bran, and Paris Green with bran. To 3 lb. of bran add 1 oz. of metaldehyde finely crushed or 2 oz. of Paris Green. Sprinkle either bait around plants liable to be attacked or place in small heaps where the slugs can get at it. The Paris Green bait has the disadvantage of being poisonous to human beings and domestic animals. Both baits are most effective if used in damp, warm weather. Metaldehyde can also be obtained in suspension. It is then mixed with water and applied to soil and plants from a watering can fitted with a rose.

SLUGWORMS. These have nothing to do with slugs. They are the larvae of certain species of sawfly and they get their popular name from the fact that they are often blackish (though sometimes yellow) and somewhat like a small, thin slug in appearance. A closer examination will show that they have legs (a slug has none, of course). Slugworms have the curious habit of eating the surface of a leaf while leaving a transparent 'skeleton' intact. Roses, cherries and pears are favourite subjects for attack. The best killing agent is nicotine but derris, DDT or BHC can be used if there is any danger in applying a poisonous insecticide.

SOFT ROT. Every grower of cabbages or celery is likely to meet this troublesome disease sooner or later. It also attacks carrots, onions, seakale and even bearded irises and arum lilies. It is caused by a bacterium which is far too small to be seen with the naked eye or even a hand lens, but its effect, a soft, slimy decay proceeding from the centre of the plant outwards, is all too obvious.

This disease attacks plants through wounds so one method of controlling it is to avoid all possible causes of injury, as for example by clearing the ground of slugs and keeping down caterpillars. There is no remedy once the disease starts and affected plants should always be burnt at once.

SOOTY MOULD. This very descriptive name describes a disease which is often widespread, especially in greenhouses and on plants that have been heavily attacked by aphides or scale insects. It appears as a black, dirty looking film on the surface of the leaf and is, in the main, growing on the sticky substance left on the leaf by the insects that have preceded it. It can be sponged off with warm, soapy water but it is most important to take the appropriate steps to rid the plants of the pests which have given the mould a chance to grow.

SPRINGTAILS. The name is given to tiny, whitish insects which are sometimes found in great numbers on the roots of all kinds of plants, even large trees. When disturbed some of them appear to jump by means of a rapid movement of the rear part of the body. In the main springtails, like millepedes, follow in the wake of other troubles, feeding on matter already dead or decaying, but also like millepedes, they seem to be capable of carrying the damage still further themselves or perhaps sometimes even initiating it. Good cultivation and drainage will help to eliminate them, as will correct liming. It is also wise to avoid the use of half rotted dung and compost if these pests have proved troublesome. In bad cases use a DDT or BHC soil insecticide.

SPUR BLIGHT. A disfiguring fungal disease of raspberries, loganberries and blackberries which attacks the canes, usually at or near to the base of a leaf, producing a large purplish blotch which may eventually completely encircle the cane. Though the canes themselves are seldom killed, the buds in the leaf axils where infection occurs are destroyed. All infected canes should be removed and burnt and young canes should be well thinned so that each gets plenty of light and air. In addition two sprayings with lime sulphur may be given as for Cane Spot (q.v.).

STREAK. A troublesome disease of sweet peas and tomatoes which is most likely to occur under conditions of high cultivation. This is because it is caused by various viruses which thrive most readily in tissue that has been rendered soft by overfeeding. One of the few preventives is to avoid the use of too much food containing nitrogen and to give plenty of potash to ensure firm, disease-resistant growth. Streak is well-named for it causes long, sunken brown or blackish streaks on stems and leaves and, in the case of tomatoes, brown sunken spots on the fruits as well. Badly affected plants should always be burned.

TARSONEMID MITE. Many gardeners will dismiss the tarsonemid mite as just another red spider. It does not much matter really as the same treatment will do for either. Nevertheless as the name is sure to be met sooner or later it is as well to know what it stands for and how it differs from the true red spider. There are several tarsonemid mites and each has its favourite plant, one attacking strawberries, another begonias, a third cyclamen and so on. Like red spiders they belong to the mite family, are very small and found mostly on the undersides of leaves. They are whitish or pale brown rather than reddish, and leaves which are attacked become deep purple in colour and very brittle. Flower buds wither and blooms are distorted. Young strawberry plants that are attacked may be immersed before planting for ten minutes in water at a steady temperature of 115° Fahr. A petroleum emulsion spray is effective but will cause leaf injury to some delicate plants. Sponging with nicotine and soft soap is useful in the case of greenhouse plants.

THRIPS. Outdoors and under glass thrips are ever ready to give trouble especially when the weather gets hot and the atmosphere dry. In fact precisely the conditions which favour red spiders also encourage thrips and the two may often be found together. The thrips is small, very narrow in proportion to its length, yellow to black and almost always running about actively. A very few thrips seem able to do a quite disproportionate amount of damage. Leaves and stems become distorted and develop silvery or brown streaks. Flower buds turn brown and refuse to open. When thrips are suspected it is always a good plan to shake a plant or flower over a sheet of paper. It is almost certain that a few will be dislodged and be seen scuttling away to safety.

The remedy outdoors is to spray frequently with malathion, nicotine or BHC insecticide. Under glass fumigation with napthalene is effective but requires the use of a special lamp for vaporisation. It is simpler to use a BHC smoke generator.

VIRUS DISEASES. These have proved both the most difficult class of disease to investigate and the most troublesome to treat. Viruses are so minute that they cannot be seen with ordinary microscopes, however powerful, nor can they be trapped in the finest of filters. Their presence can be detected by the peculiar symptoms they produce and the fact that they can be inoculated from one plant to another. This is, in fact, how many of them are spread, the inoculations being carried out by sucking insects such as aphides and thrips.

Viruses are seldom killers in the sense that many fungus diseases can be, but they gradually weaken the plants which they attack and they disfigure them by causing their foliage to become mottled, or to develop dry brown spots, or to become distorted or stunted. Some plants have a considerable degree of tolerance to certain viruses and may show no signs of ill-health even when heavily infected. Such plants can be a potential source of danger in the garden by acting as unsuspected carriers of disease.

So far no satisfactory methods of curing virus infected plants have been discovered and all such plants must be destroyed as soon as noted to prevent the disease being passed on. Any measures taken to keep down sucking insects will also help to limit the spread of viruses and care should also be taken in the use of pruning implements, such as knives and sécateurs. Virus infection may be carried on the blades of these and so, if they are used on any doubtful plants they should be dipped in boiling water or a solution of Lysol before being used.

WART DISEASE. Fortunately this is not a common disease and most readers will probably never see it but I mention it here because it is one of the most serious diseases of the potato, notifiable to the Ministry of Agriculture and, in consequence, one which gets much publicity. Attacked tubers develop large, warty outgrowths which may eventually encompass the whole of the potato, reducing it to a shapeless, cancerous-looking mass. This disease must not be confused with scab which causes no more than rusty-looking scabs on the skin and leaves the flesh untouched. There is no remedy for wart disease but fortunately many varieties are immune to it. These are indicated in catalogues by the single word 'immune' after the name and should always be planted in districts in which wart disease is known to have occurred.

WEEVILS. A number of weevils can prove troublesome in the garden but four are of such outstanding importance as pests that even the beginner should learn something about them. They are the Apple Blossom Weevil, the Pea and Bean Weevil, the Clay Coloured Weevil and the Vine Weevil.

The first, as its name suggests, attacks the flowers of apples. The adult weevil is a small, dark beetle-like creature but it is its white grub which does the damage. It feeds within the opening flower causing it to turn brown and become 'capped'. DDT or BHC, applied when the buds are first bursting in March or early April and the most

The Amateur Gardener

forward are at the 'mouse-ear' stage, are by far the most effective remedies.

The Pea and Bean Weevil also conveniently confines its attentions to the plants indicated by its name, broad beans being a particular favourite. The plants are usually attacked when still quite small and the leaf edges only are eaten so that they quickly acquire a distinctive, scalloped appearance. This time it is the grey, beetle-like adult which does the damage, though it is so active and cunning that as likely as not it will never be seen. Foliage should be dusted occasionally with DDT or derris.

The Clay Coloured and Vine Weevils are so similar from the gardener's standpoint that they can be considered together. Both are destructive in both the adult and larval (grub) stages. The grubs are small, whitish and fond of attacking roots, bulbs, corms, etc. in which they may be found curled up. The adults are beetle-like with the long snouts characteristic of weevils. The Clay Coloured is ashen-grey, the Vine Weevil black. They eat ragged holes in foliage and the damage is often mistaken for that caused by caterpillars or slugs. A great variety of plants is attacked both outdoors and under glass. If plants are shaken after dark over tarred sacks or papers many feeding weevils will fall off and be trapped. Spraying or dusting with DDT may do some good. When pot plants are attacked by the larvae of these weevils the only remedy as a rule is to unpot the plants and remove the grubs by hand.

WHITE FLY. With red spider and thrips white fly shares the doubtful honour of being the most troublesome pest under glass. There is also a related but distinct form which lives outdoors and has a special fancy for brassicas. In the greenhouse white fly seems to live on anything, though tomatoes are always singled out for early attention. It is not really a fly at all and does not look like one. It is very small, winged and pure white. It flies out when disturbed and, if there is a heavy infestation, the effect is like a cloud of smoke. Scales, representing a stage in the life cycle of the insect, are formed on the leaves and eggs are also laid in great numbers. The white fly and the scales suck sap from the plant and cover it with a sticky grey excrement.

Fumigation with DDT or lindane is effective if repeated two or three times at intervals of about a fortnight. Outdoor plants should be sprayed with BHC or DDT or with a combined nicotine and summer petroleum emulsion insecticide.

WILT. A number of quite unrelated diseases pass under the name 'wilt'.

794

Common Pests and Diseases

The two most important for the gardener are Aster Wilt, which is confined to annual asters and has very much the appearance of damping off disease (see p. 775) except that the main stem may be attacked well above soil level; and Spotted Wilt.

Aster wilt is best controlled by sterilising the soil in which the plants are raised and growing them in a different part of the garden each year. Wilt resistant varieties can be obtained.

Spotted wilt is a disease of many greenhouse plants, including tomatoes, gloxinias and arum lilies. The first symptom is the appearance of ring-like spots on the leaves. Plants are stunted and the heads of tomato plants become bunched and have a bronzed appearance. This is a virus disease and, as it is incurable and very catching, infected plants should be burned. Thrips are often active in spreading infection, so appropriate steps should be taken against these pests (see p. 792).

WINTER MOTHS.—See CATERPILLARS p. 772.

WIREWORMS. These are amongst the most destructive soil pests in the garden. They are to be found everywhere, being the larvae of certain species of small brown beetles, known as 'click beetles' because, if they are rolled over on their backs, they right themselves with a jerk and a distinct clicking noise. The wireworms themselves are yellow, shiny-skinned, up to an inch long and no thicker than a piece of ordinary string. They are not very active and have only three pairs of small legs near the head, points which serve to distinguish them from the very active and many legged centipedes. Wireworms live on the roots of plants and on large seeds such as peas and beans. They are particularly fond of potatoes and carrots, and are usually found in great numbers in rough grassland. Often damage is most severe the second year after such land is broken up, the explanation apparently being that the first year they continue to feed on the decaying grass roots and only turn their attention seriously to garden plants when their original source of food is gone.

Good cultivation will reduce the wireworm population by exposing the grubs to birds. Many wireworms can be trapped in sliced potatoes or carrots buried just beneath the surface of the soil and examined every day or so. Potting and seed soil may be sterilised by heat or with one of the advertised chemical sterilisers.

A dust containing lindane may be applied to the soil according to manufacturer's instructions. On ground that is to be used for root crops this dust should be applied the autumn prior to cropping.

WOODLICE. Everyone is familiar with the hard-skinned, grey or black-ish woodlice, with its habit of rolling itself into a ball when disturbed which has given it the name of 'pillbug' in some localities. It feeds mainly on decaying matter but will also attack soft-stemmed plants, and particularly tiny seedlings which may be eaten off so cleanly that they have the appearance of being mown. Many can be trapped in the same way as earwigs (see p. 776) and they can also be poisoned with a mixture of Paris Green and bran as advised for slugs (see p. 790), or Paris Green 1 oz. mixed with dried blood 3 lb. Another effective remedy is 5 per cent. DDT or BHC dust sprinkled where they are seen. In greenhouses fumigation with BHC or DDT is effective. Decaying refuse should be removed as it provides a hiding place and breeding ground.

WOOLLY APHIS. This form of aphis attacks apples and has several peculiarities, notably the habit of completely covering itself with a white, wool-like protective material, so that a tree heavily infested appears to be covered with pieces of cotton wool. This makes it difficult to get an ordinary spray into contact with the insects. It is usually best to apply the insecticide direct to the patches with a stiff, old paint brush. Nicotine or malathion may be used or methylated spirits, the latter having the advantage of being particularly penetrating. March spraying with thiocyanate winter wash will also help to clear trees. Buds are often so severely damaged by woolly aphis that they become blind and develop large gall-like swellings. The pest is also known as American Blight.

CHAPTER XXXIV

Useful Remedies

I MAKE NO pretence that the following list of remedies or preventives for diseases and pests is in any way complete, or even that it necessarily represents the best for each and every purpose. Improvements, both in formulae and in methods of manufacture, are constantly being made and every maker has the natural, and occasionally justified, feeling that his own products are the best. But I can say that I have at one time or another used all the preparations here described and found them effective for the purposes and within the limits described. Most of them are what might be regarded as everyday remedies which should be in the gardener's store cupboard as a matter of course.

AZOBENZENE. A chemical which is very effective in destroying red spider in the greenhouse. It must be purchased as a proprietary aerosol or smoke, the former to be discharged in the greenhouse, usually by means of a special apparatus, the latter to be ignited like a firework. Manufacturer's instructions regarding application must be followed. The temperature should be maintained at or above 75° during use.

BHC. The abbreviation commonly used for a chemical named benzene hexachloride. It is used as an insecticide against a wide range of insects including aphides, caterpillars, cutworms, weevils and their larvae, scale insects, wireworms and leatherjackets. The active insecticidal portion of BHC is what is known as its gamma isomer and for some purposes this is separated from the other isomers which are apt to impart a musty taint to treated crops particularly roots and fruits. This extraction is sometimes known as gamma-BHC and, when at least 99% pure, as Lindane.

BORDEAUX MIXTURE. This excellent fungicide was developed in the Bordeaux district of France to deal with a troublesome disease of the vineyards. It has proved to be one of the most useful fungus killers with a very wide range of application in the garden. It is particularly valuable as a preventive of potato blight both on potatoes and tomatoes. It will also check or cure most mildews and many rust and leaf spot diseases. It is liable to scorch the foliage of some plants but this can be checked by using rather more lime and water in its preparation.

The standard mixture is prepared by dissolving 6 oz. copper sulphate and 8 oz. of quicklime (or fresh hydrated lime) in 5 gallons of water. Dissolve the copper sulphate first in 4 gallons of water. Then dissolve the lime by pouring the other gallon of water on to it slowly. Finally add lime solution to copper sulphate solution, stir well and use at once. The solution can be tested for acidity by dipping a piece of blue litmus paper in it. If this turns pink a little more lime should be added until there is no reaction. This spray must always be mixed in wooden, copper or thoroughly enamelled vessels. It will react with iron or tin. Prepared Bordeaux Mixture in powder form can also be purchased ready for mixing with water. In this case manufacturer's instructions regarding strength must be followed.

CALOMEL. This mercuric compound has proved an excellent remedy for onion and cabbage root fly and a useful check for club root disease. It is sold, ready for use, as a 4 per cent. dust mixed with a non-active carrier. A little is sprinkled around each plant to be protected, or, in the case of small seedlings, down each side of the seeds row in a narrow but continuous band. Its effect is to kill the eggs laid by the root flies in the soil. For club root a small quantity of the dust is sprinkled into each hole prepared for a brassica plant before it is placed in position.

CAPTAN. A synthetic chemical used as a fungicide. It is particularly recommended for the control of apple and pear scab as it does not scorch leaves or russet or crack fruits. It is purchased as a powder which must be mixed in water according to manufacturer's instructions and kept stirred while it is applied as a spray. Its effect does not last long and so it may be necessary to spray every 10 days from April to September to secure complete control. Captan does not control apple mildew but will control many other diseases including rose black spot, grey mould, peach leaf curl, various storage rots and damping off.

CHESHUNT COMPOUND. A mixture of two parts by weight copper sulphate and one part ammonium carbonate which can either be purchased ready for use or be manufactured at home in a glass-stoppered bottle, simply by mixing the two chemicals together very thoroughly and leaving them well stoppered for at least twenty-four hours. The purchased article or the home-made product should be dissolved in water at the rate of $\frac{1}{2}$ oz. per gallon. It can then be watered on soil as a fungicide even when small seedlings are growing in it. Cheshunt Compound is an excellent preventive of damping-off disease.

Useful Remedies

CHLORDANE. Useful as a worm killer on lawns. It is watered on after dilution according to manufacturers' instructions. The worms are killed in the soil and do not come to the surface.

COLLOIDAL COPPER. This fungicide must be purchased as a manufactured article ready for mixing with water. It is comparable with Bordeaux mixture in character and use but is claimed to give a more even cover of leaves and stems and to be a more effective killer of resistant fungi such as those causing many of the rusts and the black spot disease of roses. The usual strength is 2 fluid oz. to 5 gallons of water, but manufacturer's instructions should be obtained whenever possible.

COLLOIDAL SULPHUR. This is a similar manufactured article to the last named but with sulphur instead of copper as its active, fungus-killing element. It is used in the same way, the usual strength being 3 fluid oz. to 5 gallons of water but manufacturer's instructions should be consulted where possible. It is particularly useful against mildews and has been preferred by some growers to lime sulphur for the treatment of apple and pear scab.

COPPER SULPHATE. This chemical should always be in the gardener's store cupboard if only because it is an essential ingredient of Bordeaux Mixture and Cheshunt Compound. By itself it can only be used on hard-wooded plants while they are completely dormant and leafless in winter, as it will scorch foliage severely. It is occasionally used on roses in December or January to kill the resting spores of the fungi which cause black spot and orange rose rust diseases. For this purpose it is dissolved in water at the rate of 1 oz. per gallon.

COPPER WHITE OIL EMULSION. A proprietary fungicide which has been found very useful in controlling diseases caused by fungi, notably black spot of roses. The fungicide should be mixed with water according to manufacturer's instructions and applied to the roses as a fine, wetting spray once a fortnight during July, August and September.

CRESYLIC ACID. To most readers this chemical will be more familiar as carbolic acid. It is sometimes used as a soil steriliser at the rate of 1 gall. 97 to 99 per cent. purity cresylic acid to 39 gall. water. This makes sufficient sterilising fluid to treat about 12 sq. yd. of moderately light soil or 9 sq. yd. of heavy soil. It is simply poured on from a watering can and then the soil is dug or forked over to mix the chemical in as thoroughly as possible. Nothing should be sown or planted until the soil has completely lost the smell of the acid.

DDT. This insecticide was developed very rapidly during the war as an alternative to derris for killing lice and bugs. It proved to have considerable possibilities as an insect killer in the garden and is now offered in a variety of forms. The most generally useful are the dusts, mixed with a non-active carrier for application dry; the wettable powders for solution in water and use as a spray, and the oil emulsion, also for spray application after suitable dilution. In all cases manufacturer's instructions must be followed.

DDT dust has proved very effective in combating weevils and beetles, particularly the turnip flea beetle (see p. 778), and the apple blossom weevil (see p. 793). It can also be used to kill woodlice, leatherjackets and cockroaches. The wettable powder gives good control of most caterpillars, while the oil emulsion is excellent for use against thrips, scale insects and white fly.

DDT is rather slow in effect but very lasting. In consequence a combination of DDT with the much quicker acting pyrethrum (see p. 805) has many possibilities.

DERRIS. One of the most useful insect and mite killers. It is fairly effective against both biting and sucking insects, particularly caterpillars and aphides and also red spiders. Purchasable as a dust mixed with a non-active carrier, or as a powder or liquid to be mixed with water. The powder should be used at 1–2 oz. to 5 gallons of water with 4 oz. soft soap or a suitable 'spreader' added. The liquid must be used according to manufacturer's instructions. Derris is relatively non-poisonous.

DIAZINON. A comparatively new insecticide and acaricide chiefly used for the control of aphides, capsid bugs, thrips, and red spider, particularly under glass, but also possibly useful in the control of fly maggots (e.g. cabbage root fly, onion fly, carrot fly) outdoors.

DIMETHOATE. A systemic insecticide, i.e. the chemical enters into the plant and renders it poisonous to insects, including bees. It is effective against aphids, capsid bugs, leaf hoppers, thrips and red spider mite. It should not be used on chrysanthemums.

DINOCAP. A fungicide effective against powdery mildews. It should be sprayed on roses etc. at the first sign of mildew or if conditions are such that an attack by mildew is likely.

DNC (*Dinitro-ortho-cresol*). This is a winter wash mainly for use on fruit trees. In commercial orchards it has, to a very large extent, taken the place of the older tar oil winter wash as it has at least as great an effect on the eggs of aphides and caterpillars and considerably more effect on capsid bugs, red spider and apple sucker. It is not quite so popular in private gardens because it is rather unpleasant to use, staining flesh and nails a bright yellow and causing soreness of the eyes. Workers should protect themselves with plenty of vaseline which effectively stops staining and enables the chemical to be removed with warm water and soap when the work is completed.

DNC is purchased as a manufactured emulsion ready for mixing with water, the normal strength being 1 quart to 3 gallons of water. It is used at half strength on plums. It can be applied later than tar oil wash and is most effective at the delayed dormant stage, i.e. when the bud scales are already well loosened but before the first small leaves give them a 'mouse-eared' appearance.

FORMALDEHYDE. The most generally useful chemical soil steriliser. For this purpose the commercial grade known as 'formalin' is commonly used. This has an analysis of 40 per cent. formaldehyde and it is diluted at the rate of 1 part by volume formalin to 49 parts water. The soil to be treated should be spread out on a hard floor soaked with the diluted formalin (75 gallons is sufficient to treat 1 ton of soil) and then immediately thrown into a heap and covered with sacks or tarpaulins to trap the fumes. After twenty-four hours the covering is removed and the soil spread out again to let the fumes escape. The soil should not be used until it has lost all smell of formalin, which takes two or three weeks.

LIME SULPHUR. A very popular fungicide which is much used by fruit growers to prevent apple and pear scab, gooseberry mildew and raspberry cane spot. It is also effective against mites, including currant big bud mite.

Lime sulphur must be purchased as a manufactured fluid. This is used at several different strengths according to season and purpose. Two common dilutions are 11 fluid oz. to 2 gallons of water (known as winter strength) and 3 fluid oz. to 2 gallons of water (known as summer strength). The first can be used on fruit trees up to the stage at which the fruit buds commence to show petal colour (pink bud in apples, white bud in pears). After this stage winter strength lime sulphur may cause severe leaf scorching. Summer strength lime sulphur should be used from petal fall onwards.

Exceptions to these general instructions must be made to deal with black currant big bud and raspberry cane spot. For the former one application of lime sulphur at 1 pint to 2 gallons of water is made in March when the most forward leaves are as big as shillings. Consider-- able scorching may result but the bushes should recover after a few weeks. For cane spot lime sulphur is used at 1 pint per gallon in mid-March and at 6 fluid oz. to 2 gallons of water in mid-May.

LINDANE.—*See* BHC, p. 797.

LIVER OF SULPHUR (*Potassium sulphide*). An old-fashioned remedy for mildews and other fungus diseases and one which has been superseded to a considerable extent by modern sprays such as colloidal sulphur and lime sulphur. Nevertheless it is still a good standby and may, on occasion, prove effective when other remedies have failed. It is used at the rate of 1 oz. to 3 gallons of water and is much more effective if 3 or 4 oz. of soft soap is added. Liver of sulphur must be stored in a tightly stoppered jar.

MALATHION. One of the organo-phosphorus insecticides of which parathion and schradan are other examples. It is, however, much safer to handle than these and, though poisonous, it can be used without special protective clothing when diluted to the recommended strength for spraying. It is effective against all kinds of aphis and apple sucker as well as red spider mites, thrips, whiteflies, leaf hoppers, scale insects and mealy bug. Manufacturer's instructions must be obtained concerning dilution. Once mixed, malathion should be used without delay as it quickly decomposes. It can be mixed with most fungicides and insecticides but lime sulphur and other alkaline chemicals may shorten its period of effectiveness.

MENAZON. A useful aphis killer (i.e. for use against greenfly, blackfly, etc.) which has a very low toxicity to human beings, mammals and birds and is absorbed into the plant so that there is no danger of it being washed off by rain or of it hurting insects which do not eat the plant or suck its sap. It is effective for a month or more and is most usefully applied in spring or summer immediately aphides are seen or immediately before an expected attack by aphides.

METALDEHYDE. Originally this substance was sold exclusively as a solid fuel but later it was discovered to be an excellent slug poison. For this purpose it should be powdered as finely as possible and mixed with any suitable bait. A mixture of 1 oz. metaldehyde to 3 lb. of very slightly moistened bran is excellent. Place in small heaps where slugs are likely to feed. It is most effective if used in damp, warm weather.

Useful Remedies

MOWRAH MEAL. This is still one of the best worm killers for lawns. Its one drawback is that very large quantities of water are needed to wash it in. The mowrah meal is first broadcast over the lawn at the rate of from 4 to 8 oz. per sq. yd. Is is then washed in as freely as possible, preferably with a hose. The worms come to the surface after a few hours and can be swept up. Treatment is most effective in spring and autumn.

NAPHTHALENE. Used as a fumigant both in soil and greenhouses. For the former purpose finely powdered naphthalene is simply forked or raked in at the rate of 4 oz. per sq. yd. on vacant ground or 2 oz. per sq. yd. if crops are growing. The fumes from it will drive out many soil pests and kill some. A surface sprinkling of naphthalene in May and June will keep away egg-laying flies such as carrot fly, onion fly and cabbage root fly.

For greenhouse work the naphthalene must be vaporised and for this purpose a special lamp is required. Grade 16 naphthalene is commonly used, the correct dose being 4 to 6 oz. per 1,000 cubic feet. It is particularly effective against thrips and red spider but needs to be used with care as poor vaporisation or an overdose may cause serious damage to plants.

NICOTINE. This remains the best aphis killer and it is also very effective against capsid bugs and thrips and to a lesser extent against leaf-mining maggots, caterpillars, etc. Its two drawbacks are that it is very poisonous to human beings and that, after use, it loses its insect-killing properties fairly quickly. For the former reason it should never be used on vegetables or fruits which are to be eaten raw within a week or so. Because of its volatility it is necessary to repeat applications fairly frequently if the attack persists.

Liquid nicotine can be used as a spray, the 'pure' product being employed at the strength of $\frac{1}{4}$ to $\frac{1}{2}$ fluid oz. to 5 gallons of water. However, most nicotine sold by horticultural sundriesmen is already diluted considerably and with these brands manufacturer's instructions should always be followed. Nicotine sprays are more effective if combined with soft soap, 1 oz. per gallon, or one of the advertised spreaders.

Nicotine dust can be purchased ready for application dry. Nicotine can also be obtained in several forms for glasshouse fumigation. For this purpose liquid nicotine is vaporised over a small spirit lamp, or shreds or cones impregnated with nicotine may be ignited and allowed to burn in the house. In all cases manufacturer's instructions should be consulted.

PARADICHLORBENZENE. An alternative to naphthalene as a soil fumigant. It is used at the rate of ½ oz. per sq. yd. either forked in or dropped into dibber holes made 6 or 8 in. deep and 9 to 12 in. apart.

PARATHION. One of the most powerful of the newer synthetic insecticides and one of the best for killing red spider. Unfortunately parathion is so very poisonous to warm blooded animals, including human beings, that it cannot be recommended for general garden use. When parathion is used great care should be taken not to get it on the skin or to inhale it. Protective rubber clothing should be worn including rubber gloves and a gas mask. Parathion is a liquid which should be diluted with water at the rate of ¼ fluid oz. to 12 gallons to prepare it for use unless manufacturer's instructions state otherwise. In addition to red spider it will kill a wide range of pests including aphides, capsid bugs, thrips and caterpillars.

PARIS GREEN. An arsenical poison which is useful as a killer of slugs, cutworms, leatherjackets and woodlice. It must be mixed with a suitable bait, bran being most effective for the first three mentioned and dried blood for woodlice. Suitable proportions are ¼ lb. Paris Green to 7 lb. of very slightly moistened bran or 2 oz. Paris Green to 7 lb. of dried blood. Place in small heaps where the pests are likely to feed, or broadcast thinly over the surface of the soil.

PETROLEUM OIL. This is prepared in several ways for dilution with water and use as a spray. It is particularly effective against scale insects, capsid bugs and aphides and can also be used to kill red spiders, thrips and, in combination with nicotine, white fly. It is essentially a manufactured spray and for this reason manufacturer's instructions should always be consulted if possible. Usual strengths are 3 pints petroleum oil or emulsion to 5 gallons of water for winter and very early spring use, and 6 to 8 fluid oz. of petroleum emulsion to 5 gallons of water for later spring and summer use.

PYRETHRUM. Nowadays this insecticide is more often used with other substances than by itself. It is a good aphis killer and has some effect on most insects. Particularly important is its rapid action, which contrasts with the much slower operation of some other insecticides such as DDT. A mixture of these two substances has many possibilities, giving both the 'knock down' result and the lasting effect which is so desirable. Pyrethrum can be purchased in both liquid and dust form and as there is no standard strength manufacturer's instructions should always be consulted. It is non-poisonous to domestic animals and human beings.

SCHRADAN. This name has been coined for a complicated organic chemical which is used as a systemic insecticide. The term 'systemic' means that the chemical is actually absorbed into the sap of the plant and distributed in the sap to every part of it, even the roots. This makes the whole plant poisonous to any insects that may attempt to feed on it, but contrariwise, the chemical does no harm to useful insects which do not feed on the plants. For this reason systemic insecticides are often described as selective, i.e. killing foe but sparing friend. The drawback to insecticides of this type is that they may make the plants poisonous to warm blooded animals including human beings. This schradan does, but as it is decomposed fairly quickly within the plant, some parts of it actually being used as plant food, the danger ceases to exist after a time. One month is regarded as a safe period to elapse between application of chemical and use of crop.

Schradan is a liquid which should be diluted with water according to manufacturer's instructions and then should be sprayed on the plants in the usual way. Great care should be taken not to swallow any of the fluid or get it on the skin.

Schradan is effective against a wide range of insects, particularly aphides, capsid bugs, red spider and thrips.

SOFT SOAP. Good grade soft soap, once freely employed as an insecticide, is now more frequently used as a spreader for more powerful substances. Its effect is to help the liquid to spread in a thin, even film all over the surface of the plant sprayed thus giving a complete protection against pest or disease. For this purpose 1 oz. of soft soap per gallon of spray is usually enough but more may be needed if the water is very hard, while less will be required if rain water is used.

SULPHUR. Ordinary flowers of sulphur, which can be purchased from any chemist, is an excellent fungicide for use as a dust directly on the foliage of plants. It will do no harm, even to tender greenhouse plants, and can be used on grapes, even when ripening, to check the spread of mildew. Special brands of green horticultural sulphur are used in precisely the same way.

TAR OIL WINTER WASH. One of the most powerful winter cleansers for fruit trees. Not only will it kill aphis and caterpillar eggs but will also clear the bark of lichens and green, scummy growths. Tar oil is very damaging to leaves and even to swelling buds so must only be used when the trees are quite dormant in December or January. It is a manufactured article but usually prepared to a standard strength, the correct dilution of which is 5 pints concentrated tar oil to 10 gallons of water.

THIRAM. The name given to zinc oxide, a fungicide that has proved particularly effective in controlling rose black spot, tulip fire and tomato leaf mould, as well as some mildews and rusts, including those of roses and chrysanthemums. It is used as a spray and should be mixed according to manufacturer's instructions.

WASHING SODA. Ordinary household washing soda can be used with soft soap to make a useful fungicide. The proportions are 12 oz. washing soda and 8 oz. soft soap to 5 gallons of water. This mixture is particularly effective against gooseberry mildew provided frequent applications are made during spring and summer. It has the twin merits of being non-poisonous and non-staining.

INDEX

Figures in italics indicate references to illustrations

807

3A

daboëcia, 275
daffodil, 359
dahlia, 100, 343
  dividing, *244*
  from seed, 100, 346
  types, 346
daisy, 93
dalapon, 30
damping down, *431*
damping off, *759*, 775
danaë, 275
daphne, 200, 275, 461
datura, 461
day lily, 159
DDT, 392, 751, 764, 765,
  771, 774, 776, 778,
  781, 782, 787, 790,
  791, 793, 794, 796,
  800
  and red-spider, 786
deciduous, 238
deficiency disease, 773
delphinium, 151, 200
derris, 668, 751, 765,
  768, 781, 785, 786,
  800
desfontainea, 462
deutzia, 276, 462
dianthus, 101, 151, 201
diazinon, 800
dicentra, 152, 462
dictamnus, 152
didiscus, 463
die back, 775
dieffenbachia, 463
dielytra, 152
dierama, 346
diervilla, 276
digging, *18*, 31
digitalis, 152
dimethoate, 800
dimorphotheca, 101
dinocap, 783, 800
diplacus, 463
dipladenia, 463
disbudding, *246*
  chrysanthemums, 510
diseases, 747, *756–760*
  bacterial, 752, 761
  description of, 749
  fungal, 752

physiological, 761
  soil, 761
  virus, 752, 761
division, *244*
  trees and shrubs, 252
DNC, 668, 766, 772, 789,
  800
dodecatheon, 202, 380
doronicum, 153
douglas fir, 303
draba, 202
dracaena, 457, 464
dracocephalum, 170
drainage, 38–41
drains, land, 39
  herring-bone, *40*
  laying, *21*
dryas, 203
dry walls, 183
dry set, 776

earthworms, 776
earwigs, 776
  trap, *753*
Eccremocarpus scaber, 102
echeveria, 464
echinacea, 153
echinops, 153
echium, 102
edelweiss, 212
edraianthus, 203
eelworms, *755*, 777
egg plant, 562
elder, 312
electrical heating, 412
elaeagnus, *276*
elm, 319
elodea, 375
embothrium, 277
endive, 586
enkianthus, 277
epacris, 464
epilobium, 203
epimedium, 153
eranthis, 346
eremurus, 347
erica, 277, 465
erigeron, 154
erinus, 204
eriophorum, 375
eritrichium, 204

erodium, 204
eryngium, 154
erysimum, 102, 205
erythrina, 465
erythronium, 348
escallonia, 255, 278
eschscholzia, 102
espalier, *652*
eucalyptus, 466
eucharis, 466
eucryphia, 279
euonymus, 279
eupatorium, 466
euphorbia, 154, 205, 466
evening primrose, 115,
  167, 217
evergreen, 238
everlasting flowers, 87,
  105, 120, 122
exacum, 467
exochorda, 280

fabiana, 280
fairy rings, 394
fatshedera, 524
fatsia, 280, 467
feathers, 55
feeding, 48
felicia, 103
ferns, 395–400
  as house plants, 399
  greenhouse, 397
  hardy, 395
fertilisers, 46–51
  analysis, 50
  complete, 50
  mixing, 50
fertility rules in fruit
  garden, 631
ficus, 467
figs, 703–706
fir, Douglas, 303
fire, 778
fire thorn, 304
fish and pools, 372
fish guano, 56
  manure, 56
fish waste, 55
fittonia, 524
flea beetle, 778
flowering rush, 373